William of Malmesbury's Chronicle of the kings of England. From the earliest period to the reign of King Stephen

William, John Sharpe, John Allen Giles D.C.L.

Copyright © BiblioLife, LLC

This book represents a historical reproduction of a work originally published before 1923 that is part of a unique project which provides opportunities for readers, educators and researchers by bringing hard-to-find original publications back into print at reasonable prices. Because this and other works are culturally important, we have made them available as part of our commitment to protecting, preserving and promoting the world's literature. These books are in the "public domain" and were digitized and made available in cooperation with libraries, archives, and open source initiatives around the world dedicated to this important mission.

We believe that when we undertake the difficult task of re-creating these works as attractive, readable and affordable books, we further the goal of sharing these works with a global audience, and preserving a vanishing wealth of human knowledge.

Many historical books were originally published in small fonts, which can make them very difficult to read. Accordingly, in order to improve the reading experience of these books, we have created "enlarged print" versions of our books. Because of font size variation in the original books, some of these may not technically qualify as "large print" books, as that term is generally defined; however, we believe these versions provide an overall improved reading experience for many.

WILLIAM OF MALMESBURY'S

CHRONICLE

OF THE

KINGS OF ENGLAND.

FROM THE EARLIEST PERIOD TO THE REIGN OF KING STEPHEN

With Notes and Illustrations.

BY J. A. GILES, D.C.L,
LATE FELLOW OF CORPUS CHRISTI COLLEGE, OXFORD.

LONDON:
HENRY G. BOHN, YORK STREET, COVENT GARDEN.
M.DCCC.XLVII.

EDITOR'S PREFACE.

"WILLIAM of MALMESBURY," according to archbishop Usher, "is the chief of our historians;" Leland records him "as an elegant, learned, and faithful historian;" and Sir Henry Saville is of opinion, that he is the only man of his time who has discharged his trust as an historian. His History of the Kings of England was translated into English by the Rev. John Sharpe, and published in quarto, in 1815.

Though the language of Mr. Sharpe's work is by no means so smooth as the dialect of the present day would require, yet the care with which he examined MSS., and endeavoured to give the exact sense of his author, seemed so important a recommendation, that the editor of the present volume has gladly availed himself of it as a ground-work for his own labours. The result of this plan is, that the public are enabled to purchase without delay and at an insignificant expense, the valuable contemporary historian, who has hitherto been like a sealed book to the public, or only accessible through a bulky volume, the scarcity of which served to exclude it from all but public libraries or the studies of the wealthy.

But the translation of Mr. Sharpe has by no means been reprinted verbatim. Within the last ten years a valuable edition of the original text, with copious collations of MSS., has been published by the English Historical Society. This edition has been compared with the translation, and numerous passages retouched and improved. Some charters, also, have been added, and a large number of additional notes appended at the foot of the pages, together with a few other improvements and additions calculated to render this interesting history more acceptable to the reading public.

J. A. G.

Bampton, June, 1847.

THE
TRANSLATOR'S PREFACE.

The author whose work is here presented to the public in an English dress, has, unfortunately, left few facts of a personal nature to be recorded of him; and even these can only be casually gleaned from his own writings. It is indeed much to be regretted that he who wrote so well on such a variety of topics, should have told so little to gratify the curiosity of his readers with respect to himself. Every notice of such an ardent lover of literature as Malmesbury, must have been interesting to posterity, as a desire to be acquainted with the history of those who have contributed to our instruction or amusement seems natural to civilized man. With the exception indeed of the incidental references made by successive chroniclers, who borrowed from his history, there is nothing to be learned of him from extrinsic sources till the time of Leland, who indignantly observes, that even at Malmesbury, in his own monastery, they had nearly lost all remembrance of their brightest ornament.

To himself then we are indebted for the knowledge of his being descended from both English and Norman parents; his father having probably come hither at the conquest. The exact time of his birth cannot be ascertained; though perhaps an approximation to it may be made. In the "Commentary on Jeremiah,"* Malmesbury observes, that he "had long since, in his youthful days, amused himself with writing history, that he was now forty years of age;" and, in another place, he mentions a circumstance which occurred "in the

* "*Olim* enim *cum historias lusi*, viridioribus annis rerumque lætitiæ congruebat rerum jocunditas. Nunc ætas progressior, et fortuna detenor, aliud dicendi genus expostulant. *Quadragenarius sum hodie*," &c. Prol. in expos. Thren. Hierem. MS. Bodl. 868.

time of king Henry;"* apparently implying that Henry was then dead. Now, admitting the expression of "long since" to denote a period of ten years, this, as his "Histories of the Kings" and "of the Prelates" were completed in the year 1125, must have been written about 1135, the time of Henry's death, and would of course place his own birth about 1095 or 1096.†

The next circumstance to be noticed is, that when a boy, he was placed in the monastery whence he derived his name, where in due time he became librarian, and, according to Leland, precentor; and ultimately refused the dignity of abbat. His death is generally supposed to have taken place about 1143; though it is probable that he survived this period some time: for his "Modern History" terminates at the end of the year 1142; and it will appear, from a manuscript hereafter to be described, that he lived at least long enough after its publication to make many corrections, alterations, and insertions, in that work as well in the other portions of his History.

With these facts, meagre as they are, the personal account of him must close. But with regard to his literary bent and attainments there is ample store of information in his writings. From his earliest youth he gave his soul to study, and to the collecting of books;‡ and he visited many of the most celebrated monasteries in the kingdom, apparently in prosecution of this darling propensity. The ardour of his curiosity, and the unceasing diligence of his researches, in this respect, have perhaps been seldom surpassed. He seems to have procured every volume within his reach; and to have carefully examined and digested its contents, whether

* "Ista autem avis (struthio) membrorum grandium, pennas quidem habens, sed volatu carens. Qualem in Anglia vidimus, *tempore regis Henrici* externorum monstrorum appetentissimi." Ch iv. v. 31.

† He has afforded another notice of time, but not equally precise. Godfrey is said to have been abbat of Malmesbury from the year 1084 till 1105; and Malmesbury mentions certain transactions which took place in Godfrey's time as beyond his memory; and others which happened when he was a boy. Anglia Sacra, II. 45—7. If Malmesbury wrote the miracles of St. Andrew, a work which is attributed to him, he was born the 30th of November.

‡ He says he also collected many books for the monastic library: and mentions others which he had seen at Canterbury, Bury St. Edmunds, &c. Gale, tom. iii. pp. 376, 298.

divinity, history, biography, poetry, or classical literature. Of his acquirements as a scholar it is indeed difficult to speak in terms of sufficient commendation. That he had accurately studied nearly all the Roman authors, will be readily allowed by the classical reader of his works. From these he either quotes or inserts so appositely, as to show how thoroughly he had imbibed their sense and spirit. His adaptations are ever ready and appropriate; they incorporate with his narrative with such exactness that they appear only to occupy their legitimate place. His knowledge of Greek is not equally apparent; at least his references to the writers of Greece are not so frequent, and even these might probably be obtained from translations: from this, however, no conclusion can be drawn that he did not understand the language. With respect to writers subsequent to those deemed classics, his range was so extensive that it is no easy matter to point out many books which he had not seen, and certainly he had perused several which we do not now possess.

Malmesbury's love of learning was constitutional: he declares in one of his prefaces, that had he turned to any other than literary pursuits, he should have deemed it not only disgraceful, but even detrimental to his better interest. Again, his commendations of Bede show how much he venerated a man of congenial inclinations and studies; and how anxious he was to form himself on the same model of accurate investigation and laborious research, and to snatch every possible interval from the performance of his monastic duties, for the purposes of information and improvement.

His industry and application were truly extraordinary. Even to the moment when we reluctantly lose sight of him, he is discovered unceasingly occupied in the correction of his works.* In the MSS. of the "History of the Kings"

---

* Some notion of his diligence may perhaps be afforded by the following list of his writings.

1. *De Gestis Regum.* The History of the Kings of England. The first three books were probably written soon after the year 1120. Malmesbury intimates that he then hesitated for a time on the expediency of continuing his history; but at length having determined on prosecuting his design, he dedicated the fourth and fifth books to Robert earl of Gloucester; at whose request he afterwards composed

2. *Historiæ Novellæ.* The Modern History. This appears to have been begun after the death of Henry I; probably not long before 1140.

may be found traces of at least four several editions; and the "History of the Prelates" supplies nearly as many varieties. And though it may reasonably be imagined that

3. *De Gestis Pontificum.* The History of the Prelates of England containing, in four books, an account of the bishops, and of the principal monasteries, from the conversion of the English, by St. Augustine, to 1123; to which he added a fifth

4. *De Vita Aldhelmi.* The Life of St. Aldhelm: which was completed in 1125. It is very reasonably conjectured that this last was published separately and some time after the others; as, though there are many ancient MSS. of the first four books, one copy only has yet been discovered with the fifth. The former were published by Saville, but from very faulty and scanty MSS. The latter by H. Wharton, and by Gale; but also very defectively.

5. *De Vita S. Dunstani.* The Life of S. Dunstan, in two books. MS. Bodley Rawlinson, 263. This was written at the request of the monks of Glastonbury, for whom he had previously composed the following three:

6. *Vita S. Patricii.* The Life of S. Patrick, in two books. Leland, Collectanea, 3, 272, has extracts from it, but no MS. has hitherto occurred.

7. *Miracula S. Benigni.* The Miracles of S. Benignus. This has not occurred.

8. *Passio S. Indracti.* The Martyrdom of S Indract. MS. Bodley Digby, 112. This he translated and abridged from the Anglo-Saxon. Abbreviated in Capgrave's Legenda Nova.

9. *De Antiquitate Glastoniensis Ecclesiæ.* The History of Glastonbury. It is addressed to Henry bishop of Winchester, and was of course written after 1129. Printed in Gale's Collection, t. 3, and by Hearne, from an interpolated MS.

10. *Vita S. Wulstani Episcopi Wigorniensis.* The Life of S. Wulstan, Bishop of Worcester. A Translation from the Anglo-Saxon, addressed to Prior Guarin, between 1124 and 1140. The greater part of it has been printed. Anglia Sacra, t. 2.

11. *Chronica.* Chronicles, in three books. See p. 480. This work is probably lost.

12 *Miracula S. Elfgifæ.* The Miracles of Elfgifa, in metre. A specimen of these rhymes, there printed as prose, may be seen in the De Gestis Pontif. f. 143: they were apparently written while he was very young, as, before 1125, he says, "*quondam cecini.*"

13. *Itinerarium Joannis Abbatis Meldunensis versus Romam.* The Itinerary of John Abbat of Malmesbury to Rome. This was drawn up, after 1140, from the relation of another monk of that foundation who accompanied the abbat. Leland, Collect. 3, 272, ed. 1774, mentions it as being very curious. It does not occur, but it was formerly in the possession of Bale.

14. *Expositio Threnorum Hieremiæ.* A Commentary on the Lamentations of Jeremiah. MS. Bodley, 868. Abridged from Paschasius Radbert, probably about 1136.

15. *De Miraculis Divæ Mariæ libri quatuor Gul. Cantoris Malmsburie.* The Miracles of the Blessed Virgin, in four books. Leland, Coll. 4. 155.

a great portion of the alterations are merely verbal, and of course imperceptible in a translation, yet they contribute in an extraordinary degree to the polish and elegance of his style.*
Another excellent feature of Malmesbury's literary character is, his love of truth. He repeatedly declares that, in the remoter periods of his work, he had observed the most guarded caution in throwing all responsibility, for the facts he mentions, on the authors from whom he derived them; and in his own times he avers, that he has recorded nothing that he had not either personally witnessed, or learned from the most credible authority. Adhering closely to this principle, he seems to have been fully impressed with the difficulty of relating the transactions of the princes, his contemporaries, and on this account he repeatedly apologizes for his omissions. But here is seen his dexterous management in maintaining an equipoise between their virtues and vices; for he spares neither William the First, nor his sons who succeeded him: indeed several of his strictures in the earlier editions of this work, are so severe, that he afterwards found it necessary to modify and soften them.

His character and attainments had early acquired a high degree of reputation among his contemporaries. He was entreated by the monks of various monasteries to write either the history of their foundations, or the lives of their patron saints. He associated with persons of the highest consequence

16. *De Serie Evangelistarum, Carmine.* The Order of the Evangelists, in verse Leland, Collect. 4 157. These two have not occurred.

17. *De Miraculis B. Andreæ.* The Miracles of S. Andrew. MS. Cotton. Nero, E 1. Abridged from a very prolix work.

18. *Abbreviatio Amalarii de Ecclesiasticis Officiis.* Amalarius on Ecclesiastical Offices, abridged. MS. Lambeth. 380.

19 *Epitome Historiæ Aimonis Floriacensis.* The History of Haimo of Flory, abridged. MS. Bodley, Selden. Arch. B. 32.

Several other works are attributed to him by Tanner, on the authority of Bale and Pits.

* These remarks on the character and style of our author must be received, as they say, *cum grano salis.* They more justly evince the zeal of Mr. Sharpe than the merits of Malmesbury's composition. The classical reader will probably lament with me that our early historians should have used a style so cumbersome and uninviting. To this general censure Malmesbury is certainly no exception. His Latinity is rude and repulsive, and the true value of his writings arises from the fidelity with which he has recorded facts, which he had either himself witnessed or had obtained from eye-witnesses.

and authority; and in one instance, at least, he took a share in the important political transactions of his own times. Robert earl of Gloucester, the natural son of Henry the First, was the acknowledged friend and patron of Malmesbury. This distinguished nobleman, who was himself a profound scholar, seems to have been the chief promoter of learning at that period. Several portions of our author's work are dedicated to him, not merely through motives of personal regard, but from the conviction that his attainments as a scholar would lead him to appreciate its value as a composition, and the part which he bore in the transactions of his day, enable him to decide on the veracity of its relation.

Having thus stated the leading features of Malmesbury's life, his avocations and attainments, it may not be irrelevant to consider the form and manner which he has adopted in the history before us. A desire to be acquainted with the transactions of their ancestors seems natural to men in every stage of society, however rude or barbarous. The northern nations, more especially, had their historical traditions, and the songs of their bards, from the remotest times. Influenced by this feeling, the Anglo-Saxons turned their attention to the composition of annals very early after their settlement in Britain; and hence originated that invaluable register the SAXON CHRONICLE,* in which facts are briefly related as they arose;—in chronological order, indeed, but without comment or observation. After the Norman conquest, among other objects of studious research in England, history attracted considerable attention, and the form, as well as the matter, of the Saxon Chronicle, became the prevailing standard. It might readily be supposed that Malmesbury's genius and attainments would with difficulty submit to the shackles of a mere chronological series, which afforded no field for the exercise of genius or judgment. Accordingly, following the bent of his inclination, he struck into a different and freer path; and to a judicious selection of facts gave the added charm of wisdom and experience. It may therefore be useful to advert to the exemplification of this principle in the scope and design of the work immediately before us. His

* This valuable work has been published, together with Bede's Ecclesiastical History, in a preceding volume of this series.

first book comprises the exploits of the Anglo-Saxons, from the period of their arrival till the consolidation of the empire under the monarchy of Egbert. Herein too is separately given the history of those powerful but rival kingdoms, which alternately subjugated, or bowed down to the dominion of, each other, and deluged the country with blood, as the love of conquest or the lust of ambition prompted. The second portion of the work continues the regal series till the mighty revolution of the Norman conquest. The three remaining books are occupied with the reigns of William and his sons, including a very interesting account of the first Crusade. His Modern History carries the narrative into the turbulent reign of Stephen.

Such is the period embraced: and to show these times, " their form and pressure," Malmesbury collected every thing within his reach. His materials, as he often feelingly laments, were scanty and confined, more especially in the earlier annals. The Chronicles of that era afforded him but little, yet of that little he has made the most, through the diligence of his research and the soundness of his judgment. His discrimination in selecting, and his skill in arranging, are equally conspicuous. His inexhaustible patience, his learning, his desire to perpetuate every thing interesting or useful, are at all times evident. Sensibly alive to the deficiencies of the historians who preceded him, he constantly endeavours to give a clear and connected relation of every event. Indeed, nothing escaped his observation which could tend to elucidate the manners of the times in which he wrote. History was the darling pursuit of Malmesbury, and more especially biographical history, as being, perhaps, the most pleasing mode of conveying information. He knew the prevailing passion of mankind for anecdote, and was a skilful master in blending amusement with instruction. Few historians ever possessed such power of keeping alive the reader's attention; few so ably managed their materials, or scattered so many flowers by the way. Of his apt delineation of character, and happy mode of seizing the most prominent features of his personages, it is difficult to speak in terms of adequate commendation. He does not weary with a tedious detail, " line upon line," nor does he complete his portrait at a sitting. On the contrary, the traits are scattered, the proportions disunited, the body dismembered, as it were; but in a moment some master-stroke is applied, some vivid flash of Promethean fire animates the canvass, and the perfect figure darts into life and expression: hence we have the surly, ferocious snarl of the Conqueror, and the brutal horse-laugh of Rufus. Malmesbury's history, indeed, may be called a kind of biographical drama; where, by a skilful gradation of character and variety of personage, the story is presented entire, though the tediousness of continued narrative is avoided. Again, by saying little on uninteresting topics, and dilating on such as are important, the tale, which might else disgust from the supineness or degeneracy of some principal actor, is artfully relieved by the force of contrast: and the mind, which perhaps recoils with indignation from the stupid indifference of an Ethelred, hangs, with fond delight, on the enterprising spirit and exertion of an Ironside.

It may be superfluous, perhaps, after enumerating qualities of this varied kind, in an author, who gives a connected history of England for several centuries, to observe, that readers of every description must derive instruction and delight from his labours. Historians, antiquaries, or philosophers, may drink deeply of the stream which pervades his work, and find their thirst for information gratified. The diligent investigator of the earlier annals of his own country, finds a period of seven hundred years submitted to his inspection, and this not merely in a dry detail of events, but in a series of authentic historical facts, determined with acuteness, commented on with deliberation, and relieved by pleasing anecdote or interesting episode. When the narrative flags at home, the attention is roused by events transacting abroad, while foreign is so blended with domestic history, that the book is never closed in disgust. The antiquary here finds ample field for amusement and instruction in the various notices of arts, manners, and customs, which occur. The philosopher traces the gradual progress of man towards civilization; watches his mental improvement, his advance from barbarism to comparative refinement; and not of man alone, but of government, laws, and arts, as well as of all those attainments which serve to exalt and embellish human nature. These are topics carefully, though perhaps only incidentally, brought forward; but they are points essentially requisite in every legitimate historian. Here, however, it must be admitted, that in the volume before us, a considerable portion of the marvellous prevails; and though, perhaps, by many readers, these will be considered as among the most curious parts of the work, yet it may be objected, that the numerous miraculous tales detract, in some measure, from that soundness of judgment which has been ascribed to our author. But it should be carefully recollected, that it became necessary to conform, in some degree, to the general taste of the readers of those days, the bulk of whom derived their principal amusement from the lives of saints, and from their miracles, in which they piously believed: besides, no one ever thought of impeaching the judgment of Livy, or of any other historian of credit, for insertions of a similar nature. Even in these relations, however, Malmesbury is careful that his own veracity shall not be impeached; constantly observing, that the truth of the story must rest on the credit of his authors; and, indeed, they are always so completely separable from the main narrative, that there is no danger of mistaking the legend for history.

Having thus noticed the multifarious topics embraced by Malmesbury, it may be necessary to advert to his style: although, after what has been premised, it might seem almost superfluous to add, that it admits nearly of as much variety as his facts. This probably arises from that undeviating principle which he appears to have laid down, that his chief efforts should be exerted to give pleasure to his readers; in imitation of the rhetoricians, whose first object was to make their audience kindly disposed, next attentive, and finally anxious to receive instruction.* Of his style, therefore, generally speaking, it may not be easy to give a perfect description. To say to which Roman author it bears the nearest resemblance, when he imitated almost every one of them, from Sallust to Eutropius, would be rash indeed. How shall we bind this classical Proteus, who occasionally assumes the semblance of Persius, Juvenal, Horace, Lucan, Virgil, Lucretius; and who never appears in his proper shape so long as he can seize the form of an ancient classic?†

* See his prologue to the Life of Wulstan, Anglia Sacra, ii. 243.
† Some of these allusions are occasionally marked in the notes

Often does he declare that he purposely varies his diction, lest the reader should be disgusted by its sameness; anxiously careful to avoid repetition, even in the structure of his phrases. It may be said, however, that generally, in his earlier works, (for he was apparently very young when he wrote his History of the Kings,) his style is rather laboured; though, perhaps, even this may have originated in an anxiety that his descriptions should be full, or, to use his own expression, that posterity should be wholly and perfectly informed. That his diction is highly antithetical, and his sentences artfully poised, will be readily allowed; and perhaps the best index to his meaning, where he may be occasionally obscure, is the nicely-adjusted balance of his phrase. That he gradually improved his style, and in riper years, where he describes the transactions of his own times, became terse, elegant, and polished, no one will attempt to dispute; and it will be regretted, that this interesting portion of history should break off abruptly in the midst of the contest between the empress Maud and Stephen.

In this recapitulation perhaps enough has been said to make an attempt at translating such an author regarded with kindness and complacency. To prevent a work of such acknowledged interest and fidelity from remaining longer a sealed book to the English reader, may well justify an undertaking of this kind; and it should be remarked that a translation of Malmesbury may serve to diffuse a very different idea of the state of manners and learning in his days from that which has been too commonly entertained; and at the same time to rescue a set of very deserving men from the unjust obloquy with which they have been pursued for ages. For without the least design of vindicating the institutions of monachism or overlooking the abuses incident to it, we may assert that, in Malmesbury's time, religious houses were the grand depositaries of knowledge, and monks the best informed men of the age.

It remains briefly to speak of the mode in which the translation has been conducted. The printed text of Malmesbury*

---

* A considerable portion of the present work was printed anonymously as a continuation of Bede, at Heidelberg, in 1587. The whole, together with the History of the Prelates, was first printed by Sir Henry Savillᵉ, who appears to have consulted several copies in the "Scriptores post

was found so frequently faulty and corrupted that, on a careful perusal, it was deemed necessary to seek for authentic manuscripts. These were supplied by that noble institution, the British Museum; but one more especially, which, on an exact comparison with others, was found to possess indisputable proofs of the author's latest corrections. This, Bib. Reg. 13, D. II, has been collated throughout with the printed copy; the result has produced numerous important corrections, alterations, and insertions, which are constantly referred to in the notes. In addition to this, various other MSS. have been repeatedly consulted, so that it is presumed the text, from which the translation has been made, is, by these means, completely established.

As the plan pursued by Malmesbury did not often require him to affix dates to the several transactions, it has been deemed necessary to remedy this omission. The chronology here supplied has been constructed on a careful examination and comparison of the Saxon Chronicle and Florence of Worcester, which are considered the best authorities; although even these occasionally leave considerable doubt as to the precise time of certain events. The remoteness of the period described by Malmesbury makes notes also in some measure indispensable. These are derived as frequently as possible from contemporary authors. Their object is briefly to amend, to explain, and to illustrate. By some perhaps they may be thought too limited; by others they may occasionally be considered unnecessary; but they are such as were deemed likely to be acceptable to readers in general.

With these explanations the translator takes leave of the reader, and is induced to hope that the present work will not be deemed an unimportant accession to the stock of English literature.

Bedam," London, 1596, fol. This was reprinted, but with many additional errors, at Frankfort, 1601, fol. Saville's division into chapters, in the second book more especially, has no authority; but as it appeared sufficiently convenient, it has been adopted. the division of the sections is nearly the same throughout all the MSS.

THE AUTHOR'S EPISTLE

TO

ROBERT, EARL OF GLOUCESTER,*

SON OF KING HENRY.

To my respected Lord, the renowned Earl Robert, son of the King, health, and, as far as he is able, his prayers, from William, Monk of Malmesbury.

THE virtue of celebrated men holds forth as its greatest excellence, its tendency to excite the love of persons even far removed from it: hence the lower classes make the virtues of their superiors their own, by venerating those great actions, to the practice of which they cannot themselves aspire. Moreover, it redounds altogether to the glory of exalted characters, both that they do good, and that they gain the affection of their inferiors. To you, Princes, therefore, it is owing, that we act well; to you, indeed, that we compose anything worthy of remembrance; your exertions incite us to make you live for ever in our writings, in return for the dangers you undergo to secure our tranquillity. For this reason, I have deemed it proper to dedicate the History of the Kings of England, which I have lately published, more especially to you, my respected and truly amiable Lord.

* Robert, Earl of Gloucester, the Mecænas of his age, was a natural son of Henry I., and a man of great talents and of unshaken fidelity. He married Mabil, daughter of Robert Fitzhamon, by whom he had a numerous issue. He died October 31, A.D. 1147.

None, surely, can be a more suitable patron of the liberal arts than yourself, in whom are combined the magnanimity of your grandfather, the munificence of your uncle, the circumspection of your father ; more especially as you add to the qualities of these men, whom you alike equal in industry and resemble in person, this peculiar characteristic, a devotion to learning. Nor is this all : you condescend to honour with your notice those literary characters who are kept in obscurity, either by the malevolence of fame, or the slenderness of their fortune. And as our nature inclines us, not to condemn in others what we approve in ourselves, therefore men of learning find in you manners congenial to their own ; for, without the slightest indication of moroseness, you regard them with kindness, admit them with complacency, and dismiss them with regret. Indeed, the greatness of your fortune has made no difference in you, except that your beneficence can now almost keep pace with your inclination.

Accept, then, most illustrious Sir, a work in which you may contemplate yourself as in a glass, where your Highness's sagacity will discover that you have imitated the actions of the most exalted characters, even before you could have heard their names. The Preface to the first book declares the contents of this work ; on deigning to peruse which, you will briefly collect the whole subject-matter. Thus much I must request from your Excellency, that no blame may attach to me because my narrative often wanders wide from the limits of our own country, since I design this as a compendium of many histories, although, with a view to the larger portion of it, I have entitled it a History of the Kings of England.

PREFACE.

THE history of the English, from their arrival in Britain to his own times, has been written by Bede, a man of singular learning and modesty, in a clear and captivating style. After him you will not, in my opinion, easily find any person who has attempted to compose in Latin the history of this people. Let others declare whether their researches in this respect have been, or are likely to be, more fortunate; my own labour, though diligent in the extreme, has, down to this period, been without its reward. There, are, indeed, some notices of antiquity, written in the vernacular tongue after the manner of a chronicle,* and arranged according to the years of our Lord. By means of these alone, the times succeeding this man have been rescued from oblivion: for of Elward,† a noble and illustrious man, who attempted to arrange these chronicles in Latin, and whose intention I could applaud if his language did not disgust me, it is better to be silent. Nor has it escaped my knowledge, that there is also a work of my Lord Eadmer,‡ written with a chastened elegance of style, in which, beginning from King Edgar, he has but hastily glanced at the times down to William the First: and thence, taking a freer range, gives a narrative, copious, and of great utility to the studious, until the death of Archbishop Ralph.§ Thus from the time of Bede there is a period of two hundred and twenty-three years left unnoticed in his history; so that the regular series of time, unsupported by a connected relation, halts in the middle. This circumstance has induced me, as well out of love to my

* This alludes to those invaluable records, the Saxon Chronicles. These, as originally compiled, have been already published in the present Series of Monkish Historians.

† Elward, or Ethelwerd, was a noble Saxon, great-great-grandson of King Ethelred, brother of Alfred. He abridged and translated the Saxon Chronicle into Latin, published in the present Series. He lived apparently in the time of Edgar, towards the close of the tenth century.

‡ Eadmer, a monk and precentor of Christ-Church, Canterbury, and pupil of Archbishop Anselm, together with a variety of other works, wrote "Historia Novorum," or, a history of modern times, from A.D. 1066 to 1122.

§ MS. Anselmi. Eadmer at first brought down his history to the death of Archbishop Anselm only, A.D. 1109, but afterwards continued it to the decease of Ralph, A.D. 1122.

country, as respect for the authority of those who have enjoined on me the undertaking, to fill up the chasm, and to season the crude materials with Roman art. And that the work may proceed with greater regularity, I shall cull somewhat from Bede, whom I must often quote, glancing at a few facts, but omitting more.

The First Book, therefore, contains a succinct account of the English, from the time of their descent on Britain, till that of King Egbert, who, after the different Princes had fallen by various ways, gained the monarchy of almost the whole island.

But as among the English arose four powerful kingdoms, that is to say, of Kent, of the West Saxons, of the Northumbrians, and of the Mercians, of which I purpose severally to treat if I have leisure ; I shall begin with that which attained the earliest to maturity, and was also the first to decay. This I shall do more clearly, if I place the kingdoms of the East Angles, and of the East Saxons, after the others, as little meriting either my labours, or the regard of posterity.

The Second Book will contain the chronological series of the Kings to the coming of the Normans.

The three following Books will be employed upon the history of three successive kings, with the addition of whatever, in their times, happened elsewhere, which, from its celebrity, may demand a more particular notice. This, then, is what I purpose, if the Divine favour shall smile on my undertaking, and carry me safely by those rocks of rugged diction, on which Elward, in his search after sounding and far-fetched phrases, so unhappily suffered shipwreck. " Should any one, however," to use the poet's expression,* " peruse this work with sensible delight," I deem it necessary to acquaint him, that I vouch nothing for the truth of long past transactions, but the consonance of the time ; the veracity of the relation must rest with its authors. Whatever I have recorded of later times, I have either myself seen, or heard from credible authority However, in either part, I pay but little respect to the judgment of my contemporaries . trusting that I shall gain with posterity, when love and hatred shall be no more, if not a reputation for eloquence, at least credit for diligence.

* Virgili Ecl. VI. v. 10.

THE HISTORY

OF THE

KINGS OF ENGLAND.

BOOK I.

CHAPTER I.

Of the arrival of the Angles, and of the Kings of Kent. [A.D. 449.]

IN the year of the incarnation of our Lord 449, Angles and Saxons first came into Britain; and although the cause of their arrival is universally known, it may not be improper here to subjoin it: and, that the design of my work may be the more manifest, to begin even from an earlier period. That Britain, compelled by Julius Cæsar to submit to the Roman power, was held in high estimation by that people, may be collected from their history, and be seen also in the ruins of their ancient buildings. Even their emperors, sovereigns of almost all the world, eagerly embraced opportunities of sailing hither, and of spending their days here. Finally, Severus and Constantius, two of their greatest princes, died upon the island, and were there interred with the utmost pomp. The former, to defend this province from the incursions of the barbarians, built his celebrated and well-known wall from sea to sea. The latter, a man, as they report, of courteous manners, left Constantine, his son by Helena, a tender of cattle,* a youth of great promise, his

* Helena's origin has been much contested Gibbon decides that she was daughter of an innkeeper. The word "Stabularia," literally implies an ostler-wench; and it has been conjectured that it was applied to her, by the Jews and Gentiles, on account of her building a church on the spot where stood the stable in which our Lord was born

heir. Constantine, greeted emperor by the army, led away, in an expedition destined to the continent, a numerous force of British soldiers; by whose exertions, the war succeeding to his wishes, he gained in a short time the summit of power. For these veterans, when their toil was over, he founded a colony on the western coast of Gaul, where, to this day, their descendants, somewhat degenerate in language and manners from our own Britons, remain with wonderful increase.*

In succeeding times, in this island, Maximus, a man well-fitted for command, had he not aspired to power in defiance of his oath, assumed the purple, as though compelled by the army, and preparing immediately to pass over into Gaul, he despoiled the province of almost all its military force. Not long after also, one Constantine, who had been elected emperor on account of his name, drained its whole remaining warlike strength; but both being slain, the one by Theodosius, the other by Honorius, they became examples of the instability of human greatness. Of the forces which had followed them, part shared the fate of their leaders; the rest, after their defeat, fled to the continental Britons. Thus when the tyrants had left none but half-savages in the country, and, in the towns, those only who were given up to luxury, Britain, despoiled of the support of its youthful† population, and bereft of every useful art, was for a long time exposed to the ambition of neighbouring nations.

For immediately, by an excursion of the Scots and Picts, numbers of the people were slain, villages burnt,‡ towns destroyed, and everything laid waste by fire and sword. Part of the harassed islanders, who thought anything more advisable than contending in battle, fled for safety to the mountains; others, burying their treasures in the earth, many of which are dug up in our own times, proceeded to Rome to ask assistance. The Romans, touched with pity, and deeming it above all things important to yield succour to their oppressed allies, twice lent their aid, and defeated the enemy. But at length, wearied with the distant voyage, they declined returning in future; bidding them rather themselves not

---

* Various periods have been assigned for the British settlement in Armorica, or Bretagne; but the subject is still involved in great obscurity.

† Some MSS. read *juvenilis*, others *militaris*.

‡ Some MSS. read *succensæ*.

REIGN OF VORTIGERN.

degenerate from the martial energy of their ancestors, but learn to defend their country with spirit, and with arms. They accompanied their advice with the plan of a wall, to be built for their defence; the mode of keeping watch on the ramparts; of sallying out against the enemy, should it be necessary, together with other duties of military discipline. After giving these admonitions, they departed, accompanied by the tears of the miserable inhabitants; and Fortune, smiling on their departure, restored them to their friends and country. The Scots, learning the improbability of their return, immediately began to make fresh and more frequent irruptions against the Britons; to level their wall, to kill the few opponents they met with, and to carry off considerable booty; while such as escaped fled to the royal residence, imploring the protection of their sovereign.

At this time Vortigern was King of Britain; a man calculated neither for the field nor the council, but wholly given up to the lusts of the flesh, the slave of every vice: a character of insatiable avarice, ungovernable pride, and polluted by his lusts. To complete the picture, as we read in the History of the Britons, he had defiled his own daughter, who was lured to the participation of such a crime by the hope of sharing his kingdom, and she had borne him a son. Regardless of his treasures at this dreadful juncture, and wasting the resources of the kingdom in riotous living, he was awake only to the blandishments of abandoned women. Roused at length, however, by the clamours of the people, he summoned a council, to take the sense of his nobility on the state of public affairs. To be brief, it was unanimously resolved to invite over from Germany the Angles and Saxons, nations powerful in arms, but of a roving life. It was conceived that this would be a double advantage: for it was thought that, by their skill in war, these people would easily subdue their enemies; and, as they hitherto had no certain habitation, would gladly accept even an unproductive soil, provided it afforded them a stationary residence. Moreover, that they could not be suspected of ever entertaining a design against the country, since the remembrance of this kindness would soften their native ferocity. This counsel was adopted, and ambassadors, men of rank, and worthy to represent the country, were sent into Germany.

The Germans, hearing that voluntarily offered, which they had long anxiously desired, readily obeyed the invitation; their joy quickening their haste. Bidding adieu, therefore, to their native fields and the ties of kindred, they spread their sails to Fortune, and, with a favouring breeze, arrived in Britain in three of those long vessels which they call " ceols "* At this and other times came over a mixed multitude from three of the German nations ; that is to say, the Angles, Saxons, and Jutes. For almost all the country lying to the north of the British ocean, though divided into many provinces, is justly denominated Germany, from its germinating so many men. And as the pruner cuts off the more luxuriant branches of the tree to impart a livelier vigour to the remainder, so the inhabitants of this country assist their common parent by the expulsion of a part of their members, lest she should perish by giving sustenance to too numerous an offspring; but in order to obviate discontent, they cast lots who shall be compelled to migrate. Hence the men of this country have made a virtue of necessity, and, when driven from their native soil, they have gained foreign settlements by force of arms. The Vandals, for instance, who formerly over-ran Africa ; the Goths, who made themselves masters of Spain; the Lombards, who, even at the present time, are settled in Italy ; and the Normans, who have given their own name to that part of Gaul which they subdued. From Germany, then, there first came into Britain, an inconsiderable number indeed, but well able to make up for their paucity by their courage. These were under the conduct of Hengist and Horsa, two brothers of suitable disposition, and of noble race in their own country. They were great-grandsons of the celebrated Woden, from whom almost all the royal families of these barbarous nations deduce their origin ; and to whom the nations of the Angles, fondly deifying him, have consecrated by immemorial superstition the fourth day of the week, as they have the sixth to his wife Frea. Bede has related in what particular parts of

* These are supposed to be long vessels, somewhat like galleys, and it would appear, as well from Brompton, col. 897, as from so small a number containing a body equal to a military enterprise like that described here and in other places, that they were of considerable burden.

Britain, the Angles, Saxons, and Jutes,* fixed their habitations: my design, however, is not to dilate, though there may be abundance of materials for the purpose, but to touch only on what is necessary.

The Angles were eagerly met on all sides upon their arrival: from the king they received thanks, from the people expressions of good-will. Faith was plighted on either side, and the Isle of Thanet appropriated for their residence. It was agreed, moreover, that they should exert their prowess in arms for the service of the country; and, in return, receive a suitable reward from the people for whose safety they underwent such painful labours. Ere long, the Scots advanced, as usual, secure, as they supposed, of a great booty with very little difficulty. However, the Angles assailed them, and scarcely had they engaged, before they were put to flight, whilst the cavalry pursued and destroyed the fugitives. Contests of this kind were frequent, and victory constantly siding with the Angles, as is customary in human affairs, while success inflamed the courage of one party, and dread increased the cowardice of the other, the Scots in the end avoided nothing so cautiously as an engagement with them.

In the meantime, Hengist, not less keen in perception than ardent in the field, with consent of Vortigern, sends back some of his followers to his own country, with the secret purpose, however, of representing the indolence of the king and people, the opulence of the island, and the prospect of advantage to new adventurers. Having executed their commission adroitly, in a short time they return with sixteen ships, bringing with them the daughter of Hengist; a maiden, as we have heard, who might justly be called the master-piece of nature and the admiration of mankind. At an entertainment, provided for them on their return, Hengist commanded his daughter to assume the office of cupbearer, that she might gratify the eyes of the king as he sat at table. Nor was the design unsuccessful: for he, ever eager after female beauty, deeply smitten with the graceful-

---

* Bede i. 15. The people of Kent and of the Isle of Wight were Jutes; the East, South, and West Saxons, were Saxons; and of the Angles came the East-Angles, Mid-Angles, Mercians, and Northumbrians. For the limits of the several kingdoms of the Heptarchy, see Chap. VI. The Cottonian MS (Claud. ix.) reads, *Wichtis*.

ness of her form and the elegance of her motion, instantly conceived a vehement desire for the possession of her person, and immediately proposed marriage to her father; urging him to a measure to which he was already well inclined. Hengist, at first, kept up the artifice by a refusal; stating, that so humble a connection was unworthy of a king: but, at last, appearing to consent with reluctance, he gave way to his importunities, and accepted, as a reward, the whole of Kent, where all justice had long since declined under the administration of its Gourong (or Viceroy), who, like the other princes of the island, was subject to the monarchy of Vortigern. Not satisfied with this liberality, but abusing the imprudence of the king, the barbarian persuaded him to send for his son and brother, men of warlike talents, from Germany, pretending, that he would defend the province on the east, while they might curb the Scots on the northern frontier. The king assenting, they sailed round Britain, and arriving at the Orkney Isles, the inhabitants of which they involved in the same calamity with the Picts and Scots, at this and after times, they finally settled in the northern part of the island, now called Northumbria. Still no one there assumed the royal title or insignia till the time of Ida, from whom sprang the regal line of the Northumbrians; but of this hereafter. We will now return to the present subject.

Vortimer, the son of Vortigern, thinking it unnecessary longer to dissemble that he saw himself and his Britons circumvented by the craft of the Angles, turned his thoughts to their expulsion, and stimulated his father to the same attempt. At his suggestion, the truce was broken seven years after their arrival; and during the ensuing twenty, they frequently fought partial battles,* and, as the chronicle relates, four general actions. From the first conflict they parted on equal terms: one party lamenting the loss of Horsa, the brother of Hengist; the other, that of Katigis, another of Vortigern's sons. The Angles, having the advantage in all the succeeding encounters, peace was concluded; Vortimer, who had been the instigator of the war,

* At Aylesford, A.D. 455; at Crayford, 457, at Wippedsfleet (supposed, but very doubtful, Ebbsfleet, in Thanet), 465; and the fourth, A.D. 473, the place not mentioned. See Saxon Chronicle, A.D. 465.

and differed far from the indolence of his father, perished prematurely, or he would have governed the kingdom in a noble manner, had God permitted. When he died, the British strength decayed, and all hope fled from them ; and they would soon have perished altogether, had not Ambrosius, the sole survivor of the Romans, who became monarch after Vortigern, quelled the presumptuous barbarians by the powerful aid of warlike Arthur. It is of this Arthur that the Britons fondly tell so many fables, even to the present day ; a man worthy to be celebrated, not by idle fictions, but by authentic history. He long upheld the sinking state, and roused the broken spirit of his countrymen to war. Finally, at the siege of Mount Badon,* relying on an image of the Virgin, which he had affixed to his armour, he engaged nine hundred of the enemy, single-handed, and dispersed them with incredible slaughter. On the other side, the Angles, after various revolutions of fortune, filled up their thinned battalions with fresh supplies of their countrymen ; rushed with greater courage to the conflict, and extended themselves by degrees, as the natives retreated, over the whole island : for the counsels of God, in whose hand is every change of empire, did not oppose their career But this was effected in process of time ; for while Vortigern lived, no new attempt was made against them. About this time, Hengist, from that bad quality of the human heart, which grasps after more in proportion to what it already possesses, by a preconcerted piece of deception, invited his son-in-law, with three hundred of his followers, to an entertainment ; and when, by more than usual compotations, he had excited them to clamour, he began, purposely, to taunt them severally, with sarcastic raillery: this had the desired effect, of making them first quarrel, and then come to blows. Thus the Britons were basely murdered to a man, and breathed their last amid their cups The king himself, made captive, purchased his liberty at the price of three provinces After this, Hengist died, in the thirty-ninth year after his arrival; he

* Said to be Bannesdown, near Bath. Giraldus Cambrensis says, the image of the Virgin was fixed on the inside of Arthur's shield, that he might kiss it in battle. Bede erroneously ascribes this event to A.D 493. (Bede'. Ecclesiastical History, b. i. c. 6.)

was a man, who urging his success not less by artifice than courage, and giving free scope to his natural ferocity, preferred effecting his purpose rather by cruelty than by kindness. He left a son named Eisc,* who, more intent on defending, than enlarging, his dominions, never exceeded the paternal bounds. At the expiration of twenty-four years, he had for his successors, his son Otha, and Otha's son, Ermenric, who, in their manners, resembled him, rather than their grandfather and great grandfather. To the times of both, the Chronicles assign fifty-three years; but whether they reigned singly, or together, does not appear.

After them Ethelbert, the son of Ermenic, reigned fifty-three years according to the Chronicle; but fifty-six according to Bede. The reader must determine how this difference is to be accounted for; as I think it sufficient to have apprized him of it, I shall let the matter rest.† In the infancy of his reign, he was such an object of contempt to the neighbouring kings, that, defeated in two battles, he could scarcely defend his frontier; afterwards, however, when to his riper years he had added a more perfect knowledge of war, he quickly, by successive victories, subjugated every kingdom of the Angles, with the exception of the Northumbrians. And, in order to obtain foreign connections, he entered into affinity with the king of France, by marrying his daughter Bertha. And now by this connection with the Franks, the nation, hitherto savage and wedded to its own customs, began daily to divest itself of its rustic propensities and incline to gentler manners. To this was added the very exemplary life of bishop Luidhard, who had come over with the queen, by which, though silently, he allured the king to the knowledge of Christ our Lord. Hence it arose, that his mind, already softened, easily yielded to the preaching of the blessed Augustine; and he was the first of all his race who renounced the errors of paganism, that he might obscure, by the glory of his faith,

* According to Sprott, Hengist died in 488, and was succeeded by his son Octa, vel Osca. Osca died A.D. 408, and Esc, his son, ascended the throne. In the year 522 Ermenric, the father of king Ethelbert, reigned. Ethelbert became king of Kent in 558.

† The difference seems to have arisen from carelessness in the scribe; as the Saxon Chronicle states him to have ascended the throne A.D. 560, and to have died 616 which is exactly fifty-six years, although it asserts him to have reigned only 53.

those whom he surpassed in power. This, indeed, is spotless nobility; this, exalted virtue; to excel in worth those whom you exceed in rank. Besides, extending his care to posterity, he enacted laws, in his native tongue, in which he appointed rewards for the meritorious, and opposed severer restraints to the abandoned, leaving nothing doubtful for the future.*

Ethelbert died in the twenty-first year after he had embraced the Christian faith, leaving the diadem to his son Edbald. As soon as he was freed from the restraints of paternal awe, he rejected Christianity, and overcame the virtue of his stepmother.† But the severity of the divine mercy opposed a barrier to his utter destruction: for the princes, whom his father had subjugated, immediately rebelled, he lost a part of his dominions, and was perpetually haunted by an evil spirit, whereby he paid the penalty of his unbelief. Laurentius, the successor of Augustine, was offended at these transactions, and after having sent away his companions, was meditating his own departure from the country, but having received chastisement from God, he was induced to change his resolution ‡ The king conversing with him on the subject, and finding his assertions confirmed by his stripes, became easily converted, accepted the grace of Christianity, and broke off his incestuous intercourse. But, that posterity might be impressed with the singular punishment due to apostacy, it was with difficulty he could maintain his hereditary dominions, much less rival the eminence of his father. For the remainder of his life, his faith was sound, and he did nothing to sully his reputation. The monastery also, which his father had founded without the walls of Canterbury,§ he ennobled with large estates, and sumptuous presents. The praises and merits of both these men ought ever to be proclaimed, and had in honour by the English; because they allowed the Christian faith to acquire

* See Wilkins's "Leges Anglo-Saxonicæ," and the Textus Roffensis.

† The name of the second queen of Ethelbert is not mentioned, probably on account of this incest.

‡ St. Peter, it is said, appeared to Laurentius at night, and reproaching him for his cowardice, severely chastised him with a scourge, the marks of which had the effect here mentioned the next day. Bede ii 6 According to Sprott, St. Laurentius became archbishop of Canterbury, A.D. 610

§ St. Augustine's, Canterbury, completed, according to Sprott, A D. 663.

strength, in England, by patient listening and willingness to believe. Who can contemplate, without satisfaction, the just and amiable answer which Bede makes king Ethelbert to have given to the first preaching of Augustine? "That he could not, thus early, embrace a new doctrine and leave the accustomed worship of his country; but that, nevertheless, persons who had undertaken so long a journey for the purpose of kindly communicating to the Angles what they deemed an inestimable benefit, far from meeting with ill-treatment, ought rather to be allowed full liberty to preach, and also to receive the amplest maintenance." He fully kept his promise; and at length the truth of Christianity becoming apparent by degrees, himself and all his subjects were admitted into the number of the faithful. And what did the other? Though led away at first, more by the lusts of the flesh than perverseness of heart, yet he paid respect to the virtuous conduct of the prelates, although he neglected their faith; and lastly, as I have related, was easily converted through the sufferings of Laurentius, and became of infinite service to the propagation of Christianity. Both, then, were laudable: both deserved high encomiums; for the good work, so nobly begun by the one, was as kindly fostered by the other.

To him, after a reign of twenty-four years, succeeded Erconbert, his son, by Emma, daughter of the king of France. He reigned an equal number of years with his father, but under happier auspices; alike remarkable for piety towards God, and love to his country. For his grandfather, and father, indeed, adopted our faith, but neglected to destroy their idols; whilst he, thinking it derogatory to his royal zeal not to take the readiest mode of annihilating openly what they only secretly condemned, levelled every temple of their gods to the ground, that not a trace of their paganism might be handed down to posterity. This was nobly done: for the mass of the people would be reminded of their superstition, so long as they could see the altars of their deities. In order, also, that he might teach his subjects, who were too much given to sensual indulgence, to accustom themselves to temperance, he enjoined the solemn fast of Lent to be observed throughout his dominions. This was an extraordinary act for the king to attempt in those times:

but he was a man whom no blandishments of luxury could enervate; no anxiety for power seduce from the worship of God. Wherefore he was protected by the favour of the Almighty; every thing, at home and abroad, succeeded to his wishes, and he grew old in uninterrupted tranquillity. His daughter Ercongotha, a child worthy of such a parent, and emulating her father in virtuous qualities, became a shining light in the monastery of Kalas in Gaul.*

His son Egbert, retaining his father's throne for nine years, did nothing memorable in so short a reign; unless indeed it be ascribed to the glory of this period, that Theodoret† the archbishop, and Adrian the abbat, two consummate scholars, came into England in his reign. Were not the subject already trite, I should willingly record what light they shed upon the Britons; how on one side the Greeks, and on the other the Latins, emulously contributed their knowledge to the public stock, and made this island, once the nurse of tyrants, the constant residence of philosophy: but this and every other merit of the times of Egbert is clouded by his horrid crime, of either destroying, or permitting to be destroyed, Elbert and Egelbright, his nephews.‡

To Egbert succeeded his brother Lothere, who began his reign with unpropitious omens. For he was harassed during eleven years by Edric, the son of Egbert, and engaged in many civil conflicts which terminated with various success, until he was ultimately pierced through the body with a dart, and died while they were applying remedies to the wound. Some say, that both the brothers perished by a premature death as a just return for their cruelty; because Egbert, as I have related, murdered the innocent children of his uncle; and Lothere ridiculed the notion of holding them up as martyrs: although the former had lamented the action, and had granted a part of the Isle of Thanet to the mother of his nephews, for the purpose of building a monastery.

* Chelles, near Paris.

† Theodore, archbishop of Canterbury, was a native of Tarsus in Cilicia, and a prelate of great learning; but it being apprehended by Pope Vitalian that he might rather incline to the doctrines of the Greek Church, Adrian was sent with him, as a kind of superintendent, and was appointed abbat of St. Augustine's.

‡ See book ii. chap. 13, "but this and every other," &c. Some editions omit this passage altogether.

Nor did Edric long boast the prosperous state of his government; for within two years he was despoiled both of kingdom and of life, and left his country to be torn in pieces by its enemies. Immediately Cædwalla, with his brother Mull, in other respects a good and able man, but breathing an inextinguishable hatred against the people of Kent, made vigorous attempts upon the province; supposing it must easily surrender to his views, as it had lately been in the enjoyment of long continued peace, but at that time was torn with intestine war. He found, however, the inhabitants by no means unprepared or void of courage, as he had expected. For, after many losses sustained in the towns and villages, at length they rushed with spirit to the conflict. They gained the victory in the contest, and having put Cædwalla to flight, drove his brother Mull into a little cottage, which they set on fire. Thus, wanting courage to sally out against the enemy, the fire gained uncontrolled power, and he perished in the flames. Nevertheless Cædwalla ceased not his efforts, nor retired from the province; but consoled himself for his losses by repeatedly ravaging the district; however, he left the avenging of this injury to Ina, his successor, as will be related in its place.

In this desperate state of the affairs of Kent, there was a void of about six years in the royal succession. In the seventh, Withred, the son of Egbert, having repressed the malevolence of his countrymen by his activity, and purchased peace from his enemies by money, was chosen king by the inhabitants, who entertained great and well-founded hopes of him. He was an admirable ruler at home, invincible in war, and a truly pious follower of the Christian faith, for he extended its power to the utmost. And, to complete his felicity, after a reign of thirty-three years, he died in extreme old age, which men generally reckon to be their greatest happiness, leaving his three children his heirs. These were Egbert, Ethelbert, and Alric, and they reigned twenty-three, eleven, and thirty-four years successively, without deviation from the excellent example and institutions of their father, except that Ethelbert, by the casual burning of Canterbury, and Alric, by an unsuccessful battle with the Mercians, considerably obscured the glory of their reigns. So it is that, if any thing disgraceful occurs, it is not concealed; if any thing fortunate, it is not sufficiently noticed in the Chronicles; whether it be done designedly, or whether it arise from that bad quality of the human mind, which makes gratitude for good transient; whereas the recollection of evil remains for ever. After these men the noble stock of kings began to wither, the royal blood to flow cold. Then every daring adventurer, who had acquired riches by his eloquence, or whom faction had made formidable, aspired to the kingdom, and disgraced the ensigns of royalty. Of these, Edbert otherwise called Pren, after having governed Kent two years. over-rating his power, was taken prisoner in a war with the Mercians, and loaded with chains. But being set at liberty by his enemies, though not received by his own subjects, it is uncertain by what end he perished. Cuthred, heir to the same faction and calamity, reigned, in name only, eight years. Next Baldred, a mere abortion of a king, after having for eighteen years more properly possessed, than governed the kingdom, went into exile, on his defeat by Egbert, king of the West Saxons. Thus the kingdom of Kent, which, from the year of our Lord 449, had continued 375 years, became annexed to another. And since by following the royal line of the first kingdom which arose among the Angles, I have elicited a spark, as it were, from the embers of antiquity, I shall now endeavour to throw light on the kingdom of the West Saxons, which, though after a considerable lapse of time, was the next that sprang up. While others were neglected and wasted away, this flourished with unconquerable vigour, even to the coming of the Normans; and, if I may be permitted the expression, with greedy jaws swallowed up the rest. Wherefore, after tracing this kingdom in detail down to Egbert, I shall briefly, for fear of disgusting my readers, subjoin some notices of the two remaining; this will be a suitable termination to the first book, and the second will continue the history of the West Saxons alone.

CHAP. II.

Of the kings of the West Saxons. [A.D. 495.]

THE kingdom of the West Saxons,—and one more magnificent or lasting Britain never beheld,—sprang from Cerdic, and soon increased to great importance. He was a German by nation, of the noblest race, being the tenth from Woden, and, having nurtured his ambition in domestic broils, determined to leave his native land and extend his fame by the sword. Having formed this daring resolution he communicated his design to Cenric his son, who closely followed his father's track to glory, and with his concurrence transported his forces into Britain in five ceols. This took place in the year of our Saviour's incarnation 495, and the eighth after the death of Hengist. Coming into action with the Britons the very day of his arrival, this experienced soldier soon defeated an undisciplined multitude, and compelled them to fly. By this success he obtained perfect security in future for himself, as well as peace for the inhabitants of those parts. For they never dared after that day to attack him, but voluntarily submitted to his dominion. Nevertheless he did not waste his time in indolence; but, on the contrary, extending his conquests on all sides, by the time he had been twenty-four years in the island, he had obtained the supremacy of the western part of it, called West-Saxony. He died after enjoying it sixteen years, and his whole kingdom, with the exception of the isle of Wight, descended to his son. This, by the royal munificence, became subject to his nephew, Withgar; who was as dear to his uncle by the ties of kindred, for he was his sister's son, as by his skill in war, and formed a noble principality in the island, where he was afterwards splendidly interred. Cenric moreover, who was as illustrious as his father, after twenty-six years, bequeathed the kingdom, somewhat enlarged, to his son Ceawlin.

The Chronicles extol the singular valour of this man in battle, so as to excite a degree of envious admiration; for he was the astonishment of the Angles, the detestation of the Britons, and was eventually the destruction of both. I shall briefly subjoin some extracts from them. Attacking Ethelbert king of Kent, who was a man in other respects laudable, but at that time was endeavouring from the consciousness of his family's dignity to gain the ascendency, and, on this account, making too eager incursions on the territories of his neighbour, he routed his troops and forced him to retreat. The Britons, who, in the times of his father and grandfather, had escaped destruction either by a show of submission, or by the strength of their fortifications at Gloucester, Cirencester, and Bath, he now pursued with ceaseless rancour; ejected them from their cities, and chased them into mountainous and woody districts, as at the present day. But about this time, as some unluckly throw of the dice in the table of human life perpetually disappoints mankind, his military successes were clouded by domestic calamity: his brother Cutha met an untimely death, and he had a son of the same name taken off in battle; both young men of great expectation, whose loss he frequently lamented as a severe blow to his happiness. Finally, in his latter days, himself, banished from his kingdom, presented a spectacle, pitiable even to his enemies. For he had sounded, as it were, the trumpet of his own detestation on all sides, and the Angles as well as the Britons conspiring against him, his forces were destroyed at Wodensdike;* he lost his kingdom thirty-one years after he had gained it; went into exile, and shortly after died. The floating reins of government were then directed by his nephews, the sons of Cutha, that is to say, Celric during six, Ceolwulf during fourteen years: of these the inferior with respect to age, but the more excellent in spirit, passed all his days in war, nor ever neglected, for a moment, the protection and extension of his empire.

After him, the sons of Celric, Cynegils and Cuichelm, jointly put on the ensigns of royalty; both active, both contending with each other only in mutual offices of kindness; insomuch, that to their contemporaries they were a miracle of concord very unusual amongst princes, and to posterity a proper example. It is difficult to say whether their courage or their moderation exceeded in the numberless contests in which they engaged either against the Britons, or against Penda, king of the Mercians: a man, as will be related in its place, wonderfully expert in the subtleties of war, and who, overpassing the limits of his own territory, in an attempt to add Cirencester to his possessions, being unable to withstand the power of these united kings, escaped with only a few followers. A considerable degree of guilt indeed attaches to Cuichelm, for attempting to take off, by the hands of an assassin, Edwin king of the Northumbrians, a

* Wansdike, in Wiltshire.

man of acknowledged prudence. Yet, if the heathen maxim,

Who asks if fraud or force availed the foe?*

be considered, he will be readily excused, as having done nothing uncommon, in wishing to get rid, by whatever means, of a rival encroaching on his power. For he had formerly lopped off much from the West Saxon empire, and now receiving fresh ground of offence, and his ancient enmity reviving, he inflicted heavy calamities on that people. The kings, however, escaped, and were, not long after, enlightened with the heavenly doctrine, by the means of St. Birinus the bishop, in the twenty-fifth year of their reign, and the fortieth after the coming of the blessed Augustine, the apostle of the Angles. Cynegils, veiling his princely pride, condescended to receive immediately the holy rite of baptism: Cuichelm resisted for a time, but warned, by the sickness of his body, not to endanger the salvation of his soul, he became a sharer in his brother's piety, and died the same year. Cynegils departed six years afterwards, in the thirty-first year of his reign, enjoying the happiness of a long-extended peace.

Kenwalk his son succeeded: in the beginning of his reign, to be compared only to the worst of princes; but, in the succeeding and latter periods, a rival of the best. The moment the young man became possessed of power, wantoning in regal luxury and disregarding the acts of his father, he abjured Christianity and legitimate marriage; but being attacked and defeated by Penda, king of Mercia, whose sister he had repudiated, he fled to the king of the East Angles. Here, by a sense of his own calamities and by the perseverance of his host, he was once more brought back to the Christian faith, and after three years, recovering his strength and resuming his kingdom, he exhibited to his subjects the joyful miracle of his reformation. So valiant was he, that he who formerly was unable to defend his own territories, now extended his dominion on every side; totally defeating in two actions the Britons, furious with the recollection of their ancient liberty, and in consequence perpetually meditating resistance; first, at a place called Witgcornesburg,† and then at a mountain named

* Virgil, Æn. ii. 390.   † Bradford on Avon. See Sax. Chron. A.D. 652.

Pene;* and again, avenging the injury of his father on Wulfhere, the son of Penda, he deprived him of the greatest part of his kingdom: moreover he was so religious, that, first of all his race, he built, for those times, a most beautiful church at Winchester, on which site afterwards was founded the episcopal see with still more skilful magnificence.

But since we have arrived at the times of Kenwalk, and the proper place occurs for mentioning the monastery of Glastonbury,† I shall trace from its very origin the rise and progress of that church as far as I am able to discover it from the mass of evidences. It is related in annals of good credit that Lucius, king of the Britons, sent to Pope Eleutherius, thirteenth in succession from St. Peter, to entreat, that he would dispel the darkness of Britain by the splendour of Christian instruction. This surely was the commendable deed of a magnanimous prince, eagerly to seek that faith, the mention of which had barely reached him, at a time when it was an object of persecution to almost every king and people to whom it was offered. In consequence, preachers, sent by Eleutherius, came into Britain, the effects of whose labours will remain for ever, although the rust of antiquity may have obliterated their names. By these was built the ancient church of St. Mary of Glastonbury, as faithful tradition has handed down through decaying time. Moreover there are documents of no small credit, which have been discovered in certain places to the following effect: "No other hands than those of the disciples of Christ erected the church of Glastonbury." Nor is it dissonant from probability: for if Philip, the Apostle, preached to the Gauls, as Freculphus relates in the fourth chapter of his second book, it may be believed that he also planted the word on this side of the channel also. But that I may not seem to balk the expectation of my readers by vain imaginations, leaving all doubtful matter, I shall proceed to the relation of substantial truths.

* Pen, in Somersetshire.

† Malmesbury wrote a History of Glastonbury, which is printed in Gale's Collection, vol iii. and by Hearne, in the History of Glastonbury, and from this work he extracts this account. Sharpe gives it [from " But since," &c. to " character so munificent" in page 28, line 2], in a note as a various reading of one of the MSS. The note occupies the greater part of seven pages from 25 to 31 in Sharpe's original volume.

The church of which we are speaking, from its antiquity called by the Angles, by way of distinction, "Ealde Chirche," that is, the "Old Church," of wattle-work, at first, savoured somewhat of heavenly sanctity even from its very foundation, and exhaled it over the whole country; claiming superior reverence, though the structure was mean. Hence, here arrived whole tribes of the lower orders, thronging every path; here assembled the opulent divested of their pomp; and it became the crowded residence of the religious and the literary. For, as we have heard from men of old time, here Gildas, an historian neither unlearned nor inelegant, to whom the Britons are indebted for whatever notice they obtain among other nations, captivated by the sanctity of the place, took up his abode for a series of years.* This church, then, is certainly the oldest I am acquainted with in England, and from this circumstance derives its name. In it are preserved the mortal remains of many saints, some of whom we shall notice in our progress, nor is any corner of the church destitute of the ashes of the holy. The very floor, inlaid with polished stone, and the sides of the altar, and even the altar itself above and beneath are laden with the multitude of relics. Moreover in the pavement may be remarked on every side stones designedly interlaid in triangles and squares, and figured with lead, under which if I believe some sacred enigma to be contained, I do no injustice to religion. The antiquity, and multitude of its saints, have endued the place with so much sanctity, that, at night, scarcely any one presumes to keep vigil there, or, during the day, to spit upon its floor: he who is conscious of pollution shudders throughout his whole frame: no one ever brought hawk or horses within the confines of the neighbouring cemetery, who did not depart injured either in them or in himself. Within the memory of man, all persons who, before undergoing the ordeal † of fire or water, there put up

* There is a Life of Gildas, written not long after this history, by Caradoc of Lancarvon, in which we are told, that, while he was residing at Glastonbury, a prince of that country carried off Arthur's queen and lodged her there; that Arthur immediately besieged it, but, through the mediation of the abbat, and of Gildas, consented, at length, to receive his wife again and to depart peaceably.

† The ordeal was an appeal to heaven to decide immediately on the justice of the cause. There were many modes of this whimsical trial; as

their petitions, exulted in their escape, one only excepted: if any person erected a building in its vicinity, which by its shade obstructed the light of the church, it forthwith became a ruin. And it is sufficiently evident, that, the men of that province had no oath more frequent, or more sacred, than to swear by the Old Church, fearing the swiftest vengeance on their perjury in this respect. The truth of what I have asserted, if it be dubious, will be supported by testimony in the book which I have written, on the antiquity of the said church, according to the series of years.

In the meantime it is clear, that the depository of so many saints may be deservedly styled an heavenly sanctuary upon earth. There are numbers of documents, though I abstain from mentioning them for fear of causing weariness, to prove how extremely venerable this place was held by the chief persons of the country, who there more especially chose to await the day of resurrection under the protection of the mother of God. Willingly would I declare the meaning of those pyramids, which are almost incomprehensible to all, could I but ascertain the truth. These, situated some few feet from the church, border on the cemetery of the monks. That which is the loftiest and nearest the church, is twenty-eight feet high and has five stories: this, though threatening ruin from its extreme age, possesses nevertheless some traces of antiquity, which may be clearly read though not perfectly understood. In the highest story is an image in a pontifical habit. In the next a statue of regal dignity, and the letters, Her Sexi, and Blisperh. In the third, too, are the names, Pencrest, Bantomp, Pinepegn. In the fourth, Bate, Pulfred, and Eanfled. In the fifth, which is the lowest, there is an image, and the words as follow, Logor, Peslicas, and Bregden, Spelpes, Highingendes Bearn. The other pyramid is twenty-six feet high and has four stories, in which are read, Kentwin, Hedda the bishop, and Bregored and Beorward. The meaning of these I do not hastily decide, but I shrewdly conjecture that within, in stone coffins, are contained the

by handling hot iron, plunging the arm into hot water, throwing the accused into water, &c. If, after three days, the party exhibited no mark of burning in the two former; or if he did not sink in the latter experiment, he was considered innocent. The whole was conducted with great solemnity; the ritual may be seen in Spelman, voce Ordalium.

bones of those persons whose names are inscribed without.*
At least Logor is said to imply the person from whom Logperesbeorh formerly took its name, which is now called Montacute; Bregden, from whom is derived Brentknolle and Brentmarsh; Bregored and Beorward were abbats of that place in the time of the Britons; of whom, and of others which occur, I shall henceforward speak more circumstantially. For my history will now proceed to disclose the succession of abbats, and what was bestowed on each, or on the monastery, and by what particular king.

And first, I shall briefly mention St. Patrick, from whom the series of our records dawns. While the Saxons were disturbing the peace of the Britons, and the Pelagians assaulting their faith, St. Germanus of Auxerre assisted them against both; routing the one by the chorus of Hallelujah,† and hurling down the other by the thunder of the Evangelists and Apostles. Thence returning to his own country, he summoned Patrick to become his inmate, and after a few years, sent him, at the instance of Pope Celestine, to preach to the Irish. Whence it is written in the Chronicles, " In the year of our Lord's incarnation 425, St. Patrick is ordained to Ireland by Pope Celestine." Also, " In the year 433 Ireland is converted to the faith of Christ by the preaching of St. Patrick, accompanied by many miracles." In consequence executing his appointed office with diligence, and in his latter days returning to his own country, he landed in Cornwall, from his altar,‡ which even to this time is held in high veneration by the inhabitants for its sanctity and efficacy in restoring the infirm. Proceeding to Glastonbury, and there becoming monk, and abbat, after some years he paid the debt of nature. All doubt of the truth of this

* The Saxon mode of interment appears frequently to have been under pyramids or obelisks. See Anglia Sacra, ii. 110.

† St Germanus drew up a body of his new converts in a valley surrounded on every side by mountains, and, on the approach of their enemies, ordered that on a given signal, all should shout " Hallelujah." The sudden sound, being reverberated by the surrounding mountains, struck their foes with such a panic, that they instantly fled. See Bede, Hist. Eccl. b 1 c. 20.

‡ Patrick is said to have floated over, from Ireland, on this altar, and to have landed near Padstow in Cornwall. Gough's Camden, 1 19. Malmesbury appears to have been misled by the Glastonbury historian, so as to confound St. Patrick with St. Petrock. From the latter, the town of Padstow derives its name, as is proved by Whitaker, in his Ancient Cathedral of Cornwall.

assertion is removed by the vision of a certain brother, who, after the saint's death, when it had frequently become a question, through decay of evidence, whether he really was monk and abbat there, had the fact confirmed by the following oracle. When asleep he seemed to hear some person reading, after many of his miracles, the words which follow —"this man then was adorned by the sanctity of the metropolitan pall, but afterwards was here made monk and abbat." He added, moreover, as the brother did not give implicit credit to him, that he could show what he had said inscribed in golden letters. Patrick died in the year of his age 111, of our Lord's incarnation 472, being the forty-seventh year after he was sent into Ireland. He lies on the right side of the altar in the old church: indeed the care of posterity has enshrined his body in silver. Hence the Irish have an ancient usage of frequenting the place to kiss the relics of their patron. Wherefore the report is extremely prevalent that both St. Indract and St. Briget, no mean inhabitants of Ireland, formerly came over to this spot. Whether Briget returned home or died at Glastonbury is not sufficiently ascertained, though she left here some of her ornaments; that is to say, her necklace, scrip, and implements for embroidering, which are yet shown in memory of her sanctity, and are efficacious in curing divers diseases. In the course of my narrative it will appear that St. Indract, with seven companions, was martyred near Glastonbury, and afterwards interred in the old church.*

Benignus succeeded Patrick in the government of the abbey; but for how long, remains in doubt. Who he was, and how called in the vernacular tongue, the verses of his epitaph at Ferramere express, not inaptly:

> Beneath this marble Beon's ashes lie,
> Once rev'rend abbat of this monastery:
> Saint Patrick's servant, as the Irish frame
> The legend-tale, and Beon was his name.

The wonderful works both of his former life, and since his recent translation into the greater church, proclaim the sin-

* On their return from a pilgrimage to Rome they designed visiting Glastonbury, out of respect to St. Patrick, and filled their scrips with parsley and various other seeds, which they purposed carrying to Ireland, but their staves being tipped with brass, which was mistaken for gold, they were murdered for the supposed booty.

gular grace of God which he anciently possessed, and which he still retains.

The esteem in which David, archbishop of Menevia, held this place, is too notorious to require repeating. He established the antiquity and sanctity of the church by a divine oracle; for purposing to dedicate it, he came to the spot with his seven suffragan bishops, and every thing being prepared for the due celebration of the solemnity, on the night, as he purposed, preceding it, he gave way to profound repose. When all his senses were steeped in rest, he beheld the Lord Jesus standing near, and mildly inquiring the cause of his arrival; and on his immediately disclosing it, the Lord diverted him from his purpose by saying, "That the church had been already dedicated by himself in honour of his Mother, and that the ceremony was not to be profaned by human repetition." With these words he seemed to bore the palm of his hand with his finger, adding, "That this was a sign for him not to reiterate what himself had done before. But that, since his design savoured more of piety than of temerity, his punishment should not be prolonged: and lastly, that on the following morning, when he should repeat the words of the mass, 'With him, and by him, and in him,' his health should return to him undiminished." The prelate, awakened by these terrific appearances, as at the moment he grew pale at the purulent matter, so afterwards he hailed the truth of the prediction. But that he might not appear to have done nothing, he quickly built and dedicated another church. Of this celebrated and incomparable man, I am at a loss to decide, whether he closed his life in this place, or at his own cathedral. For they affirm that he is with St. Patrick; and the Welsh, both by the frequency of their prayers to him and by various reports, without doubt confirm and establish this opinion; openly alleging that bishop Bernard sought after him more than once, notwithstanding much opposition, but was not able to find him. But let thus much suffice of St. David.

After a long lapse of time, St. Augustine, at the instance of St. Gregory, came into Britain in the year of our Lord's incarnation 596, and the tradition of our ancestors has handed down, that the companion of his labours, Paulinus, who was bishop of Rochester after being archbishop of

York, covered the church, built, as we have before observed, of wattle-work, with a casing of boards. The dexterity of this celebrated man so artfully managed, that nothing of its sanctity should be lost, though much should accrue to its beauty: and certainly the more magnificent the ornaments of churches are, the more they incline the brute mind to prayer, and bend the stubborn to supplication.

In the year of our Lord's incarnation 601, that is, the fifth after the arrival of St. Augustine, the king of Devonshire, on the petition of abbat Worgrez, granted to the old church which is there situated the land called Ineswitrin, containing five cassates.* "I, Maworn, bishop, wrote this grant. I, Worgrez, abbat of the same place, signed it."

Who this king might be, the antiquity of the instrument prevents our knowing. But that he was a Briton cannot be doubted, because he called Glastonbury, Ineswitrin, in his vernacular tongue; and that, in the British, it is so called, is well known. Moreover it is proper to remark the extreme antiquity of a church, which, even then, was called "the old church." In addition to Worgrez, Lademund and Bregored, whose very names imply British barbarism, were abbats of this place. The periods of their presiding are uncertain, but their names and dignities are indicated by a painting in the larger church, near the altar. Blessed, therefore, are the inhabitants of this place, allured to uprightness of life, by reverence for such a sanctuary. I cannot suppose that any of these, when dead, can fail of heaven, when assisted by the virtues and intercession of so many patrons. In the year of our Lord's incarnation 670, and the 29th of his reign, Kenwalk gave to Berthwald, abbat of Glastonbury, Ferramere, two hides, at the request of archbishop Theodore. The same Berthwald, against the will of the king and of the bishop of the diocese, relinquishing Glastonbury, went to govern the monastery of Reculver. In consequence, Berthwald equally renowned for piety and high birth, being nephew to Ethelred, king of the Mercians, and residing in the vicinity of Canterbury, on the demise of archbishop Theodore, succeeded to his see. This may be sufficient for me to have inserted on the antiquity of the church of Glas-

* It is understood as synonymous with hide, or as much land as one plough could till.

tonbury. Now I shall return in course to Kenwalk, who was of a character so munificent that he never refused to give any part of his patrimony to his relations; but with noble-minded generosity conferred nearly the third of his kingdom on his nephew.* These qualities of the royal mind, were stimulated by the admonitions of those holy bishops of his province, Agilbert, of whom Bede relates many commendable things in his history of the Angles, and his nephew Leutherius, who, after him, was, for seven years, bishop of the West Saxons. This circumstance I have thought proper to mention, because Bede has left no account of the duration of his episcopacy, and to disguise a fact which I learn from the Chronicles, would be against my conscience; besides, it affords an opportunity for making mention of a distinguished man, who by a mind, clear, and almost divinely inspired, advanced the monastery of Malmesbury, where I carry on my earthly warfare, to the highest pitch. This monastery was so slenderly endowed by Maildulph, a Scot, as they say, by nation, a philosopher by erudition, and a monk by profession, that its members could scarcely procure their daily subsistence; but Leutherius, after long and due deliberation, gave it to Aldhelm,† a monk of the same place, to be by him governed with the authority then possessed by bishops. Of which matter, that my relation may obviate every doubt, I shall subjoin his own words.

"I, Leutherius, by divine permission, bishop supreme of the Saxon see, am requested by the abbats who, within the jurisdiction of our diocese, preside over the conventual assemblies of monks with pastoral anxiety, to give and to grant that portion of land called Maildulfesburgh, to Aldhelm the priest, for the purpose of leading a life according to strict rule; in which place, indeed, from his earliest infancy and first initiation in the study of learning, he has been instructed in the liberal arts, and passed his days, nurtured in the bosom of the holy mother church; and on which account fraternal love appears principally to have conceived this request. Wherefore assenting to the petition of the aforesaid abbats, I willingly grant that place to him and his successors, who shall sedulously follow the laws of the holy

* Cuthred. According to the Saxon Chronicle, he bestowed on him 3000 hides of land. † Bede, in " Chronicles of the Anglo-Saxons," p. 267.

institution. Done publicly near the river Bladon;* this eighth before the kalends of September, in the year of our Lord's incarnation 672."

But when the industry of the abbat was superadded to the kindness of the bishop, then the affairs of the monastery began to flourish exceedingly; then monks assembled on all sides; there was a general concourse to Aldhelm; some admiring the sanctity of his life, others the depth of his learning. For he was a man as unsophisticated in religion as multifarious in knowledge, whose piety surpassed even his reputation; and he had so fully imbibed the liberal arts, that he was wonderful in each of them, and unrivalled in all. I greatly err, if his works written on the subject of virginity,† than which, in my opinion, nothing can be more pleasing or more splendid, are not proofs of his immortal genius: although, such is the slothfulness of our times, they may excite disgust in some persons, not duly considering how modes of expression differ according to the customs of nations. The Greeks, for instance, express themselves impliedly, the Romans clearly, the Gauls gorgeously, the Angles turgidly. And truly, as it is pleasant to dwell on the graces of our ancestors and to animate our minds by their example, I would here, most willingly, unfold what painful labours this holy man encountered for the privileges of our church, and with what miracles he signalized his life, did not my avocations lead me elsewhere; and his noble acts appear clearer even to the eye of the purblind, than they can possibly be sketched by my pencil. The innumerable miracles which now take place at his tomb, manifest to the present race the sanctity of the life he passed. He has therefore his proper praise; he has the fame acquired by his merits.‡ We proceed with the history.

* Where this river was is not known: it has been conjectured it should be Avon. Malmesbury is also said to have been originally called Bladon.

† De Laudibus Virginitatis. His "Commendation of Virginity," was first written in prose: and was printed by H. Wharton, 4to. 1693. He afterwards versified it with occasional amplifications or omissions. Some MSS give the date as 671: others 672; and others again 675. See Canisius, Antiquæ Lectiones, t. i. 713. Ed. Basnagii. The whole works of Aldhelm have been collected for the first time by the present editor, and form vol. i. of PATRES ECCLESIÆ ANGLICANÆ.

‡ Malmesbury afterwards wrote the life of Aldhelm. It ought to form

After thirty-one years, Kenwalk dying, bequeathed the administration of the government to his wife Sexburga; nor did this woman want spirit for discharging the duties of the station. She levied new forces, preserved the old in their duty; ruled her subjects with moderation, and overawed her enemies: in short, she conducted all things in such a manner, that no difference was discernible except that of her sex. But, breathing more than female spirit, she died, having scarcely reigned a year.

Escwin passed the next two years in the government; a near relation to the royal family, being grand-nephew to Cynegils, by his brother Cuthgist. At his death, either natural or violent, for I cannot exactly find which, Kentwin, the son of Cynegils, filled the vacant throne in legitimate succession. Both were men of noted experience in war; as the one routed the Mercians, the other the Britons, with dreadful slaughter: but they were to be pitied for the shortness of their career; the reign of the latter not extending beyond nine, that of the former, more than two years, as I have already related. This is on the credit of the Chronicles. However, Bede records that they did not reign successively, but divided the kingdom between them.

Next sprang forth a noble branch of the royal stock, Cædwalla, grand-nephew of Ceawlin, by his brother Cutha: a youth of unbounded promise, who allowed no opportunity of exercising his valour to escape him. He, having long since, by his active exertions, excited the animosity of the princes of his country, was, by a conspiracy, driven into exile, Yielding to this outrage, as the means of depriving the province of its warlike force, he led away all the military population with him; for, whether out of pity to his broken fortunes, or regard for his valour, the whole of the youth accompanied him into exile. Ethelwalch, king of the South Saxons, hazarding an engagement with him, felt the first effects of his fury: for he was routed with all the forces he had collected, and too late repented his rash design.* The spirits of his followers being thus elated, Cædwalla, by a sudden and unexpected return, drove the rivals of his power from

the fifth book "*de Gentis Pontificum,*" but has never yet been printed in the same volume with the four preceding books.

* See Bede, b. iv. c. 15.

the kingdom. Enjoying his government for the space of two years, he performed many signal exploits. His hatred and hostility towards the South Saxons were inextinguishable, and he totally destroyed Edric, the successor of Ethelwalch, who opposed him with renovated boldness: he nearly depopulated the Isle of Wight, which had rebelled in confederacy with the Mercians: he also gained repeated victories over the people of Kent, as I have mentioned before in their history. Finally, as is observed above, he retired from that province, on the death of his brother, compensating his loss by the blood of many of its inhabitants. It is difficult to relate, how extremely pious he was even before his baptism, insomuch that he dedicated to God the tenth of all the spoils which he had acquired in war. In which, though we approve the intention, we condemn the example; according to the saying: "He who offers sacrifice from the substance of a poor man, is like him who immolates the son in the sight of the father." That he went to Rome to be baptized by Pope Sergius, and was called Peter; and that he yielded joyfully to the will of heaven, while yet in his initiatory robes, are matters too well known to require our illustration.

After his departure to Rome, the government was assumed by Ina, grand-nephew of Cynegils by his brother Cuthbald, who ascended the throne, more from the innate activity of his spirit, than any legitimate right of succession. He was a rare example of fortitude; a mirror of prudence; unequalled in piety. Thus regulating his life, he gained favour at home and respect abroad. Safe from any apprehensions of treachery, he grew old in the discharge of his duties for fifty-eight years, the pious conciliator of general esteem. His first expedition was against the people of Kent, as the indignation at their burning Moll had not yet subsided. The inhabitants resisted awhile: but soon finding all their attempts and endeavours fail, and seeing nothing in the disposition of Ina which could lead them to suppose he would remit his exertions, they were induced, by the contemplation of their losses, to treat of a surrender. They tempt the royal mind with presents, lure him with promises, and bargain for a peace for thirty thousand marks of gold, that, softened by so high a price, he should put an end to the war, and, bound in golden chains, sound a retreat. Accepting the money, as a sufficient atonement for their offence, he returned into his kingdom. And not only the people of Kent, but the East Angles* also felt the effects of his hereditary anger; all their nobility being first expelled, and afterwards routed in battle. But let the relation of his military successes here find a termination. Moreover how sedulous he was in religious matters, the laws he enacted to reform the manners of the people, are proof sufficient,† in which the image of his purity is reflected even upon the present times. Another proof are the monasteries nobly founded at the king's expense. But‡ more especially Glastonbury, whither he ordered the bodies of the blessed martyr, Indract, and of his associates, to be taken from the place of their martyrdom and to be conveyed into the church. The body of St. Indract he deposited in the stone pyramid on the left side of the altar, where the zeal of posterity afterwards also placed St. Hilda: the others were distributed beneath the pavement as chance directed or regard might suggest. Here, too, he erected a church, dedicated to the holy apostles, as an appendage to the ancient church, of which we are speaking, enriched it with vast possessions, and granted it a privilege to the following effect:

"In the name of our Lord Jesus Christ. I, Ina, supported in my royal dignity by God, with the advice of my queen, Sexburga, and the permission of Berthwald, archbishop of Canterbury, and of all his suffragans; and also at the instance of the princes Baltred and Athelard, to the ancient church, situate in the place called Glastonbury (which church the great high-priest and chiefest minister formerly through his own ministry, and that of angels, sanctified by many and unheard-of miracles to himself and the eternal Virgin Mary. as was formerly revealed to St David,) do grant out of those

---

* The Saxon Chronicle and Florence of Worcester mention his attacks on the South Saxons, but do not notice the East Angles.

† See Wilkins's Leges Anglo-Saxonicæ.

‡ Some manuscripts omit all that follows to "Berthwald, archbishop of Canterbury," p. 35, and insert in place of it "More especially that at Glastonbury most celebrated in our days, which he erected in a low retired situation, in order that the monks might more eagerly thirst after heavenly, in proportion as they were less affected by earthly things." Sharpe inserts the shorter passage in his text, and gives the longer in a note.

places, which I possess by paternal inheritance, and hold in my demesne, they being adjacent and fitting for the purpose, for the maintenance of the monastic institution, and the use of the monks, Brente ten hides, Sowy ten hides, Pilton twenty hides, Dulting twenty hides, Bledenhida one hide, together with whatever my predecessors have contributed to the same church :* to wit, Kenwalk, who, at the instance of archbishop Theodore, gave Ferramere, Bregarai, Coueneie, Maitineseie, Etheredseie; Kentwin, who used to call Glastonbury, "the mother of saints," and liberated it from every secular and ecclesiastical service, and granted it this dignified privilege, that the brethren of that place should have the power of electing and appointing their ruler according to the rule of St. Benedict: Hedda the bishop, with permission of Cædwalla, who, though a heathen, confirmed it with his own hand, gave Lantokay: Baltred, who gave Pennard, six hides: Athelard who contributed Poelt, sixty hides, I, Ina, permitting and confirming it. To the piety and affectionate entreaty of these people I assent, and I guard by the security of my royal grant against the designs of malignant men and snarling curs, in order that the church of our Lord Jesus Christ and the eternal Virgin Mary, as it is the first in the kingdom of Britain and the source and the fountain of all religion, may obtain surpassing dignity and privilege, and, as she rules over choirs of angels in heaven, it may never pay servile obedience to men on earth. Wherefore the chief pontiff, Gregory, assenting, and taking the mother of his Lord, and me, however unworthy, together with her, into the bosom and protection of the holy Roman church; and all the princes, archbishops, bishops, dukes, and abbats of Britain consenting, I appoint and establish, that, all lands, places, and possessions of St. Mary of Glastonbury be free, quiet, and undisturbed, from all royal taxes and works, which are wont to be appointed, that is to say, expeditions, the building of bridges or forts, and from the edicts or molestations of all archbishops or bishops, as is found to be confirmed and granted by my predecessors, Kenwalk, Kentwin, Cædwalla, Baltred, in the ancient charters of the same church And whatsoever questions shall arise, whether of homicide, sacrilege, poison, theft, rapine, the dis-

---

* See Kemble's Charters, vol. i. p. 85.

posal and limits of churches, the ordination of clerks, ecclesiastical synods, and all judicial inquiries, they shall be determined by the decision of the abbat and convent, without the interference of any person whatsoever. Moreover, I command all princes, archbishops, bishops, dukes, and governors of my kingdom, as they tender my honour and regard, and all dependants, mine as well as theirs, as they value their personal safety, never to dare enter the island of our Lord Jesus Christ and of the eternal Virgin, at Glastonbury, nor the possessions of the said church, for the purpose of holding courts, making inquiry, or seizing, or doing anything whatever to the offence of the servants of God there residing . moreover I particularly inhibit, by the curse of Almighty God, of the eternal Virgin Mary, and of the holy apostles Peter and Paul, and of the rest of the saints, any bishop on any account whatever from presuming to take his episcopal seat or celebrate divine service or consecrate altars, or dedicate churches, or ordain, or do any thing whatever, either in the church of Glastonbury itself, or its dependent churches, that is to say—Sowy, Brente, Merlinch, Sapewic, Stret, Sbudeclalech, Pilton, or in their chapels, or islands, unless he be specially invited by the abbat or brethren of that place. But if he come upon such invitation, he shall take nothing to himself of the things of the church, nor of the offerings ; knowing that he has two mansions appointed him in two several places out of this church's possessions, one in Pilton, the other in the village called Poelt, that, when coming or going, he may have a place of entertainment. Nor even shall it be lawful for him to pass the night here unless he shall be detained by stress of weather or bodily sickness, or invited by the abbat or monks, and then with not more than three or four clerks. Moreover let the aforesaid bishop be mindful every year, with his clerks that are at Wells, to acknowledge his mother church of Glastonbury with litanies on the second day after our Lord's ascension ; and should he haughtily defer it, or fail in the things which are above recited and confirmed, he shall forfeit his mansions above mentioned. The abbat or monks shall direct whom they please, celebrating Easter canonically, to perform service in the church of Glastonbury, its dependent churches, and in their chapels. Whosoever, be he of what dignity, profession, or degree, he may, shall hereafter, on any occasion whatsoever, attempt to pervert, or nullify this, the witness of my munificence and liberality, let him be aware that, with the traitor Judas, he shall perish, to his eternal confusion, in the devouring flames of unspeakable torments. The charter of this donation was written in the year of our Lord's incarnation 725, the fourteenth of the indiction, in the presence of the king Ina, and of Berthwald, archbishop of Canterbury."

What splendour he [Ina] added to the monastery, may be collected from the short treatise which I have written about its antiquities.* Father Aldhelm assisted the design, and his precepts were heard with humility, nobly adopted, and joyfully carried into effect. Lastly, the king readily confirmed the privilege which Aldhelm had obtained from pope Sergius, for the immunity of his monasteries; gave much to the servants of God by his advice, and finally honoured him, though constantly refusing, with a bishopric; but an early death malignantly cut off this great man from the world. For scarcely had he discharged the offices of his bishopric four years, ere he made his soul an offering to heaven, in the year of our Lord's incarnation 709, on the vigil of St. Augustine the apostle of the Angles, namely the eighth before the Kalends of June.† Some say, that he was the nephew of the king, by his brother Kenten; but I do not choose to assert for truth any thing which savours more of vague opinion, than of historic credibility; especially as I can find no ancient record of it, and the Chronicle clearly declares, that Ina had no other brother than Ingild, who died some few years before him. Aldhelm needs no support from fiction: such great things are there concerning him of indisputable truth, so many which are beyond the reach of doubt. The sisters, indeed, of Ina were Cuthburga and Cwenburga. Cuthburga was given in marriage to Alfrid, king of the Northumbrians, but the contract being soon after dissolved, she led a life dedicated to God, first at Barking,‡ under the abbess Hildelitha, and afterwards as superior of the convent at Wimborne; now a mean village, but formerly celebrated

---

* The Antiquities of Glastonbury were published about the same time by Gale, vol. iii and by Hearne.
† The 25th of May.   ‡ Bede, Eccl. Hist. b. iv. c. 7 – 10.

for containing a full company of virgins, dead to earthly desires, and breathing only aspirations towards heaven. She embraced the profession of holy celibacy from the perusal of Aldhelm's books on virginity, dedicated indeed to the sisterhood of Barking, but profitable to all, who aspire to that state. Ina's queen was Ethelburga, a woman of royal race and disposition: who perpetually urging the necessity of bidding adieu to earthly things, at least in the close of life, and the king as constantly deferring the execution of her advice, at last endeavoured to overcome him by stratagem. For, on a certain occasion, when they had been revelling at a country seat with more than usual riot and luxury, the next day, after their departure, an attendant, with the privity of the queen, defiled the palace in every possible manner, both with the excrement of cattle and heaps of filth; and lastly he put a sow, which had recently farrowed, in the very bed where they had lain. They had hardly proceeded a mile, ere she attacked her husband with the fondest conjugal endearments, entreating that they might immediately return thither, whence they had departed, saying, that his denial would be attended with dangerous consequences. Her petition being readily granted, the king was astonished at seeing a place, which yesterday might have vied with Assyrian luxury, now filthily disgusting and desolate: and silently pondering on the sight, his eyes at length turned upon the queen. Seizing the opportunity, and pleasantly smiling, she said, "My noble spouse, where are the revellings of yesterday? Where the tapestries dipped in Sidonian dyes? Where the ceaseless impertinence of parasites? Where the sculptured vessels, overwhelming the very tables with their weight of gold? Where are the delicacies so anxiously sought throughout sea and land, to pamper the appetite? Are not all these things smoke and vapour? Have they not all passed away? Woe be to those who attach themselves to such, for they in like manner shall consume away. Are not all these like a rapid river hastening to the sea? And woe to those who are attached to them, for they shall be carried away by the current. Reflect, I entreat you, how wretchedly will these bodies decay, which we pamper with such unbounded luxury. Must not we, who gorge so constantly, become more disgustingly putrid? The mighty must undergo mightier torments, and a severer trial awaits the strong." Without saying more, by this striking example, she gained over her husband to those sentiments, which she had in vain attempted for years by persuasion.*

For after his triumphal spoils in war ; after many successive degrees in virtue, he aspired to the highest perfection, and went to Rome. There, not to make the glory of his conversion public, but that he might be acceptable in the sight of God alone, he was shorn in secret ; and, clad in homely garb, grew old in privacy. Nor did his queen, the author of this noble deed, desert him ; but as she had before incited him to undertake it, so, afterwards, she made it her constant care to soothe his sorrows by her conversation, to stimulate him, when wavering, by her example ; in short, to omit nothing that could be conducive to his salvation. Thus united in mutual affection, in due time they trod the common path of all mankind. This was attended, as we have heard, with singular miracles, such as God often deigns to bestow on the virtues of happy couples.

To the government succeeded Ethelard, the cousin of Ina ; though Oswald, a youth of royal extraction, often obscured his opening prospects. Exciting his countrymen to rebellion, he attempted to make war on the king, but soon after perishing by some unhappy doom, Ethelard kept quiet possession of the kingdom for fourteen years, and then left it to his kinsman, Cuthred, who for an equal space of time, and with similar courage, was ever actively employed :—

" In the name of our Lord Jesus Christ, I, Cuthred, king of the West Saxons, do hereby declare that all the gifts of former kings—Kentwin, Baldred, Kedwall, Ina, Ethelard, and Ethbald king of the Mercians, in country houses, and in villages and lands, and farms, and mansions, according to the confirmations made to the ancient city of Glastonbury, and confirmed by autograph and by the sign of the cross, I do, as was before said, hereby decree that this grant of former kings shall remain firm and inviolate, as long as the revolution of the pole shall carry the lands and seas with regular move-

---

* All this passage, from " What splendour, p. 35, to persuasion," is omitted in some MSS., and is given in a note by Hardy and Sharpe ; but it seems almost necessary to the context.

ment round the starry heavens. But if any one, confiding in tyrannical pride shall endeavour on any occasion to disturb and nullify this my testamentary grant, may he be separated by the fan of the last judgment from the congregation of the righteous, and joined to the assembly of the wicked for ever, paying the penalty of his violence. But whoever with benevolent intention shall strive to approve, confirm, and defend this my grant, may he be allowed to enjoy unfailing immortality before the glory of Him that sitteth on the throne, together with the happy companies of angels and of all the saints. A copy of this grant was set forth in presence of king Cuthred, in the aforesaid monastery, and dedicated to the holy altar by the munificence of his own hand, in the wooden church, where the brethren placed the coffin of abbat Hemgils, the 30th of April, in the year of our Lord 745."

The same Cuthred, after much toil, made a successful campaign against Ethelbald, king of Mercia, and the Britons, and gave up the sovereignty after he had held it fourteen years.

Sigebert then seized on the kingdom; a man of inhuman cruelty among his own subjects, and noted for cowardice abroad; but the common detestation of all conspiring against him, he was within a year driven from the throne, and gave place to one more worthy. Yet, as commonly happens in similar cases, the severity of his misfortunes brought back some persons to his cause, and the province which is called Hampshire, was, by their exertions, retained in subjection to him. Still, however, unable to quit his former habits, and exciting the enmity of all against him by the murder of one Cumbran, who had adhered to him with unshaken fidelity, he fled to the recesses of wild beasts. Misfortune still attending him thither also, he was stabbed by a swineherd. Thus the cruelty of a king, which had almost desolated the higher ranks, was put an end to by a man of the lowest condition.

Cynewolf next undertook the guidance of the state; illustrious for the regulation of his conduct and his deeds in arms: but suffering extremely from the loss of a single battle, in the the twenty-fourth year of his reign, against Offa, king of the Mercians, near Bensington, he was also finally doomed to a disgraceful death. For after he had reigned thirty-one years,* neither indolently nor oppressively, either elated with success, because he imagined nothing could oppose him, or alarmed for his posterity, from the increasing power of Kineard, the brother of Sigebert, he compelled him to quit the kingdom. Kineard, deeming it necessary to yield to the emergency of the times, departed as if voluntarily ; but soon after, when by secret meetings he had assembled a desperate band of wretches, watching when the king might be alone, for he had gone into the country for the sake of recreation, he followed him thither with his party. And learning that he was there giving loose to improper desires, he beset the house on all sides. The king struck with his perilous situation, and holding a conference with the persons present, shut fast the doors, expecting either to appease the desperadoes by fair language, or to terrify them by threats. When neither succeeded, he rushed furiously on Kineard, and had nearly killed him ; but, surrounded by the multitude, and thinking it derogatory to his courage to give way, he fell, selling his life nobly. Some few of his attendants, who, instead of yielding, attempted to take vengeance for the loss of their lord, were slain. The report of this dreadful outrage soon reached the ears of the nobles, who were waiting near at hand. Of these Esric, the chief in age and prudence, conjuring the rest not to leave unrevenged the death of their sovereign to their own signal and eternal ignominy, rushed with drawn sword upon the conspirators. At first Kineard attempted to argue his case ; to make tempting offers ; to hold forth their relationship ; but when this availed nothing, he stimulated his party to resistance. Doubtful was the conflict, where one side contended with all its powers for life, the other for glory. And victory, wavering for a long time, at last decided for the juster cause. Thus, fruitlessly valiant, this unhappy man lost his life, unable long to boast the success of his treachery. The king's body was buried at Winchester, and the prince's at Repton ; at that time a noble monastery, but at present, as I have heard, with few, or scarcely any inmates.

* Malmesbury here perpetuates the error of the transcriber of the Saxon Chronicle, in assigning thirty-one years to Cynewolf, for as he came to the throne in 756, and was killed in 784, consequently he reigned about twenty-nine years. Perhaps he wrote, correctly, " *uno de triginta annis*," conjectures Mr. Hardy.

After him, for sixteen years, reigned Bertric: more studious of peace than of war. Skilful in conciliating friendship, affable with foreigners, and giving great allowances to his subjects, in those matters at least which could not impair the strength of the government. To acquire still greater estimation with his neighbours, he married the daughter of Offa, king of Mercia, at that time all-powerful; by whom, as far as I am acquainted, he had no issue. Supported by this alliance he compelled Egbert, the sole survivor of the royal stock, and whom he feared as the most effectual obstacle to his power, to fly into France. In fact Bertric himself, and the other kings, after Ina, though glorying in the splendour of their parentage, as deriving their origin from Cerdic, had considerably deviated from the direct line of the royal race. On Egbert's expulsion, then, he had already begun to indulge in indolent security, when a piratical tribe of the Danes, accustomed to live by plunder, clandestinely arriving in three ships, disturbed the tranquillity of the kingdom. This band came over expressly to ascertain the fruitfulness of the soil, and the courage of the inhabitants, as was afterwards discovered by the arrival of that multitude, which over-ran almost the whole of Britain. Landing then, unexpectedly, when the kingdom was in a state of profound peace, they seized upon a royal village, which was nearest them, and killed the superintendent, who had advanced with succours; but losing their booty, through fear of the people, who hastened to attack them, they retired to their ships. After Bertric, who was buried at Warham, Egbert ascended the throne of his ancestors; justly to be preferred to all the kings who preceded him. Thus having brought down our narrative to his times, we must, as we have promised, next give our attention to the Northumbrians.

CHAP. III.

Of the kings of the Northumbrians. [A.D. 450.]

WE have before related briefly, and now necessarily repeat, that Hengist, having settled his own government in Kent, had sent his brother Otha, and his son Ebusa, men of activity and tried experience, to seize on the northern parts of Britain. Sedulous in executing the command, affairs succeeded to their wishes. For frequently coming into action with the inhabitants, and dispersing those who attempted resistance, they conciliated with uninterrupted quiet such as submitted. Thus, though through their own address and the good will of their followers, they had established a certain degree of power, yet never entertaining an idea of assuming the royal title, they left an example of similar moderation to their immediate posterity. For during the space of ninety-nine years, the Northumbrian leaders, contented with subordinate power, lived in subjection to the kings of Kent. Afterwards, however, this forbearance ceased ; either because the human mind is ever prone to degeneracy, or because that race of people was naturally ambitious. In the year, therefore, of our Lord's incarnation 547, the sixtieth after Hengist's death, the principality was converted into a kingdom. The most noble Ida, in the full vigour of life and of strength, first reigned there. But whether he himself seized the chief authority, or received it by the consent of others, I by no means venture to determine, because the truth is unrevealed. However, it is sufficiently evident, that, sprung from a great and ancient lineage, he reflected much splendour on his illustrious descent, by his pure and unsullied manners. Unconquerable abroad, at home he tempered his kingly power with peculiar affability. Of this man, and of others, in their respective places, I could lineally trace the descent, were it not that the very names, of uncouth sound, would be less agreeable to my readers than I wish. It may be proper though to remark, that Woden had three sons, Weldeg, Withleg, and Beldeg ; from the first, the kings of Kent derived their origin , from the second, the kings of Mercia , and from the third, the kings of the West-Saxons and Northumbrians, with the exception of the two I am going to particularize. This Ida, then, the ninth from Beldeg, and the tenth from Woden, as I find positively declared, continued in the government fourteen years.

His successor Alla, originating from the same stock, but descending from Woden by a different branch, conducted the government, extended by his exertions considerably beyond its former bounds, for thirty years. In his time, youths from Northumbria were exposed for sale, after the common and

almost native custom of this people; so that, even as our
days have witnessed, they would make no scruple of
separating the nearest ties of relationship through the
temptation of the slightest advantage. Some of these youths
then, carried from England for sale to Rome, became the
means of salvation to all their countrymen. For exciting
the attention of that city, by the beauty of their countenances
and the elegance of their features, it happened that, among
others, the blessed Gregory, at that time archdeacon of the
apostolical see, was present. Admiring such an assemblage
of grace in mortals, and, at the same time, pitying their
abject condition, as captives, he asked the standers-by, "of
what race are these? Whence come they?" They reply, "by
birth they are Angles; by country are Deiri; (Deira being
a province of Northumbria,) subjects of King Alla, and
Pagans." Their concluding characteristic he accompanied
with heartfelt sighs: to the others he elegantly alluded,
saying, "that these Angles, *angel*-like, should be delivered
from *(de) ira*, and taught to sing *Alle-luia*." Obtaining
permission without delay from pope Benedict, the industry
of this excellent man was all alive to enter on the journey to
convert them; and certainly his zeal would have completed
this intended labour, had not the mutinous love of his
fellow citizens recalled him, already on his progress. He
was a man as celebrated for his virtues, as beloved by his
countrymen; for by his matchless worth, he had even
exceeded the expectations they had formed of him from his
youth. His good intention, though frustrated at this time,
received afterwards, during his pontificate, an honourable
termination, as the reader will find in its proper place. I
have made this insertion with pleasure, that my readers
might not lose this notice of Alla, mention of whom is
slightly made in the life of Pope Gregory, who, although he
was the primary cause of introducing Christianity among
the Angles, yet, either by the counsel of God, or some
mischance, was never himself permitted to know it. The
calling, indeed, descended to his son.

On the death of Alla, Ethelric, the son of Ida, advanced
to extreme old age, after a life consumed in penury, obtained
the kingdom, and after five years, was taken off by a sudden
death. He was a pitiable prince, whom fame would have

hidden in obscurity, had not the conspicuous energy of the son lifted up the father to notice.

When, therefore, by a long old age, he had satisfied the desire of life, Ethelfrid, the elder of his sons, ascended the throne, and compensated the greenness of his years by the maturity of his conduct. His transactions have been so displayed by graceful composition, that they want no assistance of mine, except as order is concerned. Bede has eagerly dwelt on the praises of this man and his successors; and has dilated on the Northumbrians at greater length, because they were his near neighbours: our history, therefore, will select and compile from his relation. In order, however, that no one may blame me for contracting so diffuse a narrative, I must tell him that I have done it purposely, that they who have been satiated with such high-seasoned delicacies, may respire a little on these humble remnants: for it is a saying trite by use and venerable for its age, "that the meats which cloy the least are eaten with keenest appetite." Ethelfrid then, as I was relating, having obtained the kingdom, began at first vigorously to defend his own territories, afterwards eagerly to invade his neighbours, and to seek occasion for signalizing himself on all sides. Many wars were begun by him with foresight, and terminated with success; as he was neither restrained from duty by indolence, nor precipitated into rashness by courage. An evidence of these things is Degstan,* a noted place in those parts, where Edan, king of the Scots, envying Ethelfrid's successes, had constrained him, though averse, to give battle; but, being overcome, he took to flight, though the triumph was not obtained without considerable hazard to the victor. For Tedbald, the brother of Ethelfrid, opposing himself to the most imminent dangers that he might display his zeal in his brother's cause, left a mournful victory indeed, being cut off with his whole party. Another proof of his success is afforded by the city of Carlegion, now commonly called Chester, which, till that period possessed by the Britons, fostered the pride of a people hostile to the king. When he bent his exertions to subdue this city, the townsmen preferring any extremity to a siege, and at the same confiding in their numbers, rushed out in multitudes to battle. But deceived by a stratagem, they were

* Supposed Dalston near Carlis'e, or Dawston near Ichborough.

overcome and put to flight; his fury being first vented on the monks, who came out in numbers to pray for the safety of the army. That their number was incredible to these times is apparent from so many half-destroyed walls of churches in the neighbouring monastery, so many winding porticoes, such masses of ruins as can scarcely be seen elsewhere. The place is called Bangor; at that day a noted monastery, but now changed into a cathedral.* Ethelfrid, thus, while circumstances proceeded to his wishes abroad, being desirous of warding off domestic apprehensions and intestine danger, banished Edwin, the son of Alla, a youth of no mean worth, from his kingdom and country. He, wandering for a long time without any settled habitation, found many of his former friends more inclined to his enemy than to the observance of their engagements; for as it is said,

"If joy be thine, 'tis then thy friends abound:
Misfortune comes, and thou alone art found."†

At last he came to Redwald, king of the East Angles, and bewailing his misfortunes, was received into his protection. Shortly after there came messengers from Ethelfrid, either demanding the surrender of the fugitive, or denouncing hostilities. Determined by the advice of his wife not to violate, through intimidation, the laws of friendship, Redwald collected a body of troops, rushed against Ethelfrid, and attacked him suddenly, whilst suspecting nothing less than an assault. The only remedy that courage, thus taken by surprise, could suggest, there being no time to escape, he availed himself of. Wherefore, though almost totally unprepared, though beset with fearful danger on every side, he fell not till he had avenged his own death by the destruction of Regnhere, the son of Redwald. Such an end had Ethelfrid, after a reign of twenty-four years: a man second to none in martial experience, but entirely ignorant of the holy faith. He had two sons by Acca, the daughter of Alla, sister of Edwin, Oswald aged twelve, and Oswy four years; who, upon the death of their father, fled through the management of their governors, and escaped into Scotland.

* Malmesbury here confounds the ancient monastery of Banchor, near Chester, with the more modern see of Bangor in Carnarvonshire.
† Ovid. Trist. l. 9, v. 5.

In this manner, all his rivals being slain or banished, Edwin, trained by many adversities, ascended, not meanly qualified, the summit of power. When the haughtiness of the Northumbrians had bent to his dominion, his felicity was crowned by the timely death of Redwald, whose subjects, during Edwin's exile among them, having formerly experienced his ready courage and ardent disposition, now willingly swore obedience to him. Granting to the son of Redwald the empty title of king, himself managed all things as he thought fit. At this juncture, the hopes and the resources of the Angles centred totally in him; nor was there a single province of Britain which did not regard his will, and prepare to obey it, except Kent: for he had left the Kentish people free from his incursions, because he had long meditated a marriage with Ethelburga, sister of their king. When she was granted to him, after a courtship long protracted, to the intent that he should not despise that woman when possessed whom he so ardently desired when withheld, these two kingdoms became so united by the ties of kindred, that, there was no rivalry in their powers, no difference in their manners. Moreover, on this occasion, the faith of Christ our Lord, infused into those parts by the preaching of Paulinus, reached first the king himself, whom the queen, among other proofs of conjugal affection, was perpetually instructing; nor was the admonition of bishop Paulinus wanting in its place. For a long time, he was wavering and doubtful; but once received, he imbibed it altogether. Then he invited neighbouring kings to the faith; then he erected churches, and neglected nothing for its propagation. In the meanwhile, the merciful grace of God smiled on the devotion of the king; insomuch, that not only the nations of Britain, that is to say, the Angles, Scots, and Picts, but even the Orkney and Mevanian isles, which we now call Anglesey, that is, islands of the Angles, both feared his arms, and venerated his power. At that time, there was no public robber; no domestic thief; the tempter of conjugal fidelity was far distant; the plunderer of another man's inheritance was in exile: a state of things redounding to his praise, and worthy of celebration in our times. In short, such was the increase of his power, that justice and peace willingly met and kissed each other, imparting mutual acts of kindness.

And now indeed would the government of the Angles have held a prosperous course, had not an untimely death, the stepmother of all earthly felicity, by a lamentable turn of fortune, snatched this man from his country. For in the forty-eighth year of his age, and the seventeenth of his reign, being killed, together with his son, by the princes whom he had formerly subjugated, Cadwalla of the Britons and Penda of the Mercians, rising up against him, he became a melancholy example of human vicissitude. He was inferior to none in prudence: for he would not embrace even the Christian faith till he had examined it most carefully; but when once adopted, he esteemed nothing worthy to be compared to it.

Edwin thus slain, the sons of Ethelfrid, who were also the nephews of Edwin, Oswald, and Oswy, now grown up, and in the budding prime of youth, re-sought their country, together with Eanfrid, their elder brother, whom I forgot before to mention. The kingdom, therefore, was now divided into two. Indeed, Northumbria, long since separated into two provinces, had elected Alla, king of the Deirans, and Ida, of the Bernicians. Wherefore Osric, the cousin of Edwin, succeeding to Deira, and Eanfrid, the son of Ethelfrid, to Bernicia, they exulted in the recovery of their hereditary right. They had both been baptized in Scotland, though they were scarcely settled in their authority, ere they renounced their faith: but shortly after they suffered the just penalty of their apostacy through the hostility of Cadwalla. The space of a year, passed in these transactions, improved Oswald, a young man of great hope, in the science of government. Armed rather by his faith, for he had been admitted to baptism while in exile with many nobles among the Scots, than by his military preparations, on the first onset he drove Cadwalla,* a man elated with the recollection of his former deeds, and, as he used himself to say, "born for the extermination of the Angles," from his camp, and afterwards destroyed him with all his forces. For when he had collected the little army which he was able to muster, he excited them to the conflict, in which, laying aside all thought of flight, they must determine either to conquer or die, by suggesting,

* Cadwalla, king of the Britons, having slain Eanfrid and Osric, A.D. 634, had usurped the government of Northumbria.

"that it must be a circumstance highly disgraceful for the Angles to meet the Britons on such unequal terms, as to fight against those persons for safety, whom they had been used voluntarily to attack for glory only; that therefore they should maintain their liberty with dauntless courage, and the most strenuous exertions; but, that of the impulse to flight no feeling whatever should be indulged." In consequence they met with such fury on both sides, that, it may be truly said, no day was ever more disastrous for the Britons, or more joyful for the Angles: so completely was one party routed with all its forces, as never to have hope of recovering again; so exceedingly powerful did the other become, through the effects of faith and the accompanying courage of the king. From this time, the worship of idols fell prostrate in the dust; and he governed the kingdom, extended beyond Edwin's boundaries, for eight years, peaceably and without the loss of any of his people. Bede, in his History, sets forth the praises of this king in a high style of panegyric, of which I shall extract such portions as may be necessary, by way of conclusion. With what fervent faith his breast was inspired, may easily be learned from this circumstance. If at any time Aidan the priest addressed his auditors on the subject of their duty, in the Scottish tongue, and no interpreter was present, the king himself would directly, though habited in the royal robe, glittering with gold, or glowing with Tyrian purple, graciously assume that office, and explain the foreign idiom in his native language. It is well known too, that frequently at entertainments, when the guests had whetted their appetites and bent their inclinations on the feast, he would forego his own gratification;* procuring, by his abstinence, comfort for the poor. So that I think the truth of that heavenly sentence was fulfilled even on earth, where the celestial oracle hath said, "He that dispersed abroad, he hath given to the poor, his righteousness remaineth for ever." And moreover, what the hearer must wonder at, and cannot deny, that identical royal right hand,

* When he was seated at table and just about to commence dinner, the royal almoner informed the king that a great number of poor were assembled in the street, asking relief; on which he immediately ordered the whole of the provisions to be distributed, and the silver dish also to be cut into pieces, and divided amongst them. See Bede, b. iii. c. 6.

the dispenser of so many alms, remains to this day perfect, with the arm, the skin and nerves, though the remainder of the body, with the exception of the bones, mouldering into dust, has not escaped the common lot of mortality. It is true the corporeal remains of some of the saints are unconscious altogether of decay. Wherefore let others determine by what standard they will fix their judgment; I pronounce this still more gracious and divine on account of its singular manifestation; because things ever so precious degenerate by frequency, and whatever is more unusual, is celebrated more generally. I should indeed be thought prolix were I to relate how diligent he was to address his prayers on high, and to fill the heavens with vows. This virtue of Oswald is too well known to require the support of our narrative. For at what time would that man neglect his supplications, who, in the insurrection excited by Penda king of the Mercians, his guards being put to flight and himself actually carrying a forest of darts in his breast, could not be prevented by the pain of his wounds or the approach of death, from praying for the souls of his faithful companions? In such manner this personage, of surpassing celebrity in this world, and highly in favour with God, ending a valuable life, transmitted his memory to posterity by a frequency of miracles; and indeed most deservedly. For it is not common, but even more rare than a white crow, for men to abound in riches, and not give indulgence to their vices.*

When he was slain, his arms with the hands and his head were cut off by the insatiable rage of his conqueror, and fixed on a stake. The dead trunk indeed, as I have mentioned, being laid to rest in the calm bosom of the earth, turned to its native dust; but the arms and hands, through the power of God, remain, according to the testimony of an author of veracity, without corruption. These being placed by his brother Oswy in a shrine, at the city of Bebbanburg,† so the Angles call it, and shown for a miracle, bear testimony to the fact. Whether they remain at that place at the present day, I venture not rashly to affirm, because I waver in my opinion. If other historians have precipitately recorded any matter, let them be accountable: I hold common report

* Juv. Sat. vii. 202.
† Bambrough in Northumberland. Bede iii. 6, p. 118.

at a cheaper rate, and affirm nothing but what is deserving of entire credit. The head was then buried by his beforementioned brother at Lindisfarne; but it is said now to be preserved at Durham in the arms of the blessed Cuthbert.* When Ostritha, the wife of Ethelred, king of the Mercians, daughter of king Oswy, through regard to her uncle, was anxious to take the bones of the trunk to her monastery of Bardney, which is in the country of the Mercians not far from the city of Lincoln, the monks refused her request at first; denying repose even to the bones of that man when dead whom they had hated whilst living, because he had obtained their country by right of arms. But at midnight being taught, by a miraculous light from heaven shining on the relics, to abate their haughty pride, they became converts to reason, and even entreated as a favour, what before they had rejected. Virtues from on high became resident in this place: every sick person who implored this most excellent martyr's assistance, immediately received it. The withering turf grew greener from his blood, and recovered a horse:† and some of it being hung up against a post, the devouring flames fled from it in their turn. Some dust, moistened from his relics, was equally efficacious in restoring a lunatic to his proper senses. The washings of the stake which had imbibed the blood fresh streaming from his head, restored health to one despairing of recovery. For a long time this monastery, possessing so great a treasure, flourished in the sanctity of its members and the abundance of its friends, more especially after king Ethelred received the tonsure there, where also his tomb is seen even to the present day. After many years indeed, when the barbarians infested these parts, the bones of the most holy Oswald were removed to Gloucester. This place, at that period inhabited by monks, but at the present time by canons, contains but few inmates. Oswald, therefore, was the man who yielded the first fruits of holiness to his nation; since no Angle be-

* St. Cuthbert is represented as holding the head of Oswald in his arms. Bede's bones were afterwards laid in the same coffin.

† The horse lay down under his rider in great agony; but recovered by rolling on the spot and cropping the grass. A person carried away some of the earth, which he hung up against a post in the wall: the house caught fire and was burnt with the exception of the timber to which the bag was tied. See Bede, b. iii. c. 9, 10; and for the other stories, c. 13.

fore him, to my knowledge, was celebrated for miracles. For after a life spent in sanctity, in liberally giving alms, in frequent watchings and prayer, and lastly, through zeal for the church of God, in waging war with an heathen, he poured out his spirit, according to his wishes, before he could behold, what was his greatest object of apprehension, the decline of Christianity. Nor indeed shall he be denied the praise of the martyrs, who, first aspiring after a holy life, and next opposing his body to a glorious death, certainly trod in their steps: in a manner he deserves higher commendation, since they barely consecrated themselves to God; but Oswald not only himself, but all the Northumbrians with him.

On his removal from this world, Oswy his brother assumed the dominion over the Bernicians, as did Oswin, the son of Osric, whom I have before mentioned, over the Deirans. After meeting temperately at first on the subject of the division of the provinces, under a doubtful truce, they each retired peaceably to their territories, but not long after, by means of persons who delighted in sowing the seeds of discord, the peace, of which they had so often made a mockery by ambiguous treaties, was finally broken, and vanished into air. Horrid crime! that there should be men who could envy these kings their friendly intimacy, nor abstain from using their utmost efforts to precipitate them into battle. Here then fortune, who had before so frequently caressed Oswin with her blandishments, now wounded him with her scorpion-sting. For thinking it prudent to abstain from fighting, on account of the smallness of his force, he had secretly withdrawn to a country-seat, where he was immediately betrayed by his own people, and killed by Oswy. He was a man admirably calculated to gain the favour of his subjects by his pecuniary liberality; and, as they relate, demonstrated his care for his soul by his fervent devotion. Oswy, thus sovereign of the entire kingdom, did every thing to wipe out this foul stain, and to increase his dignity, extenuating the enormity of that atrocious deed by the rectitude of his future conduct. Indeed the first and highest point of his glory is, that he nobly avenged his brother and his uncle, and gave to perdition Penda king of the Mercians, that destroyer of his neighbours, and fomenter of hostility. From this period he either governed the Mercians, as well as almost all the Angles, himself, or was supreme over those who did. Turning from this time altogether to offices of piety, that he might be truly grateful for the favours of God perpetually flowing down upon him, he proceeded to raise up and animate, with all his power, the infancy of the Christian faith, which of late was fainting through his brother's death. This faith, brought shortly after to maturity by the learning of the Scots, but wavering in many ecclesiastical observances, was now settled on canonical foundations:* first by Agilbert and Wilfrid, and next by archbishop Theodore: for whose arrival in Britain, although Egbert, king of Kent, as far as his province is concerned, takes much from his glory, the chief thanks are due to Oswy.† Moreover he built numerous habitations for the servants of God, and so left not his country destitute of this advantage also. The principal of these monasteries, at that time for females, but now for males, was situate about thirty miles north of York, and was anciently called Streaneshalch, but latterly Whitby. Begun by Hilda, a woman of singular piety, it was augmented with large revenues by Elfled, daughter of this king, who succeeded her in the government of it; in which place also she buried her father with all due solemnity, after he had reigned twenty-eight years. This monastery, like all others of the same order, was destroyed in the times of the Danish invasion, which will be related hereafter, and bereaved of the bodies of many saints. For the bones of St. Aidan the bishop, of Ceolfrid the abbat, and of that truly holy virgin Hilda, together with those of many others, were, as I have related in the book which I lately published on the Antiquity of the Church of Glastonbury, at that time removed to Glastonbury; and those of other saints to different places. Now the monastery, under another name, and somewhat restored as circumstances permitted, hardly presents a vestige of its former opulence.

To Oswy, who had two sons, the elder who was illegitimate being rejected, succeeded the younger, Egfrid, legitimately born, more valued on account of the good qualities of his most pious wife Etheldrida, than for his own; yet he

* The principal points in dispute were, the time of celebrating Easter and the form of the tonsure. See Bede, Eccl. Hist. iii. 25
† See Bede, Hist. Eccl. iii. 29.

was certainly to be commended for two things which I have read in the history of the Angles, his allowing his wife to dedicate herself to God, and his promoting the blessed Cuthbert to a bishopric, whose tears at the same time burst out with pious assent.* But my mind shudders at the bare recollection of his outrage against the holy Wilfrid, when, loathing his virtues, he deprived the country of this shining character. Overbearing towards the suppliant, a malady incident to tyrants, he overwhelmed the Irish, a race of men harmless in genuine simplicity and guiltless of every crime, with incredible slaughter. On the other hand, inactive towards the rebellious, and not following up the triumphs of his father, he lost the dominion of the Mercians, and moreover, defeated in battle by Ethelred the son of Penda, their king, he lost his brother also. Perhaps these last circumstances may be truly attributed to the unsteadiness of youth, but his conduct towards Wilfrid, to the instigation of his wife,† and of the bishops; more especially as Bede, a man who knew not how to flatter, calls him, in his book of the Lives of his Abbats, the most pious man, the most beloved by God. At length, in the fifteenth year of his reign, as he was leading an expedition against the Picts, and eagerly pursuing them as they purposely retired to some secluded mountains, he perished with almost all his forces; the few who escaped by flight carried home news of the event; and yet the divine Cuthbert, from his knowledge of future events, had both attempted to keep him back, when departing, and at the very moment of his death, enlightened by heavenly influence, declared, though at a distance, that he was slain.

While a more than common report every where noised the death of Egfrid, an intimation of it, "borne on the wings of haste," reached the ears of his brother Alfrid. Though the elder brother, he had been deemed, by the nobility, unwor-

---

* Bede's Life of St. Cuthbert, c. 24.
† Ermenburga, the second wife of Egfrid. The first, Etheldrida, was divorced from him, on account of her love of celibacy, and became a nun. Wilfrid, bishop of Hexham, was several times expelled his see. Elected bishop of York, A.D. 664, he was expelled in 678 He was recalled to Northumbria in 687, and again expelled 692. He died A.D. 709, having been reinstated by the pope. See Bede v. 19. and Sax. Chron.

thy of the government, from his illegitimacy, as I have observed, and had retired to Ireland, either through compulsion or indignation. In this place, safe from the persecution of his brother, he had, from his ample leisure, become deeply versed in literature, and had enriched his mind with every kind of learning. On which account the very persons who had formerly banished him, esteeming him the better qualified to manage the reins of government, now sent for him of their own accord. Fate rendered efficacious their entreaties; neither did he disappoint their expectations. For during the space of nineteen years, he presided over the kingdom in the utmost tranquillity and joy; doing nothing that even greedy calumny itself could justly carp at, except the persecution of that great man Wilfrid. However he held not the same extent of territory as his father and brother, because the Picts, proudly profiting by their recent victory, and attacking the Angles, who were become indolent through a lengthened peace, had curtailed his boundaries on the north.

He had for successor his son, Osred, a boy of eight years old, who disgracing the throne for eleven years, and spending an ignominious life in the seduction of nuns, was ultimately taken off by the hostility of his relations. Yet he poured out to them a draught from the same cup; for Kenred after reigning two, and Osric eleven years, left only this to be recorded of them; that they expiated by a violent death, the blood of their master, whom they supposed they had rightfully slain. Osric indeed deserved a happier end, for, as a heathen* says, he was more dignified than other shades, because, while yet living he had adopted Ceolwulf, Kenred's brother, as his successor. Then Ceolwulf ascended the giddy height of empire, seventh in descent from Ida. a man competent in other respects, and withal possessed of a depth of literature, acquired by good abilities and indefatigable attention. Bede vouches for the truth of my assertion, who, at the very juncture when Britain most abounded with scholars, offered his History of the Angles, for correction, to this prince more especially; making choice of his authority, to confirm by his high station what had been well written; and of his learning, to rectify by his talents what might be carelessly expressed.

* Virg. Æn. vi. 815.

In the fourth year of his reign, Bede, the historian, after having written many books for the holy church, entered the heavenly kingdom, for which he had so long languished, in the year of our Lord's incarnation 734 ; of his age the fifty-ninth. A man whom it is easier to admire than worthily to extol : who, though born in a remote corner of the world, was able to dazzle the whole earth with the brilliancy of his learning. For even Britain, which by some is called another world, since, surrounded by the ocean, it was not thoroughly known by many geographers, possesses, in its remotest region, bordering on Scotland, the place of his birth and education. This region, formerly exhaling the grateful odour of monasteries, or glittering with a multitude of cities built by the Romans, now desolate through the ancient devastations of the Danes, or those more recent of the Normans,* presents but little to allure the mind. Here is the river Wear, of considerable breadth and rapid tide ; which running into the sea, receives the vessels, borne by gentle gales, on the calm bosom of its haven. Both its banks† have been made conspicuous by one Benedict, ‡ who there built churches and monasteries ; one dedicated to Peter, and the other to Paul, united in the bond of brotherly love and of monastic rule. The industry and forbearance of this man, any one will admire who reads the book which Bede composed concerning his life and those of the succeeding abbats : his industry, in bringing over a multitude of books, and being the first person who introduced in England constructors of stone edifices, as well as makers of glass windows ; in which pursuits he spent almost his whole life abroad : the love of his country and his taste for elegance beguiling his painful labours, in the

* The country was laid waste by the Danes, A.D 793, and continued to be disturbed by them throughout the reigns of Alfred and Ethelred. The great devastation was made by William the Conqueror A.D. 1069.

† This is not quite correct: Jarrow, one of Benedict's monasteries, is on the river Tyne.

‡ Benedict surnamed Biscop, a noble Northumbrian, quitted the service of king Oswy, when he had attained his twenty-fifth year, and travelled to Rome five several times, occupying himself while there, either in learning the Roman ritual, or in collecting books, pictures, and ornaments of various descriptions for the monasteries he had founded at Wearmouth : he also brought over masons from France to build a church after the Roman manner ; as well as artificers in glass. See Bede's Lives of the Abbats of Wearmouth and Jarrow.

earnest desire of conveying something to his countrymen out of the common way; for very rarely before the time of Benedict were buildings of stone * seen in Britain, nor did the solar ray cast its light through the transparent glass. Again, his forbearance: for when in possession of the monastery of St. Augustine at Canterbury, he cheerfully resigned it to Adrian, when he arrived, not as fearing the severity of St. Theodore the archbishop, but bowing to his authority. And farther, while long absent abroad, he endured not only with temper, but, I may say, with magnanimity, the substitution of another abbat, without his knowledge, by the monks of Wearmouth; and on his return, admitted him to equal honour with himself, in rank and power. Moreover, when stricken so severely with the palsy that he could move none of his limbs, he appointed a third abbat, because the other, of whom we have spoken, was not less affected by the same disease. And when the disorder, increasing, was just about to seize his vitals, he bade adieu to his companion, who was brought into his presence, with an inclination of the head only; nor was he better able to return the salutation, for he was hastening to a still nearer exit, and actually died before Benedict.

Ceolfrid succeeded, under whom the affairs of the monastery flourished beyond measure. When, through extreme old age, life ceased to be desirable, he purposed going to Rome, that he might pour out, as he hoped, his aged soul an offering to the apostles his masters. But failing of the object of his desires, he paid the debt of nature at the city of Langres. The relics of his bones were in after time conveyed to his monastery; and at the period of the Danish devastation, with those of St. Hilda, were taken to Glastonbury.† The merits of these abbats, sufficiently eminent in

* "... lapidei tabulatus," this seems intended to designate buildings with courses of stone in a regular manner, which is also implied by him, De Gestis Pontif. lib. iii. f. 148. Bede, whom he here follows, affords no assistance as to the precise meaning he merely states, that Benedict caused a church to be erected after the Roman model.

† The monks of Glastonbury used all possible means to obtain relics of saints. See the curious account of a contention concerning the body of St. Dunstan, which those monks asserted they had stolen from Canterbury, after it had been burnt by the Danes, in the time of Ethelred, in Whartoni Anglia Sacra, vol. ii. p. 222.

themselves, their celebrated pupil, Bede, crowns with superior splendour. It is written indeed, "A wise son is the glory of his father:" for one of them made him a monk, the other educated him. And since Bede himself has given some slight notices of these facts, comprising his whole life in a kind of summary, it may be allowed to turn to his words, which the reader will recognize, lest any variation of the style should affect the relation. At the end then of the Ecclesiastical History of the English * this man, as praiseworthy in other respects as in this, that he withheld nothing from posterity, though it might be only a trifling knowledge of himself, says thus:

"I, Bede, the servant of Christ, and priest of the monastery of the holy apostles Peter and Paul, which is at Wearmouth, have, by God's assistance, arranged these materials for the history of Britain. I was born within the possessions of this monastery, and at seven years of age, was committed, by the care of my relations, to the most reverend abbat Benedict, to be educated, and, after, to Ceolfrid; passing the remainder of my life from that period in residence at the said monastery, I have given up my whole attention to the study of the Scriptures, and amid the observance of my regular discipline and my daily duty of singing in the church, have ever delighted to learn, to teach, or to write. In the nineteenth year of my life, I took deacon's, in the thirtieth, priest's orders; both, at the instance of abbat Ceolfrid, by the ministry of the most reverend bishop John :† from which time of receiving the priesthood till the fifty-ninth year of my age, I have been employed for the benefit of myself or of my friends, in making these extracts from the works of the venerable fathers, or in making additions, according to the form of their sense or interpretation." Then enumerating thirty-six volumes which he published in seventy-eight books, he proceeds, "And I pray most earnestly, O merciful Jesus, that thou wouldst grant me, to whom thou hast already given the knowledge of thyself, finally to come to thee, the fountain of all wisdom, and to appear for ever in thy presence. Moreover I humbly entreat all persons,

* Eccles. Hist., book v. ch. 24.
† John of Beverley, bishop of Hexham, A.D 686. He was made bishop of York, A.D. 705, and died 7th of May, 722. See Bede, b. v. c. 2—6.

whether readers or hearers, whom this history of our nation shall reach, that they be mindful to intercede with the divine clemency for my infirmities both of mind and of body, and that, in their several provinces, they make me this grateful return; that I, who have diligently laboured to record, of every province, or of more exalted places, what appeared worthy of preservation or agreeable to the inhabitants, may receive, from all, the benefit of their pious intercessions."

Here my abilities fail, here my eloquence falls short: ignorant which to praise most, the number of his writings, or the gravity of his style. No doubt he had imbibed a large portion of heavenly wisdom, to be able to compose so many volumes within the limits of so short a life. Nay, they even report, that he went to Rome for the purpose either of personally asserting that his writings were consistent with the doctrines of the church; or of correcting them by apostolical authority, should they be found repugnant thereto. That he went to Rome I do not however affirm for fact: but I have no doubt in declaring that he was invited thither, as the following epistle will certify, as well as that the see of Rome so highly esteemed him as greatly to desire his presence.

"*Sergius the bishop, servant of the servants of God, to Ceolfrid the holy abbat sendeth greeting:—*

"With what words, and in what manner, can we declare the kindness and unspeakable providence of our God, and return fit thanks for his boundless benefits, who leads us, when placed in darkness, and the shadow of death, to the light of knowledge?" And below, "Know, that we received the favour of the offering which your devout piety hath sent by the present bearer, with the same joy and goodwill with which it was transmitted. We assent to the timely and becoming prayers of your laudable anxiety with deepest regard, and entreat of your pious goodness, so acceptable to God, that, since there have occurred certain points of ecclesiastical discipline, not to be promulgated without farther examination, which have made it necessary for us to confer with a person skilled in literature, as becomes an assistant of God's holy universal mother-church, you would not delay paying ready obedience to this, our admonition; but would send without loss of time. to our lowly presence, at the church of the chief apostles, my lords Peter and Paul, your friends and protectors, that religious servant of God, Bede, the venerable priest of your monastery; whom, God willing, you may expect to return in safety, when the necessary discussion of the above-mentioned points shall be, by God's assistance, solemnly completed: for whatever may be added to the church at large, by his assistance, will, we trust, be profitable to the things committed to your immediate care "

So extensive was his fame then, that even the majesty of Rome itself solicited his assistance in solving abstruse questions, nor did Gallic conceit ever find in this Angle any thing justly to blame. All the western world yielded the palm to his faith and authority; for indeed he was of sound faith, and of artless, yet pleasing eloquence: in all elucidations of the holy scriptures, discussing those points from which the reader might imbibe the love of God, and of his neighbour, rather than those which might charm by their wit, or polish a rugged style. Moreover the irrefragable truth of that sentence, which the majesty of divine wisdom proclaimed to the world forbids any one to doubt the sanctity of his life, " Wisdom will not enter the malevolent soul, nor dwell in the person of the sinful;" which indeed is said not of earthly wisdom, which is infused promiscuously into the hearts of men, and in which, even the wicked, who continue their crimes until their last day, seem often to excel, according to the divine expression, " The sons of this world are in their generation wiser than the children of light;" but it rather describes that wisdom which needs not the assistance of learning, and which dismisses from its cogitations those things which are void of understanding, that is to say, of the understanding of acting and speaking properly. Hence Seneca in his book, " De Causis,"* appositely relates that Cato, defining the duty of an orator, said, "An orator is a good man, skilled in speaking." This ecclesiastical orator, then, used to purify his knowledge, that so he might, as far as possible, unveil the meaning of mystic writings. How indeed could that man be enslaved to vice who gave his whole soul and spirit to elucidate the scriptures? For, as he confesses in his third book on Samuel, if his expositions were productive of no advantage to his readers, yet were they of con-

---

* Seneca, Controvers lib. 1.

siderable importance to himself, inasmuch as, while fully intent upon them, he escaped the vanity and empty imaginations of the times. Purified from vice, therefore, he entered within the inner veil, divulging in pure diction the sentiments of his mind.

But the unspotted sanctity and holy purity of his heart were chiefly conspicuous on the approach of death. Although for seven weeks successively, from the indisposition of his stomach, he nauseated all food, and was troubled with such a difficulty of breathing that his disorder confined him to his bed, yet he by no means abandoned his literary avocations. During whole days he endeavoured to mitigate the pressure of his disorder and to lose the recollection of it by constant lectures to his pupils, and by examining and solving abstruse questions, in addition to his usual task of psalmody. Moreover the gospel of St. John, which from its difficulty exercises the talents of its readers even to the present day, was translated by him into the English language, and accommodated to those who did not understand Latin. Occasionally, also, would he admonish his disciples, saying, "Learn, my children, while I am with you, for I know not how long I shall continue; and although my Maker should very shortly take me hence, and my spirit should return to him that sent and granted it to come into this life, yet have I lived long, God hath rightly appointed my portion of days, I desire to be dissolved and to be with Christ."

Often too when the balance was poised between hope and fear, he would remark "It is a fearful thing to fall into the hands of the living God.* I have not passed my life among you in such manner as to be ashamed to live, neither do I fear to die, because we have a kind Master;" thus borrowing the expression of St. Ambrose when dying. Happy man! who could speak with so quiet a conscience as neither being ashamed to live, nor afraid to die; on the one hand not fearing the judgment of men, on the other waiting with composure the hidden will of God. Often, when urged by extremity of pain, he comforted himself with these remarks, "The furnace tries the gold, and the fire of temptation the just man: the sufferings of this present time are not worthy

* Hebrews x. 31.

to be compared to the future glory which shall be revealed in us."* Tears and a difficulty of breathing accompanied his words. At night, when there were none to be instructed or to note down his remarks, he passed the whole season in giving thanks and singing psalms, fulfilling the saying of that very wise man,† "that he was never less alone than when alone." If at any time a short and disturbed sleep stole upon his eye-lids, he immediately shook it off, and showed that his affections were always intent on God, by exclaiming "Lift me up, O Lord, that the proud calumniate me not. Do with thy servant according to thy mercy." These and similar expressions which his shattered memory suggested, flowed spontaneously from his lips whenever the pain of his agonizing disorder became mitigated. But on the Tuesday before our Lord's ascension his disease rapidly increased, and there appeared a small swelling in his feet, the sure and certain indication of approaching death. Then the congregation being called together, he was anointed and received the sacrament. Kissing them all, and requesting from each that they would bear him in remembrance, he gave a small present, which he had privately reserved, to some with whom he had been in closer bonds of friendship. On Ascension day, when his soul, tired of the frail occupation of the body, panted to be free, lying down on a hair-cloth near the oratory, where he used to pray, with sense unimpaired and joyful countenance, he invited the grace of the Holy Spirit, saying, "O King of glory, Lord of virtue, who ascendedst this day triumphant into the heavens, leave us not destitute, but send upon us the promise of the Father, the Spirit of truth." This prayer ended, he breathed his last, and immediately the senses of all were pervaded by an odour such as neither cinnamon nor balm could give, but coming, as it were, from paradise, and fraught with all the joyous exhalations of spring. At that time he was buried in the same monastery, but at present, report asserts that he lies at Durham with St. Cuthbert

With this man was buried almost all knowledge of history down to our times, inasmuch as there has been no English-

* Romans viii 18.
† Scipio Africanus was accustomed to observe, "that he was never less idle than when unoccupied, nor never less alone than when by himself." *Cicero de Offic.* l. 3.

man either emulous of his pursuits, or a follower of his graces, who could continue the thread of his discourse, now broken short. Some few indeed, "whom the mild Jesus loved," though well skilled in literature, have yet observed an ungracious silence throughout their lives; others, scarcely tasting of the stream, have fostered a criminal indolence. Thus to the slothful succeeded others more slothful still, and the warmth of science for a long time decreased throughout the island. The verses of his epitaph will afford sufficient specimen of this indolence; they are indeed contemptible, and unworthy the tomb of so great a man:

> "Presbyter hic Beda, requiescit carne sepultus,
> Dona, Christe, animam in cœlis gaudere per ævum:
> Daque illi sophiæ debriari fonte, cui jam
> Suspiravit ovans, intento semper amore."*

Can this disgrace be extenuated by any excuse, that there was not to be found even in that monastery, where during his lifetime the school of all learning had flourished, a single person who could write his epitaph, except in this mean and paltry style? But enough of this: I will return to my subject.

Ceolwulf thinking it beneath the dignity of a Christian to be immersed in earthly things, abdicated the throne after a reign of eight years, and assumed the monastic habit at Lindisfarne, in which place how meritoriously he lived, is amply testified by his being honourably interred near St. Cuthbert, and by many miracles vouchsafed from on high.

He had made provision against the state's being endangered, by placing his cousin, Eadbert,† on the throne, which he filled for twenty years with singular moderation and virtue. Eadbert had a brother of the same name, archbishop of York, who, by his own prudence and the power of the king, restored that see to its original state. For, as is well known to any one conversant in the history of the Angles,‡

* These lines are thus rendered into English:

> "Beneath this stone Bede's mortal body lies;
> God grant his soul may rest amid the skies.
> May he drink deeply, in the realms above,
> Of wisdom's fount, which he on earth did love!"

† Called Egbert by some writers. ‡ Paulinus had departed from Northumbria, in consequence of the confusion which prevailed on the death of Edwin. Bede, b. ii. c. 20. He died Oct. 10, 644.

Paulinus, the first prelate of the church of York, had been forcibly driven away, and died at Rochester, where he left that honourable distinction of the pall which he had received from pope Honorius. After him, many prelates of this august city, satisfied with the name of a simple bishopric, aspired to nothing higher: but when Eadbert was seated on the throne, a man of loftier spirit, and one who thought, that, "as it is over-reaching to require what is not our due, so is it ignoble to neglect our right," he reclaimed the pall by frequent appeals to the pope. This personage, if I may be allowed the expression, was the depository and receptacle of every liberal art, and founded a most noble library at York. For this I cite Alcuin,* as competent witness; who was sent from the kings of England to the emperor Charles the Great, to treat of peace, and being hospitably entertained by him, observes, in a letter to Eanbald, third in succession from Eadbert, "Praise and glory be to God, who hath preserved my days in full prosperity, that I should rejoice in the exaltation of my dearest son, who laboured in my stead, in the church where I had been brought up and educated, and presided over the treasures of wisdom, to which my beloved master, archbishop Egbert, left me heir." Thus too to Charles Augustus:† "Give me the more polished volumes of scholastic learning, such as I used to have in my own country, through the laudable and ardent industry of my master, archbishop Egbert. And, if it please your wisdom, I will send some of our youths, who may obtain thence whatever is necessary, and bring back into France the flowers of Britain; that the garden of Paradise may not be confined to York, but that some of its scions may be transplanted to Tours."

This is the same Alcuin, who, as I have said, was sent into France to treat of peace, and during his abode with Charles, captivated either by the pleasantness of the country or the kindness of the king, settled there; and being held in high estimation, he taught the king, during his leisure from

* Alcuin, a native of Northumbria, and educated at York, through his learning and talents became the intimate friend and favourite of Charlemagne, for whom he transcribed, with his own hand, the Holy Scriptures. This relic is now preserved in the British Museum.
† See this epistle at length in Alcuini Op. vol. i. p. 52. Epist. 38.

the cares of state, a thorough knowledge of logic, rhetoric, and astronomy. Alcuin was, of all the Angles, of whom I have read, next to St. Aldhelm and Bede, certainly the most learned, and has given proof of his talents in a variety of compositions. He lies buried in France, at the church of St Paul, of Cormaric,* which monastery Charles the Great built at his suggestion: on which account, even at the present day, the subsistence of four monks is distributed in alms, for the soul of our Alcuin, in that church.

But since I am arrived at that point where the mention of Charles the Great naturally presents itself, I shall subjoin a true statement of the descent of the kings of France, of which antiquity has said much: nor shall I depart widely from my design; because to be unacquainted with their race, I hold as a defect in information; seeing that they are our near neighbours, and to them the Christian world chiefly looks up: and, perhaps, to glance over this compendium may give pleasure to many who have not leisure to wade through voluminous works.

The Franks were so called, by a Greek appellative, from the ferocity of their manners, when, by order of the emperor Valentinian the First, they ejected the Alani, who had retreated to the Mæotian marshes. It is scarcely possible to believe how much this people, few and mean at first, became increased by a ten years' exemption from taxes: such, before the war, being the condition on which they engaged in it. Thus augmenting wonderfully by the acquisition of freedom, and first seizing the greatest part of Germany, and next the whole of Gaul, they compelled the inhabitants to list under their banners. Hence the Lotharingi and Allamanni, and other nations beyond the Rhine, who are subject to the emperor of Germany, will have themselves more properly to be called Franks; and those whom we suppose Franks, they call by an ancient appellative Galwalæ, that is to say, Gauls. To this opinion I assent; knowing that Charles the Great, whom none can deny to have been king of the Franks, always used the same vernacular language with the Franks on the other side of the Rhine. Any one who shall read the

* Others say he was buried at St Martin's, at Tours, where he died, April 18, 804. His works will be included in PATRES ECCLESIÆ ANGLICANÆ.

life of Charles will readily admit the truth of my assertion.*
In the year then of the Incarnate Word 425 the Franks
were governed by Faramund, their first king. The grandson of Faramund was Meroveus, from whom all the succeeding kings of the Franks, to the time of Pepin, were
called Merovingians. In like manner the sons of the kings
of the Angles took patronymical appellations from their
fathers. For instance ; Eadgaring the son of Edgar ; Eadmunding the son of Edmund, and the rest in like manner ;
commonly, however, they are called ethelings. The native
language of the Franks, therefore, partakes of that of the
Angles, by reason of both nations originating from Germany.
The Merovingians reigned successfully and powerfully till
the year of our Lord's incarnation, 687. At that period
Pepin, son of Ansegise, was made mayor of the palace †
among the Franks, on the other side of the Rhine. Seizing
opportunities for veiling his ambitious views, he completely
subjugated his master Theodoric, the dregs as it were of the
Merovingians, and to lessen the obloquy excited by the
transaction, he indulged him with the empty title of king,
while himself managed every thing, at home and abroad,
according to his own pleasure. The genealogy of this Pepin,
both to and from him, is thus traced : Ausbert, the senator,
on Blithilde, the daughter of Lothaire, the father of Dagobert, begot Arnold : Arnold begot St. Arnulph, bishop of
Metz : Arnulph begot Flodulph, Walcthise, Anschise : Flodulph begot duke Martin, whom Ebroin slew : Walcthise
begot the most holy Wandregesil the abbat : duke Anschise
begot Ansegise : Ansegise begot Pepin. The son of Pepin
was Carolus Tudites, whom they also call Martel, because he
beat down the tyrants who were raising up in every part of
France, and nobly defeated the Saracens, at that time infesting Gaul. Following the practice of his father, whilst he
was himself satisfied with the title of earl, he kept the kings

* The Life of Charlemagne, by Eginhard, who was secretary to that
monarch. Du Chesne Script. Franc. tom. ii. It is one of the most amusing books of the period.

† The mayors of the palace seem originally to have merely regulated
the king's household, but by degrees they acquired so much power, that
Pepin the elder, maternal grandfather of him here mentioned, had already
become in effect, king of France. They first appear to have usurped
the regal power under Clovis II. A. D. 638.

in a state of pupilage. He left two sons, Pepin and Caroloman. Caroloman, from some unknown cause, relinquishing the world, took his religious vows at Mount Cassin. Pepin was crowned king of the Franks, and patrician of the Romans, in the church of St. Denys, by pope Stephen, the successor of Zachary. For the Constantinopolitan emperors, already much degenerated from their ancient valour, giving no assistance either to Italy or the church of Rome, which had long groaned under the tyranny of the Lombards, this pope bewailed the injuries to which they were exposed from them to the ruler of the Franks; wherefore Pepin passing the Alps, reduced Desiderius, king of the Lombards, to such difficulties, that he restored what he had plundered to the church of Rome, and gave surety by oath that he would not attempt to resume it. Pepin returning to France after some years, died, leaving his surviving children, Charles and Caroloman, his heirs. In two years Caroloman departed this life. Charles obtaining the name of "Great" from his exploits, enlarged the kingdom to twice the limits which it possessed in his father's time, and being contented for more than thirty years with the simple title of king, abstained from the appellation of emperor, though repeatedly invited to assume it by pope Adrian. But when, after the death of this pontiff, his relations maimed the holy Leo, his successors in the church of St. Peter, so as to cut out his tongue, and put out his eyes, Charles hastily proceeded to Rome to settle the state of the church. Justly punishing these abandoned wretches, he stayed there the whole winter, and restored the pontiff, now speaking plainly and seeing clearly, by the miraculous interposition of God, to his customary power. At that time the Roman people, with the privity of the pontiff, on the day of our Lord's nativity, unexpectedly hailed him with the title of Augustus; which title, though, from its being unusual, he reluctantly admitted, yet afterwards he defended with proper spirit against the Constantinopolitan emperors, and left it, as hereditary, to his son Louis. His descendants reigned in that country, which is now properly called France, till the time of Hugh, surnamed Capet, from whom is descended the present Louis. From the same stock came the sovereigns of Germany and Italy, till the year of our Lord 912, when Conrad, king of the Teutonians, seized that empire. The grandson of this personage was Otho the Great, equal in every estimable quality to any of the emperors who preceded him. Thus admirable for his valour and goodness, he left the empire hereditary to his posterity; for the present Henry, son-in-law of Henry, king of England, derives his lineage from his blood.

To return to my narrative. Alcuin, though promoted by Charles the Great to the monastery of St. Martin in France, was not unmindful of his countrymen, but exerted himself to retain the emperor in amity with them, and stimulated them to virtue by frequent epistles. I shall here subjoin many of his observations, from which it will appear clearly how soon after the death of Bede the love of learning declined even in his own monastery: and how quickly after the decease of Eadbert the kingdom of the Northumbrians came to ruin, through the prevalence of degenerate manners.

He says thus to the monks of Wearmouth, among whom Bede had both lived and died, obliquely accusing them of having done the very thing which he begs them not to do, "Let the youths be accustomed to attend the praises of our heavenly King, not to dig up the burrows of foxes, or pursue the winding mazes of hares; let them now learn the Holy Scriptures, that, when grown up, they may be able to instruct others. Remember the most noble teacher of our times, Bede, the priest, what thirst for learning he had in his youth, what praise he now has among men, and what a far greater reward of glory with God." Again, to those of York he says, "The Searcher of my heart is witness that it was not for lust of gold that I came to France or continued there, but for the necessities of the church." And thus to Offa, king of the Mercians, "I was prepared to come to you with the presents of king Charles and to return to my country, but it seemed more advisable to me, for the peace of my nation, to remain abroad, not knowing what I could have done among those persons, with whom no one can be secure, or able to proceed in any laudable pursuit. Behold every holy place is laid desolate by Pagans, the altars are polluted by perjury, the monasteries dishonoured by adultery, the earth itself stained with the blood of rulers and of princes." Again, to king Ethelred, third in the sovereignty after Eadbert, "Behold the church of St. Cuthbert is sprinkled with the blood of God's priests, despoiled of all its ornaments, and the holiest spot in Britain given up to Pagan nations to be plundered; and where, after the departure of St. Paulinus from York, the Christian religion first took its rise in our own nation, there misery and calamity took their rise also. What portends that shower of blood which in the time of Lent, in the city of York, the capital of the whole kingdom, in the church of St. Peter, the chief of the apostles, we saw tremendously falling on the northern side of the building from the summit of the roof, though the weather was fair? Must not blood be expected to come upon the land from the northern regions?" Again, to Osbert, prince of the Mercians, "Our kingdom of the Northumbrians has almost perished through internal dissensions and perjury." So also to Athelard, archbishop of Canterbury, "I speak this on account of the scourge which has lately fallen on that part of our island which has been inhabited by our forefathers for nearly three hundred and forty years. It is recorded in the writings of Gildas, the wisest of the Britons, that those very Britons ruined their country through the avarice and rapine of their princes, the iniquity and injustice of their judges, their bishops' neglect of preaching, the luxury and abandoned manners of the people Let us be cautious that such vices become not prevalent in our times, in order that the divine favour may preserve our country to us in that happy prosperity for the future which it has hitherto in its most merciful kindness vouchsafed us."

It has been made evident, I think, what disgrace and what destruction the neglect of learning and the immoral manners of degenerate men brought upon England! These remarks obtain this place in my history merely for the purpose of cautioning my readers.

Eadbert, then, rivalling his brother in piety, assumed the monastic habit, and gave place to Oswulph, his son, who being, without any cause on his part, slain by his subjects, was, after a twelvemonth's reign, succeeded by Moll. Moll carried on the government with commendable diligence for eleven years,* and then fell a victim to the treachery of

* Malmesbury differs from all the best authorities, who assign only six years to his reign. He ascended the throne A.D. 759, and was expelled A.D. 765.

Alcred. Alcred in his tenth year was compelled by his countrymen to retire from the government which he had usurped. Ethelred too, the son of Moll, being elected king, was expelled by them at the end of five years. Alfwold was next hailed sovereign: but he also, at the end of eleven years, experienced the perfidy of the inhabitants, for he was cut off by assassination, though guiltless, as his distinguished interment at Hexham and divine miracles sufficiently declare. His nephew, Osred,* the son of Alcred, succeeding him, was expelled after the space of a year, and gave place to Ethelred, who was also called Ethelbert. He was the son of Moll, also called Ethelwald, and, obtaining the kingdom after twelve years of exile, held it during four, at the end of which time, unable to escape the fate of his predecessors, he was cruelly murdered. At this, many of the bishops and nobles greatly shocked, fled from the country. Some indeed affirm that he was punished deservedly, because he had assented to the unjust murder of Osred, whereas he had it in his power to quit the sovereignty and restore him to his throne. Of the beginning of this reign Alcuin thus speaks: "Blessed be God, the only worker of miracles, Ethelred, the son of Ethelwald, went lately from the dungeon to the throne, from misery to grandeur; by the infancy of whose reign we are detained from coming to you."† Of his death he writes‡ thus to Offa king of the Mercians: "Your esteemed kindness is to understand that my lord, king Charles, often speaks to me of you with affection and sincerity, and in him you have the firmest friend. He therefore sends becoming presents to your love, and to the several sees of your kingdom. In like manner he had appointed presents for king Ethelred, and for the sees of his bishops, but, oh, dreadful to think, at the very moment of despatching these gifts and letters there came a sorrowful account, by the

---

* Osred, through a conspiracy of his nobles, had been deposed, and, after receiving the tonsure, was compelled to go into exile. Two years after, induced by the promises and oaths of certain of the Northumbrian chiefs, he returned, but being deserted by his forces, he was made prisoner and put to death by the order of Ethelred. Sim. Dunelm. A.D. 790—2. Osred was expelled from his kingdom, A.D. 790, and Ethelred was restored after an exile of twelve years.—*Hardy.*

† This letter is not yet published in Alcuini Opera.

‡ Epist. xlii. Op. tom 1 p. 57.

ambassadors who returned out of Scotland through your country, of the faithlessness of the people, and the death of the king. So that Charles, withholding his liberal gifts, is so highly incensed against that nation as to call it perfidious and perverse, and the murderer of its sovereigns, esteeming it worse than pagan; and had I not interceded he would have already deprived them of every advantage within his reach, and have done them all the injury in his power."

After Ethelred no one durst ascend the throne;* each dreading the fate of his predecessor, and preferring a life of safety in inglorious ease, to a tottering reign in anxious suspense: for most of the Northumbrian kings had ended their reigns by a death which was now become almost habitual. Thus being without a sovereign for thirty-three years, that province became an object of plunder and contempt to its neighbours. For when the Danes, who, as I have before related from the words of Alcuin, laid waste the holy places, on their return home represented to their countrymen the fruitfulness of the island, and the indolence of its inhabitants; these barbarians came over hastily, in great numbers, and obtained forcible possession of that part of the country, till the time we are speaking of: indeed they had a king of their own for many years, though he was subordinate to the authority of the king of the West Saxons. However, after the lapse of these thirty-three years, king Egbert obtained the sovereignty of this province, as well as of the others, in the year of our Lord's incarnation 827, and the twenty-eighth of his reign. And since we have reached his times, mindful of our engagement, we shall speak briefly of the kingdom of the Mercians; and this, as well because we admire brevity in relation, as that there is no great abundance of materials.

* This is not quite correct. Osbald was elected by a party to succeed him; but after a very short period he was deposed, and the government devolved on Eardulf. Eardulf after a few years was driven into exile, went to Rome, and, it would seem, was restored to his kingdom, by the influence of Charlemagne, A D. 808. V. Sim. Dunelm. col. 117, and Eginhardi Annales, Duchesne, 2, 255.

CHAPTER IV.

Of the kings of the Mercians. [A.D. 626—874.]

In the year of our Lord's incarnation 626, and the hundred and thirty-ninth after the death of Hengist, Penda the son of Pybba, tenth in descent of Woden, of noble lineage, expert in war, but at the same time an irreligious heathen, at the age of fifty assumed the title* of king of the Mercians, after he had already fostered his presumption by frequent incursions on his neighbours. Seizing the sovereignty, therefore, with a mind loathing quiet and unconscious how great an enormity it was even to be victorious in a contest against his own countrymen, he began to attack the neighbouring cities, to invade the confines of the surrounding kings, and to fill everything with terror and confusion. For what would not that man attempt, who, by his lawless daring, had extinguished those luminaries of Britain, Edwin and Oswald, kings of the Northumbrians, Sigebert, Ecgric, and Anna, kings of the East Angles; men, in whom nobility of race was equalled by sanctity of life? Kenwalk also, king of the West Saxons, after being frequently harassed by him, was driven into exile; though, perhaps, he deservedly paid the penalty of his perfidy towards God, in denying his faith; and towards Penda himself, in repudiating his sister. It is irksome to relate, how eagerly he watched opportunities of slaughter, and as a raven flies greedily at the scent of a carcase, so he joined Cadwalla,† and was of infinite service to him, in recovering his dominions. In this manner, for thirty years, he attacked his countrymen, but did nothing worthy of record against strangers. His insatiable desires, however, at last found an end suitable to their deserts; for being routed, with his allies, by Oswy, who had succeeded his brother Oswald, more through the assistance

* It would appear that Penda was not the first king, but the first of any note. Hen Huntingdon assigns the origin of the kingdom to about the year 584 under Crida, who was succeeded, in the year 600, by Pybba; Ceorl came to the throne in 610, and Penda in 626. See H. Hunt. f. 181, 184—b.

† King of the Britons, see Bede, b. ii. ch. 20. It was by his assistance that Cadwalla defeated Edwin, king of Northumbria, at Hatfield, Oct. 12, A D. 633.

of God than his military powers, Penda increased the number of infernal spirits. By his queen Kyneswith his sons were Peada, Wulfhere, Ethelred, Merwal, and Mercelin: his daughters, Kyneburg, and Kyneswith; both distinguished for inviolable chastity. Thus the parent, though ever rebellious towards God, produced a most holy offspring for Heaven.

His son Peada succeeded him in a portion of the kingdom, by the permission of Oswy, advanced to the government of the South Mercians; a young man of talents, and even in his father's lifetime son-in-law to Oswy. For he had received his daughter, on condition of renouncing paganism and embracing Christianity; in which faith he would soon have caused the province of participate, the peaceful state of the kingdom and his father-in-law's consent tending to such a purpose, had not his death, hastened, as they say, by the intrigues of his wife, intercepted these joyful prospects. Then Oswy resumed the government, which seemed rightly to appertain to him from his victory over the father, and from his affinity to the son. The spirit, however, of the inhabitants could not brook his authority more than three years; for they expelled his generals, and Wulfhere, the son of Penda, being hailed as his successor, the province recovered its liberty.

Wulfhere, that he might not disappoint the hopes of the nation, began to act with energy, to show himself an efficient prince by great exertions both mental and personal, and finally to afford Christianity, introduced by his brother and yet hardly breathing in his kingdom, every possible assistance. In the early years of his reign he was heavily oppressed by the king of the West Saxons, but in succeeding times, repelling the injury by the energy of his measures, he deprived him of the sovereignty of the Isle of Wight; and leading it, yet panting after heathen rites, into the proper path, he soon after bestowed it on his godson, Ethelwalch, king of the South Saxons, as a recompence for his faith. But these and all his other good qualities are stained and deteriorated by the dreadful brand of simony; because he, first of the kings of the Angles, sold the sacred bishopric of London to one Wini, an ambitious man. His wife was Ermenhilda, the daughter of Erconbert, king of Kent, of whom he begat Kinred, and Wereburga, a most holy virgin who lies buried at Chester. His brother Merewald married Ermenburga, the daughter of Ermenred, brother of the same Erconbert; by her he had issue, three daughters; Milburga, who lies at Wencloch; Mildritha in Kent, in the monastery of St. Augustine; and Milgitha: and one son, Merefin. Alfrid king of the Northumbrians married Kyneburg, daughter of Penda: who, after a time, disgusted with wedlock, took the habit of a nun in the monastery which her brothers, Wulfhere and Ethelred, had founded.

Wulfhere died at the end of nineteen years, and his brother Ethelred ascended the throne; more famed for his pious disposition than his skill in war. Moreover he was satisfied with displaying his valour in a single but illustrious expedition into Kent, and passed the remainder of his life in quiet, except that attacking Egfrid, king of the Northumbrians, who had passed beyond the limits of his kingdom, he admonished him to return home, by the murder of his brother Elfwin. He atoned however for this slaughter, after due deliberation, at the instance of St. Theodore, the archbishop, by giving Egfrid a large sum of money.* Subsequently to this, in the thirtieth year of his reign, he took the cowl, and became a monk at Bardney, of which monastery he was ultimately promoted to be abbat. This is the same person who was contemporary with Ina, king of the West Saxons, and confirmed by his authority also the privilege which St. Aldhelm brought from Rome. His wife was Ostritha, sister of Egfrid, king of the Northumbrians, by whom she had issue a son named Ceolred.

He appointed Kenred, the son of his brother Wulfhere his successor, who, equally celebrated for piety to God and uprightness towards his subjects, ran his mortal race with great purity of manners, and proceeding to Rome in the fifth year of his reign, passed the remainder of his life there in the offices of religion; chiefly instigated to this by the melancholy departure of a soldier, who, as Bede relates,†

* This was by paying to his relatives his weregild, or the legal price of his blood; for all, from the king to the slave, had their established value. One moiety, only, of the weregild went to the family of the murdered person; the other went into the public purse.

† Ethelbald had been frequently exhorted by the king to make confession of his transgressions, but had constantly declined it. At last being

disdaining to confess his crimes when in health, saw, manifestly, when at the point of death, those very demons coming to punish him to whose vicious allurements he had surrendered his soul.

After him reigned Ceolred, the son of Ethelred his uncle, as conspicuous for his valour against Ina, as pitiable for an early death, for not filling the throne more than eight years, he was buried at Lichfield, leaving Ethelbald, the grand-nephew of Penda by his brother Alwy, his heir. This king, enjoying the sovereignty in profound and long-continued peace, that is, for the space of forty-one years, was ultimately killed by his subjects, and thus met with a reverse of fortune. Bernred, the author of his death, left nothing worthy of record, except that afterwards, being himself put to death by Offa, he received the just reward of his treachery. To this Ethelbald, Boniface,[*] archbishop of Mentz, an Angle by nation, who was subsequently crowned with martyrdom, sent an epistle, part of which I shall transcribe, that it may appear how freely he asserts those very vices to have already gained ground among the Angles of which Alcuin in after times was apprehensive. It will also be a strong proof, by the remarkable deaths of certain kings, how severely God punishes those guilty persons for whom his long-suspended anger mercifully waits.

[†] *"To Ethelbald, my dearest lord, and to be preferred to all other kings of the Angles, in the love of Christ, Boniface the archbishop, legate to Germany from the church of Rome,*

---

seized with sickness, he appears to have imagined that he saw two angels approach with a very small volume, in which were written the few good actions he had ever performed; when immediately a large company of demons advancing, display another book of enormous bulk and weight, containing all his evil deeds, which are read to him; after which, asserting their claim to the sinner against the angels, they strike him on the head and feet, as symptoms of his approaching end. Bede, b. v. c. 13.

[*] Boniface, whose original name was Winfred, after unwearied labour in the conversion of various nations in Germany, by which he acquired the honourable appellation of Apostle of the Germans, at length suffered martyrdom in Friesland. A collected edition of his works forms volumes xv. and xvi. of PATRES ECCLESIÆ ANGLICANÆ by the editor of this work. One of the original churches, built by him in Saxony, still exists in the Duchy of Gotha, at a little village called Gierstedt.

[†] See this epistle at length in Spelmanni Concilia, vol. i. page 232, and reprinted by Wilkins, Concilia, i. 87, also in Bonifacii Opera, &c.

wisheth perpetual health in Christ. We confess before God that when we hear of your prosperity, your faith, and good works, we rejoice; and if at any time we hear of any adversity befallen you, either in the chance of war or the jeopardy of your soul, we are afflicted. We have heard that, devoted to almsgiving, you prohibit theft and rapine, are a lover of peace, a defender of widows, and of the poor; and for this we give God thanks. Your contempt for lawful matrimony, were it for chastity's sake, would be laudable; but since you wallow in luxury and even in adultery with nuns, it is disgraceful and damnable; it dims the brightness of your glory before God and man, and transforms you into an idolater, because you have polluted the temple of God. Wherefore, my beloved son, repent, and remember how dishonourable it is, that you, who, by the grant of God, are sovereign over many nations, should yourself be the slave of lust to his disservice. Moreover, we have heard that almost all the nobles of the Mercian kingdom, following your example, desert their lawful wives and live in guilty intercourse with adultresses and nuns. Let the custom of a foreign country teach you how far distant this is from rectitude. For in old Saxony, where there is no knowledge of Christ, if a virgin in her father's house, or a married woman under the protection of her husband, should be guilty of adultery, they burn her, strangled by her own hand, and hang up her seducer over the grave where she is buried; or else, cutting off her garments to the waist, modest matrons whip her and pierce her with knives, and fresh tormentors punish her in the same manner as she goes from town to town, till they destroy her. Again the Winedi,* the basest of nations, have this custom—the wife, on the death of her husband, casts herself on the same funeral pile to be consumed with him. If then the gentiles, who know not God, have so zealous a regard for chastity, how much more ought you to possess, my beloved son, who are both a Christian and a king? Spare therefore your own soul, spare a multitude of people, perishing by your example, for whose souls you must give account. Give heed to this too, if the nation of the Angles, (and we are reproached in France and

* The Winedi were seated on the western bank of the Vistula, near the Baltic. In Wilkins, it is "apud Persas," among the Persians.

in Italy and by the very pagans for it,) despising lawful matrimony, give free indulgence to adultery, a race ignoble and despising God must necessarily proceed from such a mixture, which will destroy the country by their abandoned manners, as was the case with the Burgundians, Provençals, and Spaniards, whom the Saracens harassed for many years on account of their past transgressions. Moreover, it has been told us, that you take away from the churches and monasteries many of their privileges, and excite, by your example, your nobility to do the like. But recollect, I entreat you, what terrible vengeance God hath inflicted upon former kings, guilty of the crime we lay to your charge. For Ceolred, your predecessor, the debaucher of nuns, the infringer of ecclesiastical privileges, was seized, while splendidly regaling with his nobles, by a malignant spirit, who snatched away his soul without confession and without communion, while in converse with the devil and despising the law of God. He drove Osred also, king of the Deirans and Bernicians, who was guilty of the same crimes, to such excess that he lost his kingdom and perished in early manhood by an ignominious death. Charles also, governor of the Franks, the subverter of many monasteries and the appropriator of ecclesiastical revenues to his own use, perished by excruciating pain and a fearful death." And afterwards, "Wherefore, my beloved son, we entreat with paternal and fervent prayers that you would not despise the counsel of your fathers, who, for the love of God, anxiously appeal to your highness. For nothing is more salutary to a good king than the willing correction of such crimes when they are pointed out to him; since Solomon says 'Whoso loveth instruction, loveth wisdom.' Wherefore, my dearest son, showing you good counsel, we call you to witness, and entreat you by the living God, and his Son Jesus Christ, and by the Holy Spirit, that you would recollect how fleeting is the present life, how short and momentary is the delight of the filthy flesh, and how ignominious for a person of transitory existence to leave a bad example to posterity. Begin therefore to regulate your life by better habits, and correct the past errors of your youth, that you may have praise before men here, and be blest with eternal glory hereafter. We wish your Highness health and proficiency in virtue."

I have inserted in my narrative portions of this epistle, to give sufficient knowledge of these circumstances, partly in the words of the author and partly in my own, shortening the sentences as seemed proper, for which I shall easily be be excused, because there was need of brevity for the sake of those who were eager to resume the thread of the history. Moreover, Boniface transmitted an epistle of like import to archbishop Cuthbert, adding that he should remonstrate with the clergy and nuns on the fineness and vanity of their dress. Besides, that he might not wonder at his interfering in that in which he had no apparent concern, that is to say, how or with what manners the nation of the Angles conducted itself, he gave him to understand, that he had bound himself by oath to pope Gregory the Third, not to conceal the conduct of the nations near him from the knowledge of the apostolical see ; wherefore, if mild measures failed of success, he should take care to act in such manner, that vices of this kind should not be kept secret from the pope. Indeed, on account of the fine texture of the clerical vestments, Alcuin obliquely glances at Athelard the archbishop, Cuthbert's successor, reminding him that, when he should come to Rome to visit the emperor Charles the Great, the grandson of Charles of whom Boniface was speaking above, he should not bring the clergy or monks dressed in party-coloured or gaudy garments, for the clergy amongst the Franks dressed only in ecclesiastical habits.

Nor could the letters of so great a man, which he was accustomed to send from watchful regard to his legation and pure love of his country, be without effect. For both Cuthbert, the archbishop, and king Ethelbald summoned a council for the purpose of retrenching the superfluities which he had stigmatised. The acts of this synod, veiled in a multiplicity of words, I shall forbear to add, as I think they will better accord with another part of my work, when I come to the succession of the bishops : but as I am now on the subject of kingly affairs, I shall subjoin a charter of Ethelbald's, as a proof of his devotion, because it took place in the same council.

"It often happens, through the uncertain change of times, that those things which have been confirmed by the testimony and advice of many faithful persons, have been made of none effect by the contumacy of very many, or by the artifices of deceit, without any regard to justice, unless they have been committed to eternal memory by the authority of writing and the testimony of charters. Wherefore I Ethelbald, king of the Mercians, out of love to heaven and regard for my own soul, have felt the necessity of considering how I may, by good works, set it free from every tie of sin. For since the Omnipotent God, through the greatness of his clemency, without any previous merit on my part, hath bestowed on me the sceptre of government, therefore I willingly repay him out of that which he hath given. On this account I grant, so long as I live, that all monasteries and churches of my kingdom shall be exempted from public taxes, works, and impositions, except the building of forts and bridges, from which none can be released. And moreover the servants of God shall have perfect liberty in the produce of their woods and lands, and the right of fishing, nor shall they bring presents either to king or princes except voluntarily, but they shall serve God without molestation."

Lullus* succeeded Boniface, an Englishman by birth also; of whose sanctity mention is made in the life of St. Goar, and these verses, which I remember to have heard from my earliest childhood, bear witness:

> "Lullus, than whom no holier prelate lives,
> By God's assistance healing medicine gives,
> Cures each disorder by his powerful hand,
> And with his glory overspreads the land."

However, to return to my history, Offa, descended from Penda in the fifth degree, succeeded Ethelbald. He was a a man of great mind, and one who endeavoured to bring to effect whatever he had preconceived; he reigned thirty-nine years. When I consider the deeds of this person, I am doubtful whether I should commend or censure. At one time, in the same character, vices were so palliated by virtues, and at another virtues came in such quick succession upon vices that it is difficult to determine how to characterize the changing Proteus. My narrative shall give examples of each. Engaging in a set battle with Cynewulf, king of the

* Lullus was appointed his successor by Boniface, on setting out for Friesland, in 755; he died A.D. 785.

West Saxons, he easily gained the victory, though the other was a celebrated warrior. When he thought artifice would better suit his purpose, this same man beheaded king Ethelbert, who had come to him through the allurement of great promises, and was at that very time within the walls of his palace, soothed into security by his perfidious attentions, and then unjustly seized upon the kingdom of the East Angles which Ethelbert had held.

The relics of St. Alban, at that time obscurely buried, he ordered to be reverently taken up and placed in a shrine, decorated to the fullest extent of royal munificence, with gold and jewels; a church of most beautiful workmanship was there erected, and a society of monks assembled. Yet rebellious against God, he endeavoured to remove the archiepiscopal see formerly settled at Canterbury, to Lichfield, envying, forsooth, the men of Kent the dignity of the archbishopric: on which account he at last deprived Lambert, the archbishop, worn out with continual exertion, and who produced many edicts of the apostolical see, both ancient and modern, of all possessions within his territories, as well as of the jurisdiction over the bishoprics. From pope Adrian, therefore, whom he had wearied with plausible assertions for a long time, as many things not to be granted may be gradually drawn and artfully wrested from minds intent on other occupations, he obtained that there should be an archbishopric of the Mercians at Lichfield, and that all the prelates of the Mercians should be subject to that province. Their names were as follow: Denebert, bishop of Worcester, Werenbert, of Leicester, Edulph, of Sidnacester, Wulpheard, of Hereford; and the bishops of the East Angles, Alpheard, of Elmham, Tidfrid, of Dunwich; the bishop of Lichfield was named Aldulph. Four bishops however remained suffragan to Lambert, archbishop of Canterbury, London, Winchester, Rochester, and Selsey. Some of these bishoprics are now in being, some are removed to other places, others consolidated by venal interest, for Leicester, Sidnacester, and Dunwich, from some unknown cause, are no longer in existence. Nor did Offa's rapacity stop here, for he showed himself a downright public pilferer, by converting to his own use the lands of many churches, of which Malmesbury was one. But this iniquity did not long deform canonical institutions, for soon after Kenulf, Offa's successor, inferior to no preceding king in power or in faith, transmitted a letter to Leo, the successor of Adrian, and restored Athelard who had succeeded Lambert, to his former dignity. Hence Alcuin, in an epistle to the same Athelard, says " Having heard of the success of your journey, and your return to your country, and how you were received by the pope, I give thanks with every sentiment of my heart to the Lord our God, who, by the precious gift of his mercy, directed your way with a prosperous progress, gave you favour in the sight of the pope, granted you to return home with the perfect accomplishment of your wishes, and hath condescended, through you, to restore the holiest seat of our first teacher to its pristine dignity." I think it proper to subjoin part of the king's epistle and also of the pope's, though I may seem by so doing to anticipate the regular order of time ; but I shall do it on this account, that it is a task of greater difficulty to blend together disjointed facts than to despatch those I had begun.

" To the most holy and truly loving lord Leo, pontiff of the sacred and apostolical see, Kenulf, by the grace of God king of the Mercians, with the bishops, princes, and every degree of dignity under our authority, sendeth the salutation of the purest love in Christ.

" We give thanks ever to God Almighty, who is wont, by the means of new guides, the former being taken to the life eternal, to guide the church, purchased by his precious blood, amid the diverse storms of this world, to the haven of salvation, and to shed fresh light upon it, in order that it be led into no error of darkness, but may pursue the path of truth without stumbling ; wherefore the universal church justly rejoices, that when the true rewarder of all good men took the most glorious pastor of his flock, Adrian, to be eternally rewarded in heaven, still his kind providence gave a shepherd to his flock, not less skilled, to conduct the sheep of God into the fold of life. We also, who live on the farthest confines of the world, justly boast, beyond all other things, that the church's exaltation is our safety, its prosperity our constant ground of joy ; since your apostolical dignity and our true faith originate from the same source. Whentfore I deem it fitting to incline the ear of our obedience, with all due humility, to your holy commands, and to fulfil, with every possible endeavour, what shall seem just to your piety for us to accomplish : but to avoid, and utterly reject, all that shall be found inconsistent with right. But now, I, Kenulf, by the grace of God king, humbly entreat your excellence that I may address you as I wish, without offence, on the subject of our progress, that you may receive me with peaceful tranquillity into the bosom of your piety, and that the liberal bounty of your benediction may qualify me, gifted with no stock of merit, to rule my people ; in order that God may deign, through your intercession, to defend the nation, which, together with me, your apostolical authority has instructed in the rudiments of the faith, against all attacks of adversaries, and to extend that kingdom which he hath given. This benediction all the Mercian kings before me were, by your predecessors, deemed worthy to obtain. This, I humbly beg, and this, O most holy man, I desire to receive, that you would more especially accept me as a son by adoption, as I love you as my father, and always honour you with all possible obedience. For among such great personages faith ever should be kept inviolate, as well as perfect love, because paternal love is to be looked upon as filial happiness in God, according to the saying of Hezekiah, ' A father will make known thy truth to his sons, O Lord.' In which words I implore you, O loved father, not to deny to your unworthy son the knowledge of the Lord in your holy words, in order that, by your sound instruction, I may deserve, by the assistance of God, to come to a better course of life. And moreover, O most affectionate father, we beg, with all our bishops, and every person of rank among us, that, concerning the many inquiries on which we have thought it right to consult your wisdom, you would courteously reply, lest the traditions of the holy fathers and their instructions should, through ignorance, be misunderstood by us ; but let your reply reach us in charity and meekness, that, through the mercy of God, it may bring forth fruit in us. The first thing our bishops and learned men allege is, that, contrary to the canons and papal constitutions enacted for our use by the direction of the most holy father Gregory, as you know, the jurisdiction of the metropolitan of Canterbury is divided into two provinces, to whose power, by the same father's command, twelve bishops ought to be subject, as is read throughout our churches, in the letter which he directed to his brother and fellow bishop, Augustine, concerning the two metropolitans of London and York, which letter doubtlessly you also possess. But that pontifical dignity, which was at that time destined to London, with the honour and distinction of the pall, was, for his sake, removed and granted to Canterbury. For since Augustine, of blessed memory, who, at the command of St. Gregory, preached the word of God to the nation of the Angles, and so gloriously presided over the church of the Saxons, died in that city, and his body was buried in the church of St. Peter, the chief of apostles, which his successor St. Laurentius consecrated, it seemed proper to the sages of our nation, that the metropolitan dignity should reside in that city where rests the body of the man who planted the true faith in these parts. The honour of this pre-eminence, as you know, king Offa first attempted to take away and to divide it into two provinces, through enmity against the venerable Lambert and the Kentish people; and your pious brother and predecessor, Adrian, at the request of the aforesaid king, first did what no one had before presumed, and honoured the prelate of the Mercians with the pall. But yet we blame neither of these persons, whom, as we believe, Christ crowns with eternal glory. Nevertheless we humbly entreat your excellence, on whom God hath deservedly conferred the key of wisdom, that you would consult with your counsellors on this subject, and condescend to transmit to us what may be necessary for us to observe hereafter, and what may tend to the unity of real peace, as we wish, through your sound doctrine, lest the coat of Christ, woven throughout without seam, should suffer any rent among us. We have written this to you, most holy father, with equal humility and regard, earnestly entreating your clemency, that you would kindly and justly reply to those things which have been of necessity submitted to you. Moreover we wish that you would examine, with pious love, that epistle which, in the presence of all our bishops, Athelard the archbishop wrote to you more fully on the subject of his own affairs and necessities, as well as on those of all Britain; that whatever the rule of faith requires in those matters which are contained therein, you would condescend truly to explain. Wherefore last year I sent my own embassy, and that of the bishops by Wada the abbat, which he received, but idly and foolishly executed. I now send you a small present as a token of regard, respected father, by Birine the priest, and Fildas and Ceolbert, my servants, that is to say, one hundred and twenty mancuses,* together with letters, begging that you would condescend to receive them kindly, and give us your blessing. May God Almighty long preserve you safe to the glory of his holy church."

"*To the most excellent prince, my son Kenulf, king of the Mercians, of the province of the Saxons, pope Leo sendeth greeting.* Our most holy and reverend brother Athelard, archbishop of Canterbury, arriving at the holy churches of the blessed apostles Peter and Paul, as well for the faithful performance of his vow of prayer as to acquaint us with the cause of his ecclesiastical mission to the apostolical see, hath brought to us the enclosures of your royal excellence, where finding, in two epistles filled with true faith, your great humility, we return thanks to Almighty God, who hath taught and inclined your most prudent excellence to have due regard with us in all things towards St. Peter, the chief of apostles, and to submit with meekness to all apostolical constitutions. Moreover, in one of these epistles we find that, were it requisite, you would even lay down your life for us, for the sake of our apostolical office. And again, you confess that you rejoice much in the Lord at our prosperity, and that when these our letters of kindest admonition reach the ears of your cordiality, you will receive them with all humility and spiritual joy of heart, as sons do the gift of a father. It is added too that you had ordered a small present out of your abundance to be offered to us, an hundred and twenty mancuses, which, with ardent desire for the salvation of your soul, we have accepted. The aforesaid archbishop, with his attendants, has been honourably and kindly received by us, and has been rendered every necessary assistance. In the meantime, trusting to your most prudent excellence when you observe, even in your own royal letters, that no Christian can presume to run counter to our aposto-

* The value of the mancus is doubtful; sometimes it appears to mean the same with the mark, at others it is supposed equal to thirty pence of the money of that time. The gold manca is supposed to be eight to the pound, which was probably the coin sent to the pope.

lical decisions, we therefore endeavour, with all possible diligence, to transmit and ordain what shall be of service to your kingdom, that as a canonical censure enjoins your royal excellence, and all the princes of your nation, and the whole people of God, to observe all things which the aforesaid archbishop Athelard our brother, or the whole body of the evangelical and apostolical doctrine and that of the holy fathers and of our predecessors the holy pontiffs ordain, you ought by no means to resist their orthodox doctrine in any thing, as our Lord and Saviour says in the Gospel, "He who receiveth you receiveth me," and "he who receives a prophet, in the name of a prophet, shall receive a prophet's reward." And how much more do we praise the Almighty for this same lord archbishop, whom you have so highly commended to us as being, what he really is, honourable, and skilful, and prudent, of good morals, worthy before God and men. O loving son and excellent king, we praise God, that hath pointed out to you a prelate who, like a true shepherd, is able to prescribe due penance, according to the doctrine of the holy Scriptures, and to rescue the souls of those who are under his sacerdotal authority from the nethermost hell, snatching them from inextinguishable fire, bringing them into the haven of salvation, and offering for them to God Almighty a sacrifice, fit and pure in the sight of the Divine Majesty. And since the aforesaid archbishop hath pleased us extremely in every respect, in all holiness and conversation of life, confiding much to him, we give him such prelatical power by the authority of St. Peter, the chief of the apostles, whose office, though unworthily, we fill, that if any in his province, as well kings and princes as people, shall transgress the commandments of the Lord, he shall excommunicate him until he repent ; and if he remain impenitent, let him be to you as an heathen and a publican. But with respect to the aforesaid Athelard, archbishop of Canterbury, since your excellent prelates have demanded from us that we do him justice concerning the jurisdiction which he lately held, as well of bishops as monasteries, and of which he has been unjustly deprived, as you know, and which have been taken from his venerable see: we, making most diligent search, have found in our sacred depository, that St. Gregory, our predecessor, delivered that diocese to his deputed archbishop St. Augustine, with the right of consecrating bishops, to the full number of twelve. Hence we also, having ascertained the truth, have, by our apostolical authority, placed all ordinations or confirmations on their ancient footing, and do restore them to him entire, and we deliver to him the grant of our confirmation, to be duly observed by his church, according to the sacred canons."

In the meantime Offa, that the outrages against his countrymen might not secretly tend to his disadvantage, in order to conciliate the favour of neighbouring kings, gave his daughter Eadburga in marriage to Bertric, king of the West Saxons; and obtained the amity of Charles the Great, king of the Franks, by repeated embassies, though he could find little in the disposition of Charles to second his views. They had disagreed before, insomuch that violent feuds having arisen on both sides, even the intercourse of traders was prohibited. There is an epistle of Alcuin to this effect, part of which I shall subjoin, as it affords a strong proof of the magnanimity and valour of Charles, who spent all his time in war against the Pagans, rebels to God. He says,[*] "The ancient Saxons and all the Friesland nations were converted to the faith of Christ through the exertions of king Charles, urging some with threats, and others with rewards. At the end of the year the king made an attack upon the Sclavonians and subjugated them to his power. The Avares, whom we call Huns, made a furious attempt upon Italy, but were conquered by the generals of the aforesaid most Christian king, and returned home with disgrace. In like manner they rushed against Bavaria, and were again overcome and dispersed by the Christian army. Moreover the princes and commanders of the same most Christian king took great part of Spain from the Saracens, to the extent of three hundred miles along the sea coast: but, O shame! these accursed Saracens, who are the Hagarens, have dominion over the whole of Africa, and the larger part of Asia Major. I know not what will be our destination, for some ground of difference, fomented by the devil, has arisen between king Charles and king Offa, so that, on both sides,

[*] See this entire, Usserii Veterum Epistolarum Hibernicarum Sylloge, epist. 18. p. 36; and Alcuini Opera, tom. 1. p. 6, epist. 3.

all navigation is prohibited the merchants. Some say that we are to be sent into those parts to treat of peace."

In these words, in addition to what I have remarked above, any curious person may determine how many years have elapsed since the Saracens invaded Africa and Asia Major. And indeed, had not the mercy of God animated the native spirit of the emperors of the Franks, the pagans had long since subjugated Europe also. For, holding the Constantinopolitan emperors in contempt, they possessed themselves of Sicily and Sardinia, the Balearic isles, and almost all the countries surrounded by the sea, with the exception of Crete, Rhodes, and Cyprus. In our time however they have been compelled to relinquish Sicily by the Normans, Corsica and Sardinia by the Pisans, and great part of Asia and Jerusalem itself by the Franks and other nations of Europe. But, as I shall have a fitter place to treat largely of these matters hereafter, I shall now subjoin, from the words of Charles himself, the treaty which was ratified between him and Offa king of the Mercians.

"*Charles, by the grace of God king of the Franks and Lombards, and patrician of the Romans, to his esteemed and dearest brother Offa king of the Mercians, sendeth health:*—
First, we give thanks to God Almighty for the purity of the Catholic faith, which we find laudably expressed in your letters. Concerning pilgrims, who for the love of God or the salvation of their souls, wish to visit the residence of the holy apostles, let them go peaceably without any molestation; but if persons, not seeking the cause of religion, but that of gain, be found amongst them, let them pay the customary tolls in proper places. We will, too, that traders have due protection within our kingdom, according to our mandate, and if in any place they suffer wrongful oppression, let them appeal to us or to our judges, and we will see full justice done. Let your kindness also be apprized that we have sent some token of our regard, out of our dalmatics* and palls, to each episcopal see of your kingdom or of Ethelred's, as an

---

* The dalmatic was a garment worn by the clergy, and sometimes by princes. Its name is said to have been derived from its invention in Dalmatia. The pall here apparently signifies an upper vesture also, in form resembling a cloak without sleeves; but it has a variety of meanings. See Du Cange, and note at p. 44, of Bede's Eccles. History.

almsgiving, on account of our apostolical lord Adrian, earnestly begging that you would order him to be prayed for, not as doubting that his blessed soul is at rest, but to show our esteem and regard to our dearest friend. Moreover we have sent somewhat out of the treasure of those earthly riches, which the Lord Jesus hath granted to us of his unmerited bounty, for the metropolitan cities, and for yourself a belt, an Hungarian sword, and two silk cloaks."

I have inserted these brief extracts from the epistle that posterity may be clearly acquainted with the friendship of Offa and Charles; confiding in which friendly intercourse, although assailed by the hatred of numbers, he passed the rest of his life in uninterrupted quiet, and saw Egfert his son anointed to succeed him. This Egfert studiously avoided the cruel path trod by his father, and devoutly restored the privileges of all the churches which Offa had in his time abridged. The possessions also which his father had taken from Malmesbury he restored into the hands of Cuthbert, then abbat of that place, at the admonition of the aforesaid Athelard archbishop of Canterbury, a man of energy and a worthy servant of God, and who is uniformly asserted to have been its abbat before Cuthbert, from the circumstance of his choosing there to be buried. But while the hopes of Egfert's noble qualities were ripening, in the first moments of his reign, untimely death cropped the flower of his youthful prime; on which account Alcuin writing to the patrician Osbert, says, "I do not think that the most noble youth Egfert died for his own sins, but because his father, in the establishment of his kingdom, shed a deluge of blood." Dying after a reign of four months, he appointed Kenulf, nephew of Penda in the fifth degree by his brother Kenwalk, to succeed him.

Kenulf was a truly great man, and surpassed his fame by his virtues, doing nothing that malice could justly find fault with. Religious at home, victorious abroad, his praises will be deservedly extolled so long as an impartial judge can be found in England. Equally to be admired for the extent of his power and for the lowliness of his mind; of which he gave an eminent proof in restoring, as we have related, its faltering dignity to Canterbury, he little regarded earthly grandeur in his own kingdom at the expense of deviating from anciently-enjoined canons. Taking up Offa's hatred against the Kentish people, he sorely afflicted that province, and led away captive their king Eadbert, surnamed Pren; but not long after, moved with sentiments of pity, he released him. For at Winchelcombe, where he had built a church to God, which yet remains, on the day of its dedication he freed the captive king at the altar, and consoled him with liberty; thereby giving a memorable instance of his clemency. Cuthred,* whom he had made king over the Kentish people, was present to applaud this act of royal munificence. The church resounded with acclamations, the street shook with crowds of people, for in an assembly of thirteen bishops and ten dukes, no one was refused a largess, all departed with full purses. Moreover, in addition to those presents of inestimable price and number in utensils, clothes, and select horses, which the chief nobility received, he gave to all who did not possess landed property† a pound of silver, to each presbyter a marca of gold, to every monk a shilling, and lastly he made many presents to the people at large. After he had endowed the monastery with such ample revenues as would seem incredible in the present time, he honoured it by his sepulture, in the twenty-fourth year of his reign. His son Kenelm, of tender age, and undeservedly murdered by his sister Quendrida, gained the title and distinction of martyrdom, and rests in the same place.

After him the kingdom of the Mercians sank from its prosperity, and becoming nearly lifeless, produced nothing worthy to be mentioned in history. However, that no one may accuse me of leaving the history imperfect, I shall glance over the names of the kings in succession. Ceolwulf, the brother of Kenulf, reigning one year was expelled in the second by Bernulf; who in the third year of his reign being overcome and put to flight by Egbert, king of the West Saxons, was afterwards slain by the East Angles, because he had attempted to seize on East Anglia, as a kingdom subject to the Mercians from the time of Offa. Ludecan, after

* Kenulf made Cuthred king of Kent, A.D. 798. Eadbert had been dreadfully mutilated by having his eyes put out and his hands cut off. See chap. i.

† "Qui agros non habebant." These words refer to an inferior class of gentry, as he mentions the people at large, "populus," afterwards.

a reign of two years, was despatched by these Angles, as he was preparing to avenge his predecessor: Withlaf, subjugated in the commencement of his reign by the before-mentioned Egbert, governed thirteen years, paying tribute to him and to his son, both for his person and his property: Berthwulf reigning thirteen years on the same conditions, was at last driven by the Danish pirates beyond the sea: Burhred marrying Ethelswith, the daughter of king Ethelwulf, the son of Egbert, exonerated himself, by this affinity, from the payment of tribute and the depredations of the enemy, but after twenty-two years, driven by them from his country, he fled to Rome, and was there buried at the school of the Angles, in the church of St. Mary; his wife, at that time continuing in this country, but afterwards following her husband, died at Pavia. The kingdom was next given by the Danes to one Celwulf, an attendant of Burhred's, who bound himself by oath that he would retain it only at their pleasure: after a few years it fell under the dominion of Alfred, the grandson of Egbert. Thus the sovereignty of the Mercians, which prematurely bloomed by the overweening ambition of an heathen, altogether withered away through the inactivity of a driveller king, in the year of our Lord's incarnation eight hundred and seventy-five.

CHAP. V.

Of the kings of the East Angles. [A D. 520—905.]

As my narrative has hitherto treated of the history of the four more powerful kingdoms in as copious a manner, I trust, as the perusal of ancient writers has enabled me, I shall now, as last in point of order, run through the governments of the East Angles and East Saxons, as suggested in my preface. The kingdom of the East Angles arose anterior to the West Saxons, though posterior to the kingdom of Kent. The first* and also the greatest king of the East Angles was Redwald, tenth in descent from Woden as they affirm; for all the southern provinces of the Angles and Saxons on this side of

* Redwald was not the first king of East Anglia, but the first who became distinguished. In the year 571, Uffa assumed the title of king: he was succeeded by his son, Titil, in 578 who was followed by Redwald, his son. See Bede, b. ii. c. 15.

the river Humber, with their kings, were subject to his authority. This is the person whom I have formerly mentioned as having, out of regard for Edwin, killed Ethelfrid, king of the Northumbrians. Through the persuasion of Edwin too he was baptized; and after, at the instigation of his wife, abjured the faith. His son, Eorpwald, embraced pure Christianity, and poured out his immaculate spirit to God, being barbarously murdered by the heathen Richbert. To him succeeded Sigebert, his brother by the mother's side, a worthy servant of the Lord, polished from all barbarism by his education among the Franks. For, being driven into banishment by Redwald, and for a long time associating with them, he had received the rites of Christianity, which, on his coming into power he graciously communicated to the whole of his kingdom, and also instituted schools of learning in different places. This ought highly to be extolled: as men heretofore uncivilized and irreligious, were enabled, by his means, to taste the sweets of literature. The promoter of his studies and the stimulator of his religion was Felix the bishop, a Burgundian by birth, who now lies buried at Ramsey. Sigebert moreover renouncing the world and taking the monastic vow, left the throne to his relation, Ecgric, with whom, being attacked in intestine war by Penda, king of the Mercians, he met his death, at the moment when, superior to his misfortunes, and mindful of his religious profession, he held only a wand in his hand. The successor of Ecgric was Anna, the son of Eni, the brother of Redwald, involved in similar destruction by the same furious Penda; he was blessed with a numerous and noble offspring, as the second book will declare in its proper place. To Anna succeeded his brother Ethelhere, who was justly slain by Oswy king of the Northumbrians, together with Penda, because he was an auxiliary to him, and was actually supporting the very army which had destroyed his brother and his kinsman. His brother Ethelwald, in due succession, left the kingdom to Adulf and Elwold, the sons of Ethelhere. Next came Bernred. After him Ethelred. His son was St. Ethelbert, whom Offa king of the Mercians killed through treachery, as has already been said, and will be repeated hereafter. After him, through the violence of the Mercians, few kings reigned in Eastern Anglia till the time of St. Edmund, and he was despatched in the sixteenth year of his reign, by Hingwar, a heathen; from which time the Angles ceased to command in their own country for fifty years. For the province was nine years without a king, owing to the continued devastations of the pagans; afterwards both in it and in East Saxony, Gothrun, a Danish king, reigned for twelve years, in the time of king Alfred. Gothrun had for successor a Dane also, by name Eohric, who, after he had reigned fourteen years, was taken off by the Angles, because he conducted himself with cruelty towards them. Still, however, liberty beamed not on this people, for the Danish earls continued to oppress them, or else to excite them against the kings of the West Saxons, till Edward, the son of Alfred, added both provinces to his own West Saxon empire, expelling the Danes and freeing the Angles. This event took place in the fiftieth year after the murder of St. Edmund, king and martyr, and in the fifteenth * of his own reign.

CHAP. VI.
Of the kings of the East Saxons. [A. D. 520—823.

NEARLY co-eval with the kingdom of the East Angles, was that of the East Saxons; which had many kings in succession, though subject to others, and principally to those of the Mercians. First, then, Sleda,† the tenth from Woden, reigned over them; whose son, Sabert, nephew of St. Ethelbert, king of Kent, by his sister Ricula, embraced the faith of Christ at the preaching of St. Mellitus, first bishop of London; for that city belongs to the East Saxons. On the death of Sabert, his sons, Sexred and Seward, drove Mellitus into banishment, and soon after, being killed by the West Saxons, they paid the penalty of their persecution against Christ. Sigbert, surnamed the Small, the son of Seward, succeeding, left the kingdom to Sigebert, the son of Sigebald,

* According to the Saxon Chronicle, A.D. 921, that is, the 21st of Edward the Elder, and the fiftieth from the murder of king Edmund. Now following this statement, as Edward succeeded his father, Alfred A.D. 901, the expulsion of the Danes would be the twentieth of his reign. In Florence of Worcester the union of the kingdoms under Edward the Elder is assigned to the year 918.—*Hardy.*

† Sleda was not the first, but their times are uncertain. See Florence of Worcester, who calls him the son of Escwine, whom Henry of Huntingdon considers to have been the first king of Essex.

who was the brother of Sabert. This Sigebert, at the exhortation of king Oswy, was baptized in Northumbria by bishop Finan, and brought back to his nation, by the ministry of bishop Cedd,* the faith which they had expelled together with Mellitus. After gloriously governing the kingdom, he left it in a manner still more glorious; for he was murdered by his near relations, merely because, in conformity to the gospel-precept, he used kindly to spare his enemies, nor regard with harsh and angry countenance, if they were penitent, those who had offended him. His brother Suidelm, baptized by the same Cedd in East Anglia, succeeded. On his death, Sighere, the son of Sigbert the Small, and Sebbi, the son of Seward, held the sovereignty. Sebbi's associate dying, he himself voluntarily retired from the kingdom in his thirtieth year, becoming a monk, as Bede relates. His sons Sighard and Suefred reigned after him. On their decease Offa, the son Sighere, governed the kingdom for a short time; a youth of engaging countenance and disposition, in the flower of his age, and highly beloved by his subjects. He, through the persuasion of Kyneswith, daughter of king Penda, whom he had anxiously sought in marriage, being taught to aspire after heavenly affections, went to Rome with Kenred king of the Mercians, and St. Edwin bishop of Worcester; and there taking the vow, in due time entered the heavenly mansions. To him succeeded Selred, son of Sigebert the Good, during thirty-eight years; who being slain, Swithed assumed the sovereignty of the East Saxons;† but in the same year that Egbert king of the West Saxons subdued Kent, being expelled by him, he vacated the kingdom; though London, with the adjacent country, continued subject to the kings of the Mercians as long as they held their sovereignty.

The kings of Kent, it is observed, had dominion peculiarly in Kent, in which are two sees; the archbishopric of Canterbury, and the bishopric of Rochester.

* Brother to St. Chad, bishop of Lichfield. See Bede, b. iii. c. 22.

† Here seems an oversight which may be supplied from Florence of Worcester. "Swithed succeeded Selred, and held the sovereignty some years; after whom few native kings ruled in Essex, for in the same year that Egbert conquered Kent, they surrendered to his power." Selred died 746; their submission took place 823. It would appear, however, from the authorities adduced by Mr. Turner, Hist of Anglo-Saxons, vol. i. p. 318, that Selred was in fact king of East-Anglia.

The kings of the West Saxons ruled in Wiltshire, Berkhire, and Dorsetshire; in which there is one bishop, whose see is now at Sarum or Salisbury; formerly it was at Ramsbury, or at Sherborne: in Sussex, which for some little time possessed a king of its own;* the episcopal see of this county was anciently in the island of Selsey, as Bede relates, where St. Wilfrid built a monastery; the bishop now dwells at Chichester: in the counties of Southampton and Surrey; which have a bishop, whose see is at Winchester: in the county of Somerset, which formerly had a bishop at Wells, but now at Bath: and in Domnonia, now called Devonshire, and Cornubia, now Cornwall; at that time there were two bishoprics, one at Crediton, the other at St. German's; now there is but one, and the see is at Exeter.

The kings of the Mercians governed the counties of Gloucester, Worcester, and Warwick; in these is one bishop whose residence is at Worcester: in Cheshire, Derbyshire, and Staffordshire; these have one bishop, who has part of Warwickshire and Shropshire; his residence is at the city of Legions, that is Chester or Coventry; formerly it was at Lichfield: in Herefordshire; and there is a bishop having half Shropshire and part of Warwickshire, and Gloucestershire; whose residence is at Hereford: in Oxfordshire, Buckinghamshire, Hertfordshire, Huntingdonshire, half of Bedfordshire, Northamptonshire, Leicestershire, Lincolnshire; which counties are under the jurisdiction of a bishop now resident at Lincoln, but formerly at Dorchester in the county of Oxford: in Leicestershire and Nottinghamshire, which belong to the diocese of York; formerly they had their own bishop, whose seat was at Leicester.

The kings of the East Angles had dominion over the county of Cambridge; there is a bishop, whose seat is at Ely: and in Norfolk and Suffolk: whose see is at Norwich; formerly at Elmham or Thetford.

The kings of the East Saxons ruled in Essex, in Middle-

* The kingdom of Sussex was founded by Ælla, who arrived in Britain with three vessels, and accompanied by his three sons, A.D. 477. He seems to have attained a very high degree of power, and was succeeded by his son Cissa.—The affairs of this kingdom are extremely obscure; it appears to have been sometimes dependent on Kent and sometimes on Wessex until finally united to the latter by Egbert, A.D. 823.

sex, and half of Hertfordshire ; where there anciently was, and still remains, the bishop of London.

The kings of the Northumbrians governed all the country which is beyond the river Humber, even into Scotland ; and there were the archbishop of York, the bishops of Hexham, of Ripon, of Lindisfarne, and of Candida Casa [Whitherne]; Hexham and Ripon are no more ; Lindisfarne is translated to Durham.

Such were the divisions of the kingdom of England, although the kings, according to the vicissitude of the times, now one, and then the other, would exceed their boundaries through their courage, or lose them by their indolence ; but all these several kingdoms Egbert subjugated by his abilities, and consolidated into one empire, reserving to each their own laws. Wherefore, since I have passed beyond his times, fulfilling my promise in a review of the different periods, I will here fix the limits of my first volume, that the various tracks of the different kingdoms may unite in the general path of the West Saxon Empire.

BOOK II.

PROLOGUE.

A LONG period has elapsed since, as well through the care of my parents as my own industry, I became familiar with books. This pleasure possessed me from my childhood : this source of delight has grown with my years. Indeed I was so instructed by my father, that, had I turned aside to other pursuits, I should have considered it as jeopardy to my soul and discredit to my character. Wherefore mindful of the adage "covet what is necessary," I constrained my early age to desire eagerly that which it was disgraceful not to possess. I gave, indeed, my attention to various branches of literature, but in different degrees. Logic, for instance, which gives arms to eloquence, I contented myself with barely hearing. Medicine, which ministers to the health of the body, I studied with somewhat more attention. But now, having scrupulously examined the several branches of

Ethics, I bow down to its majesty, because it spontaneously unveils itself to those who study it, and directs their minds to moral practice; History more especially; which, by an agreeable recapitulation of past events, excites its readers, by example, to frame their lives to the pursuit of good, or to aversion from evil. When, therefore, at my own expense, I had procured some historians of foreign nations, I proceeded, during my domestic leisure, to inquire if any thing concerning our own country could be found worthy of handing down to posterity. Hence it arose, that, not content with the writings of ancient times, I began, myself, to compose; not indeed to display my learning, which is comparatively nothing, but to bring to light events lying concealed in the confused mass of antiquity. In consequence rejecting vague opinions, I have studiously sought for chronicles far and near, though I confess I have scarcely profited any thing by this industry. For perusing them all, I still remained poor in information; though I ceased not my researches as long as I could find any thing to read. However, what I have clearly ascertained concerning the four kingdoms, I have inserted in my first book, in which I hope truth will find no cause to blush, though perhaps a degree of doubt may sometimes arise. I shall now trace the monarchy of the West Saxon kingdom, through the line of successive princes, down to the coming of the Normans: which if any person will condescend to regard with complacency, let him in brotherly love observe the following rule: "If before, he knew only these things, let him not be disgusted because I have inserted them; if he shall know more, let him not be angry that I have not spoken of them;" but rather let him communicate his knowledge to me, while I yet live, that at least, those events may appear in the margin of my history, which do not occur in the text.

CHAP. I.

The history of king Egbert. [A.D. 800—839.]

My former volume terminated where the four kingdoms of Britain were consolidated into one. Egbert, the founder of this sovereignty, grand-nephew of king Ina, by his brother Ingild, of high rank in his own nation, and liberally educated, had been conspicuous among the West Saxons from his childhood. His uninterrupted course of valour begat envy, and as it is almost naturally ordained that kings should regard with suspicion whomsoever they see growing up in expectation of the kingdom, Bertric, as before related, jealous of his rising character, was meditating how to destroy him. Egbert, apprised of this, escaped to Offa, king of the Mercians. While Offa concealed him with anxious care, the messengers of Bertric arrived, demanding the fugitive for punishment, and offering money for his surrender. In addition to this they solicited his daughter in marriage for their king, in order that the nuptial tie might bind them in perpetual amity. In consequence Offa, who would not give way to hostile threats, yielded to flattering allurements, and Egbert, passing the sea, went into France; a circumstance which I attribute to the counsels of God, that a man destined to rule so great a kingdom might learn the art of government from the Franks; for this people has no competitor among all the Western nations in military skill or polished manners. This ill-treatment Egbert used as an incentive to "rub off the rust of indolence," to quicken the energy of his mind, and to adopt foreign customs, far differing from his native barbarism. On the death, therefore, of Bertric, being invited into Britain by frequent messages from his friends, he ascended the throne, and realized the fondest expectations of his country. He was crowned in the year of our Lord's incarnation 800, and in the thirty-fourth year of the reign of Charles the Great, of France, who survived this event twelve years. In the meantime Egbert, when he had acquired the regard of his subjects by his affability and kindness, first manifested his power against those Britons who inhabit that part of the island which is called Cornwall, and having subjugated them, he proceeded to make the Northern Britons,* who are separated from the others by an arm of the sea, tributary to him. While the fame of these victories struck terror into the rest, Bernulf king of the Mercians, aiming at something great, and supposing it would redound to his glory if he could remove the terror of others by his own audacity, proclaimed war

* The early adventures of Egbert are found only in Malmesbury. He does not observe the order in which these events happened.

against Egbert. Deeming it disgraceful to retreat, Egbert met him with much spirit, and on then coming into action, Bernulf was defeated and fled. This battle took place at Hellendun, A.D. 824.* Elated with this success, the West Saxon king, extending his views, in the heat of victory, sent his son Ethelwulf, with Alstan, bishop of Sherborne, and a chosen band, into Kent, for the purpose of adding to the West Saxon dominions that province, which had either grown indolent through long repose, or was terrified by the fame of his valour. These commanders observed their instructions effectually, for they passed through every part of the country, and driving Baldred its king, with little difficulty, beyond the river Thames, they subjugated to his dominion, in the twenty-fourth year of his reign, Kent, Surrey, the South Saxons, and the East Saxons, who had formerly been under the jurisdiction of his predecessors. Not long after the East Angles, animated by the support of Egbert, killed by successive stratagems, Bernulf and Ludecan, kings of the Mercians. The cause of their destruction was, their perpetual incursions, with their usual insolence, on the territories of others. Withlaf their successor, first driven from his kingdom by Egbert, and afterwards admitted as a tributary prince, augmented the West Saxon sovereignty. In the same year the Northumbrians perceiving that themselves only remained and were a conspicuous object, and fearing lest he should pour out his long-cherished anger on them, at last, though late, gave hostages, and yielded to his power. When he was thus possessed of all Britain, the rest of his life, a space of nine years, passed quietly on, except that, nearly in his latter days, a piratical band of Danes made a descent, and disturbed the peace of the kingdom. So changeable is the lot of human affairs, that he, who first singly governed all the Angles, could derive but little satisfaction from the obedience of his countrymen, for a foreign enemy was perpetually harassing

* The printed text of the former editions places the battle of Hellendun, A.D. 806. Several MSS. have 826, one 825, and two only appear to adopt the correct year 824, as inserted above. These are—The Arundel MS. No. 35, Brit. Mus. and the MS. in Trinity Coll. Cam. R. 14. The place is variously conjectured: Wilton in Wiltshire; Hillingdon in Middlesex; and near Highworth in Wilts.

him and his descendants. Against these invaders the forces of the Angles made a stand, but fortune no longer flattered the king with her customary favours, but deserted him in the contest: for, when, during the greater part of the day, he had almost secured the victory, he lost the battle as the sun declined; however, by the favour of darkness, he escaped the disgrace of being conquered. In the next action, with a small force, he totally routed an immense multitude. At length, after a reign of thirty-seven years and seven months, he departed this life, and was buried at Winchester; leaving an ample field of glory for his son, and declaring, that he must be happy, if he was careful not to destroy, by the indolence natural to his race, a kingdom that himself had consolidated with such consummate industry.

CHAP. II.

Of king Ethelwulf. [A.D. 839—858.]

In the year of our Lord's incarnation 837,* Ethelwulf, whom some call Athulf, the son of Egbert, came to the throne, and reigned twenty years and five months. Mild by nature he infinitely preferred a life of tranquillity to dominion over many provinces; and, finally, content with his paternal kingdom, he bestowed all the rest, which his father had subjugated, on his son Ethelstan; of whom it is not known when, or in what manner, he died. He assisted Burhred, king of the Mercians, with an army against the Britons, and highly exalted him by giving him his daughter in marriage. He frequently overcame the piratical Danes, who were traversing the whole island and infesting the coast with sudden descents, both personally and by his generals; although, according to the chance of war, he himself experienced great and repeated calamities; London and almost the whole of Kent being laid waste. Yet these disasters were ever checked by the alacrity of the king's advisers, who suffered not the enemy to trespass with impunity, but fully avenged themselves on them by the effect of their united counsels. For he possessed at that time, two most excellent prelates,

* Malmesbury, in following the Saxon Chronicle, is two years earlier than the Northern Chronicles.

St. Swithun of Winchester, and Ealstan of Sherborne, who perceiving the king to be of heavy and sluggish disposition, perpetually stimulated him, by their admonitions, to the knowledge of governing. Swithun, disgusted with earthly, trained his master to heavenly pursuits; Ealstan, knowing that the business of the kingdom ought not to be neglected, continually inspirited him against the Danes: himself furnishing the exchequer with money, as well as regulating the army. Any peruser of the Annals* will find many affairs of this kind, both entered on with courage, and terminated with success through his means. He held his bishopric fifty years, happy in living for so long a space in the practice of good works. I should readily commend him, had he not been swayed by worldly avarice, and usurped what belonged to others, when by his intrigues he seized the monastery of Malmesbury for his own use. We feel the mischief of this shameful conduct even to the present day, although the monastery has baffled all similar violence from the time of his death till now, when it has fallen again into like difficulty.† Thus the accursed passion of avarice corrupts the human soul, and forces men, though great and illustrious in other respects, into hell.

Ethelwulf, confiding in these two supporters, provided effectually for external emergencies, and did not neglect the interior concerns of his kingdom. For after the subjugation of his enemies, turning to the establishment of God's worship, he granted every tenth hide of land within his kingdom to the servants of Christ, free from all tribute, exempt from all services. But how small a portion is this of his glory? Having settled his kingdom, he went to Rome, and there offered to St. Peter that tribute which England pays to this day,‡ before pope Leo the fourth, who had also, formerly,

* See Saxon Chronicle, A.D 823—825.

† Roger, bishop of Salisbury, seized it in like manner to his own use, A.D. 1118, and held it till his death, 1159.

‡ Alluding to the Rome-scot, or Peter's-pence, a penny from each house, paid on the festival of St. Peter. Its origin and application seem obscure: Higden interpolates Malmesbury, as assigning its first grant to Ina · Henry of Huntingdon says, Offa. This grant is supposed by Spelman to have been made in a General Council of the nation. A similar payment appears to have been made by other nations. It is to be observed that Asser mentions only Ethelwulf's donation of three hundred mancuses.

honourably received, and anointed as king, Alfred,* his son, whom Ethelwulf had sent to him. Continuing there a whole year, he nobly repaired the School of the Angles, which, according to report, was first founded by Offa, king of the Mercians, and had been burned down the preceding year.†
Returning home through France, he married Judith, daughter of Charles, king of the Franks.

OF THE SUCCESSORS OF CHARLEMAGNE.

For Louis the Pious, son of Charles the Great, had four sons; Lothaire, Pepin, Louis, and Charles, surnamed the Bald; of these Lothaire, even in his father's life-time, usurping the title of emperor, reigned fifteen years in that part of Germany situated near the Alps which is now called Lorraine, that is, the kingdom of Lothaire, and in all Italy together with Rome. In his latter days, afflicted with sickness, he renounced the world. He was a man by far more inhuman than all who preceded him; so much so, as even frequently to load his own father with chains in a dungeon. Louis indeed was of mild and simple manners, but he was unmercifully persecuted by Lothaire, because Ermengarda, by whom he had his first family, being dead, he was doatingly fond of Charles, his son by his second wife Judith.

* Asser relates that pope Leo stood sponsor for, and confirmed Alfred, who had been sent to Rome by his father the preceding year.

† The conflagration here named seems that mentioned by Anastasius, who tells us, that, shortly after the accession of Pope Leo the fourth, a fire broke out in the Saxon street, but the pope, making the sign of the cross with his fingers, put a stop to it. (Anastas. Biblioth. p. 319.) From this author's account it appears to have been a street or quarter of considerable extent, and near to St. Peter's. There were schools of this kind belonging to various nations at Rome. Matt. Westminster says it was founded by Ina, with the consent and approbation of Pope Gregory, that priests, nobles, prelates, or kings, of the English nation, might be entertained there during their stay for the purpose of being thoroughly instructed in the Catholic faith; for that, from the time of Augustine, the doctrine and schools of the English had been interdicted by the popes on account of the various heresies which had sprung up among them; that, moreover, Ina bestowed a penny from each house, or Rome-scot, for the support of these persons. (Matt. West. A.D. 727.) It was destroyed by fire in the year 816, and partially again A.D. 854. Our text, therefore, is at variance with the account given by Anastasius, and the latter is probably incorrect.

Pepin, another son of Louis, had dominion in Aquitaine* and Gascony. Louis, the third son of Louis, in addition to Norica, which he had already, possessed the kingdoms which his father had given him, that is to say, Alemannia, Thuringia, Austrasia, Saxony, and the kingdom of the Avares, that is, the Huns. Charles obtained the half of France on the west, and all Neustria, Brittany, and the greatest part of Burgundy, Gothia, Gascony, and Aquitaine, Pepin the son of Pepin being ejected thence and compelled to become a monk in the monastery of St. Methard; who afterwards escaping by flight, and returning into Aquitaine, remained there in concealment a long time; but being again treacherously deceived by Ranulph the governor, he was seized, brought to Charles at Senlis, and doomed to perpetual exile. Moreover, after the death of the most pious emperor, Louis, Lothaire, who had been anointed emperor eighteen years before his father's decease, being joined by Pepin with the people of Aquitaine, led an army against his brothers, that is, Louis, the most pious king of the Bavarians, and Charles, into the county of Auxerre to a place called Fontenai.† where, when the Franks with all their subject nations had been overwhelmed by mutual slaughter, Louis and Charles ultimately triumphed; Lothaire being put to flight. After this most sanguinary conflict, however, peace was made between them, and they divided the sovereignty of the Franks, as has been mentioned above. Lothaire had three sons by Ermengarda the daughter of Hugo: first, Louis, to whom he committed the government of the Romans and of Italy; next, Lothaire, to whom he left the imperial crown; lastly, Charles, to whom he gave Provence. Lothaire died in the year of our Lord's incarnation 855, of his reign the

* The divisions of France were liable to considerable variation but it may be sufficient to observe, that Aquitaine lay between the Garonne and Loire; Vasconia, from the Garonne to the Pyrenees; Gothia, from the Pyrenees along the coast to the eastward; Austrasia or East France, besides various tracts beyond the Rhine, lay between that river and the Meuse; Neustria or West France, from the Channel to the Loire with the exception of Brittany.

† The battle of Fontenai is considered as the most calamitous in the French annals; more than one hundred thousand men having, it is said, perished in it. It was fought on the 25th of June, A.D. 841, a memorable month in the annals of France.

thirty-third. Charles his son, who governed Provence, survived him eight years, and then Louis, emperor of the Romans, and Lothaire his brother, shared his kingdom of Provence. But Louis king of the Norici, that is, of the Bavarians, the son of Louis the emperor, in the year of our Lord's incarnation 865, after the feast of Easter, divided his kingdom between his sons. To Caroloman he gave Norica, that is, Bavaria, and the marches bordering on the Sclavonians and the Lombards; to Louis, Thuringia, the Eastern Franks, and Saxony; to Charles he left Alemannia, and Curnwalla, that is, the county of Cornwall.* Louis himself reigned happily over his sons, in full power for ten years, and then died in the year of our Lord's incarnation 876, when he had reigned fifty-four years. Charles king of the West Franks, in the thirty-sixth year of his reign, entering Italy, came to offer up his prayers in the church of the apostles, and was there elected emperor by all the Roman people, and consecrated by pope John on the 25th of December, in the year of our Lord's incarnation 875. Thence he had a prosperous return into Gaul. But in the thirty-eighth year of his reign, and the beginning of the third of his imperial dignity, he went into Italy again, and held a conference with pope John; and returning into Gaul, he died, after passing Mount Cenis, on the 13th of October, in the tenth of the Indiction, in the year of our Lord 877, and was succeeded by his son Louis. Before the second year of his reign was completed this Louis died in the palace at Compeigne, on the sixth before the Ides of April, in the year of our Lord 879, the twelfth of the Indiction. After him his sons, Louis and Caroloman, divided his kingdom. Of these, Louis gained a victory over the Normans in the district of Vimeu, and died soon after on the 12th of August, in the year of our Lord 881, the fifteenth of the Indiction, having reigned two years, three months, and twenty-four days. He was succeeded in his government by his brother Caroloman, who, after reigning three years and six days, was wounded by a wild boar† in the forest of Iveline, in Mount Ericus.

* Cornu-guallia, i.e. the Horn of Gaul from the projection of Brittany.

† Some pretend that he was accidentally wounded by Bertholde, one of his attendants; and that the story of the boar was invented in order to

He departed this life in the year of our Lord 884, the second of the Indiction, the 24th of December. Next Charles king of the Suavi, the son of Louis king of the Norici, assumed the joint empire of the Franks and Romans, in the year of the Incarnate Word 885, the third of the Indiction; whose vision, as I think it worth preserving, I here subjoin:

"In the name of God most high, the King of kings. As I, Charles by the free gift of God, emperor, king of the Germans, patrician of the Romans, and emperor of the Franks, on the sacred night of the Lord's day, after duly performing the holy service of the evening, went to the bed of rest and sought the sleep of quietude, there came a tremendous voice to me, saying, 'Charles, thy spirit shall shortly depart from thee for a considerable time:' immediately I was rapt in the spirit, and he who carried me away in the spirit was most glorious to behold. In his hand he held a clue of thread emitting a beam of purest light, such as comets shed when they appear. This he began to unwind, and said to me, 'Take the thread of this brilliant clue and bind and tie it firmly on the thumb of thy right hand, for thou shalt be led by it through the inextricable punishments of the infernal regions.' Saying this, he went before me, quickly unrolling the thread of the brilliant clue, and led me into very deep and fiery valleys which were full of pits boiling with pitch, and brimstone, and lead, and wax, and grease. There I found the bishops of my father and of my uncles: and when in terror I asked them why they were suffering such dreadful torments? they replied, 'We were the bishops of your father and of your uncles, and instead of preaching, and admonishing them and their people to peace and concord, as was our duty, we were the sowers of discord and the fomenters of evil. On this account we are now burning in these infernal torments, together with other lovers of slaughter and of rapine; and hither also will your bishops and ministers come, who now delight to act as we did.' While I was fearfully listening to this, behold the blackest demons came flying about me, with fiery claws endeavouring to snatch away the thread of life which I held in my hand, and to draw it to them; but repelled by the rays of the clue, they were unable

screen him from punishment. Malmesbury, however, follows Asser, the Saxon Chron., &c.

to touch it. Next running behind me, they tried to gripe me in their claws and cast me headlong into those sulphureous pits: but my conductor, who carried the clue, threw a thread of light over my shoulders, and doubling it, drew me strongly after him, and in this manner we ascended lofty fiery mountains, from which arose lakes, and burning rivers, and all kinds of burning metals, wherein I found immersed innumerable souls of the vassals and princes of my father and brothers, some up to the hair. others to the chin, and others to the middle, who mournfully cried out to me, 'While we were living, we were, together with you, and your father, and brothers, and uncles, fond of battle, and slaughter, and plunder, through lust of earthly things: wherefore we now undergo punishment in these boiling rivers, and in various kinds of liquid metal' While I was, with the greatest alarm, attending to these, I heard some souls behind me crying out, 'The great will undergo still greater torment.' I looked back and beheld on the banks of the boiling river, furnaces of pitch and brimstone, filled with great dragons, and scorpions, and different kinds of serpents, where I also saw some of my father's nobles, some of my own, and of those of my brothers and of my uncles, who said, 'Alas, Charles, you see what dreadful torments we undergo on account of our malice, and pride, and the evil counsel which we gave to our kings and to you, for lust's sake.' When I could not help groaning mournfully at this, the dragons ran at me with open jaws filled with fire, and brimstone, and pitch, and tried to swallow me up. My conductor then tripled the thread of the clue around me, which by the splendour of its rays overcame their fiery throats: he then pulled me with greater violence, and we descended into a valley, which was in one part dark and burning like a fiery furnace, but in another so extremely enchanting and glorious, that I cannot describe it. I turned myself to the dark part which emitted flames, and there I saw some kings of my race in extreme torture; at which, affrighted beyond measure and reduced to great distress, I expected that I should be immediately thrown into these torments by some very black giants, who made the valley blaze with every kind of flame. I trembled very much, and, the thread of the clue of light assisting my eyes, I saw, on the side of the valley, the light somewhat brightening, and two fountains flowing out thence: one was extremely hot; the other clear and luke-warm; two large casks were there besides. When, guided by the thread of light, I proceeded thither, I looked into the vessel containing boiling water, and saw my father Louis, standing therein up to his thighs. He was dreadfully oppressed with pain and agony, and said to me, 'Fear not, my lord Charles; I know that your spirit will again return into your body, and that God hath permitted you to come hither, that you might see for what crimes myself and all whom you have beheld, undergo these torments. One day I am bathed in the boiling cask, next I pass into that other delightful water; which is effected by the prayers of St. Peter and St. Remigius, under whose patronage our royal race has hitherto reigned. But if you, and my faithful bishops and abbats, and the whole ecclesiastical order will quickly assist me with masses, prayers and psalms, and alms, and vigils, I shall shortly be released from the punishment of the boiling water. For my brother Lothaire and his son Louis have had these punishments remitted by the prayers of St. Peter and St. Remigius, and have now entered into the joy of God's paradise.' He then said to me, 'Look on your left hand;' and when I had done so, I saw two very deep casks boiling furiously. 'These,' said he, 'are prepared for you, if you do not amend and repent of your atrocious crimes.' I then began to be dreadfully afraid, and when my conductor saw my spirit thus terrified, he said to me, 'Follow me to the right of that most resplendent valley of paradise.' As we proceeded, I beheld my uncle Lothaire sitting in excessive brightness, in company with glorious kings, on a topaz-stone of uncommon size, crowned with a precious diadem: and near him, his son Louis crowned in like manner. Seeing me near at hand he called me to him in a kind voice, saying, 'Come to me, Charles, now my third successor in the empire of the Romans; I know that you have passed through the place of punishment where your father, my brother, is placed in the baths appointed for him; but, by the mercy of God, he will be shortly liberated from those punishments as we have been, by the merits of St. Peter and the prayers of St Remigius, to whom God hath given a special charge over the kings and people of the Franks, and unless he shall continue to favour and assist the dregs of our family, our race must shortly cease both from the kingdom and the empire. Know, moreover, that the rule of the empire will be shortly taken out of your hand, nor will you long survive. Then Louis turning to me, said, 'The empire which you have hitherto held by hereditary right, Louis the son of my daughter is to assume.' So saying, there seemed immediately to appear before me a little child, and Lothaire his grandfather looking upon him, said to me, 'This infant seems to be such an one as that which the Lord set in the midst of the disciples, and said, "Of such is the kingdom of God, I say unto you, that their angels do always behold the face of my father who is in heaven." But do you bestow on him the empire by that thread of the clue which you hold in your hand.' I then untied the thread from the thumb of my right hand, and gave him the whole monarchy of the empire by that thread, and immediately the entire clue, like a brilliant sun-beam, became rolled up in his hand. Thus, after this wonderful transaction, my spirit, extremely wearied and affrighted, returned into my body. Therefore, let all persons know willingly or unwillingly, forasmuch as, according to the will of God, the whole empire of the Romans will revert into his hands, and that I cannot prevail against him, compelled by the conditions of this my calling, that God, who is the ruler of the living and the dead, will both complete and establish this ; whose eternal kingdom remains for ever and ever, amen."

The vision itself, and the partition of the kingdoms, I have inserted in the very words I found them in.* This Charles, then, had scarcely discharged the united duties of the empire and kingdom for two years, when Charles, the son of Louis who died at Compeigne, succeeded him: this is the Charles who married the daughter of Edward, king of England, and gave Normandy to Rollo with his daughter Gisla, who was the surety of peace and pledge of the treaty. To this Charles, in the empire, succeeded Arnulph ; a king of the imperial line, tutor of that young Louis of whom the vision above recited speaks. Arnulph dying after fifteen years, this Louis succeeded him, at whose death, one Conrad, king of the

* This vision is copied from Hariulfe's Chronicle, lib. iii cap. 21 The Annals ascribed to Asser also recite the vision, sub anno 886.—*See Mr. Hardy's Note*, vol. 1. p. 160.

Teutonians, obtained the sovereignty. His son Henry, who succeeded him, sent to Athelstan king of the Angles, for his two sisters, Aldgitha and Edgitha, the latter of whom he married to his son Otho, the former to a certain duke near the Alps. Thus the empire of the Romans and the kingdom of the Franks being severed from their ancient union, the one is governed by emperors and the other by kings. But as I have wandered wide from my purpose, whilst indulging in tracing the descent of the illustrious kings of the Franks, I will now return to the course I had begun, and to Ethelwulf.

On his return after his year's peregrination and marriage with the daughter of Charles the Bald, as I have said, he found the dispositions of some persons contrary to his expectations. For Ethelbald his son, and Ealstan bishop of Sherborne, and Enulph earl of Somerset conspiring against him, endeavoured to eject him from the sovereignty; but through the intervention of maturer counsel, the kingdom was divided between the father and his son. This partition was extremely unequal; for malignity was so far successful that the western portion, which was the better, was allotted to the son, the eastern, which was the worse, fell to the father. He, however, with incredible forbearance, dreading "a worse than civil war," calmly gave way to his son, restraining, by a conciliatory harangue, the people who had assembled for the purpose of asserting his dignity. And though all this quarrel arose on account of his foreign wife, yet he held her in the highest estimation, and used to place her on the throne near himself, contrary to the West Saxon custom. For that people never suffered the king's consort either to be seated by the king or to be honoured with the appellation of queen, on account of the depravity of Eadburga, daughter of Offa, king of the Mercians; who, as we have before mentioned, being married to Bertric, king of the West Saxons, used to persuade him, a tender-hearted man, as they report, to the destruction of the innocent, and would herself take off by poison those against whom her accusations failed. This was exemplified in the case of a youth much beloved by the king, whom she made away with in this manner: and immediately afterwards Bertric fell sick, wasted away and died, from having previously drunk of the same potion, unknown to the queen. The rumour of this getting abroad, drove the poisoner from the kingdom. Proceeding to Charles the Great, she happened to find him standing with one of his sons, and after offering him presents, the emperor, in a playful, jocose manner, commanded her to choose which she liked best, himself, or his son. Eadburga choosing the young man for his blooming beauty, Charles replied with some emotion, "Had you chosen me, you should have had my son, but since you have chosen him, you shall have neither." He then placed her in a monastery where she might pass her life in splendour; but, soon after, finding her guilty of incontinence he expelled her.* Struck with this instance of depravity, the Saxons framed the regulation I have alluded to, though Ethelwulf invalidated it by his affectionate kindness. He made his will a few months before he died, in which, after the division of the kingdom between his sons Ethelbald and Ethelbert, he set out the dowry of his daughter, and ordered, that, till the end of time, one poor person should be clothed and fed from every tenth hide of his inheritance, and that every year, three hundred mancas of gold† should be sent to Rome, of which one-third should be given to St. Peter, another to St. Paul for lamps, and the other to the pope for distribution. He died two years after he came from Rome, and was buried at Winchester in the cathedral. But that I may return from my digression to my proposed series, I shall here subjoin the charter of ecclesiastical immunities which he granted to all England.

"Our Lord Jesus Christ reigning for evermore. Since we perceive that perilous times are pressing on us, that there are in our days hostile burnings, and plunderings of our wealth, and most cruel depredations by devastating enemies, and many tribulations of barbarous and pagan nations, threatening even our destruction: therefore I Ethelwulf king of the West Saxons, with the advice of my bishops and nobility, have established a wholesome counsel

* Asser had conversed with many persons who afterwards saw her begging for a subsistence in Pavia, where she died.

† One hundred were for the pope, and the other two hundred to be divided between the churches of St. Peter and St. Paul, to provide lights on Easter-eve

and general remedy. I have decided that there shall be given to the servants of God, whether male or female or laymen,* a certain hereditary portion of the lands possessed by persons of every degree, that is to say, the tenth manse,† but where it is less than this, then the tenth part; that it may be exonerated from all secular services, all royal tributes great and small, or those taxes which we call Witereden. And let it be free from all things, for the release of our souls, that it may be applied to God's service alone, exempt from expeditions, the building of bridges, or of forts; in order that they may more diligently pour forth their prayers to God for us without ceasing, inasmuch as we have in some measure alleviated their service. Moreover it hath pleased Ealstan bishop of Sherborne, and Swithun bishop of Winchester, with their abbats and the servants of God, to appoint that all our brethren and sisters at each church, every week on the day of Mercury, that is to say, Wednesday, should sing fifty psalms, and every priest two masses, one for king Ethelwulf, and another for his nobility, consenting to this gift, for the pardon and alleviation of their sins; for the king while living, they shall say, 'Let us pray: O God, who justifiest.' For the nobility while living, 'Stretch forth, O Lord.' After they are dead; for the departed king, singly: for the departed nobility, in common: and let this be firmly appointed for all the times of Christianity, in like manner as that immunity is appointed, so long as faith shall increase in the nation of the Angles This charter of donation was written in the year of our Lord's incarnation 844,‡ the fourth of the indiction, and on the nones, i. e. the fifth day of November, in the city of Winchester, in the church of St. Peter, before the high altar, and they have done this for the honour of St. Michael

* Ingulf, who likewise gives this charter, reads, "laicis miseris," the poor laity.

† Manse implies generally a dwelling and a certain quantity of land annexed: sometimes it is synonymous with a hide, or plough-land

‡ Ingulf has A.D. 855 3 indict which agrees with Asser, who assigns that year for the grant. It appears to be the charter which Malmesbury before referred to on the king's going to Rome, and has given rise to much controversy; some holding that it conveyed the tithes of the land only, while others maintain that it was an actual transfer of the tenth part of all lands in the kingdom. See Carte, vol. 1. 293. Both opinions are attended

the archangel, and of St. Mary the glorious queen, the mother of God, and also for the honour of St. Peter the chief of the apostles, and of our most holy father pope Gregory, and all saints. And then, for greater security, king Ethelwulf placed the charter on the altar of St. Peter, and the bishops received it in behalf of God's holy faith, and afterwards transmitted it to all churches in their dioceses according to the above-cited form."

From this king the English chronicles trace the line of the generation of their kings upwards, even to Adam, as we know Luke the evangelist has done with respect to our Lord Jesus; and which, perhaps, it will not be superfluous for me to do, though it is to be apprehended, that the utterance of barbarous names may shock the ears of persons unused to them. Ethelwulf was the son of Egbert, Egbert of Elmund, Elmund of Eafa, Eafa of Eoppa, Eoppa was the son of Ingild, the brother of king Ina, who were both sons of Kenred; Kenred of Ceolwald, Ceolwald of Cutha, Cutha of Cuthwin, Cuthwin of Ceawlin, Ceawlin of Cynric, Cynric of Creoding, Creoding of Cerdic, who was the first king of the West Saxons; Cerdic of Elesa, Elesa of Esla, Esla of Gewis, Gewis of Wig, Wig of Freawin, Freawin of Frithogar, Frithogar of Brond, Brond of Beldeg, Beldeg of Woden, and from him, as we have often remarked, proceeded the kings of many nations. Woden was the son of Frithowald, Frithowald of Frealaf, Frealaf of Finn, Finn of Godwulf, Godwulf of Geat, Geat of Tætwa, Tætwa of Beaw, Beaw of Sceldi, Sceldi of Sceaf; who, as some affirm, was driven on a certain island in Germany, called Scamphta, (of which Jornandes,[*] the historian of the Goths, speaks,) a little boy in a skiff, without any attendant, asleep, with a handful of corn at his head, whence he was called Sceaf; and, on account of his singular appearance, being well received by

---

with considerable difficulties. Mr Carte very inadvertently imagines this charter and the copy in Ingulf to be distinct grants: the latter being, he says, a confirmation and extension of the former, after Ethelwulf's return from Rome: but the false date in Malmesbury is of no importance, some MSS. having even 814, and 855 was the year of his departure, not of his return.

[*] Jordanes, or Jornandes, was secretary to the kings of the Goths in Italy. He was afterwards bishop of Ravenna, and wrote, *De Rebus Gothicis*; and also, *De Regnorum et Temporum Successione*.—*Hardy.*

the men of that country, and carefully educated, in his riper age he reigned in a town which was called Slaswic, but at present Haitheby; which country, called old Anglia, whence the Angles came into Britain, is situated between the Saxons and the Gioths. Sceaf was the son of Heremod, Heremod of Itermon, Itermon of Hathra, Hathra of Guala, Guala of Bedwig, Bedwig of Streaf, and he, as they say, was the son of Noah, born in the Ark.*

CHAPTER III.

Of Ethelbald, Ethelbert, and Ethelred, sons of Ethelwulf.
[A.D. 858—872.]

IN the year of our Lord 857,† the two sons of Ethelwulf divided their paternal kingdom; Ethelbald reigned in West Saxony, and Ethelbert in Kent. Ethelbald, base and perfidious, defiled the bed of his father by marrying, after his decease, Judith his step-mother. Dying, however, at the end of five years, and being interred at Sherborne, the whole government devolved upon his brother. In his time a band of pirates landing at Southampton, proceeded to plunder the populous city of Winchester, but soon after being spiritedly repulsed by the king's generals, and suffering considerable loss, they put to sea, and coasting round, chose the Isle of Thanet, in Kent, for their winter quarters. The people of Kent, giving hostages, and promising a sum of money, would have remained quiet, had not these pirates, breaking the treaty, laid waste the whole district by nightly predatory excursions, but roused by this conduct they mustered a force and drove out the truce-breakers. Moreover Ethelbert, having ruled the kingdom with vigour and with mildness,

* A similar list of the genealogy of the West Saxon kings, will be found in the Saxon Chronicle, A.D. 855.

† Malmesbury's Chronology to the accession of Edward the Elder, is a year later than the Saxon Chronicle, Asser, and Florence of Worcester. His computation rests on fixing the death of Ethelwulf in 857, who went to Rome in 855, stayed there a year, and died in the second year after his return. Allowing ten years for Ethelbald and Ethelbert, it brings the accession of Ethelred to 867, and five years added to this give 872 for Alfred's accession. After the death of Ethelbald Judith returned to France. She left no children, but marrying afterwards Baldwin, count of Flanders, she bore him Matilda, wife of William the Conqueror.

paid the debt of nature after five years, and was buried at Sherborne.

In the year of our Lord 867, Ethelred, the son of Ethelwulf, obtained his paternal kingdom, and ruled it for the same number of years as his brothers. Surely it would be a pitiable and grievous destiny, that all of them should perish by an early death, unless it is, that in such a tempest of evils, these royal youths should prefer an honourable end to a painful government. Indeed, so bravely and so vigorously did they contend for their country, that it was not to be imputed to them that their valour did not succeed in its design. Finally, it is related, that this king was personally engaged in hostile conflict against the enemy nine times in one year, with various success indeed, but for the most part victor, besides sudden attacks, in which, from his skill in warfare, he frequently worsted those straggling depredators. In these several actions the Danes lost nine earls and one king, besides common people innumerable.

One battle memorable beyond all the rest was that which took place at Eschendun.* The Danes, having collected an army at this place, divided it into two bodies; their two kings commanded the one, all their earls the other. Ethelred drew near with his brother Alfred. It fell to the lot of Ethelred to oppose the kings, while Alfred was to attack the earls. Both armies eagerly prepared for battle, but night approaching deferred the conflict till the ensuing day. Scarcely had the morning dawned ere Alfred was ready at his post, but his brother, intent on his devotions, had remained in his tent; and when urged on by a message, that the pagans were rushing forward with unbounded fury, he declared that he should not move a step till his religious services were ended. This piety of the king was of infinite advantage to his brother, who was too impetuous from the thoughtlessness of youth, and had already far advanced. The battalions of the Angles were now giving way, and even bordering on flight, in consequence of their adversaries pressing upon them from the higher ground, for the Christians were fighting in an unfavourable situation, when the

* Supposed Aston, near Wallingford, Berks. Others think Ashendon in Bucks. The Latin and Saxon names, *Mons Fraxini*, and Eschen-dun, seem to favour the latter.

king himself, signed with the cross of God, unexpectedly hastened forward, dispersing the enemy, and rallying his subjects. The Danes, terrified equally by his courage and the divine manifestation, consulted their safety by flight. Here fell Oseg their king, five earls, and an innumerable multitude of common people.

The reader will be careful to observe that during this time, the kings of the Mercians and of the Northumbrians, eagerly seizing the opportunity of the arrival of the Danes, with whom Ethelred was fully occupied in fighting, and somewhat relieved from their bondage to the West Saxons, had nearly regained their original power. All the provinces, therefore, were laid waste by cruel depredations, because each king chose rather to resist the enemy within his own territories, than to assist his neighbours in their difficulties; and thus preferring to avenge injury rather than to prevent it, they ruined their country by their senseless conduct. The Danes acquired strength without impediment, whilst the apprehensions of the inhabitants increased, and each successive victory, from the addition of captives, became the means of obtaining another. The country of the East Angles, together with their cities and villages, was possessed by these plunderers; its king, St. Edmund, slain by them in the year of our Lord's incarnation 870, on the tenth of November, purchased an eternal kingdom by putting off this mortal life. The Mercians, often harassed, alleviated their afflictions by giving hostages. The Northumbrians, long embroiled in civil dissensions, made up their differences on the approach of the enemy. Replacing Osbert their king, whom they had expelled, upon the throne, and collecting a powerful force, they went out to meet the foe; but being easily repelled, they shut themselves up in the city of York, which was presently after set on fire by the victors; and when the flames were raging to the utmost and consuming the very walls, they perished for their country in the conflagration. In this manner Northumbria, the prize of war, for a considerable time after, felt the more bitterly, through a sense of former liberty, the galling yoke of the barbarians. And now Ethelred, worn down with numberless labours, died and was buried at Wimborne.

CHAP. IV.

Of king Alfred. [A.D. 872—901.]

IN the year of our Lord's incarnation 872, Alfred, the youngest son of Ethelwulf, who had, as has been related before, received the royal unction and crown from pope Leo the fourth at Rome, acceded to the sovereignty and retained it with the greatest difficulty, but with equal valour, twenty-eight years and a half. To trace in detail the mazy labyrinth of his labours was never my design; because a recapitulation of his exploits in their exact order of time would occasion some confusion to the reader. For, to relate how a hostile army, driven by himself or his generals, from one part of a district, retreated to another; and, dislodged thence, sought a fresh scene of operation and filled every place with rapine and slaughter; and, if I may use the expression, "to go round the whole island with him," might to some seem the height of folly: consequently I shall touch on all points summarily. For nine successive years battling with his enemies, sometimes deceived by false treaties, and sometimes wreaking his vengeance on the deceivers, he was at last reduced to such extreme distress, that scarcely three counties, that is to say, Hampshire, Wiltshire, and Somersetshire, stood fast by their allegiance, as he was compelled to retreat to a certain island called Athelney, which from its marshy situation was hardly accessible. He was accustomed afterwards, when in happier circumstances, to relate to his companions, in a lively and agreeable manner, his perils there, and how he escaped them by the merits of St. Cuthbert;* for it frequently happens that men are pleased with the recollection of those circumstances, which formerly they dreaded to encounter. During his retreat in this island, as he was one day in the house alone, his companions being dispersed on the river side for the purpose of fishing, he endeavoured to refresh his weary frame with sleep: and behold! Cuthbert, formerly bishop of Lindisfarne, addressed

---

* This legend will be found in the curious "account of the translation of the body of St. Cuthbert from Lindisfarne to Durham," which we shall give in "Anglo-Saxon Letters, Biographies," &c. It is taken from the Acta Sanctorum, iii. March, p. 127.

him, while sleeping, in the following manner:—"I am Cuthbert, if ever you heard of me; God hath sent me to announce good fortune to you; and since England has already largely paid the penalty of her crimes, God now, through the merits of her native saints, looks upon her with an eye of mercy. You too, so pitiably banished from your kingdom, shall shortly be again seated with honour on your throne; of which I give you this extraordinary token: your fishers shall this day bring home a great quantity of large fish in baskets; which will be so much the more extraordinary because the river, at this time hard-bound with ice, could warrant no such expectation; especially as the air now dripping with cold rain mocks the art of the fisher. But, when your fortune shall succeed to your wishes, you will act as becomes a king, if you conciliate God your helper, and me his messenger, with suitable devotion." Saying thus, the saint divested the sleeping king of his anxiety; and comforted his mother also, who was lying near him, and endeavouring to invite some gentle slumbers to her hard couch to relieve her cares, with the same joyful intelligence. When they awoke, they repeatedly declared that each had had the self-same dream, when the fishermen entering, displayed such a multitude of fishes as would have been sufficient to satisfy the appetite of a numerous army.

Not long after, venturing from his concealment, he hazarded an experiment of consummate art. Accompanied only by one of his most faithful adherents, he entered the tent of the Danish king under the disguise of a minstrel;* and being admitted, as a professor of the mimic art, to the banqueting room, there was no object of secrecy that he did not minutely attend to both with eyes and ears. Remaining there several days, till he had satisfied his mind on every matter which he wished to know, he returned to Athelney: and assembling his companions, pointed out the indolence of the enemy and the easiness of their defeat. All were eager for the enterprise, and himself collecting forces from every side, and learning exactly the situation of the barbarians from scouts he had sent out for that purpose, he suddenly attacked and routed them with incredible slaughter. The

* This story rests upon the authority of Ingulf and William of Malmesbury. Asser does not notice it.

remainder, with their king, gave hostages that they would embrace Christianity and depart from the country; which they performed. For their king, Gothrun, whom our people call Gurmund, with thirty nobles and almost all the commonalty, was baptized, Alfred standing for him; and the provinces of the East Angles, and Northumbrians * were given up to him, in order that he might, under fealty to the king, protect with hereditary right, what before he had overrun with predatory incursion. However, as the Ethiopian cannot change his skin, he domineered over these tributary provinces with the haughtiness of a tyrant for eleven years, and died in the twelfth, transmitting to his posterity the inheritance of his disloyalty, until subdued by Athelstan, the grandson of Alfred, they were, though reluctantly, compelled to admit one common king of England, as we see at the present day. Such of the Danes as had refused to become Christians, together with Hastings, went over sea, where the inhabitants are best able to tell what cruelties they perpetrated. For overrunning the whole maritime coasts to the Tuscan sea, they unpeopled Paris and Tours, as well as many other cities seated on the Seine and Loire, those noted rivers of France. At that time the bodies of many saints being taken up from the spot of their original interment and conveyed to safer places, have ennobled foreign churches with their relics even to this day. Then also the body of St. Martin, venerated, as Sidonius says, over the whole earth, in which virtue resides though life be at an end, was taken to Auxerre, by the clergy of his church, and placed in that of St. German, where it astonished the people of that district by unheard-of miracles. And when they who came thither, out of gratitude for cures performed, contributed many things to requite the labours of those who had borne him to this church, as is commonly the case, a dispute arose about the division of the money; the Turonians claiming the whole, because their patron had called the contributors together by his miracles: the natives, on the other hand, alleging that St. German was not unequal in merit, and was of equal

* This seems a mistake as far relates to Northumbria. The Saxon Chronicle has "Northerna," and Florence of Worcester "Rex Northmanicus," which at a first glance might easily be converted into Northumbria.

kindness; that both indeed had the same power, but that the prerogative of their church preponderated. To solve this knotty doubt, a leprous person was sought, and placed, nearly at the last gasp, wasted to a skeleton, and already dead, as it were, in a living carcass, between the bodies of the two saints. All human watch was prohibited for the whole night: the glory of Martin alone was vigilant; for the next day, the skin of the man on his side appeared clear, while on that of German, it was discoloured with its customary deformity. And, that they might not attribute this miracle to chance, they turned the yet diseased side to Martin. As soon as the morning began to dawn, the man was found by the hastening attendants with his skin smooth, perfectly cured, declaring the kind condescension of the resident patron, who yielded to the honour of such a welcome stranger. Thus the Turonians, both at that time and afterwards, safely filled their common purse by the assistance of their patron, till a more favourable gale of peace restored them to their former residence. For these marauders infesting France for thirteen years, and being at last overcome by the emperor Ernulph and the people of Brittany in many encounters, retreated into England as a convenient receptacle for their tyranny. During this space of time Alfred had reduced the whole island to his power, with the exception of what the Danes possessed. The Angles had willingly surrendered to his dominion, rejoicing that they had produced a man capable of leading them to liberty. He granted London, the chief city of the Mercian kingdom, to a nobleman named Ethered, to hold in fealty, and gave him his daughter Ethelfled in marriage. Ethered conducted himself with equal valour and fidelity; defended his trust with activity, and kept the East Angles and Northumbrians, who were fomenting rebellion against the king, within due bounds, compelling them to give hostages. Of what infinite service this was, the following emergency proved. After England had rejoiced for thirteen years in the tranquillity of peace and in the fertility of her soil, the northern pest of barbarians again returned. With them returned war and slaughter; again arose conspiracies of the Northumbrians and East Angles: but neither strangers nor natives experienced the same fortune as in former years; the one party, diminished by foreign contests, were less alert in their invasions; while the other, now experienced in war and animated by the exhortations of the king, were not only more ready to resist, but also to attack. The king himself was, with his usual activity, present in every action, ever daunting the invaders, and at the same time inspiriting his subjects, with the signal display of his courage. He would oppose himself singly to the enemy; and by his own personal exertions rally his declining forces The very places are yet pointed out by the inhabitants where he felt the vicissitudes of good and evil fortune. It was necessary to contend with Alfred even after he was overcome, after he was prostrate; insomuch that when he might be supposed altogether vanquished, he would escape like a slippery serpent, from the hand which held him, glide from his lurking-place, and, with undiminished courage, spring on his insulting enemies : he was insupportable after flight, and became more circumspect from the recollection of defeat, more bold from the thirst of vengeance. His children by Elswitha, the daughter of earl Athelred, were Ethelswitha, Edward who reigned after him; Ethelfled who was married to Ethered earl of the Mercians; Ethelwerd, whom they celebrate as being extremely learned; Elfred and Ethelgiva, virgins. His health was so bad that he was constantly disquieted either by the piles or some disorder of the intestines. It is said, however, that he entreated this from God, in his supplications, in order that, by the admonition of pain, he might be less anxious after earthly delights.

Yet amid these circumstances the private life of the king is to be admired and celebrated with the highest praise. For although, as some one has said, "Laws must give way amid the strife of arms," yet he, amid the sound of trumpets and the din of war, enacted statutes by which his people might equally familiarise themselves to religious worship and to military discipline. And since, from the example of the barbarians, the natives themselves began to lust after rapine, insomuch that there was no safe intercourse without a military guard, he appointed centuries, which they call "hundreds," and decennaries, that is to say, "tythings," so that every Englishman, living according to law, must be a member of both. If any one was accused of a crime, he was obliged immediately to produce persons from the hundred and tything to become his surety; and whosoever was unable to find such surety, must dread the severity of the laws. If any who was impleaded made his escape either before or after he had found surety, all persons of the hundred and tything paid a fine to the king. By this regulation he diffused such peace throughout the country, that he ordered golden bracelets, which might mock the eager desires of the passengers while no one durst take them away, to be hung up on the public causeways, where the roads crossed each other. Ever intent on almsgiving, he confirmed the privileges of the churches, as appointed by his father, and sent many presents over sea to Rome and to St. Thomas in India. Sighelm, bishop of Sherborne, sent ambassador for this purpose, penetrated successfully into India, a matter of astonishment even in the present time. Returning thence, he brought back many brilliant exotic gems and aromatic juices in which that country abounds, and a present more precious than the finest gold, part of our Saviour's cross, sent by pope Marinus to the king. He erected monasteries wherever he deemed it fitting; one in Athelney, where he lay concealed, as has been above related, and there he made John abbat, a native of Old Saxony; another at Winchester, which is called the New-minster, where he appointed Grimbald abbat, who, at his invitation, had been sent into England by Fulco archbishop of Rheims, known to him, as they say, by having kindly entertained him when a child on his way to Rome. The cause of his being sent for was that by his activity he might awaken the study of literature in England, which was now slumbering and almost expiring. The monastery of Shaftesbury also he filled with nuns, where he made his daughter Ethelgiva abbess. From St. David's he procured a person named Asser,* a man of skill in literature, whom he made bishop of Sherborne. This man explained the meaning of the works of Boethius, on the Consolation of Philosophy, in clearer terms, and the king himself translated them into the English language. And since there was no good scholar in his own kingdom, he sent for Werefrith

---

* Asser, the faithful friend and biographer of this great king. His Life of Alfred, alike honourable to his master and himself, is free from flattery. It is given in one of the volumes of our Series.

bishop of Worcester out of Mercia, who by command of the king rendered into the English tongue the books of Gregory's Dialogues. At this time Johannes Scotus is supposed to have lived; a man of clear understanding and amazing eloquence. He had long since, from the continued tumult of war around him, retired into France to Charles the Bald, at whose request he had translated the Hierarchia of Dionysius the Areopagite, word for word, out of the Greek into Latin. He composed a book also, which he entitled περὶ φύσεων μερισμοῦ, or Of the Division of Nature,* extremely useful in solving the perplexity of certain indispensable inquiries, if he be pardoned for some things in which he deviated from the opinions of the Latins, through too close attention to the Greeks. In after time, allured by the munificence of Alfred, he came into England, and at our monastery, as report says, was pierced with the iron styles of the boys whom he was instructing, and was even looked upon as a martyr; which phrase I have not made use of to the disparagement of his holy spirit, as though it were matter of doubt, especially as his tomb on the left side of the altar, and the verses of his epitaph, record his fame.† These, though rugged and deficient in the polish of our days, are not so uncouth for ancient times:

> "Here lies a saint, the sophist John, whose days
> On earth were grac'd with deepest learning's praise:
> Deem'd meet at last by martyrdom to gain
> Christ's kingdom, where the saints for ever reign."

Confiding in these auxiliaries, the king gave his whole soul to the cultivation of the liberal arts, insomuch that no Englishman was quicker in comprehending, or more elegant in translating. This was the more remarkable, because until twelve years of age he absolutely knew nothing of literature.‡

* It has been printed by Gale, Oxon, 1681.

† John the Scot is generally supposed to have died in France before A.D. 877, as the letter of Anastasius (Usher's Sylloge, Ep. 24,) addressed to Charles the Bald, who died in that year, seems strongly to imply that he was not then living. There is, however, no positive notice of the time of his death. The story indeed has so much the air of one told in Asser of John abbat of Athelney, that one would almost suspect it was formed from it: especially as Malmesbury seems to speak in a very hesitating manner on the subject. V. Asser, à Wise, p. 62.

‡ Asser says he first began his literary education, Nov. 11, 887.

At that time, lured by a kind mother, who under the mask of amusement promised that he should have a little book which she held in her hand for a present if he would learn it quickly, he entered upon learning in sport indeed at first, but afterwards drank of the stream with unquenchable avidity. He translated into English the greater part of the Roman authors, bringing off the noblest spoil of foreign intercourse for the use of his subjects; of which the chief books were Orosius, Gregory's Pastoral, Bede's History of the Angles, Boethius Of the Consolation of Philosophy, his own book, which he called in his vernacular tongue "Handboc," that is, a manual.* Moreover he infused a great regard for literature into his countrymen, stimulating them both with rewards and punishments, allowing no ignorant person to aspire to any dignity in the court. He died just as he had begun a translation of the Psalms. In the prologue to "The Pastoral" he observes, "that he was incited to translate these books into English because the churches which had formerly contained numerous libraries had, together with their books, been burnt by the Danes." And again, "that the pursuit of literature had gone to decay almost over the whole island, because each person was more occupied in the preservation of his life than in the perusal of books; wherefore he so far consulted the good of his countrymen, that they might now hastily view what hereafter, if peace should ever return, they might thoroughly comprehend in the Latin language." Again, "That he designed to transmit this book, transcribed by his order, to every see, with a golden style in which was a mancus of gold; that there was nothing of his own opinions inserted in this or his other translations, but that everything was derived from those celebrated men Plegmund† archbishop of Canterbury, Asser the bishop, Grimbald and John the priests." But, in short, I may thus briefly elucidate his

* Alfred's Manual, from the description which Asser gives of it, appears to have contained psalms, prayers, texts of Scripture, etc.: Malmesbury, however, in his Lives of the Bishops, quotes anecdotes of Aldhelm from it also.

† Plegmund is said to have written part of the Saxon Chronicle; Asser was archbishop of St. David's, and biographer of Alfred; Grimbald, abbat of St. Omers; and John of Corvey, a German Saxon, whom Alfred invited into England.

whole life: he so divided the twenty-four hours of the day and night as to employ eight of them in writing, in reading, and in prayer, eight in the refreshment of his body, and eight in dispatching the business of the realm. There was in his chapel a candle consisting of twenty-four divisions, and an attendant, whose peculiar province it was to admonish the king of his several duties by its consumption. One half of all revenues, provided they were justly acquired, he gave to his* monasteries, all his other income he divided into two equal parts, the first was again subdivided into three, of which the first was given to the servants of his court, the second to artificers whom he constantly employed in the erection of new edifices, in a manner surprising and hitherto unknown to the English, the third he gave to strangers. The second part of the revenue was divided in such a mode that the first portion should be given to the poor of his kingdom, the second to the monasteries, the third to scholars,† the fourth to foreign churches. He was a strict inquirer into the sentences passed by his magistrates, and a severe corrector of such as were unjust. He had one unusual and unheard of custom, which was, that he always carried in his bosom a book in which the daily order of the Psalms was contained, for the purpose of carefully perusing it, if at any time he had leisure. In this way he passed his life, much respected by neighbouring princes, and gave his daughter Ethelswitha in marriage to Baldwin earl of Flanders, by whom he had Arnulf and Ethelwulf; the former received from his father the county of Boulogne, from the other at this day are descended the earls of Flanders.‡

Alfred, paying the debt of nature, was buried at Winchester, in the monastery which he had founded; to build the offices of which Edward, his son, purchased a sufficient space of ground from the bishop and canons, giving, for every foot, a mancus of gold of the statute weight. The endurance of

* Asser says he devoted one half of his income "to God;" which part was afterwards subdivided for the poor, for the two monasteries he had founded, for the school he had established, for other monasteries and churches, domestic and foreign.

† This proportion was for both teachers and pupils in the school he founded for the young nobility.—*Lappenberg*, vol. i. p. 340.

‡ Matilda, queen of William the First, was daughter of Baldwin earl of Flanders, the fifth in descent from Ethelswitha. See note, p. 110.

the king was astonishing, in suffering such a sum to be extorted from him; but he did not choose to offer a sacrifice to God from the robbery of the poor. These two churches were so contiguous, that, when singing, they heard each others' voices; on this and other accounts an unhappy jealousy was daily stirring up causes of dissension, which produced frequent injuries on either side. For this reason that monastery was lately removed out of the city, and became a more healthy, as well as a more conspicuous, residence. They report that Alfred was first buried in the cathedral, because his monastery was unfinished, but that afterwards, on account of the folly of the canons, who asserted that the royal spirit, resuming its carcass, wandered nightly through the buildings, Edward, his son and successor, removed the remains of his father, and gave them a quiet resting-place in the new minster.* These and similar superstitions, such as that the dead body of a wicked man runs about, after death, by the agency of the devil, the English hold with almost inbred credulity,† borrowing them from the heathens, according to the expression of Virgil,

" Forms such as flit, they say, when life is gone."‡

CHAP. V.

Of Edward the son of Alfred. [A.D. 901—924.]

IN the year of our Lord's incarnation, 901, Edward, the son of Alfred, succeeded to the government, and held it twenty three years: he was much inferior to his father in literature, but greatly excelled in extent of power. For Alfred, indeed, united the two kingdoms of the Mercian and West Saxons, holding that of the Mercians only nominally, as he had assigned it to prince Ethelred: but at his death Edward first brought the Mercians altogether under his power, next, the West§ and East Angles, and Northumbrians, who had

* On its removal called Hyde Abbey.
† The popular notion was, that the devil re-animated the corpse, and played a variety of pranks by its agency; and that the only remedy was to dig up and consume the body with fire. See Will. Neubrig v 22.
‡ Virg Æneid, x. 641.
§ By West-Angles he probably intends the people of Essex or East-Saxons. See Florence of Worcester.

become one nation with the Danes; the Scots, who inhabit the northern part of the island; and all the Britons, whom we call Welsh, after perpetual battles, in which he was always successful. He devised a mode of frustrating the incursions of the Danes; for he repaired many ancient cities, or built new ones, in places calculated for his purpose, and filled them with a military force, to protect the inhabitants and repel the enemy. Nor was his design unsuccessful; for the inhabitants became so extremely valorous in these contests, that if they heard of an enemy approaching, they rushed out to give them battle, even without consulting the king or his generals, and constantly surpassed them, both in number and in warlike skill. Thus the enemy became an object of contempt to the soldiery and of derision to the king. At last some fresh assailants, who had come over under the command of Ethelwald, the son of the king's uncle, were all, together with himself, cut off to a man; those before, settled in the country, being either destroyed or spared under the denomination of Angles. Ethelwald indeed had attempted many things in the earlier days of this king; and, disdaining subjection to him, declared himself his inferior neither in birth nor valour; but being driven into exile by the nobility, who had sworn allegiance to Edward, he brought over the pirates; with whom, meeting his death, as I have related, he gave proof of the folly of resisting those who are our superiors in power. Although Edward may be deservedly praised for these transactions, yet, in my opinion, the palm should be more especially given to his father, who certainly laid the foundation of this extent of dominion. And here indeed Ethelfled, sister of the king and relict of Ethered, ought not to be forgotten, as she was a powerful accession to his party, the delight of his subjects, the dread of his enemies, a woman of an enlarged soul, who, from the difficulty experienced in her first labour, ever after refused the embraces of her husband; protesting that it was unbecoming the daughter of a king to give way to a delight which, after a time, produced such painful consequences. This spirited heroine assisted her brother greatly with her advice, was of equal service in building cities, nor could you easily discern, whether it was more owing to fortune or her own exertions, that a woman should be able to protect men at home, and to intimidate them abroad. She died five years before her brother, and was buried in the monastery of St. Peter's, at Gloucester; which, in conjunction with her husband, Ethered, she had erected with great solicitude. Thither too she had transferred the bones of St. Oswald, the king, from Bardney; but this monastery being destroyed in succeeding time by the Danes, Aldred, archbishop of York, founded another, which is now the chief in that city.

As the king had many daughters, he gave Edgiva to Charles, king of France, the son of Lewis the Stammerer, son of Charles the Bald, whose daughter, as I have repeatedly observed, Ethelwulf had married on his return from Rome; and, as the opportunity has now presented itself, the candid reader will not think it irrelevant, if I state the names of his wives and children. By Egwina, an illustrious lady, he had Athelstan, his first-born, and a daughter, whose name I cannot particularise, but her brother gave her in marriage to Sihtric, king of the Northumbrians. The second son of Edward was Ethelward, by Elfleda, daughter of earl Etheline; deeply versed in literature, much resembling his grandfather Alfred in features and disposition, but who departed, by an early death, soon after his father. By the same wife he had Edwin, of whose fate what the received opinion is I shall hereafter describe, not with confidence, but doubtingly. By her too he had six daughters; Edfleda, Edgiva, Ethelhilda, Ethilda, Edgitha, Elgifa: the first and third vowing celibacy to God, renounced the pleasure of earthly nuptials; Edfleda in a religious, and Ethelhilda in a lay habit: they both lie buried near their mother, at Winchester. Her father gave Edgiva, as I have mentioned, to king Charles,* and her brother, Athelstan, gave Ethilda to Hugh:† this same brother also sent Edgitha and Elgifa to Henry,‡ emperor of Germany, the second of whom he gave to his son Otho, the other to a certain duke, near the Alps.

* Charles the Simple had one son by her, Louis II., surnamed D'Outremer.
† Surnamed the Great. father of Hugh Capet: she had no issue by him.
‡ Henry, surnamed the Fowler, father of Otho the Great She had a son and daughter by him. One of Edward's daughters, called Adela, is said to have been married to Ebles, earl of Poitiers, by whom she had two sons. See L'Art de Verifier les Dates, n. 312.

Again; by his third wife, named Edgiva, he had two sons, Edmund and Edred, each of whom reigned after Athelstan: two daughters, Eadburga, and Edgiva; Eadburga, a virgin, dedicated to Christ, lies buried at Winchester; Edgiva, a lady of incomparable beauty, was united, by her brother Athelstan, to Lewis, prince of Aquitaine.* Edward had brought up his daughters in such wise, that in childhood they gave their whole attention to literature, and afterwards employed themselves in the labours of the distaff and the needle, that thus they might chastely pass their virgin age. His sons were so educated, as, first, to have the completest benefit of learning, that afterwards they might succeed to govern the state, not like rustics, but philosophers.

Charles, the son-in-law of Edward, constrained thereto by Rollo, through a succession of calamities, conceded to him that part of Gaul which at present is called Normandy. It would be tedious to relate for how many years, and with what audacity, the Normans disquieted every place from the British ocean, as I have said, to the Tuscan sea. First Hasten, and then Rollo; who, born of noble lineage among the Norwegians, though obsolete from its extreme antiquity, was banished, by the king's command, from his own country, and brought over with him multitudes, who were in danger, either from debt or consciousness of guilt, and whom he had allured by great expectations of advantage. Betaking himself therefore to piracy, after his cruelty had raged on every side at pleasure, he experienced a check at Chartres. For the townspeople, relying neither on arms nor fortifications, piously implored the assistance of the blessed Virgin Mary. The shift too of the virgin, which Charles the Bald had brought with other relics from Constantinople, they displayed to the winds on the ramparts, thronged by ·the garrison, after the fashion of a banner. The enemy on seeing it began to laugh, and to direct their arrows at it. This, however, was not done with impunity; for presently their eyes became dim, and they could neither retreat nor advance. The townsmen, with joy perceiving this, indulged

* This seems to have been Lewis the Blind, king of Arles: and if so, she must have been one of the elder daughters, as he appears not to have survived A.D. 930. She had, at least, one son by him, Charles Constantine, earl of Vienne. See L'Art de Verifier les Dates, ii. 429.

themselves in a plentiful slaughter of them, as far as fortune permitted. Rollo, however, whom God reserved for the true faith, escaped, and soon after gained Rouen and the neighbouring cities by force of arms, in the year of our Lord 876, and one year before the death of Charles the Bald, whose grandson Lewis, as is before mentioned, vanquished the Normans, but did not expel them: but Charles, the brother of that Lewis, grandson of Charles the Bald, by his son Lewis, as I have said above, repeatedly experiencing, from unsuccessful conflicts, that fortune gave him nothing which she took from others, resolved, after consulting his nobility, that it was advisable to make a show of royal munificence, when he was unable to repel injury; and, in a friendly manner, sent for Rollo. He was at this time far advanced in years; and, consequently, easily inclined to pacific measures. It was therefore determined by treaty, that he should be baptized, and hold that country of the king as his lord. The inbred and untameable ferocity of the man may well be imagined, for, on receiving this gift, as the by standers suggested to him, that he ought to kiss the foot of his benefactor, disdaining to kneel down, he seized the king's foot and dragged it to his mouth as he stood erect. The king falling on his back, the Normans began to laugh, and the Franks to be indignant; but Rollo apologized for his shameful conduct, by saying that it was the custom of his country. Thus the affair being settled, Rollo returned to Rouen, and there died.

The son of this Charles was Lewis: he being challenged by one Isembard, that had turned pagan, and renounced his faith, called upon his nobility for their assistance: they not even deigned an answer; when one Hugh, son of Robert, earl of Mont Didier, a youth of no great celebrity at the time, voluntarily entered the lists for his lord and killed the challenger. Lewis, with his whole army pursuing to Ponthieu, gained there a glorious triumph; either destroying or putting to flight all the barbarians whom Isembard had brought with him. But not long after, weakened by extreme sickness, the consequence of this laborious expedition, he appointed this Hugh, a young man of noted faith and courage, heir to the kingdom. Thus the lineage of Charles the Great ceased with him, because either his wife was barren, or else did not live long enough to have issue. Hugh married one of the daughters of Edward,* and begot Robert; Robert begot Henry; Henry, Philip; and Philip, Lewis, who now reigns in France. But to return to our Edward: I think it will be pleasing to relate what in his time pope Formosus commanded to be done with respect to filling up the bishoprics, which I shall insert in the very words I found it.†

"In the year of our Lord's nativity 904, pope Formosus sent letters into England, by which he denounced excommunication and malediction to king Edward and all his subjects, instead of the benediction which St. Gregory had given to the English nation from the seat of St. Peter, because for seven whole years the entire district of the Gewissæ, that is, of the West-Saxons, had been destitute of bishops. On hearing this, king Edward assembled a council of the senators of the English, over which presided Plegmund, archbishop of Canterbury, interpreting carefully the words of the apostolic legation. Then the king and the bishops chose for themselves and their followers a salutary council, and, according to our Saviour's words, 'The harvest truly is plenteous, but the labourers are few,'‡ they elected and appointed one bishop to every province of the Gewissæ, and that district which two formerly possessed they divided into five. The council

* This is a mistake: Hugh is confounded with his father, who married Edward's daughter. There is no notice of this exploit of Hugh's in Bouquet, though Isembard is mentioned as the nephew of Lewis, who, being unjustly banished, returns accompanied by a large body of Danes and Normans, but is defeated. Bouquet, Recueil, &c. tom. ix. 58. Lewis, however, left issue, and it was on the death of his grandson Lewis, that Hugh Capet became king of France.

† This story of pope Formosus and the seven bishops is to be found verbatim in a MS. (Bodley, 579) which was given to the cathedral of Exeter by bishop Leofric, who died A.D. 1073. Its difficulties therefore are not to be imputed to our author. But though it may not be easy to assign a rational motive for the invention of such an instrument, it is a decided forgery; and all the ecclesiastical writers, from Baronius to Wilkins, [See Concilia, i. p. 201,] have utterly failed in their conjectural attempts to uphold it: even the temperate, the acute, the learned Henry Wharton [Anglia Sacra, i. 554, 5], who rejects decidedly the epistle, gives but an unsatisfactory solution of the seven vacant sees. Its repugnancies will be seen at a glance, when it is recollected, that Formosus died A.D. 896; Edward did not reign till A.D. 901; and Frithstan did not become bishop of Winchester before A.D. 910.

‡ Matt. ix. 37.

being dissolved, the archbishop went to Rome with splendid presents, appeased the pope with much humility, and related the king's ordinance, which gave the pontiff great satisfaction. Returning home, in one day he ordained in the city of Canterbury seven bishops to seven churches:—Frithstan to the church of Winchester; Athelstan to Cornwall; Werstan to Sherborne; Athelelm to Wells; Aidulf to Crediton in Devonshire: also to other provinces he appointed two bishops; to the South-Saxons, Bernegus, a very proper person; and to the Mercians, Cenulph, whose see was at Dorchester, in Oxfordshire. All this the pope established, in such wise, that he who should invalidate this decree should be damned everlastingly."

Edward, going the way of all flesh, rested in the same monastery with his father, which he had augmented with considerable revenues, and in which he had buried his brother Ethelward four years before.

CHAP. VI.

Of Athelstan, the son of Edward. [A.D. 924—940.]

IN the year of our Lord's incarnation 924, Athelstan, the son of Edward, began to reign, and held the sovereignty sixteen years. His brother, Ethelward, dying a few days after his father, had been buried with him at Winchester. At this place, therefore, Athelstan, being elected king by the unanimous consent of the nobility, he was crowned at a royal town, which is called Kingston; though one Elfred, whose death we shall hereafter relate in the words of the king, with his factious party, as sedition never wants adherents, attempted to prevent it. The ground of his opposition, as they affirm, was, that Athelstan was born of a concubine. But having nothing ignoble in him, except this stain, if after all it be true, he cast all his predecessors into the shade by his piety, as well as the glory of all their triumphs, by the splendour of his own. So much more excellent is it to have that for which we are renowned inherent, than derived from our ancestors; because the former is exclusively our own, the latter is imputable to others. I forbear relating how many new and magnificent monasteries he founded; but I will not conceal that there was scarcely an old one in England which he did not embellish, either with buildings, or ornaments, or books, or possessions. Thus he ennobled the new ones expressly, but the old, as though they were only casual objects of his kindness. With Sihtric, king of the Northumbrians, who married, as I have before said, one of his sisters, he made a lasting covenant; he dying after a year, Athelstan took that province under his own government, expelling one Aldulph, who resisted him. And as a noble mind, when once roused, aspires to greater things, he compelled Jothwel, king of all the Welsh, and Constantine, king of the Scots, to quit their kingdoms; but not long after, moved with commiseration, he restored them to their original state, that they might reign under him, saying, "it was more glorious to make than to be a king." His last contest was with Anlaf, the son of Sihtric, who, with the beforenamed Constantine, again in a state of rebellion, had entered his territories under the hope of gaining the kingdom. Athelstan purposely retreating, that he might derive greater honour from vanquishing his furious assailants, this bold youth, meditating unlawful conquests, had now proceeded far into England, when he was opposed at Bruneford* by the most experienced generals, and most valiant forces. Perceiving, at length, what danger hung over him, he assumed the character of a spy. Laying aside his royal ensigns, and taking a harp in his hand, he proceeded to our king's tent: singing before the entrance, and at times touching the trembling strings in harmonious cadence, he was readily admitted, professing himself a minstrel, who procured his daily sustenance by such employment. Here he entertained the king and his companions for some time with his musical performance, carefully examining everything while occupied in singing. When satiety of eating had put an end to their sensual enjoyments, and the business of war was resumed among the nobles, he was ordered to depart, and received the recompence of his song; but disdaining to take it away, he hid it beneath him in the earth. This circumstance was remarked by a person, who had formerly served under him, and immediately related it to Athelstan. The king, blaming him

* In the Saxon Chronicle it is called Brumby. [See Chronicles of the Anglo-Saxons, in Bohn's Antiquarian Library, pp. 376, 377.] Its site is not exactly known, but it was probably not far from the Humber.

extremely for not having detected his enemy as he stood before them, received this answer: "The same oath, which I have lately sworn to you, O king, I formerly made to Anlaf; and had you seen me violate it towards him, you might have expected similar perfidy towards yourself: but condescend to listen to the advice of your servant, which is, that you should remove your tent hence, and remaining in another place till the residue of the army come up, you will destroy your ferocious enemy by a moderate delay." Approving this admonition, he removed to another place. Anlaf advancing, well prepared, at night, put to death, together with the whole of his followers, a certain bishop,* who had joined the army only the evening before, and, ignorant of what had passed, had pitched his tent there on account of the level turf. Proceeding farther, he found the king himself equally unprepared; who, little expecting his enemy capable of such an attack, had indulged in profound repose. But, when roused from his sleep by the excessive tumult, and urging his people, as much as the darkness of the night would permit, to the conflict, his sword fell by chance from the sheath; upon which, while all things were filled with dread and blind confusion, he invoked the protection of God and of St. Aldhelm, who was distantly related to him; and replacing his hand upon the scabbard, he there found a sword, which is kept to this day, on account of the miracle, in the treasury of the kings. Moreover, it is, as they say, chased in one part, but can never be inlaid either with gold or silver. Confiding in this divine present, and at the same time, as it began to dawn, attacking the Norwegian, he continued the battle unwearied through the day, and put him to flight with his whole army. There fell Constantine, king of the Scots, a man of treacherous energy and vigorous old age, five other kings, twelve earls, and almost the whole assemblage of barbarians. The few who escaped were preserved to embrace the faith of Christ.

Concerning this king a strong persuasion is prevalent among the English, that one more just or learned never governed the kingdom. That he was versed in literature, I

* Said to be Werstan, bishop of Sherborne. See Malmesbury's Gesta Pontificum; or, Lives of the Bishops, to be hereafter translated and published in this series.

discovered a few days since, in a certain old volume, wherein the writer struggles with the difficulty of the task, unable to express his meaning as he wished. Indeed I would subjoin his words for brevity's sake, were they not extravagant beyond belief in the praises of the king, and just in that style of writing which Cicero, the prince of Roman eloquence, in his book on Rhetoric, denominates "bombast." The custom of that time excuses the diction, and the affection for Athelstan, who was yet living, gave countenance to the excess of praise. I shall subjoin, therefore, in familiar language, some few circumstances which may tend to augment his reputation.

King Edward, after many noble exploits, both in war and peace, a few days before his death subdued the contumacy of the city of Chester, which was rebelling in confederacy with the Britons; and placing a garrison there, he fell sick and died at Faringdon, and was buried, as I before related, at Winchester. Athelstan, as his father had commanded in his will, was then hailed king, recommended by his years,—for he was now thirty,—and the maturity of his wisdom. For even his grandfather Alfred, seeing and embracing him affectionately when he was a boy of astonishing beauty and graceful manners, had most devoutly prayed that his government might be prosperous: indeed, he had made him a knight* unusually early, giving him a scarlet cloak, a belt studded with diamonds, and a Saxon sword with a golden scabbard. Next he had provided that he should be educated in the court of Ethelfled his daughter, and of his son-in-law Ethered; so that, having been brought up in expectation of succeeding to the kingdom, by the tender care of his aunt and of this celebrated prince, he repressed and destroyed all envy by the lustre of his good qualities; and, after the death of his father, and decease of his brother, he was crowned at Kingston. Hence, to celebrate such splendid events, and the joy of that illustrious day, the poet justly exclaims:

* This passage is thought to prove the existence of knights as a distinct order among the Saxons; and, coupled with the case of Hereward, it has very much that air. See Mr. Turner's Anglo-Saxons, 4, 171, et inf. But perhaps in the present instance, it may amount to nothing more than bestowing his first arms on him. Lewis the Debonnaire received his arms, "ense accinctus est," at thirteen years old —Duchesne, t. ii. 289.

Of royal race a noble stem
Hath chased our darkness like a gem.
Great Athelstan, his country's pride,
Whose virtue never turns aside;
Sent by his father to the schools,
Patient, he bore their rigid rules,
And drinking deep of science mild,
Passed his first years unlike a child.
Next clothed in youth's bewitching charms,
Studied the harsher lore of arms,
Which soon confessed his knowledge keen,
As after in the sovereign seen.
Soon as his father, good and great,
Yielded, though ever famed, to fate,
The youth was called the realm to guide,
And, like his parent, well preside.
The nobles meet, the crown present,
On rebels, prelates curses vent;
The people light the festive fires,
And show by turns their kind desires.
Their deeds their loyalty declare,
Though hopes and fears their bosoms share.
With festive treat the court abounds;
Foams the brisk wine, the hall resounds.
The pages run, the servants haste,
And food and verse regale the taste.
The minstrels sing, the guests commend,
Whilst all in praise to Christ contend.
The king with pleasure all things sees,
And all his kind attentions please.

The solemnity of the consecration being finished, Athelstan, that he might not deceive the expectation of his subjects, and fall below their opinion, subdued the whole of England, except Northumbria, by the single terror of his name. One Sihtric, a relation of that Gothrun who is mentioned in the history of Alfred, presided over this people, a barbarian both by race and disposition, who, though he ridiculed the power of preceding kings, humbly solicited affinity with Athelstan, sending messengers expressly for the purpose; and himself shortly following confirmed the proposals of the ambassadors. In consequence, honoured by a union with his sister, and by various presents, he laid the basis of a perpetual treaty. But, as I have before observed, dying at the end of a year, he afforded Athelstan an opportunity for uniting Northumbria, which belonged to him both by ancient right and recent affinity, to his sovereignty. Anlaf, the son of Sihtric, then fled into Ireland, and his brother Guthferth into Scotland. Messengers from the king immediately followed to Constantine, king of the Scots, and Eugenius, king of the Cumbrians, claiming the fugitive under a threat of war. The barbarians had no idea of resistance, but without delay coming to a place called Dacor, they surrendered themselves and their kingdoms to the sovereign of England. Out of regard to this treaty, the king himself stood for the son of Constantine, who was ordered to be baptized, at the sacred font. Guthferth, however, amid the preparations for the journey, escaped by flight with one Turfrid, a leader of the opposite party; and afterwards laying siege to York, where he could succeed in bringing the townsmen to surrender neither by entreaties nor by threats, he departed. Not long after, being both shut up in a castle, they eluded the vigilance of the guards, and escaped. Turfrid, losing his life quickly after by shipwreck, became a prey to fishes. Guthferth, suffering extremely both by sea and land, at last came a suppliant to court. Being amicably received by the king, and sumptuously entertained for four days, he resought his ships; an incorrigible pirate, and accustomed to live in the water like a fish. In the meantime Athelstan levelled with the ground the castle which the Danes had formerly fortified in York, that there might be no place for disloyalty to shelter in; and the booty which had been found there, which was very considerable, he generously divided, man by man, to the whole army. For he had prescribed himself this rule of conduct, never to hoard up riches; but liberally to expend all his acquisition either on monasteries or on his faithful followers. On these, during the whole of his life, he expended his paternal treasures, as well as the produce of his victories. To the clergy he was humble and affable; to the laity mild and pleasant; to the nobility rather reserved, from respect to his dignity; to the lower classes, laying aside the stateliness of power, he was kind and condescending. He was, as we have heard, of becoming stature, thin in person, his hair flaxen, as I have seen by his remains, and beautifully wreathed with golden threads. Extremely beloved by his subjects from admiration of his fortitude and humility, he was terrible to those who rebelled against him, through his invincible courage. He compelled the rulers of the northern

Welsh, that is, of the North Britons, to meet him at the city of Hereford, and after some opposition to surrender to his power. So that he actually brought to pass what no king before him had even presumed to think of: which was, that they should pay annually by way of tribute, twenty pounds of gold, three hundred of silver, twenty-five thousand oxen, besides as many dogs as he might choose, which from their sagacious scent could discover the retreats and hiding places of wild beasts; and birds, trained to make prey of others in the air. Departing thence, he turned towards the Western Britons, who are called the Cornwallish, because, situated in the west of Britain, they are opposite to the extremity of Gaul.* Fiercely attacking, he obliged them to retreat from Exeter, which, till that time, they had inhabited with equal privileges with the Angles, fixing the boundary of their province on the other side of the river Tamar, as he had appointed the river Wye to the North Britons. This city then, which he had cleansed by purging it of its contaminated race, he fortified with towers and surrounded with a wall of squared stone. And, though the barren and unfruitful soil can scarcely produce indifferent oats, and frequently only the empty husk without the grain, yet, owing to the magnificence of the city, the opulence of its inhabitants, and the constant resort of strangers, every kind of merchandise is there so abundant that nothing is wanting which can conduce to human comfort. Many noble traces of him are to be seen in that city, as well as in the neighbouring district, which will be better described by the conversation of the natives, than by my narrative.

On this account all Europe resounded with his praises, and extolled his valour to the skies: foreign princes with justice esteemed themselves happy if they could purchase his friendship either by affinity or by presents. Harold king of Norway sent him a ship with golden beak and a purple sail, furnished within with a compacted fence of gilded shields. The names of the persons sent with it, were Helgrim and Offrid: who, being received with princely magnificence in the city of York, were amply compensated, by rich presents, for the labour of their journey. Henry the First, for there were many of the name, the son of Conrad, king of the

* Cornu Galliæ, a fanciful etymology.

Teutonians and emperor of the Romans, demanded his sister, as I have before related, for his son Otho: passing over so many neighbouring kings, but contemplating from a distance Athelstan's noble descent, and greatness of mind. So completely indeed had these two qualities taken up their abode with him, that none could be more noble or illustrious in descent; none more bold or prompt in disposition. Maturely considering that he had four sisters, who were all equally beautiful, except only as their ages made a difference, he sent two to the emperor at his request; and how he disposed of them in marriage has already been related: Lewis prince of Aquitania, a descendant of Charles the Great, obtained the third in wedlock: the fourth, in whom the whole essence of beauty had centred, which the others only possessed in part, was demanded from her brother by Hugh king of the Franks.* The chief of this embassy was Adulph, son of Baldwin earl of Flanders by Ethelswitha daughter of king Edward.† When he had declared the request of the suitor in an assembly of the nobility at Abingdon, he produced such liberal presents as might gratify the most boundless avarice: perfumes such as never had been seen in England before: jewels, but more especially emeralds, the greenness of which, reflected by the sun, illumined the countenances of the bystanders with agreeable light: many fleet horses with their trappings, and, as Virgil says, "Champing their golden bits:" an alabaster vase so exquisitely chased, that, the cornfields really seemed to wave, the vines to bud, the figures of men actually to move, and so clear and polished, that it reflected the features like a mirror; the sword of Constantine the Great, on which the name of its original possessor was read in golden letters; on the pommel, upon thick plates of gold, might be seen fixed an iron spike, one of the four which the Jewish faction prepared for the crucifixion of our Lord: the spear of Charles the Great, which whenever that invincible emperor hurled in his expeditions against the Saracens, he always came off conqueror; it was reported to be the same, which, driven into the side of our Saviour by

* Improperly called king: it was Hugh the Great, father of Hugh Capet. Malmesbury was probably deceived by a blunder of Ingulf's.
† This is a mistake, she was daughter of Alfred. See chap. iv. p. 117.

the hand of the centurion,* opened, by that precious wound, the joys of paradise to wretched mortals: the banner of the most blessed martyr Maurice, chief of the Theban legion;† with which the same king, in the Spanish war, used to break through the battalions of the enemy however fierce and wedged together, and put them to flight: a diadem, precious from its quantity of gold, but more so for its jewels, the splendour of which threw the sparks of light so strongly on the beholders, that the more stedfastly any person endeavoured to gaze, so much the more he was dazzled, and compelled to avert his eyes; part of the holy and adorable cross enclosed in crystal; where the eye, piercing through the substance of the stone, might discern the colour and size of the wood; a small portion of the crown of thorns, enclosed in a similar manner, which, in derision of his government, the madness of the soldiers placed on Christ's sacred head. The king, delighted with such great and exquisite presents, made an equal return of good offices; and gratified the soul of the longing suitor by a union with his sister. With some of these presents he enriched succeeding kings: but to Malmesbury he gave part of the cross and crown; by the support of which, I believe, that place even now flourishes, though it has suffered so many shipwrecks of its liberty, so many attacks of its enemies.‡ In this place he ordered Elwin and Ethelwin, the sons of his uncle Ethelward, whom he had lost in the battle against Anlaf, to be honourably buried, expressing his design of resting here himself: of which battle it is now proper time to give the account of that poet, from whom I have taken all these transactions.

> His subjects governing with justest sway,
> Tyrants o'eraw'd, twelve years had pass'd away,

* The legend of St. Longinus makes the centurion mentioned in the Gospel, the person who pierced the side of our Lord; with many other fabulous additions. See Jac. a Voragine, Legenda Sanctorum.

† The Theban legion refusing, in the Diocletian persecution, to bring the Christians to execution, were ordered to be decimated; and on their persisting in the same resolution at the instigation of Maurice, the commander of the legion, they were, together with him, put to cruel deaths. V. Acta Sanctor. 22 Sept.

‡ He has, apparently, the oppressions of bishop Roger constantly before him.

When Europe's noxious pestilence stalk'd forth,
And poured the barbarous legions from the north.
The pirate Anlaf now the briny surge
Forsakes, while deeds of desperation urge.
Her king consenting, Scotia's land receives
The frantic madman, and his host of thieves:
Now flush'd with insolence they shout and boast,
And drive the harmless natives from the coast.
Thus, while the king, secure in youthful pride,
Bade the soft hours in gentle pleasures glide,
Though erst he stemmed the battle's furious tide,
With ceaseless plunder sped the daring horde,
And wasted districts with their fire and sword.
The verdant crops lay withering on the fields
The glebe no promise to the rustic yields.
Immense the numbers of barbarian force,
Countless the squadrons both of foot and horse.
At length fame's rueful moan alarmed the king,
And bade him shun this ignominious sting,
That arms like his to ruffian bands should bend:
'Tis done . delays and hesitations end.
High in the air the threatening banners fly,
And call his eager troops to victory,
His hardy force, a hundred thousand strong
Whom standards hasten to the fight along.
The martial clamour scares the plund'ring band,
And drives them bootless tow'rds their native land.
The vulgar mass a dreadful carnage share,
And shed contagion on the ambient air,
While Anlaf, only, out of all the crew
Escapes the meed of death, so justly due,
Reserved by fortune's favor, once again
When Athelstan was dead, to claim our strain.

This place seems to require that I should relate the death of Elfred in the words of the king, for which I before pledged the faith of my narrative. For as he had commanded the bodies of his relations to be conveyed to Malmesbury, and interred at the head of the sepulchre of St. Aldhelm; he honoured the place afterwards to such a degree, that he esteemed none more desirable or more holy. Bestowing many large estates upon it, he confirmed them by charters, in one of which, after the donation, he adds : "Be it known to the sages of our kingdom, that I have not unjustly seized the lands aforesaid, or dedicated plunder to God ; but that I have received them, as the English nobility, and even John, the pope of the church of Rome himself, have judged fitting on the death of Elfred. He was the jealous rival both of my happiness and life, and consented to the wickedness of my enemies, who, on my father's decease, had not God in his mercy delivered me, wished to put out my eyes in the city of Winchester: wherefore, on the discovery of their infernal contrivances, he was sent to the church of Rome to defend himself by oath before pope John. This he did at the altar of St. Peter; but at the very instant he had sworn, he fell down before it, and was carried by his servants to the English School, where he died the third night after. The pope immediately sent to consult with us, whether his body should be placed among other Christians. On receiving this account the nobility of our kingdom, with the whole body of his relations, humbly entreated that we would grant our permission for his remains to be buried with other Christians. Consenting, therefore, to their urgent request, we sent back our compliance to Rome, and with the pope's permission he was buried, though unworthy, with other Christians. In consequence all his property of every description was adjudged to be mine. Moreover, we have noted this in writing, that, so long as Christianity reigns, it may never be abrogated, whence the aforesaid land, which I have given to God and St. Peter, was granted me; nor do I know any thing more just, than that I should bestow this gift on God and St. Peter, who caused my rival to fall in the sight of all persons, and conferred on me a prosperous reign."

In these words of the king, we may equally venerate his wisdom, and his piety in sacred matters: his wisdom, that so young a man should perceive that a sacrifice obtained by rapine could not be acceptable to God: his piety in so gratefully making a return to God, out of a benefit conferred on him by divine vengeance. Moreover, it may be necessary to observe, that at that time the church of St. Peter was the chief of the monastery, which now is deemed second only: the church of St. Mary, which the monks at present frequent, was built afterwards in the time of king Edgar, under abbat Elfric. Thus far relating to the king I have written from authentic testimony: that which follows I have learned more from old ballads, popular through succeeding times, than from books written expressly for the information of

BIRTH OF ATHELSTAN.

posterity. I have subjoined them, not to defend their veracity, but to put my reader in possession of all I know. First, then, to the relation of his birth.

There was in a certain village, a shepherd's daughter, a girl of exquisite beauty, who gained through the elegance of her person what her birth could never have bestowed. In a vision she beheld a prodigy: the moon shone from her womb, and all England was illuminated by the light. When she sportively related this to her companions in the morning, it was not so lightly received, but immediately reached the ears of the woman who had nursed the sons of the king. Deliberating on this matter, she took her home and adopted her as a daughter, bringing up this young maiden with costlier attire, more delicate food, and more elegant demeanour. Soon after, Edward, the son of king Alfred, travelling through the village, stopped at the house which had been the scene of his infantine education. Indeed, he thought it would be a blemish on his reputation to omit paying his salutations to his nurse. He became deeply enamoured of the young woman from the first moment he saw her, and passed the night with her. In consequence of this single intercourse, she brought forth her son Athelstan, and so realized her dream. For at the expiration of his childish years, as he approached manhood, he gave proof by many actions what just expectations of noble qualities might be entertained of him. King Edward, therefore, died, and was shortly followed by his legitimate son Ethelward. All hopes now centred in Athelstan: Elfred alone, a man of uncommon insolence, disdaining to be governed by a sovereign whom he had not voluntarily chosen, secretly opposed with his party to the very utmost. But he being detected and punished, as the king has before related, there were some who even accused Edwin, the king's brother, of treachery. Base and dreadful crime was it thus to embroil fraternal affection by sinister constructions. Edwin, though imploring, both personally and by messengers, the confidence of his brother, and though invalidating the accusation by an oath, was nevertheless driven into exile. So far, indeed, did the dark suggestions of some persons prevail on a mind distracted with various cares, that, forgetful of a brother's love, he expelled the youth, an object of pity even to strangers. The mode adopted too was cruel in the extreme: he was compelled to go on board a vessel, with a single attendant, without a rower, without even an oar, and the bark crazy with age. Fortune laboured for a long time to restore the innocent youth to land, but when at length he was far out at sea, and sails could not endure the violence of the wind, the young man, delicate, and weary of life under such circumstances, put an end to his existence by a voluntary plunge into the waters. The attendant wisely determining to prolong his life, sometimes by shunning the hostile waves, and sometimes by urging the boat forward with his feet, brought his master's body to land, in the narrow sea which flows between Wissant and Dover. Athelstan, when his anger cooled, and his mind became calm, shuddered at the deed, and submitting to a seven years' penance, inflicted severe vengeance on the accuser of his brother: he was the king's cup-bearer, and on this account had opportunity of enforcing his insinuations. It so happened on a festive day, as he was serving wine, that slipping with one foot in the midst of the chamber, he recovered himself with the other. On this occasion, he made use of an expression which proved his destruction: "Thus brother," said he, "assists brother." The king on hearing this, ordered the faithless wretch to be put to death, loudly reproaching him with the loss of that assistance he might have had from his brother, were he alive, and bewailing his death.

The circumstances of Edwin's death, though extremely probable, I the less venture to affirm for truth, on account of the extraordinary affection he manifested towards the rest of his brothers; for, as his father had left them very young, he cherished them whilst children with much kindness, and, when grown up, made them partakers of his kingdom; it is before related to what dignity he exalted such of his sisters as his father had left unmarried and unprovided for. Completing his earthly course, and that a short one, Athelstan died at Gloucester. His noble remains were conveyed to Malmesbury and buried under the altar. Many gifts, both in gold and silver, as well as relics of saints purchased abroad in Brittany, were carried before the body: for, in such things, admonished. as they say, in a dream, he expended the treasures which his father had long since amassed, and had left untouched. His years, though few, were full of glory.

CHAP. VII.

Of kings Edmund, Edred, and Edwy. [A.D. 940—955.]

In the year of our Lord's incarnation 940, Edmund the brother of Athelstan, a youth of about eighteen, received and held the government for six years and a half. In his time the Northumbrians, meditating a renewal of hostilities, violated the treaty which they had made with Athelstan, and created Anlaf, whom they had recalled from Ireland, their king. Edmund, who thought it disgraceful not to complete his brother's victorious course, led his troops against the delinquents; who presently retreating, he subjugated all the cities on this side the river Humber. Anlaf, with a certain prince, Reginald,* the son of that Gurmund of whom we have spoken in the history of Alfred, sounding the disposition of the king, offered to surrender himself, proffering his conversion to Christianity as a pledge of his fidelity, and receiving baptism. His savage nature, however, did not let him remain long in this resolution, for he violated his oath, and irritated his lord. In consequence of which, the following year he suffered for his crimes, being doomed to perpetual exile. The province which is called Cumberland Edmund assigned to Malcolm, king of the Scots, under fealty of an oath.

Among the many donations which the king conferred on different churches, he exalted that of Glastonbury, through his singular affection towards it, with great estates and honours, and granted it a charter in these words:

"In the name of our Lord Jesus Christ, I Edmund, king of the Angles, and governor and ruler of the other surrounding nations, with the advice and consent of my nobility, for the hope of eternal retribution, and remission of my transgressions, do grant to the church of the holy mother of God, Mary of Glastonbury, and the venerable Dunstan, whom I have there constituted abbat, the franchise and jurisdiction,

---

* Reginald was not the son of Gurmund, but of Guthferth, who was driven out of Northumberland by Athelstan. See Saxon Chronicle, A.D. 927—944.

rights, customs, and all the forfeitures of all their possessions; that is to say,* burhgeritha, and hundred-setena. athas and ordelas, and infangenetheofas, hamsocne, and fridebrice, and forestel and toll, and team, throughout my kingdom, and their lands shall be free to them, and released from all exactions, as my own are. But more especially shall the town of Glastonbury, in which is situated that most ancient church of the holy mother of God, together with its bounds, be more free than other places. The abbat of this place, alone, shall have power, as well in causes known as unknown; in small and in great; and even in those which are above, and under the earth; on dry land, and in the water; in woods and in plains; and he shall have the same authority of punishing or remitting the crimes of delinquents perpetrated within it, as my court has; in the same manner as my predecessors have granted and confirmed by charter; to wit, Edward my father, and Elfred his father, and Kentwin, Ina, and Cuthred, and many others, who more peculiarly honoured and esteemed that noble place. And that any one, either bishop, or duke,† or prince, or any of their servants, should dare to enter it for the purpose of holding courts, or distraining, or doing any thing contrary to the will of the servants of God there, I inhibit under God's curse. Whosoever therefore shall benevolently augment my donation, may his life be prosperous in this present world; long may he enjoy his happiness: but whosoever shall presume to invade it through his own rashness, let him know for certain that he shall be compelled with fear and trembling to give account before the tribunal of a rigorous judge, unless he shall first atone for his offence by proper satisfaction."

The aforesaid donation was granted in the year of our

* The exact meaning of some of these terms is not easily attainable, but they are generally understood to imply—jurisdiction over the burgh, or town—hundred court—oaths and ordeals—thieves taken within the jurisdiction—housebreakers—breach of peace—offences committed on the highways, or forestalling—tolls—warranty, or a right of reclaiming villains who had absconded. The charter therefore conveys a right to hold various courts, and consequently to try, and receive all mulcts arising from the several offences enumerated, which being generally redeemable by fine, produced considerable sums; besides, what was perhaps of more importance, exemption from the vexations of the king's officers.

† Duke is often used in charters, &c. as synonymous with earl.

Lord Jesus Christ's incarnation 944, in the first of the indiction, and was written in letters of gold in the book of the Gospels, which he presented to the same church elegantly adorned. Such great and prosperous successes, however, were obscured by a melancholy death. A certain robber named Leofa, whom he had banished for his crimes, returning after six years' absence totally unexpected, was sitting, on the feast of St. Augustine, the apostle of the English, and first archbishop of Canterbury, among the royal guests at Puckle-church,* for on this day the English were wont to regale in commemoration of their first preacher; by chance too, he was placed near a nobleman whom the king had condescended to make his guest. This, while the others were eagerly carousing, was perceived by the king alone; when, hurried with indignation and impelled by fate, he leaped from the table, caught the robber by the hair, and dragged him to the floor; but he secretly drawing a dagger from its sheath plunged it with all his force into the breast of the king as he lay upon him. Dying of the wound, he gave rise over the whole kingdom to many fictions concerning his decease. The robber was shortly torn limb from limb by the attendants who rushed in, though he wounded some of them ere they could accomplish their purpose. St. Dunstan, at that time abbat of Glastonbury, had foreseen his ignoble end, being fully persuaded of it from the gesticulations and insolent mockery of a devil dancing before him. Wherefore, hastening to court at full speed, he received intelligence of the transaction on the road. By common consent then it was determined, that his body should be brought to Glastonbury and there magnificently buried in the northern part of the tower. That such had been his intention, through his singular regard for the abbat, was evident from particular circumstances. The village also where he was murdered was made an offering for the dead, that the spot which had witnessed his fall might ever after minister aid to his soul.

In his fourth year, that is, in the year of our Lord 944, William, the son of Rollo, duke of Normandy, was treacherously killed in France, which old writers relate as having been done with some degree of justice. Rinulph, one of the Norman nobility, owing William a grudge from some un-

* In Gloucestershire.

known cause, harassed him with perpetual aggressions. His son, Anschetil, who served under the earl, to gratify his lord durst offer violence to nature for taking his father in battle: he delivered him into the power of the earl, relying on the most solemn oath, that he should suffer nothing beyond imprisonment. As wickedness, however, constantly discovers pretences for crime, the earl, shortly after feigning an excuse, sends Anschetil to Pavia bearing a letter to the duke of Italy, the purport of which was his own destruction. Completing his journey, he was received, on his entrance into the city, in the most respectful manner; and delivering the letter, the duke, astonished at the treachery, shuddered, that a warrior of such singular address should be ordered to be despatched. But as he would not oppose the request of so renowned a nobleman, he laid an ambush of a thousand horsemen, as it is said, for Anschetil when he left the city. For a long time, with his companions whom he had selected out of all Normandy, he resisted their attack; but at last he fell nobly, compensating his own death by slaying many of the enemy. The only survivor on either side was Balso, a Norman, a man of small size, but of incredible courage; although some say that he was ironically called short. This man, I say, alone hovered round the city, and by his single sword terrified the townspeople as long as he thought proper. No person will deem this incredible, who considers what efforts the desperation of a courageous man will produce, and how little military valour the people of that region possess. Returning thence to his own country, he laid his complaint of the perfidy of his lord before the king of France. Fame reported too, that Rinulph, in addition to his chains, had had his eyes put out. In consequence the earl being cited to his trial at Paris, was met, under the pretence of a conference, as they assert, and killed by Balso; thus making atonement for his own perfidy, and satisfying the rage of his antagonist in the midst of the river Seine. His death was the source of long discord between the French and Normans, till by the exertions of Richard his son it had a termination worthy such a personage. A truer history[*] indeed relates, that being at enmity with Ernulph, earl of Flanders, he had possessed himself of one of his castles, and that being invited

[*] See Will. Gemeticensis, lib. iii. c. 11.

out by him to a conference, on a pretended design of making a truce, he was killed by Balso, as they were conversing in a ship : that a key was found at his girdle, which being applied to the lock of his private cabinet, discovered certain monastic habiliments ;* for he ever designed, even amid his warlike pursuits, one day to become a monk at Jumiéges ; which place, deserted from the time of Hasten, he cleared of the overspreading thorns, and with princely magnificence exalted to its present state.

In the year of our Lord 946, Edred, Edward's third son, assuming the government, reigned nine years and a half. He gave proof that he had not degenerated in greatness of soul from his father and his brothers ; for he nearly exterminated the Northumbrians and the Scots, laying waste the whole province with sword and famine, because, having with little difficulty compelled them to swear fidelity to him, they broke their oath, and made Iricius their king. He for a long time kept Wulstan, archbishop of York, who, it was said, connived at the revolt of his countrymen, in chains, but afterwards, out of respect to his ecclesiastical dignity, released and pardoned him. In the meantime, the king himself, prostrate at the feet of the saints, devoted his life to God and to Dunstan, by whose admonition he endured with patience his frequent bodily pains,† prolonged his prayers, and made his palace altogether the school of virtue. He died accompanied with the utmost grief of men, but joy of angels ; for Dunstan, learning by a messenger that he was sick, while urging his horse in order to see him, heard a voice thundering over his head, "Now king Edred sleeps in the Lord." He lies buried in the cathedral at Winchester.

In the year of our Lord 955, Edwy, son of Edmund, the brother of Athelstan the former king, taking possession of the kingdom, retained it four years : a wanton youth, who abused the beauty of his person in illicit intercourse. Finally, taking a woman nearly related to him as his wife, he doated on her beauty, and despised the advice of his coun-

* These were a woollen shirt and cowl. Will. Gemet. lib. iii. c. 12.

† Edred is described by Bridferth as being constantly oppressed with sickness ; and of so weak a digestion, as to be unable to swallow more than the juices of the food he had masticated, to the great annoyance of his guests. Vita Dunstani, Act. Sanct. 19 Mau.

sellors. On the very day he had been consecrated king, in full assembly of the nobility, when deliberating on affairs of importance and essential to the state, he burst suddenly from amongst them, darted wantonly into his chamber, and rioted in the embraces of the harlot. All were indignant of the shameless deed, and murmured among themselves. Dunstan alone, with that firmness which his name implies,* regardless of the royal indignation, violently dragged the lascivious boy from the chamber, and on the archbishop's compelling him to repudiate the strumpet,† made him his enemy for ever. Soon after, upheld by most contemptible supporters, he afflicted with undeserved calamities all the members of the monastic order throughout England,—who were first despoiled of their property, and then driven into exile. He drove Dunstan himself, the chief of monks, into Flanders. At that time the face of monachism was sad and pitiable. Even the monastery of Malmesbury, which had been inhabited by monks for more than two hundred and seventy years, he made a sty for secular canons. But thou, O Lord Jesus, our creator and redeemer, gracious disposer, art abundantly able to remedy our defects by means of those irregular and vagabond men. Thou didst bring to light thy treasure, hidden for so many years—I mean the body of St. Aldhelm, which they took up and placed in a shrine. The royal generosity increased the fame of the canons; for the king bestowed on the saint an estate, very convenient both from its size and vicinity. But my recollection shudders even at this time, to think how cruel he was to other monasteries, equally on account of the giddiness of youth, and the pernicious counsel of his concubine, who was perpetually poisoning his uninformed mind. But let his soul, long since placed in rest by the interposition of Dunstan,‡

* A quibble on his name, as compounded of "hill" and "stone."
† Much variation prevails among the earliest writers concerning Elfgiva. Bridferth (Act. Sanct. 19 Maii) says, there were two women, mother and daughter, familiar with Edwy. A contemporary of Bridferth (MS. Cott. Nero, E I.) asserts, that he was married, but fell in love with, and carried off, another woman. A MS. Saxon Chron. (Cott. Tib. b. iv) says, they were separated, as being of kin. Osberne, Edmer, and Malmesbury, in his Life of Dunstan (MS.), all repeat the story of the two women.
‡ Dunstan, learning that he was dead, and that the devils were about to carry off his soul in triumph by his prayers obtained his release. A curious

pardon my grief: grief, I say, compels me to condemn him, "because private advantage is not to be preferred to public loss, but rather public loss should outweigh private advantage." He paid the penalty of his rash attempt even in this life, being despoiled of the greatest part of his kingdom;* shocked with which calamity, he died, and was buried in the new minster at Winchester.

CHAP. VIII.

Of king Edgar, son of king Edmund. [A.D. 959—975.]

In the year of our Lord's incarnation 959, Edgar, the honour and delight of the English, the son of Edmund, the brother of Edwy, a youth of sixteen years old, assuming the government, held it for about a similar period. The transactions of his reign are celebrated with peculiar splendour even in our times. The Divine love, which he sedulously procured by his devotion and energy of counsel, shone propitious on his years. It is commonly reported, that at his birth Dunstan heard an angelic voice, saying, "Peace to England so long as this child shall reign, and our Dunstan survives." The succession of events was in unison with the heavenly oracle; so much while he lived did ecclesiastical glory flourish, and martial clamour decay. Scarcely does a year elapse in the chronicles, in which he did not perform something great and advantageous to his country; in which he did not build some new monastery. He experienced no internal treachery, no foreign attack. Kinad, king of the Scots, Malcolm, of the Cambrians, that prince of pirates, Maccus, all the Welsh kings, whose names were Dufnal, Giferth, Huval, Jacob, Judethil, being summoned to his court, were bound to him by one, and that a lasting oath; so that meeting him at Chester, he exhibited them on the river Dee in triumphal ceremony. For putting them all on board the same vessels he compelled them to row him as he sat at the prow: thus displaying his regal magnificence, who held so many kings in subjection. Indeed, he is reported to have said, that henceforward his successors might truly boast of being kings

colloquy between the abbat and the devils on the subject, may be found in Osberne's Life of Dunstan, Anglia Sacra, ii. 108.

* The Mercians had revolted, and chosen Edgar king.

of England, since they would enjoy so singular an honour. Hence his fame being noised abroad, foreigners, Saxons, Flemings, and even Danes, frequently sailed hither, and were on terms of intimacy with Edgar, though their arrival was highly prejudicial to the natives: for from the Saxons they learned an untameable ferocity of mind; from the Flemings an unmanly delicacy of body; and from the Danes drunkenness; though they were before free from such propensities, and disposed to observe their own customs with native simplicity rather than admire those of others. For this history justly and deservedly blames him; for the other imputations which I shall mention hereafter have rather been cast on him by ballads.

At this time the light of holy men was so resplendent in England, that you would believe the very stars from heaven smiled upon it. Among these was Dunstan, whom I have mentioned so frequently, first, abbat of Glastonbury, next, bishop of Worcester; and lastly, archbishop of Canterbury · of great power in earthly matters, in high favour with God; in the one representing Martha, in the other Mary. Next to king Alfred, he was the most extraordinary patron of the liberal arts throughout the whole island; the munificent restorer of monasteries; terrible were his denunciations against transgressing kings and princes; kind was his support of the middling and poorer classes. Indeed, so extremely anxious was he to preserve peace ever in trivial matters, that, as his countrymen used to assemble in taverns, and when a little elevated quarrel as to the proportions of their liquor, he ordered gold or silver pegs to be fastened in the pots, that whilst every man knew his just measure, shame should compel each neither to take more himself, nor oblige others to drink beyond their proportional share. Osberne,* precentor of Canterbury, second to none of these times in composition, and indisputably the best skilled of all in music, who wrote his life with Roman elegance, forbids me to relate farther praiseworthy anecdotes of him. Besides, in addition to this, if the divine grace shall accompany my design, I intend after the succession of the kings at least to particularize the names of all the bishops of each province in England, and to offer them to the knowledge of my countrymen, if I shall be able

* Osberne's Life of St. Dunstan is published in the Anglia Sacra, vol. ii.

to coin anything worth notice out of the mintage of antiquity. How powerful indeed the sanctity and virtue of Dunstan's disciples were, is sufficiently evidenced by Ethelwold, made abbat of Abingdon from a monk of Glastonbury, and afterwards bishop of Winchester, who built so many and such great monasteries, as to make it appear hardly credible how the bishop of one see should be able to effect what the king of England himself could scarcely undertake. I am deceived, and err through hasty opinion, if what I assert be not evident. How great are the monasteries of Ely, Peterborough, and Thorney, which he raised from the foundations, and completed by his industry; which though repeatedly reduced by the wickedness of plunderers, are yet sufficient for their inhabitants. His life was composed in a decent style by Wulstan,* precentor of Winchester, who had been his attendant and pupil: he wrote also another very useful work, "On the Harmony of Sounds," a proof that he was a learned Englishman, a man of pious life and correct eloquence. At that time too Oswald, nephew of Odo, who had been archbishop before Dunstan, from a monk of Flory becoming bishop of Worcester and archbishop of York, claimed equal honours with the others. Treading the same paths, he extended the monastic profession by his authority, and built a monastery at Ramsey in a marshy situation. He filled the cathedral of Worcester with monks, the canons not being driven out by force, but circumvented by pious fraud.† Bishop Ethelwold, by the royal command, had before expelled the canons from Winchester, who, upon the king's giving them an option either to live according to rule, or depart the place, gave the preference to an easy life, and were at that time without fixed habitations wandering over the whole island. In this manner these three persons, illuminating England, as it were, with a triple light, chased away the thick darkness of error. In consequence, Edgar advanced the monastery of Glastonbury, which he ever loved beyond all others, with great possessions, and was anxiously vigilant

* Wulstan's Life of Ethelwold is printed by Mabillon, and in the Acta Sanctorum, Antwerp. Aug. tome i.

† He erected another church at Worcester, in which he placed monks. The canons finding the people desert them in order to obtain the favour of the new comers, by degrees took the monastic habit. See Malmesbury de Gest. Pontif. lib. iii

in all things pertaining either to the beauty or convenience of the church, whether internally or externally. It may be proper here to subjoin to our narrative the charter he granted to the said church, as I have read it in their ancient chartulary.*

* Some MSS. omit from "Edgar of glorious memory, &c." to "spoken of another. The monastic order," &c in page 155, and insert the charter at length, together with what follows it, thus:

"In the name of our Lord Jesus Christ: although the decrees of pontiffs and the decisions of priests are fixed by irrevocable bonds, like the foundations of the mountains, yet, nevertheless, through the storms and tempests of secular matters, and the corruptions of reprobate men, the institutions of the holy church of God are often convulsed and broken. Wherefore I perceive that it will be advantageous to posterity that I should confirm by writing what has been determined by wholesome counsel and common consent. In consequence, it seems proper that the church of the most blessed mother of God, the eternal virgin Mary, of Glastonbury, inasmuch as it has always possessed the chief dignity in my kingdom, should be honoured by us with some especial and unusual privilege. Dunstan, therefore, and Oswald, archbishops of Canterbury and York, exhorting thereto, and Brithelm, bishop of Wells, and other bishops, abbats, and chiefs assenting and approving, I, Edgar, by the grace of God, king of the English, and ruler and governor of the adjacent nations, in the name of the blessed Trinity, for the soul of my father who reposes there, and of my predecessors, do by this present privilege decree, appoint, and establish, that the aforesaid monastery and all its possessions shall remain free and exonerated from all payments to the Exchequer now and for ever : they shall have soc and sac, on stronde and on wude, on felde, on grithbrice, on burgbrice, hundredsetena, and mortheras, athas, and ordelas, ealle hordas bufan eorthan, and beneothan : infangenetheof, utfangenetheof, flemenefertha, hamsocne, friderbrice, foresteal, toll and team, just as free and peaceably as I have in my kingdom · let the same liberty and power also as I have in my own court, as well in forgiving as in punishing, and in every other matter, be possessed by the abbat and monks of the aforesaid monastery within their court. And should the abbat, or any monk of that place, upon his journey, meet a thief going to the gallows, or to any other punishment of death, they shall have power of rescuing him from the impending danger throughout my kingdom. Moreover, I confirm and establish what has hitherto been scrupulously observed by all my predecessors, that the bishop of Wells and his ministers shall have no power whatever over this monastery, or its parish-churches ; that is to say, Street, Mincling [Merlinge], Budecal, Shapwick, Sowy, or their chapels, or even over those contained in the islands, that is to say, Beokery, otherwise called Little Ireland, Godney, Martensia, Patheneberga, Adredseia, and Ferramere, except only when summoned by the abbat for dedications or ordinations, nor shall they cite their priests to their synods or chapters, or to any of their courts, nor shall they suspend them from their holy office, or presume to exercise any right over them whatever. The abbat shall cause any bishop of the same province he pleases to ordain his monks, and the clerks of the aforesaid

"Edgar of glorious memory, king of the Angles, son of king Edmund, whose inclinations were ever vigilantly bent on divine matters, often coming to the monastery of the churches, according to the ancient custom of the church of Glastonbury, and the apostolical authority of archbishop Dunstan, and of all the bishops of my kingdom; but the dedications of the churches we consign to the bishop of Wells, if he be required by the abbat At Easter let him receive the chrism of sanctification, and the oil from the bishop of Wells, according to custom, and distribute them to his before mentioned churches. This too I command above all other things: on the curse of God, and by my authority, saving the right of the holy Roman church, and that of Canterbury, I inhibit all persons, of whatever dignity, be they king, or bishop, or earl, or prince, or any of my dependants, from daring to enter the bounds of Glastonbury, or of the above named parishes, for the purpose of searching, seizing, holding courts, or doing any thing to the prejudice of the servants of God there residing The abbat and convent shall alone have power in causes known and unknown, in small and in great, and in every thing as we have before related And whosoever, upon any occasion, whatever be his dignity, whatever his order, whatever his profession, shall attempt to pervert or nullify the pre-eminence of this my privilege by sacrilegious boldness, let him be aware that he must without a doubt give account thereof, with fear and trembling, before a severe Judge, unless he first endeavour to make reparation by proper satisfaction" The charter of this privilege the aforesaid king Edgar confirmed by his own signature at London, in the twelfth year of his reign, with the common consent of his nobles; and in the same year, which was the 965th of our Lord's incarnation, and the 14th of the indiction, pope John, in a general assembly, authorized it at Rome, and made all the men of chief dignity who presided at that council confirm it, and also, from motives of paternal regard, sent a letter to the following effect to earl Alfric, who was then grievously persecuting the aforesaid church:—

"Bishop John, servant of the servants of God, to Alfric the distinguished earl, and our dearly beloved son in the Spirit, perpetual health and apostolical benediction We have learned, from the report of certain faithful people, that you commit many enormities against the church of the holy mother of God, called Mary of Glastonbury, which is acknowledged to belong solely to, and to be under the protection of, the Roman Pontiff, from the earliest times; and that you have seized with boundless rapacity upon its estates and possessions, and even the churches of Brent and Pilton, which, by the gift of king Ina, it legally possesses, together with other churches, that is to say, Sowy, Martine, Budecal, Shapwick, and that on account of your near residence you are a continual enemy to its interests It would, however, have been becoming, from your living so near, that by your assistance the holy church of God might have been much benefited and enriched; but, horrible to say! it is impoverished by your hostility, and injured by your deeds of oppression; and since we doubt not that we, though unworthily, have received from St. Peter the apostle the care of all the churches, and solicitude for all things; we therefore admonish your affection, to abstain from plundering it, for the love of the apostles Peter

holy mother of God at Glastonbury, and studying to honour this place with dignity superior to others, hath by the common consent of the bishops, abbats, and nobility, conferred on it many and very splendid privileges;—the first of which is, that no person, unless a monk of that place, shall there be abbat, either in name or in office, nor any other, except such as the common consent of the meeting shall have chosen according to the tenor of the rule. But should necessity so ordain, that an abbat or monk of another monastery be made president of this place, then he deems it proper that none shall be appointed, but such as the congregation of the monastery may elect, to preside over them in the fear of the Lord; nor shall this be done, if any, even the lowest of the congregation, can be there found fit for the office. He hath appointed too, that the election of their abbat shall rest for ever in the monks, reserving only to himself and his heirs the power of giving the pastoral staff to the elected brother. He hath ordained also, that so often as the abbat or the monks of this place shall appoint any of their society to be dignified with holy orders, they shall cause any bishop canonically ordained, either in his own cathedral, or in the monastery of St Mary at Glastonbury, to ordain such monks and clerks as they deem fit to the church of St. Mary. He hath granted moreover, that as he himself decides in his own dominions, so the abbat or the convent shall decide the causes of their entire island,* in all matters ecclesiastical or secular, without the contradiction of any one. Nor shall it be lawful for any person to enter that island which bore witness to his birth, whether he be bishop, duke, or prince, or person of whatever order, for the purpose of there doing any thing prejudicial to the servants of God: this he forbids altogether, in the same manner as his predecessors have sanctioned and confirmed by their privileges; that is to say, Kentwin, Ina, Ethelard, Cuthred, Alfred, Edward, Athelstan, and Edmund. When, therefore, by the common con-

and Paul, and respect to us, invading none of its possessions, churches, chapels, places, and estates; but if you persist, remember, that by the authority of the chief of the apostles, committed unto us, you shall be excommunicated and banished from the company of the faithful, subjected to a perpetual curse, and doomed to eternal fire with the traitor Judas."

* Glastonbury is situated on land which was once an island formed by a stagnation of inland waters, in a low situation.

sent, as has been said, of his prelates, abbats, and nobility, he determined to grant these privileges to the place aforesaid, he laid his own horn, beautifully formed of ivory and adorned with gold, upon the altar of the holy mother of God, and by that donation confirmed them to the same holy mother of God, and her monks, to be possessed for ever. Soon after he caused this horn to be cut in two in his presence, that no future abbat might give or sell it to any one, commanding part of it to be kept upon the spot for a testimony of the aforesaid donation. Recollecting, however, how great is the temerity of human inconstancy, and on whom it is likely to creep, and fearing lest any one hereafter should attempt to take away these privileges from this place, or eject the monks, he sent this charter of royal liberality to the renowned lord, pope John, who had succeeded Octavian in the honour of the pontificate, begging him to corroborate these grants by an apostolical bull. Kindly receiving the legation, the pope, with the assenting voice of the Roman council, confirmed what had been already ordained, by writing an apostolical injunction, terribly hurling on the violators of them, should any be so daring, the vengeance of a perpetual curse. This confirmation therefore of the aforesaid pope, directed to the same place, king Edgar, of worthy memory, laid upon the altar of the holy mother of God for a perpetual remembrance, commanding it to be carefully kept in future for the information of posterity. We have judged it proper to insert both these instruments, lest we should be supposed to invent such things against those persons who seek to enter into the fold of St. Mary, not like shepherds, by the door, but like thieves and robbers, some other way. "Be it known to all the faithful, that I, John the twelfth, through the mercy of God unworthy pope of the holy Roman See, am intreated by the humble request of the noble Edgar, king of the Angles, and of Dunstan, archbishop of the holy church of Canterbury, for the monastery of St. Mary, Glastonbury ; which, induced by the love of the heavenly King, they have endowed with many great possessions, increasing in it the monastic order, and having confirmed it by royal grant, they pray me also so to do. Wherefore assenting to their affectionate request, I take that place into the bosom of the Roman church, and the protection of the holy apostles, and support and confirm its immunities as long as it shall remain in the same conventual order in which it now flourishes. The monks shall have power to elect their own superior; ordination, as well of monks as of clerks, shall be at the will of the abbat and convent. We ordain, moreover, that no person shall have liberty to enter this island, either to hold courts, to make inquiry, or to correct; and should any one attempt to oppose this, or to take away, retain, diminish, or harass with vexatious boldness, the possessions of the same church, he shall become liable to a perpetual curse, by the authority of God the Father, Son, and Holy Spirit, the holy mother of God, the holy apostles Peter and Paul, and all saints, unless he recant. But the peace of our Lord Jesus Christ be with all who maintain the rights of the place aforesaid. Amen. And let this our deed remain unshaken. Done in the time of Edward, abbat of the said monastery." The aforesaid king Edgar confirmed these things at London, by his solemn charter, in the twelfth year of his reign; and in the same year, that is, of our Lord 965,* the pope aforesaid allowed them in a general synod at Rome, and commanded all members of superior, dignity who were present at the said general council, to confirm them likewise. Let the despisers then of so terrible a curse consider well what an extensive sentence of excommunication hangs over their heads: and indeed to St. Peter the apostle, the chief of apostles, Christ gave the office either of binding or loosing, as well as the keys of the kingdom of heaven. But to all the faithful it must be plain and evident, that the head of the Roman church must be the vicar of this apostle, and the immediate inheritor of his power. Over this church then John of holy memory laudably presided in his lifetime, as he lives to this day in glorious recollection, promoted thereto by the choice of God and of all the people. If then the ordinance of St. Peter the apostle be binding, consequently that of John the pope must be so likewise; but not even a madman would deny the ordinance of Peter the apostle to be binding, consequently no one in his sober senses can say that the ordinance of John the pope is invalid. Either, therefore, acknowledging the power conferred by Christ on St. Peter and his successors, they will abstain from transgressing against the authority of so dread-

* The twelfth of Edgar was 971.

ful an interdict, or else contemning it, they will, with the devil and his angels, bring upon themselves the eternal duration of the curse aforewritten. In consequence, it is manifest that no stranger ever seized this monastery for himself, who did not, as shall appear, disgracefully lose it again ; and that this occurred, not by any concerted plan of the monks, but by the judgment of God, for the avenging his holy authority. Wherefore let no man reading this despise it, nor make himself conspicuous by being angry at it ; for should he, perhaps he will confess that to be said of himself which was designed to be spoken of another. The monastic order, for a long time depressed, now joyfully reared its head, and hence it came to pass that our monastery also resumed its ancient liberties : but this I think will be more suitably related in the words of the king himself.

"I, Edgar, king of all Albion, and exalted, by the subjection of the surrounding kings maritime or insular, by the bountiful grace of God, to a degree never enjoyed by any of my progenitors, have often, mindful of so high an honour, diligently considered what offering I should more especially make from my earthly kingdom, to the King of kings. In aid of my pious devotion, heavenly love suddenly insinuated to my watchful solicitude, that I should rebuild all the holy monasteries throughout my kingdom, which, as they were outwardly ruinous, with mouldering shingles and worm-eaten boards, even to the rafters, so, what was still worse, they had become internally neglected, and almost destitute of the service of God ; wherefore, ejecting those illiterate clerks, subject to the discipline of no regular order, in many places I have appointed pastors of an holier race, that is, of the monastic order, supplying them with ample means out of my royal revenues to repair their churches wherever ruinated. One of these pastors, by name Elfric, in all things a true priest, I have appointed guardian of that most celebrated monastery which the Angles call by a twofold name Maldelmes-burgh. To which, for the benefit of my soul, and in honour of our Saviour, and the holy mother of God the virgin Mary, and the apostles Peter and Paul, and the amiable prelate Aldhelm, I have restored, with munificent liberality, a portion of land : and more especially a piece of ground,*

* Here is an omission, apparently, which may be supplied from the Ang.

with meadows and woods. This, leased out by the aforesaid priest, was unjustly held by the contentious Edelnot; but his vain and subtle disputation being heard by my counsellors, and his false defence being, in my presence, nullified, by them, I have restored it to the use of the monastery in the year of our Lord 974, in the fourteenth of my reign, and the first of my royal consecration."

And here I deem it not irrelevant to commit to writing what was supernaturally shown to the king. He had entered a wood abundant in game, and, as usually happens, while his associates were dispersed in the thicket for the purpose of hunting, he was left alone. Pursuing his course, he came to the outlet of the wood, and stopping there waited for his companions. Shortly after, seized with an irresistible desire to sleep, he alighted from his horse, that the enjoyment of a short repose might assuage the fatigue of the past day. He lay down, therefore, under a wild apple-tree, where the clustering branches had formed a shady canopy all around. A river, flowing softly beside him, adding to his drowsiness, by its gentle murmur soothed him to sleep; when a bitch, of the hunting breed, pregnant, and lying down at his feet, terrified him in his slumbers. Though the mother was silent, yet the whelps within her womb barked in various sonorous tones, incited, as it were, by a singular delight in the place of their confinement. Astonished at this prodigy, as he lifted up his eyes towards the summit of the tree, he saw, first one apple, and then another, fall into the river, by the collision of which, the watery bubbles being put in commotion, a voice articulately sounded, "Well is thee." Soon after, driven by the rippling wave, a little pitcher appeared upon the stream, and after that a larger vessel, overflowing with water, for the former was empty: and although by the violence of the stream the greater vessel pressed upon the lesser that it might discharge its waters into it; yet it ever happened that the pitcher escaped, still empty, and again, as in a haughty and insulting manner, attacked the larger. Returning home, as the Psalmist says, "He thought upon what had been done, and sought out his spirit." His mother addressed him, however, that she might cheer both his counte-

Sac. ii p 33. "A piece of ground, to wit, of ten farms (or manors), called Estotun," &c. G. Malm. de Vita Adhelmi.

nance and his heart; saying, it should be her care to entreat God, who knew how to explain mysteries by the light of his inspiration. With this admonition he dispelled his grief and dismissed his anxiety, conscious of his mother's sanctity, to whom God had vouchsafed many revelations. Her name was Elfgiva, a woman intent on good works, and gifted with such affection and kindness, that she would even secretly discharge the penalties of those culprits whom the sad sentence of the judges had publicly condemned. That costly clothing, which, to many women, is the pander of vice, was to her the means of liberality; as she would give a garment of the most beautiful workmanship to the first poor person she saw. Even malice itself, as there was nothing to carp at, might praise the beauty of her person and the work of her hands. Thoroughly comprehending the presage, she said to her son next morning, "The barking of the whelps while the mother was sleeping, implies, that after your death, those persons who are now living and in power, dying also, miscreants yet unborn will bark against the church of God. And whereas one apple followed the other, so that the voice, 'Well is thee,' seemed to proceed from the dashing of the second against the first, this implies that from you, who are now a tree shading all England, two sons will proceed; the favourers of the second will destroy the first, when the chiefs of the different parties will say to each of the boys, 'Well is thee,' because the dead will reign in heaven, the living on earth, Forasmuch as the greater pitcher could not fill the smaller, this signifies, that the Northern nations, which are more numerous than the English, shall attack England after your death; and, although they may recruit their deficiencies by perpetual supplies of their countrymen, yet they shall never be able to fill this Angle of the world, but instead of that, our Angles, when they seem to be completely subjugated, shall drive them out, and it shall remain under its own and God's governance, even unto the time before appointed by Christ. Amen."

Farther perusal will justify the truth of the presage. The manifest sanctity both of parent and child ought here to be considered; that the one should see a mystery when broad awake without impediment, and that the other should be able to solve the problem by the far-discerning eye of prophecy.

The rigour of Edgar's justice was equal to the sanctity of his manners, so that he permitted no person, be his dignity what it might, to elude the laws with impunity. In his time there was no private thief, no public freebooter, unless such as chose to risk the loss of life for their attacks upon the property of others.* How, indeed, can it be supposed that he would pass over the crimes of men when he designed to exterminate every beast of prey from his kingdom; and commanded Judwall, king of the Welsh, to pay him yearly a tribute of three hundred wolves? This he performed for three years, but omitted in the fourth, declaring that he could find no more.

Although it is reported that he was extremely small both in stature and in bulk, yet nature had condescended to enclose such strength in that diminutive body, that he would voluntarily challenge any person, whom he knew to be bold and valiant, to engage with him, and his greatest apprehension was, lest they should stand in awe of him in these encounters. Moreover, at a certain banquet, where the prating of coxcombs generally shows itself very freely, it is reported that Kinad, king of the Scots, said in a sportive manner, that it seemed extraordinary to him how so many provinces should be subject to such a sorry little fellow. This was caught up with malignant ear by a certain minstrel, and afterwards cast in Edgar's teeth, with the customary raillery of such people. But he, concealing the circumstance from his friends, sent for Kinad, as if to consult him on some secret matter of importance, and leading him aside far into the recesses of a wood, he gave him one of two swords, which he had brought with him. "Now," said he, "as we are alone, I shall have an opportunity of proving your strength; I will now make it appear which ought deservedly to command the other; nor shall you stir a foot till you try the matter with me, for it is disgraceful in a king to prate at a banquet, and not to be prompt in action." Confused, and not daring to utter a word, he fell at the feet of his sovereign

* Edgar's laws for the punishment of offenders were horribly severe. The eyes were put out, nostrils slit, ears torn off, hands and feet cut off, and, finally, after the scalp had been torn off, the miserable wretches were left exposed to birds or beasts of prey. V. Acta Sanctor. Jul 2, in Vita Swythuni.

lord, and asked pardon for what was merely a joke; which he immediately obtained. But what of this? Every summer, as soon as the festival of Easter was passed, he ordered his ships to be collected on each coast; cruising to the western part of the island with the eastern fleet; and, dismissing that, with the western to the north; and then again with the northern squadron towards the east, carefully vigilant lest pirates should disturb the country. During the winter and spring, travelling through the provinces, he made inquiry into the decisions of men in power, severely avenging violated laws, by the one mode advancing justice, by the other military strength; and in both consulting public utility. There are some persons, indeed, who endeavour to dim his exceeding glory by saying, that in his earlier years he was cruel to his subjects, and libidinous in respect of virgins. Their first accusation they exemplify thus. There was, in his time, one Athelwold, a nobleman of celebrity and one of his confidants. The king had commissioned him to visit Elfthrida, daughter of Ordgar, duke of Devonshire, (whose charms had so fascinated the eyes of some persons that they commended her to the king), and to offer her marriage, if her beauty were really equal to report. Hastening on his embassy, and finding everything consonant to general estimation, he concealed his mission from her parents and procured the damsel for himself. Returning to the king, he told a tale which made for his own purpose; that she was a girl nothing out of the common track of beauty, and by no means worthy such transcendent dignity. When Edgar's heart was disengaged from this affair, and employed on other amours, some tattlers acquainted him, how completely Athelwold had duped him by his artifices. Paying him in his own coin, that is, returning him deceit for deceit, he showed the earl a fair countenance, and, as in a sportive manner, appointed a day when he would visit his far-famed lady. Terrified, almost to death, with this dreadful pleasantry, he hastened before to his wife, entreating that she would administer to his safety by attiring herself as unbecomingly as possible: then first disclosing the intention of such a proceeding. But what did not this woman dare? She was hardy enough to deceive the confidence of her first lover, her first husband; to call up every charm by art, and to omit nothing which could stimulate the desire of a young and powerful man. Nor did events happen contrary to her design. For he fell so desperately in love with her the moment he saw her, that, dissembling his indignation, he sent for the earl into a wood at Warewelle,* called Harewood, under pretence of hunting, and ran him through with a javelin: and when the illegitimate son of the murdered nobleman approached with his accustomed familiarity, and was asked by the king how he liked that kind of sport, he is reported to have said, "Well, my sovereign liege, I ought not to be displeased with that which gives you pleasure." This answer so assuaged the mind of the raging monarch, that, for the remainder of his life, he held no one in greater estimation than this young man; mitigating the offence of his tyrannical deed against the father, by royal solicitude for the son. In expiation of this crime, a monastery which was built on the spot by Elfthrida is inhabited by a large congregation of nuns.

To this instance of cruelty, they add a second of lust. Hearing of the beauty of a certain virgin, who was dedicated to God, he carried her off from a monastery by force, ravished her, and repeatedly made her the partner of his bed. When this circumstance reached the ears of St. Dunstan, he was vehemently reproved by him, and underwent a seven years' penance; though a king, submitting to fast and to forego the wearing of his crown for that period.† They add a third, in which both vices may be discovered King Edgar coming to Andover, a town not far from Winchester, ordered the daughter of a certain nobleman, the fame of whose beauty had been loudly extolled, to be brought to him. The mother of the young lady, shocked at the proposed concubinage of her daughter, assisted by the darkness of night placed an attendant in his bed; a maiden indeed neither deficient in elegance nor in understanding. The night having passed, when aurora was hastening into day, the woman attempted to rise; and being asked, "why in such haste?" she replied, "to perform the daily labour of her mistress." Retained though with difficulty, on her knees she bewailed her wretched situation to the king, and entreated her freedom as

* Whorwell, Hants.
† This seems to have been founded on the singular circumstance of his not having been crowned till within two years of his death.

the recompence of her connexion with him; saying, "that it became his greatness, not to suffer one who had ministered to his royal pleasure, any longer to groan under the commands of cruel masters." His indignation being excited, and sternly smiling, while his mind was wavering between pity to the girl, and displeasure to her mistress, he, at last, as if treating the whole as a joke, released her from servitude, and dismissed his anger. Soon after, he exalted her with great honour, to be mistress of her former tyrants, little consulting how they liked it, loved her entirely, nor left her bed till he took Elfthrida, the daughter of Ordgar, to be his legitimate wife. Elfthrida bore him Edmund, who dying five years before his father, lies buried at Romsey, and Ethelred, who reigned after him. Besides, of Egelfleda, surnamed the fair, the daughter of the most powerful duke, Ordmer, he begot Edward; and St. Editha of Wulfritha, who it is certain was not a nun at that time, but being a lay virgin had assumed the veil through fear of the king, though she was immediately afterwards forced to the royal bed; on which, St. Dunstan, offended that he should desire lustfully a person who had been even the semblance of a nun, exerted the pontifical power against him. But however these things may be, this is certain, that from the sixteenth year of his age, when he was appointed king, till the thirtieth, he reigned without the insignia of royalty; for at that time, the princes and men of every order assembling generally, he was crowned with great pomp at Bath, survived only three years, and was buried at Glastonbury. Nor is it to be forgotten, that when abbat Ailward opened his tomb in the year of our Lord 1052, he found the body unconscious of corruption; which instead of inclining him to reverence, served only to increase his audacity. For when the receptacle which he had prepared, seemed too small to admit the body, he profaned the royal corpse by cutting it. Whence the blood immediately gushing out in torrents, shook the hearts of the bystanders with horror. In consequence his royal remains were placed upon the altar in a shrine, which he had himself given to this church, with the head of St. Apollinaris, and the relics of Vincent the martyr; which purchased, at a great price, he had added to the beauty of the house of God. The violator of the sacred body presently became distracted, and not long after, going out of the church, met his death by a broken neck. Nor did the display of royal sanctity stop thus; it proceeded still further, a man, lunatic and blind, being there cured. Deservedly then does the report prevail among the English, that no king, either of his own or former times in England, could be justly and fairly compared to Edgar: for nothing could be more holy than his life, nothing more praiseworthy than his justice; those vices excepted which he afterwards obliterated by abundant virtues: a man who rendered his country illustrious through his distinguished courage, and the brilliancy of his actions, as well as by the increase of the servants of God. After his departure, the state and the hopes of the English met with a melancholy reverse.*

CHAP. IX.

Of St. Edward king and martyr the son of Edgar. [A.D 975—978.]

In the year of our Lord 975, Edward the son of Edgar began to reign, and enjoyed the sovereignty for three years and a half. Dunstan, in common consent with the other bishops, elevated him to the royal dignity, in opposition, as it is said, to the will of some of the nobility, and of his stepmother; who was anxious to advance her son Ethelred, a child scarcely seven years of age, in order that herself might govern under colour of his name. Then, from the increasing malice of men, the happiness of the kingdom was impaired; then too, comets were seen, which were asserted certainly to portend either pestilence to the inhabitants, or a change in the government. Nor was it long ere there followed a scarcity of corn; famine among men; murrain among cattle; and an extraordinary accident at a royal town called Calne. For as soon as Edgar was dead, the secular canons who had been for some time expelled their monasteries, rekindled the former feuds, alleging, that it was a great and serious disgrace, for new comers to drive the ancient inmates from their dwellings; that it could not be esteemed grateful to God, who had granted them their ancient habitations: neither could it be so to any considerate man, who might dread that

* Virg. Æn. ii. 169.

injustice as likely to befall himself, which he had seen overtake others. Hence they proceeded to clamour and rage, and hastened to Dunstan; the principal people, as is the custom of the laity, exclaiming more especially, that the injury which the canons had wrongfully suffered, ought to be redressed by gentler measures. Moreover, one of them, Elferius, with more than common audacity, had even overturned almost all the monasteries which that highly revered monk Ethelwold, bishop of Winchester, had built throughout Mercia. On this account a full synod being convened, they first assembled at Winchester. What was the issue of the contest of that place, other writings declare;[*] relating, that the image of our Saviour, speaking decidedly, confounded the canons and their party. But men's minds being not yet at rest on the subject, a council was called at Calne; where, when all the senators of England, the king being absent on account of his youth, had assembled in an upper chamber, and the business was agitated with much animosity and debate; while the weapons of harsh reproach were directed against that firmest bulwark of the church, I mean Dunstan, but could not shake it; and men of every rank were earnestly defending their several sides of the question; the floor with its beams and supporters gave way suddenly and fell to the ground. All fell with it except Dunstan, who alone escaped unhurt by standing on a single rafter which retained its position: the rest were either killed, or subjected to lasting infirmity. This miracle procured the archbishop peace on the score of the canons; all the English, both at that time and afterwards, yielding to his sentiments.

Meanwhile king Edward conducted himself with becoming affection to his infant brother and his step-mother; he retained only the name of king, and gave them the power; following the footsteps of his father's piety, and giving both his attention and his heart to good council. The woman, however, with that hatred which a step-mother only can entertain, began to meditate a subtle stratagem, in order that not even the title of king might be wanting to her child, and to lay a treacher-

[*] When the question was agitated, whether the monks should be supported or the canons restored, the crucifix is said to have exclaimed, "Far be it from you: you have done well; to change again would be wrong." See Edmer, and Osberne, Angl. Sacra, ii. 219, 112

ous snare for her son-in-law, which she accomplished in the following manner. He was returning home, tired with the chase and gasping with thirst from the exercise, while his companions were following the dogs in different directions as it happened, when hearing that they dwelt in a neighbouring mansion, the youth proceeded thither at full speed, unattended and unsuspecting, as he judged of others by his own feelings. On his arrival, alluring him to her with female blandishment, she made him lean forward, and after saluting him while he was eagerly drinking from the cup which had been presented, the dagger of an attendant pierced him through. Dreadfully wounded, with all his remaining strength he clapped spurs to his horse in order to join his companions; when one foot slipping, he was dragged by the other through the trackless paths and recesses of the wood, while the streaming blood gave evidence of his death to his followers. Moreover, they then commanded him to be ingloriously interred at Wareham; envying him even holy ground when dead, as they had envied him his royal dignity while living. They now publicly manifested their extreme joy as if they had buried his memory with his body; but God's all-seeing eye was there, who ennobled the innocent victim by the glory of miracles. So much is human outweighed by heavenly judgment. For there lights were shown from above; there the lame walked; there the dumb resumed his faculty of speech; there every malady gave way to health. The fame of this pervading all England, proclaimed the merits of the martyr. The murderess excited by it, attempted a progress thither; and was already urging forward the horse she had mounted, when she perceived the manifest anger of God; for the same creature which she had heretofore constantly ridden, and which was used to outstrip the very wind in speed, now by command of God, stood motionless. The attendants, both with whips and clamours, urged him forward that he might carry his noble mistress with his usual readiness; but their labour was in vain. They changed the horse; and the same circumstance recurred. Her obdurate heart, though late, perceived the meaning of the miracle; wherefore, what she was not herself permitted to do, she suffered to be performed by another: for that Elferius, whom I before blamed for destroying the monasteries, repenting of his rashness, and being deeply distressed in mind, took up the sacred corpse from its unworthy burial-place, and paid it just and distinguished honours at Shaftesbury. He did not escape unpunished, however, for, within a year afterwards, he was eaten of the vermin which we call lice. Moreover, since a mind unregulated is a torment to itself, and a restless spirit endures its own peculiar punishment in this life, Elfthrida declining from her regal pride, became extremely penitent; so that at Werewell, for many years, she clothed her pampered body in hair-cloth, slept at night upon the ground without a pillow; and mortified her flesh with every kind of penance. She was a beautiful woman; singularly faithful to her husband; but deserving punishment from the commission of so great a crime. It is believed and commonly reported, that from her violence to Edward, the country for a long time after groaned under the yoke of barbarian servitude.

At Shaftesbury, truly shines a splendid proof of royal sanctity; for to his merit must it be attributed, that there a numerous choir of women dedicated to God, not only enlighten those parts with the blaze of their religion, but even reach the very heavens. There reside sacred virgins wholly unconscious of contamination, there, continent widows, ignorant of a second flame after the extinction of the first; in all whose manner, graceful modesty is so blended with chastened elegance, that nothing can exceed it. Indeed it is matter of doubt which to applaud most, their assiduity in the service of God or their affability in their converse with men: hence assent is justly given to those persons who say that, the world, which has long tottered with the weight of its sins, is entirely supported by their prayers.

CHAP. X.

Of king Ethelred and king Edmund. [A.D. 979—1017.]

In the year of our Lord's incarnation 979, Ethelred, son of Edgar and Elfthrida, obtaining the kingdom, occupied, rather than governed it for thirty-seven years. The career of his life is said to have been cruel in the beginning, wretched in the middle, and disgraceful in the end. Thus, in the murder to which he gave his concurrence, he was cruel; base in his flight, and effeminacy; miserable in his death. Dunstan, indeed, had foretold his worthlessness, having discovered it by a very filthy token: for when quite an infant, the bishops standing round, as he was immersed in the baptismal font, he defiled the sacrament by a natural evacuation: at which Dunstan, being extremely angered, exclaimed, "By God, and his mother, this will be a sorry fellow." I have read, that when he was ten years of age, hearing it noised abroad that his brother was killed, he so irritated his furious mother by his weeping, that not having a whip at hand, she beat the little innocent with some candles she had snatched up: nor did she desist, till herself bedewed him, nearly lifeless, with her tears. On this account he dreaded candles during the rest of his life, to such a degree that he would never suffer the light of them to be brought into his presence. The nobility being assembled by the contrivance of his mother, and the day appointed for Dunstan, in right of his see, to crown him, he, though he might be ill-affected to them, forbore to resist, being a prelate of mature age, and long versed in secular matters. But, when placing the crown on his head he could not refrain from giving vent with a loud voice, to that prophetic spirit which he had so deeply imbibed. "Since," said he, "thou hast aspired to the kingdom by the death of thy brother, hear the word of God; thus saith the Lord God: the sin of thy abandoned mother, and of the accomplices of her base design, shall not be washed out but by much blood of the wretched inhabitants; and such evils shall come upon the English nation as they have never suffered from the time they came to England until then." Nor was it long after, that is, in his third year, that seven piratical vessels came to Southampton, a port near Winchester, and having ravaged the coast fled back to the sea: this I think right to mention because many reports are circulated among the English, concerning these vessels.

A quarrel between the king and the bishop of Rochester had arisen from some unknown cause; in consequence of which he led an army against that city. It was signified to him by the archbishop, that he should desist from his fury, and not irritate St. Andrew, under whose guardianship that bishopric was; for as he was ever ready to pardon, so was he equally formidable to avenge. This simple message being held in contempt, he graced the intimation with money, and sent him a hundred pounds, as a bribe, that he should raise the siege and retire. He therefore took the money, retreated, and dismissed his army. Dunstan, astonished at his avarice, sent messengers to him with the following words, "Since you have preferred silver to God, money to the apostle, and covetousness to me; the evils which God has pronounced will shortly come upon you; but they will not come while I live, for this also hath God spoken." Soon after the death of this holy man, which was in the tenth year of his reign, the predictions speedily began to be fulfilled, and the prophecies to have their consummation. For the Danes infested every port, and made descents on all sides with great activity, so that it was not known where they could be opposed. But Siric, the second archbishop after Dunstan, advised that money should repel those whom the sword could not: thus a payment of ten thousand pounds satisfied the avarice of the Danes. This was an infamous precedent, and totally unworthy the character of men, to redeem liberty, which no violence can ever extirpate from a noble mind, by money. They now indeed abstained a short time from their incursions; but as soon as their strength was recruited by rest, they returned to their old practices. Such extreme fear had seized the English, that there was no thought of resistance: if any indeed, mindful of their ancient glory, made an attempt to oppose, or engage them, they were unsuccessful, from the multitude of their enemies, and the desertion of their allies. The leader of revolt was one Elfric, whom the king had appointed to command the fleet: he, instead of trying his fortune, as he ought, in a naval conflict, went over, on the night preceding the battle, a base deserter to the enemy, whom he had apprised, by messengers, what preparations to make; and though the king, for this perfidious crime, ordered his son's eyes to be put out, yet he returned again, and again deserted. All Northumbria being laid waste, the enemy was met in battle and worsted. London was besieged, but honourably defended by its citizens. In consequence, the besiegers, after suffering severely and despairing of taking the city, retired; and devastating the whole province to the eastward, compelled the king to pay a sum of money, amounting to sixteen thousand pounds. Moreover, hostages being given, he caused their king Anlaf to come to him, stood for him at the font, and soothing him with royal munificence, bound him by an oath that he should never return into England again. The evil however was not thus put to rest. For they could never provide against their enemies from Denmark, springing up afresh, like the heads of the hydra. The province in the west of England, called Devonshire, was laid waste, the monasteries destroyed, and the city of Exeter set on fire: Kent was given up to plunder; the metropolitan city and seat of the patriarchs, burnt; the holy patriarch himself, the most reverend Elphege, carried away and bound in chains: and at last, when required to plunder his tenants in order to ransom himself, and refusing to do so, he was stoned, struck with a hatchet, and glorified heaven with his soul. After he was murdered, God exalted him; insomuch, that when the Danes, who had been instrumental to his death, saw that dead wood besmeared with his blood miraculously grew green again in one night, they ran eagerly to kiss his remains, and to bear them on their shoulders. Thus they abated their usual pride, and suffered his sacred corpse to be carried to London. There it was honorably buried; and when taken up, ten years afterwards, free from every taint of corruption, it conferred honour on his cathedral at Canterbury.* To the present moment both its blood remains fresh, and its soundness unimpaired, and it is considered a miracle, that a carcass should be divested of life, and yet not decay. That I may not be tedious in mentioning severally all the provinces which the Danes laid waste, let it be briefly understood, that out of thirty-two counties, which are reckoned in England, they had already overrun sixteen; the names of which I forbear to enumerate on account of the harshness of the language. In the meantime, the king, admirably calculated for sleeping, did nothing but postpone and hesitate, and if ever he recovered his senses enough to raise himself upon his elbow, he quickly relapsed into his original wretchedness, either from the oppression of indolence, or the adverseness of fortune. His brother's ghost also, demanding dire expiation, tormented him. Who can tell how often he collected his

* The life of Elphege, by Osberne, is in the Anglia Sacra, ii. 122.

army? how often he ordered ships to be built? how frequently he called out commanders from all quarters? and yet nothing was ever effected. For the army, destitute of a leader and ignorant of military discipline, either retreated before it came into action, or else was easily overcome. The presence of the leader is of much avail in battle; courage manifested by him avails also; experience, and more especially, discipline avail much; and as I have said, the want of these, in an army, must be an irreparable injury to its countrymen, as well as a pitiable object of contempt to an enemy. For soldiers are a kind of men, who, if not restrained before the battle, are eager to plunder; and if not animated during it, are prone to flight. When the ships, built for the defence of the sea-coast, were lying at anchor, a tempest suddenly arising dashed them together, and rendered them useless by the destruction of their tackling: a few, fitted from the wrecks of the others, were, by the attack of one Wulnod, whom the king had banished, either sunk, or burnt, and consequently disappointed the expectations of all England. The commanders, if ever they met to confer, immediately chose different sides, and rarely or never united in one good plan; for they gave more attention to private quarrels, than to public exigences: and, if in the midst of pressing danger, they had resolved on any eligible secret design, it was immediately communicated to the Danes by traitors. For besides Elfric, the successor of Elfere who had murdered the late king, there was one Edric, a man infamously skilled in such transactions, whom the king had made governor of the Mercians. This fellow was the refuse of mankind, the reproach of the English; an abandoned glutton, a cunning miscreant; who had become opulent, not by nobility, but by specious language and impudence. This artful dissembler, capable of feigning anything, was accustomed, by pretended fidelity, to scent out the king's designs, that he might treacherously divulge them. Often, when despatched to the enemy as the mediator of peace, he inflamed them to battle. His perfidy was sufficiently conspicuous in this king's reign, but much more so in the next; of which I shall have occasion to speak hereafter. Ulfkytel, earl of the East Angles, was the only person who, at that time, resisted the invaders with any degree of spirit; insomuch that although the enemy had nominally the victory, yet the conquerors suffered much more than the conquered:* nor were the barbarians ashamed to confess this truth, while they so frequently bewailed that victory. The valour of the earl was more conspicuously eminent, after the death of Ethelred, in that battle which mowed down the whole flower of the province; where, when he was surrounded from the rear, deeming it disgraceful to fly, he gave fresh confidence to the king by his blood; but this happened some time after.† At this juncture, that the measure of king Ethelred's misery might be full, a famine ravaged all England, and those whom war had spared perished from want. The enemy over-ran the country with such freedom, that they would carry off their booty to their ships through a space of fifty miles, without fearing any resistance from the inhabitants. In the midst of these pressing evils, the expedient of buying off hostilities by money was again debated and adopted; for first twenty-four, and soon after, thirty thousand pounds were given to the Danes: with what advantage, succeeding times will show. To me, indeed, deeply reflecting upon the subject, it seems wonderful, how a man, as we have been taught to suppose, neither very foolish, nor excessively heartless, should pass his life in the wretched endurance of so many calamities. Should any one ask me the reason of this, I could not easily answer, except by saying, that the revolt of the generals proceeded from the haughtiness of the king. Their perfidy has been spoken of before: I now hasten to instances of his violence, which was so intolerable, that he spared not even his own relations. For, besides the English, whom he despoiled of their hereditary possessions without any cause, or defrauded of their property for supposititious crimes: besides the Danes, whom, from light suspicion only, he ordered to be all butchered on the same day throughout England; which was a dreadful spectacle to behold; each one compelled to betray his dearest guests, now become dearer from the tenderest connexions of

* Ulfkytel attacked the Danes near Thetford, A.D. 1004, and though compelled to retreat, yet occasioned so severe a loss to the enemy, that they are said to have acknowledged that they had never endured a more powerful attack. See Flor. Wigorn., and the Saxon Chronicle, A.D. 1004.
† At Assingdon in Essex, A.D. 1016.

affinity, and to cut short their embraces with the sword: yet besides all this, I say, he was so inconstant towards his wife, that he scarcely deigned her his bed, and degraded the royal dignity by his intercourse with harlots. She too, a woman, conscious of her high descent, became indignant at her husband, as she found herself endeared to him neither by her blameless modesty nor her fruitfulness; for she had borne him two children, Elfred and Edward. She was the daughter of Richard, earl of Normandy, the son of William, who, after his father, presided over that earldom for fifty-two years, and died in the twenty-eighth year of this king. He lies at the monastery of Fescamp, which he augmented with certain revenues, and which he adorned with a monastic order, by means of William, formerly abbat of Dijon. Richard was a distinguished character, and had also often harassed Ethelred: which, when it became known at Rome, the holy see, not enduring that two Christians should be at enmity, sent Leo, bishop of Treves, into England, to restore peace: the epistle describing this legation was as follows:—

"John the fifteenth, pope of the holy Roman church, to all faithful people, health. Be it known to all the faithful of the holy mother church, and our children spiritual and secular, dispersed through the several climates of the world, that inasmuch as we had been informed by many of the enmity between Ethelred, king of the West-Saxons, and Richard the marquis, and were grieved sorely at this, on account of our spiritual children; taking, therefore, wholesome counsel, we summoned one of our legates, Leo, bishop of the holy church of Treves, and sent him with our letters, admonishing them, that they should return from their ungodliness. He, passing vast spaces, at length crossed the sea, and, on the day of the Lord's nativity, came into the presence of the said king; whom, having saluted on our part, he delivered to him the letters we had sent. And all the faithful people of his kingdom, and senators of either order, being summoned, he granted, for love and fear of God Almighty, and of St. Peter, the chief of the apostles, and on account of our paternal admonition, the firmest peace for all his sons and daughters, present and future, and all his faithful people, without deceit. On which account he sent Edelsin, prelate of the holy church of Sherborne, and Leofstan, son of Alfwold, and Edelnoth, son of Wulstan, who passed the maritime boundaries, and came to Richard, the said marquis. He, peaceably receiving our admonitions, and hearing the determination of the said king, readily confirmed the peace for his sons and daughters, present and future, and for all his faithful people, with this reasonable condition, that if any of their subjects, or they themselves, should commit any injustice against each other, it should be duly redressed; and that peace should remain for ever unshaken and confirmed by the oath of both parties: on the part of king Ethelred, to wit, Edelsin, prelate of the holy church of Sherborne; Leofstan, the son of Alfwold; Edelnoth, the son of Wulstan. On the part of Richard, Roger, the bishop; Rodolph, son of Hugh; Truteno, the son of Thurgis.

"Done at Rouen, on the kalends of March, in the year of our Lord 991, the fourth of the indiction. Moreover, of the king's subjects, or of his enemies, let Richard receive none, nor the king of his, without their respective seals."

After the death of this John, Gregory succeeded; after whom came John XVI.; then Silvester, also called Gerbert, about whom it will not be absurd, in my opinion, if I commit to writing those facts which are generally related about him.* Born in Gaul, from a lad he grew up a monk at Flory; afterwards, when he arrived at the double path of Pythagoras,† either disgusted at a monastic life or seized by lust of glory, he fled by night into Spain, chiefly designing to learn astrology and other sciences of that description from the Saracens. Spain, formerly for many years possessed by the Romans, in the time of the emperor Honorius, fell under the power of the Goths. The Goths were Arians down to the days of St. Gregory, when that people were united to the Catholic church by Leander bishop of Seville, and by king Recared, brother of Hermengildus,‡ whom his father

---

* In several of the manuscripts there is an omission of several words which has made nonsense of the whole paragraph Its restoration is due to Mr. Hardy, in whose edition of William of Malmesbury it is given correctly from MS. authority.

† That is, when he had attained that age when a man settles, or chooses his future line of conduct; or, to years of discretion. This Pythagoras represented by the form of the letter Y, or the Greek *gamma*.

‡ Hermenegild the eldest son of Leovigild. He was invested by his

slew on Easter night for professing the true faith. To Leander succeeded Isidore,* celebrated for learning and sanctity, whose body purchased, for its weight in gold, Aldefonsus king of Gallicia in our times conveyed to Toledo. The Saracens, who had subjugated the Goths, being conquered in their turn by Charles the Great, lost Gallicia and Lusitania, the largest provinces of Spain; but to this day they possess the southern parts. As the Christians esteem Toledo, so do they hold Hispalis, which in common they call Seville, to be the capital of the kingdom; there practising divinations and incantations, after the usual mode of that nation. Gerbert then, as I have related, coming among these people, satisfied his desires. There he surpassed Ptolemy with the astrolabe,† and Alcandræus in astronomy, and Julius Firmicus in judicial astrology; there he learned what the singing and the flight of birds portended; there he acquired the art of calling up spirits from hell: in short, whatever, hurtful or salutary, human curiosity has discovered. There is no necessity to speak of his progress in the lawful sciences of arithmetic and astronomy, music and geometry, which he imbibed so thoroughly as to show they were beneath his talents, and which, with great perseverance, he revived in Gaul, where they had for a long time been wholly obsolete. Being certainly the first who seized on the abacus‡ from the Saracens,

father with the royal diadem and the principality of Bœtica, and contracted an alliance with Ingundis, daughter of Sigebert, king of Austrasia. Ingundis was persecuted, and at length killed by her husband's mother, on account of her Catholic faith. Leander, archbishop of Seville, easily persuaded Hermenegild to resent the treatment of his bride, and assisted him in an attempt to dethrone his father. Hermenegild was taken and sentenced to death for his rebellion. The inflexible constancy, with which he refused to accept the Arian communion, from which he had been converted by Leander, as the price of his safety, procured for him the honour of being enrolled among the saints of the Romish church.—HARDY.

* Isidore was bishop of Seville in the sixth century.

† An instrument for making celestial observations. The reader who is conversant with the Arabian Nights' Entertainments will remember its being frequently mentioned in that amusing book.

‡ The abacus was a counting table: here it seems used metaphorically for arithmetic, Gerbert having written a treatise on arithmetic with that title. The authors of the Hist. Litt. de la France, t. vi. understand him literally, as stealing a book containing the principles of the science, and then confound this supposed book with the conjuring treatise mentioned below. They also seem very much displeased with Malmesbury for relating these

he gave rules which are scarcely understood even by laborious computers. He resided with a certain philosopher of that sect, whose good will he had obtained, first by great liberality, and then by promises. The Saracen had no objection to sell his knowledge; he frequently associated with him; would talk with him of matters at times serious, at others trivial, and lend him books to transcribe. There was however one volume, containing the knowledge of his whole art, which he could never by any means entice him to lend. In consequence Gerbert was inflamed with anxious desire to obtain this book at any rate, "for we ever press more eagerly towards what is forbidden, and that which is denied is always esteemed most valuable."* Trying, therefore, the effect of entreaty, he besought him for the love of God, and by his friendship; offered him many things, and promised him more. When this failed he tried a nocturnal stratagem. He plied him with wine, and, with the help of his daughter, who connived at the attempt through the intimacy which Gerbert's attentions had procured, stole the book from under his pillow and fled. Waking suddenly, the Saracen pursued the fugitive by the direction of the stars, in which art he was well versed. The fugitive too, looking back, and discovering his danger by means of the same art, hid himself under a wooden bridge which was near at hand; clinging to it, and hanging in such a manner as neither to touch earth nor water.† In this manner the eagerness of the pursuer being eluded, he returned home. Gerbert, then quickening his pace, arrived at the sea-coast. Here, by his incantations, he called up the devil, and made an agreement with him to be under his dominion for ever, if he would defend him from the Saracen, who was again pursuing, and transport him to the opposite coast: this was accordingly done.

Probably some may regard all this as a fiction, because the vulgar are used to undermine the fame of scholars, saying that the man who excels in any admirable science, holds converse with the devil. Of this, Boethius, in his book, On

tales of their countryman, and attribute them to cardinal Benno, but there is nothing of this kind in his work published by Goldastus, and in Brown's Fasciculus, t. i.

* Ovid Amor. iii. iv. 17.

† This was perhaps a necessary precaution, according to the rules of the necromantic art.

the Consolation of Philosophy, complains; and affirms, that he had the discredit of such practices on account of his ardent love of literature, as if he had polluted his knowledge by detestable arts for the sake of ambition. "It was hardly likely," says he, "that I, whom you dress up with such excellence as almost to make me like God, should catch at the protection of the vilest spirits; but it is in this point that we approach nearest to a connection with them, in that we are instructed in your learning, and educated in your customs." So far Boethius. The singular choice of his death confirms me in the belief of his league with the devil; else, when dying, as we shall relate hereafter, why should he, gladiator-like, maim his own person, unless conscious of some unusual crime? Accordingly, in an old volume, which accidentally fell into my hands, wherein the names and years of all the popes are entered, I found written to the following purport, "Silvester, who was also called Gerbert, ten months; this man made a shameful end."

Gerbert, returning into Gaul, became a public professor in the schools, and had as brother philosophers and companions of his studies, Constantine, abbat of the monastery of St. Maximin, near Orleans, to whom he addressed the Rules of the Abacus;* and Ethelbald bishop, as they say, of Winteburg, who himself gave proof of ability, in a letter which he wrote to Gerbert, on a question concerning the diameter in Macrobius,† and in some other points. He had as pupils, of exquisite talents and noble origin, Robert, son of Hugh surnamed Capet, and Otho, son of the emperor Otho. Robert, afterwards king of France, made a suitable return to his master, and appointed him archbishop of Rheims. In that church are still extant, as proofs of his science, a clock constructed on mechanical principles: and an hydraulic organ, in which the air escaping in a surprising manner, by the force of heated water, fills the cavity of the instrument, and the brazen pipes emit modulated tones through the multifarious apertures. The king himself, too, was well skilled in sacred music, and in this and many other respects, a liberal benefactor to the church: moreover, he composed that beautiful sequence, "The grace of the Holy Spirit be with

* His treatise so called. † Macrob. in Somn. Scip. i. 20.

us;" and the response, "He hath joined together Judah and Jerusalem;" together with more, which I should have pleasure in relating, were it not irksome to others to hear. Otho, emperor of Italy after his father, made Gerbert archbishop of Ravenna, and finally Roman pontiff. He followed up his fortune so successfully by the assistance of the devil, that he left nothing unexecuted which he had once conceived. The treasures formerly buried by the inhabitants, he discovered by the art of necromancy, and removing the rubbish, applied to his own lusts. Thus viciously disposed are the wicked towards God, and thus they abuse his patience, though he had rather that they repent than perish. At last, he found where his master would stop, and as the proverb says, "in the same manner as one crow picks out another crow's eyes," while endeavouring to oppose his attempts with art like his own.

There was a statue in the Campus Martius near Rome, I know not whether of brass or iron, having the forefinger of the right hand extended, and on the head was written, "Strike here." The men of former times supposing this should be understood as if they might find a treasure there, had battered the harmless statute by repeated strokes of a hatchet. But Gerbert convicted them of error by solving the problem in a very different manner. Marking where the shadow of the finger fell at noon-day, when the sun was on the meridian, he there placed a post; and at night proceeded thither, attended only by a servant carrying a lanthorn. The earth opening by means of his accustomed arts, displayed to them a spacious entrance. They see before them a vast palace with golden walls, golden roofs, every thing of gold, golden soldiers amusing themselves, as it were, with golden dice; a king of the same metal, at table with his queen; delicacies set before them, and servants waiting: vessels of great weight and value, where the sculpture surpassed nature herself. In the inmost part of the mansion, a carbuncle of the first quality, though small in appearance, dispelled the darkness of night. In the opposite corner stood a boy, holding a bow bent, and the arrow drawn to the head. While the exquisite art of every thing ravished the eyes of the spectators, there was nothing which might be handled though it might be seen: for immediately, if any one stretched forth his hand to touch any thing, all these figures appeared to rush forward and repel such presumption. Alarmed at this, Gerbert repressed his inclination: but not so the servant. He endeavoured to snatch off from a table, a knife of admirable workmanship; supposing that in a booty of such magnitude, so small a theft could hardly be discovered. In an instant, the figures all starting up with loud clamour, the boy let fly his arrow at the carbuncle, and in a moment all was in darkness; and if the servant had not, by the advice of his master, made the utmost despatch in throwing back the knife, they would have both suffered severely. In this manner, their boundless avarice unsatiated, they departed, the lantern directing their steps. That he performed such things by unlawful devices is the generally received opinion. Yet, however, if any one diligently investigate the truth, he will see that even Solomon, to whom God himself had given wisdom, was not ignorant of these arts: for, as Josephus relates,* he, in conjunction with his father, buried vast treasures in coffers, which were hidden, as he says, in a kind of necromantic manner, under ground: neither was Hyrcanus, celebrated for his skill in prophecy and his valour; who, to ward off the distress of a siege, dug up, by the same art, three thousand talents of gold from the sepulchre of David, and gave part of them to the besiegers; with the remainder building an hospital for the reception of strangers. But Herod, who would make an attempt of the same kind, with more presumption than knowledge, lost in consequence many of his attendants, by an eruption of internal fire. Besides, when I hear the Lord Jesus saying, "My father worketh hitherto, and I work;" I believe, that He, who gave to Solomon power over demons to such a degree, as the same historian declares, that he relates there were men, even in his time, who could eject them from persons possessed, by applying to the nostrils of the patient a ring having the impression pointed out by Solomon: I believe, I say, that he could give, also, the same science to this man: but I do not affirm that he did give it.

But leaving these matters to my readers, I shall relate what I recollect having heard, when I was a boy, from a certain monk of our house, a native of Aquitaine, a man in

* Josephus Antiq. Jud. l. vii. c. 15. viii. 2.

years, and a physician by profession. "When I was seven years old," said he, "despising the mean circumstances of my father, a poor citizen of Barcelona, I surmounted the snowy Alps, and went into Italy. There, as was to be expected in a boy of that age, having to seek my daily bread in great distress, I paid more attention to the food of my mind than of my body. As I grew up I eagerly viewed many of the wonders of that country and impressed them on my memory. Among others I saw a perforated mountain, beyond which the inhabitants supposed the treasures of Octavian were hidden. Many persons were reported to have entered into these caverns for the purpose of exploring them, and to have there perished, being bewildered by the intricacy of the ways. But, as hardly any apprehension can restrain avaricious minds from their intent, I, with my companions, about twelve in number, meditated an expedition of this nature, either for the sake of plunder, or through curiosity. Imitating therefore the ingenuity of Dædalus, who brought Theseus out of the labyrinth by a conducting clue, we, also carrying a large ball of thread, fixed a small post at the entrance. Tying the end of the thread to it, and lighting lanterns, lest darkness, as well as intricacy, should obstruct us, we unrolled the clue; and fixing a post at every mile, we proceeded on our journey along the caverns of the mountain, in the best manner we were able. Every thing was dark, and full of horrors; the bats, flitting from holes, assailed our eyes and faces: the path was narrow, and made dreadful on the left-hand by a precipice, with a river flowing beneath it. We saw the way strewed with bare bones: we wept over the carcasses of men yet in a state of putrefaction, who, induced by hopes similar to our own, had in vain attempted, after their entrance, to return. After some time, however, and many alarms, arriving at the farther outlet, we beheld a lake of softly murmuring waters, where the wave came gently rolling to the shores. A bridge of brass united the opposite banks. Beyond the bridge were seen golden horses of great size, mounted by golden riders, and all those other things which are related of Gerbert. The mid-day beams of Phœbus darting upon them, with redoubled splendour, dazzled the eyes of the beholders. Seeing these things at a distance, we should have been delighted with a nearer view, meaning, if fate would permit, to carry off some portion of the precious metal. Animating each other in turn, we prepared to pass over the lake. All our efforts, however, were vain : for as soon as one of the company, more forward than the rest, had put his foot on the hither edge of the bridge, immediately, wonderful to hear, it became depressed, and the farther edge was elevated, bringing forward a rustic of brass with a brazen club, with which, dashing the waters, he so clouded the air, as completely to obscure both the day and the heavens. The moment the foot was withdrawn, peace was restored. The same was tried by many of us, with exactly the same result. Despairing, then, of getting over, we stood there some little time ; and, as long as we could, at least glutted our eyes with the gold. Soon after returning by the guidance of the thread, we found a silver dish, which being cut in pieces and distributed in morsels only irritated the thirst of our avidity without allaying it. Consulting together the next day, we went to a professor, of that time, who was said to know the unutterable name of God. When questioned, he did not deny his knowledge, adding, that, so great was the power of that name, that no magic, no witchcraft could resist it. Hiring him at a great price, fasting and confessed, he led us, prepared in the same manner, to a fountain. Taking up some water from it in a silver vessel, he silently traced the letters with his fingers, until we understood by our eyes, what was unutterable with our tongues. We then went confidently to the mountain, but we found the farther outlet beset, as I believe, with devils, hating, forsooth, the name of God because it was able to destroy their inventions. In the morning a Jew-necromancer came to me, excited by the report of our attempt ; and, having inquired into the matter, when he heard of our want of enterprise, "You shall see," said he, venting his spleen with loud laughter, "how far the power of my art can prevail." And immediately entering the mountain, he soon after came out again, bringing, as a proof of his having passed the lake, many things which I had noted beyond it : indeed some of that most precious dust, which turned every thing that it touched into gold : not that it was really so, but only retained this appearance until washed with water ; for nothing effected by necromancy can, when put into water, deceive the sight of the beholders. The truth of my assertion is confirmed by a circumstance which happened about the same time.

"There were in a public street leading to Rome, two old women, the most drunken and filthy beings that can be conceived ; both living in the same hut, and both practising witchcraft. If any lone stranger happened to come in their way, they used to make him appear either a horse, or a sow, or some other animal ; expose him for sale to dealers, and gluttonize with the money. By chance, on a certain night, taking in a lad to lodge who got his livelihood by stagedancing, they turned him into an ass : and so possessed a creature extremely advantageous to their interests, who caught the eyes of such as passed by the strangeness of his postures. In whatever mode the old woman commanded, the ass began to dance, for he retained his understanding, though he had lost the power of speech. In this manner the women had accumulated much money ;" for there was, daily, a large concourse of people, from all parts, to see the tricks of the ass. The report of this induced a rich neighbour to purchase the quadruped for a considerable sum ; and he was warned, that, if he would have him as a constant dancer, he must keep him from water. The person who had charge of him rigidly fulfilled his orders. A long time elapsed ; the ass sometimes gratified his master by his reeling motions, and sometimes entertained his friends with his tricks. But, however, as in time all things surfeit, he began at length to be less cautiously observed. In consequence of this negligence, breaking his halter, he got loose, plunged into a pool hard by, and rolling for a long time in the water, recovered his human form. The keeper, inquiring of all he met, and pursuing him by the track of his feet, asked him if he had seen an ass ; he replied that himself had been an ass, but was now a man : and related the whole transaction. The servant astonished told it to his master, and the master to pope Leo, the holiest man in our times. The old women were convicted, and confessed the fact. The pope doubting this, was assured by Peter Damian, a learned man, that it was not wonderful that such things should be done : he produced the example of Simon Magus,* who caused Faustini-

* In the fabulous Itinerary of St. Peter, falsely attributed to Clemens Romanus, Simon is represented as causing Faustinianus to assume his

anus to assume the figure of Simon, and to become an object of terror to his sons, and thus rendered his holiness better skilled in such matters for the future."

I have inserted this narrative of the Aquitanian to the intent that what is reported of Gerbert should not seem wonderful to any person; which is, that he cast, for his own purposes, the head of a statue, by a certain inspection of the stars when all the planets were about to begin their courses, which spake not unless spoken to, but then pronounced the truth, either in the affirmative or negative. For instance, when Gerbert would say, "Shall I be pope?" the statute would reply, "Yes." "Am I to die, ere I sing mass at Jerusalem?" "No." They relate, that he was so much deceived by this ambiguity, that he thought nothing of repentance: for when would he think of going to Jerusalem, to accelerate his own death? Nor did he foresee that at Rome there is a church called Jerusalem, that is, "the vision of peace," because whoever flies thither finds safety, whatsoever crime he may be guilty of. We have heard, that this was called an asylum in the very infancy of the city, because Romulus, to increase the number of his subjects, had appointed it to be a refuge for the guilty of every description. The pope sings mass there on three Sundays, which are called "The station at Jerusalem" Wherefore upon one of those days Gerbert, preparing himself for mass, was suddenly struck with sickness; which increased so that he took to his bed: and consulting his statue, he became convinced of his delusion and of his approaching death. Calling, therefore, the cardinals together, he lamented his crimes for a long space of time. They, being struck with sudden fear were unable to make any reply, whereupon he began to rave, and losing his reason through excess of pain, commanded himself to be maimed, and cast forth piecemeal, saying, "Let him have the service of my limbs, who before sought their homage; for my mind never consented to that abominable oath."

And since I have wandered from my subject, I think it may not be unpleasant to relate what took place in Saxony

countenance, by rubbing his face with a medicated unguent, to the great alarm of his sons, who mistook him for Simon, and fled until recalled by St. Peter.

in the time of this king, in the year of our Lord 1012, and is not so generally known. It is better to dilate on such matters than to dwell on Ethelred's indolence and calamities: and it will be more pleasing certainly, and nearer the truth, if I subjoin it in the original language of the person who was a sufferer, than if I had clothed it in my own words. Besides, I think it ornamental to a work, that the style should be occasionally varied.

"I Ethelbert,* a sinner, even were I desirous of concealing the divine judgment which overtook me, yet the tremor of my limbs would betray me, wherefore I shall relate circumstantially how this happened, that all may know the heavy punishment due to disobedience. We were, on the eve of our Lord's nativity, in a certain town of Saxony, in which was the church of Magnus the martyr, and a priest named Robert had begun the first mass. I was in the churchyard with eighteen companions, fifteen men and three women, dancing, and singing profane songs to such a degree that I interrupted the priest, and our voices resounded amid the sacred solemnity of the mass. Wherefore, having commanded us to be silent, and not being attended to, he cursed us in the following words, 'May it please God and St. Magnus, that you may remain singing in that manner for a whole year.' His words had their effect. The son of John the priest seized his sister who was singing with us, by the arm, and immediately tore it from her body, but not a drop of blood flowed out. She also remained a whole year with us, dancing and singing. The rain fell not upon us; nor did cold, nor heat, nor hunger, nor thirst, nor fatigue assail us: we neither wore our clothes nor shoes, but we kept on singing as though we had been insane. First we sank into the ground up to our knees: next to our thighs; a covering was at length, by the permission of God, built over us to keep off the rain. When a year had elapsed, Herbert, bishop of the city of Cologne, released us from the tie wherewith our hands were bound, and reconciled us before the altar of St. Magnus. The daughter of the priest, with the other two women, died immediately; the rest of us slept three whole days and nights: some died afterwards, and are famed for miracles: the remainder betray their punishment by the trembling of

* Other MSS. read Otbert.

their limbs. This narrative was given to us by the lord Peregrine, the successor of Herbert, in the year of our Lord 1013."

In that city, which formerly was called Agrippina, from Agrippa the son-in-law of Augustus, but afterwards named Colonia by the emperor Trajan, because being there created emperor he founded in it a colony of Roman citizens; in this city, I repeat, there was a certain bishop, famed for piety, though to a degree hideous in his person, of whom I shall relate one miracle, which he predicted when dying, after having first recorded what a singular chance elevated him to such an eminent station. The emperor of that country going to hunt on Quinquagesima Sunday, came alone, for his comcompanions were dispersed, to the edge of a wood, where this rural priest, deformed and almost a monster, had a church. The emperor, feigning himself a soldier, humbly begs a mass, which the priest immediately begins. The other in the meantime was revolving in his mind why God, from whom all beautiful things proceed, should suffer so deformed a man to administer his sacraments. Presently, when that verse in the tract occurred, "Know ye that the Lord himself is God," the priest looked behind him, to chide the inattention of an assistant, and said with a louder voice, as if in reply to the emperor's thoughts, "He made us; and not we ourselves." Struck with this expression, the emperor esteeming him a prophet, exalted him, though unwilling and reluctant, to the archbishopric of Cologne, which, when he had once assumed, he dignified by his exemplary conduct; kindly encouraging those who did well, and branding with the stigma of excommunication such as did otherwise, without respect of persons. The inhabitants of that place proclaim a multitude of his impartial acts; one of which the reader will peruse in that abbreviated form which my work requires. In a monastery of nuns in that city, there was a certain virgin who had there grown up, more by the kindness of her parents than through any innate wish for a holy life: this girl, by the attraction of her beauty and her affable language to all, allured many lovers; but while others, through fear of God or the censure of the world, restrained their desires, there was one who, excited to wantonness by the extent of his wealth and the nobility of his descent, broke through the bounds of law and of justice, and despoiled her of her virginity; and carrying her off kept her as his lawful wife. Much time elapsed while the abbess entreated, and his friends admonished him not to persevere in so dreadful a crime. Turning a deaf ear, however, to his advisers, he continued as immoveable as a rock. By chance at this time the prelate was absent, occupied in business at Rome, but on his return the circumstance was related to him. He commands the sheep to be returned to the fold directly; and after much altercation the woman was restored to the monastery. Not long after, watching an opportunity when the bishop was absent, she was again carried away. Excommunication was then denounced against the delinquent, so that no person could speak to, or associate with him. This, however, he held in contempt, and retired to one of his estates afar off, not to put the command in force, but to elude its power: and there, a turbulent and powerful man, he lived in company with his excommunicated paramour. But when it pleased God to take the bishop to himself, and he was lying in extreme bodily pain upon his bed, the neighbours flocked around him that they might partake the final benediction of this holy man. The offender alone not daring to appear, prevailed on some persons to speak for him. The moment the bishop heard his name he groaned, and then, I add his very words, spoke to the following effect, "If that wretched man shall desert that accursed woman, he shall be absolved; but if he persist, let him be ready to give account before God, the following year, at the very day and hour on which I shall depart: moreover, you will see me expire when the bell shall proclaim the sixth hour." Nor were his words vain; for he departed at the time which he had predicted; and the other, together with his mistress, at the expiration of the year, on the same day, and at the same hour, was killed by a stroke of lightning.

But king Ethelred, after the martyrdom of Elphege, as we have related, gave his see to a bishop named Living.* Moreover, Turkill, the Dane, who had been the chief cause of the archbishop's murder, had settled in England, and held the East Angles in subjection. For the other Danes, exacting

* "Living, formerly called Elfstan, was translated from Wells to Canterbury in the year 1013; he died, 12th June, 1020."—HARDY.

from the English a tribute of eight thousand pounds, had distributed themselves, as best suited their convenience, in the towns, or in the country; and fifteen of their ships, with the crews, had entered into the king's service. In the meantime Thurkill sent messengers to Sweyn, king of Denmark, inviting him to come to England; telling him that the land was rich and fertile, but the king a driveller; and that, wholly given up to wine and women, his last thoughts were those of war: that in consequence he was hateful to his own people and contemptible to foreigners: that the commanders were jealous of each other, the people weak, and that they would fly the field, the moment the onset was sounded.

Sweyn* was naturally cruel, nor did he require much persuasion; preparing his ships, therefore, he hastened his voyage. Sandwich was the port he made, principally designing to avenge his sister Gunhilda. This woman, who possessed considerable beauty, had come over to England with her husband Palling, a powerful nobleman, and by embracing Christianity, had made herself a pledge of the Danish peace. In his ill-fated fury, Edric had commanded her, though proclaiming that the shedding her blood would bring great evil on the whole kingdom, to be beheaded with the other Danes. She bore her death with fortitude; and she neither turned pale at the moment, nor, when dead, and her blood exhausted, did she lose her beauty; her husband was murdered before her face, and her son, a youth of amiable disposition, was transfixed with four spears. Sweyn then proceeding through East Anglia against the Northumbrians. received their submission without resistance: not indeed, that the native ardour of their minds, which brooked no master. had grown cool, but because Utred, their prince, was the first to give example of desertion. On their submission all the other people who inhabit England on the north, gave him tribute and hostages. Coming southward, he compelled those of Oxford and Winchester, to obey his commands; the Londoners alone, protecting their lawful sovereign within their walls, shut their

* Malmesbury seems to have fallen into some confusion here. The murder of the Danes took place on St. Brice's day, A D. 1002, and accordingly we find Sweyn infesting England in 1003 and the following year (see Saxon Chronicle): but this his second arrival took place, A.D. 1013: so that the avenging the murder of his sister Gunhilda could hardly be the object of his present attack.

gates against him. The Danes, on the other hand, assailing with greater ferocity, nurtured their fortitude with the hope of fame; the townsmen were ready to rush on death for freedom, thinking they ought never to be forgiven, should they desert their king, who had committed his life to their charge. While the conflict was raging fiercely on either side, victory befriended the juster cause; for the citizens made wonderful exertions, every one esteeming it glorious to show his unwearied alacrity to his prince, or even to die for him. Part of the enemy were destroyed, and part drowned in the river Thames, because in their headlong fury, they had not sought a bridge. With his shattered army Sweyn retreated to Bath, where Ethelmer, governor of the western district, with his followers, submitted to him. And, although all England was already bending to his dominion, yet not even now would the Londoners have yielded, had not Ethelred withdrawn his presence from among them. For being a man given up to indolence, and, through consciousness of his own misdeeds, supposing none could be faithful to him, and at the same time wishing to escape the difficulties of a battle and a siege, he by his departure left them to their own exertions. However, they applied the best remedy they could to their exigencies, and surrendered after the example of their countrymen. They were men laudable in the extreme, and such as Mars himself would not have disdained to encounter, had they possessed a competent leader. Even while they were supported by the mere shadow of one, they risked every chance of battle, nay even a siege of several months' continuance. He in the meantime giving fresh instance of his constitutional indolence, fled from the city, and by secret journeys came to Southampton, whence he passed over to the Isle of Wight. Here he addressed those abbats and bishops who, even in such difficulties, could not bring themselves to desert their master, to the following effect: "That they must perceive in what dreadful state his affairs, and those of his family were; that he was banished from his paternal throne by the treachery of his generals, and that he, in whose hands their safety was formerly vested, now required the assistance of others; that though lately a monarch and a potentate, he was now an outcast and a fugitive; a melancholy change for him, because it certainly is more tolerable never to have had power, than to have lost it when possessed; and more especially disgraceful to the English, as this instance of deserting their prince would be noised throughout the world; that through mere regard to him they had exposed their houses and property to plunderers, and, unprovided, taken to a voluntary flight; food was matter of difficulty to all; many had not even clothing; he commended their fidelity indeed, but still could find no security from it; the country was now so completely subdued, the coast so narrowly watched, that there was no escape unattended with danger: that they should, therefore, confer together, what was to be done: were they to remain, greater peril was to be apprehended from their countrymen, than from their enemies, for perhaps they might purchase the favour of their new master by joining to distress them; and certainly to be killed by an enemy was to be ascribed to fortune, to be betrayed by a fellow citizen was to be attributed to want of exertion; were they to fly to distant nations, it would be with the loss of honour; if to those who knew them, the dread would be, lest their dispositions should take a tinge from their reverse of fortune; for many great and illustrious men had been killed on similar occasions; but, however, he must make the experiment, and sound the inclinations of Richard, duke of Normandy, who, if he should kindly receive his sister and nephews, might probably not unwillingly afford him his protection. His favour shown to my wife and children," continued he, "will be the pledge of my own security. Should he oppose me, I am confident, nay fully confident, I shall not want spirit to die here with honour, in preference to living there with ignominy. Wherefore this very month of August, while milder gales are soothing the ocean, let Emma make a voyage to her brother, and take our children, our common pledges, to be deposited with him. Let their companions be the bishop of Durham and the abbat of Peterborough; I myself will remain here till Christmas, and should he send back a favourable answer, I will follow directly."

On the breaking up of the conference, all obeyed; they set sail for Normandy, while he remained anxiously expecting a favourable report. Shortly after he learned from abroad, that Richard had received his sister with great affection, and that he invited the king also to condescend to become his inmate. Ethelred, therefore, going into Normandy, in the month of January, felt his distresses soothed by the attentions of his host. This Richard was son of Richard the first, and equalled his father in good fortune and good qualities; though he certainly surpassed him in heavenly concerns. He completed the monastery at Feschamp, which his father had begun. He was more intent on prayer and temperance, than you would require in any monk, or hermit. He was humble to excess, in order that he might subdue by his patience, the petulance of those who attacked him. Moreover it is reported, that at night, secretly escaping the observation of his servants, he was accustomed to go unattended to the matins* of the monks, and to continue in prayer till day-light. Intent on this practice, one night in particular, at Feschamp, he was earlier than customary, and finding the door shut, he forced it open with unusual violence, and disturbed the sleep of the sacristan. He, astonished at the noise of a person knocking in the dead of night, got up, that he might see the author of so bold a deed; and finding only a countryman in appearance, clothed in rustic garb, he could not refrain from laying hands on him; and, moved with vehement indignation, he caught hold of his hair, and gave this illustrious man a number of severe blows, which he bore with incredible patience, and without uttering a syllable. The next day, Richard laid his complaint before the chapter,† and with counterfeited anger, summoned the monk to meet him at the town of Argens, threatening that, " he would take such vengeance for the injury, so that all France should talk of it." On the day appointed, while the monk stood by, almost dead with fear, he detailed the matter to the nobility, largely exaggerating the enormity of the transaction, and keeping the culprit in suspense, by crafty objections to what he urged in mitigation. Finally, after he had been mercifully judged by the nobility, he pardoned him, and to make his forgiveness more acceptable, he annexed all that town, with its appurtenances, reported to be abundant in the best wine, to the office of this sacristan: saying, " That he was an admirable monk, who

* Matins were sometimes performed shortly after midnight
† It was customary to hold a chapter immediately after primes.

properly observed his appointed charge, and did not break silence, though roused with anger." In the twenty-eighth year of his dukedom, he died, having ordered his body to be buried at the door of the church, where it would be subjected to the feet of such as passed by, and to the spouts of water which streamed from above. In our time, however, William, third abbat of that place, regarding this as disgraceful, removed the long-continued reproach, and taking up the body, placed it before the high altar. He had a brother, Robert, whom he made archbishop of Rouen, though by this he tarnished his reputation. For he, cruelly abusing this honour, at first, committed many crimes and many atrocious acts; but growing in years, he certainly wiped off some of them by his very liberal almsgiving. After Richard, his son of the same name obtained the principality, but lived scarcely a year. A vague opinion indeed has prevailed, that, by the connivance of his brother Robert, whom Richard the second begat on Judith, daughter of Conan, earl of Brittany, a certain woman, skilled in poisons, took the young man off. In atonement for his privity to this transaction he departed for Jerusalem, after the seventh year of his earldom; venturing on an undertaking very meritorious at that time, by commencing, with few followers, a journey, exposed to incursions of barbarians, and strange, by reason of the customs of the Saracens. He persevered nevertheless, and did not stop, but safely completed the whole distance, and purchasing admission at a high price, with bare feet, and full of tears, he worshipped at that glory of the Christians, the sepulchre of our Lord. Conciliating the favour of God, as we believe, by this labour, on his return homewards he ended his days at Nice, a city of Bithynia; cut off, as it is said, by poison. This was administered by his servant Ralph, surnamed Mowin, who had wrought himself up to the commission of this crime, from a hope of obtaining the dukedom. But on his return to Normandy, the matter becoming known to all, he was detested as a monster, and retired to perpetual exile. To Robert succeeded William, his son, then a child, of whom as I shall have to speak hereafter, I shall now return to my narrative.

In the meantime Sweyn, as I have before related, oppressed England with rapine and with slaughter: the inhabitants were first plundered of their property, and then proscribed. In every city it was matter of doubt what should be done: if revolt was determined on, they had none to take the lead; if submission was made choice of, they would have a harsh ruler to deal with. Thus their public and private property, together with their hostages, was carried to the fleet; as he was not a lawful sovereign, but a most cruel tyrant. The Deity, however, was too kind to permit England to fluctuate long in such keen distress, for the invader died shortly after, on the purification of St. Mary,* though it is uncertain by what death. It is reported, that while devastating the possessions of St. Edmund,† king and martyr, he appeared to him in a vision, and gently addressed him on the misery of his people; that on Sweyn's replying insolently, he struck him on the head; and that, in consequence of the blow, he died, as has been said, immediately after. The Danes then elected Canute, the son of Sweyn, king; while the Angles, declaring that their natural sovereign was dearer to them, if he could conduct himself more royally than he had hitherto done, sent for king Ethelred out of Normandy. He despatched Edward, his son, first, to sound the fidelity of the higher orders and the inclination of the people, on the spot; who, when he saw the wishes of all tending in his favour, went back in full confidence for his father. The king returned, and, being flattered by the joyful plaudits of the Angles, that he might appear to have shaken off his constitutional indolence, he hastened to collect an army against Canute, who was at that time in Lindsey, where his father had left him with the ships and hostages, and was levying fresh troops and horses, that, mustering a sufficient force, he might make a vigorous attack upon his enemies unprepared: vowing most severe vengeance, as he used to say, on the deserters. But, circumvented by a contrivance similar to his own, he retreated. Escaping at that time with much difficulty, and putting to sea with his remaining forces, he coasted the British ocean from east to south, and landed at Sandwich. Here, setting all divine and human laws at defiance, he mutilated his hostages, who were young men of great nobility and elegance, by depriving them

* Sweyn died Feb. 3, A.D. 1014.
† The monastery of St. Edmundbury.

of their ears, and nostrils, and some even of their manhood. Thus tyrannizing over the innocent, and boasting of the feat, he returned to his own country. In the same year the sea-flood, which the Greeks call Euripus, and we Ledo,* rose to so wonderful a height, that none like it was recollected in the memory of man, for it overflowed the villages, and destroyed their inhabitants, for many miles.

The year following a grand council of Danes and English was assembled at Oxford, where the king commanded two of the noblest Danes, Sigeferth, and Morcar, accused of treachery to him by the impeachment of the traitor Edric, to be put to death. He had lured them, by his soothing expressions, into a chamber, and deprived them, when drunk to excess, of their lives, by his attendants who had been prepared for that purpose. The cause of their murder was said to be, his unjustifiable desire for their property. Their dependants, attempting to revenge the death of their lords by arms, were worsted, and driven into the tower of St. Frideswide's church at Oxford, where, as they could not be dislodged, they were consumed by fire: however, shortly after, the foul stain was wiped out by the king's penitence, and the sacred place repaired. I have read the history of this transaction, which is deposited in the archives of that church. The wife of Sigeferth, a woman remarkable for her rank and beauty, was carried prisoner to Malmesbury; on which account, Edmund, the king's son, dissembling his intention, took a journey into those parts. Seeing her, he became enamoured; and becoming enamoured, he made her his wife; cautiously keeping their union secret from his father, who was as much an object of contempt to his family as to strangers. This Edmund was not born of Emma, but of some other person, whom fame has left in obscurity. With that exception, he was a young man in every respect of noble disposition; of great strength both of mind and person, and, on this account, by the English, called "Ironside:" he would have shrouded the indolence of his father, and the meanness of his mother, by his own conspicuous virtue, could the fates have spared him. Soon after, at the instigation of his wife, he asked of his father the

* He here considers Ledo to imply the spring tide; but others say it means the neap, and express the former by Malina. See Du Cange.

possessions of Sigeferth, which were of large extent among the Northumbrians, but could not obtain them, by his own exertions, however, he procured them at last, the inhabitants of that province willingly submitting to his power.

The same summer Canute, having settled his affairs in Denmark, and entered into alliance with the neighbouring kings, came to England, determined to subdue it or perish in the attempt. Proceeding from Sandwich into Kent, and thence into West Saxony, he laid every thing waste with fire and slaughter, while the king was lying sick at Cosham.* Edmund indeed attempted to oppose him, but being thwarted by Edric, he placed his forces in a secure situation. Edric, however, thinking it unnecessary longer to dissemble, but that he might, now, openly throw off the mask, revolted to Canute with forty ships, and all West Saxony following his example, delivered hostages, and gave up their arms. Yet the Mercians repeatedly assembling stood forward to resist: and if the king would but come, and command whither they were to march, and bring with him the leading men of London, they were ready to shed their blood for their country. But he, accustomed to commit his safety to fortifications, and not to attack the enemy, remained in London; never venturing out, for fear, as he said, of traitors. On the contrary, Canute was gaining towns and villages over to his party; and was never unemployed; for he held consultations by night, and fought battles by day. Edmund, after long deliberation, esteeming it best, in such an emergency, to recover, if possible, the revolted cities by arms, brought over Utred, an earl, on the other side of the Humber, to the same sentiments. They imagined too, that such cities as were yet doubtful which side to take, would determine at once, if they would only inflict signal vengeance on those which had revolted. But Canute, possessed of equal penetration, circumvented them by a similar contrivance. Giving over the West Saxons and that part of Mercia which he had subjugated, to the custody of his generals, he proceeded himself against the Northumbrians; and, by depopulating the country, compelled Utred to retire, to defend his own possessions; and notwithstanding he surrendered himself, yet with inhuman levity he ordered him to

* Corsham, in Wiltshire?

be put to death. His earldom was given to Eric, whom
Canute afterwards expelled England, because he pretended
to equal power with himself. Thus all being subdued, he
ceased not pursuing Edmund, who was gradually retreating,
till he heard that he was at London with his father. Canute
then remained quiet till after Easter, that he might attack
the city with all his forces. But the death of Ethelred
preceded the attempt: for in the beginning of Lent, on St.
Gregory's day,* he breathed out a life destined only to
labours and misery : he lies buried at St. Paul's in London.
The citizens immediately proclaimed Edmund king, who,
mustering an army, routed the Danes at Penn,† near
Gillingham, about Rogation-day. After the festival of St.
John, engaging them again at Sceorstan,‡ he retired from a
drawn-battle. The English had begun to give way, at the
instance of Edric ; who being on the adversaries' side, and
holding in his hand a sword stained with the blood of a
fellow whom he had dexterously slain, exclaimed. " Fly,
wretches ! fly ! behold, your king was slain by this sword!"
The Angles would have fled immediately, had not the king,
apprised of this circumstance, proceeded to an eminence, and
taking off his helmet, shown his face to his comrades. Then
brandishing a dart with all his forces, he launched it at Edric;
but being seen, and avoided, it missed him, and struck a
soldier standing near ; and so great was its violence, that it
even transfixed a second. Night put a stop to the battle, the
hostile armies retreating as if by mutual consent, though the
English had well-nigh obtained the victory.

After this the sentiments of the West Saxons changed,
and they acknowledged their lawful sovereign. Edmund
proceeded to London, that he might liberate those deserving
citizens whom a party of the enemy had blocked up immediately after his departure ; moreover they had surrounded
the whole city, on the parts not washed by the river Thames,
with a trench , and many men lost their lives on both sides
in the skirmishes. Hearing of the king's approach, they

---

* March 12th, but the Saxon Chronicle says St George's day, 23d April
† In Somersetshire ?
‡ Sceorstan is conjectured to be near Chipping Norton.—Sharp Sup-
posed to be a stone which divided the four counties of Oxford, Gloucester,
Worcester and Warwick.—Hardy

precipitately took to flight; while he pursuing directly, and passing the ford called Brentford, routed them with great slaughter. The remaining multitude which were with Canute, while Edmund was relaxing a little and getting his affairs in order, again laid siege to London both on the land and river side; but being nobly repulsed by the citizens, they wreaked their anger on the neighbouring province of Mercia, laying waste the towns and villages, with plunder, fire, and slaughter. The best of the spoil was conveyed to their ships assembled in the Medway; which river flowing by the city of Rochester, washes its fair walls with a strong and rapid current. They were attacked and driven hence also by the king in person; who suddenly seizing the ford, which I have before mentioned at Brentford,* dispersed them with signal loss.

While Edmund was preparing to pursue, and utterly destroy the last remains of these plunderers, he was prevented by the crafty and abandoned Edric, who had again insinuated himself into his good graces; for he had come over to Edmund, at the instigation of Canute, that he might betray his designs. Had the king only persevered, this would have been the last day for the Danes; but misled by the insinuations of a traitor, who affirmed that the enemy would make no farther attempt, he brought swift destruction upon himself, and the whole of England. Being thus allowed to escape, they again assembled; attacked the East Angles, and, at Assandun,† compelled the king himself, who came to their assistance, to retreat. Here again, the person I am ashamed to mention so frequently, designedly gave the first example of flight. A small number, who, mindful of their former fame, and encouraging each other, had formed a compact body, were cut off to a man. On this field of battle Canute gained the kingdom; the glory of the Angles fell; and the whole flower of the country withered. Amongst these was Ulfkytel, earl of East Anglia, who had gained immortal honour in the time of Sweyn, when first attacking the pirates, he showed that they might be overcome: here

* He passed the Thames at Brentford, followed them into Kent, and defeated them at Aylesford. Saxon Chron.
† Thought to be either Assingdon, Ashdown in Essex, or Aston in Berkshire.

fell, too, the chief men of the day, both bishops and abbats. Edmund flying hence almost alone, came to Gloucester, in order that he might there re-assemble his forces, and attack the enemy, indolent, as he supposed, from their recent victory. Nor was Canute wanting in courage to pursue the fugitive. When everything was ready for battle, Edmund demanded a single combat; that two individuals might not, for the lust of dominion, be stained with the blood of so many subjects, when they might try their fortune without the destruction of their faithful adherents: and observing, that it must redound greatly to the credit of either to have obtained so vast a dominion at his own personal peril. But Canute refused this proposition altogether; affirming that his courage was surpassing, but that he was apprehensive of trusting his diminutive person against so bulky an antagonist: wherefore, as both had equal pretensions to the kingdom, since the father of either of them had possessed it, it was consistent with prudence that they should lay aside their animosity, and divide England.* This proposition was adopted by either army, and confirmed with much applause, both for its equity and its beneficent regard to the repose of the people who were worn out with continual suffering. In consequence, Edmund, overcome by the general clamour, made peace, and entered into treaty with Canute, retaining West Saxony himself and giving Mercia to the other. He died soon after on the festival of St. Andrew,† though by what mischance is not known, and was buried at Glastonbury near his grandfather Edgar. Fame asperses Edric, as having, through regard for Canute, compassed his death by means of his servants: reporting that there were two attendants on the king to whom he had committed the entire care of his person, and, that Edric seducing them by promises, at length made them his accomplices, though at first they were struck with horror at the enormity of the crime; and that, at his suggestion, they drove an iron hook into his posteriors, as he was sitting down for a necessary

---

* Henry Huntingdon says they actually engaged, and that Canute finding himself likely to be worsted, proposed the division.—H. Hunt l. 6

† "Florence of Worcester and the Saxon Chronicle place his death on the 30th of November, 1016. Florence, however, adds the year of the indiction, which corresponds with A.D. 1017."—HARDY.

purpose. Edwin, his brother on the mother's side, a youth of amiable disposition, was driven from England by Edric, at the command of Canute, and suffering extremely for a considerable time, "both by sea and land," his body, as is often the case, became affected by the anxiety of his mind, and he died in England, where he lay concealed after a clandestine return, and lies buried at Tavistock. His sons, Edwy and Edward, were sent to the king of Sweden to be put to death; but being preserved by his mercy, they went to the king of Hungary, where, after being kindly treated for a time, the elder died; and the younger married Agatha, the sister of the queen. His brothers by Emma, Alfred and Edward, lay securely concealed in Normandy for the whole time that Canute lived.

I find that their uncle Richard took no steps to restore them to their country: on the contrary, he married his sister Emma to the enemy and invader; and it may be difficult to say, whether to the greater ignominy of him who bestowed her, or of the woman who consented to share the nuptial couch of that man who had so cruelly molested her husband, and had driven her children into exile. Robert, however, whom we have so frequently before mentioned as having gone to Jerusalem, assembling a fleet and embarking soldiers, made ready an expedition, boasting that he would set the crown on the heads of his grand-nephews; and doubtlessly he would have made good his assertion, had not, as we have heard from our ancestors, an adverse wind constantly opposed him: but assuredly this was by the hidden counsel of God, in whose disposal are the powers of all kingdoms. The remains of the vessels, decayed through length of time, were still to be seen at Rouen in our days.

CHAP. XL

Of king Canute. [A.D. 1017—1031.]

CANUTE began to reign in the year of our Lord 1017, and reigned twenty years. Though he obtained the sovereignty unjustly, yet he conducted himself with great affability and firmness. At his entrance on the government, dividing the kingdom into four parts, himself took the West Saxons, Edric the Mercians, Thurkill the East Angles, and Eric the Northumbrians. His first care was to punish the murderers of Edmund, who had, under expectation of great recompence, acknowledged the whole circumstances: he concealed them for a time, and then brought them forward in a large assembly of the people, where they confessed the mode of their attack upon him, and were immediately ordered to execution. The same year, Edric, whom words are wanting to stigmatize as he deserved, being, by the king's command, entrapped in the same snare which he had so frequently laid for others, breathed out his abominable spirit to hell. For a quarrel arising, while they were angrily discoursing, Edric, relying on the credit of his services, and amicably, as it were, reproaching the king, said, "I first deserted Edmund for your sake, and afterwards even despatched him in consequence of my engagements to you." At this expression the countenance of Canute changed with indignation, and he instantly pronounced this sentence: "Thou shalt die," said he, "and justly; since thou art guilty of treason both to God and me, by having killed thy own sovereign, and my sworn brother; thy blood be upon thy head, because thy mouth hath spoken against thee, and thou hast lifted thy hand against the Lord's anointed." and immediately, that no tumult might be excited, the traitor was strangled in the chamber where they sat, and thrown out of the window into the river Thames: thus meeting the just reward of his perfidy. In process of time, as opportunities occurred, Thurkill and Eric were driven out of the kingdom, and sought their native land. The first, who had been the instigator of the murder of St. Elphege, was killed by the chiefs the moment he touched the Danish shore * When all England, by these means, became subject to Canute alone, he began to conciliate the Angles with unceasing diligence; allowing them equal rights with the Danes, in their assemblies, councils, and armies: on which account, as I have before observed, he sent for the wife of the late king out of Normandy, that, while they were paying obedience to their accustomed sovereign, they should the less repine at the dominion of the Danes. Another design he had in view by this, was, to acquire favour with Richard; who would think

* The Danish chiefs were apprehensive that he would excite commotions in their country; in consequence of which he was ultimately despatched.—Ang. Sac. ii. 144.

little of his nephews, so long as he supposed he might have others by Canute. He repaired, throughout England, the monasteries, which had been partly injured, and partly destroyed by the military incursions of himself, or of his father; he built churches in all the places where he had fought, and more particularly at Assingdon, and appointed ministers to them, who, through the succeeding revolutions of ages, might pray to God for the souls of the persons there slain. At the consecration of this edifice, himself was present, and the English and Danish nobility made their offerings · it is now, according to report, an ordinary church, under the care of a parish priest. Over the body of the most holy Edmund, whom the Danes of former times had killed, he built a church with princely magnificence, appointed to it an abbat, and monks: and conferred on it many large estates. The greatness of his donation, yet entire, stands proudly eminent at the present day; for that place surpasses almost all the monasteries of England. He took up, with his own hands, the body of St. Elphege, which had been buried at St. Paul's in London, and sending it to Canterbury, honoured it with due regard. Thus anxious to atone for the offences of himself or of his predecessors, perhaps he wiped away the foul stain of his former crimes with God: certainly he did so with man. At Winchester, he displayed all the magnificence of his liberality: here he gave so largely, that the quantity of precious metals astonished the minds of strangers; and the glittering of jewels dazzled the eyes of the beholders: this was at Emma's suggestion, who with pious prodigality exhausted his treasures in works of this kind, while he was meditating fierce attacks on foreign lands. For his valour, incapable of rest, and not contented with Denmark, which he held from his father, and England, which he possessed by right of war, transferred its rage against the Swedes. These people are contiguous to the Danes, and had excited the displeasure of Canute by their ceaseless hostility. At first he fell into an ambush, and lost many of his people, but afterwards recruiting his strength, he routed his opponents, and brought the kings of that nation, Ulf and Eglaf, to terms of peace. The English, at the instance of earl Godwin, behaved nobly in this conflict. He exhorted them, not to forget their ancient fame, but clearly to display their valour to their new lord:

telling them, that it must be imputed to fortune, that they had formerly been conquered by him, but it would be ascribed to their courage, if they overcame those who had overcome him. In consequence, the English put forth all their strength, and gaining the victory, obtained an earldom for their commander, and honour for themselves. Thence, on his return home, he entirely subdued the kingdom of Norway, putting Olave, its king, to flight; who, the year following, returning with a small party into his kingdom, to try the inclinations of the inhabitants, found them faithless, and was slain with his adherents.

In the fifteenth year of his reign, Canute went to Rome, and after remaining there some time, and atoning for his crimes by giving alms to the several churches, he sailed back to England.* Soon after, with little difficulty, he subdued Scotland, then in a state of rebellion, and Malcolm her king, by leading an army thither. I trust it will not appear useless, if I subjoin the epistle, which he transmitted to the English, on his departure from Rome, by the hands of Living, abbat of Tavistock, and afterwards bishop of Crediton, to exemplify his reformation of life, and his princely magnificence.

"*Canute, king of all England, Denmark, Norway, and part of the Swedes, to Ethelnoth, metropolitan, and Elfric archbishop of York, and to all bishops, nobles, and to the whole nation of the English high and low, health.* I notify to you, that I have lately been to Rome, to pray for the forgiveness of my sins; for the safety of my dominions, and of the people under my government. I had long since vowed such a journey to God, but, hitherto hindered by the affairs of my kingdom, and other causes preventing, I was unable to accomplish it sooner. I now return thanks most humbly to my Almighty God, for suffering me, in my lifetime, to approach the holy apostles Peter and Paul, and all the holy saints within and without the city of Rome, wherever I could discover them, and there, present, to worship and adore according to my desire. I have been the more diligent in the performance of this, because I have learned from the wise, that St. Peter, the apostle, has received from God, great power in binding and in loosing: that he carries the key of the kingdom of heaven; and consequently I have judged

* He returned by the way of Denmark. Florence of Worcester.

it matter of special importance to seek his influence with God. Be it known to you, that at the solemnity of Easter, a great assembly of nobles was present with pope John, and the emperor Conrad, that is to say, all the princes of the nations from mount Garganus* to the neighbouring sea. All these received me with honour, and presented me with magnificent gifts. But more especially was I honoured by the emperor, with various gifts and offerings, in gold and silver vessels, and palls and costly garments. Moreover, I spoke with the emperor himself, and the sovereign pope and the nobles who were there, concerning the wants of all my people, English as well as Danes; observing that there ought to be granted to them more equitable regulations, and greater security on their passage to Rome; that they should not be impeded by so many barriers† on the road, nor harassed with unjust exactions. The emperor assented to my request, as did Rodolph the king, who has the chief dominion over those barriers; and all the princes confirmed by an edict, that my subjects, traders, as well as those who went on a religious account, should peaceably go and return from Rome, without any molestation from warders of barriers, or tax-gatherers. Again I complained before the pope, and expressed my high displeasure, that my archbishops were oppressed by the immense sum of money which is demanded from them when seeking, according to custom, the apostolical residence to receive the pall: and it was determined that it should be so no longer. Moreover, all things which I requested for the advantage of my kingdom, from the sovereign pope, and the emperor, and king Rodolph, and the other princes, through whose territories our road to Rome is situated, they have freely granted, and confirmed by oath, under the attestation of four archbishops, and twenty bishops, and an innumerable multitude of dukes and nobles who were present. Wherefore I give most hearty thanks to God Almighty, for having successfully completed all that I had wished, in the manner I had designed, and fully satisfied my intentions. Be it known then, that since I have vowed to God himself, henceforward to reform my life in all things,

---

* St. Angelo in Calabria.

† The several princes, through whose territories their passage lay, exacted large sums for permission to pass; apparently in the defiles of the Alps.

and justly, and piously to govern the kingdoms and the people subject to me, and to maintain equal justice in all things, and have determined, through God's assistance, to rectify any thing hitherto unjustly done, either through the intemperance of my youth, or through negligence; therefore I call to witness, and command my counsellors, to whom I have entrusted the counsels of the kingdom, that they by no means, either through fear of myself, or favour to any powerful person, suffer, henceforth, any injustice, or cause such, to be done in all my kingdom. Moreover, I command all sheriffs, or governors throughout my whole kingdom, as they tender my affection, or their own safety, not to commit injustice towards any man, rich or poor, but to allow all, noble and ignoble, alike to enjoy impartial law, from which they are never to deviate, either on account of royal favour, the person of any powerful man, or for the sake of amassing money for myself: for I have no need to accumulate money by unjust exaction. Be it known to you therefore, that returning by the same way that I went, I am now going to Denmark, through the advice of all the Danes, to make peace and firm treaty with those nations, who were desirous, had it been possible, to deprive me both of life and of sovereignty: this, however, they were not able to perform, God, who by his kindness preserves me in my kingdom and in my honour, and destroys the power of all my adversaries, bringing their strength to nought. Moreover, when I have established peace with the surrounding nations, and put all our sovereignty here in the East in tranquil order, so that there shall be no fear of war or enmity on any side, I intend coming to England, as early in the summer as I shall be able to get my fleet prepared. I have sent this epistle before me, in order that my people may rejoice at my prosperity; because, as yourselves know, I have never spared, nor will I spare, either myself or my pains for the needful service of my whole people. I now therefore adjure all my bishops, and governors, throughout my kingdom, by the fidelity they owe to God and me, to take care that, before I come to England, all dues owing by ancient custom be discharged: that is to say, plough-alms,* the tenth of animals born in the

---

* A penny for every plough, that is, for as much land as a plough could

current year,* and the pence owing to Rome for St. Peter, whether from cities or villages: and in the middle of August, the tenth of the produce of the earth: and on the festival of St. Martin, the first fruits of seeds, to the church of the parish where each one resides, which is called in English 'Circscet.'† If these and such like things are not paid before I come to England, all who shall have offended will incur the penalty of a royal mulct,‡ to be exacted without remission, according to law." Nor was this declaration without effect; for he commanded all the laws which had been enacted by ancient kings, and chiefly by his predecessor Ethelred, to be observed for ever, under the penalty of a royal mulct: in the observance of which,§ the custom even at the present day, in the time of good kings, is to swear by the name of king Edward, not that he indeed appointed, but that he observed them.

At that time there were in England very great and learned men, the principal of whom was Ethelnoth, archbishop after Living. He was appointed primate from being dean,‖ and performed many works truly worthy to be recorded: encouraging even the king himself in his good actions by the authority of his sanctity, and restraining him in his excesses: he first exalted the archiepiscopal cathedral by the presence of the body of St. Elphege, and afterwards personally at Rome, restored it to its pristine dignity.¶ Returning home, he transmitted to Coventry the arm of St. Augustine** the teacher, which he had purchased at Pavia, for an hundred talents of silver, and a talent of gold. Moreover, Canute took a journey to the church of Glastonbury, that he might visit the remains of his brother Edmund, as he used to call

till, to be distributed to the poor: it was payable in fifteen days from Easter. * Payable at Whitsuntide.

† A certain quantity of corn. Though it also implies, occasionally, other kinds of offerings.

‡ A forfeiture to the king, but varying according to the nature of the offence.

§ This seems to be the meaning: he has probably in view the practice of the early princes of the Norman line, who swore to observe the laws of king Edward ‖ Dean of Canterbury.

¶ This appears merely intended to express that he received the pall from the pope. The two transactions are inverted; he went to Rome A.D. 1021, and translated Elphege's body A.D. 1023.

** Augustine, bishop of Hippo.

him; and praying over his tomb, he presented a pall, interwoven, as it appeared, with party-coloured figures of peacocks. Near the king stood the before-named Ethelnoth, who was the seventh monk of Glastonbury that had become archbishop of Canterbury: first Berthwald: second Athelm, first bishop of Wells: third his nephew Dunstan: fourth Ethelgar, first abbat of the New-minster at Winchester, and then bishop of Chichester:* fifth Siric, who, when he was made archbishop, gave to this his nursing-mother seven palls, with which, upon his anniversary, the whole ancient church is ornamented: sixth Elphege, who from prior of Glastonbury was, first, made abbat of Bath, and then bishop of Winchester: seventh Ethelnoth, who upon showing to the king the immunities of predecessors, asked, and obtained from the king's own hand a confirmation of them, which was to the following effect.

"The Lord reigning for evermore, who disposes and governs all things by his unspeakable power, who wonderfully determines the changes of times and of men, and justly brings them to an uncertain end, according to his pleasure; and who from the secret mysteries of nature mercifully teaches us, how lasting, instead of fleeting and transitory, kingdoms are to be obtained by the assistance of God: wherefore I Canute king of England, and governor and ruler of the adjacent nations, by the counsel and decree of our archbishop Ethelnoth, and of all the priests of God, and by the advice of our nobility, do, for the love of heaven, and the pardon of my sins, and the remission of the transgressions of my brother, king Edmund, grant to the church of the holy mother of God, Mary, at Glastonbury, its rights and customs throughout my kingdom, and all forfeitures throughout its possessions, and that its lands shall be free from all claim and vexation as my own are. Moreover, I inhibit more especially, by the authority of the Almighty Father, Son, and Holy Spirit, and the curse of the eternal Virgin, and so command it to be observed by the judges and primates of my kingdom as they tender their safety, every person, be they of what order or dignity they may, from entering, on

* He was bishop of Selsey, which see was afterwards removed to Chichester.

any account, that island;* but all causes, ecclesiastical as well as secular, shall await the sole judgment of the abbat and convent, in like manner as my predecessors have ratified and confirmed by charters; that is to say, Kentwin, Ina, Cuthred, Alfred, Edward, Ethelred, Athelstan, the most glorious Edmund, and the equally glorious Edgar. And should any one hereafter endeavour, on any occasion, to break in upon, or make void the enactment of this grant, let him be driven from the communion of the righteous by the fan of the last judgment; but should any person endeavour diligently, with benevolent intention, to perform these things, to approve, and defend them, may God increase his portion in the land of the living, through the intercession of the most holy mother of God, Mary, and the rest of the saints. The grant of this immunity was written and published in the Wooden Church, in the presence of king Canute, in the year of our Lord 1032, the second indiction."

By the advice of the said archbishop also, the king, sending money to foreign churches, very much enriched Chartres, where at that time flourished bishop Fulbert, most renowned for sanctity and learning. Who, among other demonstrations of his diligence, very magnificently completed the church of our lady St. Mary, the foundations of which he had laid: and which moreover, in his zeal to do every thing he could for its honour, he rendered celebrated by many musical modulations. The man who has heard his chants, breathing only celestial vows, is best able to conceive the love he manifested in honour of the Virgin. Among his other works, a volume of epistles is extant; in one of which,† he thanks that most magnificent king Canute, for pouring out the bowels of his generosity in donations to the church of Chartres.

In the fifteenth year of Canute's reign, Robert king of France, of whom we have before briefly spoken, departed this life: a man so much given to alms, that when, on festival days, he was either dressing, or putting off the royal robes, if he had nothing else at hand, he would give even

* The whole country round Glastonbury is flat and marshy, bearing evident marks of having formerly been covered by water.

† "See the letter of Fulbert to king Canute (an. 1020 aut 1021.) No. xliv, p. 466. tom. x. Rec des Hist. de la France Fulberti Carnot. Episc. Op. Var. 8vo. par. 1608 Epist xcvii. p. 92."—HARDY.

these to the poor, if his attendants did not purposely drive away the needy who were importuning him. He had two sons, Odo, and Henry: the elder, Odo,* was dull: the other crafty and impetuous. Each parent had severally divided their affections on their children: the father loved the firstborn, often saying that he should succeed him: the mother regarded the younger, to whom the sovereignty was justly due, if not for his age, yet certainly for his ability. It happened, as women are persevering in their designs, that she did not cease until, by means of presents, and large promises, she had gotten to her side all the chief nobility who are subject to the power of France. In consequence, Henry, chiefly through the asssistance of Robert the Norman, was crowned ere his father had well breathed his last. Mindful of this kindness, when, as I before related, Robert went to Jerusalem, Henry most strenuously espoused the cause of William, his son, then a youth, against those who attempted to throw off his yoke. In the meantime Canute, finishing his earthly career, died at Shaftesbury, and was buried at Winchester.

CHAP. XII.

Of king Harold and Hardecanute. [A.D 1036—1042.]

In the year of our Lord's incarnation 1036,† Harold, whom fame ‡ reported to be the son of Canute, by the daughter of earl Elfelm, succeeded, and reigned four years and as many months. He was elected by the Danes and the citizens of London, who, from long intercourse with these barbarians, had almost entirely adopted their customs. The English resisted for a long time, rather wishing to have one of the sons of Ethelred, who were then in Normandy, or else Hardecanute, the son of Canute by Emma, at that time in Den-

* Though several French chronicles give nearly the same account of Odo being the elder brother, the learned editors of the Recueil des Historiens de France insist that the assertion is false.

† "After the death of Canute, the kingdom was at first divided: the northern part fell to the share of Harold, and Hardecanute obtained the southern division. In the year 1037, Harold was chosen to reign over all England, (Flor Wigorn.)"—Hardy.

‡ This he notices, because there was a suspicion that she had imposed the children of a priest and of a cobbler on Canute as her own. V. Flor. Wigorn.

mark, for their king. The greatest stickler for justice, at this juncture, was earl Godwin; who professing himself the defender of the fatherless, and having queen Emma and the royal treasures in his custody, for some time restrained his opponents by the power of his name: but at last, overcome by numbers and by violence, he was obliged to give way. Harold, secure in his sovereignty, drove his mother-in-law into exile. Not thinking she should be safe in Normandy, where, her brother and nephews being dead, disgust at the rule of a deserted orphan created great disorders, she passed over into Flanders, to earl Baldwin, a man of tried integrity: who afterwards, when king Henry died leaving a young son, Philip, for some years nobly governed the kingdom of France, and faithfully restored it to him, for he had married his aunt, when he came of age. Emma passed three years securely under the protection of this man, at the expiration of which, Harold dying at Oxford, in the month of April,* was buried at Westminster. The Danes and the English then uniting in one common sentiment of sending for Hardecanute, he came, by way of Normandy, into England in the month of August. For Ethelred's sons were held in contempt nearly by all, more from the recollection of their father's indolence, than the power of the Danes. Hardecanute, reigning two years except ten days, lost his life amid his cups at Lambeth nigh London, and was buried near his father at Winchester: a young man who evinced great affection towards his brother and sister. For his brother, Edward, wearied with continual wandering, revisiting his native land in the hope of fraternal kindness, was received by him with open arms, and entertained most affectionately. He was rash, however, in other respects, and at the instigation of Elfric, archbishop of York, and of others whom I am loath to name, he ordered the dead body of Harold to be dug up, the head to be cut off, and thrown into the Thames, a pitiable spectacle to men! but it was dragged up again in a fisherman's net, and buried in the cemetery of the Danes at London. He imposed a rigid, and intolerable tribute upon England, in order that he might pay, according to his promise, twenty marks to the soldiers

* The Saxon Chronicle says March 17: it also makes Hardecanute arrive on the 18th of June.

of each of his vessels. While this was harshly levied throughout the kingdom, two of the collectors, discharging their office rather too rigorously, were killed by the citizens of Worcester; upon which, burning and depopulating the city by means of his commanders, and plundering the property of the citizens, he cast a blemish on his fame and diminished the love of his subjects. But here I will not pass over in silence, what tattlers report of Alfred the firstborn of Ethelred. Doubtful what to do between Harold's death and the arrival of Hardecanute, he came into the kingdom, and was deprived of his eyes by the treachery of his countrymen, and chiefly of Godwin, at Gillingham: from thence being sent to the monastery of Ely, he supported, for a little time, a wretched subsistence upon homely food; all his companions, with the exception of the tenth, being beheaded: for by lot every tenth man was saved.* I have mentioned these circumstances, because such is the report; but as the Chronicles are silent, I do not assert them for fact. For this reason, Hardecanute, enraged against Living, bishop of Crediton, whom public opinion pointed out as author of the transaction, expelled him from his see: but, soothed with money, he restored him within the year. Looking angrily too upon Godwin, he obliged him to clear himself by oath; but he, to recover his favour entirely, added to his plighted oath a present of the most rich and beautiful kind; it was a ship beaked with gold, having eighty soldiers on board, who had two bracelets on either arm, each weighing sixteen ounces of gold; on their heads were gilt helmets; on their left shoulder they carried a Danish axe, with an iron spear in their right hand; and, not to enumerate everything, they were equipped with such arms, as that splendour vying with terror, might conceal the steel beneath the gold. But farther, as I had begun to relate, his sister Gunhilda, the daughter of Canute by Emma, a young woman of exquisite beauty, who was sighed for, but not obtained, by many lovers in her father's time, was by Hardecanute given in marriage to Henry, emperor of the

* The printed Saxon Chronicle has no mention of this transaction, but there are two manuscripts which relate it. The story appears true in the main, but it is told with so much variety of time, place, &c., that it is difficult to ascertain its real circumstances. See MSS. Cott. Tib. b 1. and iv.

Germans. The splendour of the nuptial pageant was very striking, and is even in our times frequently sung in ballads about the streets: where while this renowned lady was being conducted to the ship, all the nobility of England were crowding around and contributing to her charges whatever was contained in the general purse, or royal treasury. Proceeding in this manner to her husband, she cherished for a long time the conjugal tie; at length being accused of adultery, she opposed in single combat to her accuser, a man of gigantic size, a young lad of her brother's[*] establishment, whom she had brought from England, while her other attendants held back in cowardly apprehension. When, therefore, they engaged, the impeacher, through the miraculous interposition of God, was worsted, by being ham-strung. Gunhilda, exulting at her unexpected success, renounced the marriage contract with her husband; nor could she be induced either by threats or by endearments again to share his bed: but taking the veil of a nun, she calmly grew old in the service of God.

This emperor possessed many and great virtues; and nearly surpassed in military skill all his predecessors: so much so, that he subdued the Vindelici and the Leutici,[†] and the other nations bordering on the Suevi, who alone, even to the present day, lust after pagan superstitions: for the Saracens and Turks worship God the Creator, looking upon Mahomet not as God, but as his prophet. But the Vindelici worship fortune, and putting her idol in the most eminent situation, they place a horn in her right hand, filled with that beverage, made of honey and water, which by a Greek term we call "hydromel." St. Jerome proves, in his eighteenth book on Isaiah, that the Egyptians and almost all the eastern nations do the same. Wherefore on the last day of November, sitting round in a circle, they all taste it; and if they find the horn full, they applaud with loud clamours: because in the ensuing year, plenty with her

[*] It seems to mean a page, or personal attendant: some MSS. read "alumnus sturni," apparently the keeper of her starling. There appears to have been a sort of romance on this subject. The youth is said to have been a dwarf, and therefore named Mimicon: his gigantic adversary was Roddingar. V. Matt. West. and Joh. Brompton.

[†] These people inhabited the country on and near the southern coast of the Baltic.

brimming horn will fulfil their wishes in everything: but if it be otherwise, they lament. Henry made these nations in such wise tributary to him, that upon every solemnity on which he wore his crown, four of their kings were obliged to carry a cauldron in which flesh was boiled, upon their shoulders, to the kitchen, by means of levers passed through rings.

Frequently, when disengaged from the turmoils of his empire, Henry gave himself up to good fellowship and merriment, and was replete with humour; this may be sufficiently proved by two instances. He was so extremely fond of his sister, who was a nun, that he never suffered her to be from his side, and her chamber was always next his own. As he was on a certain time, in consequence of a winter remarkable for severe frost and snow, detained for a long while in the same place, a certain clerk * about the court, became too familiar with the girl, and often passed the greatest part of the night in her chamber. And although he attempted to conceal his crime by numberless subterfuges, yet some one perceived it, for it is difficult not to betray guilt either by look or action, and the affair becoming notorious, the emperor was the only person in ignorance, and who still believed his sister to be chaste. On one particular night, however, as they were enjoying their fond embraces, and continuing their pleasures longer than usual, the morning dawned upon them, and behold snow had completely covered the ground. The clerk fearing that he should be discovered by his track in the snow, persuades his mistress to extricate him from his difficulty by carrying him on her back. She, regardless of modesty so that she might escape exposure, took her paramour on her back, and carried him out of the palace. It happened at that moment, that the emperor had risen for a necessary purpose, and looking through the window of his chamber, beheld the clerk mounted. He was stupified at the first sight, but observing still more narrowly, he became mute with shame and indignation. While he was hesitating whether he should pass over the crime unpunished,

* Clerk was a general term including every degree of orders, from the bishop downwards to the chanter. A story near similar has been told of the celebrated Eginhard and the daughter of Charlemagne. V. Du Chesne, Script. Franc. T. ii.

or openly reprehend the delinquents, there happened an opportunity for him to give a vacant bishopric to the clerk, which he did: but at the same time whispered in his ear, "Take the bishopric, but be careful you do not let women carry you any more." At the same time he gave his sister the rule over a company of nuns, "Be an abbess," said he, "but carry clerks no longer." Both of them were confused, and feeling themselves grievously stricken by so grave an injunction, they desisted from a crime which they thought revealed by God.

He had also a clergyman about his palace, who abused the depth of his learning and the melody of his voice by the vicious propensities of the flesh, being extremely attached to a girl of bad character, in the town; with whom having passed one festival night, he stood next morning before the emperor at mass, with countenance unabashed. The emperor concealing his knowledge of the transaction, commanded him to prepare himself to read the gospel, that he might be gratified with the melody of his voice: for he was a deacon. Conscious of his crime, he made use of a multitude of subterfuges, while the emperor, to try his constancy, still pressed him with messages. Refusing, however, to the very last, the emperor said, "Since you will not obey me in so easy a command, I banish you from the whole of my territories." The deacon, yielding to the sentence, departed directly. Servants were sent to follow him, and in case he should persist in going, to bring him back after he had left the city. Gathering, therefore, immediately all his effects together, and packing them up, he had already gone a considerable distance, when he was brought back, not without extreme violence, and placed in the presence of Henry, who smiled and said · "You have done well, and I applaud your integrity for valuing the fear of God more than your country, and regarding the displeasure of heaven more than my threats. Accept, therefore, the first bishopric, which shall be vacant in my empire; only renounce your dishonourable amour."

As nothing however is lasting in human enjoyments, I shall not pass over in silence a certain dreadful portent which happened in his time. The monastery of Fulda, in Saxony, is celebrated for containing the body of St. Gall, and is enriched with very ample territories. The abbat of this place furnishes the emperor with sixty thousand warriors against his enemies; and possesses from ancient times the privilege of sitting at his right hand on the most distinguished festivals. This Henry we are speaking of was celebrating Pentecost at Mentz. A little before mass, while the seats were preparing in the church, a quarrel arose between the attendants of the abbat, and those of the archbishop, which of their masters should sit next the sovereign: one party alleging the dignity of the prelate, the other ancient usage. When words made but little for peace, as the Germans and Teutonians possess untractable spirits, they came to blows. Some snatched up staves, others threw stones, while the rest unsheathed their swords: finally each used the weapon that his anger first supplied. Thus furiously contending in the church, the pavement soon streamed with blood: but the bishops hastening forward, peace was restored amid the remains of the contending parties. The church was cleansed, and mass performed with joyful sound. But now comes the wonder: when the sequence was chanted, and the choir paused at that verse, "Thou hast made this day glorious:" a voice in the air replied aloud, "I have made this day contentious." All the others were motionless with horror, but the emperor the more diligently attended to his occupation, and perceiving the satisfaction of the enemy: "You," said he, "the inventor and also the instigator of all wickedness, have made this day contentious and sorrowful to the proud; but we, by the grace of God, who made it glorious, will make it gracious to the poor." Beginning the sequence afresh, they implored the grace of the Holy Spirit by solemn lamentation. You might suppose he had come upon them, for some were singing, others weeping, and all beating their breasts. When mass was over, assembling the poor by means of his officers, he gave them the whole of the entertainment which had been prepared for himself and his courtiers: the emperor placing the dishes before them, standing at a distance according to the custom of servants, and clearing away the fragments.

In the time of his father, Conrad, he had received a silver pipe, such as boys in sport spirt water with, from a certain clerk, covenanting to give him a bishopric, when he should become emperor. This, when he was of man's estate, on his application he readily gave to him. Soon after he was confined to his bed with severe sickness: his malady increasing, he lay for three days insensible and speechless, while the vital breath only palpitated in his breast: nor was there any other sign of life, than the perception of a small degree of breathing, on applying the hand to his nostrils. The bishops being present, enjoined a fast for three days, and entreated heaven with tears and vows, for the life of the king. Recovering by these remedies, as it is right to think, he sent for the bishop whom he had so improperly appointed, and deposed him by the judgment of a council: confessing, that for three whole days he saw malignant demons blowing fire upon him through a pipe; fire so furious that ours in comparison would be deemed a jest, and have no heat: that afterwards there came a young man half scorched, bearing a golden cup of immense size, full of water; and that being soothed by the sight of him, and bathed by the water, the flame was extinguished, and he recovered his health: that this young man was St. Laurence, the roof of whose church he had restored when gone to decay; and, among other presents, had honoured it with a golden chalice.

Here many extraordinary things occur, which are reported of this man; for instance, of a stag, which took him on its back, when flying from his enemies, and carried him over an unfordable river: and some others which I pass by because I am unwilling to go beyond the reader's belief. He died when he had completed the eighteenth year of his empire, and was buried at Spires, which he re-built, and called by that name, on the site of the very ancient and ruined Nemetum: his epitaph is as follows:

> Cæsar, as was the world once great,
> Lies here, confin'd in compass straight
> Hence let each mortal learn his doom;
> No glory can escape the tomb.
> The flower of empire, erst so gay,
> Falls with its Cæsar to decay,
> And all the odours which it gave
> Sink prematurely to the grave
> The laws which sapient fathers made,
> A listless race had dared evade,
> But thou reforming by the school
> Of Rome, restor'dst the ancient rule.

> Nations and regions, wide and far,
> Whom none could subjugate by war,
> Quell'd by thy sword's resistless strife,
> Turn'd to the arts of civil life.
> What grief severe must Rome engross,
> Widow'd at first by Leo's loss,
> And next by Cæsar's mournful night,
> Reft of her other shining light;
> Living, what region did not dread,
> What country not lament thee, dead?
> So kind to nations once subdued,
> So fierce to the barbarians rude,
> That, those who fear'd not, must bewail,
> And such as griev'd not, fears assail.
> Rome, thy departed glory moan,
> And weep thy luminaries gone.

This Leo, of whom the epitaph speaks, had been Roman pontiff, called to that eminence from being Bruno bishop of Spires. He was a man of great and admirable sanctity; and the Romans celebrate many of his miracles. He died before Henry, when he had been five years pope.

CHAP. XIII.

Of St. Edward, son of king Ethelred. [A.D. 1042—1066.]

In the year of our Lord's incarnation 1042, St. Edward, the son of Ethelred, assumed the sovereignty, and held it not quite twenty-four years; he was a man from the simplicity of his manners little calculated to govern; but devoted to God, and in consequence directed by him. For while he continued to reign, there arose no popular commotions, which were not immediately quelled; no foreign war; all was calm and peaceable both at home and abroad; which is the more an object of wonder, because he conducted himself so mildly, that he would not even utter a word of reproach to the meanest person. For when he had once gone out to hunt, and a countryman had overturned the standings by which the deer are driven into the toils, struck with noble indignation he exclaimed, "By God and his mother, I will serve you just such a turn, if ever it come in my way." Here was a noble mind, who forgot that he was a king, under such circumstances, and could not think himself allowed to injure a man even of the lowest condition. In the meantime, the regard his subjects entertained for him was extreme, as was also the fear of foreigners; for God assisted his simplicity, that he might be feared, for he knew not how to be angry. But however indolent or unassuming himself might be esteemed, he had nobles capable of elevating him to the highest pitch: for instance, Siward, earl of the Northumbrians; who, at his command, engaging with Macbeth, the Scottish king, deprived him both of life and of his kingdom, and placed on the throne Malcolm, who was the son of the king of Cumbria:* again, Leofric, of Hereford; he, with liberal regard, defended him against the enmity of Godwin, who trusting to the consciousness of his own merits, paid little reverence to the king. Leofric and his wife Godifa, generous in their deeds towards God, built many monasteries, as, Coventry, St. Mary's at Stow, Wenlock, Leon, and some others; to the rest he gave ornaments and estates; to Coventry he consigned his body, with a very large donation of gold and silver. Harold too, of the West Saxons, the son of Godwin; who by his abilities destroyed two brothers, kings of the Welsh, Rees and Griffin; and reduced all that barbarous country to the state of a province under fealty to the king. Nevertheless, there were some things which obscured the glory of Edward's times: the monasteries were deprived of their monks, false sentences were passed by depraved men; his mother's property, at his command, was almost entirely taken from her. But the injustice of these transactions was extenuated by his favourers in the following manner: the ruin of the monasteries, and the iniquity of the judges, are said to have taken place without his knowledge, through the insolence of Godwin and his sons, who used to laugh at the easiness of the king: but afterwards, on being apprised of this, he severely avenged it by their banishment. his mother had for a long time mocked at the needy state of her son, nor ever assisted him; transferring her hereditary hatred of the father to the child; for she had both loved Canute more when living, and more commended him when dead: besides, accumulating money by every method, she had hoarded it, regardless of the poor, to whom she would give nothing, for fear of diminishing her heap. Wherefore that which had

* This brief allusion to Macbeth rather disproves the historical accuracy of Shakespere. See the Saxon Chronicle.

been so unjustly gathered together, was not improperly taken away, that it might be of service to the poor, and replenish the king's exchequer. Though much credit is to be attached to those who relate these circumstances, yet I find her to have been a religiously-disposed woman, and to have expended her property on ornaments for the church of Winchester, and probably upon others.* But to return : Edward receiving the mournful intelligence of the death of Hardecanute, was lost in uncertainty what to do, or whither to betake himself. While he was revolving many things in his mind, it occurred as the better plan to submit his situation to the opinion of Godwin. To Godwin therefore he sent messengers, requesting, that he might in security have a conference with him. Godwin, though for a long time hesitating and reflecting, at length assented, and when Edward came to him and endeavoured to fall at his feet, he raised him up ; and when relating the death of Hardecanute, and begging his assistance to effect his return to Normandy, Godwin made him the greatest promises. He said, it was better for him to live with credit in power, than to die ingloriously in exile : that he was the son of Ethelred, the grandson of Edgar : that the kingdom was his due : that he was come to mature age, disciplined by difficulties, conversant in the art of well-governing from his years, and knowing, from his former poverty, how to feel for the miseries of the people : if he thought fit to rely on him, there could be no obstacle ; for his authority so preponderated in England, that wherever he inclined, there fortune was sure to favour : if he assisted him, none would dare to murmur ; and just so was the contrary side of the question : let him then only covenant a firm friendship with himself ; undiminished honours for his sons, and a marriage with his daughter, and he who was now shipwrecked almost of life and hope, and imploring the assistance of another, should shortly see himself a king.

There was nothing which Edward would not promise, from the exigency of the moment : so, pledging fidelity on both sides, he confirmed by oath every thing which was demanded. Soon after convening an assembly at Gillingham, Godwin,

* This seems the foundation of the fable of Emma and the Ploughshares : as the first apparent promulgator of it was a constant reader and amplifier of Malmesbury. See Ric. Divisiensis, MS. C. C. C. Cant. No. 339

unfolding his reasons, caused him to be received as king, and homage was paid to him by all. He was a man of ready wit, and spoke fluently in the vernacular tongue; poweiful in speech, powerful in bringing over the people to whatever he desired. Some yielded to his authority; some were influenced by presents; others admitted the right of Edward; and the few who resisted in defiance of justice and equity, were carefully marked, and afterwaids driven out of England.

Edward was crowned with great pomp at Winchester, on Easter-day, and was instructed by Eadsine,* the archbishop, in the sacred duties of governing. This, at the time, he treasured up with readiness in his memory, and afterwards displayed in the holiness of his conduct. The above-mentioned Eadsine, in the following year, falling into an incurable disease, appointed as his successor Siward, abbat of Abingdon; communicating his design only to the king and the earl, lest any improper person should aspire to so great an eminence, either by solicitation or by purchase. Shortly after the king took Edgitha. the daughter of Godwin, to wife; a woman whose bosom was the school of every liberal art, though little skilled in earthly matters: on seeing her, if you were amazed at her erudition, you must absolutely languish for the purity of her mind, and the beauty of her person. Both in her husband's life-time, and afterwards, she was not entirely free from suspicion of dishonour; but when dying, in the time of king William, she voluntarily satisfied the by-standers of her unimpaired chastity, by an oath. When she became his wife, the king acted towards her so delicately, that he neither removed her from his bed, nor knew her after the manner of men. I have not been able to discover, whether he acted thus from dislike to her family, which he prudently dissembled from the exigency of the times, or out of pure regard to chastity: yet it is most notoriously affirmed, that he never violated his purity by connexion with any woman.

But since I have gotten thus far, I wish to admonish my reader, that the track of my history is here but dubious,

* " Eadsine was translated from Winchester to Canterbury in 1038. The Saxon Chronicle (p. 416) states, that he consecrated Edward, at Winchester, on Easter day, and before all people well admonished him "—HARDY.

because the truth of the facts hangs in suspense. It is to be observed, that the king had sent for several Normans, who had formerly slightly ministered to his wants when in exile. Among these was Robert, whom, from being a monk of Jumièges, he had appointed bishop of London, and afterwards archbishop of Canterbury. The English of our times vilify this person, together with the rest, as being the impeacher of Godwin and his sons; the sower of discord; the purchaser of the archbishopric: they say too, that Godwin and his sons were men of liberal mind, the stedfast promoters and defenders of the government of Edward; and that it was not to be wondered at, if they were hurt at seeing men of yesterday, and strangers, preferred to themselves: still, that they never uttered even a harsh word against the king, whom they had formerly exalted to the throne. On the opposite hand the Normans thus defended themselves: they allege, that both himself and his sons acted with the greatest want of respect, as well as fidelity, to the king and his party; aiming at equal sovereignty with him; often ridiculing his simplicity; often hurling the shafts of their wit against him: that the Normans could not endure this, but endeavoured to weaken their power as much as possible; and that God manifested, at last, with what kind of purity Godwin had served him. For, after his piratical ravages, of which we shall speak hereafter, when he had been reinstated in his original favour, and was sitting with the king at table, the conversation turning on Alfred, the king's brother, "I perceive," said he, "O king, that on every recollection of your brother, you regard me with angry countenance; but God forbid that I should swallow this morsel, if I am conscious of any thing which might tend, either to his danger or your disadvantage." On saying this, he was choked with the piece he had put into his mouth, and closed his eyes in death: being dragged from under the table by Harold his son, who stood near the king, he was buried in the cathedral of Winchester.

On account of these feuds, as I have observed, my narrative labours under difficulties, for I cannot precisely ascertain the truth, by reason either of the natural dislike of these nations for each other, or because the English disdainfully bear with a superior, and the Normans cannot endure an equal. In the following book, however, when the opportunity occurs for relating the arrival of the Normans in England, I shall proceed to speak of their habits; at present I shall glance, with all possible truth, at the grudge of the king against Godwin and his sons.

Eustace,* earl of Boulogne, the father of Godfrey and Baldwin, who, in our times, were kings of Jerusalem, had married the king's sister, Goda, who had borne a son, named Ralph, to her former husband, Walter of Mantes. This son, at that time earl of Hereford, was both indolent and cowardly; he had been beaten in battle by the Welsh, and left his county and the city, together with the bishop, to be consumed with fire by the enemy; the disgrace of which transaction was wiped off by the valour of Harold, who arrived opportunely. Eustace, therefore, crossing the channel, from Whitsand to Dover, went to king Edward on some unknown business. When the conference was over, and he had obtained his request, he was returning through Canterbury,† where one of his harbingers, dealing too fiercely with a citizen, and demanding quarters with blows, rather than entreaty or remuneration, irritated him to such a degree, that he put him to death. Eustace, on being informed of the fact, proceeded with all his retinue to revenge the murder of his servant, and killed the perpetrator of the crime, together with eighteen others: but the citizens flying to arms, he lost twenty-one of his people, and had multitudes wounded; himself and one more with difficulty making their escape during the confusion. Thence returning to court and procuring a secret audience, he made the most of his own story, and excited the anger of the king against the English. Godwin, being summoned by messengers, arrived at the palace.

* Eustace II, surnamed *Aux Grenons*. He succeeded his father, Eustace I, in 1049; and married, in 1050, Goda, daughter of king Ethelbert, and widow of Gauthier comte de Mantes, by whom he had no issue; but by his wife Ida he left three sons; Eustace, who succeeded him, Godefroi, created, in 1076, marquis d'Anvers by the emperor Henry IV, and afterwards duc de Bouillon, was elected king of Jerusalem in 1099, (23rd July); and, dying 18th July, 1100, was succeeded by his brother Baudouin, comte d'Edesse.—HARDY.

† He means Dover, according to the Saxon Chronicle, from which he borrows the account. Eustace stopped at Canterbury to refresh himself, and his people, and afterwards set out for Dover.—Sax. Chron. page 421:

When the business was related, and the king was dwelling more particularly on the insolence of the citizens of Canterbury, this intelligent man perceived that sentence ought not to be pronounced, since the allegations had only been heard on one side of the question. In consequence, though the king ordered him directly to proceed with an army into Kent, to take signal vengeance on the people of Canterbury, still he refused: both because he saw with displeasure, that all foreigners were gaining fast upon the favour of the king; and because he was desirous of evincing his regard to his countrymen. Besides, his opinion was more accordant, as it should seem, with equity, which was, that the principal people of that town should be mildly summoned to the king's court, on account of the tumult; if they could exculpate themselves, they should depart unhurt; but if they could not, they must make atonement, either by money, or by corporal punishment, to the king, whose peace they had broken, and to the earl, whom they had injured: moreover, that it appeared unjust to pass sentence on those people unheard, who had a more especial right to protection. After this the conference broke up; Godwin paying little attention to the indignation of the king, as merely momentary. In consequence of this, the nobility of the whole kingdom were commanded to meet at Gloucester, that the business might there be canvassed in full assembly. Thither came those, at that time, most renowned Northumbrian earls, Siward and Leofric, and all the nobility of England. Godwin and his sons alone, who knew that they were suspected, not deeming it prudent to be present unarmed, halted with a strong force at Beverstone, giving out that they had assembled an army to restrain the Welsh, who, meditating independence on the king, had fortified a town in the county of Hereford, where Sweyn, one of the sons of Godwin, was at that time in command. The Welsh, however, who had come beforehand to the conference, had accused them of a conspiracy, and rendered them odious to the whole court; so that a rumour prevailed, that the king's army would attack them in that very place. Godwin, hearing this, sounded the alarm to his party; told them that they should not purposely withstand their sovereign lord; but if it came to hostilities, they should not retreat without avenging themselves. And, if better counsels had not intervened, a dreadful scene of misery, and a worse than civil war, would have ensued. Some small share of tranquillity, however, being restored, it was ordered that the council should be again assembled at London; and that Sweyn, the son of Godwin, should appease the king's anger by withdrawing himself: that Godwin and Harold should come as speedily as possible to the council, with this condition: that they should be unarmed, bring with them only twelve men, and deliver up to the king the command of the troops which they had throughout England. This on the other hand they refused; observing, that they could not go to a party-meeting without sureties and pledges; that they would obey their lord in the surrender of the soldiers, as well as in every thing else, except risking their lives and reputation: should they come unarmed, the loss of life might be apprehended; if attended with few followers, it would detract from their glory. The king had made up his mind too firmly, to listen to the entreaties of those who interceded with him; wherefore an edict was published, that they should depart from England within five days. Godwin and Sweyn retired to Flanders, and Harold to Ireland. His earldom was given to Elgar, the son of Leofric, a man of active habits; who, receiving, governed it with ability, and readily restored it to him on his return; and afterwards, on the death of Godwin, when Harold had obtained the dukedom of his father, he boldly reclaimed it, though, by the accusation of his enemies, he was banished for a time. All the property of the queen was seized, and herself delivered into the custody of the king's sister at Wherwell, lest she alone should be void of care, whilst all her relations were sighing for their country.

The following year, the exiles, each emerging from his station, were now cruising the British sea, infesting the coast with piracy, and carrying off rich booty from the substance of their countrymen. Against these, on the king's part, more than sixty sail lay at anchor. Earls Odo and Ralph, relations of the king, were commanders of the fleet. Nor did this emergency find Edward himself inactive; since he would pass the night on ship-board, and watch the sallies of the plunderers; diligently compensating, by the wisdom of his counsel, for that personal service which age and infirmity denied. But when they had approached each other, and the conflict was on the eve of commencing, a very thick mist arose, which in a moment obscured the sight of the opponents, and repressed the pitiable audacity of men. At last Godwin and his companions were driven, by the impetuosity of the wind, to the port they had left; and not long after returning to their own country with pacific dispositions, they found the king at London, and were received by him on soliciting pardon. The old man, skilled in leading the minds of his audience by his reputation and his eloquence, dexterously exculpated himself from every thing laid to his charge; and in a short time prevailed so far, as to recover his honours, undiminished, for himself and for his children; to drive all the Normans, branded with ignominy, from England; and to get sentence passed on Robert, the archbishop, and his accomplices, for disturbing the order of the kingdom and stimulating the royal mind against his subjects. But he, not waiting for violent measures, had fled of his own accord while the peace was in agitation, and proceeding to Rome, and appealing to the apostolical see on his case, as he was returning through Jumièges, he died there, and was buried in the church of St. Mary, which he chiefly had built at vast expense. While he was yet living, Stigand, who was bishop of Winchester, forthwith invaded the archbishopric of Canterbury: a prelate of notorious ambition, who sought after honours too keenly, and who, through desire of a higher dignity, deserting the bishopric of the South Saxons, had occupied Winchester, which he held with the archbishopric. For this reason he was never honoured with the pall by the papal see, except that one Benedict, the usurper, as it were, of the papacy, sent him one; either corrupted by money to grant a thing of this kind, or else because bad people are pleased to gratify others of the same description. But he, through the zeal of the faithful, being expelled by Nicholas, who legally assumed the papacy from being bishop of Florence, laid aside the title he so little deserved. Stigand, moreover, in the time of king William, degraded by the Roman cardinals and condemned to perpetual imprisonment, could not fill up the measure of his insatiable avidity even in death. For on his decease, a small key was discovered among his secret recesses, which on being applied to the lock of a chamber-cabinet, gave evidence of papers, describing immense treasures, and in which were noted both the quality and the quantity of the precious metals which this greedy pilferer had hidden on all his estates: but of this hereafter: I shall now complete the history of Godwin which I had begun.

When he was a young man he had Canute's sister to wife, by whom he had a son, who in his early youth, while proudly curveting on a horse which his grandfather had given him, was carried into the Thames, and perished in the stream: his mother, too, paid the penalty of her cruelty; being killed by a stroke of lightning. For it is reported, that she was in the habit of purchasing companies of slaves in England, and sending them into Denmark; more especially girls, whose beauty and age rendered them more valuable, that she might accumulate money by this horrid traffic. After her death, he married another wife,* whose descent I have not been able to trace; by her he had Harold, Sweyn, Wulnod, Tosty, Girth, and Leofwine. Harold became king for a few months after Edward; and being overcome by William at Hastings, there lost his life and kingdom, together with his two younger brothers. Wulnod, given by his father as an hostage, was sent over to Normandy by king Edward, where he remained all that king's time in inextricable captivity; and being sent back into England during William's reign, grew old in confinement at Salisbury: Sweyn being of an obstinate disposition, and faithless to the king, frequently revolted from his father, and his brother Harold, and turning pirate, tarnished the virtues of his forefathers, by his depredations on the coast: at last struck with remorse for the murder of Bruno,† a relation, or as some say, his brother, he went to Jerusalem, and returning thence was surprised by the Saracens, and put to death: Tosty, after the death of Siward, was preferred to the earldom of Northumbria by king Ed-

* Earl Godwin's second wife's name was Gytha. (Saxon Chron. and Flor. Wigorn.)—HARDY

† Sweyn had debauched an abbess, and being enraged that he was not allowed to retain her as his wife, he fled to Flanders. Shortly after he returned, and intreated Bruno or Beorn to accompany him to the king, and to intercede for his pardon: but it should seem this was a mere pretence; as he forced him on ship-board, and then put him to death. V. Flor. Wigorn, A.D. 1049. Chron Sax A D. 1046, p. 419

ward, and presided over that province for nearly ten years; at the end of which he impelled the Northumbrians to rebel, by the asperity of his manners. For finding him unattended, they drove him from the district; not deeming it proper to kill him, from respect to his dignity: but they put to death his attendants both English and Danes, appropriating to their own use, his horses, his arms, and his effects. As soon as this rumour, and the distracted state of the country reached the king, Harold set forward to avenge the outrage. The Northumbrians, though not inferior in point of numbers, yet preferring peace, excused themselves to him for the transaction; averring, that they were a people free-born, and freely educated, and unable to put up with the cruelty of any prince; that they had been taught by their ancestors either to be free, or to die; did the king wish them to be obedient, he should appoint Morcar, the son of Elgar, to preside over them, who would experience how cheerfully they could obey, provided they were treated with gentleness. On hearing this, Harold, who regarded the quiet of the country more than the advantage of his brother, recalled his army, and, after waiting on the king, settled the earldom on Morcar. Tosty, enraged against every one, retired with his wife and children to Flanders, and continued there till the death of Edward: but this I shall delay mentioning, while I record what, as I have learned from ancient men, happened in his time at Rome.

Pope Gregory the Sixth,* first called Gratian, was a man of equal piety and strictness. He found the power of the Roman pontificate so reduced by the negligence of his predecessors, that, with the exception of a few neighbouring towns, and the offerings of the faithful, he had scarcely anything whereon to subsist. The cities and possessions at a distance, which were the property of the church, were forcibly seized by plunderers; the public roads and highways throughout all Italy were thronged with robbers to such a degree, that no pilgrim could pass in safety unless strongly

* "Pagi places the commencement of Gregory's papacy in May 1044, but Ughelli cites a charter in which the month of August, 1045, is stated to be in the first year of his pontificate. He was deposed at a council held at Sutri, on Christmas-day, A. D. 1046, for having obtained the holy see by simony. Mr. Sharpe remarks that Malmesbury's character of this pope is considered as apocryphal. Compare Rodul Glaber, lib. v. c. 5."—HARDY.

guarded. Swarms of thieves beset every path, nor could the traveller devise any method of escaping them. Their rage was equally bent against the poor and the rich; entreaty or resistance were alike unavailing. The journey to Rome was discontinued by every nation, as each had much rather contribute his money to the churches in his own country, than feed a set of plunderers with the produce of his labours. And what was the state of that city which of old was the only dwelling-place of holiness? Why there an abandoned set of knaves and assassins thronged the very forum. If any one by stratagem eluded the people who lay in wait upon the road, from a desire even at the peril of destruction to see the church of the apostle; yet then, encountering these robbers, he was never able to return home without the loss either of property or of life. Even over the very bodies of the holy apostles and martyrs, even on the sacred altars were swords unsheathed, and the offerings of pilgrims, ere well laid out of their hands, were snatched away and consumed in drunkenness and fornication. By such evils was the papacy of Gregory beset. At first he began to deal gently with his subjects; and, as became a pontiff, rather by love than by terror; he repressed the delinquents more by words than by blows; he entreated the townsmen to abstain from the molestation of pilgrims, and the plunder of sacred offerings. The one, he said, was contrary to nature, that the man who breathed the common air could not enjoy the common peace; that Christians surely ought to have liberty of proceeding whither they pleased among Christians, since they were all of the same household, all united by the tie of the same blood, redeemed by the same price: the other, he said, was contrary to the command of God, who had ordained, that "they who served at the altar, should live by the altar;" moreover, that "the house of God ought to be the house of prayer, not a den of thieves," nor an assembly of gladiators; that they should allow the offerings to go to the use of the priests, or the support of the poor; that he would provide for those persons whom want had compelled to plunder, by giving them some honest employment to procure their subsistence; that such as were instigated by avaricious desire, should desist immediately for the love of God and the credit of the world. He invited, by mandates and epistles, those who had invaded the patrimony of the church, to restore what did not belong to them, or else to prove in the Roman senate, that they held it justly; if they would do neither, they must be told that they were no longer members of the church, since they opposed St. Peter, the head of the church, and his vicar. Perpetually haranguing to this effect, and little or nothing profiting by it, he endeavoured to cure the inveterate disorder by having recourse to harsher remedies. He then separated from the body of the church, by the brand of excommunication, all who were guilty of such practices, and even those who associated or conversed with the delinquents. Though he acted strictly according to his duty, yet his diligence in this business had well nigh proved his destruction; for as one says, "He who accuses a mocker, makes himself an enemy," so the abandoned crew began to kick against this gentle admonition; to utter their threats aloud; to clash their arms around the walls of the city, so as nearly even to kill the pope. Finding it now absolutely necessary to cut short the evil, he procured arms and horses from every side, and equipped troops of horse and foot. Taking possession, in the first place, of the church of St. Peter, he either killed or put to flight the plunderers of the oblations. As fortune appeared to favour his designs, he proceeded farther; and despatching all who dared resist, restored to their original jurisdiction all the estates and towns which had been for a considerable time lost. In this manner, peace, which had been long driven into banishment by the negligence of many, was restored to the country by the exertions of an individual. Pilgrims now began securely to travel on the public ways, which had been deserted; they feasted their eyes with pleasure on the ancient wonders within the city; and, having made their offerings, they returned home with songs of joy. In the meantime the common people of Rome, who had been accustomed to live by theft, began to call him sanguinary, and not worthy to offer sacrifice to God, since he was stained by so many murders; and, as it generally happens that the contagion of slander spreads universally, even the cardinals themselves joined in the sentiments of the people; so that, when this holy man was confined by the sickness which proved his death, they, after consulting among themselves, with matchless insolence recommended him not to think of ordering himself to be buried in the church of St. Peter with the rest of the popes, since he had polluted his office by being accessory to the death of so many men. Resuming spirit, however, and sternly regarding them, he addressed them in the following manner:

"If you possessed either a single spark of human reason, or of the knowledge of divine truth, you would hardly have approached your pontiff with so inconsiderate an address; for, throughout my whole life, I have dissipated my own patrimony for your advantage, and at last have sacrificed the applause of the world for your rescue. If any other persons were to allege what you urge in defamation of me, it would become you to silence them by explaining away the false opinions of fools. For whom, I pray you, have I laid up treasure? For myself perhaps? and yet I already possessed the treasures of my predecessors, which were enough for any man's covetousness. To whom have I restored safety and liberty? You will reply, to myself perhaps? And yet I was adored by the people, and did, without restraint, whatever I pleased; entire orations teemed with my praises; every day resounded my applause. These praises and these applauses have been lost to me, through my concern for your poverty. Towards you I turned my thoughts; and found that I must adopt severer measures. A sacrilegious robber fattened on the produce of your property, while your subsistence was only from day to day. He, from the offerings belonging to you, was clad in costly silk; while you, in mean and tattered clothing, absolutely grieved my sight. In consequence, when I could endure this no longer, I acted with hostility to others, that I might get credit for the clergy, though at the loss of the citizens. However, I now find I have lavished my favours on the ungrateful; for you publicly proclaim what others mutter only in secret. I approve, indeed, your freedom, but I look in vain for your affection. A dying parent is persecuted by his sons concerning his burial. Will you deny me the house common to all living? The harlot, the usurer, the robber, are not forbidden an entrance to the church, and do you refuse it to the pope? What signifies it whether the dead or the living enter the sanctuary, except it be, that the living is subject to many temptations, so that he cannot be free from spot even in the church; often finding matter of sin in the very place where he had come to wash it away; whereas the dead knows not how, nay, he who wants only his last sad office, has not the power to sin. What savage barbarity then is it to exclude from the house of God him in whom both the inclination and the power of sinning have ceased! Repent, then, my sons, of your precipitate boldness, if perchance God may forgive you this crime, for you have spoken both foolishly and bitterly even to this present hour. But that you may not suppose me to rest merely on my own authority, listen to reason. Every act of man ought to be considered according to the intention of his heart, that the examination of the deed may proceed to that point whence the design originated; I am deceived if the Truth does not say the same; 'If thine eye be simple thy whole body shall be full of light; if evil, all thy body shall be dark.' A wretched pauper hath often come to me to relieve his distress. As I knew not what was about to happen, I have presented him with divers pieces of money, and dismissed him. On his departure he has met with a thief on the public road, has incautiously fallen into conversation with him, proclaimed the kindness of the apostolical see, and, to prove the truth of his words, produced the purse. On their journey the way has been beguiled with various discourse, until the dissembler, loitering somewhat behind, has felled the stranger with a club, and immediately despatched him; and, after carrying off his money, has boasted of a murder which his thirst for plunder had excited. Can you, therefore, justly accuse me for giving that to a stranger which was the cause of his death? for even the most cruel person would not murder a man unless he hoped to fill his pockets with the money. What shall I say of civil and ecclesiastical laws? By these is not the selfsame fact both punished and approved under different circumstances? The thief is punished for murdering a man in secret, whereas the soldier is applauded who destroys his enemy in battle; the homicide, then, is ignominious in one and laudable in the other, as the latter committed it for the safety of his country, the former for the gratification of his desire for plunder. My predecessor Adrian the First, of renowned memory, was applauded for giving up the investiture of the churches to

Charles the Great, so that no person elected could be consecrated by the bishop till the king had first dignified him with the ring and staff: on the other hand the pontiffs of our time have got credit for taking away these appointments from the princes. What at that time, then, might reasonably be granted, may at the present be reasonably taken away. But why so? Because the mind of Charles the Great was not assailable by avarice, nor could any person easily find access unless he entered by the door. Besides, at so vast a distance, it could not be required of the papal see to grant its consent to each person elected, so long as there was a king at hand who disposed of nothing through avarice, but always appointed religious persons to the churches, according to the sacred ordinances of the canons. At the present time luxury and ambition have beset every king's palace; wherefore the spouse of Christ deservedly asserts her liberty, lest a tyrant should prostitute to an ambitious usurper. Thus, on either side, may my cause be denied or affirmed; it is not the office of a bishop either himself to fight, or to command others to do so; but it belongs to a bishop's function, if he see innocence made shipwreck of, to oppose both hand and tongue. Ezekiel accuses the priests for not strongly opposing and holding forth a shield for the house of Israel in the day of the Lord. Now there are two persons in the church of God, appointed for the purpose of repressing crimes; one who can rebuke sharply, the other, who can wield the sword. I, as you can witness for me, have not neglected my part; as far as I saw it could profit, I did rebuke sharply. I sent a message to him whose business it was to bear the sword; he wrote me word back, that he was occupied in his war with the Vandals, entreating me not to spare my labour nor his expense in breaking up the meetings of the plunderers. If I had refused, what excuse could I offer to God after the emperor had delegated his office to me? Could I see the murder of the townspeople, the robbery of the pilgrims, and slumber on? But he who spares a thief, kills the innocent. Yet it will be objected that it is not the part of a priest to defile himself with the blood of any one · I grant it. But he does not defile himself, who frees the innocent by the destruction of the guilty. Blessed, truly blessed, are they who always keep judgment and do justice. Phineas and Mattathias were priests most renowned in fame, both crowned with the sacred mitre, and both habited in sacerdotal garb; and yet they both punished the wicked with their own hands. The one transfixed the guilty couple with a javelin: the other mingled the blood of the sacrificer with the sacrifice. If then those persons, regarding, as it were, the thick darkness of the law, were, through divine zeal, transported for mysteries, the shadows only of those which were to be; shall we, who see the truth with perfect clearness, suffer our sacred things to be profaned? Azarias the priest drove away king Ozias, when offering incense, and no doubt would have killed him, had he not quickly departed; the divine vengeance, however, anticipated the hand of the priest, for a leprosy preyed on the body of the man whose mind had coveted unlawful things; the devotion of a king was disturbed, and shall not the desires of a thief be so? It is not enough to excuse, I even applaud this my conduct; indeed I have conferred a benefit on the very persons I seem to have destroyed. I have diminished their punishment in accelerating their deaths. The longer a wicked man lives the more he will sin, unless he be such as God hath graciously reserved for a singular example. Death in general is good for all; for by it the just man finds repose in heaven,—the unjust ceases from his crimes,—the bad man puts an end to his guilt,—the good proceeds to his reward,—the saint approaches to the palm,—the sinner looks forward to pardon, because death has fixed a boundary to his transgressions They then surely ought to thank me, who through my conduct have been exempted from so many sufferings. I have urged these matters in my own defence, and to invalidate your assertions however, since both your reasoning and mine may be fallacious, let us commit all to the decision of God. Place my body, when laid out in the manner of my predecessors, before the gates of the church; and let them be secured with locks and bars. If God be willing that I should enter, you will hail a miracle; if not, do with my dead body according to your inclination."

Struck by this address, when he had breathed his last, they carried out the remains of the departed prelate before the doors, which were strongly fastened; and presently a whirlwind, sent by God, broke every opposing bolt, and drove the very doors, with the utmost violence, against the walls. The surrounding people applaud with joy, and the body of the pontiff was interred, with all due respect, by the side of the other popes.

At the same time something similar occurred in England, not by divine miracle, but by infernal craft; which when I shall have related, the credit of the narrative will not be shaken, though the minds of the hearers should be incredulous; for I have heard it from a man of such character, who swore he had seen it, that I should blush to disbelieve. There resided at Berkeley a woman addicted to witchcraft, as it afterwards appeared, and skilled in ancient augury: she was excessively gluttonous, perfectly lascivious, setting no bounds to her debaucheries, as she was not old, though fast declining in life. On a certain day, as she was regaling, a jack-daw, which was a very great favourite, chattered a little more loudly than usual. On hearing which the woman's knife fell from her hand, her countenance grew pale, and deeply groaning, "This day," said she, "my plough has completed its last furrow; to-day I shall hear of, and suffer, some dreadful calamity." While yet speaking, the messenger of her misfortunes arrived; and being asked, why he approached with so distressed an air? "I bring news," said he, "from that village," naming the place, "of the death of your son, and of the whole family, by a sudden accident." At this intelligence, the woman, sorely afflicted, immediately took to her bed, and perceiving the disorder rapidly approaching the vitals, she summoned her surviving children, a monk, and a nun, by hasty letters; and, when they arrived, with faltering voice, addressed them thus: "Formerly, my children, I constantly administered to my wretched circumstances by demoniacal arts: I have been the sink of every vice, the teacher of every allurement: yet, while practising these crimes, I was accustomed to soothe my hapless soul with the hope of your piety. Despairing of myself, I rested my expectations on you; I advanced you as my defenders against evil spirits, my safeguards against my strongest foes. Now, since I have approached the end of my life, and shall have those eager to punish, who lured me to sin, I entreat you by your mother's breasts, if you have any regard, any affection, at least to endeavour to alleviate my torments; and, although you cannot revoke the sentence already passed upon my soul, yet you may, perhaps, rescue my body, by these means: sew up my corpse in the skin of a stag; lay it on its back in a stone coffin; fasten down the lid with lead and iron; on this lay a stone, bound round with three iron chains of enormous weight; let there be psalms sung for fifty nights, and masses said for an equal number of days, to allay the ferocious attacks of my adversaries. If I lie thus secure for three nights, on the fourth day bury your mother in the ground; although I fear, lest the earth, which has been so often burdened with my crimes, should refuse to receive and cherish me in her bosom." They did their utmost to comply with her injunctions: but alas! vain were pious tears, vows, or entreaties; so great was the woman's guilt, so great the devil's violence. For on the first two nights, while the choir of priests was singing psalms around the body, the devils, one by one, with the utmost ease bursting open the door of the church, though closed with an immense bolt, broke asunder the two outer chains; the middle one being more laboriously wrought, remained entire. On the third night, about cock-crow, the whole monastery seemed to be overthrown from its very foundation, by the clamour of the approaching enemy. One devil, more terrible in appearance than the rest, and of loftier stature, broke the gates to shivers by the violence of his attack. The priests grew motionless with fear,* their hair stood on end, and they became speechless. He proceeded, as it appeared, with haughty step towards the coffin, and calling on the woman by name, commanded her to rise. She replying that she could not on account of the chains. "You shall be loosed," said he, "and to your cost:" and directly he broke the chain, which had mocked the ferocity of the others, with as little exertion as though it had been made of flax. He also beat down the cover of the coffin with his foot, and taking her by the hand, before them all, he dragged her out of the church. At the doors appeared a black horse, proudly neighing, with iron hooks projecting over his whole back; on which the wretched creature was placed, and, immediately, with the whole party, vanished from the eyes of the

* "Steteruntque comæ, et vox faucibus hæsit."—Virgil, Æneid iii. 48.

beholders; her pitiable cries, however, for assistance, were heard for nearly the space of four miles. No person will deem this incredible, who has read St. Gregory's Dialogues;* who tells, in his fourth book, of a wicked man that had been buried in a church, and was cast out of doors again by devils. Among the French also, what I am about to relate is frequently mentioned. Charles Martel, a man of renowned valour, who obliged the Saracens, when they had invaded France, to retire to Spain, was, at his death, buried in the church of St. Denys; but as he had seized much of the property of almost all the monasteries in France for the purpose of paying his soldiers, he was visibly taken away from his tomb by evil spirits, and has nowhere been seen to his day. At length this was revealed to the bishop of Orleans, and by him publicly made known.

But to return to Rome: there was a citizen of this place, youthful, rich, and of senatorial rank, who had recently married; and, who calling together his companions, had made a plentiful entertainment. After the repast, when by moderate drinking they had excited hilarity, they went out into the field to promote digestion, either by leaping, or hurling, or some other exercise. The master of the banquet, who was leader of the game, called for a ball to play with, and in the meantime placed the wedding ring on the outstretched finger of a brazen statue which stood close at hand. But when almost all the others had attacked him alone, tired with the violence of the exercise, he left off playing first, and going to resume his ring, he saw the finger of the statue clenched fast in the palm. Finding, after many attempts, that he was unable either to force it off, or to break the finger, he retired in silence; concealing the matter from his companions, lest they should laugh at him at the moment, or deprive him of the ring when he was gone. Returning thither with some servants in the dead of night, he was surprised to find the finger again extended, and the ring taken away. Dissembling his loss, he was soothed by the blandishments of his bride. When the hour of rest arrived, and he had placed himself by the side of his spouse, he was conscious of something dense, and cloud-like, rolling between them, which might be felt, though not seen,

* There are various stories of this kind in Gregory's Dialogues.

and by this means was impeded in his embraces: he heard a voice too, saying, "Embrace me, since you wedded me to-day; I am Venus, on whose finger you put the ring; I have it, nor will I restore it." Terrified at such a prodigy, he had neither courage, nor ability to reply, and passed a sleepless night in silent reflection upon the matter. A considerable space of time elapsed in this way: as often as he was desirous of the embraces of his wife, the same circumstance ever occurred; though in other respects, he was perfectly equal to any avocation, civil or military. At length, urged by the complaints of his consort, he detailed the matter to her parents; who, after deliberating for a time, disclosed it to one Palumbus, a suburban priest. This man was skilled in necromancy, could raise up magical figures, terrify devils, and impel them to do anything he chose. Making an agreement, that he should fill his purse most plentifully, provided he succeeded in rendering the lovers happy, he called up all the powers of his art, and gave the young man a letter which he had prepared; saying, "Go, at such an hour of the night, into the high road, where it divides into four several ways, and stand there in silent expectation. There will pass by human figures of either sex, of every age, rank, and condition; some on horseback, some on foot; some with countenances dejected, others elated with full-swollen insolence; in short, you will perceive in their looks and gestures, every symptom both of joy and of grief: though these should address you, enter into conversation with none of them. This company will be followed by a person taller, and more corpulent than the rest, sitting in a chariot; to him you will, in silence, give the letter to read, and immediately your wish will be accomplished, provided you act with resolution." The young man took the road he was commanded; and, at night, standing in the open air, experienced the truth of the priest's assertion by everything which he saw; there was nothing but what was completed to a tittle. Among other passing figures, he beheld a woman, in meretricious garb, riding on a mule; her hair, which was bound above in a golden fillet, floated unconfined on her shoulders; in her hand was a golden wand, with which she directed the progress of her beast; she was so thinly clad, as to be almost naked, and her gestures were wonderfully indecent. But what need of more? At last came the chief, in appearance, who, from his chariot adorned with emeralds and pearls, fixing his eyes most sternly on the young man, demanded the cause of his presence. He made no reply, but stretching out his hand, gave him the letter. The demon, not daring to despise the well-known seal, read the epistle, and immediately, lifting up his hands to heaven, "Almighty God," said he, "in whose sight every transgression is as a noisome smell, how long wilt thou endure the crimes of the priest Palumbus?" The devil then directly sent some of those about him to take the ring by force from Venus, who restored it at last, though with great reluctance. The young man thus obtaining his object, became possessed of his long desired pleasures without farther obstacle; but Palumbus, on hearing of the devil's complaint to God concerning him, understood that the close of his days was predicted. In consequence, making a pitiable atonement by voluntarily cutting off all his limbs, he confessed unheard-of crimes to the pope in the presence of the Roman people.

At that time the body of Pallas, the son of Evander, of whom Virgil speaks, was found entire at Rome, to the great astonishment of all, for having escaped corruption so many ages. Such, however, is the nature of bodies embalmed, that, when the flesh decays, the skin preserves the nerves, and the nerves the bones. The gash which Turnus had made in the middle of his breast measured four feet and a half. His epitaph was found to this effect,

> Pallas, Evander's son, lies buried here
> In order due, transfix'd by Turnus' spear.

Which epitaph I should not think made at the time, though Carmentis the mother of Evander is reported to have discovered the Roman letters, but that it was composed by Ennius, or some other ancient poet.* There was a burning lamp at his head, constructed by magical art; so that no

---

* The original is as follows:

> Filius Evandri Pallas, quem lancea Turni
> Militis occidit, more suo jacet hic.

I am unable to say who was the author of this epigram, but it is not too hazardous to assert that it was not composed either by Ennius or by any other ancient poet.

violent blast, no dripping of water could extinguish it. While many were lost in admiration at this, one person, as there are always some people expert in mischief, made an aperture beneath the flame with an iron style, which introducing the air, the light vanished. The body, when set up against the wall, surpassed it in height, but some days afterwards, being drenched with the drip of the eves, it acknowledged the corruption common to mortals; the skin and the nerves dissolving.

At that time too, on the confines of Brittany and Normandy, a prodigy was seen in one, or more properly speaking, in two women: there were two heads, four arms, and every other part two-fold to the navel; beneath, were two legs, two feet, and all other parts single. While one was laughing, eating, or speaking, the other would cry, fast, or remain silent: though both mouths ate, yet the excrement was discharged by only one passage. At last, one dying, the other survived, and the living carried about the dead, for the space of three years, till she died also, through the fatigue of the weight, and the stench of the dead carcass.* Many were of opinion, and some even have written, that these women represented England and Normandy, which, though separated by position, are yet united under one master. Whatever wealth these countries greedily absorb, flows into one common receptacle, which is either the covetousness of princes, or the ferocity of surrounding nations. England, yet vigorous, supports with her wealth Normandy now dead and almost decayed, until she herself perhaps shall fall through the violence of spoilers. Happy, if she shall ever again breathe that liberty, the mere shadow of which she has long pursued! She now mourns, borne down with calamity, and oppressed with exactions; the causes of which misery I shall relate, after I have despatched some things pertaining to my subject. For since I have hitherto recorded the civil and military transactions of the kings of England, I

---

* There seems no reason to doubt the truth of this circumstance, since the exhibition of the Siamese twins, the most extraordinary *lusus naturæ* that has occurred in the nineteenth century. Medical science, aided by comparative anatomy, has ascertained that the bodies of both man and the brute creation are susceptible of combinations—not usually occurring in the course of nature,—which in former times were thought impossible, and as such were universally disbelieved.

may be allowed to expatiate somewhat on the sanctity of certain of them; and at the same time to contemplate what splendour of divine love beamed on this people, from the first dawning of their faith: since I believe you can no where find the bodies of so many saints entire after death, typifying the state of final incorruption. I imagine this to have taken place by God's agency, in order that a nation, situated, as it were, almost out of the world, should more confidently embrace the hope of a resurrection from the contemplation of the incorruption of the saints. There are, altogether, five which I have known of, though the residents in many places boast of more; Saint Etheldrida,* and Werburga, virgins; king Edmund; archbishop Elphege;† Cuthbert the ancient father: who with skin and flesh unwasted, and their joints flexile, appear to have a certain vital warmth about them, and to be merely sleeping. Who can enumerate all the other saints, of different ranks and professions? whose names and lives, singly to describe, I have neither intention nor leisure: yet oh that I might hereafter have leisure! But I will be silent, lest I should seem to promise more than I can perform. In consequence, it is not necessary to mention any of the commonalty, but merely, not to go out of the path of my subject history, the male and female scions of the royal stock, most of them innocently murdered; and who have been consecrated martyrs, not by human conjecture, but by divine acknowledgment. Hence may be known how little indulgence they gave to the lust of pleasure, who inherited eternal glory by means of so easy a death.

In the former book, my history dwelt for some time on the praises of the most holy Oswald, king and martyr; among whose other marks of sanctity, was this, which, according to some copies, is related in the History of the Angles.‡ In the monastery at Selsey, which Wilfrid of holy memory had

* Sometimes called St. Audry. She was abbess of Ely monastery. St. Werburga was patroness of Chester monastery.

† Archbishop of Canterbury, from A.D. 1006 to 1012. See Sax. Chronicle, pp 402, 403.

‡ Bede, book IV chap. 14. There are some MSS. which want this chapter. The former editor of Bede accounts for it very satisfactorily; stating that a very ancient MS in the Cotton Collection has a note marking that a leaf was here wanting; and that those which want the chapter were transcripts of this imperfect MS.

filled with Northumbrian monks, a dreadful malady broke out, and destroyed numbers; the remainder endeavoured to avert the pestilence by a fast of three days. On the second day of the fast, the blessed apostles Peter and Paul, appearing to a youth who was sick with the disorder, animated him by observing: "That he should not fear approaching death, as it would be a termination of his present illness, and an entrance into eternal life; that no other person of that monastery would die of this disorder, because God had granted this to the merits of the noble king Oswald, who was that very day supplicating for his countrymen: for it was on this day that the king, murdered by the faithless, had in a moment ascended to the heavenly tribunal: that they should search, therefore, in the scroll, in which the names of the dead were written, and if they found it so, they should put an end to the fast, give loose to security and joy, and sing solemn masses to God, and to the holy king." This vision being quickly followed by the death of the boy, and the anniversary of the martyr being found in the martyrology, and at the same time the cessation of the disorder being attested by the whole province, the name of Oswald was from that period inserted among the martyrs, which before, on account of his recent death, had only been admitted into the list of the faithful. Deservedly, I say, then, deservedly is he to be celebrated, whose glory the divine approbation so signally manifested, as to order him to be dignified with masses, in a manner, as I think, not usual among men. The undoubted veracity of the historian precludes the possibility of supposing this matter to be false; as does also the blessed bishop Acca,* who was the friend of the author.

Egbert, king of Kent, the son of Erconbert, whom I have mentioned before, had some very near relations, descended from the royal line; their names were Ethelred† and Ethelbert, the sons of Ermenred his uncle. Apprehensive that they might grow up with notions of succeeding to the kingdom, and fearful for his safety, he kept them about him for some time, with very homely entertainment: and, at last, grudging them his regards, he removed them from his court.

* Acca, bishop of Hexham, A.D 710, and a great friend of venerable Bede, who inscribed to him many of his works.
† Or Elbert. See b. i. c. i. p. 15.

Soon after, when they had been secretly despatched by one of his servants named Thunre, which signifies Thunder, he buried them under heaps of rubbish, thinking that a murder perpetrated in privacy would escape detection. The eye of God however, which no secrets of the heart can deceive, brought the innocents to light, vouchsafing many cures upon the spot; until the neighbours, being roused, dug up the unsightly heaps of turf and rubbish cast upon their bodies, and forming a trench after the manner of a sepulchre, they erected a small church over it. There they remained till the time of king Edgar, when they were taken up by St. Oswald, archbishop* of Worcester, and conveyed to the monastery of Ramsey; from which period, granting the petitions of the suppliant, they have manifested themselves by many miracles.

Offa king of the Mercians murdered many persons of consequence for the security, as he supposed, of his kingdom, without any distinction of friend or foe; among these was king Ethelbert;† thereby being guilty of an atrocious outrage against the suitor of his daughter. His unmerited death, however, is thought to have been amply avenged by the short reign of Offa's son. Indeed God signalised his sanctity by such evident tokens, that at this very day the episcopal church of Hereford is consecrated to his name. Nor should any thing appear idle or irrelevant, which our pious and religious ancestors have either tolerated by their silence, or confirmed by their authority.

What shall my pen here trace worthy of St. Kenelm, a youth of tender age? Kenulf, king of the Mercians, his father, had consigned him, when seven years old, to his sister Quendrida, for the purpose of education. But she, falsely entertaining hopes of the kingdom for herself, gave her little brother in charge to a servant of her household, with an order to despatch him. Taking out the innocent, under pretence of hunting for his amusement or recreation, he murdered and hid him in a thicket. But strange to tell, the crime which had been so secretly committed in England, gained publicity in Rome, by God's agency: for a dove, from heaven, bore a parchment scroll to the altar of St. Peter, containing an exact account both of his death and

* He was at the same time bishop of Worcester, and archbishop of York.
See b. i. c. 4, p. 78.

place of burial. As this was written in the English language it was vainly attempted to be read by the Romans and men of other nations who were present. Fortunately, however, and opportunely, an Englishman was at hand, who translated the writing to the Roman people, into Latin, and gave occasion to the pope to write a letter to the kings of England, acquainting them with the martyrdom of their countryman. In consequence of this the body of the innocent was taken up in presence of a numerous assembly, and removed to Winchcomb. The murderous woman was so indignant at the vocal chaunt of the priests and loud applause of the laity, that she thrust out her head from the window of the chamber where she was standing, and, by chance, having in her hands a psalter, she came in course of reading to the psalm "O God my praise," which, for I know not what charm, reading backwards, she endeavoured to drown the joy of the choristers. At that moment, her eyes, torn by divine vengeance from their hollow sockets, scattered blood upon the verse which runs, "This is the work of them who defame me to the Lord, and who speak evil against my soul." The marks of her blood are still extant, proving the cruelty of the woman, and the vengeance of God. The body of the little saint is very generally adored, and there is hardly any place in England more venerated, or where greater numbers of persons attend at the festival ; and this arising from the long-continued belief of his sanctity, and the constant exhibition of miracles.

Nor shall my history be wanting in thy praise, Wistan,[*] blessed youth, son of Wimund, son of Withlaf king of the Mercians, and of Elfleda, daughter of Ceolwulf, who was the uncle of Kenelm ; I will not, I say, pass thee over in silence, whom Berfert thy relation so atrociously murdered. And let posterity know, if they deem this history worthy of perusal, that there was nothing earthly more praiseworthy than your disposition ; at which a deadly assassin becoming irritated, despatched you : nor was there any thing more innocent than your purity towards God ; invited by which, the secret Judge deemed it fitting to honour you : for a pillar of light, sent down from heaven, piercing the sable robe of night,

[*] "Concerning St. Wistan, consult MSS. Harl. 2253. *De Martyrio S. Wistani.*"—HARDY.

revealed the wickedness of the deep cavern, and brought to view the crime of the murderer. In consequence, Wistan's venerable remains were taken up, and by the care of his relations conveyed to Rependun;* at that time a famous monastery, now a villa belonging to the earl of Chester, and its glory grown obsolete with age; but at present thou dwellest at Evesham, kindly favouring the petitions of such as regard thee.

Bede has related many anecdotes of the sanctity of the kings of the East Saxons, and East Angles, whose genealogy I have in the first book of this work traced briefly; because I could no where find a complete history of the kings. I shall however, dilate somewhat on St. Edmund, who held dominion in East Anglia, and to whom the time of Bede did not extend. This province, on the south and east, is surrounded by the ocean; on the north, by deep lakes, and stagnant pools, which, stretching out a vast distance in length, with a breadth of two or three miles, afford abundance of fish for the use of the inhabitants; on the west it is continuous with the rest of the island, but defended by the earth's being thrown up in the form of a rampart.† The soil is admirable for pasture, and for hunting; it is full of monasteries, and large bodies of monks are settled on the islands of these stagnant waters; the people are a merry, pleasant, jovial race, though apt to carry their jokes to excess. Here, then, reigned Edmund; a man devoted to God, ennobled by his descent from ancient kings, and though he presided over the province in peace for several years, yet never through the effeminacy of the times did he relax his virtue. Hingwar and Hubba, two leaders of the Danes, came over to depopulate the provinces of the Northumbrians and East Angles. The former of these seized the unresisting king, who had cast away his arms and was lying on the ground in prayer, and, after the infliction of tortures,‡ beheaded him. On the death of this saintly man, the purity of his past life was evidenced by unheard-of miracles. The Danes had cast away the head, when severed from the body

* Repton. † Thought to be the Devil's Dyke, on Newmarket Heath.
‡ He was tied to a tree, and shot to death with arrows. Abbo Floriacensis.

by the cruelty of the executioners, and it had been hidden in a thicket. While his subjects, who had tracked the footsteps of the enemy as they departed, were seeking it, intending to solemnize with due honour the funeral rites of their king, they were struck with the pleasing intervention of God: for the lifeless head uttered a voice, inviting all who were in search of it to approach. A wolf, a beast accustomed to prey upon dead carcasses, was holding it in its paws, and guarding it untouched; which animal also, after the manner of a tame creature, gently followed the bearers to the tomb, and neither did nor received any injury. The sacred body was then, for a time, committed to the earth; turf was placed over it, and a wooden chapel, of trifling cost, erected. The negligent natives, however, were soon made sensible of the virtue of the martyr, which excited their listless minds to reverence him, by the miracles which he performed. And though perhaps the first proof of his power may appear weak and trivial, yet nevertheless I shall subjoin it. He bound, with invisible bands, some thieves who had endeavoured to break into the church by night: this was done in the very attempt; a pleasant spectacle enough, to see the plunder hold fast the thief, so that he could neither desist from the enterprise, nor complete the design. In consequence, Theodred bishop of London, who lies at St. Paul's, removed the lasting disgrace of so mean a structure, by building a nobler edifice over those sacred limbs, which evidenced the glory of his unspotted soul, by surprising soundness, and a kind of milky whiteness. The head, which was formerly divided from the neck, is again united to the rest of the body showing only the sign of martyrdom by a purple seam. One circumstance indeed surpasses human miracles, which is, that the hair and nails of the dead man continue to grow: these, Oswen, a holy woman, used yearly to clip and cut, that they might be objects of veneration to posterity. Truly this was a holy temerity, for a woman to contemplate and handle limbs superior to the whole of this world. Not so Leofstan, a youth of bold and untamed insolence, who, with many impertinent threats, commanded the body of the martyr to be shown to him; for he was desirous, as he said, of settling the uncertainty of report by the testimony of his own eyesight. He paid dearly, however, for his audacious experiment; for he became insane, and shortly after, died, swarming with vermin. He felt indeed that Edmund was now capable of doing, what he before used to do; that is,

"To spare the suppliant, but confound the proud,"

by which means he so completely engaged the inhabitants of all Britain to him, that every person looked upon himself as particularly happy, in contributing either money or gifts to St. Edmund's monastery: even kings themselves, who rule others, used to boast of being his servants, and sent him their royal crown; redeeming it, if they wished to use it, at a great price. The exactors of taxes also, who, in other places, gave loose to injustice, were there suppliant, and ceased their cavilling at St. Edmund's boundary,* admonished thereto by the punishment of others who had presumed to overpass it.

My commendations shall also glance at the names of some maidens of the royal race, though I must claim indulgence for being brief upon the subject, not through fastidiousness, but because I am unacquainted with their miracles. Anna king of the East Angles had three daughters, Etheldrida, Ethelberga, and Sexberga. Etheldrida, though married to two husbands, yet by means of saintly continence, as Bede relates, without any diminution of modesty, without a single lustful inclination, triumphantly displayed to heaven the palm of perpetual virginity. Ethelberga, first a nun, and afterwards abbess, in a monastery in France called Brigis,† was celebrated for unblemished chastity; and it is well worthy of remark, that as both sisters had subdued the lusts of the flesh while living, so, when dead, their bodies remained uncorrupt, the one in England, and the other in France; insomuch, that their sanctity, which is abundantly resplendent, may suffice

"To cast its radiance over both the poles."

Sexberga was married to Erconbert king of Kent, and, after his death, took the veil in the same monastery where her sister Etheldrida was proclaimed a saint. She had two daughters by king Erconbert, Earcongota and Ermenhilda.

---

* This boundary is said to have been formed by Canute, in consequence of his father Sweyn having been killed by St Edmund in a vision for attempting to plunder his territory. See Malm. de Gest. Pontif. lib. ii. f. 136, b. edit. Lond. † Faremoutier in Brie.

Of Ercongota, such as wish for information will find it in Bede;* Ermenhilda married Wulfhere, king of the Mercians, and had a daughter, Werburga, a most holy virgin. Both are saints: the mother, that is to say, St. Ermenhilda, rests at Ely, where she was abbess after her mother, Sexberga; and the daughter lies at Chester, in the monastery of that city, which Hugo earl of Chester, ejecting a few canons who resided there in a mean and irregular manner, has recently erected. The praises and miracles of both these women, and particularly of the younger, are there extolled and held in veneration, and though they are favourable to all petitions without delay, yet are they more especially kind and assistant to the supplications of women and youths.

Merewald the brother of Wulfhere, by Ermenburga, the daughter of Ermenred brother of Erconbert king of Kent, had two daughters: Mildritha and Milburga. Mildritha, dedicating herself to celibacy, ended her days in the Isle of Thanet in Kent, which king Egbert had given to her mother, to atone for the murder of her brothers, Ethelred and Ethelbert.† In after times, being transferred to St. Augustine's monastery at Canterbury, she is there honoured by the marked attention of the monks, and celebrated equally for her kindness and affability to all, as her name‡ implies. And although almost every corner of that monastery is filled with the bodies of saints of great name and merit, any one of which would be of itself sufficient to irradiate all England, yet no one is there more revered, more loved, or more gratefully remembered; and she, turning a deaf ear to none who love her, is present to them in the salvation of their souls.

Milburga reposes at Wenlock:§ formerly well known to the neighbouring inhabitants; but for some time after the arrival of the Normans, through ignorance of the place of her burial, she was neglected. Lately, however, a convent of

* Hist. Eccl. b. iii. c. 8, p. 122.

† In b. 1, c. 1, p. 15, it is said the compensation for their murder was made to their mother; but here she is called their sister, which is the general account. When it was left to her to estimate this compensation (i. e. their weregild), she asked as much land as her stag should compass, at one course, in the Isle of Thanet; where she founded the monastery of Minster. Vide W. Thorn. col 1910, and Natale S. Mildrythæ (Saxonicè), MS. Cott. Calig. A. xiv. 4.   ‡ "Mild" gentle.   § In Shropshire.

Clugniac monks being established there, while a new church was erecting, a certain boy running violently along the pavement, broke into the hollow of the vault, and discovered the body of the virgin; when a balsamic odour pervading the whole church, she was taken up, and performed so many miracles, that the people flocked thither in great multitudes. Large spreading plains could hardly contain the troops of pilgrims, while rich and poor came side by side, one common faith impelling all. Nor did the event deceive their expectations: for no one departed, without either a perfect cure, or considerable abatement of his malady, and some were even healed of the king's evil, by the merits of this virgin, when medical assistance was unavailing.

Edward the Elder, of whom I have before spoken at large, had by his wife Edgiva, several daughters. Among these was Eadburga, who, when she was scarcely three years old, gave a singular indication of her future sanctity. Her father was inclined to try whether the little girl was inclined to God, or to the world, and had placed in a chamber the symbols of different professions; on one side a chalice, and the gospels; on the other, bracelets and necklaces. Hither the child was brought in the arms of her indulgent attendant, and, sitting on her father's knee, was desired to choose which she pleased. Rejecting the earthly ornaments with stern regard, she instantly fell prostrate before the chalice and the gospels, and worshipped them with infant adoration. The company present exclaimed aloud, and fondly hailed the prospect of the child's future sanctity; her father embraced the infant in a manner still more endearing. "Go," said he, "whither the Divinity calls thee; follow with prosperous steps the spouse whom thou hast chosen, and truly blessed shall my wife and myself be, if we are surpassed in holiness by our daughter." When clothed in the garb of a nun, she gained the affection of all her female companions, in the city of Winchester, by the marked attention she paid them. Nor did the greatness of her birth elevate her; as she esteemed it noble to stoop to the service of Christ. Her sanctity increased with her years, her humility kept pace with her growth; so that she used secretly to steal away the socks of the several nuns at night, and, carefully washing and anointing them, lay them again upon their beds. Wherefore, though God signalized her, while living, by many miracles, yet I more particularly bring forward this circumstance, to show that charity began all her works, and humility completed them : and finally, many miracles in her life-time, and since her death, confirm the devotion of her heart and the incorruptness of her body, which the attendants at her churches at Winchester and Pershore relate to such as are unacquainted with them.

St. Editha, the daughter of king Edgar, ennobles, with her relics, the monastery of Wilton, where she was buried, and cherishes that place with her regard, where, trained from her infancy in the school of the Lord, she gained his favour by unsullied virginity, and constant watchings : repressing the pride of her high birth by her humility. I have heard one circumstance of her, from persons of elder days, which greatly staggered the opinions of men : for she led them into false conclusions from the splendour of her costly dress; being always habited in richer garb than the sanctity of her profession seemed to require. On this account, being openly rebuked by St. Ethelwold, she is reported to have answered with equal point and wit, that the judgment of God was true and irrefragable, while that of man, alone, was fallible ; for pride might exist even under the garb of wretchedness : wherefore, "I think," said she, "that a mind may be as pure beneath these vestments, as under your tattered furs." The bishop was deeply struck by this speech ; admitting its truth by his silence, and blushing with pleasure that he had been chastised by the sparkling repartee of the lady, he held his peace. St. Dunstan had observed her, at the consecration of the church of St. Denys, which she had built out of affection to that martyr, frequently stretching out her right thumb, and making the sign of the cross upon her forehead ; and being extremely delighted at it, "May this finger," he exclaimed, "never see corruption:" and immediately, while celebrating mass, he burst into such a flood of tears, that he alarmed with his faltering voice an assistant standing near him ; who inquiring the reason of it, "Soon," said he, "shall this blooming rose wither ; soon shall this beloved bird take its flight to God, after the expiration of six weeks from this time." The truth of the prelate's prophecy was very shortly fulfilled ; for on the appointed day, this noble, firmly-minded lady, expired in her prime, at the age of twenty-three years. Soon after, the same saint saw, in a dream, St. Denys kindly taking the virgin by the hand, and strictly enjoining, by divine command, that she should be honoured by her servants on earth, in the same manner as she was venerated by her spouse and master in heaven. Miracles multiplying at her tomb, it was ordered, that her virgin body should be taken up, and exalted in a shrine ; when the whole of it was found resolved into dust, except the finger, with the abdomen and parts adjacent. In consequence of which, some debate arising, the virgin herself appeared, in a dream, to one of those who had seen her remains, saying, "It was no wonder, if the other parts of the body had decayed, since it was customary for dead bodies to moulder to their native dust, and she, perhaps, as a girl, had sinned with those members ; but it was highly just, that the abdomen should see no corruption which had never felt the sting of lust ; as she had been entirely free from gluttony or carnal copulation."

Truly both these virgins support their respective monasteries by their merits ; each of them being filled with large assemblies of nuns, who answer obediently to the call of their mistresses and patronesses, inviting them to virtue. Happy the man, who becomes partaker of those virgin orisons which the Lord Jesus favours with kind regard. For, as I have remarked of the nuns of Shaftesbury, all virtues have long since quitted the earth, and retired to heaven ; or, if any where, (but this I must say with the permission of holy men,) are to be found only in the hearts of nuns ; and surely those women are highly to be praised, who, regardless of the weakness of their sex, vie with each other in the preservation of their continence, and by such means ascend, triumphant, to heaven.

I think it of importance to have been acquainted with many of the royal family of either sex ; as it may be gathered from thence that king Edward, concerning whom I was speaking before I digressed, by no means degenerated from the virtues of his ancestors. In fact he was famed both for miracles, and for the spirit of prophecy, as I shall hereafter relate. In the exaction of taxes he was sparing, and he abominated the insolence of collectors: in eating and drinking he was free from the voluptuousness which his state allowed · on the more solemn festivals, though dressed in robes interwoven with gold, which the queen had most splendidly embroidered, yet still he had such forbearance, as to be sufficiently majestic, without being haughty; considering in such matters, rather the bounty of God, than the pomp of the world. There was one earthly enjoyment in which he chiefly delighted; which was, hunting with fleet hounds, whose opening in the woods he used with pleasure to encourage: and again, with the pouncing of birds, whose nature it is to prey on their kindred species. In these exercises, after hearing divine service in the morning, he employed himself whole days. In other respects he was a man by choice devoted to God, and lived the life of an angel in the administration of his kingdom. To the poor and to the stranger, more especially foreigners and men of religious orders, he was kind in invitation, munificent in his presents, and constantly exciting the monks of his own country to imitate their holiness. He was of a becoming stature; his beard and hair milk-white; his countenance florid; fair throughout his whole person; and his form of admirable proportion.

The happiness of his times had been revealed in a dream to Brithwin bishop of Wilton, who had made it public. For in the time of Canute, when, at Glastonbury, he was once intent on heavenly watchings, and the thought of the near extinction of the royal race of the Angles, which frequently distressed him, came into his mind, sleep stole upon him thus meditating; when behold! he was rapt on high, and saw Peter, the chief of the apostles, consecrating Edward, who at that time was an exile in Normandy, king; his chaste life too was pointed out, and the exact period of his reign, twenty-four years, determined; and, when inquiring about his posterity, it was answered, "The kingdom of the English belongs to God; after you he will provide a king according to his pleasure."

But now to speak of his miracles. A young woman had married a husband of her own age, but having no issue by the union, the humours collecting abundantly about her neck, she had contracted a sore disorder; the glands swelling in a dreadful manner. Admonished in a dream to have the part affected washed by the king, she entered the palace, and the king himself fulfilled this labour of love, by rubbing the woman's neck with his fingers dipped in water. Joyous health followed his healing hand: the lurid skin opened, so that worms flowed out with the purulent matter, and the tumour subsided. But as the orifice of the ulcers was large and unsightly, he commanded her to be supported at the royal expense till she should be perfectly cured. However, before a week was expired, a fair, new skin returned, and hid the scars so completely, that nothing of the original wound could be discovered: and within a year becoming the mother of twins, she increased the admiration of Edward's holiness. Those who knew him more intimately, affirm that he often cured this complaint in Normandy: whence appears how false is their notion, who, in our times assert, that the cure of this disease does not proceed from personal sanctity, but from hereditary virtue in the royal line.

A certain man, blind from some unknown mischance, had persisted in asserting about the palace, that he should be cured, if he could touch his eyes with the water in which the king's hands had been washed. This was frequently related to Edward, who derided it, and looked angrily on the persons who mentioned it; confessing himself a sinner, and that the works of holy men did not belong to him. But the servants, thinking this a matter not to be neglected, tried the experiment when he was ignorant of it, and was praying in church. The instant the blind man was washed with the water, the long-enduring darkness fled from his eyes, and they were filled with joyful light; and the king, inquiring the cause of the grateful clamour of the by-standers, was informed of the fact. Presently afterwards, when, by thrusting his fingers towards the eyes of the man he had cured, and perceiving him draw back his head to avoid them, he had made proof of his sight, he, with uplifted hands, returned thanks to God. In the same way he cured a blind man at Lincoln, who survived him many years, a proof of the royal miracle.

That you may know the perfect virtue of this prince, in the power of healing more especially, I shall add something which will excite your wonder. Wulwin, surnamed Spillecorn, the son of Wulmar of Nutgareshale, was one day cutting timber in the wood of Bruelle, and indulging in a long sleep after his labour, he lost his sight for seventeen years, from the blood, as I imagine, stagnating about his eyes: at the end of this time, he was admonished in a dream to go round to eighty-seven churches, and earnestly entreat a cure of his blindness from the saints. At last he came to the king's court, where he remained for a long time, in vain, in opposition to the attendants, at the vestibule of his chamber. He still continued importunate, however, without being deterred, till at last, after much difficulty, he was admitted by order of the king. When he had heard the dream, he mildly answered, "By my lady St. Mary, I shall be truly grateful, if God, through my means, shall choose to take pity upon a wretched creature." In consequence, though he had no confidence in himself, with respect to miracles, yet, at the instigation of his servants, he placed his hand, dipped in water, on the blind man. In a moment the blood dripped plentifully from his eyes, and the man, restored to sight, exclaimed with rapture, "I see you, O king! I see you, O king!" In this recovered state, he had charge of the royal palace at Windsor, for there the cure had been performed, for a long time; surviving his restorer several years. On the same day, from the same water, three blind men, and a man with one eye, who were supported on the royal arms, received a cure; the servants administering the healing water with perfect confidence.

On Easter-day, he was sitting at table at Westminster, with the crown on his head, and surrounded by a crowd of nobles. While the rest were greedily eating, and making up for the long fast of Lent by the newly provided viands, he, with mind abstracted from earthly things, was absorbed in the contemplation of some divine matter, when presently he excited the attention of the guests by bursting into profuse laughter: and as none presumed to inquire into the cause of his joy, he remained silent as before, till satiety had put an end to the banquet. After the tables were removed, and as he was unrobing in his chamber, three persons of rank followed him; of these earl Harold was one, the second was an abbat, and the third a bishop, who presuming on their intimacy asked the cause of his laughter, observing, that it seemed just matter of astonishment to see him, in such perfect tranquillity both of time and occupation, burst into a vulgar laugh, while all others were silent. "I saw something wonderful," said he, "and therefore I did not laugh without a cause." At this, as is the custom of mankind, they began to inquire and search into the matter more earnestly, entreating that he would condescend to disclose it to them. After much reluctance, he yielded to their persevering solicitations, and related the following wonderful circumstance, saying, that the Seven Sleepers in mount Cœlius had now lain for two hundred years on their right side, but that, at the very hour of his laughter, they turned upon their left; that they would continue to lie in this manner for seventy-four years, which would be a dreadful omen to wretched mortals. For every thing would come to pass, in these seventy-four years, which the Lord had foretold to his disciples concerning the end of the world; nation would rise against nation, and kingdom against kingdom; earthquakes would be in divers places; pestilence and famine, terrors from heaven and great signs; changes in kingdoms; wars of the gentiles against the Christians, and also victories of the Christians over the pagans. Relating these matters to his wondering audience, he descanted on the passion of these sleepers, and the make of their bodies, though totally unnoticed in history, as readily as though he had lived in daily intercourse with them. On hearing this the earl sent a knight; the bishop a clergyman; and the abbat a monk, to Maniches the Constantinopolitan emperor, to investigate the truth of his declaration; adding letters and presents from the king. After being kindly entertained, Maniches sent them to the bishop of Ephesus, giving them at the same time what is called a holy letter, that the martyr-relics of the Seven Sleepers should be shown to the delegates of the king of England.* It fell out that

---

* The Seven Sleepers were inhabitants of Ephesus; six were persons of some consequence, the seventh their servant. During the Decian persecution they retired to a cave, whence they despatched their attendant occasionally to purchase food for them. Decius, hearing this, ordered the mouth of the cave to be stopped up while the fugitives were sleeping. After a lapse of some hundred years, a part of the masonry at the mouth of the cave falling, the light flowing in awakened them. Thinking they had enjoyed a good night's rest, they despatched their servant to buy provision. He finds all appear strange in Ephesus, and a whimsical dialogue takes place, the citizens accusing him of having found hidden treasure, he persisting that he offered the current coin of the empire. At length the attention of the emperor

the presage of king Edward was proved by all the Greeks, who could swear they had heard from their fathers that the men were lying on their right side; but after the entrance of the English into the vault, they published the truth of the foreign prophecy to their countrymen. Nor was it long before the predicted evils came to pass; for the Hagarens, and Arabs, and Turks, nations averse to Christ, making havoc of the Christians, overran Syria, and Lycia, and Asia Minor altogether, devastating many cities too of Asia Major, among which was Ephesus, and even Jerusalem itself. At the same time, on the death of Maniches emperor of Constantinople, Diogenes, and Michaelius, and Bucinacius, and Alexius, in turn hurled each other headlong from the throne; the last of whom, continuing till our time, left for heir his son John more noted for cunning and deceit than worth. He contrived many hurtful plots against the pilgrims on their sacred journey; but venerating the fidelity of the English, he showed them every civility, and transmitted his regard for them to his son.* In the next seven years were three popes, Victor, Stephen, Nicholas,† who diminished the vigour of the papacy by their successive deaths. Almost immediately afterwards too died Henry, the pious emperor of the Romans, and had for successor Henry his son, who brought many calamities on the city of Rome by his folly and his wickedness. The same year Henry, king of France, a good and active warrior, died by poison. Soon after a comet, a star denoting, as they say, change in kingdoms, appeared trailing its extended and fiery train along the sky. Wherefore a certain monk of our monastery,‡ by name Elmer, bowing down with terror at the sight of the brilliant star, wisely exclaimed, "Thou art come! a matter of lamentation to many a mother art thou come; I have seen

is excited, and he goes in company with the bishop to visit them. They relate their story and shortly after expire. In consequence of the miracle they were considered as martyrs. See Capgrave, Legenda Nova.

* On the Norman conquest many English fled to Constantinople, where they were eagerly received by Alexius, and opposed to the Normans under Robert Guiscard. Orderic. Vitalis, p. 508.

† Victor II. succeeded Leo IX. in 1056, and died in 1057. Stephen or Frederic, brother of duke Godefroi, succeeded Victor II. on the second of August, 1057, and Nicolaus became pope in 1059.

‡ That is, of Malmesbury. This Elmer is not to be confounded with Elmer or Ailmer prior of Canterbury.

thee long since; but I now behold thee much more terrible, threatening to hurl destruction on this country." He was a man of good learning for those times, of mature age, and in his early youth had hazarded an attempt of singular temerity. He had by some contrivance fastened wings to his hands and feet, in order that, looking upon the fable as true, he might fly like Dædalus, and collecting the air on the summit of a tower, had flown for more than the distance of a furlong; but, agitated by the violence of the wind and the current of air, as well as by the consciousness of his rash attempt, he fell and broke his legs, and was lame ever after. He used to relate as the cause of his failure, his forgetting to provide himself a tail.

Another prophecy similar to this, Edward uttered when dying, which I shall here anticipate. When he had lain two days speechless, on the third, sadly and deeply sighing as he awoke from his torpor, "Almighty God," said he, "as this shall be a real vision, or a vain illusion, which I have seen, grant me the power of explaining it, or not, to the bystanders" Soon after speaking fluently, "I saw just now," continued he, "two monks near me, whom formerly, when a youth in Normandy, I knew both to have lived in a most religious manner, and to have died like perfect Christians. These men, announcing themselves as the messengers of God, spake to the following effect : ' Since the chiefs of England, the dukes, bishops, and abbats, are not the ministers of God, but of the devil, God, after your death, has delivered this kingdom for a year and a day, into the hand of the enemy, and devils shall wander over all the land.' And when I said that I would show these things to my people ; and promised that they should liberate themselves by repentance, after the old example of the Ninevites ; ' Neither of these,' said they, ' shall take place ; for they will not repent, nor will God have mercy on them.' When then, said I, may cessation from such great calamities be hoped for ? They replied, ' Whenever a green tree shall be cut through the middle, and the part cut off, being carried the space of three acres from the trunk, shall, without any assistance, become again united to its stem, bud out with flowers, and stretch forth its fruit, as before, from the sap again uniting ; then may a cessation of such evils be at last expected.' "

Though others were apprehensive of the truth of this prediction, yet Stigand, at that time archbishop, received it with laughter ; saying, that the old man doted through disease. We, however, find the truth of the presage experimentally ; for England is become the residence of foreigners, and the property of strangers : at the present time, there is no Englishman, either earl, bishop, or abbat ; strangers all, they prey upon the riches and vitals of England ; nor is there any hope of a termination to this misery. The cause of which evil, as I have long since promised, it is now high time that my narrative should endeavour briefly to disclose.

King Edward declining into years, as he had no children himself, and saw the sons of Godwin growing in power, despatched messengers to the king of Hungary, to send over Edward, the son of his brother Edmund, with all his family : intending, as he declared, that either he, or his sons, should succeed to the hereditary kingdom of England, and that his own want of issue should be supplied by that of his kindred. Edward came in consequence, but died almost immediately at St. Paul's* in London : he was neither valiant, nor a man of abilities. He left three surviving children ; that is to say, Edgar, who, after the death of Harold, was by some elected king ; and who, after many revolutions of fortune, is now living wholly retired in the country, in extreme old age : Christina, who grew old at Romsey in the habit of a nun . Margaret, whom Malcolm king of the Scots espoused. Blessed with a numerous offspring, her sons were Edgar, and Alexander, who reigned in Scotland after their father in due succession : for the eldest, Edward, had fallen in battle with his father ; the youngest, David, noted for his meekness and discretion, is at present king of Scotland. Her daughters were, Matilda, whom in our time king Henry has married, and Maria, whom Eustace the younger, earl of Boulogne, espoused. The king, in consequence of the death of his relation, losing his first hope of support, gave the succession of England to William earl of Normandy.† He was well worthy of such a gift, being a young man of superior mind, who had raised himself to the highest eminence by his un-

* Died and was buried at St Paul's. Sax. Chron. A. 1057.

† It is hardly necessary to observe, that the succession of William is one of the most obscure points in our history.

wearied exertion : moreover, he was his nearest relation by consanguinity, as he was the son of Robert, the son of Richard the second, whom we have repeatedly mentioned as the brother of Emma, Edward's mother. Some affirm that Harold himself was sent into Normandy by the king for this purpose : others, who knew Harold's more secret intentions, say, that being driven thither against his will, by the violence of the wind, he imagined this device, in order to extricate himself. This, as it appears nearest the truth, I shall relate. Harold being at his country-seat at Boseham,* went for recreation on board a fishing boat, and, for the purpose of prolonging his sport, put out to sea ; when a sudden tempest arising, he was driven with his companions on the coast of Ponthieu. The people of that district, as was their native custom, immediately assembled from all quarters ; and Harold's company, unarmed and few in number, were, as it easily might be, quickly overpowered by an armed multitude, and bound hand and foot. Harold, craftily meditating a remedy for this mischance, sent a person, whom he had allured by very great promises, to William, to say, that he had been sent into Normandy by the king, for the purpose of expressly confirming, in person, the message which had been imperfectly delivered by people of less authority ; but that he was detained in fetters by Guy earl of Ponthieu, and could not execute his embassy : that it was the barbarous and inveterate custom of the country, that such as had escaped destruction at sea, should meet with perils on shore : that it well became a man of his dignity, not to let this pass unpunished : that to suffer those to be laden with chains, who appealed to his protection, detracted somewhat from his own greatness : and that if his captivity must be terminated by money, he would gladly give it to earl William, but not to the contemptible Guy. By these means, Harold was liberated at William's command, and conducted to Normandy by Guy in person. The earl entertained him with much respect, both in banqueting and in vesture, according to the custom of his country ; and the better to learn his disposition, and at the same time to try his courage, took him with him in an expedition he at that time led against Brittany. There, Harold, well proved both in ability and courage, won the

* Near Chichester.

heart of the Norman; and, still more to ingratiate himself, he of his own accord, confirmed to him by oath the castle of Dover, which was under his jurisdiction, and the kingdom of England, after the death of Edward. Wherefore, he was honoured both by having his daughter, then a child, betrothed to him, and by the confirmation of his ample patrimony, and was received into the strictest intimacy. Not long after his return home, the king was crowned* at London on Christmas-day, and being there seized with the disorder of which he was sensible he should die, he commanded the church of Westminster to be dedicated on Innocents-day.† Thus, full of years and of glory, he surrendered his pure spirit to heaven, and was buried on the day of the Epiphany, in the said church, which he, first in England, had erected after that kind of style which, now, almost all attempt to rival at enormous expense. The race of the West Saxons, which had reigned in Britain five hundred and seventy-one years, from the time of Cerdic, and two hundred and sixty-one from Egbert, in him ceased altogether to rule. For while the grief for the king's death was yet fresh, Harold, on the very day of the Epiphany, seized the diadem, and extorted from the nobles their consent; though the English say, that it was granted him by the king: but I conceive it alleged, more through regard to Harold, than through sound judgment, that Edward should transfer his inheritance to a man of whose power he had always been jealous. Still, not to conceal the truth, Harold would have governed the kingdom with prudence and with courage, in the character he had assumed, had he undertaken it lawfully. Indeed, during Edward's lifetime, he had quelled, by his valour, whatever wars were excited against him; wishing to signalize himself with his countrymen, and looking forward

* It was customary for the king to wear his crown on the solemn festivals of Easter, Whitsuntide, and Christmas: it being placed on his head in due form by the archbishop.

† "Westminster Abbey was consecrated on the 28th of December, 1065. Ailred of Rievaulx, in his Life of Edward, states that the church had been commenced some years before, in performance of a vow the king had made to go to Rome; but being dissuaded from it, he sent to the pope to obtain his dispensation from that journey; the pope granted it, on condition that Edward should, with the money he would have spent in that voyage, build a monastery in honour of St. Peter."—HARDY.

with anxious hope to the crown. He first vanquished Griffin king of the Welsh, as I have before related, in battle; and, afterwards, when he was again making formidable efforts to recover his power, deprived him of his head; appointing as his successors, two of his own adherents, that is, the brothers of this Griffin, Blegent and Rivallo, who had obtained his favour by their submission. The same year Tosty arrived on the Humber, from Flanders, with a fleet of sixty ships, and infested with piratical depredations those parts which were adjacent to the mouth of the river; but being quickly driven from the province by the joint force of the brothers, Edwin and Morcar, he set sail towards Scotland; where meeting with Harold Harfager king of Norway, then meditating an attack on England with three hundred ships, he put himself under his command. Both, then, with united forces, laid waste the country beyond the Humber; and falling on the brothers, reposing after their recent victory and suspecting no attack of the kind, they first routed, and then shut them up in York. Harold, on hearing this, proceeded thither with all his forces, and, each nation making every possible exertion, a bloody encounter followed: but the English obtained the advantage, and put the Norwegians to flight. Yet, however reluctantly posterity may believe it, one single Norwegian for a long time delayed the triumph of so many, and such great men. For standing on the entrance of the bridge, which is called Standford Brigge,* after having killed several of our party, he prevented the whole from passing over. Being invited to surrender, with the assurance that a man of such courage should experience the amplest clemency from the English, he derided those who entreated him; and immediately, with stern countenance, reproached the set of cowards who were unable to resist an individual. No one approaching nearer, as they thought it unadvisable to come to close quarters with a man who had desperately rejected every means of safety, one of the king's followers aimed an iron javelin at him from a distance; and transfixed him as he was boastfully flourishing about, and too incautious from his security, so that he yielded the victory to the English. The army immediately

* The battle of Stanford-bridge was fought on the 25th of September, 1066. See Saxon. Chron. p. 440.

passing over without opposition, destroyed the dispersed and flying Norwegians. King Harfager and Tosty were slain; the king's son, with all the ships, was kindly sent back to his own country. Harold, elated by his successful enterprise, vouchsafed no part of the spoil to his soldiers. Wherefore many, as they found opportunity, stealing away, deserted the king, as he was proceeding to the battle of Hastings. For with the exception of his stipendiary and mercenary soldiers, he had very few of the people* with him; on which account, circumvented by a stratagem of William's, he was routed, with the army he headed, after possessing the kingdom nine months and some days. The effect of war in this affair was trifling; it was brought about by the secret and wonderful counsel of God: since the Angles never again, in any general battle, made a struggle for liberty, as if the whole strength of England had fallen with Harold, who certainly might and ought to pay the penalty of his perfidy, even though it were at the hands of the most unwarlike people. Nor in saying this, do I at all derogate from the valour of the Normans, to whom I am strongly bound, both by my descent, and for the privileges I enjoy. Still† those persons appear to me to err, who augment the numbers of the English, and underrate their courage; who, while they design to extol the Normans, load them with ignominy. A mighty commendation indeed! that a very warlike nation should conquer a set of people who were obstructed by their multitude, and fearful through cowardice! On the contrary, they were few in number and brave in the extreme; and sacrificing every regard to their bodies, poured forth their spirit for their country. But, however, as these matters await a more detailed narrrative, I shall now put a period to my second book, that I may return to my composition, and my readers to the perusal of it, with fresh ardour.

* What Malmesbury here relates is highly probable, from the shortness of the time which elapsed from William's landing, to the battle of Hastings,—only fifteen days. In this period, therefore, the intelligence was to be conveyed to York, and Harold's march into Sussex to be completed; of course few could accompany him, but such as were mounted.

† Will. Pictaviensis, to whom he seems here to allude, asserts that Harold had collected immense forces from all parts of England; and that Denmark had supplied him with auxiliaries also. But the circumstances mentioned in the preceding note show the absurdity of this statement.

BOOK III.

PREFACE.

NORMANS and English, incited by different motives, have written of king William: the former have praised him to excess; extolling to the utmost both his good and his bad actions: while the latter, out of national hatred, have laden their conqueror with undeserved reproach. For my part, as the blood of either people flows in my veins, I shall steer a middle course: where I am certified of his good deeds, I shall openly proclaim them; his bad conduct I shall touch upon lightly and sparingly, though not so as to conceal it; so that neither shall my narrative be condemned as false, nor will I brand that man with ignominious censure, almost the whole of whose actions may reasonably be excused, if not commended. Wherefore I shall willingly and carefully relate such anecdotes of him, as may be matter of incitement to the indolent, or of example to the enterprising; useful to the present age, and pleasing to posterity. But I shall spend little time in relating such things as are of service to no one, and which produce disgust in the reader, as well as ill-will to the author. There are always people, more than sufficient, ready to detract from the actions of the noble: my course of proceeding will be, to extenuate evil, as much as can be consistently with truth, and not to bestow excessive commendation even on good actions. For this moderation, as I imagine, all true judges will esteem me neither timid, nor unskilful. And this rule too, my history will regard equally, with respect both to William and his two sons; that nothing shall be dwelt on too fondly; nothing untrue shall be admitted. The elder of these did little worthy of praise, if we except the early part of his reign; gaining, throughout the whole of his life, the favour of the military at the expense of the people. The second, more obsequious to his father than to his brother, possessed his spirit, unsubdued either by prosperity or adversity: on regarding his warlike expeditions, it is matter of doubt, whether he was more cautious or more bold; on contemplating their event, whether he was more fortunate, or unsuccessful. There will be a time, however, when the reader may judge for himself. I am now about to begin my third volume; and I think I have said enough to make him attentive, and disposed to receive instruction: his own feelings will persuade him to be candid.

Of William the First. [A D 1066—1087.]

ROBERT, second son of Richard the Second, after he had, with great glory, held the duchy of Normandy for seven years, resolved on a pilgrimage to Jerusalem. He had, at that time, a son seven years of age, born of a concubine, whose beauty he had accidentally beheld, as she was dancing, and had become so smitten with it, as to form a connexion with her: after which, he loved her exclusively, and, for some time, regarded her as his wife. He had by her this boy, named, after his great-great-grandfather, William, whose future glory was portended to his mother by a dream; wherein she imagined her intestines were stretched out, and extended over the whole of Normandy and England: and, at the very moment, also, when the infant burst into life and touched the ground, he filled both hands with the rushes strewed upon the floor, firmly grasping what he had taken up. This prodigy was joyfully witnessed by the women, gossipping on the occasion; and the midwife hailed the propitious omen, declaring that the boy would be a king.

Every provision being made for the expedition to Jerusalem,* the chiefs were summoned to a council at Feschamp, where, at his father's command, all swore fidelity to William: earl Gilbert was appointed his guardian; and the protection of the earl was assigned to Henry, king of France. While Robert was prosecuting his journey, the Normans, each in his several station, united in common for the defence of their country, and regarded their infant lord with great affection. This fidelity continued till the report was spread of Robert's death, upon which their affection changed with his fortune; and then they began severally to fortify their towns, to build castles, to carry in provisions,

* "Robert's expedition to Jerusalem was in 1035," (Bouq. 14, 420.)

and to seek the earliest opportunities of revolting from the child. In the meantime, however, doubtlessly by the special aid of God who had destined him to the sovereignty of such an extended empire, he grew up uninjured; while Gilbert, almost alone, defended by arms what was just and right: the rest being occupied by the designs of their respective parties. But Gilbert being at this time killed by his cousin Rodulph, fire and slaughter raged on all sides. The country, formerly most flourishing, was now torn with intestine broils, and divided at the pleasure of the plunderers; so that it was justly entitled to proclaim, "Woe to the land whose sovereign is a child."*

William, however, as soon as his age permitted, receiving the badge of knighthood from the king of France, inspirited the inhabitants to hope for quiet. The sower of dissension was one Guy, a Burgundian on his father's side, and grandson to Richard the Second by his daughter. William and Guy had been children together, and at that time were equally approaching to manhood. Mutual intercourse had produced an intimacy between them which had ripened into friendship. Moreover, thinking, as they were related, that he ought to deny him nothing, he had given him the castles of Briony and Vernon. The Burgundian, unmindful of this, estranged himself from the earl, feigning sufficient cause of offence to colour his conduct. It would be tedious, and useless, to relate what actions were performed on either side, what castles were taken; for his perfidy had found abettors in Nigel, viscount of Coutances, Ralph, viscount of Bayeux, and Haimo Dentatus, grandfather of Robert, who was the occupier of many estates in England in our time. With these persons, this most daring plunderer, allured by vain expectation of succeeding to the earldom, was devastating the whole of Normandy. A sense of duty, however, compelled the guardian-king to succour the desperate circumstances of his ward. Remembering, therefore, the kindness of his father, and that he had, by his influence, exalted him to the kingdom, he rushed on the revolters at Walesdun. Many thousands of them were there slain; many drowned in the river Orne, by its rapidity, while, being hard-pressed, they spurred their horses to ford the

* Ecclesiast x. 16.

current. Guy, escaping with difficulty, betook himself to Briony; but was driven thence by William, and unable to endure this disgrace, he retired, of his own accord, to Burgundy, his native soil. Here too his unquiet spirit found no rest; for being expelled thence by his brother, William, earl of that province, against whom he had conceived designs, it appears not what fate befell him. Nigel and Ralph were admitted to fealty: Haimo fell in the field of battle; after having become celebrated by his remarkable daring for having unhorsed the king himself; in consequence of which he was despatched by the surrounding guards, and, in admiration of his valour, honourably buried at the king's command. King Henry received a compensation for this favour, when the Norman lord actively assisted him against Geoffrey Martel at Herle-Mill, which is a fortress in the country of Anjou. For William had now attained his manly vigour; an object of dread even to his elders, and though alone, a match for numbers. Unattended he would rush on danger; and when unaccompanied, or with only a few followers, dart into the thickest ranks of the enemy. By this expedition he gained the reputation of admirable bravery, as well as the sincerest regard of the king; so that, with parental affection, he would often admonish him not to hold life in contempt by encountering danger so precipitately; a life, which was the ornament of the French, the safeguard of the Normans, and an example to both.

At that time Geoffrey* was earl of Anjou, who had boastingly taken the surname of Martel, as he seemed, by a certain kind of good fortune, to beat down all his opponents. Finally, he had made captive, in open battle, his liege lord, the earl of Poitou; and, loading him with chains, had compelled him to dishonourable terms of peace; namely, that he should yield up Bourdeaux and the neighbouring cities, and pay an annual tribute for the rest. But he, as it is thought, through the injuries of his confinement and want of food, was, after three days, released from eternal ignominy by a timely death. Martel then, that his effrontery might be complete, married the stepmother of the deceased; taking his brothers under his protection until they should be capa-

* Geoffrey II., son of Foulques III., earl of Anjou, whom he succeeded, A D 1040.

ble of governing the principality. Next entering the territories of Theobald, earl of Blois, he laid siege to the city of Tours, and while he was hastening to the succour of his subjects, made him participate in their afflictions; for being taken, and shut up in prison, he ceded the city from himself and his heirs for ever. Who shall dare cry shame on this man's cowardice, who, for the enjoyment of a little longer life, defrauded his successors for ever of the dominion of so great a city? for although we are too apt to be severe judges of others, yet we must know, that we should consult our own safety, if we were ever to be placed in similar circumstances. In this manner Martel, insolent from the accession of so much power, obtained possession of the castle of Alençon, even from the earl of Normandy; its inhabitants being faithlessly disposed. Irritated at this outrage, William retaliated, and invested Danfrunt, which at that time belonged to the earl of Anjou. Geoffrey, immediately, excited by the complaints of the besieged, hastily rushed forward with a countless force. Hearing of his approach, William sends Roger Montgomery* and William Fitz-Osberne to reconnoitre. They, from the activity of youth, proceeding many miles in a short time, espied Martel on horseback, and apprized him of the dauntless boldness of their lord. Martel immediately began to rage, to threaten mightily what he would do; and said that he would come thither the next day, and show to the world at large how much an Angevin could excel a Norman in battle: at the same time, with unparalleled insolence, describing the colour of his horse, and the devices on the arms he meant to use. The Norman nobles, with equal vanity, relating the same of William, return and stimulate their party to the conflict. I have described these things minutely, for the purpose of displaying the arrogance of Martel. On this occasion, however, he manifested none of his usual magnanimity, for he retreated without coming to battle; on hearing which, the inhabitants

* "He was the son of Hugh de Montgomery and Jemima his wife, daughter of Turolf of Pont-Andomare, by Wora, sister of Gunnora, great-grandmother to the Conqueror. He led the centre of the army at the battle of Hastings, and was afterwards governor of Normandy. William the Conqueror gave him the earldoms of Arundel and Shrewsbury. See more of him in Sir H. Ellis's Introduction to Domesday, vol. 1. p. 479."—HARDY.

of Alençon surrendered, covenanting for personal safety; and, afterwards, those of Danfrunt also, listed under the more fortunate standard.

In succeeding years William, earl of Arches, his illegitimate uncle, who had always been faithless and fluctuating from his first entrance on the duchy, rebelled against him; for, even during the siege of Danfrunt, he had unexpectedly stolen away, and had communicated to many persons the secrets of his soul. In consequence of this, William had committed the keeping of his castle to some men, whom he had erroneously deemed faithful; but the earl, with his usual skill in deception, had seduced even these people to his party, by giving them many things, and promising them more. Thus possessed of the fortress, he declared war against his lord. William, with his customary alacrity, contrary to the advice of his friends, laid siege to Arches, declaring publicly, that the miscreants would not dare attempt any thing, if they came into his sight. Nor was his assertion false: for more than three hundred soldiers who had gone out to plunder and forage, the instant they beheld him, though almost unattended, fled back into their fortifications. Being inclined to settle this business without bloodshed, he fortified a castle in front of Arches, and turned to matters of hostile operation which required deeper attention, because he was aware that the king of France, who had already become adverse to him from some unknown cause, was hastening to the succour of the besieged. He here gave an instance of very laudable forbearance; for though he certainly appeared to have the juster cause, yet he was reluctant to engage with that person, to whom he was bound both by oath and by obligation. He left some of his nobility, however, to repress the impetuosity of the king; who, falling into an ambush laid by their contrivance, had most deservedly to lament Isembard, earl of Ponthieu, who was killed in his sight, and Hugh Bardulf, who was taken prisoner. Not long after, in consequence of his miscarriage, retiring to his beloved France, the earl of Arches, wasted with hunger, and worn to a skeleton, consented to surrender, and was preserved, life and limb, an example of clemency, and a proof of perseverance. During the interval of this siege, the people of the fortress called Moulin, becoming disaffected, at the instigation of one Walter, went over to the king's side. An active party of soldiers was placed there, under the command of Guy, brother of the earl of Poitou, who diligently attended for some time to his military duties: but on hearing the report of the victory at Arches, he stole away into France, and contributed, by these means, considerably to the glory of the duke.

King Henry, however, did not give indulgence to inactivity, but, muttering that his armies had been a laughing-stock to William, immediately collected all his forces, and, dividing them into two bodies, he over-ran the whole of Normandy. He himself headed all the military power which came from that part of Celtic Gaul which lies between the rivers Garonne and Seine, and gave his brother Odo the command over such as came from that part of Belgic Gaul which is situated between the Rhine and the Seine. In like manner William divided his army, with all the skill he possessed; approaching by degrees the camp of the king, which was pitched in the country of Briony, in such a manner, as neither to come to close engagement, nor yet suffer the province to be devastated in his presence. His generals were Robert, earl of Aux; Hugo de Gournay, Hugo de Montfort, and William Crispin, who opposed Odo at a town called Mortemar. Nor did he, relying on the numerous army which he commanded, at all delay coming to action; yet making only slight resistance at the beginning, and afterwards being unable to withstand the attack of the Normans, he retreated, and was himself the first to fly. And here, while Guy, earl of Ponthieu, was anxiously endeavouring to revenge his brother, he was made captive, and felt, together with many others surpassing in affluence and rank, the weight of that hand which was so fatal to his family. When William was informed of this success by messengers, he took care that it should be proclaimed in the dead of night, near the king's tent. On hearing which he retired, after some days spent in Normandy, into France; and, soon after, ambassadors passing between them, it was concluded, by treaty, that the king's partizans should be set at liberty, and that the earl should become legally possessed of all that had been, or should hereafter be, taken from Martel.

It would be both tedious and useless, to relate their perpetual contentions, or how William always came off conqueror. What shall we say besides, when, magnanimously despising the custom of modern times, he never condescended to attack him suddenly, or without acquainting him of the day. Moreover, I pass by the circumstance of king Henry's again violating his friendship, his entering Normandy, and proceeding through the district of Hiesmes to the river Dive, boasting that the sea was the sole obstacle to his farther progress. But William now perceiving himself reduced to extremities by the king's perfidy, at length brandished the arms of conscious valour, and worsted the royal forces which were beyond the river—for part of them, hearing of his arrival, had passed over some little time before—with such entire loss, that henceforth France had no such object of dread as that of irritating the ferocity of the Normans. The death of Henry soon following, and, shortly after, that of Martel, put an end to these broils. The dying king delegated the care of his son Philip, at that time extremely young, to Baldwin earl of Flanders. He was a man equally celebrated for fidelity and wisdom; in the full possession of bodily strength, and also ennobled by a marriage with the king's sister. His daughter, Matilda, a woman who was a singular mirror of prudence in our time, and the perfection of virtue, had been already married to William. Hence it arose, that being mediator between his ward, and his son-in-law, Baldwin restrained, by his wholesome counsels, the feuds of the chiefs, and of the people.

But since the mention of Martel has so often presented itself, I shall briefly trace the genealogy of the earls of Anjou,* as far as the knowledge of my informant reaches. Fulk the elder, presiding over that county for many years, until he became advanced in years, performed many great and prudent actions. There is only one thing for which I have heard him branded: for, having induced Herbert earl of Maine to come to Saintes, under the promise of yielding him that city, he caused him, in the midst of their conversation, to be surrounded by his attendants, and compelled him to submit to his own conditions: in other respects he was

* "For an account of the earls of Anjou consult the Gesta Consulum Andegavensium, auctore Monacho Benedictino Majoris Monasterii (apud Acherium, tom. iii.)"—HARDY.

a man of irreproachable integrity. In his latter days, he ceded his principality to Geoffrey his son so often mentioned. Geoffrey conducted himself with excessive barbarity to the inhabitants, and with equal haughtiness even to the person who had conferred this honour upon him: on which, being ordered by his father to lay down the government and ensigns of authority, he was arrogant enough to take up arms against him. The blood of the old man, though grown cold and languid, yet boiled with indignation; and in the course of a few days, by adopting wiser counsels, he so brought down the proud spirit of his son, that after carrying his saddle* on his back for some miles, he cast himself with his burden at his father's feet. He, fired once more with his ancient courage, rising up and spurning the prostrate youth with his foot, exclaimed, "You are conquered at last! you are conquered!" repeating his words several times. The suppliant had still spirit enough to make this admirable reply, "I am conquered by you alone, because you are my father; by others I am utterly invincible." With this speech his irritated mind was mollified, and having consoled the mortification of his son by paternal affection, he restored him to the principality, with admonitions to conduct himself more wisely: telling him that the prosperity and tranquillity of the people were creditable to him abroad, as well as advantageous at home. In the same year the old man, having discharged all secular concerns, made provisions for his soul, by proceeding to Jerusalem; where compelling two servants by an oath to do whatever he commanded, he was by them publicly dragged naked, in the sight of the Turks, to the holy sepulchre. One of them had twisted a withe about his neck, the other with a rod scourged his bare back, whilst he cried out, "Lord, receive the wretched Fulk, thy perfidious, thy runagate; regard my repentant soul, O Lord Jesu Christ." At this time he obtained not his request; but, peacefully returning home, he died some few years after. The precipitate boldness of his

* To carry a saddle was a punishment of extreme ignominy for certain crimes. See another instance in W Gemeticensis, Du Chesne, p 259, and Du Cange, in voce "Sella;" who very justly supposes the disgrace to arise from the offender acknowledging himself a brute, and putting himself entirely in the power of the person he had offended.

son Geoffrey has been amply displayed in my preceding history. He dying, bequeathed to Geoffrey, his sister's son, his inheritance, but his worldly industry he could not leave him. For being a youth of simple manners, and more accustomed to pray in church, than to handle arms, he excited the contempt of the people of that country, who knew not how to live in quiet. In consequence, the whole district becoming exposed to plunderers, Fulk, his brother, of his own accord, seized on the duchy. Fulk was called Rhechin, from his perpetual growling at the simplicity of his brother, whom he finally despoiled of his dignity, and kept in continual custody. He had a wife, who, being enticed by the desire of enjoying a higher title, deserted him and married Philip king of France; who so desperately loved her, regardless of the adage,

> "Majesty and love
> But ill accord, nor share the self-same seat,"

that he patiently suffered himself to be completely governed by her, though he was at the same time desirous of ruling over every other person. Lastly, for several years, merely through regard for her, he suffered himself to be pointed at like an idiot, and to be excommunicated from the whole Christian world. The sons of Fulk were Geoffrey and Fulk. Geoffrey obtaining the hereditary surname of Martel, ennobled it by his exertions: for he procured such peace and tranquillity in those parts, as no one ever had seen, or will see in future. On this account being killed by the treachery of his people, he forfeited the credit of his consummate worth. Fulk succeeding to the government, is yet living;[*] of whom as I shall perhaps have occasion to speak in the times of king Henry, I will now proceed to relate what remains concerning William.

When, after much labour, he had quelled all civil dissension, he meditated an exploit of greater fame, and determined to recover those countries anciently attached to Normandy, though now disunited by long custom. I allude to

---

[*] "From this passage it is clear that Foulques IV. was still the reigning earl of Anjou, which therefore proves that Malmesbury had finished this work before 1129, in which year Geoffrey le Bel, better known as Geoffrey Plantagenet, son of Foulques, became earl of Anjou."—HARDY.

the counties of Maine and Brittany; of which Mans, long since burnt by Martel and deprived of its sovereign Hugo, had lately experienced some little respite under Herbert the son of Hugo; who, with a view to greater security against the earl of Anjou, had submitted, and sworn fidelity to William: besides, he had solicited his daughter in marriage, and had been betrothed to her, though he died by disease ere she was marriageable. He left William his heir, adjuring his subjects to admit no other; telling them, they might have, if they chose, a mild and honourable lord; but, should they not, a most determined assertor of his right. On his decease, the inhabitants of Maine rather inclined to Walter of Mantes, who had married Hugo's sister: but at length, being brought to their senses by many heavy losses, they acknowledged William. This was the time, when Harold was unwillingly carried to Normandy by an unpropitious gale; whom, as is before mentioned, William took with him in his expedition to Brittany, to make proof of his prowess, and, at the same time, with the deeper design of showing to him his military equipment, that he might perceive how far preferable was the Norman sword to the English battle-axe. Alan, at that time, earl of Brittany, flourishing in youth, and of transcendent strength, had overcome his uncle Eudo, and performed many famous actions; and so far from fearing William, had even voluntarily irritated him. But he, laying claim to Brittany as his hereditary territory, because Charles had given it with his daughter, Gisla, to Rollo, shortly acted in such wise, that Alan came suppliantly to him, and surrendered himself and his possessions. And since I shall have but little to say of Brittany hereafter, I will here briefly insert an extraordinary occurrence, which happened about that time in the city of Nantes.

There were in that city two clerks, who though not yet of legal age, had obtained the priesthood from the bishop of that place, more by entreaty than desert: the pitiable death of one of whom, at length taught the survivor, how near they had before been to the brink of hell As to the knowledge of literature, they were so instructed, that they wanted little of perfection. From their earliest infancy, they had in such wise vied in offices of friendship, that according to the expression of the comic writer,* "To serve each other they would not only stir hand and foot, but even risk the loss of life itself." Wherefore, one day, when they found their minds more than usually free from outward cares, they spoke their sentiments, in a secret place, to the following effect: "That for many years they had given their attention sometimes to literature, and sometimes to secular cares; nor had they satisfied their minds, which had been occupied rather in wrong than proper pursuits, that in the meanwhile, the bitter day was insensibly approaching, which would burst the bond of union which was indissoluble while life remained: wherefore they should provide in time, that the friendship which united them while living should accompany him who died first to the place of the dead." They agreed, therefore, that whichever should first depart, should certainly appear to the survivor, either waking or sleeping, if possible within thirty days, to inform him, that, according to the Platonic tenet, death does not extinguish the spirit, but sends it back again, as it were from prison, to God its author. If this did not take place, then they must yield to the sect of the Epicureans, who hold, that the soul, liberated from the body, vanishes into air, or mingles with the wind. Mutually plighting their faith, they repeated this oath in their daily conversation. A short time elapsed, and behold a violent death suddenly deprived one of them of life. The other remained, and seriously revolving the promise of his friend, and constantly expecting his presence, during thirty days, found his hopes disappointed. At the expiration of this time, when, despairing of seeing him, he had occupied his leisure in other business, the deceased, with that pale countenance which dying persons assume, suddenly stood before him, when awake, and busied on some matter. The dead first addressing the living man, who was silent: "Do you know me?" said he; "I do," replied the other; "nor am I so much disturbed at your unusual presence, as I wonder at your prolonged absence." But when he had accounted for the tardiness of his appearance; "At length," said he, "at length, having overcome every impediment, I am present; which presence, if you please, my friend, will be advantageous to you, but to me totally unprofitable; for I am doomed, by a sentence

* Terent. Andr. iv. 1.

which has been pronounced and approved, to eternal punishment." When the living man promised to give all his property to monasteries, and to the poor, and to spend days and nights in fasting and prayer, for the release of the defunct; he replied, "What I have said is fixed; for the judgments of God, by which I am plunged in the sulphureous whirlpool of hell, are without repentance. There I shall be tossed for my crimes, as long as the pole whirls round the stars, or ocean beats the shores. The rigour of this irreversible sentence remains for ever, devising lasting and innumerable kinds of punishment: now, therefore, let the whole world seek for availing remedies! And that you may experience some little of my numberless pains, behold," said he, stretching out his hand, dripping with a corrupted ulcer, "one of the very smallest of them; does it appear trifling to you?" When the other replied, that it did appear so; he bent his fingers into the palm, and threw three drops of the purulent matter upon him; two of which touching his temples, and one his forehead, penetrated the skin and flesh, as if with a burning cautery, and made holes of the size of a nut. When his friend acknowledged the acuteness of the pain, by the cry he uttered, "This," said the dead man, "will be a strong proof to you, as long as you live, of my pains; and, unless you neglect it, a singular token for your salvation. Wherefore, while you have the power; while indignation is suspended over your head; while God's lingering mercy waits for you; change your habit, change your disposition; become a monk at Rennes, in the monastery of St. Melanius." When the living man was unwilling to agree to these words, the other, sternly glancing at him, "If you doubt, wretched man," said he, "turn and read these letters;" and with these words, he stretched out his hand, inscribed with black characters, in which, Satan, and all the company of infernals sent their thanks, from hell, to the whole ecclesiastical body; as well for denying themselves no single pleasure, as for sending, through neglect of their preaching, so many of their subject-souls to hell, as no former age had ever witnessed. With these words the speaker vanished; and the hearer distributing his whole property to the church and to the poor, went to the monastery; admonishing all, who heard or saw him, of his sudden conversion, and extraordinary interview, so that they exclaimed, "It is the right hand of the Almighty that has done this."

I feel no regret at having inserted this for the benefit of my readers: now I shall return to William. For since I have briefly, but I hope not uselessly, gone over the transactions in which he was engaged, when only earl of Normandy, for thirty years, the order of time now requires a new series of relation; that I may, as far as my inquiries have discovered, detect fallacy, and declare the truth relating to his regal government.

When king Edward had yielded to fate, England, fluctuating with doubtful favour, was uncertain to which ruler she should commit herself: to Harold, William, or Edgar: for the king had recommended him also to the nobility, as nearest to the sovereignty in point of birth; concealing his better judgment from the tenderness of his disposition. Wherefore, as I have said above, the English were distracted in their choice, although all of them openly wished well to Harold. He, indeed, once dignified with the diadem, thought nothing of the covenant between himself and William: he said, that he was absolved from his oath, because his daughter, to whom he had been betrothed, had died before she was marriageable. For this man, though possessing numberless good qualities, is reported to have been careless about abstaining from perfidy, so that he could, by any device, elude the reasonings of men on this matter. Moreover, supposing that the threats of William would never be put into execution, because he was occupied in wars with neighbouring princes, he had, with his subjects, given full indulgence to security. For indeed, had he not heard that the king of Norway was approaching, he would neither have condescended to collect troops, nor to array them. William, in the meantime, began mildly to address him by messengers; to expostulate on the broken covenant; to mingle threats with entreaties; and to warn him, that ere a year expired, he would claim his due by the sword, and that he would come to that place, where Harold supposed he had firmer footing than himself. Harold again rejoined what I have related, concerning the nuptials of his daughter, and added, that he had been precipitate on the subject of the kingdom, in having confirmed to him by oath another's right, without the universal consent and edict of the general meeting, and of the people: again, that a rash oath ought to be broken; for if the oath, or vow, which a maiden, under her father's roof, made concerning her person, without the knowledge of her parents, was adjudged invalid; how much more invalid must that oath be, which he had made concerning the whole kingdom, when under the king's authority, compelled by the necessity of the time, and without the knowledge of the nation.* Besides it was an unjust request, to ask him to resign a government which he had assumed by the universal kindness of his fellow subjects, and which would neither be agreeable to the people, nor safe for the military.

In this way, confounded either by true, or plausible, arguments, the messengers returned without success. The earl, however, made every necessary preparation for war during the whole of that year; retained his own soldiers with increased pay, and invited those of others: ordered his ranks and battalions in such wise, that the soldiers should be tall and stout; that the commanders and standard-bearers, in addition to their military science, should be looked up to for their wisdom and age; insomuch, that each of them, whether seen in the field or elsewhere, might be taken for a prince, rather than a leader. The bishops and abbats of those days vied so much in religion, and the nobility in princely liberality, that it is wonderful,† within a period of less than sixty‡ years, how either order should have become so unfruitful in goodness, as to take up a confederate war against justice: the former, through desire of ecclesiastical promotion, embracing wrong in preference to right and equity; and the latter, casting off shame, and seeking every occasion

* "These words seem to imply that the Great Council of the kingdom had never agreed to any settlement of the crown on the duke; and without such sanction no oath made by Harold in favour of William would have been binding."—HARDY.

† Some copies omit from "it is wonderful," to "But," and substitute as follows:— . . . . . "that in the course of a very few years, many, if not all, things were seen changed in either order. The former became, in some respects, more dull but more liberal; the latter, more prudent in every thing, but more penurious; yet both, in defending their country, valiant in battle, provident in counsel; prepared to advance their own fortune, and to depress that of their enemies."

‡ This passage enables us to ascertain nearly the year in which William of Malmesbury's work was written.

for begging money as for their daily pay. But at that time the prudence of William, seconded by the providence of God, already anticipated the invasion of England; and that no rashness might stain his just cause, he sent to the pope, formerly Anselm, bishop of Lucca, who had assumed the name of Alexander, alleging the justice of the war which he meditated with all the eloquence he was master of. Harold omitted to do this, either because he was proud by nature, or else distrusted his cause; or because he feared that his messengers would be obstructed by William and his partisans, who beset every port. The pope, duly examining the pretensions of both parties, delivered a standard to William, as an auspicious presage of the kingdom: on receiving which, he summoned an assembly of his nobles, at Lillebourne, for the purpose of ascertaining their sentiments on this attempt. And when he had confirmed, by splendid promises, all who approved his design, he appointed them to prepare shipping, in proportion to the extent of their possessions. Thus they departed at that time; and, in the month of August, re-assembled in a body at St. Vallery,* for so that port is called by its new name. Collecting, therefore, ships from every quarter, they awaited the propitious gale which was to carry them to their destination. When this delayed blowing for several days, the common soldiers, as is generally the case, began to mutter in their tents, "that the man must be mad, who wished to subjugate a foreign country; that God opposed him, who withheld the wind; that his father purposed a similar attempt, and was in like manner frustrated; that it was the fate of that family to aspire to things beyond their reach, and find God for their adversary." In consequence of these things, which were enough to enervate the force of the brave, being publicly noised abroad, the duke held a council with his chiefs, and ordered the body of St. Vallery to be brought forth, and to be exposed to the open air, for the purpose of imploring a

---

* "There are two places called St Valeri; one in Picardy, situated at the mouth of the Somme, and formerly called Leugonaus; the other is a large sea-port town, situated in Normandy, in the diocese of Rouen, and was formerly called S. Valeri les Plains, but now S. Valeri en Caux. It seems to be the former place to which Malmesbury here refers, 'In Pontivo apud S Walericum in ancoris congrue stare fecit,' writes William of Jumieges."—HARDY.

wind. No delay now interposed, but the wished-for gale filled their sails. A joyful clamour then arising, summoned every one to the ships. The earl himself first launching from the continent into the deep, awaited the rest, at anchor, nearly in mid-channel. All then assembled round the crimson sail of the admiral's ship; and, having first dined, they arrived, after a favourable passage, at Hastings. As he disembarked he slipped down, but turned the accident to his advantage; a soldier who stood near calling out to him, "you hold England,* my lord, its future king." He then restrained his whole army from plundering; warning them, that they should now abstain from what must hereafter be their own;† and for fifteen successive days he remained so perfectly quiet, that he seemed to think of nothing less than of war.

In the meantime Harold returned from the battle with the Norwegians; happy, in his own estimation, at having conquered, but not so in mine, as he had secured the victory by parricide. When the news of the Norman's arrival reached him, reeking as he was from battle, he proceeded to Hastings, though accompanied by very few forces. No doubt the fates urged him on, as he neither summoned his

* This was said in allusion to the feudal investiture, or formal act of taking possession of an estate by the delivery of certain symbols "This story, however, is rendered a little suspicious by these words being in exact conformity with those of Cæsar, when he stumbled and fell in his landing in Africa, *Teneo te, Africa.* The silence of William of Poitou, who was the duke's chaplain, and with him at his landing, makes the truth of it still more doubtful"—HARDY.

† "Whatever may have been the conqueror's orders, to restrain his army from plundering, it is conclusive, from the Domesday Survey, that they were of no avail. The whole of the country, in the neighbourhood of Hastings, appears to have been laid waste. Sir Henry Ellis, in the last edition of his General Introduction to Domesday, observes, that the destruction occasioned by the conqueror's army on its first arrival, is apparent more particularly under Hollington, Bexhill, &c The value of each manor is given as it stood in the reign of the conqueror; afterwards it is said, ' vastatum fuit,' and then follows the value at the time of the survey. The situation of those manors evidently shows their devastated state to have been owing to the army marching over it; and this clearly evinces another circumstance relating to the invasion, which is, that William did not land his army at one particular spot, at Bulwerhithe, or Hastings, as is supposed,—but at all the several proper places for landing along the coast, from Bexhill to Winchelsea."—HARDY.

troops, nor, had he been willing to do so, would he have found many ready to obey his call; so hostile were all to him, as I have before observed, from his having appropriated the northern spoils entirely to himself. He sent out some persons, however, to reconnoitre the number and strength of the enemy: these, being taken within the camp, William ordered to be led amongst the tents, and, after feasting them plentifully, to be sent back uninjured to their lord. On their return, Harold inquired what news they brought: when, after relating at full, the noble confidence of the general, they gravely added, that almost all his army had the appearance of priests, as they had the whole face, with both lips, shaven. For the English leave the upper lip unshorn, suffering the hair continually to increase; which Julius Cæsar, in his treatise on the Gallic War,* affirms to have been a national custom with the ancient inhabitants of Britain. The king smiled at the simplicity of the relators, observing, with a pleasant laugh, that they were not priests, but soldiers, strong in arms, and invincible in spirit. His brother, Girth, a youth, on the verge of manhood, and of knowledge and valour surpassing his years, caught up his words: "Since," said he, "you extol so much the valour of the Norman, I think it ill-advised for you, who are his inferior in strength and desert, to contend with him. Nor can you deny being bound to him, by oath, either willingly, or by compulsion. Wherefore you will act wisely, if, yourself withdrawing from this pressing emergency, you allow us to try the issue of a battle. We, who are free from all obligation, shall justly draw the sword in defence of our country. It is to be apprehended, if you engage, that you will be either subjected to flight or to death: whereas, if we only fight, your cause will be safe at all events: for you will be able both to rally the fugitives, and to avenge the dead."

His unbridled rashness yielded no placid ear to the words of his adviser, thinking it base, and a reproach to his past ilfe, to turn his back on danger of any kind; and, with similar impudence, or to speak more favourably, imprudence, he drove away a monk, the messenger of William, not deigning him even a complacent look; imprecating only, that God would decide between him and the earl. He was the bearer

* Lib. v. c. 14.

of three propositions: either that Harold should relinquish the kingdom, according to his agreement, or hold it of William; or decide the matter by single combat in the sight of either army. For William* claimed the kingdom, on the ground that king Edward, by the advice of Stigand, the archbishop, and of the earls Godwin and Siward, had granted it to him, and had sent the son and nephew of Godwin to Normandy, as sureties of the grant. If Harold should deny this, he would abide by the judgment of the pope, or by battle: on all which propositions, the messenger being frustrated by the single answer I have related, returned, and communicated to his party fresh spirit for the conflict.

The courageous leaders mutually prepared for battle, each according to his national custom. The English, as we have heard, passed the night without sleep, in drinking and singing, and, in the morning, proceeded without delay towards the enemy; all were on foot, armed with battle-axes, and covering themselves in front by the junction of their shields, they formed an impenetrable body, which would have secured their safety that day, had not the Normans, by a feigned flight, induced them to open their ranks, which till that time, according to their custom, were closely compacted. The king himself on foot, stood, with his brother, near the standard; in order that, while all shared equal danger, none might think of retreating. This standard William sent, after the victory, to the pope; it was sumptuously embroidered, with gold and precious stones, in the form of a man fighting.

On the other side, the Normans passed the whole night in confessing their sins, and received the sacrament in the morning: their infantry, with bows and arrows, formed the vanguard, while their cavalry, divided into wings, were thrown back. The earl, with serene countenance, declaring aloud, that God would favour his, as being the righteous side, called for his arms; and presently, when, through the

---

* This is from W. Pictaviensis, who puts it in the mouth of the conqueror, but it is evidently false; for Godwin died A.D. 1053, Siward A.D. 1055, and in 1054 we find Edward the Confessor sending for his nephew from Hungary, to make him his successor in the kingdom, who, accordingly, arrives in A.D. 1057, and dies almost immediately after. He could not, therefore, have made the settlement as here asserted

hurry of his attendants, he had put on his hauberk the hind part before,* he corrected the mistake with a laugh; saying, "My dukedom shall be turned into a kingdom." Then beginning the song of Roland,† that the warlike example of that man might stimulate the soldiers, and calling on God for assistance, the battle commenced on both sides. They fought with ardour, neither giving ground, for great part of the day. Finding this, William gave a signal to his party, that, by a feigned flight, they should retreat. Through this device, the close body of the English, opening for the purpose of cutting down the straggling enemy, brought upon itself swift destruction; for the Normans, facing about, attacked them thus disordered, and compelled them to fly. In this manner, deceived by a stratagem, they met an honourable death in avenging their country; nor indeed were they at all wanting to their own revenge, as, by frequently making a stand, they slaughtered their pursuers in heaps: for, getting possession of an eminence, they drove down the Normans, when roused with indignation and anxiously striving to gain the higher ground, into the valley beneath, where, easily hurling their javelins and rolling down stones on them as they stood below, they destroyed them to a man. Besides, by a short passage, with which they were acquainted, avoiding a deep ditch, they trod under foot such a multitude of their enemies in that place, that they made the hollow level with the plain, by the heaps of carcasses. This vicissitude of first one party conquering, and then the other, prevailed as long as the life of Harold continued; but when he fell, from having his brain pierced with an arrow, the flight of the English ceased not until night. The valour of both leaders was here eminently conspicuous.

Harold, not merely content with the duty of a general in exhorting others, diligently entered into every soldier-like office; often would he strike the enemy when coming to close quarters, so that none could approach him with impunity; for immediately the same blow levelled both horse and rider. Wherefore, as I have related, receiving the fatal

* As the armour of that time was of mail, this might easily happen.

† What this was is not known; but it is supposed to have been a ballad or romance, commemorating the heroic achievements of the pretended nephew of Charlemagne.

arrow from a distance, he yielded to death. One of the soldiers with a sword gashed his thigh, as he lay prostrate; for which shameful and cowardly action, he was branded with ignominy by William, and dismissed the service.

William too was equally ready to encourage by his voice and by his presence; to be the first to rush forward; to attack the thickest of the foe. Thus everywhere raging, everywhere furious, he lost three choice horses, which were that day pierced under him. The dauntless spirit and vigour of the intrepid general, however, still persisted, though often called back by the kind remonstrance of his body-guard; he still persisted, I say, till approaching night crowned him with complete victory. And no doubt, the hand of God so protected him, that the enemy should draw no blood from his person, though they aimed so many javelins at him.

This was a fatal day to England, a melancholy havoc of our dear country, through its change of masters. For it had long since adopted the manners of the Angles, which had been very various according to the times: for in the first years of their arrival, they were barbarians in their look and manners, warlike in their usages, heathens in their rites; but, after embracing the faith of Christ, by degrees, and in process of time, from the peace they enjoyed, regarding arms only in a secondary light, they gave their whole attention to religion. I say nothing of the poor, the meanness of whose fortune often restrains them from overstepping the bounds of justice: I omit men of ecclesiastical rank, whom sometimes respect to their profession, and sometimes the fear of shame, suffer not to deviate from the truth: I speak of princes, who from the greatness of their power might have full liberty to indulge in pleasure; some of whom, in their own country, and others at Rome, changing their habit, obtained a heavenly kingdom, and a saintly intercourse. Many during their whole lives in outward appearance only embraced the present world, in order that they might exhaust their treasures on the poor, or divide them amongst monasteries. What shall I say of the multitudes of bishops, hermits, and abbats? Does not the whole island blaze with such numerous relics of its natives, that you can scarcely pass a village of any consequence but you hear the name of some new saint, besides the numbers of whom all notices have perished through the want of records? Nevertheless, in process of time, the desire after literature and religion had decayed, for several years before the arrival of the Normans. The clergy, contented with a very slight degree of learning, could scarcely stammer out the words of the sacraments, and a person who understood grammar, was an object of wonder and astonishment. The monks mocked the rule of their order by fine vestments, and the use of every kind of food. The nobility, given up to luxury and wantonness, went not to church in the morning after the manner of Christians, but merely, in a careless manner, heard matins and masses from a hurrying priest in their chambers, amid the blandishments of their wives. The commonalty, left unprotected, became a prey to the most powerful, who amassed fortunes, by either seizing on their property, or by selling their persons into foreign countries, although it be an innate quality of this people, to be more inclined to revelling, than to the accumulation of wealth. There was one custom, repugnant to nature, which they adopted; namely, to sell their female servants, when pregnant by them and after they had satisfied their lust, either to public prostitution, or foreign slavery. Drinking in parties was a universal practice, in which occupation they passed entire nights as well as days. They consumed their whole substance in mean and despicable houses; unlike the Normans and French, who, in noble and splendid mansions, lived with frugality. The vices attendant on drunkenness, which enervate the human mind, followed; hence it arose that engaging William, more with rashness, and precipitate fury, than military skill, they doomed themselves, and their country to slavery, by one, and that an easy, victory. "For nothing is less effective than rashness; and what begins with violence, quickly ceases, or is repelled." In fine, the English at that time, wore short garments reaching to the mid-knee; they had their hair cropped, their beards shaven; their arms laden with golden bracelets; their skin adorned with punctured designs. They were accustomed to eat till they became surfeited, and to drink till they were sick. These latter qualities they imparted to their conquerors, as to the rest, they adopted their manners. I would not, however, have these bad propensities universally ascribed to the English. I know that many of the clergy, at that day, trod the path of sanctity, by a blameless life; I know that many of the laity, of all ranks and conditions, in this nation, were well-pleasing to God. Be injustice far from this account; the accusation does not involve the whole indiscriminately. "But, as in peace, the mercy of God often cherishes the bad and the good together; so, equally, does his severity, sometimes, include them both in captivity."

Moreover, the Normans, that I may speak of them also, were at that time, and are even now, proudly apparelled, delicate in their food, but not excessive. They are a race inured to war, and can hardly live without it; fierce in rushing against the enemy, and where strength fails of success, ready to use stratagem, or to corrupt by bribery. As I have related, they live in large edifices with economy; envy their equals; wish to excel their superiors; and plunder their subjects, though they defend them from others; they are faithful to their lords, though a slight offence renders them perfidious. They weigh treachery by its chance of success, and change their sentiments with money. They are, however, the kindest of nations, and they esteem strangers worthy of equal honour with themselves. They also intermarry with their vassals. They revived, by their arrival, the observances of religion, which were everywhere grown lifeless in England. You might see churches rise in every village, and monasteries in the towns and cities, built after a style unknown before; you might behold the country flourishing with renovated rites; so that each wealthy man accounted that day lost to him, which he had neglected to signalize by some magnificent action. But having enlarged sufficiently on these points, let us pursue the transactions of William.

When his victory was complete, he caused his dead to be interred with great pomp; granting the enemy the liberty of doing the like, if they thought proper. He sent the body of Harold* to his mother, who begged it, unransomed; though

* There seems to have been a fabulous story current during the twelfth century, that Harold escaped from the battle of Hastings. Giraldus Cambrensis asserts, that it was believed Harold had fled from the battle-field, pierced with many wounds, and with the loss of his left eye; and that he ended his days piously and virtuously, as an anchorite, at Chester. Both

she proffered large sums by her messengers. She buried it, when thus obtained, at Waltham; a church which he had built at his own expense, in honour of the Holy Cross, and had endowed for canons. William then, by degrees proceeding, as became a conqueror, with his army, not after an hostile, but a royal manner, journeyed towards London, the principal city of the kingdom; and shortly after, all the citizens came out to meet him with gratulations. Crowds poured out of every gate to greet him, instigated by the nobility, and principally by Stigand, archbishop of Canterbury, and Aldred, of York. For, shortly before, Edwin and Morcar, two brothers of great expectation, hearing, at London, the news of Harold's death, solicited the citizens to exalt one of them to the throne: failing, however, in the attempt, they had departed for Northumberland, conjecturing, from their own feelings, that William would never come thither. The other chiefs would have chosen Edgar, had the bishops supported them; but, danger and domestic broils closely impending, neither did this take effect. Thus the English, who, had they united in one opinion, might have repaired the ruin of their country, introduced a stranger, while they were unwilling to choose a native, to govern them. Being now decidedly hailed king, he was crowned on Christmas-day by archbishop Aldred; for he was careful not to accept this office from Stigand, as he was not canonically an archbishop.

Of the various wars which he carried on, this is a summary. Favoured by God's assistance, he easily reduced the city of Exeter,* when it had rebelled; for part of the wall

Knighton and Brompton quote this story. W. Pictaviensis says, that William refused the body to his mother, who offered its weight in gold for it, ordering it to be buried on the sea-coast. In the Harleian MS. 3776, before referred to, Girth, Harold's brother, is said to have escaped alive: he is represented, in his interview with Henry II. to have spoken mysteriously respecting Harold, and to have declared that the body of that prince was not at Waltham. Sir H. Ellis, quoting this MS., justly observes, that the whole was, probably, the fabrication of one of the secular canons, who were ejected at the re-foundation of Waltham Abbey in 1177."—HARDY.

* Four manuscripts read *Exoniam*, and one, namely, that which was used by Savile, read *Oxoniam*. But Matthew Paris also seems to have read *Exoniam*, for such is the text of the two best MSS. of that author. (Reg. 14. c. vii. and Cott. Nero, D. v.) Upon a passage in the Domesday Survey, describing Oxford as containing 478 houses, which were so

fell down accidentally, and made an opening for him. Indeed he had attacked it with the more ferocity, asserting that those irreverent men would be deserted by God's favour, because one of them, standing upon the wall, had bared his posteriors, and had broken wind, in contempt of the Normans. He almost annihilated the city of York, that sole remaining shelter for rebellion, and destroyed its citizens with sword and famine. For there Malcolm, king of the Scots, with his party; there Edgar, and Morcar, and Waltheof, with the English and Danes, often brooded over the nest of tyranny; there they frequently killed his generals; whose deaths, were I severally to commemorate, perhaps I should not be superfluous, though I might risk the peril of creating disgust; while I should be not easily pardoned as an historian, if I were led astray by the falsities of my authorities.

Malcolm willingly received all the English fugitives, affording to each every protection in his power, but more especially to Edgar, whose sister he had married, out of regard to her noble descent On his behalf he burnt and plundered the adjacent provinces of England; not that he supposed, by so doing, he could be of any service to him, with respect to the kingdom; but merely to distress the mind of William, who was incensed at his territories being subject to Scottish incursions. In consequence, William, collecting a body of foot and horse, repaired to the northern parts of the island, and first of all received into subjection the metropolitan city, which English, Danes, and Scots obstinately defended; its citizens being wasted with continued want. He destroyed also in a great and severe battle, a considerable number of the enemy, who had come to the succour of the besieged; though the victory was not bloodless on his side, as he lost

desolated that they could not pay gold, Sir H. Ellis remarks: " The extraordinary number of houses specified as desolated at Oxford, requires explanation. If the passage is correct, Matthew Paris probably gives us the cause of it, under the year 1067, when William the Conqueror subdued *Oxford* in his way to York :—' Eodem tempore rex Willielmus urbem Oxoniam sibi rebellem obsidione vallavit. Super cujus murum quidam, stans, nudato inguine, sonitu partis inferioris auras turbavit, in contemptum videlicet Normannorum; unde Willielmus in iram conversus, civitatem levi negotio subjugavit' (Matt. P. ed. Watts, sub ann. 1067, p 4.) The siege of Exeter in 1067 is also mentioned by Simeon of Durham, col. 197; Hoveden, col. 258; Ralph de Diceto, col. 482; Flor. of Worces. fol. Franc 1601, p. 635; and by Ordericus Vitalis, p 510."—HARDY.

many of his people. He then ordered both the towns and fields of the whole district to be laid waste; the fruits and grain to be destroyed by fire or by water, more especially on the coast, as well on account of his recent displeasure, as because a rumour had gone abroad, that Canute, king of Denmark, the son of Sweyn, was approaching with his forces. The reason of such a command, was, that the plundering pirate should find no booty on the coast to take with him, if he designed to depart again directly; or should be compelled to provide against want, if he thought proper to stay. Thus the resources of a province,* once flourishing, and the nurse of tyrants, were cut off by fire, slaughter, and devastation; the ground, for more than sixty miles, totally uncultivated and unproductive, remains bare to the present day. Should any stranger now see it, he laments over the once-magnificent cities; the towers threatening heaven itself with their loftiness; the fields abundant in pasturage, and watered with rivers: and, if any ancient inhabitant remains, he knows it no longer.

Malcolm surrendered himself, without coming to an engagement, and for the whole of William's time passed his life under treaties, uncertain, and frequently broken. But when in the reign of William, the son of William, he was attacked in a similar manner, he diverted the king from pursuing him by a false oath. He was slain soon after, together with his son, by Robert Mowbray, earl of Northumberland, while, regardless of his faith, he was devastating the province with more than usual insolence. For many years, he lay buried at Tynemouth: lately he was conveyed by Alexander his son, to Dunfermlin, in Scotland.

* Domesday Book bears ample testimony to this statement; and that which closely follows, viz. that the resources of this once-flourishing province were cut off by fire, slaughter, and devastation; and the ground, for more than sixty miles, totally uncultivated and unproductive, remains bare to the present day. The land, which had belonged to Edwin and Morcar in Yorkshire, almost everywhere in the Survey is stated to be *wasta;* and in Amunderness, after the enumeration of no fewer than sixty-two places, the possessions in which amounted to one hundred and seventy carucates, it is said, 'Omnes hæ villæ jacent ad Prestune, et tres ecclesiæ. Ex his 16 a paucis incoluntur, sed quot sint habitantes ignoratur. Reliqua sunt wasta.' Moreover, *wasta* is added to numerous places belonging to the archbishop of York, St. John of Beverley, the bishop of Durham, and to those lands which had belonged to Waltheof, Gospatric, Siward, and Merlesweyne!—HARDY.

Edgar, having submitted to the king with Stigand and Aldred the archbishops, violated his oath the following year, by going over to the Scot: but after living there some years, and acquiring no present advantage, no future prospects, but merely his daily sustenance, being willing to try the liberality of the Norman, who was at that time beyond the sea, he sailed over to him. They say this was extremely agreeable to the king, that England should be thus rid of a fomenter of dissension. Indeed it was his constant practice, under colour of high honour, to carry over to Normandy all the English he suspected, lest any disorders should arise in the kingdom during his absence. Edgar, therefore, was well received, and presented with a considerable largess: and remaining at court for many years, silently sunk into contempt through his indolence, or more mildly speaking, his simplicity. For how great must his simplicity be, who would yield up to the king, for a single horse, the pound of silver, which he received as his daily stipend? In succeeding times he went to Jerusalem with Robert, the son of Godwin,* a most valiant knight. This was the time when the Turks besieged king Baldwin, at Rama; who, unable to endure the difficulties of a siege, rushed through the midst of the enemy, by the assistance of Robert alone, who preceded him, and hewed down the Turks, on either hand, with his drawn sword; but, while excited to greater ferocity by his success, he was pressing on with too much eagerness, his sword dropped from his hand, and when stooping down to recover it, he was surrounded by a multitude, and cast into chains. Taken thence to Babylon, as they report, when he refused to deny Christ, he was placed as a mark in the middle of the market-place, and being transfixed with darts, died a martyr. Edgar, having lost his companion, returned, and received many gifts from the Greek

* Fordun has a story of Edgar's being cleared from an accusation of treason against W. Rufus, by one Godwin, in a duel; whose son, Robert, is afterwards described as one of Edgar's adherents in Scotland. L. v. c 27—34. "The Saxon Chronicle states, that in the year 1106, he was one of the prisoners taken at the battle of Tinchebrai, in Normandy. Edgar is stated, by Dr. Sayers, in his Disquisitions, 8vo, 1808, p. 296, upon the authority of the Spelman MSS., to have again visited Scotland at a very advanced period of life, and died in that kingdom in the year 1120. If this date can be relied upon, the passage above noted would prove that Malmesbury had written this portion of his history before the close of that year."—HARDY.

and German emperors; who, from respect to his noble descent, would also have endeavoured to retain him with them; but he gave up every thing, through regard to his native soil. "For, truly, the love of their country deceives some men to such a degree, that nothing seems pleasant to them, unless they can breathe their native air." Edgar, therefore, deluded by this silly desire, returned to England; where, as I have before said, after various revolutions of fortune, he now grows old in the country in privacy and quiet.

Edwin and Morcar were brothers; the sons of Elfgar, the son of Leofric. They had received charge of the county of Northumberland, and jointly preserved it in tranquillity. For, as I have before observed, a few days previous to the death of St. Edward the king, the inhabitants of the north had risen in rebellion and expelled Tosty, their governor; and, with Harold's approbation, had requested, and received, one of these brothers, as their lord. These circumstances, as we have heard from persons acquainted with the affair, took place against the inclination of the king, who was attached to Tosty; but being languid through disease, and worn down with age, he become so universally disregarded, that he could not assist his favourite. In consequence, his bodily ailments increasing from the anxiety of his mind, he died shortly after. Harold persisted in his resolution of banishing his brother: wherefore, first tarnishing the triumphs of his family by piratical excursions, he was, as I have above written, afterwards killed with the king of Norway. His body being known by a wart between the shoulders, obtained burial at York. Edwin and Morcar, by Harold's command, then conveyed the spoils of war to London, for he himself was proceeding rapidly to the battle of Hastings; where, falsely presaging, he looked upon the victory as already gained. But, when he was there killed, the brothers, flying to the territories they possessed, disturbed the peace of William for several years; infesting the woods with secret robberies, and never coming to close or open engagement. Often were they taken captive, and as often surrendered themselves, but were again dismissed with impunity, from pity to their youthful elegance, or respect to their nobility. At last, murdered, neither by the force nor craft of their enemies, but by the treachery of their partisans, their fate drew tears from the king, who would even long since have granted them matches with his relations, and the honour of his friendship, would they have acceded to terms of peace.

Waltheof, an earl of high descent, had become extremely intimate with the new king, who had forgotten his former offences, and attributed them rather to courage, than to disloyalty. For Waltheof, singly, had killed many of the Normans in the battle of York, cutting off their heads, one by one, as they entered the gate. He was muscular in the arms, brawny in the chest, tall and robust in his whole person; the son of Siward, a most celebrated earl, whom, by a Danish term, they called "Digera," which implies Strong. But after the fall of his party, he voluntarily surrendered himself, and was honoured by a marriage with Judith, the king's neice, as well as with his personal friendship. Unable however to restrain his evil inclinations, he could not preserve his fidelity. For all his countrymen, who had thought proper to resist, being either slain, or subdued, he became a party even in the perfidy of Ralph de Waher; but the conspiracy being detected,* he was taken, kept in chains for some time, and at last, being beheaded, was buried at Croyland. though some assert, that he joined the league of treachery, more through circumvention than inclination. This is the excuse the English make for him, and those, of the greater credit, for the Normans affirm the contrary, to whose decision the Divinity itself appears to assent, showing many and very great miracles at his tomb: for they declare, that during his captivity, he wiped away his transgressions by his daily penitence.

On this account perhaps the conduct of the king may reasonably be excused, if he was at any time rather severe against the English; for he scarcely found any one of them faithful. This circumstance so exasperated his ferocious mind, that he deprived the more powerful, first of their wealth, next of their estates, and finally, some of them of their lives. Moreover, he followed the device of Cæsar, who

---

* " Earl Wa'theof, or Wallef, as he is always styled in Domesday Book, was, according to the Saxon Chronicle, beheaded at Winchester on the 31st May, 1076. The Chronicle of Mailros and Florence of Worcester, however, assign this event to the preceding year."—HARDY.

drove out the Germans, concealed in the vast forest of Ardennes, whence they harassed his army with perpetual irruptions, not by means of his own countrymen, but by the confederate Gauls; that, while strangers destroyed each other, he might gain a bloodless victory. Thus, I say, William acted towards the English. For, allowing the Normans to be unemployed, he opposed an English army, and an English commander, to those, who, after the first unsuccessful battle, had fled to Denmark and Ireland, and had returned at the end of three years with considerable force: forseeing that whichever side might conquer, it must be a great advantage to himself. Nor did this device fail him; for both parties of the English, after some conflicts between themselves, without any exertion on his part, left a victory for the king; the invaders being driven to Ireland, and the royalists purchasing the empty title of conquest, at their own special loss, and that of their general. His name was Ednoth,* equally celebrated, before the arrival of the Normans, both at home and abroad. He was the father of Harding, who yet survives: a man more accustomed to kindle strife by his malignant tongue, than to brandish arms in the field of battle. Thus having overturned the power of the laity, he made an ordinance, that no monk, or clergyman, of that nation, should be suffered to aspire to any dignity whatever; excessively differing from the gentleness of Canute the former king, who restored their honours, unimpaired, to the conquered: whence it came to pass, that at his decease, the natives easily expelled the foreigners, and reclaimed their original right. But William, from certain causes, canonically deposed some persons, and in the place of such as might die, appointed diligent men of any nation, except English. Unless I am deceived, their inveterate frowardness towards the king, required such a measure; since, as I have said before, the Normans are by nature kindly disposed to strangers who live amongst them.

Ralph, whom I mentioned before, was, by the king's gift, earl of Norfolk and Suffolk; a Breton on his father's side; of a disposition foreign to every thing good. This man, in

* "Harold's master of the horse. He was killed in 1068, in opposing the sons of Harold, when they came upon their expedition from Ireland."—Hardy.

consequence of being betrothed to the king's relation, the daughter of William Fitz-Osberne, conceived a most unjust design, and meditated attack on the sovereignty. Wherefore, on the very day of his nuptials, whilst splendidly banqueting, for the luxury of the English had now been adopted by the Normans, and when the guests had become intoxicated and heated with wine, he disclosed his intention in a copious harangue. As their reason was entirely clouded by drunkenness, they loudly applauded the orator. Here Roger earl of Hereford, brother to the wife of Ralph, and here Waltheof, together with many others, conspired the death of the king. Next day, however, when the fumes of the wine had evaporated, and cooler thoughts influenced the minds of some of the party, the larger portion, repenting of their conduct, retired from the meeting. Among these is said to have been Waltheof, who, at the recommendation of archbishop Lanfranc, sailing to Normandy, related the matter to the king; concealing merely his own share of the business. The earls, however, persisted in their design, and each incited his dependents to rebel. But God opposed them, and brought all their machinations to nought. For immediately the king's officers, who were left in charge, on discovering the affair, reduced Ralph to such distress, that seizing a vessel at Norwich, he committed himself to the sea. His wife, covenanting for personal safety, and delivering up the castle. followed her husband. Roger being thrown into chains by the king, visited, or rather inhabited, a prison, during the remainder of his life; a young man of abominable treachery, and by no means imitating his father's conduct.

His father, indeed, William Fitz-Osberne,* might have been compared, nay, I know not if he might not even have been preferred, to the very best princes. By his advice, William had first been inspirited to invade, and next, assisted by his valour, to keep possession of England. The energy of his mind was seconded by the almost boundless liberality of his hand. Hence it arose, that by the multitude of soldiers, to whom he gave extravagant pay, he repelled the rapacity of the enemy, and ensured the favour of the people. In con-

* "W Fitz-Osberne was only the father-in-law of Ralph de Guader.' —Hardy

sequence, by this boundless profusion, he incurred the king's severe displeasure ; because he had improvidently exhausted his treasures. The regulations which he established in his county of Hereford, remain in full force at the present day ; that is to say, that no knight* should be fined more than seven shillings for whatever offence : whereas, in other provinces, for a very small fault in transgressing the commands of their lord, they pay twenty or twenty-five Fortune, however, closed these happy successes by a dishonourable termination, when the supporter of so great a government, the counsellor of England and Normandy, went into Flanders, through fond regard for a woman, and there died by the hands of his enemies. For the elder Baldwin, of whom I have before spoken, the father of Matilda, had two sons : Robert, who marrying the countess of Frisia, while his father yet lived, took the surname of Friso : Baldwin, who, after his father, presided some years over Flanders, and died prematurely. His two children by his wife Richelda surviving he had entrusted the guardianship of them to Philip king of France, whose aunt was his mother, and to William Fitz-Osberne. William readily undertook this office, that he might increase his dignity by an union with Richelda. But she, through female pride, aspiring to things beyond her sex, and exacting fresh tributes from the people, excited them to rebellion. Wherefore despatching a messenger to Robert Friso, they entreat him to accept the government of the country ; and abjure all fidelity to Arnulph, who was already called earl. Nor indeed were there wanting persons to espouse the party of the minor : so that for a long time, Flanders was disturbed by intestine commotion This, Fitz-Osberne, who was desperately in love with the lady, could not endure, but entered Flanders with a body of troops ; and, being immediately well received by the persons he came to defend, after some days, he rode securely from castle to castle, in a hasty manner with few attendants. On the other hand, Friso, who was acquainted with this piece of folly, en-

---

* There is considerable difficulty in distinguishing exactly the various meanings of the term "miles." Sometimes it is, in its legitimate sense, a soldier generally, sometimes it implies a horseman, and frequently it is to be taken in its modern acceptation for a knight ; the latter appears to be the meaning here.

trapped him unawares by a secret ambush, and killed him, fighting bravely but to no purpose, together with his nephew Arnulph.

Thus possessed of Flanders, he often irritated king William, by plundering Normandy. His daughter married Canute king of the Danes, of whom was born Charles,* who now rules in Flanders. He made peace with king Philip, giving him his daughter-in-law in marriage, by whom he had Lewis, who at present reigns in France; but not long after, being heartily tired of the match, because his queen was extremely corpulent, he removed her from his bed, and in defiance of law and equity, married the wife of the earl of Anjou. Robert, safe by his affinity with these princes, encountered nothing to distress him during his government; though Baldwin, the brother of Arnulph, who had an earldom in the province of Hainault and in the castle of Valenciennes, by William's assistance made many attempts for that purpose. Three years before his death, when he was now hoary-headed, he went to Jerusalem, for the mitigation of his transgressions. After his return he renounced the world, calmly awaiting his dissolution with Christian earnestness. His son was that Robert so universally famed in the expedition into Asia, which, in our times, Europe undertook against the Turks; but through some mischance, after his return home, he tarnished that noble exploit, being mortally wounded in a tournament, as they call it. Nor did a happier fate attend his son Baldwin, who, voluntarily harassing the forces of Henry king of England, in Normandy, paid dearly for his youthful temerity: for, being struck on the head with a pole, and deceived by the professions of several physicians, he lost his life, the principality devolving on Charles, of whom we have spoken before.

Now, king William conducting himself with mildness towards the obedient but with severity to the rebellious, possessed the whole of England in tranquillity, holding all the Welsh tributary to him. At this time too, beyond sea, being never unemployed, he nearly annihilated the county of Maine,

* "Charles, called the Good. He was the son of Canute IV, king of Denmark, and Adele, daughter of Robert le Frison. He succeeded Boudouin VII, as earl of Flanders (17th June, 1119,) and died 2nd March, 1127."—HARDY.

leading thither an expedition composed of English; who, though they had been easily conquered in their own, yet always appeared invincible in a foreign country. He lost multitudes of his men at Dol,* a town of Brittany, whither, irritated by some broil, he had led a military force. He constantly found Philip king of France, the daughter of whose aunt he had married, unfaithful to him; because he was envious of the great glory of a man who was vassal both to his father and to himself. But William did not the less actively resist his attempts, although his first-born son Robert, through evil counsel, assisted him in opposition to his father. Whence it happened, that in an attack at Gerborni, the son became personally engaged with his father; wounded him and killed his horse: William, the second son, departed with a hurt also, and many of the king's party were slain. In all other respects, during the whole of his life, he was so fortunate, that foreign and distant nations feared nothing more than his name. He had subdued the inhabitants so completely to his will, that without any opposition, he first caused an account to be taken of every person; compiled a register of the rent of every estate throughout England,† and made all free men, of every description, take the oath of fidelity to him. Canute, king of the Danes, who was most highly elevated both by his affinity to Robert Friso and by his own power, alone menaced his dignity; a rumour being generally prevalent, that he would invade England, a country due to him from his relationship to the ancient Canute: and indeed he would have effected it, had not God counteracted his boldness by an unfavourable wind. But this circumstance

* "King William now went over sea, and led his army to Brittany, and beset the castle of Dol; but the Bretons defended it, until the king came from France; whereupon king William departed thence, having lost there both men and horses, and many of his treasures, (Sax. Chron A.D. 1076.) This event is more correctly attributed by Florence and others to the preceding year."—HARDY.

† Domesday book. This invaluable record, which has been printed by order of the House of Commons, contains a survey of the kingdom, noting, generally, for there are some variations in different counties, the proprietors and value of lands, both at the time of the survey and during the reign of Edward the Confessor, the quantity of arable, wood, and pasture, &c. the various kinds of tenants and slaves on each estate, and, in some instances, the stock; also the number of hides at which it was rated, for the public service, with various other particulars.

reminds me briefly to trace the genealogy of the Danish kings, who succeeded after our Canute ; adding at the same time, somewhat concerning the Norwegians

As it has been before observed, Harold succeeded in England; Hardecanute, and his sons, in Denmark: for Magnus the son of Olave, whom I have mentioned in the history of our Canute, as having been killed by his subjects, had recovered Norway, which Canute had subdued. Harold dying in England, Hardecanute held both kingdoms for a short time. On his decease, Edward the Simple succeeded, who, satisfied with his paternal kingdom, despised his foreign dominions as burdensome and barbarous One Sweyn, doubtlessly a most exalted character, was then made king of the Danes.* When his government had prospered for several years, Magnus, king of the Norwegians, with the consent of some of the Danes, expelled him by force, and subjected the land to his own will. Sweyn, thus expelled, went to the king of Sweden, and collecting, by his assistance, Swedes, Vandals, and Goths, he returned, to regain the kingdom: but, through the exertions of the Danes, who were attached to the government of Magnus, he experienced a repetition of his former ill-fortune. This was a great and memorable battle among those barbarous people: on no other occasion did the Danes ever experience severer conflict, or happier success. Indeed, to this very time, they keep unbroken the vow, by which they had bound themselves, before the contest, that they would consecrate to future ages the vigil of St. Lawrence, for on that day the battle was fought, by fasting and alms, and then also Sweyn fled, but soon after, on the death of Magnus, he received his kingdom entire.

To Magnus, in Norway, succeeded one Sweyn, surnamed Hardhand; not elevated by royal descent, but by boldness and cunning ; to him Olave, the uncle of Magnus, whom they call a saint; to Olave, Harold Harvagre, the brother of Olave, who had formerly, when a young man, served under the emperor of Constantinople. Being, at his command, exposed to a lion, for having debauched a woman of quality, he strangled the huge beast by the bare vigour of his arms. He was slain in England by Harold, the son of

* Sweyn succeeded to the kingdom of Denmark on the death of Magnus in 1047

Godwin. His sons, Olave and Magnus, divided the kingdom of their father; but Magnus dying prematurely, Olave seized the whole. To him succeeded his son Magnus, who was lately miserably slain in Ireland, on which he had rashly made a descent. They relate, that Magnus, the elder son of Harold, was, after the death of his father, compassionately sent home by Harold, king of England; and that in return for this kindness, he humanely treated Harold, the son of Harold, when he came to him after William's victory: tha he took him with him, in an expedition he made to England, in the time of William the younger, when he conquered the Orkney and Mevanian Isles,* and meeting with Hugo, earl of Chester, and Hugo, earl of Shrewsbury, put the first to flight, and the second to death. The sons of the last Magnus, Hasten and Siward, yet reign conjointly, having divided the empire: the latter, a seemly and spirited youth, shortly since went to Jerusalem, passing through England, and performed many famous exploits against the Saracens; more especially in the siege of Sidon, whose inhabitants raged furiously against the Christians through their connection with the Turks.

But Sweyn, as I have related, on his restoration to the sovereignty of the Danes, being impatient of quiet, sent his son Canute twice into England; first with three hundred, and then with two hundred, ships. His associate in the former expedition was Osbern, the brother of Sweyn; in the latter, Hacco: but, being each of them bribed, they frustrated the young man's designs, and returned home without effecting their purpose. In consequence, becoming highly disgraced by king Sweyn for bartering their fidelity for money, they were driven into banishment. Sweyn, when near his end, bound all the inhabitants by oath, that, as he had fourteen sons, they should confer the kingdom on each of them in succession, as long as his issue remained. On his decease, his son Harold succeeded for three years: to him Canute, whom his father had formerly sent into England. Remembering his original failure, he prepared, as we have heard, more than a thousand vessels against England: his father-in-law, Robert Friso, the possessor of six hundred more, supporting him. But being detained, for almost two

* Man and Anglesey.

years, by the adverseness of the wind, he changed his design, affirming, that it must be by the determination of God, that he could not put to sea: but afterwards, misled by the suggestions of some persons, who attributed the failure of their passage to the conjurations of certain old women, he sentenced the chiefs, whose wives were accused of this transgression, to an intolerable fine; cast his brother, Olave, the principal of the suspected faction into chains, and sent him into exile to his father-in-law. The barbarians, in consequence, resenting this attack upon their liberty, killed him while in church, clinging to the altar, and promising reparation. They say that many miracles were shown from heaven at that place; because he was a man strictly observant of fasting and almsgiving, and pursued the transgressors of the divine laws more rigorously than those who offended against himself; from which circumstance, he was consecrated a martyr by the pope of Rome. After him, the murderers, that they might atone for their crime by some degree of good, redeemed Olave from captivity, for ten thousand marks. After ignobly reigning during eight years, he left the government to his brother Henry: who living virtuously for twenty-nine years, went to Jerusalem, and breathed his last at sea. Nicholas, the fifth in the sovereignty, still survives.*

The king of Denmark then, as I have said, was the only obstacle to William's uninterrupted enjoyment: on whose account he enlisted such an immense multitude of stipendiary soldiers out of every province on this side the mountains, that their numbers oppressed the kingdom. But he, with his usual magnaminity, not regarding the expense, had engaged even Hugo the Great, brother to the king of France, with his bands to serve in his army. He was accustomed to stimulate and incite his own valour, by the remembrance of Robert Guiscard; saying it was disgraceful to yield, in courage, to him whom he surpassed in rank. For Robert, born of middling parentage in Normandy, that is, neither very low nor very high, had gone, a few years before William's arrival in England, with fifteen knights, into Apulia, to remedy the narrowness of his own circum-

* Nicolas reigned from A.D 1105 to A.D. 1135, June 25, when he was murdered.

stances, by entering into the service of that inactive race of people. Not many years elapsed, ere, by the stupendous assistance of God, he reduced the whole country under his power. For where his strength failed, his ingenuity was alert: first receiving the towns, and after, the cities into confederacy with him. Thus he became so successful, as to make himself duke of Apulia and Calabria; his brother Richard, prince of Capua; and his other brother, Roger, earl of Sicily. At last, giving Apulia to his son Roger, he crossed the Adriatic with his other son Boamund, and taking Durazzo, was immediately proceeding against Alexius, emperor of Constantinople, when a messenger from pope Hildebrand stopped him in the heat of his career. For Henry, emperor of Germany, son of that Henry we have before mentioned, being incensed against the pope, for having excommunicated him on account of the ecclesiastical investitures, led an army against Rome; besieged it; expelled Hildebrand, and introduced Guibert of Ravenna. Guiscard learning this by the letter of the expelled pope, left his son Boamund, with the army, to follow up his designs, and returned to Apulia; where quickly getting together a body of Apulians and Normans, he proceeded to Rome. Nor did Henry wait for a messenger to announce his approach; but, affrighted at the bare report, fled with his pretended pope. Rome, freed from intruders, received its lawful sovereign; but soon after again lost him by similar violence. Then too, Alexius, learning that Robert was called home by the urgency of his affairs, and hoping to put a finishing hand to the war, rushed against Boamund, who commanded the troops which had been left. The Norman youth, however, observant of his native spirit, though far inferior in number, turned to flight, by dint of military skill, the undisciplined Greeks and the other collected nations. At the same time, too, the Venetians, a people habituated to the sea, attacking Guiscard, who having settled the object of his voyage was now sailing back, met with a similar calamity: part were drowned or killed, the rest put to flight. He, continuing his intended expedition, induced many cities, subject to Alexius, to second his views. The emperor took off, by crime, the man he was unable to subdue by arms: falsely promising his wife an imperial match. By her artifices, he drank poison,* which she had prepared, and died; deserving, had God so pleased, a nobler death: for he was unconquerable by the sword of an enemy, but fell a victim to domestic treachery. He was buried at Venusium in Apulia, having the following epitaph:

> Here Guiscard lies, the terror of the world,
> Who from the Capitol Rome's sovereign hurl'd.
> No band collected could Alexis free,
> Flight only; Venice, neither flight nor sea.

And since mention has been made of Hildebrand, I shall relate some anecdotes of him, which I have not heard trivially, but from the sober relation of a person who would swear that he had learned them from the mouth of Hugo abbat of Clugny; whom I admire and commend to notice, from the consideration, that he used to declare the secret thoughts of others by the prophetic intuition of his mind. Pope Alexander, seeing the energetic bent of his disposition, had made him chancellor† of the holy see. In consequence, by virtue of his office, he used to go through the provinces to correct abuses. All ranks of people flocked to him, requiring judgment on various affairs; all secular power was subject to him, as well out of regard to his sanctity as his office. Whence it happened, one day, when there was a greater concourse on horseback than usual, that the abbat aforesaid, with his monks, was gently proceeding in the last rank; and beholding at a distance the distinguished honour of this man, that so many earthly rulers awaited his nod, he was revolving in his mind sentiments to the following effect: "By what dispensation of God was this fellow, of diminutive stature and obscure parentage, surrounded by a retinue of so many rich men? Doubtless, from having such a crowd of attendants, he was vain-glorious, and conceived loftier notions than were becoming." Scarcely, as I have said, had he imagined this in his heart, when the archdeacon, turning back his horse, and spurring him, cried out from a distance, beckoning the abbat, "You," said he, "you have imagined falsely, wrongly deeming me guilty of a thing of which I am innocent altogether; for I neither impute this as glory to

* "Hoveden, who follows Malmesbury, adds that Alexius married, crowned, and then burnt alive his female accomplice."—HARDY.
† Archdeacon, and afterwards chancellor. Baronius, x. 289.

myself, if glory that can be called which vanishes quickly, nor do I wish it to be so imputed by others, but to the blessed apostles, to whose servant it is exhibited." Reddening with shame, and not daring to deny a tittle, he replied only, "My lord, I pray thee, how couldst thou know the secret thought of my heart which I have communicated to no one?" "All that inward sentiment of yours," said he, "was brought from your mouth to my ears, as though by a pipe."

Again, entering a country church, in the same province, they prostrated themselves before the altar, side by side. When they had continued their supplications for a long period, the archdeacon looked on the abbat with an angry countenance. After they had prayed some time longer, he went out, and asking the reason of his displeasure, received this answer, "If you love me, do not again attack me with an injury of this kind, my Lord Jesus Christ, beautiful beyond the sons of men, was visibly present to my entreaties, listening to what I said and kindly looking assent; but, attracted by the earnestness of your prayer, he left me and turned to you. I think you will not deny it to be a species of injury to take from a friend the author of his salvation. Moreover, you are to know that mortality of mankind and destruction hang over this place, and the token by which I formed such a conclusion was my seeing the angel of the Lord standing upon the altar with a naked sword, and waving it to and fro. I possess a more manifest proof of the impending ruin, from the thick, cloudy air which, as you see, already envelopes that province. Let us make haste to escape, then, lest we perish with the rest." Having said this, they entered an inn for refreshment; but, as soon as food was placed before them, the lamentations of the household took away their famished appetites: for first one, and then another, and presently many of the family suddenly lost their lives by some unseen disaster. The contagion then spreading to the adjoining houses, they mounted their mules, and departed, fear adding wings to their flight.

Hildebrand had presided for the pope at a council in Gaul, where many bishops being degraded, for having formerly acquired their churches by simony, gave place to better men. There was one, to whom a suspicion of this apostacy attached, but he could neither be convicted by any witnesses, nor confuted by any argument. When it was supposed he must be completely foiled, still like the slippery snake he eluded detection; so skilled was he in speaking, that he baffled all. Then said the archdeacon, "Let the oracle of God be resorted to, let man's eloquence cease; we know for certain that episcopal grace is the gift of the Holy Spirit, and that whosoever purchases a bishopric, supposes the gift of the Holy Ghost may be procured by money. Before you then, who are assembled by the will of the Holy Ghost, let him say, 'Glory be to the Father, and to the Son, and to the Holy Ghost,' and if he shall speak it articulately, and without hesitation, it will be manifest to me that he has obtained his office, not by purchase, but legally." He willingly accepted the condition, supposing nothing less than any difficulty in these words, and indeed he perfectly uttered, "Glory be to the Father, and to the Son," but he hesitated at the "Holy Ghost." A clamour arose on all sides, but he was never able, by any exertion, either at that time or for the remainder of his life, to name the Holy Spirit. The abbat so often mentioned was a witness of this miracle; who taking the deprived bishop with him into different places, often laughed at the issue of the experiment. Any person doubting the certainty of this relation, must be confuted by all Europe, which is aware that the numbers of the Clugniac order were increased by this abbat.

On the death of Alexander, therefore, Hildebrand, called Gregory the Seventh, succeeded.* He openly asserted what others had whispered, excommunicating those persons who, having been elected, should receive the investiture† of their churches, by the ring and staff, through the hands of the laity. On this account Henry, emperor of Germany, being incensed that he should so far presume without his concurrence, expelled him from Rome, as I observed, after the expiration of eleven years, and brought in Guibert. Not long after, the pope, being seized with that fatal disease which he had no doubt would be mortal, was requested by the cardinals

* He was elected pope the 22nd of April, 1073, and died 25th May, 1085 —HARDY.
† Investiture was a symbolical mode of receiving possession of a benefice, dignity, or office.

to appoint his successor; referring him to the example of St. Peter, who, in the church's earliest infancy, had, while yet living, nominated Clement. He refused to follow this example, because it had anciently been forbidden by councils: he would advise, however, that if they wished a person powerful in worldly matters, they should choose Desiderius, abbat of Cassino, who would quell the violence of Guibert successfully and opportunely by a military force; but if they wanted a religious and eloquent man, they should elect Odo bishop of Ostia. Thus died a man, highly acceptable to God, though perhaps rather too austere towards men. Indeed it is affirmed, that in the beginning of the first commotion between him and the emperor, he would not admit him within his doors, though barefooted, and carrying shears* and scourges, despising a man guilty of sacrilege, and of incest with his own sister. The emperor, thus excluded, departed, vowing that this repulse should be the death of many a man. And immediately doing all the injury he was able to the Roman see, he excited thereby the favourers of the pope, on every side, to throw off their allegiance to himself; for one Rodulph, revolting at the command of the pope, who had sent him a crown in the name of the apostles, he was immersed on all sides in the tumult of war. But Henry, ever superior to ill fortune, at length subdued him and all others faithlessly rebelling. At last, driven from his power, not by a foreign attack, but the domestic hatred of his son, he died miserably. To Hildebrand succeeded Desiderius, called Victor, who at his first mass fell down dead, though from what mischance is unknown, the cup, if it be possible to credit such a thing, being poisoned. The election then fell upon Odo, a Frenchman by birth, first archdeacon of Rheims, then prior of Clugny, afterwards bishop of Ostia, lastly pope by the name of Urban.

Thus far I shall be pardoned, for having digressed, as from the mention of William's transactions, some things occurred which I thought it improper to omit: now, the

* This seems intended to denote his absolute submission, and willingness to undergo any kind of penance which might be enjoined upon him. Sometimes excommunicated persons wore a halter about their necks; sometimes they were shorn or scourged prior to receiving absolution. Vide Basnage, pref. in Canisium, p. 69, 70.

reader, who is so inclined, shall learn the more common habits of his life, and his domestic manners. Above all then, he was humble to the servants of God; affable to the obedient; inexorable to the rebellious. He attended the offices of the Christian religion, as much as a secular was able; so that he daily was present at mass, and heard vespers and matins. He built one monastery in England, and another in Normandy; that at Caen * first, which he dedicated to St. Stephen, and endowed with suitable estates, and most magnificent presents. There he appointed Lanfranc, afterwards archbishop of Canterbury, abbat: a man worthy to be compared to the ancients, in knowledge, and in religion: of whom it may be truly said, "Cato the third is descended from heaven;" so much had an heavenly savour tinctured his heart and tongue; so much was the whole Western world excited to the knowledge of the liberal arts, by his learning; and so earnestly did the monastic profession labour in the work of religion, either from his example, or authority. No sinister means profited a bishop in those days; nor could an abbat procure advancement by purchase. He who had the best report for undeviating sanctity, was most honoured, and most esteemed both by the king and by the archbishop. William built another monastery near Hastings, dedicated to St. Martin, which was also called Battle, because there the principal church stands on the very spot, where, as they report, Harold was found in the thickest heaps of the slain. When little more than a boy, yet gifted with the wisdom of age, he removed his uncle Malger, from the archbishopric of Rouen. He was a man not ordinarily learned, but, through his high rank, forgetful of his profession, he gave too much attention to hunting and hawking; and consumed the treasures of the church in riotous living. The fame of this getting abroad, he never, during his whole life-time, obtained the pall, because the holy see refused the distinction of that honour, to a man who neglected his sacred office. Wherefore being frequently cited, his nephew

* "The abbey of St. Stephen's, Caen, is stated to have been completed in 1064, but when it was dedicated is not accurately known: some fix the dedication in 1073, others in 1081, and Orderic in 1077. There was, however, a foundation charter granted subsequently to 1066, for in it William styles himself king."—HARDY.

reprehending his offences, and still conducting himself in the same manner, he was, from the urgency of the case, ultimately degraded. Some report that there was a secret reason for his being deprived · that Matilda, whom William had married, was very nearly related to him : that Malger, in consequence, through zeal for the Christian faith, could not endure that they should riot in the bed of consanguinity; and that he hurled the weapon of excommunication against his nephew, and his consort : that, when the anger of the young man was roused by the complaints of his wife, an occasion was sought out, through which the persecutor of their crime might be driven from his see : but that afterwards, in riper years, for the expiation of their offence, he built the monastery to St. Stephen at Caen ; and she also one, in the same town, to the Holy Trinity ;[*] each of them choosing the inmates according to their own sex.

To Malger succeeded Maurilius of Feschamp ; a monk commendable for many virtues, but principally for his abstinence. After a holy and well-spent life, when he came, by the call of God, to his end, bereft of vital breath, he lay, as it were, dead for almost half a day. Nevertheless, when preparation was made to carry him into the church, recovering his breath, he bathed the by-standers in tears of joy, and comforted them, when lost in amazement, with this address : "Let your minds be attentive while you hear the last words of your pastor. I have died a natural death, but I am come back, to relate to you what I have seen ; yet shall I not continue with you long, because it delights me to sleep in the Lord. The conductors of my spirit were adorned with every elegance both of countenance and attire ; the gentleness of their speech accorded with the splendour of their garments; so much so, that I could wish for nothing more than the attentions of such men. Delighted therefore with their soothing approbation, I went, as it appeared to me, towards the east. A seat in paradise was promised me, which I was shortly to enter. In a moment, passing over Europe and

---

[*] "The convent of the Holy Trinity was founded by Matilda 1066, and its church dedicated on the 18th of June in that year. Duke William on the same day, presenting at the altar his infant daughter Cecilia, devoted her to the service of God in this monastery, where she became the second abbess".—HARDY.

entering Asia, we came to Jerusalem; where, having worshipped the saints, we proceeded to Jordan. The residents on the hither bank joining company with my conductors, made a joyful party. I was now hastening to pass over the river, through longing desire to see what was beyond it, when my companions informed me, that God had commanded, that I must first be terrified by the sight of the demons; in order that the venial sins, which I had not wiped out by confession, might be expiated, by the dread of terrific forms. As soon as this was said, there came opposite to me, such a multitude of devils, brandishing pointed weapons, and breathing out fire, that the plain appeared like steel, and the air like flame. I was so dreadfully alarmed at them, that had the earth clave asunder, or the heaven opened, I should not have known whither to have betaken myself for safety. Thus panic-struck, and doubting whither to go, I suddenly recovered my life, though instantaneously about to lose it again, that by this relation I might be serviceable to your salvation, unless you neglect it:" and almost as soon as he had so said, he breathed out his soul. His body, then buried under ground, in the church of St. Mary, is now, by divine miracle, as they report, raised up more than three feet above the earth.

Moreover, William, following up the design he had formerly begun in Normandy, permitted Stigand, the pretended and false archbishop, to be deposed by the Roman cardinals and by Ermenfred bishop of Sion. Walkelin succeeded him at Winchester, whose good works, surpassing fame, will resist the power of oblivion, as long as the episcopal see shall there continue: in Kent succeeded Lanfranc, of whom I have before spoken, who was, by the gift of God, as resplendent in England,

> As Lucifer, who bids the stars retire,
> Day's rosy harbinger with purple fire;

so much did the monastic germ sprout by his care, so strongly grew the pontifical power while he survived. The king was observant of his advice in such wise, that he deemed it proper to concede whatever Lanfranc asserted ought to be done. At his instigation also was abolished the infamous custom of those ill-disposed people who used to sell their slaves into Ireland. The credit of this action, I know not exactly whether to attribute to Lanfranc, or to Wulstan bishop of Worcester; who would scarcely have induced the king, reluctant from the profit it produced him, to this measure, had not Lanfranc commended it, and Wulstan, powerful from his sanctity of character, commanded it by episcopal authority: Wulstan, than whom none could be more just; nor could any in our time equal him in the power of miracles, or the gift of prophecy: of which I propose hereafter to relate some particulars, should it meet his most holy approbation.

But since the die of fortune is subject to uncertain casts, many adverse circumstances happened during those times. There was a disgraceful contention* between the abbat of Glastonbury and his monks; so that after altercation they came to blows. The monks being driven into the church, bewailed their miseries at the holy altar. The soldiers, rushing in, slew two of them, wounded fourteen, and drove away the rest. Nay the rage of the military had even bristled the crucifix with arrows. The abbat, rendered infamous by such a criminal outrage, was driven into exile during the whole of the king's life; but, upon his decease, he was restored to his honours, a sum of money being paid to such as interceded for him, for the expiation of his transgression.

Again, a cruel and ignominious end overtook Walker bishop of Durham, whom the Northumbrians, a people ever ripe for rebellion, throwing off all respect for his holy orders, put to death, after having severely insulted him. A considerable number of Lorrainers were killed there also, for the bishop was of that country. The cause of the murder was this. The bishop, independently of his see, was warder† of the whole county: over public business he had set his relation Gilbert, and over domestic, the canon Leobin; both men of diligence in their respective employments, but rash. The bishop endured their want of moderation in this respect, out of regard to their activity; and, as he had placed them in office,

---

* "This disgraceful contention happened in the year 1083. It seems to have arisen from the abbat (Thurstan) attempting to introduce a new chant, brought from Feschamp, instead of the Gregorian, to which the monks had been accustomed."--HARDY.

† Bracton says (lib. ii. c. 8, sec. 4), that the bishop of Durham had as full power in the county of Durham as the king in his own palace. The privileges of the see of Durham trace back to the time of St. Cuthbert.

treated them with great kindness. "For our nature ever indulges itself, and favourably regards its own kind works." This Leobin caused Liwulph, a servant so dearly beloved by St. Cuthbert that the saint himself used to appear to him, even when waking, and prescribe his decisions; him, I say, he caused to be killed by Gilbert; smitten with envy at his holding the higher place in the prelate's esteem for his knowledge and equity in legal determinations. Walker, terrified with this intelligence, offered the furious family of the deceased the result of a legal inquiry,* affirming that Leobin would be the cause of his death and of that of his friends. When the matter came to a trial, this ferocious race of people were not to be soothed by reasons of any kind, on the contrary, they threw the whole blame on the bishop, because they had seen both the murderers familiarly entertained in his court after the death of Liwulph. Hence arose clamour and indignation, and Gilbert, as he was of his own accord, going out of the church, where he had been sitting with the bishop, that he might, at his personal peril, save the life of his master, was impiously slain. The bishop, while making overtures of peace before the gates, next glutted the rage of the people with his blood; the fomenter of the crime, too, Leobin, was half-burnt, as he would not quit the church till it was set on fire, and when he rushed out he was received on a thousand spears. This had been predicted by Edgitha, relict of king Edward; for when she had formerly seen Walker, with his milk-white hair, rosy countenance, and extraordinary stature, conducted to Winchester to be consecrated; "We have here," said she, "a noble martyr:" being led to form such a presage by reflecting on the mutinous disposition of that people. To him succeeded William, abbat of St. Carilef, who established monks at Durham.

Moreover, the year before the king's death, there was a mortality both among men and cattle, and severe tempests, accompanied with such thunder and lightning, as no person before had ever seen or heard. And in the year he died, a contagious fever destroyed more than half the people; indeed the attack of the disease killed many, and then, from the unseasonableness of the weather, a famine following, it

* Walker offered to purge himself by oath from all participation in the murder. See Flor. Wig. A.D 1080.

spread universally and cut off those whom the fever had spared.

In addition to his other virtues he, more especially in early youth, was observant of chastity; insomuch that it was very commonly reported that he was impotent. Marrying, however, at the recommendation of the nobility, he conducted himself, during many years, in such wise, as never to be suspected of any criminal intercourse. He had many children by Matilda, whose obedience to her husband and fruitfulness in children excited in his mind the tenderest regard for her, although there are not wanting persons who prate about his having renounced his former chastity; and that, after he had acceded to the royal dignity, he was connected with the daughter of a certain priest, whom the queen caused to be removed, by being hamstrung by one of her servants; on which account he was exiled, and Matilda was scourged to death with a bridle. But I esteem it folly to believe this of so great a king; though I decidedly assert that a slight disagreement arose between them, in latter times, on account of their son Robert, whom his mother was said to supply with a military force out of her revenues. Nevertheless, he proved that his conjugal affection was not in the least diminished by this circumstance, as he buried her with great magnificence, on her death, four years before his own; and weeping most profusely for many days showed how keenly he felt her loss: moreover, from that time, if we give credit to report, he refrained from every gratification. The queen* was buried at Caen, in the monastery of the Holy Trinity. The same proof of regard was evident in the care he took of the funeral of queen Edgitha; who, placed by his attention near her husband at Westminster, has a tomb richly wrought with gold and silver.

His sons were Robert, Richard, William, and Henry. The two last reigned after him successively in England: Robert, irritated that Normandy was refused him during his father's life-time, went indignantly to Italy, that by marrying the daughter of Boniface the marquis, he might procure

* "Matilda died 2nd Nov. 1083. She bequeathed to this monastery her crown, sceptre, and ornaments of state. A copy of her will may be seen in the Essais Historiques, by the Abbé de la Rue, tom. ii. p. 437."—HARDY.

assistance in those parts, to oppose the king: but failing of this connexion, he excited Philip king of France against his father. Wherefore, disappointed of his paternal blessing and inheritance, at his death, he missed England, retaining with difficulty the duchy of Normandy: and pawning even this, at the expiration of nine years, to his brother William, he joined the expedition into Asia, with the other Christians. From thence, at the end of four years, he returned with credit for his military exploits; and without difficulty sat himself down in Normandy, because his brother William being recently dead, king Henry, unsettled on account of his fresh-acquired power, deemed it enough to retain England under his command: but as I must speak of this in another place, I will here pursue the relation I had begun concerning the sons of William the Great.

Richard afforded his noble father hopes of his future greatness; a fine youth and of aspiring disposition, considering his age: but an untimely death quickly withered the bud of this promising flower. They relate that while hunting deer in the New-forest, he contracted a disorder from a stream of infected air. This is the place which William his father, desolating the towns and destroying the churches for more than thirty miles, had appropriated for the nurture and refuge of wild beasts;* a dreadful spectacle, indeed, that where before had existed human intercourse and the worship of God, there deer, and goats, and other animals of that kind, should now range unrestrained, and these not subjected to the general service of mankind. Hence it is truly asserted that, in this very forest, William his son, and his grandson Richard, son of Robert, earl of Normandy, by the severe judgment of God, met their deaths, one by a wound in the breast by an arrow, the other by a wound in the neck, or as some say, from being suspended by the jaws on the branch of a tree, as his horse passed beneath it.

His daughters were five; first, Cecilia, abbess of Caen, who still survives: the second, Constantia, married to Alan

* Some MSS. omit from "a dreadful spectacle," to the end of the paragraph, and substitute thus, " Here he willingly passed his time, here he delighted to follow the chase. I will not say for days but even months together. Here, too, many accidents befell the royal race, which the recent recollection of the inhabitants supplies to inquirers."

Fergant, earl of Brittany, excited the inhabitants, by the severity of her justice, to administer a poisonous potion to her: the third, Adela, the wife of Stephen, earl of Blois, a lady celebrated for secular industry, lately took the veil at Marcigny. The names of the two others have escaped me.* One of these, as we have said, was betrothed to Harold, and died ere she was marriageable: the other was affianced, by messengers, to Alphonso, king of Gallicia, but obtained, from God, a virgin death. A hard substance, which proved the frequency of her prayers, was found upon her knees after her decease.

Honouring the memory of his father, by every practicable method, in the latter part of his life, he caused his bones, formerly interred at Nicea, to be taken up by means of a person sent for that purpose, in order to convey them elsewhere; who, successfully returning, stopped in Apulia, on hearing of the death of William, and there buried this illustrious man's remains. He treated his mother, who, before the death of his father, had married one Herlewin de Conteville, a man of moderate wealth, with singular indulgence as long as she lived. William's brothers, by this match, were Robert, a man of heavy, sluggish disposition, whom he made earl of Moreton; and Odo, whom, while he was earl, he made bishop of Bayeux; and when king, created him earl of Kent. Being of quicker talents than the other, he was governor of all England, under the king, after the death of William Fitz-Osberne. He had wonderful skill in accumulating treasure; possessed extreme craft in dissembling: so that, though absent, yet, stuffing the scrips of the pilgrims with letters and money, he had nearly purchased the Roman papacy from the citizens. But when, through the rumour of his intended journey, soldiers eagerly flocked to him from all parts of the kingdom, the king, taking offence, threw him into confinement; saying, that he did not seize the bishop of Bayeux, but the earl of Kent. His partisans being intimidated by threats, discovered such quantities of gold, that the heap of precious metal would surpass the belief of the present age; and, at last, many sackfuls of wrought gold were also taken out of the rivers, which he had secretly buried in cer-

* Agatha and Adeliza were their names, according to Ordericus Vitalis, (lib. iv. 512.)

tain places When released, at the death of his brother, he joined Robert's party, as he was averse to his nephew William: but then too matters turning out unfavourably, he was banished England, and went over to his nephew and his bishopric in Normandy. Afterwards, proceeding with him on his enterprize to Jerusalem, he died at Antioch while it was besieged by the Christians.

King William kindly admitted foreigners to his friendship; bestowed honours on them without distinction, and was attentive to almsgiving; he gave many possessions in England to foreign churches, and scarcely did his own munificence, or that of his nobility, leave any monastery unnoticed, more especially in Normandy, so that their poverty was mitigated by the riches of England. Thus, in his time, the monastic flock increased on every side; monasteries arose, ancient in their rule, but modern in building: but here I perceive the muttering of those who say, it would have been better that the old should have been preserved in their original state, than that new ones should have been erected from their plunder.

He was of just stature, extraordinary corpulence, fierce countenance; his forehead bare of hair: of such great strength of arm, that it was often matter of surprise, that no ne was able to draw his bow, which himself could bend when his horse was on full gallop: he was majestic, whether sitting or standing, although the protuberance of his belly deformed his royal person: of excellent health, so that he was never confined with any dangerous disorder, except at the last: so given to the pleasures of the chase, that, as I have before said, ejecting the inhabitants, he let a space of many miles grow desolate, that, when at liberty from other avocations, he might there pursue his pleasures. He gave sumptuous and splendid entertainments, at the principal festivals; passing, during the years he could conveniently remain in England, Christmas at Gloucester; Easter at Winchester; Pentecost at Westminster. At these times a royal edict summoned thither all the principal persons of every order, that the ambassadors from foreign nations might admire the splendour of the assemblage, and the costliness of the banquets. Nor was he at any time more affable or indulgent; in order that the visitants might proclaim universally, that his generosity kept pace with his riches. This mode of banqueting was constantly observed by his first successor; the second omitted it.

His anxiety for money is the only thing for which he can deservedly be blamed.* This he sought all opportunities of scraping together, he cared not how; he would say and do some things, and, indeed, almost any thing, unbecoming such great majesty, where the hope of money allured him. I have here no excuse whatever to offer, unless it be, as one has said, that, " Of necessity, he must fear many, whom many fear." For, through dread of his enemies, he used to drain the country of money, with which he might retard or repel their attacks; very often, as it happens in human affairs, where strength failed, purchasing the forbearance of his enemies with gold. This disgraceful calamity is still prevalent, and every day increases, so that both towns and churches are subjected to contributions: nor is this done with firm-kept faith on the part of the imposers, but whoever offers more, carries the prize; all former agreements being disregarded.

Residing in his latter days in Normandy, when enmity had arisen between him and the king of France, he, for a short period, was confined to the house: Philip, scoffing at this forbearance, is reported to have said, " The king of England is lying-in at Rouen, and keeps his bed, like a woman after her delivery;" jesting on his belly, which he had been reducing by medicine. Cruelly hurt at this sarcasm, he replied, " When I go to mass, after my confinement, I will make him an offering of a hundred thousand candles."† He swore this, " by the Resurrection and Glory of God." for he was wont to swear such oaths as, by the very form of his mouth, would strike terror into the minds of his hearers.

* Some MSS omit from " money," to " I have," and substitute, This he sought all opportunities of collecting, provided he could allege that they were honourable, and not unbecoming the royal dignity. But he will readily be excused, because a new government cannot be administered without large revenues. I have, &c.

† The Romish ritual directs the woman to kneel, with a lighted taper in her hand, at the church door, where she is sprinkled with holy water, and afterwards conducted into the church The practice seems connected with the festival of the Purification. Vide Durand, lib. vii. c. 7.

Not long after, in the end of the month of August, when the corn was ripe on the ground, the clusters on the vines, and the orchards laden with fruit in full abundance, collecting an army, he entered France in a hostile manner, trampling down, and laying every thing waste: nothing could assuage his irritated mind, so determined was he to revenge this injurious taunt at the expense of multitudes. At last he set fire to the city of Mantes, where the church of St. Mary was burnt, together with a recluse who did not think it justifiable to quit her cell even under such an emergency; and the whole property of the citizens was destroyed. Exhilarated by this success, while furiously commanding his people to add fuel to the conflagration, he approached too near the flames, and contracted a disorder from the violence of the fire and the intenseness of the autumnal heat. Some say, that his horse leaping over a dangerous ditch, ruptured his rider, where his belly projected over the front of the saddle. Injured by this accident, he sounded a retreat, and returning to Rouen, as the malady increased he took to his bed. His physicians, when consulted, affirmed, from an inspection of his urine, that death was inevitable. On hearing this, he filled the house with his lamentations, because death had suddenly seized him, before he could effect that reformation of life which he had long since meditated. Recovering his fortitude, however, he performed the duties of a Christian in confession and receiving the communion. Reluctantly, and by compulsion, he bestowed Normandy on Robert; to William he gave England; while Henry received his maternal possessions. He ordered all his prisoners to be released and pardoned: his treasures to be brought forth, and distributed to the churches: he gave also a certain sum of money to repair the church which had been burnt. Thus rightly ordering all things, he departed on the eighth of the ides of September, [Sept. 6,] in the fifty-ninth year of his age: the twenty-second of his reign: the fifty-second of his duchy: and in the year of our Lord 1087. This was the same year, in which Canute, king of Denmark, as we have before related, was killed; and in which the Spanish Saracens raging against the Christians, were shortly compelled to retire to their own territories by Alphonso, king of Gallicia; unwillingly evacuating even the cities they had formerly occupied.

The body, enbalmed after royal custom, was brought down the river Seine to Caen, and there consigned to the earth, a large assembly of the clergy attending, but few of the laity. Here might be seen the wretchedness of earthly vicissitude; for that man who was formerly the glory of all Europe, and more powerful than any of his predecessors, could not find a place of everlasting rest, without contention. For a certain knight, to whose patrimony the place pertained, loudly exclaiming at the robbery, forbade his burial; saying, that the ground belonged to himself by paternal right; and that the king had no claim to rest in a place which he had forcibly invaded. Whereupon, at the desire of Henry, the only one of his sons who was present, a hundred pounds of silver* were paid to this brawler, and quieted his audacious claim: for at that time, Robert his elder born was in France, carrying on a war against his own country: William had sailed for England, ere the king had well breathed his last; thinking it more advantageous to look to his future benefit, than to be present at the funeral of his father. Moreover, in the dispersion of money, neither slow, nor sparing, he brought forth from its secret hoard, all that treasure which had been accumulated at Winchester, during a reign of so many years: to the monasteries he gave a piece of gold; to each parish church five shillings in silver: to every county a hundred pounds to be divided to each poor man severally. He also very splendidly adorned the tomb of his father, with a large mass of gold and silver and the refulgence of precious stones.

At this time lived Berengar, the heresiarch of Tours, who denied, that the bread and wine, when placed on the altar and consecrated by the priest, were, as the holy church affirms, the real and substantial body of the Lord. Already was the whole of Gaul infected with this his doctrine, disseminated by means of poor scholars, whom he allured by daily hire. On this account pope Leo, of holiest memory, alarmed for the catholic faith, calling a council against him at Vercelli, dispersed the darkness of this misty error, by the effulgence of evangelical testimony. But when, after his death, the poison of heresy again burst forth from the bosoms of some worthless people where it had long been nurtured, Hildebrand, in councils, when he was archdeacon, at Tours,

* Sixty shillings down, and as much more afterwards. Orderic. Vital.

and after, when pope, at Rome, compelled him, after being convicted, to the abjuration of his opinion; which matters, any person desirous of seeing will find recorded in their proper place. Archbishop Lanfranc and Guimund, the most eloquent man of our times, first monk of St. Leofrid, in Normandy, afterwards bishop of Aversa in Apulia, confuted him; but principally and most forcibly the latter. And, indeed, though Berengar disgraced the earlier part of his life by defending certain heresies, yet he came so much to his senses in riper age, that without hesitation, he was by some esteemed a saint; admired for innumerable good qualities, but especially for his humility and alms-giving: showing himself master of his large possessions, by dispersing, not their slave by hoarding and worshipping them. He was so guarded with respect to female beauty, that he would never suffer a woman to appear before him, lest he should seem to enjoy that beauty with his eye, which he did not desire in his heart. He was used neither to despise the poor nor flatter the rich: to live by nature's rule, "and having food and raiment," in the language of the apostle, "therewith to be content." In consequence, Hildebert, bishop of Mans, a first-rate poet, highly commends him; whose words I have purposely inserted, that I may show this celebrated bishop's regard to his master; and at the same time his opinion will serve for an example to posterity, how he thought a man ought to live: although, perhaps, from the strength of his affection, he may have exceeded the bounds of just commendation.

> Fame, which the world allows his due,
> Shall Berengar, when dead, pursue.
> Whom, plac'd on faith's exalted height
> The fifth day ravish'd with fell spite:
> Sad was that day, and fatal too,
> Where grief and loss united grew,
> Wherein the church's hope and pride,
> The law, with its supporter, died.
> What sages taught, or poets sung
> Bow'd to his wit, and honey'd tongue.
> Then holier wisdom's path he trod,
> And fill'd his heart and lips with God.
> His soul, his voice, his action prov'd
> The great Creator's praise he lov'd,
> So good, so wise, his growing fame
> Shall soar above the greatest name:

Whose rank preserv'd his honours gain'd,
Preferr'd the poor to rich : maintain'd
The sternest justice. Wealth's wide power
Ne'er gave to sloth, or waste, an hour,
Nor could repeated honours, high,
Seduce him from humility;
Who ne'er on money set his mind,
But griev'd he could no object find
Where he might give : and help'd the poor
Till poverty assail'd his door.
His life by nature's laws to guide,
His mind from vice, his lips from pride,
Still was his care : to false, the true
Prefer, and nothing senseless do :
Evil to none, but good impart,
And banish lucre, hand and heart.
Whose dress was coarse, and temperance just
Awaited appetite's keen gust :
Was chastity's perpetual guest,
Nor let rank lust disturb his rest.
When nature form'd him, "See," said she,
"While others fade, one born for me."
Ere justice sought her place of rest
On high, he lock'd her in his breast.
A saint from boyhood, whose great name
Surpasses his exceeding fame,
Which, though the wide world it may fill,
Shall never reach his merit still.
Pious and grave, so humble yet,
That envy ne'er could him beset ;
For envy weeps, whom still before
She hated, prone now to adore ;
First for his life, but now his fate
She moans, laments his frail estate.
Man truly wise and truly blest !
Thy soul and body both at rest,
May I, when dead, abide with you,
And share the self-same portion too.

You may perceive in these verses, that the bishop exceeded the just measure of praise; but eloquence is apt to recommend itself in such wise; thus a brilliant style proceeds in graceful strain; thus

"Bewitching eloquence sheds purple flowers."

But though Berengar himself changed his sentiments, yet was he unable to convert all whom he had infected throughout the world; "so dreadful a thing it is to seduce others from what is right, either by example or by word; as, perhaps, in consequence, you must bear the sins of others after having atoned for your own." Fulbert, bishop of Chartres, whom Mary, the mother of our Lord, was seen to cure when sick, by the milk of her breasts, is said to have predicted this; for, when lying in the last extremity, he was visited by many persons, and the house was scarcely large enough to hold the company, he darted his eye through the throng, and endeavoured to drive away Berengar, with all the force he had remaining; protesting that an immense devil stood near him, and attempted to seduce many persons to follow him, by beckoning with his hand, and whispering some enticement. Moreover, Berengar himself, when about to expire on the day of the Epiphany, sadly sighing, at the recollection of the wretched people whom, when a very young man, in the heat of error, he had infected with his opinions, exclaimed, " To-day, in the day of his manifestation, my Lord Jesus Christ will appear to me, either to glorify me, as I hope, for my repentance; or to punish me, as I fear, for the heresy I have propagated on others."

We indeed believe, that after ecclesiastical benediction, those mysteries are the very body and blood of the Saviour; induced to such an opinion, by the authority of the ancient church, and by many miracles recently manifested. Such as that which St. Gregory exhibited at Rome; and such as Paschasius relates to have taken place in Germany; that the priest Plegild visibly touched the form of a boy, upon the altar, and that after kissing him he partook of him, turned into the similitude of bread, after the custom of the church: which, they relate, Berengar used arrogantly to cavil at, and to say, that " it was the treacherous covenant of a scoundrel, to destroy with his teeth, him whom he had kissed with his mouth." Such, too, is that concerning the Jewish boy, who by chance running playfully into a church, with a Christian of the same age, saw a child torn to pieces on the altar, and severally divided to the people; which when, with childish innocence, he related as truth to his parents, they placed him in a furnace, where the fire was burning and the door closed: whence, after many hours, he was snatched by the Christians, without injury to his person, clothes, or hair; and being asked how he could escape the devouring flames, he replied, " That beautiful woman whom I saw sitting in the chair, whose son was divided among the people, always stood at my right hand in the furnace, keeping off the threatening flames and fiery volumes with her garments."

At that time, in a province of Wales, called Ros, was found the sepulchre of Walwin, the noble nephew of Arthur; he reigned, a most renowned knight, in that part of Britain which is still named Walwerth; but was driven from his kingdom by the brother and nephew of Hengist, (of whom I have spoken in my first book,) though not without first making them pay dearly for his expulsion. He deservedly shared, with his uncle, the praise of retarding, for many years, the calamity of his falling country. The sepulchre of Arthur is no where to be seen, whence ancient ballads fable that he is still to come. But the tomb of the other, as I have suggested, was found in the time of king William, on the sea-coast, fourteen feet long: there, as some relate, he was wounded by his enemies, and suffered shipwreck; others say, he was killed by his subjects at a public entertainment. The truth consequently is doubtful; though neither of these men was inferior to the reputation they have acquired.

This, too, was the period in which Germany, for fifty years, bewailed the pitiable, and almost fatal government of Henry, of whom I have spoken in the history of William. He was neither unlearned nor indolent; but so singled out by fate for every person to attack, that whoever took up arms against him seemed, to himself, to be acting for the good of religion. He had two sons, Conrad and Henry: the first, not violating the rights of nature towards his father, having subjugated Italy, died at Arezzo, a city of Tuscany: the other, in his early age, attacking his parent when he was somewhat at rest from external molestation, compelled him to retire from the empire, and when he died shortly after, honoured him with an imperial funeral. He still survives, obstinately adhering to those very sentiments, on account of which he thought himself justified in persecuting his father; for he grants the investiture of churches by the staff and ring; and looks upon the pope as not legally elected without his concurrence; although Calixtus, who now presides over the papal see, has greatly restrained this man's inordinate ambition: but let the reader wait my farther relation of these matters in their proper order.

Moreover, pope Hildebrand dying, as I have said, and Urban being elected by the cardinals, the emperor persisted in his intention of preferring Guibert, of proclaiming him pope, and of bringing him to Rome, by the expulsion of the other. The army, however, of the marchioness Matilda, a woman, who, forgetful of her sex, and comparable to the ancient Amazons, used to lead forth her hardy troops to battle, espoused the juster cause, as it seemed, by her assistance, in succeeding time, Urban obtaining the papal throne, held quiet possession of it for eleven years. After him Paschal was appointed by the Romans, who held Henry's concurrence in contempt. Guibert yet burdened the earth with his existence, the only sower of sedition, who never, during his whole life, laid aside his obstinacy, nor conformed to justice; saying, that the decision of the emperor ought to be observed; not that of the assassins, or parchment-mongers of Rome.* In consequence, both of them being excommunicated in several councils, they treated the sentence with ridicule. Notwithstanding these circumstances, there were many things praiseworthy in the emperor: he was eloquent, of great abilities, well read, actively charitable; had many good qualities, both of mind and person: was ever prepared for war, insomuch that he was sixty-two times engaged in battle; was equitable in adjusting differences; and when matters were unsuccessful, he would prefer his griefs to heaven, and wait for redress from thence. Many of his enemies perished by untimely deaths.

I have heard a person of the utmost veracity relate, that one of his adversaries, a weak and factious man, while reclining at a banquet, was, on a sudden, so completely surrounded by mice, as to be unable to escape. So great was the number of these little animals, that there could scarcely be imagined more in a whole province. It was in vain, that they were attacked with clubs and fragments of the benches which were at hand: and though they were for a long time assailed by all, yet they wreaked their deputed curse on no

* .... lanistarum vel pellificum. It seems a sneer at the sanguinary disposition of the Roman people, and at the bulls of the pope. In a dispute on the credibility of evidence adduced, it is observed, that the oral testimony of three bishops was certainly to be preferred "to sheep-skins blackened with ink and loaded with a leaden seal." Edmer. Hist. Nov. p 65.

one else; pursuing him only with their teeth, and with a kind of dreadful squeaking. And although he was carried out to sea about a javelin's cast by the servants, yet he could not by these means escape their violence; for immediately so great a multitude of mice took to the water, that you would have sworn the sea was strewed with chaff. But when they began to gnaw the planks of the ship, and the water, rushing through the chinks, threatened inevitable shipwreck, the servants turned the vessel to the shore. The animals, then also swimming close to the ship, landed first. Thus the wretch, set on shore, and soon after entirely gnawed in pieces, satiated the dreadful hunger of the mice.

I deem this the less wonderful, because it is well known, that in Asia, if a leopard bite any person, a party of mice approach directly, to discharge their urine on the wounded man; and that a filthy deluge of their water attends his death; but if, by the care of servants driving them off, the destruction can be avoided during nine days; then medical assistance, if called in, may be of service. My informant had seen a person wounded after this manner, who, despairing of safety on shore, proceeded to sea, and lay at anchor; when immediately more than a thousand mice swam out, wonderful to relate, in the rinds of pomegranates, the insides of which they had eaten; but they were drowned through the loud shouting of the sailors. "For the Creator of all things has made nothing destitute of sagacity; nor any pest without its remedy."

During this emperor's reign flourished Marianus Scotus,* first a monk of Fulda, afterwards a recluse at Mentz, who, by renouncing the present life, secured the happiness of that which is to come. During his long continued leisure, he examined the writers on Chronology, and discovered the disagreement of the cycles of Dionysius the Little with the evangelical computation. Wherefore reckoning every year from the beginning of the world, he added twenty-two, which were wanting, to the above mentioned cycles; but he had few, or no followers of his opinion. Wherefore I am often led to wonder, why such unhappiness should

* Marianus was born in Ireland A.D. 1028, and was compiler of a celebrated chronicle, which is the basis of Florence of Worcester. His imagined correction of Dionysius is founded in error.

attach to the learned of our time, that in so great a number of scholars and students, pale with watching, scarcely one can obtain unqualified commendation for knowledge. So much does ancient custom please, and so little encouragement, though deserved, is given to new discoveries, however consistent with truth. All are anxious to grovel in the old track, and everything modern is contemned; and therefore, as patronage alone can foster genius, when that is withheld, every exertion languishes.

But as I have mentioned the monastery of Fulda, I will relate what a reverend man, Walker, prior of Malvern, whose words if any disbelieve he offends against holiness, told me had happened there. "Not more than fifteen years have elapsed," said he, "since a contagious disease attacked the abbat of that place, and afterwards destroyed many of the monks. The survivors, at first, began each to fear for himself, and to pray, and give alms more abundantly than usual. In process of time, however, for such is the nature of man, their fear gradually subsiding, they began to omit them; the cellarer more especially: who publicly and absurdly exclaimed, that the stock of provision was not adequate to such a consumption; that he had lately hoped for some reduction of expense from so many funerals, but that his hopes were at an end, if the dead consumed what the living could not. It happened on a certain night, when, from some urgent business, he had deferred going to rest for a long time, that having at length despatched every concern, he went towards the dormitory. And now you shall hear a strange circumstance: he saw in the chapter-house, the abbat, and all who had died that year, sitting in the order they had departed: when affrighted and endeavouring to escape, he was detained by force. Being reproved and corrected, after the monastic manner, with a scourge, he heard the abbat speak precisely to the following effect: that it was foolish to look for advantage by another's death, when all were subject to one common fate; that it was an impious thing, that a monk who had passed his whole life in the service of the church should be grudged the pittance of a single year after his death; that he himself should die very shortly, but that whatever others might do for him, should redound only to the advantage of those whom he had defrauded; that he might now go and correct, by his example, those whom he had corrupted by his expressions." He departed, and demonstrated that he had seen nothing imaginary, as well by his recent stripes, as by his death, which shortly followed.

In the meantime, while employed on other subjects, both matter and inclination have occurred for the relation of what was determined in William's time, concerning the controversy still existing between the archbishops of Canterbury and York. And that posterity may be fully informed of this business, I will subjoin the opinions of the ancient fathers.

Pope Gregory to Augustine, first archbishop of Canterbury.

"Let your jurisdiction not only extend over the bishops you shall have ordained, or such as have been ordained by the bishop of York, but also over all the priests of Britain, by the authority of our Lord Jesus Christ."

Boniface to Justus, archbishop of Canterbury.

"Far be it from every Christian, that anything concerning the city of Canterbury be diminished or changed, in present or future times, which was appointed by our predecessor pope Gregory, however human circumstances may be changed: but more especially, by the authority of St. Peter the prince of apostles, we command and ordain, that the city of Canterbury shall ever hereafter be esteemed the metropolitan see of all Britain; and we decree and appoint, immutably, that all the provinces of the kingdom of England shall be subject to the metropolitan church of the aforesaid see. And if any one attempt to injure this church, which is more especially under the power and protection of the holy Roman church, or to lessen the jurisdiction conceded to it, may God expunge him from the book of life; and let him know, that he is bound by the sentence of a curse."

Alexander to William, king of England.

"The cause of Alric, formerly called bishop of Chichester, we have entrusted to our brother bishop, Lanfranc, to be by him diligently reconsidered and determined. We have also commended to him the labour of deciding the dispute which has arisen between the archbishop of York, and the bishop of Dorchester, on matters belonging to their dioceses; strictly ordering him to examine this cause most diligently and bring it to a just termination. Besides, we have so fully committed to him the authority of our personal and pontifical power in considering and settling causes, that whatever he shall, according to justice, have determined, shall be regarded as firm and indissoluble hereafter, as though it had been adjudged in our presence."

"In the year of our Lord Jesus Christ's incarnation 1072, of the pontificate of pope Alexander the eleventh, and of the reign of William, glorious king of England, and duke of Normandy, the sixth; by the command of the said pope Alexander, and permission of the same king, in presence of himself, his bishops, and abbats, the question was agitated concerning the primacy which Lanfranc,[*] archbishop of Canterbury, claimed in right of his church, over that of York; and concerning the ordination of certain bishops, of which it was not clearly evident, to whom they especially pertained; and at length, after some time it was proved and shown by the distinct authority of various writings, that the church of York ought to be subject to that of Canterbury, and to be obedient to the appointments of its archbishop, as primate of all England, in all such matters as pertained to the Christian religion. But the homage of the bishop of Durham, that is of Lindisfarne, and of all the countries beyond the limits of the bishop of Lichfield, and the great river Humber, to the farthest boundaries of Scotland, and whatever on this side of the aforesaid river justly pertains to the diocese of the church of York, the metropolitan of Canterbury allowed for ever to belong to the archbishop of York and his successors: in such sort, that if the archbishop of Canterbury chose to call a council, wherever he deemed fit, the archbishop of York was bound to be present at his command, with all his suffragan bishops, and be obedient to his canonical injunctions. And Lanfranc the archbishop proved from the ancient custom of his predecessors, that the archbishop of York was bound to make profession, even with an oath, to the archbishop of Canterbury; but through

[*] See the letters which passed on this subject between Lanfranc and Thomas archbishop of York in Lanfranci Opera, ed. J. A. Giles, 2 vols. 8vo. forming vols. 21 and 22 of Patres Ecclesiæ Anglicanæ.

regard to the king, he dispensed with the oath from Thomas, archbishop of York; and received his written profession only: but not forming a precedent for his successors who might choose to exact the oath, together with the profession, from Thomas's successors. If the archbishop of Canterbury should die, the archbishop of York shall come to Canterbury; and, with the other bishops of the church aforesaid, duly consecrate the person elect as his lawful primate. But if the archbishop of York shall die, his successor, accepting the gift of the archbishopric from the king, shall come to Canterbury, or where the archbishop of Canterbury shall appoint, and shall from him receive canonical ordination. To this ordinance consented the king aforesaid, and the archbishops, Lanfranc of Canterbury, and Thomas of York; and Hubert subdeacon of the holy Roman church, and legate of the aforesaid pope Alexander; and the other bishops and abbats present. This cause was first agitated at the festival of Easter in the city of Winchester, in the royal chapel, situated in the castle; afterwards in the royal town called Windsor, where it received its termination, in the presence of the king, the bishops, and abbats of different orders, who were assembled at the king's court on the festival of Pentecost.

"The signature of William the king: the signature of Matilda the queen.

"I Hubert, subdeacon of the holy Roman church, and legate from pope Alexander, have signed.

"I Lanfranc, archbishop of Canterbury, have signed.
"I Thomas, archbishop of York, have signed.
"I William, bishop of London, have assented.
"I Herman, bishop of Sherborne, have signed.
"I Wulstan, bishop of Worcester, have signed.
"I Walter, bishop of Hereford, have assented.
"I Giso, bishop of Wells, have assented.
"I Remigius, bishop of Dorchester, have signed.
"I Walkelin, bishop of Winchester, have signed.
"I Herefast, bishop of Helmham, have signed.
"I Stigand, bishop of Chichester, have assented.
"I Siward, bishop of Rochester, have assented.
"I Osberne, bishop of Exeter, have assented.
"I Odo, bishop of Bayeux and earl of Kent, have assented.

"I Gosfrith, bishop of Coutances and one of the nobles of England, have assented.

"I Scotland, abbat of St. Augustine's monastery, have assented.

"I Thurstan, abbat of the monastery which is situated in the isle of Ely, have assented.

"I Ailnoth, abbat of Glastonbury, have assented.

"I Elfwin, abbat of the monastery of Ramsey, have assented.

"I Wulnoth, abbat of Chertsey, have assented.

"I Ailwyn, abbat of Evesham, have assented.

' I Frederic, abbat of St. Alban's, have assented.

"I Goffrid, abbat of the monastery of St. Peter, near London, have assented.

"I Baldwin, abbat of St. Edmund's monastery, have assented.

"I Turald, abbat of Burgh, have assented.

"I Adelelm, abbat of Abingdon, have assented.

"I Ruald, abbat of the New minster at Winchester, have assented.

"It becomes every Christian to be subject to Christian laws, and by no means to run counter to those things which have been wholesomely enacted by the holy fathers. For hence arise strifes, dissensions, envyings, contentions, and other things, which plunge the lovers of them into eternal punishment. And the more exalted the rank of any person is, so much the more exact should be his obedience to divine commands: wherefore I Thomas, now ordained metropolitan bishop of the church of York, hearing and knowing your authorities, make unlimited profession of canonical obedience to you, Lanfranc, archbishop of Canterbury, and your successors; and I promise to observe whatever shall be canonically enjoined me, either by you or them. Of this matter I was doubtful, while I was yet about to be ordained by you: wherefore I promised obedience unconditionally to you, but conditionally to your successors."

The archbishop of Canterbury, as I remember to have observed in my first book, originally had subject to him, these bishops: London, Winchester, Rochester, Sherborne, Worcester, Hereford, Lichfield, Selsey, Leicester, Helmham, Sidnacester, Dunwich; in the time of king Edward the

Elder were added, Cornwall, Crediton, Wells in West Saxony, and Dorchester in Mercia, as I noticed in my second book.

The archbishop of York had all the bishops on the farther side of the Humber subject to him, as Ripon, Hexham, Lindisfarne, Candida Casa, which is now called Whitherne; and all the bishops of Scotland and the Orkneys; as the archbishop of Canterbury had those of Ireland and Wales. The bishoprics of Ripon and Hexham have long since perished by hostile ravages; Leicester, Sidnacester, and Dunwich, by means that I cannot account for; and, in the time of king Edward the Simple, Cornwall and Crediton were united, and the bishopric translated to Exeter. In king William's time, at this council, it was determined that, according to the decrees of the canons, the bishops should quit the villages, and fix their abode in the cities of their dioceses; Lichfield therefore migrated to Chester, which was anciently called the City of Legions; Selsey to Chichester; Helmham first to Thetford, and now, by bishop Herbert, to Norwich; Sherborne to Salisbury; Dorchester to Lincoln. For Lindisfarne had long before passed to Durham, and lately Wells to Bath.

In this assembly Lanfranc, who was yet uninstructed in English matters, inquired of the elder bishops, what was the order of sitting in council, as originally appointed. They, alleging the difficulty of the question, deferred their answer till the next day; when, carefully calling circumstances to mind, they asserted that they had seen the arrangement as follows: that the archbishop of Canterbury, presiding at the council, should have, on the right hand, the archbishop of York, and next him the bishop of Winchester; and on his left, the bishop of London. But should it ever happen, through necessity, that the primate of Canterbury should be absent, or should he be dead, the archbishop of York, presiding at the council, should have the bishops of London on his right hand, and of Winchester on his left; and the rest should take their seats according to the time of their ordination.

At that time, too, the claim of the archbishop of York on the see of Worcester and Dorchester was decided and set at rest. For he said that they ought to be subject to his jurisdiction; which, after having pondered for some time in secret, when he proceeded to Rome with Lanfranc to receive their palls from the pope, he brought publicly before the Roman court. Lanfranc, though for the most part unmoved by injury, could not help betraying, by his countenance, his emotion at such a wanton and unheard-of attack, though he for some time refrained from speaking. But pope Alexander, who felt much for Lanfranc's distress, for he had even condescendingly risen from his seat when he approached, professing that he paid him this mark of respect, not from honour to the archbishop but regard to his learning, removed from himself the unpleasant task of deciding, and referred the adjudication of it to an English council. In consequence, as I have related, the matter, after deep investigation, came to this termination in the present council; that, as these bishops were on this side of the Humber, they should belong to Canterbury, but all beyond that river to York.

Here the pious simplicity of St. Wulstan, bishop of Worcester, and his noble confidence in God, demand praise and approbation. For when called in question as well concerning this business, as on his slender attainments in learning, he had retired to consider more carefully what answer he should make, his mind undisturbed by tumult: "Believe me," said he, "we have not yet sung the service for the sixth hour: let us sing the service therefore." And, on his companions suggesting the necessity of first expediting the business they had met upon; that there was ample time for singing, and that the king and the nobility would laugh at them, if they heard of it: "Truly," said he, "let us first do our duty towards God, and afterwards settle the disputes of men." Having sung the service, he directly proceeded towards the council-chamber, without devising any subterfuge, or any attempt to disguise the truth. To his dependents, who were desirous of withholding him, and who could not be persuaded but their cause was in danger, he said, "Know for certain, that I here visibly perceive those holy archbishops, Dunstan of Canterbury, and Oswald of York; who, defending me this day with their prayers, will darken the understandings of my gainsayers." Then giving his benediction to a monk, a man of little eloquence, but somewhat acquainted with the Norman language, on summing up his cause, he obtained that he, who was before thought unworthy of the management of his own diocese, should be humbly entreated by the archbishop of York, to condescend to visit those parts of his province, which himself, through dread of enemies, or ignorance of the language, had refrained from approaching. But I will no longer torture the patience of my readers, who perhaps do not regard this matter with pleasure, as they are in expectation of the history of William's successors; though, if I am not too partial to myself, a variety of anecdote can be displeasing to no one, unless he be morose enough to rival the superciliousness of Cato. But whoever is so inclined, will find such other matters in the fourth and fifth book, for here the third shall terminate.*

BOOK IV.

PREFACE.

I AM aware, that many persons think it unwise in me, to have written the history of the kings of my own time; alleging, that in such a work, truth is often made shipwreck of, while falsehood meets with support: because to relate the crimes of contemporaries, is attended with danger; their good actions with applause. Whence it arises, say they, that, as all things have, now, a natural tendency to evil rather than to good, the historian passes over any disgraceful transaction, however obvious, through timidity; and, for the sake of approbation, feigns good qualities, when he cannot find them. There are others, who, judging of us by their own indolence, deem us unequal to so great a task, and brand our undertaking with malignant censure. Wherefore, impelled by the reasoning of the one, or the contempt of the other, I had long since voluntarily retired to leisure and to silence: but, after indulging in them for a time, the accustomed inclination for study again strongly beset me; as it was impossible for me to be unoccupied, and I knew not how to give myself up to those forensic avocations, which are beneath the notice of a literary character. To this was to be added the

* Two of the MSS, used by Mr. Hardy, place here the dedicatory epistle of the author to Robert Earl of Gloucester, which we have placed at the commencement of the work.

incitements of my friends, to whose suggestions, though only implied, I ought to pay regard : and they indeed gently urged me, already sufficiently disposed, to prosecute my undertaking. Animated, therefore, by the advice of those whom I love most affectionately, I advance to give them a lasting pledge of friendship from the stores of my research. Grateful also to those who are in fear for me, lest I should either excite hatred, or disguise the truth, I will, by the help of Christ, make such a return for their kindness, as neither to become odious, nor a falsifier. For I will describe, both what has been done well, or otherwise, in such wise, and so safely steer between Scylla and Charybdis, that my opinions shall not be concealed, though some matters may be omitted in my history. Moreover, to those who undervalue the labours of others, I make the same answer as St. Jerome formerly did to his critics ; "Let them read if they like : if not, let them cast it aside ; because I do not obtrude my work on the fastidious, but I dedicate it, if any think it worth their notice, to the studious;" which even these men will readily pronounce to be consonant to equity, unless they are of the number of those, of whom it is said ; "Fools are easy to confute, but not so easy to restrain." I will relate, then, in this, the fourth book of my work, every thing which may be said of William, son of William the Great, in such manner that neither shall the truth suffer, nor shall the dignity of the prince be obscured. Some matters also will be inserted in these pages, which in his time were calamitous in this country, or glorious elsewhere, as far as my knowledge extends. More especially, the pilgrimage of the Christians to Jerusalem, which it will be proper to annex in this place ; because an expedition, so famous in these times, is well worth hearing, and will also be an incitement to valour. Not indeed that I have any confidence these transactions will be better treated by me than by others who have written on the subject, but that, what many write, many may read. Yet, lest so long a preface should disgust my reader, I will immediately enter on my work.

CHAP. I.

Of William the Second. [A.D. 1087—1100.]

WILLIAM then, the son of William, was born in Normandy many years before his father came to England; and being educated with extreme care by his parents, as he had naturally an ambitious mind, he at length reached the summit of dignity. He would no doubt have been a prince incomparable in our time, had not his father's greatness eclipsed him; and had not the fates cut short his years too early for his maturer age to correct errors, contracted by the licentiousness of power, and the impetuosity of youth. When childhood was passed, he spent the period of youth in military occupations; in riding, throwing the dart, contending with his elders in obedience, with those of his own age in action: and he esteemed it injurious to his reputation, if he was not the foremost to take arms in military commotions; unless he was the first to challenge the adversary, or when challenged, to overcome him. To his father he was ever dutiful; always exerting himself in his sight in battle, ever at his side in peace. His hopes gradually expanding, he already aspired after the succession, especially on the rejection of his elder brother, while the tender age of the younger gave him no uneasiness. Thus, adopted as his successor by his father during his last illness, he set out to take possession of the kingdom ere the king had breathed his last: where being gladly received by the people, and obtaining the keys of the treasury, he by these means subjected all England to his will. Archbishop Lanfranc, the grand mover of every thing, had educated him, and made him a knight,[*] and now he favoured his pretensions to the throne; by his authority and assistance William was crowned on the day of the saints Cosmas and Damian,[†] and passed the remainder of the winter quietly and with general favour.

At the expiration of this period, in the beginning of spring, his first contention was with his uncle, Odo, bishop of

---

[*] "At this period the custom of receiving knighthood from the hands of bishops or abbats yet obtained. There is a law of Henry I., prohibiting abbats from making knights."—HARDY.

[†] The 27th of September.

Bayeux. For when Odo, on his release from confinement, as I have related, had firmly established his nephew, Robert, in the duchy of Normandy, he came to England, and received from the king the earldom of Kent. But when he saw every thing in the kingdom managed, not at his own pleasure, as formerly, for the administration of public affairs was now committed to William, bishop of Durham, he was moved with envy, and having revolted from the king, he tainted many others by insinuating, that the kingdom belonged to Robert, who was of gentler disposition, and whose youthful follies had been corrected by many adversities; that William, delicately brought up, and overbearing from that ferocity of mind which was manifest in his countenance, would dare every thing, in defiance of right and equity: that it must soon come to pass, that they would lose the honours they had already obtained with so much difficulty: that nothing was gained by the father's death, if those whom he had cast into prison, were to be killed by the son. To this effect he used, at first, secretly to mutter, together with Roger Montgomery, Gosfrith, bishop of Coutances, with his nephew Robert earl of Northumberland, and others; afterwards they were more open in their clamours, repeating and disseminating them by letters and by emissaries. Moreover, even William, bishop of Durham, the confidential minister of the king, had joined in their treachery. This was matter of great concern to William, it is said; because, together with the breach of friendship, he was disappointed of the resources of the distant provinces. Odo now carried off booty of every kind to Rochester, plundering the king's revenues in Kent, and especially the lands of the archbishop; breathing eternal hatred against him, because, he said, it was by his advice, that his brother had cast him into chains. Nor was this assertion false: for when William the elder formerly complained to Lanfranc, that he was deserted by his brother: "Seize, and cast him into chains," said he. "What!" replied the king, "he is a clergyman!" Then the archbishop with playful archness, as Persius says, "balancing the objection with nice antithesis,"* rejoined, "you will not seize the bishop of Bayeux, but confine the earl of Kent."

* Persius, Sat. i. 85.

Bishop Gosfrith with his nephew, depopulating Bath, and Berkeley, and part of the county of Wilts, treasured up their spoils at Bristol. Roger Montgomery sending out his army with the Welsh from Shrewsbury, plundered Worcestershire. They had now hostilely approached Worcester, when the king's soldiers who guarded it, relying on the blessing of bishop Wulstan, to whom the custody of the castle was committed, though few in number, dispersed this multitude; and after wounding and killing many, took some of them prisoners. Moreover, Roger Bigod at Norwich, and Hugo de Grentmeisnil at Leicester, each with their party, were plundering in their respective neighbourhoods. In vain, however, did the whole power of revolt rage against a man, who was deficient neither in prudence nor in good fortune. For seeing almost all the Normans leagued in one furious conspiracy, he sent alluring letters, summoning to him such brave and honest English as yet remained; and complaining to them on the subject of his wrongs, he bound them to his party, by promising them wholesome laws, a diminution of tribute, and free leave to hunt.* With equal cunning he circumvented Roger Montgomery, when riding with him, with dissembled perfidy; for taking him aside, he loaded him with odium, saying, that he would willingly retire from the government, if it seemed meet to him and to the rest whom his father had left as his guardians; that he could not understand, why they were so outrageous; if they wanted money, they might have what they pleased; if an increase of their estates, they might have that also; in short, they might have whatever they chose; only let them be careful that the judgment of his father was not called in question: for, if they thought it ought to be disregarded in the instance of himself, it might be a bad example for them: for the same person made him king, who had made them earls. Excited by these words and promises, the earl, who, next to Odo, had been the chief leader of the faction, was the first to desert. Proceeding, therefore, immediately against the rebels, he laid siege to the castles of his uncle at Tunbridge and at Pevensey, and seizing him in the latter compelled him to swear, as he dictated, that he would depart England, and deliver up Rochester. To fulfil this promise he sent him

* On their own lands, it should seem from Sax. Chron., p. 465.

forward with a party he could rely on, intending to follow at his leisure. At that time almost all the young nobility of England and Normandy were at Rochester: three sons of earl Roger, Eustace the younger of Boulogne, and many others not deserving notice. The royal party, accompanying the bishop, were few and unarmed, for who could fear treachery where he was present? and going round the walls, they called the townsmen to open the gates; for so the bishop in person, and the absent king commanded. Observing from the wall, however, that the countenance of the bishop ill agreed with the language of the speakers, they suddenly sallied out, took horse in an instant, and carried off, together with the bishop, the whole party, captive. The report of this transaction quickly reached the king. Fierce from the injury, and smothering his indignation, he calls together his faithful English subjects, and orders them to summon all their countrymen to the siege, unless any wished to be branded with the name of "Nidering,"[*] which implies "abandoned." The English who thought nothing more disgraceful than to be stigmatised by such an appellation, flocked in troops to the king, and rendered his army invincible. Nor could the townsmen longer delay submission; experiencing, that a party, however noble, or however numerous, could avail nothing against the king of England. Odo, now taken a second time, abjured England for ever: the bishop of Durham of his own accord retired beyond sea, the king allowing him to escape uninjured out of regard to his former friendship: the rest were all admitted to fealty. During the interval of this siege, some of the king's fleet destroyed a party which the earl of Normandy had sent to assist the traitors, partly by slaughter, and partly by shipwreck; the remainder, intent on escaping, endeavoured to make sail; but being soon after disappointed by its falling calm, they became matter for laughter to our people, but their own destruction; for, that they might not be taken alive, they leaped from their vessels into the sea.

[*] Nidering is supposed by Somner to denote such as were infamous enough to rifle a dead body. Gavelk. 65. Lye renders it, nequam, exlex, —infamous, outlaw. MS. Nithing. Spelman derives it from nidus: but there is no authority for either interpretation; and in such cases it is safer, to confess ignorance than to mislead the reader by fanciful etymologies.

The next year, as the sense of injuries ever grows keener from reconsideration, the king began carefully to examine, how he might revenge his griefs, and repay his brother for this insult. In consequence, by his practices, he bribed the garrison, and obtained possession of the castle of St. Vallery, the adjoining port, and the town which is called Albemarle. The earl had not the courage to resist, but, by means of ambassadors, acquainted his lord, the king of France, with the violence of his brother, and begged his assistance. The French king, inactive, and surfeited with daily gluttony, came hiccupping, through repletion, to the war : but, as he was making great professions, the money of the king of England met him by the way ; with which his resolution being borne down, he unbuckled his armour, and went back to his gormandizing. In this manner, Normandy, for a long time, groaned under intestine war, sometimes one party, sometimes the other being victorious: the nobility, men of fickle temper, and faithful to neither brother, exciting their mutual fury. A few, better advised, attentive to their own advantage, for they had possessions in both countries, were mediators of a peace : the basis of which was, that the king should get possession of Maine for the earl ; and the earl should cede to the king those castles which he already held, and the monastery of Feschamp. The treaty was ratified and confirmed by the oath of the nobles on both sides.

Not long after the king went abroad to execute these conditions. Each leader made great efforts to invade Maine ; but when they had completed their preparations, and were just ready to proceed, an obstacle arose, through the spirit of Henry, the younger brother, loudly remonstrating against their covetousness, which had shared their paternal possessions between themselves, and blushed not at having left him almost destitute. In consequence he took possession of Mount St. Michael, and harassed, with constant sallies, the besieging forces of his brothers. During this siege, a noble specimen of disposition was exhibited, both by the king and by the earl : of compassion in the one, and of magnanimity in the other. I shall subjoin these instances, for the information of my readers.

The king, going out of his tent, and observing the enemy at a distance, proudly prancing, rushed unattended against a large party; spurred on by the impetuosity of his courage, and at the same time confident that none would dare resist him. Presently his horse, which he had that day purchased for fifteen marks of silver, being killed under him, he was thrown down, and for a long time dragged by his foot; the strength of his mail, however, prevented his being hurt. The soldier who had unhorsed him, was at this instant drawing his sword to strike him, when, terrified at the extremity of his danger, he cried out, "Hold, rascal, I am the king of England." The whole troop trembled at the well-known voice of the prostrate monarch, and immediately raised him respectfully from the ground, and brought him another horse. Leaping into the saddle without waiting assistance, and darting a keen look on the by-standers: "Who unhorsed me?" said he. While the rest were silent through fear, the bold perpetrator of the deed readily defended himself, saying, "'Twas I, who took you, not for a king, but for a soldier." The king, soothed, and regaining the serenity of his countenance, exclaimed, "By the crucifix* at Lucca," for such was his oath, "henceforth thou shalt be mine, and, placed on my roll, shalt receive the recompence of this gallant service." Nobly done, magnanimous king! what encomium shall I pass on this speech! Equal to Alexander the Great in glory; who, through admiration of his courage, preserved, unhurt, a Persian soldier, who had attempted to strike him from behind, but was frustrated in his design by the treachery of his sword.

But now to relate the compassion of the earl. When the blockade had so far proceeded that the besieged were in want of water, Henry sent messengers to Robert, to expostulate with him on the thirst he endured, and to represent, that it was impious to deprive him of water, the common right of mankind: let him try his courage another way if he chose; and not employ the violence of the elements, but the valour of a soldier. On which, wrought upon by the natural tenderness of his disposition, he ordered his party to be more remiss in their duty where they kept guard, that his thirsty

* This crucifix was very celebrated; it being pretended that it was the work of Nicodemus. "See further on this subject in the Rev. J. E. Tyler's interesting volume, entitled, 'Oaths, their origin, nature, and history.' London: 8vo, pp. 289—296."—HARDY.

brother might not be deprived of water. This circumstance, when related to the king, who was always inclined to warmth of temper, made him say to the earl, "You well know how to carry on war indeed, who allow your enemies plenty of water: and pray, how shall we subdue them, if we indulge them in food and drink?" But he smiling, uttered this kind and truly laudable expression, "Oh, shame! should I suffer my brother to die with thirst? and where shall we find another, if we lose him?" On this the king, deriding the mild temper of the man, put an end to the war without accomplishing his design; and as the commotions of the Scots and Welsh required his presence, he retired with both his brothers to his kingdom.

Immediately he led an expedition, first against the Welsh, and then against the Scots, in which he performed nothing worthy of his greatness; but lost many of his soldiers, and had his sumpter-horses intercepted. And, not only at that time, but frequently, in Wales, was fortune unfavourable to him; which may seem strange to any one, when the chance of war was generally on his side in other places. But it appears to me that the unevenness of the country, and the badness of the weather, as it assisted their rebellion, was also an impediment to his valour. But king Henry, who now reigns, a man of excellent talents, discovered a mode of counteracting their designs: which was, by stationing in their country the Flemings, to be a barrier to them, and constantly keep them within bounds. At that time, by the industry of earl Robert, who had long since gained the good graces of the Scot, the basis of a peace was laid between Malcolm and William. But various grounds of difference still existing on both sides, and justice wavering through their mutual animosity, Malcolm came of his own accord to Gloucester, a hearty solicitor for peace, so that it were on equitable conditions. He obtained, however, nothing more than permission to return uninjured to his kingdom: for the king disdained to take a man by subtlety, whom he might have conquered by arms. But the next winter he was dispatched by the party of Robert, earl of Northumberland, rather through stratagem than force. When his wife, Margaret, a woman distinguished for alms-giving and for chastity, heard of his death, disgusted with the continuance of life, she earnestly entreated of God to die. They were both remarkable for piety, but the queen more especially. For during her whole life, wherever she might be, she had twenty-four poor persons whom she supplied with meat and clothing. In Lent, waiting for the singing of the priests, she used to watch all night in the church, herself assisting at triple matins, of the Trinity, of the Cross, of St. Mary, and afterwards repeating the Psalter; with tears bedewing her garments, and agitating her breast. Departing from the church, she used to feed the poor; first three, then nine, then twenty-four, at last three hundred: herself standing by with the king, and pouring water on their hands. Edgar his son, when expelled by his uncle, was restored by William, assuredly with a noble compassion, and worthy of so great a personage, who, forgetting the injuries of the father, replaced the son, when suppliant, on his throne.

Greatness of soul was pre-eminent in the king, which, in process of time, he obscured by excessive severity; vices, indeed, in place of virtues, so insensibly crept into his bosom, that he could not distinguish them. The world doubted, for a long time, whither he would incline; what tendency his disposition would take. At first, as long as archbishop Lanfranc survived, he abstained from every crime; so that it might be hoped, he would be the very mirror of kings. After his death, for a time, he showed himself so variable, that the balance hung even betwixt vices and virtues. At last, however, in his latter years, the desire after good grew cold, and the crop of evil increased to ripeness: his liberality became prodigality; his magnanimity pride; his austerity cruelty. I may be allowed, with permission of the royal majesty, not to conceal the truth; for he feared God but little, man not at all. If any one shall say this is undiscerning, he will not be wrong; because wise men should observe this rule, "God ought to be feared at all times; man, according to circumstances." He was, when abroad, and in public assemblies, of supercilious look, darting his threatening eye on the by-stander; and with assumed severity and ferocious voice, assailing such as conversed with him. From apprehension of poverty, and of the treachery of others, as may be conjectured, he was too much given to lucre, and to cruelty. At home and at table, with his intimate companions, he gave loose to levity and to mirth. He was a most facetious railer at any thing he had himself done amiss, in order that he might thus do away obloquy, and make it matter of jest. But I shall dilate somewhat on that liberality, in which he deceived himself; and afterwards on his other propensities, that I may manifest what great vices sprang up in him under the semblance of virtues.

For, in fact, there are two kinds of givers: the one is denominated prodigal, the other liberal. The prodigal are such as lavish their money on those things, of which they will leave either a transient, or perhaps no memory in this world; neither will they gain mercy by them from God. The liberal, are those who redeem the captive from the plunderer, assist the poor, or discharge the debts of their friends. We must give, therefore, but with discrimination and moderation; for many persons have exhausted their patrimony by giving inconsiderately. " For what can be more silly, than to take pains to be no longer able to do that which you do with pleasure?"* Some, therefore, when they have nothing to give turn to rapine, and get more hatred from those from whom they take, than good will from those to whom they give. We lament that thus it happened to this king; for, when in the very beginning of his reign, through fear of tumults, he had assembled soldiers, and denied them nothing, promising still greater remuneration hereafter; the consequence was, that as he had soon exhausted his father's treasures, and had then but moderate revenues, his substance failed, though the spirit of giving remained, which, by habit, had almost become nature. He was a man who knew not how to take off from the price of any thing, or to judge of the value of goods; but the trader might sell him his commodity at whatever rate, or the soldier demand any pay he pleased. He was anxious that the cost of his clothes should be extravagant, and angry if they were purchased at a low price. One morning, indeed, while putting on his new boots, he asked his chamberlain what they cost; and when he replied, " Three shillings," indignantly and in a rage he cried out, " You son of a whore, how long has the king worn boots of so paltry a price? go, and bring

* Cicero de Officiis, ii. 15. Much of the argument is borrowed from the same source.

me a pair worth a mark of silver." He went, and bringing him a much cheaper pair, told him, falsely, that they cost as much as he had ordered: "Aye," said the king, "these are suitable to royal majesty." Thus his chamberlain used to charge him what he pleased for his clothes; acquiring by these means many things for his own advantage.

The fame of his generosity, therefore, pervaded all the West, and reached even to the East. Military men came to him out of every province on this side of the mountains, whom he rewarded most profusely. In consequence, when he had no longer aught to bestow, poor and exhausted, he turned his thoughts to rapine. The rapacity of his disposition was seconded by Ralph, the inciter of his covetousness; a clergyman of the lowest origin, but raised to eminence by his wit and subtilty. If at any time a royal edict issued, that England should pay a certain tribute, it was doubled by this plunderer of the rich, this exterminator of the poor, this confiscator of other men's inheritance. He was an invincible pleader, as unrestrained in his words as in his actions; and equally furious against the meek or the turbulent. Wherefore some people used to laugh,* and say, that he was the only man who knew how to employ his talents in this way, and cared for no one's hatred, so that he could please his master. At this person's suggestion, the sacred honours of the church, as the pastors died, were exposed to sale: for whenever the death of any bishop or abbat was announced, directly one of the king's clerks was admitted, who made an inventory of every thing, and carried all future rents into the royal exchequer. In the meantime some person was sought out fit to supply the place of the deceased; not from proof of morals, but of money; and, at last, if I may so say, the empty honour was conferred, and even that purchased, at a great price. These things appeared the more disgraceful, because, in his father's time, after the decease of a bishop or abbat, all rents were reserved entire, to be given up to the succeeding pastor; and persons truly meritorious, on account of their religion, were elected. But in the lapse of a very few years, every thing was changed. There was no man rich except the money-changer; no clerk, unless he was a lawyer; no priest, unless (to use a word which is hardly

* Some read, "The king used to laugh," &c.

Latin*) he was a farmer. Men of the meanest condition, or guilty of whatever crime, were listened to, if they could suggest any thing likely to be advantageous to the king: the halter was loosened from the robber's neck, if he could promise any emolument to the sovereign. All military discipline being relaxed, the courtiers preyed upon the property of the country people, and consumed their substance, taking the very meat from the mouths of these wretched creatures.† Then was there flowing hair and extravagant dress; and then was invented the fashion of shoes‡ with curved points; then the model for young men was to rival women in delicacy of person, to mince their gait, to walk with loose gesture, and half naked. Enervated and effeminate, they unwillingly remained what nature had made them; the assailers of others' chastity, prodigal of their own. Troops of pathics, and droves of harlots, followed the court; so that it was said, with justice, by a wise man, that England would be fortunate if Henry could reign;§ led to such an opinion, because he abhorred obscenity from his youth.

Here, were it necessary, I could add, that archbishop Anselm attempted to correct these abuses; but failing of the co-operation of his suffragans, he voluntarily quitted the kingdom, yielding to the depravity of the times. Anselm, than whom none ever was more tenacious of right; none in the present time so thoroughly learned; none so completely

* This is unintelligible to the English reader. The author uses the word "firmarius," which certainly would not have conveyed the idea of a "farmer" to the mind of either Cicero or Horace.

† Those who followed the court, being under no kind of control, were in the habit of plundering and devastating the country wherever they went. When they were unable to consume whatever they found in their lodgings, they would sell it to the best bidder, or destroy it with fire; or if it were liquor, after washing their horses' legs with a part, they let the remainder run. "As to their cruelty towards their hosts, or their unseemly conduct towards their wives and daughters, it is shameful even to remember."— Edmer. Hist. Nov. p. 94.

‡ These shoes, which gave occasion for various ordinances for their regulation or abolition, during several successive centuries, are said to have owed their invention to Fulk, earl of Anjou, in order to hide his ill-formed feet. Ordericus Vitalis, p. 682: who also observes, that the first improver, by adding the long curved termination, was a fellow (quidam nebulo) in the court of William Rufus, named Robert.

§ Others read, "The palace of the king was not the abode of majesty, but the stews of pathics."

spiritual; the father of his country, the mirror of the world: he, when just about to set sail, after waiting in port for a wind, was rifled, as though he had been a public robber; all his bags and packages being brought out and ransacked. Of this man's injuries I could speak farther, had the sun witnessed any thing more unjust than this single transaction, or were it not necessary to omit a relation, which has been anticipated by the eloquence of the very reverend Edmer.*

Hence may be perceived how fierce a flame of evil burst forth from what the king conceived to be liberality. In repressing which as he did not manifest so much diligence as negligence, he incurred a degree of infamy, not only great, but scarcely to be wiped out. I think undeservedly, however; because he never could have exposed himself to such disgrace, had he only recollected the dignity of his station. I pass over, therefore, these matters slightly, and hasten in my composition, because I blush to relate the crimes of so great a king; rather giving my attention to refute and extenuate them.

The Jews in his reign gave proofs of their insolence towards God. At one time, at Rouen, they endeavoured to prevail, by means of presents, on some converted Jews, to return to Judaism; † at another, at London, entering into controversy with our bishops; because the king, in jest, as I suppose, had said, that if they mastered the Christians in

* Edmer, besides constant mention of Anselm in his Historia Novorum, wrote his life also, in a separate form.

† A Jewish youth imagined that St. Stephen had appeared to him, and commanded him to be baptized: this he obeyed. His father immediately flew to the king, earnestly entreating an order for his son to be restored to the faith of his ancestors. The king not discovering any advantage as likely to accrue to himself, remained silent. on this the Jew offers him sixty marks, on condition that he would restore his son to Judaism. William then orders the youth to be brought before him; relates his father's complaint, and commands him to renounce his baptism. The lad, astonished, replies, "Your majesty is joking surely." "I joke with thee," exclaims the king, "thou son of ordure! begone, and obey my commands instantly, or by the cross at Lucca I will have your eyes torn out." The young man remaining inflexible, he drove him from his presence. The father was then ordered before the king, who desired him to pay down the money he had promised; but, on the Jew's remonstrating that he had not reconverted his son, and the king's declaring that his labour was not to go unrewarded, it was agreed that he should receive half the sum. Edmer, Hist. Novor. p. 47.

open argument, he would become one of their sect. The question therefore was agitated with much apprehension on the part of the bishops and clergy, fearful, through pious anxiety, for the Christian faith. From this contest, however, the Jews reaped nothing but confusion : though they used repeatedly to boast that they were vanquished, not by argument, but by power.

In later times, that is, about the ninth year of his reign, Robert, earl of Normandy, at the admonition of pope Urban, as will be related hereafter, took the resolution of going to Jerusalem, and pawned Normandy to his brother, for the sum of ten thousand marks. In consequence, an edict for an intolerable tax was circulated throughout England. On this the bishops and abbats, in great numbers, went to court, to complain of the injury ; observing that they could not raise so great an impost, unless they drove away their wretched husbandmen altogether. To this the courtiers, with angry countenance, as usual, replied, "Have you not shrines adorned with gold and silver, full of dead men's bones ?" deigning the petitioners no other answer. In consequence, perceiving the drift of the reply, they took off the gold from the shrines of their saints ; robbed their crucifixes, melted their chalices ; not for the service of the poor, but of the king's exchequer. For almost every thing, which the holy parsimony of their ancestors had saved, was consumed by the rapacity of these freebooters.

Just so, too, were their proceedings against their vassals : first taking their money, then their land : neither the poor man's poverty, nor the rich man's abundance, protecting him. He so restricted the right of hunting, which he had formerly allowed, that it became a capital offence to take a stag. This extreme severity, which was tempered by no affability, was the cause of many conspiracies, among the nobility, against his safety : one of whom, Robert de Mowbray earl of Northumberland, in consequence of very high words between him and the king, retired to his province, with the intention of making powerful efforts against his lord ; but William pursuing him, he was taken, and doomed to perpetual captivity. Another, William de Hou, being accused of treachery towards the king, challenged his accuser to single combat ; but being unable to justify himself in the duel, he was deprived of his sight, and of his manhood. The same accusation involved many innocent and honourable men; among whom was William de Aldrey, a man of handsome person, who had stood godfather* with the king. Being sentenced to be hanged, he made his confession to Osmund bishop of Salisbury, and was scourged at every church of the town. Parting his garments to the poor, he went naked to the gallows, often making the blood gush from his delicate flesh by falling on his knees upon the stones. He satisfied the minds of the bishop, and of the people who followed him to the place of punishment, by exclaiming, "God help my soul, and deliver it from evil, as I am free from the charge, of which I am accused · the sentence, indeed, passed upon me will not be revoked, but I wish all men to be certified of my innocence." The bishop then, commending his soul to heaven, and sprinkling him with holy water, departed. At his execution, he manifested an admirable degree of courage; neither uttering a groan before, nor even a sigh, at the moment of his death.

But still there are some proofs of noble magnanimity in the king, the knowledge of which, I will not deny posterity. As he was once engaged in hunting in a certain forest, a foreign messenger acquainted him that the city of Mans, which he had lately added to his dominions on the departure of his brother, was besieged. Unprepared as he was, he turned his horse instantly, and shaped his journey to the sea. When his nobles reminded him, that it would be necessary to call out his troops, and put them in array; "I shall see," said he, "who will follow me: do you think I shall not have people enough? If I know the temper of the young men of my kingdom, they will even brave shipwreck to come to me." In this manner he arrived, almost unattended, at the sea-coast. The sky at that time was overcast, the wind contrary, and a tempest swept the surface of the deep. When he determined to embark directly, the mariners besought him, to wait till the storm should subside, and the wind be favourable. "Why," said William, "I have never heard of a king perishing by shipwreck: no, weigh anchor immediately, and you shall see the elements conspire to obey me." When the report of his having

* "Compater" sometimes means a friend or companion.

crossed the sea reached the besiegers, they hastily retreated. One Helias, the author of the commotion, was taken; to whom, when brought before him, the king said jocularly, "I have you, master." But he, whose haughty spirit, even in such threatening danger, knew not how to be prudent, or to speak submissively, replied, "You have taken me by chance; if I could escape, I know what I would do." At this William, almost beside himself with rage, and seizing Helias, exclaimed, "You scoundrel! and what would you do? Begone, depart, fly: I give you leave to do whatever you can; and by the crucifix at Lucca, if you should conquer me, I will ask no return for this favour." Nor did he falsify his word, but immediately suffered him to escape; rather admiring than following the fugitive. Who could believe this of an unlettered man? And perhaps there may be some person, who, from reading Lucan, may falsely suppose, that William borrowed these examples from Julius Cæsar;* but he had neither inclination, nor leisure to attend to learning; it was rather the innate warmth of his temper, and his conscious valour which prompted him to such expressions. And indeed, if our religion would allow it, as the soul of Euphorbus was formerly said to have passed into Pythagoras of Samos, so might it equally be asserted, that the soul of Julius Cæsar had migrated into king William.

He began and completed one very noble edifice, the palace† in London; sparing no expense to manifest the greatness of his liberality. His disposition therefore the reader will be able to discover from the circumstances we have enumerated.

Should any one be desirous, however, to know the make of his person, he is to understand, that he was well set; his complexion florid, his hair yellow; of open countenance; different-coloured eyes, varying with certain glittering specks; of astonishing strength, though not very tall, and his belly

* Pharsalia, lib. ii. 515—v. 580.
† "It has been inferred from this passage, that Malmesbury states the tower of London was built by William Rufus. There appears, however, little doubt that the principal building, now called the White Tower, was commenced by the Conqueror, and finished by Rufus, under the superintendence of Gundulph, bishop of Rochester."—HARDY.

rather projecting; of no eloquence, but remarkable for a hesitation of speech, especially when angry. Many sudden and sorrowful accidents happened in his time, which I shall arrange singly, according to the years of his reign; chiefly vouching for their truth on the credit of the Chronicles.

In the second year of his reign, on the third before the ides of August, a great earthquake terrified all England with a horrid spectacle; for all the buildings were lifted up, and then again settled as before. A scarcity of every kind of produce followed; the corn ripened so slowly, that the harvest was scarcely housed before the feast of St. Andrew.

In his fourth year was a tempest of lightning, and a whirlwind: finally, on the ides of October, at Winchcombe, a stroke of lightning beat against the side of the tower with such force, that, shattering the wall where it joined to the roof, it opened a place wide enough to admit a man; entering there, it struck a very large beam, and scattered fragments of it over the whole church; moreover it cast down the head of the crucifix, with the right leg, and the image of St. Mary. A stench so noisome followed, as to be insufferable to human nostrils. At length, the monks, with auspicious boldness, entering, defeated the contrivances of the devil, by the sprinkling of holy water. But what could this mean? such a thing was unknown to every previous age. A tempest of contending winds, from the south-east, on the sixteenth before the kalends of November, destroyed more than six hundred houses in London. Churches were heaped on houses, and walls on partitions. The tempest proceeding yet farther, carried off altogether the roof of the church of St. Mary le Bow, and killed two men. Rafters and beams were whirled through the air, an object of surprise to such as contemplated them from a distance; of alarm, to those who stood nigh, lest they should be crushed by them. For four rafters, six and twenty feet long, were driven with such violence into the ground, that scarcely four feet of them were visible. It was curious to see how they had perforated the solidity of the public street, maintaining there the same position which they had occupied in the roof from the hand of the workman, until, on account of their inconvenience to passengers, they were cut off level with the ground, as they could not be otherwise removed.

In his fifth year, a similar thunder-storm at Salisbury entirely destroyed the roof of the church-tower, and much injured the wall, only five days after Osmund, the bishop of famed memory, had consecrated it.

In his sixth year there was such a deluge from rain, and such incessant showers as none had ever remembered. Afterwards, on the approach of winter, the rivers were so frozen, that they bore horsemen and waggons; and soon after, when the frost broke, the bridges were destroyed by the drifting of the ice.

In his seventh year, on account of the heavy tribute which the king, while in Normandy, had levied, agriculture failed; of which failure the immediate consequence was a famine. This also gaining ground a mortality ensued, so general, that the dying wanted attendance, and the dead, burial. At that time, too, the Welsh, fiercely raging against the Normans, and depopulating the county of Chester and part of Shropshire, obtained Anglesey by force of arms.

In his tenth year, on the kalends of October, a comet appeared for fifteen days, turning its larger train to the east, and the smaller to the south-east. Other stars also appeared, darting, as it were, at each other. This was the year in which Anselm, that light of England, voluntarily escaping from the darkness of error, went to Rome.

In his eleventh year, Magnus, king of Norway, with Harold, son of Harold, formerly king of England, subdued the Orkney, Mevanian, and other circumjacent isles; and was now obstinately bent against England from Anglesey. But Hugh, earl of Chester, and Hugh, earl of Shrewsbury, opposed him; and ere he could gain the continent, forced him to retire. Here fell Hugh of Shrewsbury, being struck from a distance with a fatal arrow.

In his twelfth year an excessive tide flowed up the Thames, and overwhelmed many villages, with their inhabitants.

In his thirteenth year, which was the last of his life, there were many adverse events; but the most dreadful circumstance was that the devil visibly appeared to men in woods and secret places, and spoke to them as they passed by. Moreover in the county of Berks, at the village of Finchhampstead, a fountain so plentifully flowed with blood for fifteen whole days, that it discoloured a neighbouring pool.

The king heard of it and laughed; neither did he care for his own dreams, nor for what others saw concerning him.

They relate many visions and predictions of his death, three of which, sanctioned by the testimony of credible authors, I shall communicate to my readers. Edmer, the historian of our times, noted for his veracity, says that Anselm, the noble exile, with whom all religion was also banished, came to Marcigny that he might communicate his sufferings to Hugo, abbat of Clugny. There, when the conversation turned upon king William, the abbat aforesaid observed, "Last night that king was brought before God; and by a deliberate judgment, incurred the sorrowful sentence of damnation." How he came to know this he neither explained at the time, nor did any of his hearers ask : nevertheless, out of respect to his piety, not a doubt of the truth of his words remained on the minds of any present. Hugh led such a life, and had such a character, that all regarded his discourse and venerated his advice, as though an oracle from heaven had spoken. And soon after, the king being slain as we shall relate, there came a messenger to entreat the archbishop to resume his see.

The day before the king died, he dreamed that he was let blood by a surgeon; and that the stream, reaching to heaven, clouded the light, and intercepted the day. Calling on St. Mary for protection, he suddenly awoke, commanded a light to be brought, and forbade his attendants to leave him. They then watched with him several hours until daylight. Shortly after, just as the day began to dawn, a certain foreign monk told Robert Fitz Hamon, one of the principal nobility, that he had that night dreamed a strange and fearful dream about the king: "That he had come into a certain church, with menacing and insolent gesture, as was his custom, looking contemptuously on the standers by; then violently seizing the crucifix, he gnawed the arms, and almost tore away the legs: that the image endured this for a long time, but at length struck the king with its foot in such a manner that he fell backwards: from his mouth, as he lay prostrate, issued so copious a flame that the volumes of smoke touched the very stars." Robert, thinking that this dream ought not to be neglected, as he was intimate with him, immediately related it to the king. William, repeatedly laughing, exclaimed, "He is a monk, and dreams for money like a monk: give him a hundred shillings." Nevertheless, being greatly moved, he hesitated a long while whether he should go out to hunt, as he had designed: his friends persuading him not to suffer the truth of the dreams to be tried at his personal risk. In consequence, he abstained from the chase before dinner, dispelling the uneasiness of his unregulated mind by serious business. They relate, that, having plentifully regaled that day, he soothed his cares with a more than usual quantity of wine. After dinner he went into the forest, attended by few persons; of whom the most intimate with him was Walter, surnamed Tirel, who had been induced to come from France by the liberality of the king. This man alone had remained with him, while the others, employed in the chase, were dispersed as chance directed. The sun was now declining, when the king, drawing his bow and letting fly an arrow, slightly wounded a stag which passed before him; and, keenly gazing, followed it, still running, a long time with his eyes, holding up his hand to keep off the power of the sun's rays. At this instant Walter, conceiving a noble exploit, which was while the king's attention was otherwise occupied to transfix another stag which by chance came near him, unknowingly, and without power to prevent it, Oh, gracious God! pierced his breast with a fatal arrow.* On receiving the wound, the king uttered not a word; but breaking off the shaft of the weapon where it projected from his body, fell upon the wound, by which he accelerated his death Walter immediately ran up, but as he found him senseless and speechless, he leaped swiftly upon his horse, and escaped by spurring him to his utmost speed. Indeed there was none to pursue him: some connived at his flight; others pitied him; and all

---

* "The tradition of William having met his death by the hand of Sir Walter Tirel, whilst hunting in the New Forest, is generally received; but Suger, a contemporary historian, and, as it seems, a friend of Tirel, in his Life of Louis le Gros, king of France, alluding to the death of Rufus, observes, 'Imponebatur a quibusdam cuidam nobili Gualtero Tirello quod eum sagitta perfoderat: quem, cum nec timeret nec speraret, jurejurando sæpius audivimus quasi sacrosanctum asserere, quod ea die nec in eam partem silvæ, in qua rex venebatur, venerit, nec eum in silva omnino viderit.' See also Edmer, Hist. Nov. p. 54, and Ord. Vit. Hist. Eccles. lib. x. p. 783."—HARDY.

were intent on other matters. Some began to fortify their dwellings; others to plunder; and the rest to look out for a new king. A few countrymen conveyed the body, placed on a cart, to the cathedral at Winchester; the blood dripping from it all the way. Here it was committed to the ground within the tower, attended by many of the nobility, though lamented by few. Next year,* the tower fell; though I forbear to mention the different opinions on this subject, lest I should seem to assent too readily to unsupported trifles, more especially as the building might have fallen, through imperfect construction, even though he had never been buried there. He died in the year of our Lord's incarnation 1100, of his reign the thirteenth, on the fourth before the nones of August, aged above forty years. He formed mighty plans, which he would have brought to effect, could he have spun out the tissue of fate, or broken through, and disengaged himself from, the violence of fortune. Such was the energy of his mind, that he was bold enough to promise himself any kingdom whatever. Indeed the day before his death, being asked where he would keep his Christmas, he answered, in Poitou; because the earl of Poitou, wishing anxiously to go to Jerusalem, was said to be about to pawn his territory to him. Thus, not content with his paternal possessions, and allured by expectation of greater glory, he grasped at honours not pertaining to him. He was a man much to be pitied by the clergy, for throwing away a soul which they could not save; to be beloved by stipendiary soldiers, for the multitude of his gifts; but not to be lamented by the people, because he suffered their substance to be plundered. I remember no council being held in his time, wherein the health of the church might be strengthened through the correction of abuses. He hesitated a long time ere he bestowed ecclesiastical honours, either for the sake of emolument, or of weighing desert. So that on the day he died, he held in his own hands three bishoprics, and twelve vacant abbeys. Besides, seeking occasion from the schism between Urban in Rome and Guibert at Ravenna, he forbade the payment of the tri-

* It fell A.D. 1107. An. Winton.
† By this probably is to be understood the payment of Peter-pence. Anselm had offended the king, by acknowledging Urban without consulting him.

bute† to the holy see: though he was more inclined to favour Guibert; because the ground and instigation of the discord between himself and Anselm was, that this man, so dear to God, had pronounced Urban to be pope, the other an apostate.

In his time began the Cistertian order, which is now both believed and asserted to be the surest road to heaven.* To speak of this does not seem irrelevant to the work I have undertaken, since it redounds to the glory of England to have produced the distinguished man who was the author and promoter of that rule. To us he belonged, and in our schools passed the earlier part of his life. Wherefore, if we are not envious, we shall embrace his good qualities the more kindly in proportion as we knew them more intimately. And, moreover, I am anxious to extol his praise, "because it is a mark of an ingenuous mind to approve that virtue in others, of which in yourself you regret the absence." He was named Harding, and born in England of no very illustrious parents. From his early years, he was a monk at Sherborne; but when secular desires had captivated his youth, he grew disgusted with the monastic garb, and went first to Scotland, and afterwards to France. Here, after some years' exercise in the liberal arts, he became awakened to the love of God. For, when manlier years had put away childish things, he went to Rome with a clerk who partook of his studies; neither the length and difficulty of the journey, nor the scantiness of their means of subsistence by the way, preventing them, both as they went and returned, from singing daily the whole psalter. Indeed the mind of this celebrated man was already meditating the design which soon after, by the grace of God, he attempted to put in execution. For returning into Burgundy, he was shorn at Molesmes, a new and magnificent monastery. Here he readily admitted the first elements of the order, as he had formerly seen them; but when additional matters were proposed for his observance, such as he had neither read in the rule nor seen elsewhere, he began, modestly and as became a monk, to ask the reason of them, saying: "By reason the supreme Creator has made all things; by reason he governs all things; by reason the fabric of the world revolves; by reason even the planets move; by reason the elements are directed; and

* Juvenal, Sat. i. 37.

by reason, and by due regulation, our nature ought to conduct itself. But since, through sloth, she too often departs from reason, many laws were, long ago, enacted for her use; and, latterly, a divine rule has been promulgated by St. Benedict, to bring back the deviations of nature to reason. In this, though some things are contained the design of which I cannot fathom, yet I deem it necessary to yield to authority. And though reason and the authority of the holy writers may seem at variance, yet still they are one and the same. For since God hath created and restored nothing without reason, how can I believe that the holy fathers, no doubt strict followers of God, could command anything but what was reasonable, as if we ought to give credit to their bare authority. See then that you bring reason, or at least authority, for what you devise; although no great credit should be given to what is merely supported by human reason, because it may be combated with arguments equally forcible. Therefore from that rule, which, equally supported by reason and authority, appears as if dictated by the spirit of all just persons, produce precedents, which if you fail to do, in vain shall you profess his rule, whose regulations you disdain to comply with."

Sentiments of this kind, spreading as usual from one to another, justly moved the hearts of such as feared God, "lest haply they should or had run in vain." The subject, then, being canvassed in frequent chapters, ended by bringing over the abbat himself to the opinion that all superfluous matters should be passed by, and merely the essence of the rule be scrutinized. Two of the fraternity, therefore, of equal faith and learning, were elected, who, by vicarious examination, were to discover the intention of the founder's rule; and when they had discovered it, to propound it to the rest. The abbat diligently endeavoured to induce the whole convent to give their concurrence, but "as it is difficult to eradicate from men's minds, what has early taken root, since they reluctantly relinquish the first notions they have imbibed," almost the whole of them refused to accept the new regulations, because they were attached to the old. Eighteen only, among whom was Harding, otherwise called Stephen, persevering in their holy determination, together with their abbat, left the monastery, declaring that the purity of the institution could not be preserved in a place where riches and gluttony warred against even the heart that was well inclined. They came therefore to Citeaux; a situation formerly covered with woods, but now so conspicuous from the abundant piety of its monks, that it is not undeservedly esteemed conscious of the Divinity himself. Here, by the countenance of the archbishop of Vienne, who is now pope, they entered on a labour worthy to be remembered and venerated to the end of time.

Certainly many of their regulations seem severe, and more particularly these: they wear nothing made with furs or linen, nor even that finely spun linen garment, which we call Staminium;* neither breeches, unless when sent on a journey, which at their return they wash and restore. They have two tunics with cowls, but no additional garment in winter, though, if they think fit, in summer they may lighten their garb. They sleep clad and girded, and never after matins return to their beds: but they so order the time of matins that it shall be light ere the lauds† begin ; so intent are they on their rule, that they think no jot or tittle of it should be disregarded. Directly after these hymns they sing the prime, after which they go out to work for stated hours. They complete whatever labour or service they have to perform by day without any other light. No one is ever absent from the daily services, or from complines, except the sick. The cellarer and hospitaller, after complines, wait upon the guests, yet observing the strictest silence. The abbat allows himself no indulgence beyond the others,—every where present,—every where attending to his flock; except that he does not eat with the rest, because his table is with the strangers and the poor. Nevertheless, be he where he may, he is equally sparing of food and of speech; for never more than two dishes are served either to him or to his company; lard and meat never but to the sick. From the Ides of September till Easter, through regard for whatever festival, they do not take more than one meal a day, except on Sunday. They never the leave the cloister but for the purpose of labour, nor do they ever speak, either there or elsewhere, save only to the abbat or prior. They pay unwearied attention to the

* A kind of woollen shirt.
† The concluding psalms of the matin service.

canonical* services, making no addition to them except the vigil for the defunct. They use in their divine service the Ambrosian chants† and hymns, as far as they were able to learn them at Milan. While they bestow care on the stranger and the sick, they inflict intolerable mortifications on their own bodies, for the health of their souls.

The abbat, at first, both encountered these privations with much alacrity himself, and compelled the rest to do the same. In process of time, however, the man repented;‡ he had been delicately brought up, and could not well bear such continued scantiness of diet. The monks, whom he had left at Molesmes, getting scent of this disposition, either by messages or letters, for it is uncertain which, drew him back to the monastery, by his obedience to the pope, for such was their pretext: compelling him to a measure to which he was already extremely well-disposed. For, as if wearied out by the pertinacity of their entreaties, he left the narrow confines of poverty, and resought his former magnificence. All followed him from Citeaux, who had gone thither with him, except eight. These, few in number but great in virtue, appointed Alberic, one of their party, abbat, and Stephen prior. The former not surviving more than eight years was, at the will of heaven, happily called away. Then, doubtless by God's appointment, Stephen though absent was elected abbat; the original contriver of the whole scheme; the especial and celebrated ornament of our times. Sixteen abbeys which he has already completed, and seven which he has begun, are sufficient testimonies of his abundant merit. Thus, by the resounding trumpet of God, he directs the people around him, both by word and deed, to heaven; acting fully up to his own precepts; affable in speech, pleasant in look, and with a mind always rejoicing in the Lord.

* The Horæ, or canonical services, were matins, primes, tierce, sexts, nones, vespers, and complines.

† The Ambrosian ritual prevailed pretty generally till the time of Charlemagne, who adopted the Gregorian. Durandus (lib. v. c. 1) has a curious account of an experiment, on the result of which was founded the general reception of the latter, and the confining the former chiefly to Milan, the church of St. Ambrose.

‡ The learned Mabillon appears much displeased with Malmesbury, for the motives here assigned for abbat Robert's quitting Citeaux. Vide Ann. Benedictinor

Hence, openly, that noble joy of countenance; hence, secretly, that compunction, coming from above; because, despising this state of a sojourner, he constantly desires to be in a place of rest. For these causes he is beloved by all; "For God graciously imparts to the minds of other men a love for that man whom he loves." Wherefore the inhabitant of that country esteems himself happy if, through his hands, he can transmit his wealth to God. He receives much, indeed, but expending little on his own wants, or those of his flock, he distributes the rest to the poor, or employs it immediately on the building of monasteries; for the purse of Stephen is the public treasury of the indigent. A proof of his abstinence is that you see nothing there, as in other monasteries, flaming with gold, blazing with jewels, or glittering with silver. For as a Gentile says, "Of what use is gold to a saint?" We think it not enough in our holy vases, unless the ponderous metal be eclipsed by precious stones; by the flame of the topaz, the violet of the amethyst, and the green shade of the emerald: unless the sacerdotal robes wanton with gold; and unless the walls glisten with various coloured paintings, and throw the reflexion of the sun's rays upon the ceiling. These men, however, placing those things which mortals foolishly esteem the first, only in a secondary point of view, give all their diligence to improve their morals, and love pure minds, more than glittering vestments; knowing that the best remuneration for doing well, is to enjoy a clear conscience. Moreover, if at any time the laudable kindness of the abbat either desires, or feigns a desire, to modify aught from the strict letter of the rule, they are ready to oppose such indulgence, saying, that they have no long time to live, nor shall they continue to exist so long as they have already done; that they hope to remain stedfast in their purpose to the end, and to be an example to their successors, who will transgress if they should give way. And, indeed, through human weakness, the perpetual law of which is that nothing attained, even by the greatest labour, can long remain unchanged, it will be so. But to comprise, briefly, all things which are or can be said of them,—the Cistertian monks at the present day are a model for all monks, a mirror for the diligent, a spur to the indolent.

At this time three sees in England were transferred from

their ancient situations; Wells to Bath, by John; Chester to Coventry, by Robert; Thetford to Norwich, by Herbert; all through greater ambition, than ought to have influenced men of such eminence. Finally, to speak of the last first: Herbert, from his skill in adulation, surnamed Losinga,* was first abbat of Ramsey, and then purchased the bishopric of Thetford, while his father, Robert, surnamed as himself, was intruded on the abbey of Winchester. This man, then, was the great source of simony in England; having craftily procured by means of his wealth, both an abbey and a bishopric. For he hood-winked the king's solicitude for the church by his money, and whispered great promises to secure the favour of the nobility: whence a poet of those times admirably observes,

> "A monster in the church from Losing rose,
> Base Simon's sect, the canons to oppose.
> Peter, thou'rt slow, see Simon soars on high;
> If present, soon thou'd'st hurl him from the sky.†
> Oh grief, the church is let to sordid hire,
> The son a bishop, abbat is the sire.
> All may be hoped from gold's prevailing sway,
> Which governs all things; gives and takes away;
> Makes bishops, abbats, basely in a day."

Future repentance, however, atoned for the errors of his youth: he went to Rome, when he was of a more serious age, and there resigning the staff and ring which he had acquired by simony, had them restored through the indulgence of that most merciful see; for the Romans regard it both as more holy and more fitting, that the dues from each church should rather come into their own purse, than be subservient to the use of any king whatever. Herbert thus returning home, removed the episcopal see, which had formerly been at Helmham, and was then at Thetford, to a town, celebrated for its trade and populousness, called Norwich. Here he settled a congregation of monks, famous for their numbers and their morals; purchasing everything for them out of his private fortune. For, having an eye to the probable complaints of his successors, he gave none of the

* From the French "losenge," adulation.
† Alluding to the legend of St. Peter and Simon Magnus; who having undertaken by means of enchantment, to fly, was, by the adjuration of St. Peter, dashed to the earth and killed. Vide Fabricius, Codex Apocryphus.

episcopal lands to the monastery, lest they should deprive the servants of God of their subsistence, if they found any thing given to them which pertained to their see. At Thetford, too, he settled Clugniac monks, because the members of that order, dispersed throughout the world, are rich in worldly possessions, and of distinguished piety towards God. Thus, by the great and extensive merit of his virtues, he shrouded the multitude of his former failings; and by his abundant eloquence and learning, as well as by his knowledge in secular affairs, he became worthy even of the Roman pontificate. Herbert thus changed, as Lucan observes of Curio, became the changer and mover of all things; and, as in the times of this king, he had been a pleader in behalf of simony, so was he, afterwards, its most strenuous opposer; nor did he suffer that to be done by others, which he lamented he had ever himself done through the presumption of juvenile ardour: ever having in his mouth, as they relate, the saying of St. Jerome, "We have erred when young; let us amend now we are old." Finally, who can sufficiently extol his conduct, who, though not a very rich bishop, yet built so noble a monastery; in which nothing appears defective, either in the beauty of the lofty edifice, the elegance of its ornaments, or in the piety and universal charity of its monks. These things soothed him with joyful hope while he lived, and when dead, if repentance be not in vain, conducted him to heaven.[*]

John was bishop of Wells; a native of Touraine, and an approved physician, by practice, rather than education. On the death of the abbat of Bath, he easily obtained the abbey from the king, both because all things at court were exposed to sale, and his covetousness seemed palliated by some degree of reason, that so famed a city might be still more celebrated, by becoming the see of a bishop. He at first began to exercise his severity against the monks, because they were dull, and in his estimation, barbarians; taking away all the lands ministering to their subsistence, and furnishing them with but scanty provision by his lay dependants. In process of time, however, when new monks

---

[*] His letters, long supposed to be lost, were found by the editor of this work in a MS. belonging to the Burgundian library at Brussels, and have been since published by R. Anstruther, 8vo. Bruxellis, 1845.

had been admitted, he conducted himself with more mildness; and gave a small portion of land to the prior, by which he might, in some measure, support himself and his inmates. And although he had begun austerely, yet many things were there by him both nobly begun and completed, in decorations and in books; and more especially, in a selection of monks, equally notable for their learning and kind offices. But still he could not, even at his death, be softened far enough totally to exonerate the lands from bondage; leaving, in this respect, an example not to be followed by his successors.

There was in the diocese of Chester, a monastery, called Coventry, which, as I have before related, the most noble earl Leofric, with his lady Godiva, had built; so splendid for its gold and silver, that the very walls of the church seemed too scanty to receive the treasures, to the great astonishment of the beholders. This, Robert bishop of the diocese eagerly seized on, in a manner by no means episcopal; stealing from the very treasures of the church wherewith he might fill the hand of the king, beguile the vigilance of the pope, and gratify the covetousness of the Romans. Continuing there many years, he gave no proof of worth whatever: for, so far from rescuing the nodding roofs from ruin, he wasted the sacred treasures, and became guilty of peculation; and a bishop might have been convicted of illegal exactions, had an accuser been at hand. He fed the monks on miserable fare, made no attempts to excite in them a love for their profession, and suffered them to reach only a very common degree of learning; lest he should make them delicate by sumptuous living, or strictness of rule and depth of learning should spirit them up to oppose him. Contented therefore with rustic fare, and humble literary attainments, they deemed it enough, if they could only live in peace. Moreover, at his death, paying little attention to the dictates of the canons, by which it is enacted, that bishops ought to be buried in their cathedrals, he commanded himself to be interred, not at Chester, but at Coventry; leaving to his successors by such a decision, the task, not of claiming what was not due to them, but as it were, of vindicating their proper right.

Here, while speaking of the times of William, I should be

induced to relate the translation of the most excellent Augustine, the apostle of the English and of his companions, had not the talents of the learned Joscelyn, anticipated me :* of Joscelyn, who being a monk of St. Bertin, formerly came to England with Herman bishop of Salisbury, skilled equally in literature and music. For a considerable time he visited the cathedrals and abbeys, and left proofs of uncommon learning in many places; he was second to none after Bede in the celebration of the English saints; next to Osberne† too, he bore away the palm in music. Moreover he wrote innumerable lives of modern saints, and restored, in an elegant manner, such of those of the ancients as had been lost through the confusion of the times, or had been carelessly edited. He also so exquisitely wrought the process of this translation, that he may be said to have realized it to the present race, and given a view of it to posterity. Happy that tongue, which ministered to so many saints! happy that voice, which poured forth such melody! more especially as in his life, his probity equalled his learning. But, as I have hitherto recorded disgraceful transactions of certain bishops, I will introduce others of different lives and dispositions, who were in being at the same time; that our age may not be said to have grown so negligent as not to produce one single saint. Such as are desirous, may find this promise completed in a subsequent book, after the narrative of king Henry's transactions.

CHAP. II.

The Expedition to Jerusalem. [A.D. 1095—1105.]

I SHALL now describe the expedition to Jerusalem, relating in my own words what was seen and endured by others. Besides too, as opportunity offers, I shall select from ancient writers, accounts of the situation and riches of Constantinople, Antioch, and Jerusalem; in order that he who is un-

---

* Joscelyn's "Life and Translation of St. Augustine" is printed in the "Acta Sanctor. Antwerp. 26 Maii." See the Preface to Bede, p xxxix.
† Another famous writer of Lives of Saints, several of which exist still in MS.

acquainted with these matters, and meets with this work, may have something to communicate to others. But for such a relation there needs a more fervent spirit, in order to complete effectually, what I begin with such pleasure. Invoking, therefore, the Divinity, as is usual, I begin as follows.

In the year of the incarnation 1095, pope Urban the second, who then filled the papal throne, passing the Alps, came into France. The ostensible cause of his journey, was, that, being driven from home by the violence of Guibert, he might prevail on the churches on this side of the mountains to acknowledge him. His more secret intention was not so well known ; this was, by Boamund's advice, to excite almost the whole of Europe to undertake an expedition into Asia ; that in such a general commotion of all countries, auxiliaries might easily be engaged, by whose means both Urban might obtain Rome, and Boamund, Illyria and Macedonia. For Guiscard, his father, had conquered those countries from Alexius, and also all the territory extending from Durazzo to Thessalonica ; wherefore Boamund claimed them as his due, since he obtained not the inheritance of Apulia, which his father had given to his younger son, Roger. Still nevertheless, whatever might be the cause of Urban's journey, it turned out of great and singular advantage to the Christian world. A council, therefore, was assembled at Clermont,* which is the most noted city of Auvergne. The number of bishops and abbats was three hundred and ten. Here at first, during several days, a long discussion was carried on concerning the catholic faith, and the establishing peace among contending parties.† For, in addition to those crimes in which every one indulged, all, on this side of the Alps, had arrived at such a calamitous state, as to take each other captive on little or no pretence ; nor were they suffered to

* " The council of Clermont, in Auvergne, continued from 18th to 28th of Nov. A D 1095 ; wherein the decrees of the councils held by pope Urban at Melfe, Benevento, Troie, and Plaisance, were confirmed, and many new canons made. Malmesbury's is perhaps the best account now known of that celebrated council See the acts of the council of Clermont ; Conc. tom. xii p. 829, &c."—HARDY

† The practice of private wars ; for an account of which, see Robertson's Hist of Charles V vol 1.

go free, unless ransomed at an enormous price. Again too, the snake of simony had so reared her slippery crest, and cherished, with poisonous warmth, her deadly eggs, that the whole world became infected with her mortal hissing, and tainted the honours of the church. At that time, I will not say bishops to their sees merely, but none aspired even to any ecclesiastical degree, except by the influence of money. Then too, many persons putting away their lawful wives, procured divorces, and invaded the marriage-couch of others. Wherefore, as in both these cases, there was a mixed multitude of offenders, the names of some powerful persons were singled out for punishment. Not to be tedious, I will subjoin the result of the whole council, abbreviating some parts, in my own language.

In a council at Clermont, in the presence of pope Urban, these articles were enacted. "That the catholic church shall be pure in faith; free from all servitude: that bishops, or abbats, or clergy of any rank, shall receive no ecclesiastical dignity from the hand of princes, or of any of the laity: that clergymen shall not hold prebends in two churches or cities: that no one shall be bishop and abbat at the same time: that ecclesiastical dignities shall be bought and sold by no one: that no person in holy orders shall be guilty of carnal intercourse: that such as not knowing the canonical prohibition had purchased canonries, should be pardoned: but that they should be taken from such as knew they possesed them by their own purchase, or that of their parents: that no layman from Ash-Wednesday, no clergyman from Quadragesima, to Easter, shall eat flesh: that, at all times, the first fast of the Ember Weeks, should be in the first week of Lent: that orders should be conferred, at all times, on the evening of Saturday, or on a Sunday, continuing fasting:* that on Easter-eve, service should not be celebrated till after the ninth hour: that the second fast should be observed in the week of Pentecost: that from our Lord's Advent, to the octave of the Epiphany; from Septuagesima to the octaves of Easter; from the first day of the Rogations

* If orders could not be completely conferred on Saturday, the ceremony might be performed on Sunday; and the parties continuing to fast. the two days were considered as one only —DURAND.

to the octaves of Pentecost; and from the fourth day of the week at sunset, at all times, to the second day in the following week at sunrise, the Truce of God be observed :* that whoever laid violent hands on a bishop should be excommunicated: that whoever laid violent hands on clergymen or their servants should be accursed: that whoever seized the goods of bishops or clergymen at their deaths, should be accursed: that whoever married a relation, even in the sixth degree of consanguinity, should be accursed: that none should be chosen bishop, except a priest, deacon, or subdeacon who was of noble descent, unless under pressing necessity, and licence from the pope: that the sons of priests and concubines should not be advanced to the priesthood, unless they first made their vow: that whosoever fled to the church, or the cross, should, being insured from loss of limb, be delivered up to justice; or if innocent, be released: that every church should enjoy its own tithes, nor pass them away to another: that laymen should neither buy nor sell tithes; that no fee should be demanded for the burial of the dead. In this council the pope excommunicated Philip, king of France, and all who called him king or lord, and obeyed or spoke to him, unless for the purpose of correcting him in like manner too his accursed consort, and all who called her queen or lady, till they so far reformed as to separate from each other: and also Guibert of Ravenna, who calls himself pope: and Henry, emperor of Germany, who supports him."

Afterwards, a clear and forcible discourse, such as should come from a priest, was addressed to the people, on the subject of an expedition of the Christians, against the Turks. This I have thought fit to transmit to posterity, as I have learned it from those who were present, preserving its sense unimpaired. For who can preserve the force of that eloquence? We shall be fortunate, if, treading an adjacent path, we come even by a circuitous route to its meaning.

* The Truce of God, was so called from the eagerness with which its first proposal was received by the suffering people of every degree: during the time it endured, no one dared infringe it, by attacking his fellows. See Du Cange and Robertson's Charles V. vol. i. It was blamed by some bishops as furnishing an occasion of perjury, and was rejected by the Nor-

"You recollect,"* said he, "my dearest brethren, many things which have been decreed for you, at this time; some matters, in our council, commanded; others inhibited. A rude and confused chaos of crimes required the deliberation of many days; an inveterate malady demanded a sharp remedy. For while we give unbounded scope to our clemency, our papal office finds numberless matters to proscribe; none to spare. But it has hitherto arisen from human frailty, that you have erred, and that, deceived by the speciousness of vice, you have exasperated the long suffering of God, by too lightly regarding his forbearance. It has arisen too from human wantonness, that, disregarding lawful wedlock, you have not duly considered the heinousness of adultery. From too great covetousness also, it has arisen, that, as opportunity offered, making captive your brethren, bought by the same great price, you have outrageously extorted from them their wealth. To you, however, now suffering this perilous shipwreck of sin, a secure haven of rest is offered, unless you neglect it. A station of perpetual safety will be awarded you, for the exertion of a trifling labour against the Turks. Compare, now, the labours which you underwent in the practice of wickedness, and those which you will encounter in the undertaking I advise. The intention of committing adultery, or murder, begets many fears; for, as Soloman says, 'There is nothing more timid than guilt:' many labours; for what is more toilsome than wickedness? But, 'He who walks uprightly, walks securely.' Of these labours, of these fears, the end was sin; the wages of sin is death; the death of sinners is most dreadful. Now the same labours and apprehensions are required from you, for a better consideration. The cause of these labours, will be charity; if thus warned by the command of God, you lay down your lives for the brethren: the wages of charity will be the grace of God; the grace of God is followed by eternal life. Go then prosperously: Go, then, with confidence, to attack the enemies of God. For they long since, oh sad reproach to

mans, as contrary to their privileges. The Truce of God was first established in Aquitaine, 1032.

* There are other orations, said to have been delivered by Urban in this council, remaining; and L'Abbe (Concil T. x) has printed one from a Vatican MS.; but they are all very inferior to Malmesbury.

Christians! have seized Syria, Armenia, and lastly, all Asia Minor, the provinces of which are Bithynia, Phrygia, Galatia, Lydia, Caria, Pamphylia, Isauria, Lycia, Cilicia; and, now they insolently domineer over Illyricum, and all the hither countries, even to the sea which is called the Straits of St. George. Nay, they usurp even the sepulchre of our Lord, that singular assurance of our faith; and sell to our pilgrims admissions to that city, which ought, had they a trace of their ancient courage left, to be open to Christians only. This alone might be enough to cloud our brows; but now, who except the most abandoned, or the most envious of Christian reputation, can endure that we do not divide the world equally with them? They inhabit Asia, the third portion of the world, as their native soil, which was justly esteemed by our ancestors equal, by the extent of its tracts and greatness of its provinces, to the two remaining parts. There, formerly, sprang up the first germs of our faith; there, all the apostles, except two, consecrated their deaths; there, at the present day, the Christians, if any survive, sustaining life by a wretched kind of agriculture, pay these miscreants tribute, and even with stifled sighs, long for the participation of your liberty, since they have lost their own. They hold Africa also, another quarter of the world, already possessed by their arms for more than two hundred years; which on this account I pronounce derogatory to Christian honour, because that country was anciently the nurse of celebrated geniuses, who, by their divine writings, will mock the rust of antiquity as long as there shall be a person who can relish Roman literature:* the learned know the truth of what I say. Europe, the third portion of the world remains; of which, how small a part do we Christians inhabit? for who can call all those barbarians who dwell in remote islands of the Frozen Ocean, Christians, since they live after a savage manner? Even this small portion of the world, belonging to us, is oppressed by the Turks and Saracens. Thus for three hundred years, Spain and the Balearic isles have been subjugated to them, and the possession of the remainder is eagerly anticipated by feeble men, who, not having courage to engage in close encounter, love a flying mode of warfare. For the Turk

* He alludes to St. Augustine and the fathers of the African church.

never ventures upon close fight ; but, when driven from his station, bends his bow at a distance, and trusts the winds with his meditated wound ; and as he has poisoned arrows, venom, and not valour, inflicts the death on the man he strikes. Whatever he effects, then, I attribute to fortune, not to courage, because he wars by flight, and by poison. It is apparent too, that every race, born in that region, being scorched with the intense heat of the sun, abounds more in reflexion, than in blood ; and, therefore, they avoid coming to close quarters, because they are aware how little blood they possess. Whereas the people who are born amid the polar frosts, and distant from the sun's heat, are less cautious indeed ; but, elate from their copious and luxuriant flow of blood, they fight with the greatest alacrity. You are a nation born in the more temperate regions of the world , who may be both prodigal of blood, in defiance of death and wounds ; and are not deficient in prudence. For you equally preserve good conduct in camp, and are considerate in battle. Thus endued with skill and with valour, you undertake a memorable expedition. You will be extolled throughout all ages, if you rescue your brethren from danger. To those present, in God's name, I command this ; to the absent I enjoin it. Let such as are going to fight for Christianity, put the form of the cross upon their garments, that they may, outwardly, demonstrate the love arising from their inward faith ; enjoying by the gift of God, and the privilege of St. Peter, absolution from all their crimes : let this in the meantime soothe the labour of their journey ; satisfied that they shall obtain, after death, the advantages of a blessed martyrdom. Putting an end to your crimes then, that Christians may at least live peaceably in these countries, go, and employ in nobler warfare, that valour, and that sagacity, which you used to waste in civil broils : Go, soldiers every where renowned in fame, go, and subdue these dastardly nations. Let the noted valour of the French advance, which, accompanied by its adjoining nations, shall affright the whole world by the single terror of its name. But why do I delay you longer by detracting from the courage of the gentiles ? Rather bring to your recollection the saying of God, ' Narrow is the way which leadeth to life.' Be it so then : the track to be followed is narrow, replete with death, and terrible with dangers; still this path will lead to your lost country. No doubt you must, 'by much tribulation enter into the kingdom of God.' Place then, before your imagination, if you shall be made captive, torments and chains; nay, every possible suffering that can be inflicted. Expect, for the firmness of your faith, even horrible punishments; that so, if it be necessary, you may redeem your souls at the expense of your bodies. Do you fear death? you men of exemplary courage and intrepidity. Surely human wickedness can devise nothing against you, worthy to be put in competition with heavenly glory: for the sufferings of the present time are not worthy to be compared 'to the glory which shall be revealed in us.' Know ye not, 'that for men to live is wretchedness, and happiness to die?' This doctrine, if you remember, you imbibed with your mother's milk, through the preaching of the clergy: and this doctrine your ancestors, the martyrs, held out by example. Death sets free from its filthy prison the human soul, which then takes flight for the mansions fitted to its virtues. Death accelerates their country to the good: death cuts short the wickedness of the ungodly. By means of death, then, the soul, made free, is either soothed with joyful hope, or is punished without farther apprehension of worse. So long as it is fettered to the body, it derives from it earthly contagion; or to say more truly, is dead. For, earthly with heavenly, and divine with mortal, ill agree. The soul, indeed, even now, in its state of union with the body, is capable of great efforts; it gives life to its instrument, secretly moving and animating it to exertions almost beyond mortal nature. But when, freed from the clog which drags it to the earth, it regains its proper station, it partakes of a blessed and perfect energy, communicating after some measure with the invisibility of the divine nature. Discharging a double office, therefore, it ministers life to the body when it is present, and the cause of its change, when it departs. You must observe how pleasantly the soul wakes in the sleeping body, and, apart from the senses, sees many future events, from the principle of its relationship to the Deity. Why then do ye fear death, who love the repose of sleep, which resembles death? Surely it must be madness, through lust of a transitory life, to deny yourselves that which is eternal. Rather, my dearest brethren, should it so happen, lay down your lives for the brotherhood. Rid God's sanctuary of the wicked: expel the robbers: bring in the pious. Let no love of relations detain you; for man's chiefest love is towards God. Let no attachment to your native soil be an impediment; because, in different points of view, all the world is exile to the Christian, and all the world his country. Thus exile is his country, and his country exile. Let none be restrained from going by the largeness of his patrimony, for a still larger is promised him; not of such things as soothe the miserable with vain expectation, or flatter the indolent disposition with the mean advantages of wealth, but of such as are shewn by perpetual example and approved by daily experience. Yet these too are pleasant, but vain, and which, to such as despise them, produce reward a hundred-fold. These things I publish, these I command: and for their execution I fix the end of the ensuing spring. God will be gracious to those who undertake this expedition, that they may have a favourable year, both in abundance of produce, and in serenity of season. Those who may die will enter the mansions of heaven; while the living shall behold the sepulchre of the Lord. And what can be greater happiness, than for a man, in his life-time, to see those places, where the Lord of heaven was conversant as a man? Blessed are they, who, called to these occupations, shall inherit such a recompence: fortunate are those who are led to such a conflict, that they may partake of such rewards."

I have adhered to the tenor of this address, retaining some few things unaltered, on account of the truth of the remarks, but omitting many. The bulk of the auditors were extremely excited, and attested their sentiments by a shout; pleased with the speech, and inclined to the pilgrimage. And immediately, in presence of the council, some of the nobility, falling down at the knees of the pope, consecrated themselves and their property to the service of God. Among these was Aimar, the very powerful bishop of Puy, who afterwards ruled the army by his prudence, and augmented it through his eloquence. In the month of November, then, in which this council was held, each departed to his home: and the report of this good resolution soon becoming general, it gently wafted a cheering gale over the minds of the Christians: which being universally diffused, there was no nation so remote, no people so retired, as not to contribute its portion. This ardent love not only inspired the continental provinces, but even all who had heard the name of Christ, whether in the most distant islands, or savage countries. The Welshman left his hunting; the Scot his fellowship with lice;* the Dane his drinking party; the Norwegian his raw fish. Lands were deserted of their husbandmen; houses of their inhabitants; even whole cities migrated. There was no regard to relationship; affection to their country was held in little esteem; God alone was placed before their eyes. Whatever was stored in granaries, or hoarded in chambers, to answer the hopes of the avaricious husbandman, or the covetousness of the miser, all, all was deserted; they hungered and thirsted after Jerusalem alone. Joy attended such as proceeded; while grief oppressed those who remained. But why do I say remained? You might see the husband departing with his wife, indeed, with all his family; you would smile to see the whole household laden on a carriage, about to proceed on their journey.† The road was too narrow for the passengers, the path too confined for the travellers, so thickly were they thronged with endless multitudes. The number surpassed all human imagination, though the itinerants were estimated at six millions.‡ Doubtless, never did so many nations unite in one opinion; never did so immense a population subject their unruly passions to one, and almost to no, direction. For the strangest wonder to behold was, that such a countless multitude marched gradually through various Christian countries without plundering, though there was none to restrain them. Mutual regard

* This gratuitous insult on a brave and noble people is unworthy a writer like William of Malmesbury; but the monkish historians were as deficient in taste as in style. The cloister was a useful seminary to teach the plodding accuracy which is required to write a chronicle; but for elevation of mind and diffusion of liberal sentiment, it was as inefficient as it is still.

† The rustic, observes Guibert, shod his oxen like horses, and placed his whole family on a cart; where it was amusing to hear the children, on the approach to any large town or castle, inquiring, if that were Jerusalem. Guib. Novigent Opera, p. 482

‡ Fulcher says, those who assumed the cross were estimated at that number; but that multitudes returned home ere they passed the sea. Fulcherius Carnotensis ap. Gesta Dei per Francos, p 387.

blazed forth in all; so that if any one found in his possession what he knew did not belong to him, he exposed it everywhere for several days to be owned; and the desire of the finder was suspended, till perchance the wants of the loser might be repaired.*

The long-looked for month of March was now at hand, when, the hoary garb of winter being laid aside, the world, clad in vernal bloom, invited the pilgrims to the confines of the east; nor, such was the ardour of their minds, did they seek delay. Godfrey, duke of Lorraine, proceeded by way of Hungary: second to none in military virtue, and, descended from the ancient lineage of Charles the Great, he inherited much of Charles both in blood and in mind. He was followed by the Frisons, Lorrainers, Saxons, and all the people who dwell between the Rhine and the Garonne.† Raimund, earl of St. Giles, and Aimar, bishop of Puy, nobly matched in valour, and alike noted for spirit against the enemy and piety to God, took the route of Dalmatia. Under their standard marched the Goths and Gascons, and all the people scattered throughout the Pyrenees and the Alps. Before them, by a shorter route, went Boamund, an Apulian by residence, but a Norman by descent. For embarking at Brindisi, and landing at Durazzo, he marched to Constantinople by roads with which he was well acquainted. Under his command, Italy, and the whole adjacent province, from the Tuscan sea to the Adriatic, joined in the war. All these assembling at the same time at Constantinople, partook somewhat of mutual joy. Here, too, they found Hugh the Great, brother of Philip, king of France: for having inconsiderately, and with a few soldiers, entered the territories of the emperor, he was taken by his troops, and detained in free custody. But Alexius, emperor of Constantinople, alarmed at the arrival of these chiefs, willingly, but, as it were, induced by their entreaties, released him. Alexius was a man famed for his duplicity, and never attempted any thing of importance, unless by stratagem. He had taken off Guiscard, as I before

---

* However repugnant this representation may be to the generally received opinion, it is that of an eye-witness, when describing the army assembled at Constantinople. Fulch. Carnot. p. 389.

† It should probably be the Elbe, as he appears to describe the people of northern Germany.

related, by poison, and had corrupted his wife by gold; falsely promising by his emissaries to marry her. Again, too, he allowed William, earl of Poitou, to be led into an ambush of the Turks, and, after losing sixty thousand soldiers, to escape almost unattended; being incensed at his reply, when he refused homage to the Greek. In after time, he laid repeated snares for Boamund, who was marching against him to avenge the injuries of the crusaders; and when these failed he bereaved him of his brother Guido, and of almost all his army; making use of his usual arts either in poisoning the rivers, or their garments: but of this hereafter. Now, however, removing the army from the city, and mildly addressing the chiefs, his Grecian eloquence proved so powerful, that he obtained from them all homage, and an oath, that they would form no plot against him; and that if they could subdue the cities pertaining to his empire, they would restore them to him, thus purchasing another's advantage at the expense of their own blood. The credit of maintaining his liberty appeared more estimable to Raimund alone; so that he neither did homage to him, nor took the oath. Collecting, then, all their forces, they made an attack on Nicea, a city of Bithynia: for they chose to assault this first, both as it was an obstacle to the crusaders, and as they were eager to revenge the death of those pilgrims who had recently been slain there. For one Walter, a distinguished soldier, but precipitate, (for you will scarcely see prudence and valour united in the same person, as one retards what the other advances,) incautiously roaming around the walls, had perished with a numerous party, which Peter the hermit had allured, by his preaching, from their country.

Now, too, in the month of September, Robert earl of Normandy, brother of king William whose name is prefixed to this book, earnestly desiring to enter on the expedition, had as his companions Robert of Flanders, and Stephen of Blois who had married his sister. They were earls of noble lineage and corresponding valour. Under their command were the English and Normans, the Western Franks and people of Flanders, and all the tribes which occupy the continental tract from the British Ocean to the Alps. Proceeding on their journey, at Lucca they found pope Urban, who being enraged at Guibert, as I have said, was, by the assistance of Matilda, carrying war into Italy and around the city of Rome. He had now so far succeeded that the Roman people, inclining to his party, were harassing that of Guibert, both by words and blows; nor did the one faction spare the other, either in the churches or in the streets, until Guibert, being weakest, left the see vacant for Urban, and fled to Germany.

Of Rome, formerly the mistress of the globe, but which now, in comparison of its ancient state, appears a small town; and of the Romans, once "Sovereigns over all and the gowned nation,"* who are now the most fickle of men, bartering justice for gold, and dispensing with the canons for money; of this city and its inhabitants, I say, whatever I might attempt to write, has been anticipated by the verses of Hildebert, first, bishop of Mans, and afterwards archbishop of Tours.† Which I insert, not to assume the honour acquired by another man's labour, but rather as a proof of a liberal mind, while not envying his fame, I give testimony to his charming poetry.

> Rome, still thy ruins grand beyond compare,
> Thy former greatness mournfully declare,
> Though time thy stately palaces around
> Hath strewed, and cast thy temples to the ground.
> Fall'n is the power, the power Araxes dire
> Regrets now gone, and dreaded when entire;
> Which arms and laws, and ev'n the gods on high
> Bade o'er the world assume the mastery;
> Which guilty Cæsar rather had enjoyed
> Alone, than e'er a fostering hand employed.
> Which gave to foes, to vice, to friends its care,
> Subdued, restrained, or bade its kindness share
> This growing power the holy fathers reared,
> Where near the stream the fav'ring spot appeared
> From either pole, materials, artists meet,
> And rising walls their proper station greet;
> Kings gave their treasures, fav'ring too was fate,
> And arts and riches on the structure wait.
> Fall'n is that city, whose proud fame to reach,
> I merely say, " Rome was," there fails my speech.

* Virgil, Æneid i. 281.
† "Hildebert was translated to Tours, A.D. 1125, upon the death of Gislebert, who died at Rome about the middle of December, 1124, in the same week with pope Calixtus. (Ord. Vit. lib. xii. p. 882)"—HARDY.

> Still neither time's decay, nor sword, nor fire,
> Shall cause its beauty wholly to expire.
> Human exertions raised that splendid Rome,
> Which gods in vain shall strive to overcome.
> Bid wealth, bid marble, and bid fate attend,
> And watchful artists o'er the labour bend,
> Still shall the matchless ruin art defy
> The old to rival, or its loss supply.
> Here gods themselves their sculptur'd forms admire,
> And only to reflect those forms aspire;
> Nature unable such like gods to form,
> Left them to man's creative genius warm;
> Life breathes within them, and the suppliant falls,
> Not to the God, but statues in the walls.
> City thrice blessed! were tyrants but away,
> Or shame compelled them justice to obey.

Are not these sufficient to point out in such a city, both the dignity of its former advantages, and the majesty of its present ruin? But that nothing may be wanting to its honour, I will add the number of its gates, and the multitude of its sacred relics; and that no person may complain of his being deprived of any knowledge by the obscurity of the narrative, the description shall run in an easy and familiar style.*

The first is the Cornelian gate, which is now called the gate of St. Peter, and the Cornelian way. Near it is situated the church of St. Peter, in which his body lies, decked with gold and silver, and precious stones: and no one knows the number of the holy martyrs who rest in that church. On the same way is another church, in which lie the holy virgins Rufina and Secunda. In a third church, are Marius and Martha, and Audifax and Abacuc, their sons.

The second is the Flaminian gate, which is now called the gate of St. Valentine,† and the Flaminian way, and when it arrives at the Milvian bridge, it takes the name of the Ravennanian way, because it leads to Ravenna; and there, at the first stone without the gate, St. Valentine rests in his church.

The third is called the Porcinian‡ gate, and the way the

---

* For a very interesting account of the walls and gates of Rome, see Andrew Lumisden's "Remarks on the Antiquities of Rome and its Environs, London, 4to. 1797."

† Now called Porta del Popolo. ‡ Porta Pinciana.

same; but where it joins the Salarian, it loses its name, and there, nearly in the spot which is called Cucumeris, lie the martyrs, Festus, Johannes, Liberalis, Diogenes, Blastus, Lucina, and in one sepulchre, the Two Hundred and Sixty,* in another, the Thirty.

The fourth is the Salarian † gate and way; now called St. Silvester's. Here, near the road, lie St. Hermes, and St. Vasella, and Prothus, and Jacinctus, Maxilian, Herculan, Crispus; and, in another place, hard by, rest the holy martyrs Pamphilus and Quirinus, seventy steps beneath the surface. Next is the church of St. Felicity, where she rests, and Silanus her son; and not far distant, Boniface the martyr. In another church, there are Crisantus, and Daria, and Saturninus, and Maurus, and Jason, and their mother Hilaria, and others innumerable. And in another church, St. Alexander, Vitalis, Martialis, sons of St. Felicity; and seven holy virgins, Saturnina, Hilarina, Duranda, Rogantina, Serotina, Paulina, Donata. Next the church of St. Silvester, where he lies under a marble tomb; and the martyrs, Celestinus, Philippus, and Felix; and there too, the Three Hundred and Sixty-five martyrs rest in one sepulchre; and near them lie Paulus and Crescentianus, Prisca and Semetrius, Praxides and Potentiana.

The fifth is called the Numentan ‡ gate. There lies St. Nicomede, priest and martyr; the way too is called by the same name. Near the road are the church and body of St. Agnes; in another church, St. Ermerenciana, and the martyrs, Alexander, Felix, Papias; at the seventh stone on this road rests the holy pope Alexander, with Euentius and Theodolus.

The sixth is the Tiburtine § gate and way, which is now called St. Lawrence's: near this way lies St. Lawrence in his church, and Habundius the martyr: and near this, in another church, rest these martyrs, Ciriaca, Romanus, Justinus, Crescentianus; and not far from hence the church of St. Hyppolitus, where he himself rests, and his family, eighteen in number; there too repose, St. Trifonia, the wife

---

* The Two Hundred and Sixty are said to have been shot with arrows in the amphitheatre, by order of Claudius. The Thirty suffered under Diocletian.   † Porta Salaria.
‡ Porta Pia.   § Porta di San Lorenzo.

of Decius, and his daughter Cirilla, and her nurse Concordia. And in another part of this way is the church of Agapit the martyr.

The seventh is called, at present, the Greater gate,* formerly the Seracusan, and the way the Lavicanian, which leads to St. Helena. Near this are Peter, Marcellinus, Tyburtius, Geminus, Gorgonius, and the Forty Soldiers,† and others without number; and a little farther the Four Coronati.‡

The eighth is the gate of St. John,§ which by the ancients was called Assenarica. The ninth gate is called Metrosa;|| and in front of both these runs the Latin way. The tenth is called the Latin gate,¶ and way. Near this, in one church, lie the martyrs, Gordianus and Epimachus, Sulpicius, Servilianus, Quintinus, Quartus, Sophia, Triphenus. Near this too, in another spot, Tertullinus, and not far distant, the church of St. Eugenia, in which she lies, and her mother Claudia, and pope Stephen, with nineteen of his clergy, and Nemesius the deacon.

The eleventh is called the Appian gate** and way. There lie St. Sebastian, and Quirinus, and originally the bodies of the apostles rested there. A little nearer Rome, are the martyrs, Januarius, Urbanus, Xenon, Quirinus, Agapetus, Felicissimus; and in another church, Tyburtius, Valerianus, Maximus. Not far distant is the church of the martyr Cecilia; and there are buried Stephanus, Sixtus, Zefferinus, Eusebius, Melchiades, Marcellus, Eutychianus, Dionysius, Antheros, Pontianus, pope Lucius, Optacius, Julianus, Calocerus, Parthenius, Tharsicius, Politanus, martyrs: there too is the church and body of St. Cornelius: and in another church, St. Sotheris: and not far off, rest the martyrs, Hippolytus, Adrianus, Eusebius, Maria, Martha, Paulina, Valeria, Marcellus, and near, pope Marcus in his church.

* Porta Maggiore.
† The Forty Soldiers suffered martyrdom under Licinius at Sebastia in Armenia.
‡ So called, because for a long time after they had suffered martyrdom (martyrio coronati) their names were unknown; and though afterwards their real names were revealed to a certain priest, yet they still continued to retain their former designation. § Porta di San Giovanni.
|| There is no notice of this in Lumisden: it is probably now destroyed.
¶ Porta Latina.   ** Porta di San Sebastiano.

Between the Appian and Ostiensian way, is the Ardeatine way, where are St. Marcus, and Marcellianus. And there lies pope Damasus in his church; and near him St. Petronilla, and Nereus, and Achilleus, and many more.

The twelfth gate and way is called the Ostiensian, but, at present, St. Paul's,* because he lies near it in his church. There too is the martyr Timotheus: and near, in the church of St. Tecla, are the martyrs Felix, Audactus, and Nemesius. At the Three Fountains† is the head of the martyr St. Anastasius.

The thirteenth is called the Portuan‡ gate and way; near which in a church are the martyrs, Felix, Alexander, Abdon and Sennes, Symeon, Anastasius, Polion, Vincentius, Milex, Candida, and Innocentia.

The fourteenth is the Aurelian§ gate and way, which now is called the gate of St. Pancras, because he lies near it in his church, and the other martyrs, Paulinus, Arthemius, St. Sapientia, with her three daughters, Faith, Hope, and Charity. In another church, Processus and Martinianus; and, in a third, two Felixes; in a fourth Calixtus, and Calepodius; in a fifth St. Basilides. At the twelfth milliary within the city, on Mount Celius, are the martyrs Johannes, and Paulus, in their dwelling, which was made a church after their martyrdom: and Crispin and Crispinianus, and St. Benedicta. On the same mount, is the church of St. Stephen, the first martyr; and there are buried the martyrs Primus, and Felicianus; on Mount Aventine St. Boniface; and on Mount Nola, St. Tatiana rests.

Such are the Roman sanctuaries, such the sacred pledges upon earth: and yet in the midst of this heavenly treasure, as it were, a people drunk with senseless fury, even at the very time the crusaders arrived, were disturbing everything with wild ambition, and, when unable to satisfy their lust of money, pouring out the blood of their fellow citizens over the very bodies of the saints.‖ The earls, confiding then

---

* Porta di San Paolo.

† Aquas Saluias, now Trefontane. The tradition is, that St. Paul was beheaded on this spot· that his head, on touching the ground, rebounded twice, and that a fountain immediately burst forth from each place where it fell. See Lumisden ‡ Porta Portese. § Porti di San Pancrazio.

‖ Sacred places and bodies of saints long since deceased, are but feeble safeguards against the outbreak or even moderate agency of human pasin Urban's benediction, having passed through Tuscany and Campania, came by Apulia to Calabria, and would have embarked immediately had not the seamen, on being consulted, forbade them, on account of the violence of the southerly winds. In consequence, the earls of Normandy and Blois passed the winter there; sojourning each among their friends, as convenient. The earl of Flanders, alone, ventured to sea, experiencing a prosperous issue to a rash attempt: wherefore part of this assembled multitude returned home through want; and part of them died from the unwholesomeness of the climate. The earls who remained however, when by the vernal sun's return they saw the sea sufficiently calm for the expedition, committed themselves to the ocean, and, by Christ's assistance, landed safely at two ports. Thence, through Thessaly, the metropolis of which is Thessalonica, and Thracia, they came to Constantinople. Many of the lower order perished on the march through disease and want; many lost their lives at the Devil's Ford, as it is called from its rapidity; and more indeed would have perished, had not the advanced cavalry been stationed in the river, to break the violence of the current; by which means the lives of some were saved, and the rest passed over on horseback. The whole multitude then, to solace themselves for their past labours, indulged in rest for fifteen days, pitching their camp in the suburbs of the city; of which, as the opportunity has presented itself, I shall briefly speak.

Constantinople was first called Byzantium: which name is still preserved by the imperial money called Bezants. St. Aldhelm, in his book On Virginity,* relates that it changed its appellation by divine suggestion: his words are as follow. As Constantine was sleeping in this city, he imagined that there stood before him an old woman, whose forehead was furrowed with age; but, that presently, clad in an imperial robe, she became transformed into a beautiful girl, and so fascinated his eyes, by the elegance of her youthful charms, that he could not refrain from kissing her: that Helena, his mother, being present, then said, "She shall be yours for

sions, which, in every country and under every form of superstition, act always in the same way
* Aldhelmi Opera, page 28.

ever; nor shall she die, till the end of time." The solution of this dream, when he awoke, the emperor extorted from heaven, by fasting and almsgiving. And behold, within eight days, being cast again into a deep sleep, he thought he saw pope Silvester, who died some little time before, regarding his convert* with complacency, and saying, "You have acted with your customary prudence, in waiting for a solution, from God, of that enigma which was beyond the comprehension of man. The old woman you saw, is this city, worn down by age, whose time-struck walls, menacing approaching ruin, require a restorer, But you, renewing its walls, and its affluence, shall signalize it also with your name; and here shall the imperial progeny reign for ever. You shall not, however, lay the foundations at your own pleasure; but mounting the horse on which, in the novitiate of your faith, you rode round the churches of the apostles at Rome, you shall give him the rein, and liberty to go whither he please: you shall have, too, in your hand, your royal spear,† whose point shall describe the circuit of the wall on the ground. You will be regulated, therefore, in what manner to dispose the foundations of the wall by the track of the spear on the earth."

The emperor eagerly obeyed the vision, and built a city equal to Rome; alleging that the emperor ought not to reign in Rome, where the martyred apostles, from the time of Christ, held dominion. He built in it two churches, one of which was dedicated to peace; the other to the apostles; bringing thither numerous bodies of saints, who might conciliate the assistance of God against the incursions of its enemies. He placed in the circus, for the admiration and ornament of the city, the statues of triumphal heroes, brought from Rome, and the tripods from Delphi; and the images of heathen deities to excite the contempt of the beholders. They relate that it was highly gratifying to the mind of the emperor, to receive a mandate from heaven, to found a city in that place, where the fruitfulness of the soil, and the temperature of the atmosphere conduced to the health of its inhabitants: for as he was

* The story of Silvester's having baptized Constantine is considered as altogether unfounded. See Mosheim, vol. i.
† This, in Aldhelm, is the Labarum, or imperial standard.

born in Britain,* he could not endure the burning heat of the sun. But Thracia is a province of Europe, as the poets observe, extremely cool, "From Hebrus' ice, and the Bistonian north;" and near to Mœsia, where, as Virgil remarks, "With wonder Gargara the harvest sees."† Constantinople, then, washed by the sea, obtains the mingled temperature both of Europe and of Asia; because, from a short distance, the Asiatic east tempers the severity of the northern blast. The city is surrounded by a vast extent of walls, yet the influx of strangers is so great, as to make it crowded. In consequence they form a mole in the sea, by throwing in masses of rock, and loads of sand; and the space obtained by this new device, straitens the ancient waters. The sea wonders to see fields unknown before, amid its glassy waves; and surrounds and supplies its city with all the conveniences of the earth. The town is encompassed on every side, except the north, by the ocean, and is full of angles in the circuit of its walls, where it corresponds with the windings of the sea; which walls contain a space of twenty miles in circumference. The Danube,‡ which is likewise called the Ister, flows in hidden channels under ground, into the city; and on certain days being let out by the removal of a plug, it carries off the filth of the streets into the sea. All vied with the emperor in noble zeal to give splendour to this city, each thinking he was bound to advance the work in hand: one contributing holy relics, another riches, Constantine all things.

After Constantine the Great, the following emperors reigned here. Constantine his son; Julian the Apostate; Jovinian, Valens, Theodosius the Great; Arcadius, Theodosius the Younger, Marchianus, Leo the First; Zeno, Anastasius, Justin the Great; Justinian, who, famed for his literature and his wars, built a church in Constantinople to Divine Wisdom; that is, to the Lord Jesus Christ, which he called Hagia Sophia; a work, as they report, surpassing every other

* The place of his birth is contested. † Geor. i. 103.
‡ "The Danube empties itself through six mouths into the Euxine. The river Lycus, formed by the conflux of two little streams, pours into the harbour of Constantinople a perpetual supply of fresh water, which serves to cleanse the bottom, and to invite the periodical shoals of fish to seek their retreat in the capacious port of Constantinople."—HARDY.

edifice in the world, and where ocular inspection proves it superior to its most pompous descriptions: Justin the Younger; Tiberius, Mauricius, the first Greek; Focas, Heraclius, Heracleonas, Constans, Constantine, the son of Heraclius; who, coming to Rome, and purloining all the remains of ancient decoration, stripped the churches even of their brazen tiles, anxiously wishing for triumphal honours, at Constantinople, even from such spoils as these; his covetousness, however, turned out unfortunately for him, for being shortly after killed at Syracuse, he left all these honourable spoils to be conveyed to Alexandria by the Saracens; Constantine, Leo the Second; Justinian, again Justinian, Tiberius, Anastasius, Philippicus, Theodosius, Leo the Third; all these reigned both at Constantinople and at Rome: the following in Constantinople only; Constantine, Leo, Constantine, Nicephorus, Stauratius, Michael, Theophilus, Michael, Basilius, Leo, Alexander, Constantine, two Romanuses, Nicephorus, Focas, Johannes, Basilius, Romanus, Michael, Constantine, Theodora the empress, Michael, Sachius, Constantine, Romanus, Diogenes, Nicephorus, Buthanus, Michael;[*] who, driven from the empire by Alexius, secretly fled to Guiscard in Apulia, and surrendering to him his power, imagined he had done something prejudicial to Alexius: hence Guiscard's ambition conceived greater designs; falsely persuading himself that he might acquire by industry, what the other had lost by inactivity: how far he succeeded, the preceding book hath explained. In the same city is the cross of our Saviour, brought by Helena from Jerusalem. There too rest the apostles, Andrew, James the brother of our Lord; Matthias: the prophets Elizeus, Daniel, Samuel, and many others · Luke the Evangelist: martyrs innumerable: confessors, Johannes Chrysostom, Basilius, Gregorious Nazianzen, Spiridion: virgins, Agatha, Lucia; and lastly all the saints whose bodies the emperors were able to collect thither out of every country.

The earls, then, of Normandy and Blois, did homage to the Greek. For the earl of Flanders had already passed on,

[*] After all the researches of the last fifty years, the "Decline and Fall of the Roman Empire," by Gibbon, will be found to contain the best history of these Byzantine emperors.

disdaining to perform this ceremony, from the recollection that he was freely born and educated. The others, giving and receiving promises of fidelity, proceeded in the first week of June to Nice, which the rest had already besieged from the middle of May. Uniting, therefore, their forces, much carnage ensued on either side; since every kind of weapon could easily be hurled by the townsmen on those who were beneath them; and the arm even of the weakest had effect on persons crowded together. Moreover the Turks dragged up, with iron hooks, numberless dead bodies of our people, to mangle them in mockery; or to cast them down again when stripped of their raiment. The Franks were grieved at this: nor did they cease venting their rage by slaughter, till the Turks, wearied by extremity of suffering, on the day of the summer solstice, surrendered themselves to the emperor by means of secret messengers. He, who knew only how to consult his own advantage, gave orders to the Franks to depart: choosing rather, that the city should be reserved for the undisguised disloyalty of the Turks, than the distrusted power of the Franks. He ordered, however, silver and gold to be distributed to the chiefs, and copper coin to those of inferior rank, lest they should complain of being unrewarded. Thus the Turks, who, passing the Euphrates, had now for the space of fifty years been possessed of Bithynia, which is a part of Asia Minor that is called Romania, betook themselves to flight to the eastward. Nevertheless, when the siege was ended, they attempted, at the instigation of Soliman,[*] who had been sovereign of all Romania, to harass the army on its advance. This man collecting, as is computed, three hundred and sixty thousand archers, attacked our people, expecting anything rather than hostility, with such violence, that overwhelmed with an iron shower of arrows, they were terrified and turned their backs. At that time, by chance, duke Godfrey and Hugh the Great, and Raimund, had taken another route, that they might plunder the enemies' country to a wider extent, and obtain forage with more facility. But the Norman, sensible of his extreme

---

[*] His Turkish name was Killidge-Arslan: his kingdom of Roum extended from the Hellespont to the confines of Syria, and barred the pilgrimage of Jerusalem. (See De Guignes, tom. iii. p. 2, pp. 10—30.)—HARDY.

danger, by means of expeditious messengers on a safe track, acquainted Godfrey and the rest of the approach of the Turks. They without a moment's delay, turned against the enemy, and delivered their associates from danger. For these were now indiscriminately slaughtered in their tents, unprepared for resistance, and filling the air with prayers and lamentations. Nor did the enemy take any particular aim, but trusting his arrows to the wind, he never, from the thickness of the ranks, drew his bow in vain. What alone retarded destruction was, that the attack took place near a thicket of canes, which prevented the Turks from riding full speed. At length, however, perceiving the advanced guard of the approaching chiefs, the Christians left the thicket, and shouting the military watch-word, "It is the will of God,"* they attack the scattered ranks of the enemy, making a signal to their companions, at the same time to assail them in the rear. Thus the Turks, pressed on either side, forthwith fled, shrieking with a dreadful cry, and raising a yell which reached the clouds. Nor had they recourse to their customary practice of a flying battle, but throwing down their bows, they manifested, by a flight of three successive days, something greater than mere human apprehension. Nor was there, indeed, any person to follow them; for our horses, scarce able to support life on the barren turf, were unequal to a vigorous pursuit: showing immediately their want of strength by their panting sides. Asia was formerly, it is true, a land most fruitful in corn; but, both in distant and in recent times, it had been so plundered by the savage Turks, that it could scarcely suffice for the maintenance of a small army, much less of a multitude, so vast as to threaten devouring whole harvests and drinking rivers dry. For, when they departed from Nice, they were still estimated at seven hundred thousand: of the remainder, part had been wasted by the sword, part by sickness, and still more had deserted to their homes.

---

* When Urban II addressed the multitude from a lofty scaffold in the market-place of Clermont, inciting the people to undertake the crusade, he was frequently interrupted by the shout of thousands in their rustic idiom exclaiming "Deus lo vult!" "It is indeed the will of God!" replied the pope; and let those words, the inspiration surely of the Holy Spirit, be for ever adopted as your war-cry."—HARDY.

Thence, then, they arrived at Heraclea by the route of Antioch and Iconium, cities of Pisidia. Here they beheld in the sky a portent fashioned like a flaming sword; the point of which extended towards the east. All the period from the kalends of July, when they left Nice, till the nones of October, had elapsed when they arrived at Antioch in Syria. The situation of this city, I should describe, had not my wish in this respect been anticipated by the eloquence of Ambrosius in Hegesippus :* were I not also fearful, that I may be blamed for the perpetual digressions of my narrative. Still, however, I will relate so much as the labour I have undertaken seems to require.

Antioch, which was named after his father, Antiochus, by Seleucus, king of Asia, is surrounded with a vast wall, which even contains a mountain within it. Next to Rome, and Constantinople, and Alexandria, it obtains precedence over the cities of the world. It is secure by its walls, lofty from its situation; and if ever taken, must be gained more by ingenuity than force. The nearest river to it, which I learn is now called Fervus, though originally Orontes, falls into the sea twelve miles from the city; its tide impetuous, and growing colder from its violence, ministers to the health of the inhabitants by its effect on the atmosphere. Capable too of receiving supplies by shipping for the service of its citizens, it can at all times mock the perseverance of its besiegers. Here the venerable title of Christian was first conceived: hence, first St. Paul, the spring and spur of this religion, went forth to preach; here the first pontific seat was filled by St. Peter; in honour to whom the church there founded remained uninjured through the whole domination of the Turks: and equally also did another, consecrated in honour of St. Mary, strike the eyes of beholders with its beauty, exciting wonder that they should reverence the church of him whose faith they persecuted.

This city, then, the Franks invested from October till June;† pitching their tents around the walls after they had

* Hegesippus, a Greek author of the second century, wrote an account of the Jewish war, and of the destruction of Jerusalem; said to have been translated into Latin by St. Ambrose. He also wrote an ecclesiastical history, in five books, a fragment of which only remains.

† "The siege of Antioch commenced on the 21st of October, 1097, and ended 3rd June, 1098."—HARDY.

passed the river. Foreseeing, however, the difficulty of taking it, and judging it expedient to provide against the cowardice of certain of their party, the chiefs, in common, took an oath, that they would not desist from the siege till the city should be taken by force or by stratagem. And, that they might more easily complete their design, they built many fortresses on this side of the river, in which soldiers were placed to keep guard. Aoxianus, too, the governor of the city, observing that the Franks acted neither jestingly nor coldly, but set heartily to besiege it, sent his son Sansadol to the Sultan, emperor of Persia, to make known the boldness of the Franks, and to implore assistance. Sultan among the Persians implies the same as Augustus among the Romans: Commander of all the Saracens, and of the whole east. I imagine this empire has continued so long, and still increases, because the people, as I have related, are unwarlike; and being deficient in active blood, know not how to cast off slavery, when once admitted; not being aware, as Lucan says,* that

"Arms were bestowed that men should not be slaves"

But the western nations, bold and fierce, disdain long-continued subjugation to any people whatever; often delivering themselves from servitude, and imposing it on others. Moreover, the Roman empire first declined to the Franks, and after to the Germans: the eastern continues ever with the Persians.

Sansadol therefore being despatched to the chief of this empire, hastened his course with youthful ardour, while his father was by no means wanting to the duties of a commander, in the protection of the city. The valour of the besieged was not content merely to defend their own party, but voluntarily harassed ours; frequently and suddenly attacking them when foraging or marketing: for, making a bridge of the vessels they found there, they had established a mart beyond the river. Through Christ's assistance, therefore, becoming resolute, they seized their arms, and boldly repelled their enemies, so that they never suffered them to reap the honour of the day. To revenge this disgrace, the Turks wreaked their indignation on the Syrian and Arme-

* Pharsalia, iv. 579.

nian inhabitants of the city; throwing, by means of their balistæ* and petraries, the heads of those whom they had slain into the camp of the Franks, that by such means they might wound their feelings.

And now, everything which could be procured for food being destroyed around the city, a sudden famine, which usually makes even fortresses give way, began to oppress the army; so much so, that the harvest not having yet attained to maturity, some persons seized the pods of beans before they were ripe, as the greatest delicacy: others fed on carrion, or hides soaked in water; others passed parboiled† thistles through their bleeding jaws into their stomachs. Others sold mice, or such like dainties, to those who required them; content to suffer hunger themselves, so that they could procure money. Some, too, there were, who even fed their corpse-like bodies with other corpses, eating human flesh; but at a distance, and on the mountains, lest others should be offended at the smell of their cookery. Many wandered through unknown paths, in expectation of meeting with sustenance, and were killed by robbers acquainted with the passes. But not long after the city was surrendered.

For Boamund, a man of superior talents, had, by dint of very great promises, induced a Turkish chief,‡ who had the custody of the principal tower, on the side where his station lay, to deliver it up to him. And he, too, to palliate the infamy of his treachery by a competent excuse, gave his son as an hostage to Boamund; professing that he did so by the express command of Christ, which had been communicated to him in a dream. Boamund, therefore, advanced his troops to the tower, having first, by a secret contrivance, obtained from the chiefs the perpetual government of the city, in case he could carry it. Thus the Franks, in the dead of the night, scaling the walls by rope ladders, and displaying on the top of the tower the crimson standard of Boamund, repeated with joyful accents the Christian watchword, "It is the will of God! It is the will of God!" The Turks

* The balista was a warlike engine for casting either darts or stones: the petrary, for throwing large stones only.

† Owing to the scarcity of fuel.

‡ "Phirouz, a Syrian renegade, has the infamy of this perfidious and foul treason."—HARDY.

awaking, and heavy from want of rest, took to flight through narrow passages; and our party, following with drawn swords, made dreadful slaughter of the enemy. In this flight fell Aoxianus, governor of the city, being beheaded by a certain Syrian peasant: his head, when brought to the Franks, excited both their laughter and their joy.

Not long rejoicing in this complete victory, they had the next day to lament being themselves besieged by the Turks from without. For the forces which had been solicited by Sansadol were now arrived under the command of Corbaguath, an eastern satrap, who had obtained from the emperor of Persia three hundred thousand men.* under twenty-seven commanders. Sixty thousand of these ascended over the rocks to the citadel, by desire of the Turks, who still remained in possession of it. These woefully harassed the Christians by frequent sallies: nor was there any hope left, but from the assistance of God, since want was now added to the miseries of war—want, the earliest attendant on great calamities. Wherefore, after a fast of three days, and earnest supplications, Peter the hermit was sent ambassador to the Turks, who spake with his usual eloquence to the following effect: "That the Turks should now voluntarily evacuate the Christian territory, which they had formerly unjustly invaded; that it was but right, as the Christians did not attack Persia, that the Turks should not molest Asia; that they should therefore, either by a voluntary departure, seek their own country, or expect an attack on the following morning; that they might try their fortune, by two, or four, or eight, that danger might not accrue to the whole army."

Corbaguath condescended not to honour the messenger even with a reply; but playing at chess and gnashing his teeth, dismissed him as he came; merely observing, "that the pride of the Franks was at an end." Hastily returning,

* "In describing the host of Corbaguath, most of the Latin historians, the author of the Gesta, (p. 17,) Robertus monachus, (p. 56,) Baldric, (p. 3,) Fulcherius Carnotensis, (p. 392,) Guibert, (p. 512,) William of Tyre, (lib. vi c. 3, p. 714,) Bernardus Thesaurarius, (c. 39, p 695,) are content with the vague expressions of 'infinita multitudo,' 'immensum agmen,' 'innumeræ copiæ,' 'innumeræ gentes.' The numbers of the Turks are fixed by Albertus Aquensis at two hundred thousand, (lib. iv. c. 10, p 242,) and by Radulphus Cadomensis (c. 72, p. 309) at four hundred thousand horse. (Gib. Decl Rom Emp. vii. pp 364, 5.)"—HARDY.

Peter apprised the army of the insolence of the Turk. Each then animating the other, it was publicly ordered, that every person should, that night, feed his horse as plentifully as possible, lest he should falter from the various evolutions of the following day. And now the morning dawned, when, drawn up in bodies, they proceeded, with hostile standard, against the enemy. The first band was led by the two Roberts, of Normandy and Flanders, and Hugh the Great; the second by Godfrey; the third by the bishop of Puy; the reserve by Boamund, as a support to the rest. Raimund continued in the city, to cover the retreat of our party, in case it should be necessary. The Turks, from a distance, observing their movements, were, at first, dubious what they could mean. Afterwards, recognizing the standard of the bishop, for they were extremely afraid of him, as they said he was the pope of the Christians and the fomenter of the war; and seeing our people advancing so courageously and quickly, they fled ere they were attacked. Our party, too, exhilarated with unexpected joy, slew them as they were flying, as far as the strength of the infantry, or exertion of the cavalry, would permit. They imagined, moreover, that they saw the ancient martyrs, who had formerly been soldiers, and who had gained eternal remuneration by their death, I allude to George and Demetrius, hastily approaching with upraised banner from the mountainous districts, hurling darts against the enemy, but assisting the Franks. Nor is it to be denied, that the martyrs did assist the Christians, as the angels formerly did the Maccabees, fighting for the selfsame cause. Returning, then, to the spoil, they found in their camp sufficient to satisfy, or even totally to glut, the covetousness of the greediest army. This battle took place A. D. 1098, on the fourth before the kalends of July; for the city had been taken the day before the nones of June. Soon after, on the kalends of the ensuing August, the bishop of Puy, the leader of the Christians, and chief author of this laudable enterprise, joyfully yielded to the common lot of mortals; and Hugh the Great, by permission of the chiefs, as it is said, returned to France, alleging as a reason, the perpetual racking of his bowels.

But when, by a long repose of seven months at Antioch, they had obliterated the memory of their past labours, they began to think of proceeding on their route. And first of all Raimund, ever unconscious of sloth, ever foremost in military energy; and next to him the two Roberts, and Godfrey, proceeded upon the march. Boamund alone, for a time, deferred his advance, lured by the prospect of a magnificent city and the love of wealth. A plausible reason, however, lay concealed beneath his covetousness, when he alleged, that Antioch ought not to be exposed to the Turks without a chief, as they would directly attack it. He therefore took up his residence in the city; and this harsh governor drove Raimund's followers, who occupied one of the streets, without the walls.

The others, however, passing through Tripoli,[*] and Berith, and Tyre, and Sidon, and Accaron, and Caiphas, and Cæsarea of Palestine, where they left the coast to the right hand, came to Ramula; being kindly received by some of the cities, and signalizing their valour by the subjugation of others. For their design was to delay no longer, as it was now the month of April, and the produce of the earth had become fully ripe. Ramula is a very small city, without walls: if we credit report, the place of the martyrdom of St. George; whose church, originally founded there, the Turks had somewhat defaced: but at that time, through fear of the Franks, they had carried off their property and retreated to the mountains. The next morning, at early dawn, Tancred, the nephew of Boamund, a man of undaunted courage, and some others, taking arms, proceeded to Bethlehem, desirous of exploring its vicinity. The Syrians of the place, who came out to meet them, manifested their joy with weeping earnestness, through apprehension for their safety, on account of the smallness of their numbers; for few more than a hundred horsemen were of the party. But our people having suppliantly adored the sacred edifice,[†] immediately stretch anxiously forward towards Jerusalem. The Turks, confident of their force, fiercely sallied out, and for some time skirmished with our troops, for the whole army had now

[*] The greatest part of their march is most accurately traced in Maundrell's Journey from Aleppo to Jerusalem.—HARDY.

[†] The church of St. Mary, at Bethlehem, contained within its walls a sort of grotto, in which it was pretended Christ was born.—See Bede, de Locis Sanctis.

come up; but they were soon repulsed by the exertions of the Franks, and sought security from their encircling walls.

The numbers who have already written on the subject, admonish me to say nothing of the situation and disposition of Jerusalem, nor is it necessary for my narrative to expatiate on such a field. Almost every person is acquainted with what Josephus, Eucherius, and Bede, have said: for who is not aware, that it was called Salem from Melchisedec; Jebus from the Jebusites; Jerusalem from Solomon? Who has not heard how often, falling from adverse war, it buried its inhabitants in its ruins, through the different attacks of Nabugodonosor, of Titus, or of Adrian? It was this last who rebuilt Jerusalem, called Ælia, after his surname, enclosing it with a circular wall, of greater compass, that it might embrace the site of the sepulchre of our Lord, which originally stood without: Mount Sion, too, added to the city, stands eminent as a citadel. It possesses no springs;* but water, collected in cisterns, prepared for that purpose, supplies the wants of the inhabitants: for the site of the city, beginning from the northern summit of Mount Sion, has so gentle a declivity, that the rain which falls there does not form any mire, but running like rivulets, is received into tanks, or flowing through the streets, augments the brook Kedron. Here is the church of our Lord, and the temple, which they call Solomon's, by whom built is unknown, but religiously reverenced by the Turks, more especially the church of our Lord, where they daily worshipped, and prohibited the Christians from entering, having placed there a statue of Mahomet. Here also is a church of elegant workmanship, containing the holy sepulchre, built by Constantine the Great, and which has never suffered any injury from the enemies of our faith, through fear, as I suppose, of being struck by that celestial fire which brightly shines in lamps, every year, on the Vigil† of Easter. When this miracle had

* "Jerusalem was possessed only of the torrent of Kedron, dry in summer, and of the little brook or spring of Siloe, (Reland, tom. i. pp. 294, 300). Tacitus mentions a perennial fountain, an aqueduct, and cisterns of rain-water. The aqueduct was conveyed from the rivulet Tekoe, or Etham, which is likewise mentioned by Bohadin, (in Vit. Saladin. p. 238.)" HARDY.

† It was pretended that the lamps in the church of the Holy Sepulchre were miraculously ignited on Easter Eve.

a beginning, or whether it existed before the times of the Saracens, history has left no trace. I have read in the writings of Bernard* the monk, that about two hundred and fifty years ago, that is, A. D. 870, he went to Jerusalem and saw that fire, and was entertained in the Hospital which the most glorious Charles the Great had there ordered to be built, and where he had collected a library at great expense. He relates, that both in Egypt and in that place, the Christians, under the dominion of the Turks, enjoyed such security, that if any traveller lost a beast of burden by accident, in the midst of the high road, he might leave his baggage and proceed to the nearest city for assistance, and without doubt find every thing untouched at his return. Still, from the suspicion that they might be spies, no foreign Christian could live there securely, unless protected by the signet of the emperor of Babylon. The natives purchased peace from the Turks at the expense of three talents or bezants annually. But as Bernard mentions the name of Theodosius, the then patriarch, this gives me an occasion of enumerating the whole of the patriarchs.

James the brother of our Lord and son of Joseph; Simon son of Cleophas, the cousin of Christ, for Cleophas was the brother of Joseph; Justus, Zaccheus, Tobias, Benjamin, Johannes, Maccabæus, Philip, Seneca, Justus, Levi, Effrem, Jesse, Judas; these fifteen were circumcised: Mark, Cassian, Publius, Maximus, Julian, Gaius; who first celebrated Easter and Lent after the Roman manner: Symmachus, Gaius, Julian, Capito, Maximus, Antonius, Valens, Docilianus, Narcissus, Dius, Germanio, Gordius, Alexander, Mazabanus, Irmeneus, Zabdas, Ermon, Macharius; in his time the Holy Cross was found by St. Helena: Cyriacus, Maximus, Cyrillus, who built the church of the Holy Sepulchre, and of Mount Calvary, and of Bethlehem, and of the Valley of Jehosaphat. All these were called bishops. After them

---

* Bernard, with two companions, sailed from Italy to Alexandria, and travelled thence by land to Jerusalem in the year 870. Their travels are printed in "Mabillon's Acta Benedictinorum." The account is short, but has several interesting particulars. There is also a good MS. in the British Museum, Bib. Cott. Faust. b 1, where, by a mistake of the scribe, it is dated A. D. 970, but this is clearly wrong, for Bernard mentions Lewis, king of Italy, as then living, and he died A. D. 875.

arose the patriarchs: Cyrillus the first patriarch; Johannes, Prailius, Juvenalis,* Zacharias, in whose time came Cosdroe† king of Persia to Jerusalem, and destroyed the churches of Judea and Jerusalem, and slew with his army six and thirty thousand of the Christians: Modestus, who was appointed patriarch by the emperor Heraclius, when he returned victorious from Persia: Sophronius, in whose time the Saracens came and thrust out all the Christians from Jerusalem, except the patriarch, whom they suffered to remain out of reverence to his sanctity: this was the period when the Saracens overran the whole of Egypt, and Africa, and Judea, and even Spain, and the Balearic Isles. Part of Spain was wrested from them by Charles the Great, but the remainder, together with the countries I have enumerated, they have possessed for nearly five hundred years, down to the present day: Theodorus,‡ Ilia, Georgius, Thomas, Basilius, Sergius, Salomontes, Theodosius, whom Bernard relates to have been an abbat, and that he was torn from his monastery, which was fifteen miles distant from Jerusalem, and made patriarch of that city: then too they say that Michael was patriarch in Babylon over Egypt, the patriarchate of Alexandria being removed thither: Ilia, Sergius, Leonthos, Athanasius, Christodolus, Thomas, Joseph, Orestes; in his time came Sultan Achim, the nephew of the patriarch Orestes, from Babylon, who sent his army to Jerusalem, destroyed all the churches, that is to say, four thousand, and caused his uncle, the patriarch, to be conveyed to Babylon and there slain: Theophilus, Nicephorus: he built the present church of the Holy Sepulchre, by the favour of Sultan Achim: Sophronius; in his time the Turks, coming to Jerusalem, fought with the Saracens, killed them all, and possessed the city; but the Christians continued there under the dominion of the Turks: Cuthimus, Simeon; in whose time came the Franks and laid

---

* Some MSS. insert the name of another John after Juvenalis, but no patriarch of this name is known to have lived at that period. Malmesbury has, moreover, omitted the names of eleven patriarchs, between Juvenal, who died A.D. 458, and Zacharias who died A.D. 609.

† Cosroes, or Chosroes the Second, king of Persia.

‡ "The church of Jerusalem was vacant after the death of Sophronius, A.D. 644, until the year 705, when John V succeeded, whom Theodorus followed, A.D. 754."—HARDY.

siege to Jerusalem, and rescued it from the hands of the Turks and of the king of Babylon.

In the fourth year, then, of the expedition to Jerusalem, the third after the capture of Nice, and the second after that of Antioch, the Franks laid siege to Jerusalem,—a city well able to repay the toils of war, to soothe its labours, and to requite the fondest expectation. It was now the seventh day of June, nor were the besiegers apprehensive of wanting food or drink for themselves, as the harvest was on the ground, and the grapes were ripe upon the vines; the care alone of their cattle distressed them, which, from the nature of the place and of the season, had no running stream to support them, for the heat of the sun had dried up the secret springs of the brook Siloah, which, at uncertain periods, used to shed abroad its refreshing waters. This brook, when at any time swollen with rain, increases that of Kedron; and then passes on, with bubbling current, into the valley of Jehosaphat. But this is extremely rare; for there is no certain period of its augmentation or decrease. In consequence, the enemy, suddenly darting from their caverns, frequently killed our people, when straggling abroad for the purpose of watering the cattle. In the meantime the chiefs were each observant at their respective posts, and Raymond actively employed before the tower of David.* This fortress, defending the city on the west, and strengthened, nearly half way up, by courses of squared stone soldered with lead, repels every fear of invaders when guarded by a small party within. As they saw, therefore, that the city was difficult to carry on account of the steep precipices, the strength of the walls, and the fierceness of the enemy, they ordered engines to be constructed. But before this, indeed, on the seventh day of the siege, they had tried their fortune by erecting ladders, and hurling swift arrows against their opponents: but, as the ladders were few, and perilous to those who mounted them, since they were exposed on all sides and nowhere protected from wounds, they changed their design. There was one engine which we call the Sow, the ancients, Vinea; because the machine, which is constructed of

* "The tower of David was the old tower Psephina or Neblosa; it was likewise called Castellum Pisanum, from the patriarch Daimbert. (D'Anville, pp. 19—23.)"—HARDY.

slight timbers, the roof covered with boards and wickerwork, and the sides defended with undressed hides, protects those who are within it, who, after the manner of a sow, proceed to undermine the foundations of the walls. There was another, which, for want of timber, was but a moderate sized tower, constructed after the manner of houses:* they call it Berefreid: this was intended to equal the walls in height. The making of this machine delayed the siege, on account of the unskilfulness of the workmen and the scarcity of the wood. And now the fourteenth day of July arrived, when some began to undermine the wall with the sows, others to move forward the tower. To do this more conveniently, they took it towards the works in separate pieces, and, putting it together again at such a distance as to be out of bowshot, advanced it on wheels nearly close to the wall. In the meantime, the slingers with stones, the archers with arrows, and the cross-bow-men with bolts, each intent on his own department, began to press forward and dislodge their opponents from the ramparts; soldiers, too, unmatched in courage, ascend the tower, waging nearly equal war against the enemy with missile weapons and with stones. Nor, indeed, were our foes at all remiss; but trusting their whole security to their valour, they poured down grease and burning oil upon the tower, and slung stones on the soldiers, rejoicing in the completion of their desires by the destruction of multitudes. During the whole of that day the battle was such that neither party seemed to think they had been worsted; on the following, which was the fifteenth of July, the business was decided. For the Franks, becoming more experienced from the event of the attack of the preceding day, threw faggots flaming with oil on a tower adjoining the wall, and on the party who defended it, which, blazing by the action of the wind, first seized the timber and then the stones, and drove off the garrison. Moreover the beams which the Turks had left hanging down from the walls in order that, being forcibly drawn back, they might, by their recoil, batter the tower in pieces in case it should advance too near, were by the Franks dragged to them, by cutting away the ropes; and being placed from the engine to the

* That is to say, with several floors or apartments, one above the other; each of which contained soldiers.

wall, and covered with hurdles, they formed a bridge of communication from the ramparts to the tower. Thus what the infidels had contrived for their defence became the means of their destruction; for then the enemy, dismayed by the smoking masses of flame and by the courage of our soldiers, began to give way. These advancing on the wall, and thence into the city, manifested the excess of their joy by the strenuousness of their exertions. This success took place on the side of Godfrey and of the two Roberts; Raymond knew nothing of the circumstance, till the cry of the fugitives and the alarm of the people, throwing themselves from the walls, who thus met death while flying from it, acquainted him that the city was taken. On seeing this, he rushed with drawn sword on the runaways, and hastened to avenge the injuries of God, until he had satiated his own animosity. Moreover, adverting to the advantages of quiet for the moment, he sent unhurt to Ascalon five hundred Ethiopians, who, retreating to the citadel of David, had given up the keys of the gates under promise of personal safety. There was no place of refuge for the Turks, so indiscriminately did the insatiable rage of the victors sweep away both the suppliant and the resisting. Ten thousand were slain in the temple of Solomon; more were thrown from the tops of the churches, and of the citadel. After this, the dead bodies were heaped and dissolved into the aery fluid by means of fire; lest putrifying in the open air, they should pour contagion on the heavy atmosphere. The city being thus expiated by the slaughter of the infidels, they proceeded with hearts contrite and bodies prostrate to the sepulchre of the Lord, which they had so long earnestly sought after, and for which they had undergone so many labours. By what ample incense of prayer, they propitiated heaven, or by what repentant tears they once again brought back the favour of God, none, I am confident, can describe; no, not if the splendid eloquence of the ancients could revive or Orpheus himself return; who, as it is said, bent e'en the listening rocks to his harmonious strain. Be it imagined then, rather than expressed.

So remarkable was the example of forbearance exhibited by the chiefs, that, neither on that, nor on the following day, did any of them, through lust of spoil, withdraw his mind from following up the victory. Tancred alone, beset with ill-timed covetousness, carried off some valuable effects from the temple of Solomon; but, afterwards, reproved by his own conscience, and the address of some other persons, he restored, if not the same things, yet such as were of equal value.* At that time, if any man, however poor, seized a house, or riches of any kind, he did not afterwards encounter the brawlings of the powerful, but held, what he had once possessed, as his hereditary right. Without delay, then, Godfrey, that brilliant mirror of Christian nobility, in which, as in a splendid ceiling,† the lustre of every virtue was reflected, was chosen king; ‡ all, in lively hope, agreeing, that they could in no wise better consult the advantage of the church; deferring, in the meantime, the election of a patriarch, who was to be appointed by the determination of the Roman Pontiff.§

But the emperor of Babylon, not the city built by Nimrod and enlarged by Semiramis and now said to be deserted, but that which Cambyses, son of Cyrus, built in Egypt, on the spot where Taphnis formerly stood: the emperor of Babylon, I say, venting his long-conceived indignation against the Franks, sent the commander of his forces, to drive them, as he said, out of his kingdom. Hastening to fulfil the command, when he heard that Jerusalem was taken, he redoubled his diligence, though he had by no means been indolent before. The design of the barbarian was to besiege the Christians in Jerusalem, and after the victory, which he, falsely presaging, already obtained in imagination, to destroy utterly the sepulchre of our Lord. The Christians, who desired nothing less than again to endure the miseries of a siege, taking courage through God's assistance, march out of the city towards Ascalon, to oppose the enemy; and carry with them part of the cross of Christ, which a certain Syrian, an inhabitant of

* Interested motives and conduct, it is to be observed, are several times imputed to the adventurers from Sicily and Calabria.

† In allusion to the custom of painting and gilding the ceilings.

‡ Godfrey would not, however, accept the name of king, nor wear a crown of jewels in a city where his Saviour had been crowned with thorns. He therefore contented himself with the title of "Defender and Baron of the Holy Sepulchre."

§ Pope Urban however died fourteen days after the taking of Jerusalem. Daibert was appointed patriarch of the captured city.

Jerusalem, had produced, as it had been preserved in his house, in succession from father to son. This truly was a fortunate and a loyal device, that the secret should be all along kept from the Turks. Obtaining moreover a great booty of sheep and cattle, near Ascalon, they issued a general order, to leave the whole of it in the open plain, lest it should be an impediment when engaging the next morning, as they would have spoil more than enough if they conquered, so that, free from incumbrance, they might avenge the injuries of heaven. In the morning, therefore, as the army was on its march, you might see, I believe by divine instinct, the cattle with their heads erect, proceeding by the side of the soldiers, and not to be driven away by any force. The enemy perceiving this at a distance, and their sight being dazzled by the rays of the sun, lost their confidence, ere the battle could commence, as they thought the multitude of their opponents was countless: yet were they, themselves, by no means deficient in numbers, and by long exercise, trained to battle. They endeavoured therefore to hem in the Franks, who were proceeding at a slow rate, by dividing their force into two bodies, and by curving their wings. But the leaders, and more especially Robert the Norman, who was in the advanced guard, eluding stratagem by stratagem, or rather cunning by valour, led on their archers and infantry, and broke through the centre of the heathens. Moreover the Lorraine cavalry, which was stationed with its commander in the rear, advancing by the flanks, prevented their flight, and occupied the whole plain. Thus the Turks, penetrated in the front, and hemmed in on every side, were slain at the pleasure of the victors; the remainder escaping through favour of approaching night. Many golden utensils were found in their camp; many jewels, which, though from their scarcity unknown in our country, there shine in native splendour. Nor was there ever a more joyful victory for the Christians, because they obtained the most precious spoil without loss.

Returning therefore to Jerusalem, when, by a rest of many days, they had recruited their strength, some of them, sighing for their native country, prepared to return by sea. Godfrey and Tancred only remained; princes, truly noble, and, to whose glory, posterity, if it judge rightly, never can set limits: men, who, from the intense cold of Europe, plunged into the insupportable heat of the East: prodigal of their own lives, so that they could succour suffering Christianity. Who, besides the fears of barbarous incursions, in constant apprehension from the unwholesomeness of an unknown climate, despised the security of rest and of health in their own country; and although very few, in number, kept in subjection so many hostile cities by their reputation and prowess. They were memorable patterns, too, of trust in God; not hesitating to remain in that climate, where they might either suffer from pestilential air, or be slain by the rage of the Saracens. Let the celebration of the poets then give way; nor let ancient fiction extol her earliest heroes. No age hath produced aught comparable to the fame of these men. For, if the ancients had any merit, it vanished after death with the smoke of their funeral pile; because it had been spent, rather on the vapour of earthly reputation, than in the acquisition of substantial good. But the utility of these men's valour will be felt, and its dignity acknowledged, as long as the world shall continue to revolve, or pure Christianity to flourish. What shall I say of the good order and forbearance of the whole army? There was no gluttony; no lewdness, which was not directly corrected by the authority of the commanders, or the preaching of the bishops. There was no wish to plunder as they passed through the territories of the Christians; no controversy among themselves, which was not easily settled by the examination of mediators. Wherefore, since the commendation of an army so well-ordered redounds to the glory of its conductors, I will signalize, in my narrative, the exploits and the adventures of each respective chief; nor will I subtract any thing from the truth, as I received it on the faith of my relators. But let no one who has had a fuller knowledge of these events, accuse me of want of diligence, since we, who are secluded on this side of the British ocean, hear but the faint echo of Asiatic transactions.

King Godfrey takes the lead in my commendation: he was the son of Eustace count of Boulogne, of whom I have spoken in the time of king Edward, but more ennobled maternally, as by that line he was descended from Charles the Great. For, his mother, named Ida, daughter of the ancient

Godfrey duke of Lorraine, had a brother called Godfrey after his father, surnamed Bocard. This was at the time when Robert Friso, of whom I have spoken above, on the death of Florence, duke of Friesland, married his widow Gertude; advancing Theodoric, his son-in-law, to the succession of the duchy. Bocard could not endure this; but expelling Friso, subjected the country to his own will. Friso, unable to revenge himself by war, did it by stratagem; killing Bocard through the agency of his Flemings, who drove a weapon into his posteriors, as he was sitting for a natural occasion. In this manner the son-in-law succeeded to the duchy, by the means of his father-in-law. The wife of this Godfrey was the marchioness Matilda, mentioned in the former book, who on her husband's death spiritedly retained the duchy, in opposition to the emperor; more especially in Italy, for of Lorraine and the hither-countries he got possession. Ida then, as I began to relate, animated her son Godfrey with great expectations of getting the earldom of Lorraine: for the paternal inheritance had devolved on Eustace her eldest son; the youngest, Baldwin, was yet a boy. Godfrey arriving at a sufficient age to bear arms, dedicated his services to the emperor Henry, who is mentioned in the preceding book. Acquiring his friendship, therefore, by unremitting exertions, he received from the emperor's singular liberality the whole of Lorraine as a recompence. Hence it arose, that when the quarrel broke out between the pope and Henry, he went with the latter to the siege of Rome; was the first to break through that part of the wall which was assigned for his attack, and facilitated the entrance of the besiegers. Being in extreme perspiration, and panting with heat, he entered a subterraneous vault which he found in his way, and when he had there appeased the violence of his thirst by an excessive draught of wine, he brought on a quartan fever. Others say that he fell a victim to poisoned wine, as the Romans, and men of that country, are used to infect whole casks. Others report, that a portion of the walls fell to his lot, where the Tiber flowing, exhales destructive vapours in the morning; that by this fatal pest, all his soldiers, with the exception of ten, lost their lives; and that himself, losing his nails and his hair, never entirely recovered. But be it which it might of these, it appears that he was never free from a slow fever, until hearing the report of the expedition to Jerusalem, he made a vow to go thither, if God would kindly restore his health. The moment this vow was made, the strength of the duke revived; so that, recovering apace, he shook disease from his limbs, and rising with expanded breast, as it were, from years of decrepitude, shone with renovated youth. In consequence, grateful for the mercies of God showered down upon him, he went to Jerusalem the very first, or among the first; leading a numerous army to the war. And though he commanded a hardy and experienced band, yet none was esteemed readier to attack, or more efficient in the combat than himself. Indeed it is known, that, at the siege of Antioch, with a Lorrainian sword, he cut asunder a Turk, who had demanded single combat, and that one half of the man lay panting on the ground, while the horse, at full speed, carried away the other: so firmly the miscreant sat. Another also who attacked him he clave asunder from the neck to the groin, by taking aim at his head with a sword; nor did the dreadful stroke stop here, but cut entirely through the saddle, and the back-bone of the horse. I have heard a man of veracity relate, that he had seen what I here subjoin: during the siege, a soldier of the duke's had gone out to forage; and being attacked by a lion, avoided destruction for some time, by the interposition of his shield. Godfrey, grieved at this sight, transfixed the ferocious animal with a hunting spear. Wounded, and becoming fiercer from the pain, it turned against the prince with such violence as to hurt his leg with the iron which projected from the wound; and had he not hastened with his sword to rip it up, this pattern of valour must have perished by the tusk of a wild beast. Renowned from these successes, he was exalted to be king of Jerusalem, more especially because he was conspicuous in rank and courage without being arrogant. His dominion was small and confined, containing, besides the few surrounding towns, scarcely any cities. For the king's bad state of health, which attacked him immediately after the Babylonish war, caused a cessation of warlike enterprise; so that he made no acquisitions: yet, by able management, he so well restrained the avidity of the barbarians for the whole of that year, that nothing was lost. They report that the king, from being unused to a state of indolence, fell again into his original fever; but I conjecture, that God, in his own good time, chose early to translate, to a better kingdom, a soul rendered acceptable to him and tried by so many labours, lest wickedness should change his heart, or deceit beguile his understanding. Revolving time thus completing a reign of one year, he died placidly, and was buried on Mount Golgotha;* a king as unconquerable in death, as he had formerly been in battle; often kindly repressing the tears of the by-standers. Being asked who was to succeed him, he mentioned no person by name, but said merely, "whoever was most worthy." He never would wear the ensign of royalty, saying, "it was too great arrogance for him to be crowned for glory, in that city, in which God had been crowned in mockery." He died on the fifteenth before the kalends of August.

On Godfrey's decease, Tancred and the other chiefs declared that Baldwin, his brother, who was at that time settled in Mesopotamia, should be king: for Eustace, the elder brother, who came to Jerusalem with Godfrey, had long since returned to his native land. The acts of Baldwin shall be related briefly, but with unsullied truth; supported in their credibility by the narrative of Fulcher† of Chartres, who was his chaplain, and wrote somewhat of him, in a style, not altogether unpolished, but, as we say, without elegance or correctness, and which may serve to admonish others to write more carefully. Baldwin, undertaking the holy pilgrimage with the rest, had for companions many knights of disposition similar to his own. Confiding in these associates, he began to levy fresh troops for his purpose; to watch for brilliant opportunities wherein to manifest his prowess: and, finally, not content with that commendation which was common to all, leaving the rest and departing three days' journey from Antioch, he got possession, by the consent of its inhabitants, of Tarsus, a noble city of Cilicia: Tarsus, formerly the nursing-mother of the apostle Paul, in honour of whom the cathedral there is dedicated. The Tarsians volun-

* The church of Golgotha contains within it the rock on which the cross was fixed for the crucifixion. Bede, Eccles. Hist. p. 264.

† Fulcher wrote an account of the transactions in Syria, where he was present, from A.D. to 1095 to 1124. Malmesbury condenses much of his narrative with his usual ability. It is printed in the Gesta Dei per Francos, and, ap. Duchesne Hist. Franc. Scriptor. tom. iii.

tarily submitted to his protection, as they were Christians, and hoped by his aid to be defended from the Turks. The Cilicians, therefore, eagerly yielded to his power, more especially after the surrender of Turbexhel, a town by situation impregnable, to whose sovereignty the inferior towns look up. This being yielded, as I have said, the others followed its decision. And not only Cilicia, but Armenia, and Mesopotamia, eagerly sought alliance with this chief: for these provinces were almost free from the domination of the Turks, though infested by their incursions. Wherefore the prince of the city of Edessa, who was alike pressed by the hatred of the citizens and the sword of the enemy, sent letters to Baldwin, descriptive of his difficulties, desiring him to come with all speed, and receive a compensation for the labour of his journey, by his adoption, as he had no issue of either sex. This is a city of Mesopotamia in Syria, very noted for the fruitfulness of its soil and for the resort of merchants, twenty miles distant from the Euphrates, and a hundred from Antioch. The Greeks call it Edessa; the Syrians Rothasia. Baldwin, therefore, exacting an oath of fidelity from the ambassadors, passed the Euphrates with only sixty-nine horsemen: a wonderful instance, it may be said, either of fortitude, or of rashness, in not hesitating to proceed among the surrounding nations of barbarians, whom any other person, with so small a force, would have distrusted either for their race or their unbelief. By the Armenians and Syrians, indeed, coming out to meet him on the road with crosses and torches, he was received with grateful joy, and kindly entertained. But the Turks, endeavouring to attack his rear, were frustrated in all their attempts by the skill of Baldwin: the Samosatians setting the first example of flight. Samosata is a city beyond the Euphrates, from which arose Paul of Samosata,* the confutation of whose heresy, whoever is desirous may read in the History of Eusebius. And, if I well remember, Josephus says, that Antony was laying siege

* Paul was bishop of Antioch in the third century. "He was better pleased with the title of ducenarius than with that of bishop. His heresy, like those of Noetus and Labellius in the same century, tended to confound the mysterious distinction of the Divine persons. He was degraded from his see in 270, by the sentence of eighty bishops, and altogether deprived of his office in 274 by Aurelian (Mosheim's Ecc. Hist. vol. i. p. 702, &c.)"
—Hardy.

to this city, when Herod came to him. The Turks inhabiting that city then, who were the first instigators of outrage against the Franks, were the first to give way. Thus, Baldwin, coming safely to Edessa, found nothing to disappoint his expectations : for being received with surpassing favour by the prince, and soon after, on his being killed by his faithless citizens, obtaining the lawful sovereignty of the city, for the whole time during which the Franks were labouring at Antioch and at Jerusalem, he was not free from hostilities ; worsting his opponents in repeated attacks.

But in the month of November, being reminded by Boamund, prince of Antioch, that they should enter on their progress to Jerusalem, he prepared for marching, and by the single display of the white standard, which was his ensign in battle, overthrowing the Turks who had broken the peace on his expected departure, he left Antioch to the right; and came to Laodicea. Here, by the liberality of earl Raymond, who presided over the city, getting, at a cheap rate, a sufficiency of supplies for his people, he passed Gibellum, and followed the recent track of Boamund, who had encamped and awaited him. Daibert, archbishop of Pisa, joined them for the march : he had landed his confederate party at Laodicea, as did also two other bishops. These forces when united were estimated at five and twenty thousand; many of whom, when they entered the territories of the Saracens, were, through the scarcity of commodities, overtaken by famine, and many were dismounted, from their horses being starved. Their distress was increased by an abundance of rain; for in that country it pours down like a torrent in the winter months only. In consequence, these poor wretches, having no change of garments, died from the severity of the cold; never getting under cover during several successive days. For this calamity, indeed, there was no remedy, as there was a deficiency both of tents and of wood: but they in some measure appeased their hunger, by constantly chewing the sweet reeds, which they call cannamel;* so denominated from cane and honey. Thus, twice only, obtaining neces-

* The sugar cane. "This kind of herb is annually cultivated with great labour. When ripe they pound it in a mortar, strain off the juice, and put it in vessels until it coagulates, and hardens in appearance like snow or

saries at an exorbitant price from the inhabitants of Tripoli and Cæsarea, they came to Jerusalem on the day of the winter solstice. They were met at the gates by king Godfrey with his brother Eustace, whom he had detained till this time, who showed them every degree of respect and generosity. Having performed in Bethlehem all the accustomed solemnities of our Lord's nativity, they appointed Daibert patriarch: to which transaction I doubt not, that the consent of pope Urban was obtained; for he was reverend from age, eloquent, and rich. After the circumcision of our Lord, therefore, assuming palms* in Jericho, which antiquity has made the ensign of pilgrims, each one hastily endeavoured to reach his home. The cause of their speed was the stench of the unburied dead bodies, the fumes of which exhaled in such a manner as to infect the air itself. In consequence, a contagious pestilence spreading in the atmosphere, consigned to death many who had recently arrived. The rest quickened their march, by the cities on the coast, that is to say, Tiberias and Cæsarea Philippi; for they were urged by scantiness of provision, and the fear of the enemy. Their want, as I have said, was remedied by the celerity of their march; and to the fury of three hundred soldiers who harassed them from the town of Baldac, they opposed a military stratagem. For feigning a flight for a short time, that by leaving the narrow passes themselves, they might induce the Turks to enter them, they retreated purposely, and then returning, routed the straggling enemy at their pleasure. They had supposed our people unprepared for fight, as their shields and bows were injured by the excessive rains; not being aware, that among men, victory consists not in reliance on excellence of arms, or of armour, but in the more noble power of courage, and of the well-nerved arm.

At that time, indeed, Baldwin returned safely to Edessa, and Boamund to Antioch. But in the beginning of the month of July, a vague report reached the ears of Baldwin, that the brilliant jewel of our commanders was dimmed;

---

white salt. This they use scraped and mixed with bread, or dissolved in water. The canes they call Zucra." Albertus Aquensis, ap. Gesta Dei, p. 270.

* In token of victory, or the completion of their purpose, by having visited the holy sepulchre. Vide Albert. Aquens. ubi sup. p 290.

Boamund being taken, and cast into chains, by one Danisman, a heathen, and a potentate of that country. In consequence, collecting a body of the people of Edessa and Antioch, he was in hopes of revenging this singular disgrace of the Christians. Moreover the Turk, who had taken this chieftain more by stratagem and chance than by courage or military force, as he had come with a small party to get possession of the city of Meletima, aware that the Franks would use their utmost efforts against him for the disgrace of the thing, betook himself to his own territories; marshalling his troops, not as though he intended to retreat, but rather to exhibit a triumph. Baldwin then proceeding two days' march beyond Meletima, and seeing the enemy decline the hazard of a battle, thought fit to return; but first, with the permission of Gabriel the governor, brought over the city to his own disposal. In the meantime, intelligence reaching him of his brother's death, and of the general consent of the inhabitants and chiefs to his election, he entrusted Edessa to Baldwin, his nearest relation by blood, and moreover a prudent and active man, and prepared for receiving the crown of Jerusalem. Wherefore collecting two hundred horse, and seven hundred foot, he proceeded on a march pregnant with death and danger; whence many, who were falsely supposed faithful, contemplating the boldness of the attempt, clandestinely deserted. He, with the remainder, marched forward to Antioch, where from the resources of his sagacious mind, he became the cause of great future advantage to his distressed people, by advising them to choose Tancred as their chief. Thence, he came to Tripoli, by the route of Gibesium and Laodicea. The governor of this city, a Turk by nation, but, from natural disposition, rich in bowels of mercy, afforded him the necessary provisions without the walls; at the same time, kindly intimating, that he should act cautiously, as Ducach, king of Damascus, had occupied a narrow pass through which he had heard he was to march. But he, ashamed of being moved by the threats of the Saracen, resolutely proceeded on his destination. When he came to the place, he perceived the truth of the governor's information: for about five miles on this side the city of Berith, there is a very narrow passage near the sea, so confined by steep precipices, and narrow defiles, that were a hundred men to get possession of the entrance, they might prevent any number, however great, from passing. Such as travel from Tripoli to Jerusalem have no possible means of avoiding it. Baldwin, therefore, arriving on the spot, sent out scouts to examine the situation of the place, and the strength of the enemy. The party returning, and hardly intelligible through fear, pointed out the difficulty of the pass, and the confidence of the enemy, who had occupied it. But Baldwin, who fell little short of the best soldier that ever existed, feeling no alarm, boldly drew up his army and led it against them. Ducach then despatched some to make an onset, and lure the party unguardedly forward; retaining his main body in a more advantageous position. For this purpose, at first they rushed on with great impetuosity, and then made a feint to retreat, to entice our people into the defile. This stratagem could not deceive Baldwin, who, skilled by long-continued warfare, made a signal to his men to make show of flight; and to induce a supposition that they were alarmed, he commanded the bag and baggage which they had cast down, to be again taken up, and the cattle to be goaded forward, as well as the ranks to be opened, that the enemy might attack them. The Turks at this began to exult, and, raging so horribly that you might suppose the Furies yelling, pursued our party. Some getting into vessels took possession of the shore, others riding forward began to kill such pilgrims as were incautiously loitering near the sea. The Franks continued their pretended flight till they reached a plain which they had before observed. No confusion deprived these men of their judgment; even the very emergency by which they had been overtaken nurtured and increased their daring; and though a small body, they withstood innumerable multitudes both by sea and land. For the moment it appeared they had sufficiently feigned alarm, they closed their ranks, turned their standards, and hemmed in the now-charging enemy on all sides. Thus the face of affairs was changed, the victors were vanquished, and the vanquished became victors. The Turks were hewn down with dreadful carnage; the remainder anxiously fled to their vessels, and when they had gotten more than a bow-shot out to sea, they still urged them forward as fiercely with their oars, as though they supposed they could be drawn back to land by the arm of their adversaries. And that you may not doubt of this miracle as fanciful, but as evident, feel it as it were, only four Christian soldiers fell in procuring by their blood this victory to the survivors. Wherefore I assert, that the Christians would never be conquered by the pagans, were they to implore the Divine assistance on their courage, ere they entered the conflict; and, when in battle, conciliate the friendly powers of heaven to their arms. But since, in peace they glut themselves in every kind of vice, and in battle rely only upon their courage; therefore it justly happens, that their valour is often unsuccessful. The earl then, rejoicing in his splendid victory, on returning to spoil the slain, found several Turks alive, whom he dismissed without personal injury, but despoiled them of their wealth. To avoid any hidden stratagem, he that night retreated with his party, and rested under the shelter of some olive trees. Next day, at dawn, he approached the defile, with the light troops, to be an eye-witness of the nature of the place; and, finding everything safe, and making a signal by smoke, as had been agreed upon, he intimated to his associates the departure of the enemy; for the Turks, who the day before were wantonly galloping around the hill, perceiving the carnage of their companions, had all fled in the dead of the night. Laying aside every delay, they instantly followed their commander. The governor of Berith sent them food on their march, astonished at the valour of so small a force. The Tyrians and Sidonians, and Accaronites, who are also called Ptholoamites, acted in the same manner, venerating with silent apprehension the bravery of the Franks. Nor were Tancred's party, in Caiphas, less generous, although he was absent. The ancient name of this town I am unable to discover; because all the inland cities, which we read of in Josephus as formerly existing, are either not in being, or else, changed into inconsiderable villages, have lost their names; whereas those on the coast remain entire. In this manner, by Cæsarea of Palestine, and Azotus, they came to Joppa. Here he was first congratulated on his kingdom, the citizens with great joy opening the gates to him.

Being afterwards accompanied by the inhabitants of Joppa to Jerusalem, where he was favourably received, he indulged in a repose of seven days' continuance. Then, that the Turks might be convinced that the spirit of his reign would proceed to their signal disadvantage, he led his troops towards Ascalon. When at a short distance from that city, he proudly displayed his forces, and with very little exertion compelled the attacking Ascalonites to retreat, by waiting a favourable opportunity for accomplishing his designs. Finally, conceiving his glory satisfied for that time by their repulse, he drew off to the mountains to pursue the enemy, and also at their expense to procure necessaries for his troops, who were famished with hunger from the barrenness of the land: for a scanty harvest had that year denied sustenance; deceiving the expectations of the province by a meagre produce. He ascended therefore the mountainous districts, whither the Turkish inhabitants of the country had retreated on leaving their towns, concealing the Syrians with them in sequestered caverns. The Franks, however, discovered a mode of counteracting the device of the fugitives, by letting smoke into their hiding-places; by which the miscreants were dislodged, and came out one by one. The Turks were killed to a man; the Syrians spared. The army turning aside thence, and marching towards Arabia, passed by the supulchres of the patriarchs Abraham, Isaac, and Jacob; and of their three wives, Sarah, Rebecca, and Leah. The place is in Hebron, thirteen miles distant from Jerusalem. For the body of Joseph lies at Neapolis, formerly called Sichem, covered with white marble, and conspicuous to every traveller; there, too, are seen the tombs of his brothers, but of inferior workmanship. The army then came into the valley where God formerly overthrew Sodom and Gomorrah, darting fire from heaven on the wicked. The lake there extends for eighteen miles, incapable of supporting any living creature, and so horrible to the palate, as to distort the mouths of such as drink it, and distend their jaws with its bitter taste. A hill overhangs the valley, emitting, in various places, a salt scum, and all over transparent, as it were, with congealed glass. Here is gathered what some call nitre; some call it crystal salt. Passing the lake, they came to a very opulent town, abundant in those luscious fruits which they call dates; in devouring which they were hardly able to fill the cavities of the stomach, or constrain the greediness of their palates, they were so extremely sweet. Every thing else had been taken away, through the alarm of the inhabitants, except a few Ethiopians, the dark wool of whose hair resembled smut. Our people, thinking it beneath their valour to kill persons of this description, treated them, not with indignation, but with laughter. Adjacent to this town is a valley, where to this day is seen the rock which Moses struck, to give water to the murmuring tribes. The stream yet runs so plentifully, and with such a current, as to turn the machinery of mills. On the declivity of the hill stands a church in honour of the legislator Aaron: where, through the mediation and assistance of his brother, he used to hold converse with God. Here learning from guides conversant in the roads, who from Saracens had been converted to Christianity, that from hence to Babylon was all barren country, and destitute of every accommodation, they returned to Jerusalem, to consecrate to God the first fruits of his reign, acquired in the subjugation of so many hostile countries.

The royal insignia being prepared, Baldwin was crowned with great ceremony, in Bethlehem, on Christmas-day, by Daibert the patriarch; all wishing him prosperity. For both at that time, and afterwards, he deserved, by his own exertions, and obtained, through the favour of others, every degree of royal respect, though sovereign of a very small, and I had almost said, a despicable kingdom. Wherefore the Christians ought to regard the mercy of our Lord Christ, and to walk in the contemplation of his power, through whose assistance they were objects of apprehension, though unable to do harm. For there were scarcely, in the whole service, four hundred horsemen and so many foot, to garrison Jerusalem, Ramula, Caiphas, and Joppa. For those who came thither by sea, with minds ill at ease, amid so many hostile ports, after having adored the saints, determined to return home, as there was no possibility of proceeding by land. Moreover, an additional difficulty was, that in the month of March Tancred had departed to assume the government of Antioch, nor could he or the king aid each other from the length of the journey: indeed, should necessity require it, he could not, without fear of irreparable loss, march his troops from one town to another. I pronounce it therefore to be a manifest miracle, that safe alone, through God's brotection, he was an object of dread to such a multitude of barbarians.

In this year, which was A.D. 1101, the sacred fire,* which used to signalize the Vigil of Easter, delayed its appearance longer than usual. For on the Saturday, the lessons being read, alternately in Greek and Latin, the "Kyrie eleeson"† repeated thrice and the melody of the clarions resounding, still when no fire appeared, and the setting sun induced the evening and led on the night, then all departed sorrowful to their homes. It had been determined, after mature deliberation, that on that night no person should remain in the church of the Holy Sepulchre, for fear any one of infected conscience should irritate God still more through his irreverent intrusion. But when the twilight was proceeding into day, a procession of the Latins was ordered to go to the Temple of Solomon, that by prayer they might call down the mercy of God: the same was performed around the Sepulchre of our Lord, by the Syrians plucking their beards and hair through violence of grief. The mercy of God could endure no longer, light being instantly sent into one lamp of the Sepulchre. Which, when a Syrian perceived glittering through a window, he expressed his joy by the clapping of his hands, and accelerated the advance of the patriarch. He, opening the recess of the sepulchral chamber by the keys which he carried, and lighting a taper, brought forth the celestial gift,‡ imparting it to all who crowded round him for that purpose; afterwards the whole of the lamps, throughout the church, were divinely lighted up, the one which was next to be illumined evincing its approaching ignition by emitting smoke in a miraculous manner. Thus, doubtless, the constant manner of Christ has been to terrify those he loved that he might again kindly soothe them, and that the dread of his power might redound to his praise. For since even the common gifts of God are

* See note, p. 384.
† "Lord have mercy upon us," thrice repeated, three times.
‡ Bernard the monk notices the custom of imparting the holy light, in order that the bishops and people might illuminate their several residences from it. Fulcher describes this event at great length, and observes that each person had a wax taper in his hand for the purpose of receiving the holy fire. Gesta Dei, p. 407.

lightly esteemed by men merely from their constant recurrence, he often enhances the grant of his indulgences by withholding them, that what was most ardently desired might be more gratefully regarded.

At that time a fleet of Genoese and Pisans had touched at Laodicea, and thence made a prosperous voyage to Joppa, and the crews, drawing their vessels on shore, spent Easter with the king at Jerusalem. He, bargaining for their services, engaged to give them the third of the spoil of each city they should take, and any particular street they might choose. Thus he impelled them, inconsiderate and blinded, more through lust of gold than love of God, to barter their blood, and lay siege immediately to Azotus, which they constrained to surrender after three days. Nor did the townspeople yield very reluctantly, as they feared the anger of the king should they be taken by storm: for, the preceding year, assisted by the machination of fortune, they had vigorously repulsed Godfrey when making a similar attempt. For, indeed, when by means of scaling ladders he had advanced his forces on the walls, and they, now nearly victorious, had gotten possession of the parapet, the sudden fall of a wooden tower, which stood close to the outside of the wall, deprived them of the victory and killed many, while still more were taken and butchered by the cruelty of the Saracens. Leaving Azotus, Baldwin laid siege to Cæsarea of Palestine, with his whole force, and with determined courage; but perceiving the resolution of its citizens and the difficulty of the enterprise, he ordered engines to be constructed. Petraries* were therefore made, and a great tower built of twenty cubits in height, surpassing the altitude of the wall. Our people, however, impatient of delay and of such lingering expectation, erecting their ladders and attempting to overtop the wall, arrived at the summit by the energy of their efforts, with conscious valour indignantly raging, that they had now been occupied in conflict with the Saracens during fifteen days, and had lost the whole of that time; and although the Cæsareans resisted with extreme courage, and rolled down large stones on them as they ascended, yet despising all danger, they broke through their opponents in a close body, and fought with an outstretched arm, and a drawn sword. The

* Engines made to cast stones.

Turks, unable longer to sustain the attack and taking to flight, either cast themselves down headlong, or fell by the hand of their enemies. Many were reserved for slavery; a few for ransom. Among these was the governor of the city, and a bishop named Arcadius. The scene was enough to excite laughter in a by-stander, to see a Turk disgorging bezants,* when struck on the neck by the fist of a Christian. The wretched males, through fear of extreme indigence, had hid money in their mouths; the females in parts not to be particularized: you perceive that my narrative blushes to speak plainly, but the reader understands what I wish, or rather what I wish not to speak.

Still, however, the emperor of Babylon could not be at rest, but would frequently send commanders and armies to attack the Franks. Arriving at Ascalon on ship-board, they scoured about Ramula, taking advantage of the king's occupation, who was then busied in the contest with Cæsarea. They frequently, therefore, by depopulating the country, irritated him to engage. But he, with equal subtlety, that their mad impetuosity might subside, suffered them, when eagerly advancing, to grow languid by declining battle. By this procrastination he effected that many, weary of delay, withdrew, while he attacked the remainder, consisting of eleven thousand horse and twenty-one thousand infantry, with his own two hundred and fifty cavalry and less than seven hundred foot. Addressing a few words to his soldiers, to whom he pledged victory if they persevered, and fame if they fell; and calling to their recollection that if they fled France was a great way off, he dashed first against the enemy; and the contest continuing for some time, when he saw his ranks giving way, he remedied circumstances which seemed almost bordering on desperation. Thus dismaying

---

* Fulcher relates, with great coolness, that he saw the bodies of the Turks, who were slain at Cæsarea, piled up and burned, in order to obtain the bezants which they had swallowed. Hist. Hierosol. ap. Du Chesne, tom. iv. 845. This practice of swallowing money is referred to by pope Urban, and, by his account, the merely burning dead bodies to obtain the hoard was a very humble imitation of the Saracen custom, with respect to those who visited Jerusalem before the crusades; which was to put scammony in their drink to make them vomit, and if this did not produce the desired effect, they proceeded to immediate incision! Guibert Abbas. Opera, p. 379.

the Turks by his well-known appearance, he laid their leader prostrate with his lance; on whose death the whole battalions fled. Our soldiers, who in the onset were so hemmed in as to be unable to see each other, then exercised their valour in such wise, under the ensign of the Holy Cross which preceded them, that they killed five thousand. Eighty of the cavalry and rather more of the infantry were slain on the side of the Franks. However subsequent successes consoled them, as they despatched five hundred Arabian horse. These had been traversing before Joppa for two days, but effecting little, they were returning to Ascalon, and seeing our troops at a distance, and, hoping they were their own, were approaching to congratulate them on their victory. But at length perceiving, by the weapons hurled against them, that they were Franks, they turned pale and, to use the words of the poet,* became like him who,

"With unshod foot, had trod upon a snake."

In consequence, enervated with astonishment, they exposed their backs to their destroyers. Thus the king coming to Joppa, corrected, by a true account, the falsity of the letter which had been sent to Tancred by the people of that city, erroneously declaring that the king had perished with his army. And, indeed, already had Tancred prepared for his march to Jerusalem, when a messenger arriving, and showing the royal signet, dispelled his sorrow, and restored his satisfaction.

It would be tedious, if I were to relate all his contests; to tell how he subdued Tiberias, Sidon, Accaron, that is, Ptolemais, and, ultimately, all the cities on the coast; or, how he distinguished almost each day by the slaughter of the Turks, either through secret attack or open warfare. The relation of his exploits requires the exclusive labours of a man who abounds in pompous diction, and undisturbed leisure: I have neither; and, what chiefly acts as an obstacle, want clear information on the subject. For it is by no means the part of an historian of veracity to give entire credit to flattering reports, or to deceive the credulity of his readers. Consequently, I shall only subjoin what I have found recorded, whereby this man's exalted devotion may be

* Juvenal, Sat. i. 43.

clearly proved, and his good report live for ever. This I may be bold to assert, that he often, with an inconsiderable force, engaged in mighty conflicts, and that he never fled the field, except at Ramula and at Accaron. And indeed signal victories ensued to each of these flights, because they proceeded more from rash valour, than from fear; as the reader will discover from the insertion of a few facts.

In the month of September, on the seventh before the ides of which the battle aforesaid took place, William, earl of Poitou, proceeded towards Jerusalem, leading with him troops estimated at sixty thousand horse and still more foot. There accompanied him, Stephen, earl of Burgundy, and Hugh de Lusignan, brother of earl Raymond, Hugh the Great, and Stephen of Blois, anxious to atone for the disgrace of their former desertion, by renovated and determined valour. Proceeding, therefore, by Constantinople, after he had by an insolent answer, as I before related, offended Alexius, he fell into the snares of Solyman; the emperor rather procuring than preventing his disaster. For Solyman, aware that the army was suffering from hunger and thirst, as they had been wandering about the marshes and desolate places for several days, encountered them with three hundred thousand archers. Never was there conflict more disastrous to the Franks; as it was impossible for flight to save the coward, or courage to rescue the bold from danger: for the battle was fought in a confined situation, and nothing could prevent the effect of clouds of arrows on men who were crowded together. More than a hundred thousand were slain; and all the booty carried off. Thus Solyman, obtaining splendid offerings to the manes of his countrymen from the spoils of the Franks, revenged the loss of Nice. But, as they had proceeded by many roads, all were not slain; nor was every thing plundered. For, except the Poitevin, who lost nearly whatever he possessed, the other earls had boldly defended their baggage. All, therefore, except Hugh the Great, who died, and was entombed in the city of Tarsus, collecting again their soldiers after the flight, hastened to Antioch. Tancred, a knight of celebrated kindness, gave them ample proof of his generosity; assisting them all, as far as he was able, with money: but more especially William, whom the inconstancy of Fortune had now as deeply depressed as she had formerly highly exalted, who, in addition to the loss of treasure, by which he was not so much affected as it was transitory and capable of reparation, was left almost the sole survivor of so many valorous soldiers Proceeding on their march with renovated courage, they sought every opportunity of giving battle. The city of Tortosa was the first to feel their rage; by attacking and plundering which, they in some degree compensated their former losses. Thence they came to the defile, which I have mentioned above, where the king had long awaited them, in order to give assistance in case the Turks should oppose their passage. Defended by his valour, and meeting with kind entertainment at Joppa, they proceeded the following Easter to Jerusalem, where they joyfully beheld, and reverently adored the sacred fire. Returning afterwards to Joppa, they took ship, each designing to revisit his native land. The Poitevin, from the continued favour of the wind, reached home; the rest were violently driven back.

But now, in the beginning of May, the Turks and Arabs laid siege to Ramula; recruiting the losses of their army in the former year, by making up its original numbers. The bishop of the city, prudently watching an opportunity, retired from the place and went secretly to Joppa. Baldwin had already gone out, relying on a false assertion that the enemy did not exceed five hundred; in consequence of which, he neither put his forces in order, nor called out his infantry, the trumpeters merely sounding for the cavalry to follow the king; though his friends earnestly advised him, to be on his guard against the subtlety of the Turks. The two Stephens, of Blois and of Burgundy, followed the king on horseback, that, instead of being branded as indolent and cowardly, they might return to their respective homes partakers of the credit of the triumph: far different, however, from their expectations, were the glory and the victory which the fates were preparing for them. For Baldwin, perceiving the multitude of the enemy and finding himself deceived in his opinion, filled with rage, and fierce in conscious valour, hesitated what was to be done. If he gave way, he contemplated the tarnish of his ancient glory; if he fought, the destruction of his followers.

Nevertheless, innate courage prevailed, and fear had already yielded, when, swayed by the advice of his comrades, he acquiesced in a plan of retiring, through the midst of the enemy, into a castle. The rest, following with loud clamour, broke through the thickest ranks, consecrating their souls to God, and nobly avenging their deaths. The earls, too, so wearied with striking that their hands grew stiff upon their swords, yielded to fate. The king escaping to the fortress, had some few companions remaining out of the two hundred he had led forth; who entreating that he would deign to protract his life by flight, and observing that their danger was of little consequence to the world, while his life was of advantage to many, in as much as he would be an example of valour to every age, by his singular constancy of mind though in adverse circumstances, he esteemed himself worthy to live. Wherefore, accompanied by five knights, he eluded his assailants, and escaped to the mountains. One of the five was Robert the Englishman, as I said before; the others, from the great distance, report has not brought to our knowledge: he, with three more, was taken; the fifth escaped with the king. The Turks vented the whole of their fury on those who had retired to the castle, among whom was Hugh de Lusignan and Geoffrey de Vincennes: only three survivors told their mournful tale to the people of Jerusalem. The king, concealing himself during the day, and, at night, urging his jaded courser through untrodden paths, arrived at Azotus, by the singular and miraculous protection of God; as the Turks had but just departed, after having been plundering around the city for the space of two days. Coming thence by sea to Joppa, he despatched an account of the certainty of his being still living to the people of Jerusalem. The bearer of the epistle was a low Syrian fellow, who, even had he been discovered, would have deceived the enemy, from the meanness of his garb, and his using the common language of the country. Escaping the hands of the infidels by lone paths with which he was acquainted, he arrived the third day at Jerusalem. Upon this the cavalry who garrisoned the city, taking with them the bands of auxiliary infantry, and purposing to proceed to Joppa, took a route close to the sea; avoiding the inland districts. The rear, however, of the party, were cut off, by the Turks pressing on them; as they were left unprotected either by horse or foot. Thus collecting ninety horse from Jerusalem, and eighty from Tiberias, which Hugh, that most intrepid commander, had brought to their assistance, the attendants also, through necessity, were advanced to the rank of knights. The battle was delayed only till the next day, the Turks being now so ferocious as to prepare their engines, and to meditate an attack on the walls of Joppa. This was prevented by the activity of Baldwin, and by the cross of Christ preceding them, which had been wanting in the former battle. They then, with all the force of the kingdom, rushed eagerly on the enemy, and the contest was fierce: but they, after their usual custom, surrounding our troops, thought they had completely overcome the Christians, and shouted with cheerful cry: but the Lord Jesus was present; who, at length looked down from heaven, and showering courage on the Franks, put the enemy, driven from the field, to flight. It had happened in the preceding action, that, though frequently driven from their tents, they afterwards conquered through their numbers; but now, as the infantry wounded them from a distance with their arrows, and the cavalry close at hand with their lances, they placed all their hopes in swiftness, and continued their flight.

He fought another battle in later years, in which our soldiers, pressed by the numbers of the Turks and compelled to fly, lost even their protecting standard. But after they had fled some distance they rallied; shame animating the timid to repel such ignominy. Then indeed the contest was strenuous; fighting foot to foot, and breast to breast. Our party recovered the cross, routing the enemy, and regaining the field. Many fell here with whom I had been acquainted; among these was Godfrey, Baldwin's bastard-grand-nephew, who, from a boy, manifested valour in his countenance and truth in his soul. In the beginning, indeed, both retreats, as it may be said, were the source of ignominy; but, in the end, true food for glory; the one more celebrated, the other more advantageous. Finally, to repair his losses, and also to be united with him in marriage, the countess of Sicily came shortly after to Jerusalem, pouring such treasures into the royal palace, that it was matter of surprise, whence a woman could accumulate such endless heaps of precious utensils:* and at this time, indeed, he received her to his bed, but shortly after he put her away. It is said that she was afflicted with a cancerous complaint, which preyed upon her womb.† This, however, is well known, that the king had no issue; nor is it wonderful, that a man, to whom leisure was burdensome, should be averse to the embraces of a wife, as he passed all his time in war. By these exertions he effected, that his admirable and nearly godlike valour should operate as an incitement to the present race, and be matter of astonishment to posterity. He died, during an expedition into Arabia, in the month of April, and was publicly buried at Jerusalem, near his brother, as the fourth month was adding to the seventeenth year of his reign. He was a man who gained his reputation by repeated labours, and on whose fame envy hath cast no shade, except it be, that he was too sparing of his money; though there is a ready and wellfounded excuse for such a fault, if it be considered, that the necessary largesses to such as remained with him, prevented him from purchasing the favour of those who departed.

He was succeeded by his kinsman, Baldwin, prince of Edessa, already celebrated for his former campaigns, whom he had, when dying, named as king. He bravely defended the kingdom for many years, and augmented it with the sovereignty of Antioch, which he obtained when Roger,‡ the son of Richard, was killed. He governed both countries with laudable conduct; with less presumptuous haughtiness, per-

* Among a variety of instances adduced of her wealth, it is stated, that the mast of the vessel which conveyed her to Palestine, was covered with pure gold. Alb. Aquens. ap. Gesta Dei, p 373.

† Fulcher assigns a different reason for her being divorced. The king, being extremely ill and thinking he should not survive, recollected that he had another wife living, to whom he had been previously married at Edessa. Du Chesne, t. iv. 864. He had been twice married before. His first wife, an English woman, accompanied him on the Crusade, and died in Asia. the second, daughter of Taphnuz, an Armenian nobleman, following him, by sea, to Jerusalem, was taken by pirates; and being suspected of improper conduct during her absence, was, on her arrival at Jerusalem, about A. D. 1105, repudiated, and shut up in the convent of St. Anne. Alb. Aquens. ubi sup Guib. Abbat. Opera, p. 452.

‡ "Roger, prince-regent of Antioch, son of Richard, seneschal of Apulia, married Hodierna, sister of Baldwin II. He was slain in 1119."—HARDY.

haps, but with great and consummate prudence, though there are some who wound his fair fame, accusing him of excessive parsimony. Wherefore, last year, when the Turks had taken him, while riding a short distance from Jerusalem, his people grieved but little for him, and for nearly a year it remained unknown, both to subjects and even to talebearers, whither he was taken, or whether or not he breathed the vital air. However, the people of Jerusalem, nothing discouraged on account of his absence, refused either to elect a king or to discontinue the order or command of the soldiers, till the certainty of the matter could be known. At last, the place where he lay captive being discovered, some knights of surpassing boldness, assuming the guise of merchants, and hiding weapons beneath their garments, entered the town, and rescued the king from jeopardy; protesting, that they did not act thus through respect for his niggardliness, but out of gratitude to Gozelin of Turbexhel,* who never hesitated to bestow all he possibly could upon the military. He has now lived long, a provident man, and subject to no other imputation.† The principality of Antioch pertains to the son of Boamund, of whom I proceed to speak.

Boamund‡ was the son of Robert Guiscard by a Norman woman; he had another son named Roger, born of an Apulian, who was, by his father, surnamed "Purse," because his paternal and attentive observation had discovered, that, from a mere child, he had pleasure in counting money. As to Boamund, who was somewhat older, he never could retain anything, but even gave away his childish presents. Roger, therefore, received Apulia, which seemed to belong to him

* This account appears in some measure incorrect Gozelin and the king were both confined in the same castle. On its being seized Gozelin escaped, and collected troops to liberate his friends, who were now themselves besieged. But ere his arrival, the Turks had made themselves masters of the fortress and carried off the king, who did not recover his liberty for some time, and then only by paying a considerable ransom. Fulch. Carnot. et Will. Tyr. ap. Gesta Dei

† Baldwin died 21st August, A. D. 1131.—HARDY.

‡ Boamund was baptized Mark; but his father hearing a tale related of a giant named Buamund, gave him that appellation. When, after his captivity, he returned to France, many of the nobility requested him to stand for their children; this he acquiesced in, and giving them his own name, it became frequent in these parts, though before nearly unknown in the West. Ord. Vital. p. 817

in right of his mother: Boamund went with his father to the Durazzian war. And when the towns-people, through confidence of their walls, boasted, that the city was called Durachium,* because it could endure all sieges undismayed; and "I," said Guiscard, "am called Durandus; and I will endure in besieging, until I take away the name from the city; so that, henceforth it shall no longer be called Durachium, but Mollucium." The firmness of this answer so terrified them, that they immediately opened their gates. Thus, secure in his rear, he subdued, with the less difficulty, the other cities as far as Thessalonica. He had now arrived there, and had already, both by himself and by his son, taught Alexius that he might be overcome, when, beguiled by the treachery of his wife, he failed, by death, of a noble enterprise. Boamund, then, returning to Apulia, possessed some castles through his brother's indulgence, and acquired many others by his own courage and prudence. Indeed the dukedom had fallen to his brother only in appearance; all the most warlike spirits following him. Nor was this of light importance: for, observant of his father's purpose, he was averse to Guibert, and strongly espoused the cause of Urban; urging him, when hesitating, to proceed into France to the council of Clermont, whither the letters of Raymond earl of Provence, and of the bishop of Chorges, invited him. The council being ended, he readily embraced the opportunity, and transported his forces into Greece; and thence moving forward his army, he quietly awaited Raymond and Godfrey. Joining them on their arrival, he possessed great influence from his military skill and from his courage, which was never surpassed. But, as what he performed in company with others, only entitles him to a share in the general praise; and my former narrative has related how he had been taken prisoner; it may be proper to mention in what manner he rescued himself from captivity. When Danisman perceived that no advantage resulted to him, from detaining so great a man in confinement, he changed his intentions, and began sedulously to treat of terms of peace; for he was neither inclined to put him

* There is a play here on the words Mollucium and Durachium, intended to imply soft and hard, "mollis" and "durus," which it is not easy to translate.

to death, lest he should excite the fierce hatred of the Christians against himself; nor would he set him at liberty,* without the hope of a lasting peace. Boamund, therefore, promising the infidel perpetual amity, returned to Antioch, bringing with him the silver fetters with which he had been confined; and being favourably received by his people, he took possession of Laodicea, and the other cities which Tancred, lest he should have been thought slumbering in indolence, whilst his uncle was sighing in prison, had acquired during his captivity. Not long after he came into France, offering up, in honour of St. Leonard, the chains with which he had been burdened; for this saint† is said to be so especially powerful in loosing fetters, that the captive may freely carry away his chains, even in the sight of his enemies, who dare not mutter a syllable. He then married one of the daughters of the king of France, and sending another to Tancred, went to Apulia, followed by the French nobility, who deserted their country in hope of greater advantages, as well as to be eye-witnesses of what could be effected by that energetic valour, which was so universally extolled by fame. Wherefore arranging his affairs in Apulia, he again burst forth against Alexius; alleging as a cause of attacking him, his cruelty to the crusaders, for which he was very noted. But being deceived by the subtlety of the emperor, who alienated his commanders from him by bribery, or took them off by poison, he had little or no success. Dejected at this, he returned to Apulia, where, in a few days, while purposing to proceed to Antioch, he died, not an old man, yet equal to any in prudence, leaving a son of tender age. He was a man firm in adversity, and circumspect in prosperity; for he had even provided himself an antidote, when apprehensive of poison. It was a knife, which, placed before him when eating, strange to tell, indicated, by the moistness of

* Orderic. Vital. p. 797, gives a different account of his deliverance, and which has quite a romantic air.

† Leonard was godson to Clovis king of France, and obtained, through the favour of that monarch, that, whenever he should see any one who was in chains, he should immediately be set at liberty. At length it pleased God to honour him to that degree, that, if any person in confinement invoked his name, their chains immediately fell off, and they might depart, their keepers themselves having no power to prevent them. Vide Surius, Vitæ Sanct. Nov. 6.

its handle, whenever poison was brought into the apartment. After him Tancred presided over Antioch; a nephew worthy of such an uncle. Tancred was removed from this world by an early death, and Roger the son of Richard succeeded. Though rivalling the fame of his predecessors in battle, yet he incurred the disgrace of being avaricious. In consequence of this, when the soldiery avoided him, he engaged the Turks with a trifling stipendiary, and a small native force, and fell nobly revenging his death: for being taken by them, stripped of his armour, and commanded to yield up his sword, he refused to deliver it to any but the commander, as he considered all present unworthy to receive the surrender of so dignified a character. The unhappy chief gave credit to his specious words, and taking off his helmet, stretched out his hand to receive Roger's sword. When, indignant, and mustering all his remaining powers for the effort, he cut off the Turk's head, and being immediately stabbed, escaped the disgrace of slavery by the act his courage had suggested. Baldwin the second, king of Jerusalem, revenging his death in a signal manner, faithfully reserved the dominion of the city, and his daughter, for Boamund the son of Boamund.

Raymond was the son of the most noble William,* earl of Toulouse, who, being a man of enterprise and ability, rendered his country, which had been obscured through the indolence of his predecessors, illustrious by his own good qualities. His wife Almodis was repeatedly married to different persons, and had a numerous issue by them all; a woman of such sad, unbridled lewdness, that, when one husband became disgusting to her from long intercourse, she would depart and take up her abode with another: to sum up all, she had been first united to the earl of Arles; presently, becoming weary of him, she connected herself with William; and then after bearing him two sons, she lured the earl of Barcelona to marry her. Moreover, William, when at the point of death, gave to his son of his own name but not of his own disposition, the county of Toulouse, because, though he was of slender talents, the people of Toulouse would attempt no innovation against him, as they were accustomed to the government of his family. But Raymond,

* He is called Pontius in Bouquet, Rec. 13, 7.

who was of brighter abilities, received Chorges, and increased it wonderfully by the addition of Arles, Narbonne, Provence, and Limoges. Again, he purchased Toulouse of his brother who went to Jerusalem many years previous to the grand crusade; but these things were achieved by a considerable lapse of time, and a life expended on the labour. Thus, ever engaged in war, he had no desire for a legitimate wife, enjoying himself in unrestrained concubinage. Finally, he condescended to honour with his adoption and inheritance, Bertrand, his son by one of his mistresses, as he, in some respects, resembled his father. To this son he married the niece* of Matilda the marchioness, a native of Lombardy, that by such affinity he might secure his possessions on that side. In the latter part of his life, too, he himself espoused the daughter of the king of Tarragona, covenanting for a noble dowry; namely, the perpetual peace of the adjacent provinces. Soon after this, on contemplating his grey hairs, he made a vow to go to Jerusalem, that his bodily powers, though decayed and feeble, might still, though late, enter into the service of God. The chief promoter of this was the bishop of Chorges, by whose especial exertions he had always been thwarted, and in one contest, had even lost an eye, which mark of deformity, so far from concealing, he was ever anxious to show, boasting of it as a proof of his gallantry. But now, leagued in mutual friendship, that they might employ their old age in religious services, they stimulated Urban, already inclined to preach the crusade, to pass the Alps and summon a council at Clermont, more especially as it was a city adjacent to their territories, and convenient for persons coming from every part of France. The bishop, however, died on his way to the council. To his influence succeeded the bishop of Puy, of whom we have before spoken: animated by whose advice, and protected by whose assistance, Raymond was the first layman who assumed the cross; making this addition to his vow, "that he would never return to his country, but endeavour to lessen the weight of his past offences by perpetual exertion against the Turks." He had already given many proofs of his prowess on the way,—the first to labour and the last to rest; many also of

* Helena, daughter of Otho I duke of Burgundy. Bouquet, Rec. 13, 7.

forbearance, as he readily relinquished those places he had first occupied at Antioch to Boamund, and the tower of David to Godfrey. But at length, his patience being worn out by the unreasonable demands of certain persons, he departed from his usual practice on the subject of the surrender of Ascalon. For, on the first arrival of the Franks, the townspeople, examining the disposition of our several commanders, made choice of him for their patron; because many men, who had come thither before by sea, from Montpelier to trade, had extolled his sincerity and courage to the skies. In consequence, they delivered to him their keys, and compelled him to make oath that he would never give up the command of the city to any other of the Christians, should he himself be either unwilling or unable to retain it. A murmuring then arose among the chiefs, who required the surrender of the city to the king; saying that his kingdom was of little value, unless he could hold Ascalon, which would be a receptacle for the enemy and an obstacle to our party. The king, indeed, set forth the matter mildly, as he did everything else, with a placid countenance consistent with his manners; the others rather more violently. However, he paid little attention to their words, obviating their allegations by very substantial reasons; saying that all his associates had secured a place of retreat; part of them had returned home; part were occupying the provinces they had acquired; that he alone, having abjured his native country, could neither return thither, nor did he possess a place of refuge here; that he had yielded in other points, but they must allow him to retain Ascalon, under fealty to the Holy Sepulchre, as he had taken an oath not to give it up. On hearing this, all began to clamour, and to call him interested and faithless; indeed they could scarcely abstain from laying hands on him. The earl, indignant at this reproach, failed in the duty of a just and upright man, delivering the keys to the enemies of God, and compensating the fear of perjury by the blood of many a man in after time; for to this day that city has never been taken either by force or by stratagem.

Moreover, many of his people, delighted with the unbounded affluence of the place, obtained the friendship of its citizens by denying their faith. Thus leaving Jerusalem, he came to Laodicea, and having subdued it, continued there some little time. Afterwards, when he had gone to Constantinople, Tancred obtained Laodicea, though it is dubious whether by force or favour. In the meantime, remaining at Byzantium, he contrived by his consummate prudence to insinuate himself into the favour of Alexius. Whence it happened, that, through the kindness of the emperor, getting a safe passage, he escaped sharing those calamities which, as we have before related, befell William of Poitou and the others; with whom he took the city of Tortosa, and, when the rest proceeded onwards, retained possession of it. To extend his power, he fortified a town over against Tripoli, called Pilgrim's Castle, where he appointed abbat Herbert, bishop. And that the shattered strength of his followers might recruit by repose, he made a seven years' league with the Tripolitans. Nevertheless, ere the time appointed, the peace was broken, on account of a certain townsman being found within the castle, with a poisoned dagger concealed beneath his garments. And now truly would he have put the finishing hand to the conquest of Tripoli, had not death, approaching almost immediately, bereft his vital spirit, big with great achievements. On learning his decease, William of Montpelier, and the other chiefs of the province, provided that William the Pilgrim, scarcely four years of age, whom he had begotten on a Spanish woman during the siege, should be conveyed home, to be educated for the succession, with the anxious wishes of all. Nor did Bertrand hear of this transaction with displeasure, although he had never been consulted, as it enabled him to renew his father's fame. Wherefore, heading a vast army, and chiefly supported by the Genoese and Pisans, who were allied to his wife, he attacked Tripoli by sea and land, and when exhausted by a protracted siege, reduced it to his dominion. To him succeeded Pontius, his son by the Lombard; a youth who rivalled the glory of his ancestors, and who obtained in marriage the relict of Tancred, formerly prince of Antioch. This, when dying, he had commanded; affirming, that, the youth would grow up a benefit to the Christians, and an utter destruction to the Turks. Pontius therefore reigns at Tripoli, professing himself the servant of the Holy Sepulchre, in this respect following the example of his grandfather and father.

Robert, son of William the first king of England, was born in Normandy, and already considered as a youth of excellent courage, when his father came to England: of tried prowess, though of small stature and projecting belly. He passed his early years amid the warlike troops of his father, obedient to him in every respect: but in the vigorous heat of youth, led by the suggestions of his idle companions, he supposed he could obtain Normandy from the king, during his lifetime. But when William refused this, and drove away the youth by the blustering of his terrific voice, Robert departed indignantly, and harassed his country by perpetual attacks. His father laughed at first, and then added, "By the resurrection of God, this little Robin Short-boot will be a clever fellow;" for such was his appellation, from his small stature; though there was nothing else to find fault with; as he was neither ill-made, nor deficient in eloquence, nor was he wanting in courage or resources of mind. At length, however, the king was so transported with anger, that he denied him his last blessing and the inheritance of England; and it was with difficulty, and disgrace, that he could retain even Normandy. After nine years he gave proof of his manhood in the labours of the crusade, and in many instances appeared wonderful, as neither Christian nor pagan could ever unhorse him: but more especially in the battle of Antioch, where he graced the victory by a singular achievement. For when the Turks, as we have related, were suddenly dismayed and fled, and our party vehemently attacked them in disorder, Corbanach, their leader, mindful of his native valour, checked his horse, and rallied his people; calling them base slaves, and forgetful of their ancient conquests, in suffering themselves, the former conquerors of the east, to be driven from their territories by a strange, and almost unarmed people. At this reproach, many, resuming their courage, wheeled round, attacked the Franks, and compelled the nearest to give way, while Corbanach continued to animate his men, and to assault the enemy; nobly fulfilling his duty, both as a commander and a soldier. But now the Norman earl and Philip the clerk, son of Roger, earl of Montgomery, and Warin de Taney, a castle so named in Maine, who had before made a feint of retreating, exhorting each other with mutual spirit, turned round their horses, and each attacking his man, threw them to the ground. Here Corbanach, though he knew the earl, yet estimating him merely by his size, and thinking it inglorious to fly, atoned for the boldness of attacking him, by a speedy exit ; being instantly deprived of life. The Turks, who were already clamouring with boastful joy, on seeing his fall, now lost their lately-acquired hopes, and redoubled their flight. In this contest Warin fell: Robert, with Philip, gained the victory. The latter, who acquired renown by this service, but afterwards, as they report, closed an honourable career at Jerusalem, was celebrated for his learning as well as his military prowess. Robert, thus coming to Jerusalem, tarnished his glory by an indelible stain, in refusing a kingdom,* offered to him, as a king's son, by the consent of all ; and this, as it is asserted, not through awe of its dignity, but through the fear of endless labour. However, returning home, where he had reckoned on giving himself up to the full indulgence of sensual pleasure, God mercifully visited him, as I believe, for this transgression ; every where thwarting him, and turning all his enjoyments into bitterness ; as will be manifested by the sequel.

His wife, the daughter of William de Conversano, whom he had married in Apulia on his return, and whose surpassing beauty, all endeavours to describe are vain, died after a few years, by disease ;† misled, as it is said, by the advice of the midwife, who had ordered her breasts, when in childbed, to be bound with a tight bandage, on account of the copious flow of her milk. A great consolation, however, in this extreme distress, was a son by his consort ; who, called William by presage of his grandfather's name, gave hope of noble talents hereafter. The immense sum which his father-in-law had given him, under the appellation of dowry, that

* None of the original historians of the crusade mention Robert, by name, as refusing the crown. Henry of Huntingdon however records it, and Albertus Aquensis observes, that it was first offered to Raymond, earl of Toulouse, who declining to accept it, and the other chiefs in succession following his example, Godfrey was, with difficulty, prevailed on to ascend the throne. Alb. Aquens. l. vi. c. 33. and Villehardouin, No. 136.

† " Sibilla, duchess of Normandy, died by poison, according to Ordericus Vitalis, and the Continuator of William of Jumièges. Malmesbury's account does not appear to be supported by any contemporary testimony."—HARDY.

he might with it redeem Normandy,* he lavished so profusely on buffoons, and worthless people, that, in a few days, he was pennyless. He accelerated his disgrace by his ill-advised arrival in England, to wrest the kingdom from his brother Henry; but, failing of the assistance of the traitors who had invited him, he easily yielded to his brother's terms of peace: which, by the agreement of the chiefs of either party, were, that, he should receive an annual present of three thousand marks from England. These were mere words: for the king had promised this without any design of fulfilling it; but, aware of his brother's easiness, had deluded his soft credulity, till his warlike passion should subside. And he, too, as if contending with fortune whether she should give or he squander most, discovering the mere wish of the queen, silently intreating it, kindly forgave the payment of this immense sum for ever; thinking it a very great matter, that female pride should condescend to ask a favour; for he was her godfather. Moreover he forgot offences, and forgave faults beyond what he ought to have done: he answered all who applied to him, exactly as they wished; and that he might not dismiss them in sadness, promised to give what was out of his power. By this suavity of disposition, with which he ought to have acquired the commendations and the love of his subjects, he so excited the contempt of the Normans, that they considered him as of no consequence whatever. For then, all the nobility falling at variance, plunder was universal, and the commonalty were pillaged. Although the inhabitants laid their injuries before the earl, they gained no kind of redress; for though incensed at first, yet his anger was soon appeased, either by a trifling present, or the lapse of time. Roused, however, by the extremity of their distresses, they determined to implore the assistance of king Henry to their suffering country. Henry, according to Cæsar's axiom,† "That if justice is ever to be violated, it ought to be violated in favour of the citizens, and that you may be observant of duty in other points," transported his forces several times into Normandy to succour expiring

* "Normandy was only mortgaged for 10,000 marks, about the 100th part of its present value."—HARDY.

† Cicero de Offic. 1. iii. But Malmesbury seems to have thought it necessary to soften it; as Cæsar's axiom says, "for the sake of power."

justice, and at last was successful enough to subjugate the whole country, with the exception of Rouen, Falaise, and Caen. Robert was now reduced so low, as to wander, hardly to be recognised, through these towns, obtaining a precarious subsistence from the inhabitants. Disgusted at this, the people of Caen did not long regard their fidelity, but sending messengers to the king, they closed the gates of their city, with locks and bolts. Robert learning this, and wishing to escape, was hardly allowed to depart; his attendant, with the furniture of his chamber, being detained. Thence flying to Rouen, he had a conference with his lord, the king of France, and his relation, the earl of Flanders, on the subject of assistance; but obtaining none, he determined, as his last resource, to risk a general action. In which, through the persecution of fate, being taken prisoner, he was kept, by the laudable affection of his brother, in free custody till the day of his death; for he endured no evil but solitude, if that can be called solitude where, by the attention of his keepers, he was provided with abundance both of amusement and of food. He was confined, however, till he had survived all his companions in the Crusade, nor was he liberated to the day of his death.* He was so eloquent in his native tongue, that none could be more pleasant; in other men's affairs, no counsellor was more excellent; in military skill equal to any; yet, through the easiness of his disposition, was he ever esteemed unfit to have the management of the state. But since I have already said all that I knew of Hugh the Great, and of the earls of Blois and of Flanders, I think I may, very properly here conclude my Fourth Book.

* Instead of these words "nor was he liberated, &c.," another manuscript reads, "and whether he ever will be set free, is doubtful." Upon which Mr. Hardy observes that these various readings of the MSS. seem to mark the periods when the author composed and amended his history. In other words, the reading in the text was substituted by the author, when he revised his work after Robert's death, for the reading in the note, which is copied from a MS written whilst Robert was still in prison.

BOOK V.

PREFACE.

SUMMONED by the progress of events, we have entered on the times of king Henry; to transmit whose actions to posterity, requires an abler hand than ours. For, were only those particulars recorded which have reached our knowledge, they would weary the most eloquent, and might overload a library. Who, then, will attempt to unfold in detail all his profound counsels, all his royal achievements? These are matters too deep for me, and require more leisure than I possess. Scarcely Cicero himself, whose eloquence is venerated by all the Western world, would attempt it in prose; and in verse, not even a rival of the Mantuan Bard. In addition to this, it is to be observed, that while I, who am a man of retired habits, and far from the secrets of a court, withhold my assent from doubtful relators, being ignorant of his greater achievements, I touch only on a few events. Wherefore, it is to be feared, that where my information falls beneath my wishes, the hero, whose numerous exploits I omit, may appear to suffer. However, for this, if it be a fault, I shall have a good excuse with him who shall recollect that I could not be acquainted with the whole of his transactions, nor ought I to relate even all that I did know. The insignificance of my condition effects the one; the disgust of my readers would be excited by the other. This fifth book, then, will display some few of his deeds, while fame, no doubt, will blazon the rest, and lasting memory transmit them to posterity. Nor will it deviate from the design of the preceding four, but particularise some things which happened during his time here and elsewhere, which perchance are either unrecorded, or unknown to many: they will occupy, indeed, a considerable portion of the volume, while I must claim the usual indulgence for long digressions, as well in this as in the others.

Of Henry the First. [A.D. 1100—1129.]

HENRY, the youngest son of William the Great, was born in England* the third year after his father's arrival; a child, even at that time, fondly cherished by the joint good wishes of all, as being the only one of William's sons born in royalty, and to whom the kingdom seemed to pertain. The early years of instruction he passed in liberal arts, and so thoroughly imbibed the sweets of learning, that no warlike commotions, no pressure of business, could ever erase them from his noble mind: although he neither read much openly, nor displayed his attainments except sparingly. His learning, however, to speak the truth, though obtained by snatches, assisted him much in the science of governing; according to that saying of Plato, "Happy would be the commonwealth, if philosophers governed, or kings would be philosophers." Not slenderly tinctured by philosophy, then, by degrees, in process of time, he learned how to restrain the people with lenity; nor did he ever suffer his soldiers to engage but where he saw a pressing emergency. In this manner, by learning, he trained his early years to the hope of the kingdom; and often in his father's hearing made use of the proverb, that "An illiterate king is a crowned ass." They relate, too, that his father, observing his disposition, never omitted any means of cherishing his lively prudence; and that once, when he had been ill-used by one of his brothers, and was in tears, he spirited him up, by saying, "Weep not, my boy, you too will be a king."

In the twenty-first year,† then, of his father's reign, when he was nineteen years of age, he was knighted by him at Westminster during Pentecost; and then accompanying him to Normandy, was, shortly after, present at his funeral; the other brothers departing whither their hopes led them, as my former narrative has related. Wherefore, supported by the blessing of his father, together with his maternal inheritance and immense treasures, he paid little regard to the haughti-

* "Henry was born in 1068, not in 1070, as stated by Ordericus Vitalis, (Annal. Burton, apud Fell, inter Rer. Anglic. Script. v. p. 246.)"—HARDY.
† "William the Conqueror was abroad at Pentecost in the 21st year of his reign, A.D. 1087. Henry undoubtedly received knighthood in the year 1086, in the 20th year of his father's reign."—HARDY.

ness of his brothers; assisting or opposing each of them as they merited. More attached, however, to Robert for his mildness, he took every means of stimulating his remissness by his own spirit. Robert, on the other hand, through blameable credulity, trusting to tale-bearers, injured his innocent brother in a way which it may not be irrelevant briefly to relate.

At the time when the nobility of England were rebelling against William the Second, while Robert was waiting a wind to sail over from Normandy, Henry had, by his command, departed into Brittany; when, eagerly seizing the opportunity, he expended on his troops all the large sum of money, amounting to three thousand marks, which had been bequeathed to the young man by the will of his father. Henry, on his return, though perhaps he endured this with difficulty, yet observed a cautious silence on the subject. However, hearing of the restoration of peace in England, the service was ended, and they laid aside their arms. The earl retired to his own territories: Henry to those which his brother had either given, or promised to give him. Indeed he placed his promises to account, retaining the tower of Rouen under fealty to Robert. But, by the accusation of some very infamous persons, his fidelity proved disadvantageous to him; and for no fault on his part, Henry was, in this very place, detained in free custody, lest he should escape the vigilance of his keepers. Released at the expiration of half a year, on the invitation of his brother William he offered him his services; but he, remunerating the young man no better, put him off, though in distress, with empty promises for more than a year. Wherefore, Robert, by his messengers, offering reparation for what had been done, he came to Normandy; having experienced attempts on his person from each of his brothers. For the king, angry at his departure, had in vain commanded him to be detained: and the earl, swayed by the arts of his accusers, had changed his intention; so that, when lured to him by soothing measures, he would not easily suffer him to depart. But he, escaping every danger by the providence of God and his own prudent caution, compelled his brother gladly to accede to peace, by seizing Avranches and some other castles. Soon after, William coming into Normandy to revenge himself on his brother Robert, Henry manifested his regard to the earl at Rouen. Finally, the king's party coming thither in the day time, he spiritedly expelled them, when already, through the treachery of the citizens, they had over-run the whole city; sending a message to the earl, to oppose them in front, while he pressed upon their rear. In consequence of this transaction, one Conan was accused of treachery to the earl; who designed to cast him into chains: supposing that no greater calamity could be inflicted on the wretch, than dooming him to drag out a hated existence in prison. But Henry requested to have this Conan committed to his care; which being granted, he led him to the top of the tower at Rouen, and ordering him carefully to survey the surrounding territory from the heights of the citadel, ironically declaring it should all be his, he thrust him suddenly off the ramparts into the Seine below; protesting to his companions, who at the same time assisted him, that no respite was due to a traitor; that the injuries of a stranger might be endured in some manner or other; but that the punishment of a man who with an oath had done homage, when once convicted of perfidy, never should be deferred. This action weighed little with Robert, who was a man of changeable disposition, for he immediately became ungrateful, and compelled his deserving brother to retire from the city. This was the period in which, as has been before mentioned, Henry, as well for his security as for his fame, made a stand against both Robert and William at Mount St. Michael's. Thus, though he had been faithful and serviceable to either brother, they, vouchsafing no establishment to the young man, trained him up, as he grew in years, to greater prudence, from the scantiness of his means.

But on the violent death of king William, as before related, after the solemnization of the royal funeral, he was elected king; though some trifling dissensions had first arisen among the nobility which were allayed chiefly through the exertions of Henry earl of Warwick, a man of unblemished integrity, with whom he had long been in the strictest intimacy. He immediately promulgated an edict throughout England, annulling the illegal ordinances* of his brother, and of Ranulph; he remitted taxes; released prisoners; drove the flagitious from court; restored the nightly use

* Wilkins, Leges Anglo-Saxonicæ, 233.

of lights within the palace, which had been omitted in his brother's time;* and renewed the operation of the ancient laws,† confirming them with his own oath, and that of the nobility, that they might not be eluded. A joyful day then seemed to dawn on the people, when the light of fair promise shone forth after such repeated clouds of distress. And that nothing might be wanting to the aggregate of happiness, Ranulf, the dregs of iniquity, was cast into the gloom of a prison, and speedy messengers were despatched to recall Anselm. Wherefore, all vying in joyous acclamation, Henry was crowned king at London, on the nones of August, four days after his brother's death. These acts were the more sedulously performed, lest the nobility should be induced to repent their choice; as a rumour prevailed, that Robert earl of Normandy, returning from Apulia, was just on the point of arriving. Soon after, his friends, and particularly the bishops, persuading him to give up meretricious pleasures and adopt legitimate wedlock, he married, on St. Martin's day, Matilda,‡ daughter of Malcolm king of Scotland, to whom he had long been greatly attached; little regarding the marriage portion, provided he could possess her whom he so ardently desired. For though she was of noble descent, being grand-niece of king Edward, by his brother Edmund, yet she possessed but little fortune, being an orphan, destitute of either parent; of whom there will be more ample matter of relation hereafter.

In the meantime, Robert, arriving in Normandy, recovered his earldom without any opposition; on hearing which, almost all the nobility of this country violated the fealty which they had sworn to the king: some without any cause; some feigning slight pretences, because he would not readily give them such lands as they coveted. Robert Fitz-Haymon, and Richard de Rivers, and Roger Bigod, and Robert earl of

---

* This has been taken to mean the abolition of the Curfew, by which it is said, all fires were ordered to be extinguished at eight o'clock; but it may be doubted, whether it does not rather refer to some regulation of the court merely.   † Those called the Confessor's.

‡ Matilda having taken the veil, though only for a purpose, scruples were raised as to the propriety of her entering the marriage state: a synod was therefore called at Lambeth by archbishop Anselm, and it was there determined that Matilda, not having voluntarily become a nun, might marry according to the law of God. See Edmer, pp. 56, 57.—HARDY.

Mellent, with his brother Henry, alone declared on the side of justice. But all the others either secretly sent for Robert to make him king, or openly branded their lord with sarcasms; calling him, Godric,* and his consort, Goddiva. Henry heard these taunts, and, with a terrific grin, deferring his anger, he repressed the contemptuous expressions cast on him by the madness of fools, by a studied silence; for he was a calm dissembler of his enmities, but, in due season, avenged them with fierceness. This tempest of the times was increased by the subtlety of Ranulf. For, concerting with his butler, he procured a rope to be sent him. The deceitful servant, who was water-bearer, carried him a very long one in a cask; by which he descended from the wall of the tower, but whether he hurt his arms, or grazed the skin off his hands, is a matter of no importance.† Escaping thence to Normandy, he stimulated the earl, already indignant and ripe for war, to come to England without a moment's delay.

In the second year, then, of Henry's reign, in the month of August, arriving at Portsmouth, he landed, divided and posted his forces over the whole district. Nor did the king give way to indolence, but collected an innumerable army over against him, to assert his dignity, should it be necessary. For, though the nobility deserted him, yet was his party strong; being espoused by archbishop Anselm, with his brother bishops, and all the English. In consequence, grateful to the inhabitants for their fidelity, and anxious for their safety, he frequently went through the ranks, instructing them how to elude the ferocity of the cavalry by opposing their shields, and how to return their strokes. By this he made them voluntarily demand the fight, perfectly fearless of the Normans. Men, however, of sounder counsel interfering, who observed, that the laws of natural affection must be violated should brothers meet in battle, they shaped their minds to peace; reflecting, that, if one fell, the other would be the weaker, as there was no surviving brother. Besides, a promise of three thousand marks deceived

---

* These appellations seem intended as sneers at the regular life of Henry and his queen. Godric implies God's kingdom or government.

† For the particulars of the bishop's escape, see Ordericus Vitalis p. 787.

the easy credulity of the earl; who imagined that, when he had disbanded his army, he might gratify his inclinations with such an immense sum of money: which, the very next year, he cheerfully surrendered to the queen's pleasure, because she desired it.

The following year Robert de Belesme, eldest son of Roger de Montgomery, rebelled, fortifying the castles of Bridgenorth and Arundel against the king; carrying thither corn from all the district round Shrewsbury, and every necessary which war requires. The castle of Shrewsbury, too, joined the rebellion, the Welsh being inclined to evil on every occasion. In consequence, the king, firm in mind and bearing down every adverse circumstance by valour, collecting an army, laid siege to Bridgenorth, from whence Robert had already retired to Arundel; presuming from the plenty of provision and the courage of the soldiers, that the place was abundantly secure. But, after a few days, the townsmen, impelled by remorse of conscience and by the bravery of the king's army, surrendered: on learning which, Arundel repressed its insolence; putting itself under the king's protection, with this remarkable condition; that its lord, without personal injury, should be suffered to retire to Normandy. Moreover, the people of Shrewsbury sent the keys of the castle to the king by Ralph, at that time abbat of Sees, and afterwards archbishop of Canterbury, as tokens of present submission, and pledges of their future obedience. Thus, this fire of dissension which was expected to become excessive, wasted to ashes in the course of very few days; and the avidity of the revolters, perpetually panting after innovation, was repressed. Robert, with his brothers, Ernulph, who had obtained the surname of his father, and Roger the Poitevin, so called because he had married his wife from that country, abjured England for ever; but the strictness of this oath was qualified with a proviso, "unless he should satisfy the king on some future occasion, by his obedient conduct."

The torch of war now lighted up in Normandy, receiving fresh fuel by the arrival of the traitors, blazed forth and seized every thing within its reach. Normandy, indeed, though not very wide in its extent, is a convenient and patient fosterer of the abandoned. Wherefore, for a long time, she well endures intestine broils ; and on the restoration of peace, rises soon to a state more fruitful than before ; at her pleasure ejecting her disturbers, when detected by the province, by an easy egress into France. Whereas England does not long endure the turbulent ; but when once received to her bosom, either surrenders, or puts them to death , neither, when laid waste by tumult, does she again soon rear her recovering head. Belesme, then, arriving in Normandy, had, both at that time and afterwards, accomplices in his malignity, and lest this should seem too little, inciters also. Among others was William earl of Moreton, the son of Robert, the king's uncle. He, from a boy, had been envious of Henry's fame, and had, more especially, on the arrival of the Norman, manifested his evil disposition. For not content with the two earldoms, of Moreton in Normandy, and Cornwall in England, he demanded from the king the earldom of Kent, which Odo his uncle had held ; so troublesome and presumptuous was he, that, with shameless arrogance, he vowed, that he would not put on his cloak till he could procure the inheritance derived to him from his uncle ; for such was his expression. But even then the king, with his characteristic circumspection, beguiled him by the subtlety of an ambiguous answer. The tumult, however, being allayed and tranquillity restored, he not only refused assent to his demand, but persisted in recovering what he unjustly retained ; though he did it with moderation, and the sanction of law, that none of his actions might appear illegal, or contrary to equity. William, ousted by the sentence of the law, retired, indignant and furious into Normandy. Here, in addition to his fruitless attacks upon the royal castles, he assailed Richard earl of Chester, the son of Hugh ; invading, plundering, and destroying some places which formed part of his possessions : the earl himself being at that time a minor, and under the protection and guardianship of the king.

These two persons, then, the leaders of faction and fomenters of rebellion, in conjunction with others whom I am ashamed to particularize, harassed the country, far and wide, with their devastations. Complaints from the suffering inhabitants on the subject of their injuries, though frequent, were lavished upon the earl in vain. He was moved by them, it is true ; but fearing on his own account, lest they should disturb his ease if offended, he dissembled his feelings. King Henry, however, felt deeply for his brother's infamy, carried to the highest pitch by the sufferings of the country: aware, that it was the extreme of cruelty, and far from a good king's duty, to suffer abandoned men to riot on the property of the poor. In consequence, he once admonished his brother, whom he had sent for into England, with fair words; but afterwards, arriving in Normandy, he severely reminded him, more than once, by arms, to act the prince rather than the monk. He also despoiled William, the instigator of these troubles, of every thing he had in England; razing his castles to the ground. But when he could, even thus, make no progress towards peace, the royal majesty long anxiously employed its thoughts, whether, regardless of fraternal affection, it should rescue the country from danger, or through blind regard, suffer it to continue in jeopardy. And indeed the common weal, and sense of right, would have yielded to motives of private affection, had not pope Paschal, as they say,* urged him, when hesitating, to the business by his letters: averring, with his powerful eloquence, that it would not be a civil war, but a signal benefit to a noble country. In consequence, passing over,† he, in a short time, took, or more properly speaking, received, the whole of Normandy; all flocking to his dominion, that he might provide, by his transcendent power, for the good of the exhausted province. Yet he achieved not this signal conquest without bloodshed; but lost many of his dearest associates. Among these was Roger of Gloucester, a tried soldier, who was struck on the head by a bolt from a crossbow, at the siege of Falaise; and Robert Fitz-Haymon, who receiving a blow on the temple, with a lance, and losing his faculties, survived a considerable time, almost in a state of

* "There is no vestige of this exhortation in any letter of pope Paschal to king Henry now known. Indeed Paschal, writing to archbishop Anselm, enjoins him to effect a reconciliation between the king and his brother. See Anselmi Opera, edit. nov. p. 382, col. 2."—HARDY.

† Orderic. Vital. [p. 815] relates a circumstance highly indicative of the troubled state of Normandy. Henry, on his arrival, was immediately welcomed by Serlo bishop of Sees; who, on conducting him into the church, pointed out the area nearly filled with boxes and packages brought thither for security from plunderers, by the inhabitants.

idiotcy.* They relate, that he was thus deservedly punished, because, for the sake of liberating him, king Henry had consumed the city of Bayeux, together with the principal church, with fire. Still, however, as we hope, they both atoned for it. For the king munificently repaired the damage of that church: and it is not easy to relate, how much Robert ennobled, by his favour, the monastery of Tewkesbury; where the splendour of the edifice, and the kindness of the monks, attract the eyes, and captivate the minds of the visitors. Fortune, however, to make up for the loss of these persons, put a finishing hand to the war, when at its height, and with little labour, gave his brother, when opposing him with no despicable force, together with William earl of Moreton, and Robert de Belesme, into his power. This battle was fought at Tenersebrey, a castle of the earl of Moreton's, on Saturday the Vigil of St. Michael. It was the same day, on which, about forty years before, William had first landed at Hastings: doubtless by the wise dispensation of God, that Normandy should be subjected to England on the same day that the Norman power had formerly arrived to subjugate that kingdom. Here was taken the earl of Moreton, who came thither to fulfil his promise of strenuous assistance to the townsmen, as well as in the hope of avenging his injuries. But, made captive, as I have related, he passed the residue of his life in the gloom of a prison; meriting some credit from the vivacity of his mind, and the activity of his youth, but deserving an unhappy end, from his perfidy. Then, too, Belesme† escaped death by flight at the first onset; but when, afterwards, he had irritated the king by secret faction, he also was taken; and being involved in the same jeopardy with the others, he was confined in prison as long as he lived. He was a man intolerable from the barbarity of his manners, and inexorable to the faults of others; remarkable besides for cruelty; and, among other instances, on account of some trifling fault of its father, he blinded his godchild, who was

* His daughter Mabil became the wife of Robert earl of Gloucester, to whom Malmesbury dedicated this work.

† Robert de Belesme was seized by order of king Henry in 1112, having come to him in Normandy as ambassador from the king of France to treat of peace. Robert was in the following year sent over to England, and confined in Wareham Castle until his death.—HARDY.

his hostage, tearing out the little wretch's eyes with his accursed nails: full of cunning and dissimulation, he used to deceive the credulous by the serenity of his countenance and the affability of his speech; though the same means terrified those who were acquainted with his malignity; as there was no greater proof of impending mischief, than his pretended mildness of address.

The king, thus splendidly successful, returned triumphant to his kingdom, having established such peace in Normandy as it had never known before; and such as even his father himself, with all his mighty pomp of words and actions, had never been able to accomplish. Rivalling his father also, in other respects, he restrained, by edict,* the exactions of the courtiers, thefts, rapine, and the violation of women; commanding the delinquents to be deprived of sight, as well as of their manhood. He also displayed singular diligence against the mintmasters, commonly called moneyers; suffering no counterfeiter, who had been convicted of deluding the ignorant by the practice of his roguery, to escape, without losing his hand.

Adopting the custom of his brother, he soothed the Scottish kings by his affability. For William made Duncan, the illegitimate son of Malcolm, a knight; and, on the death of his father, appointed him king of Scotland. When Duncan was taken off by the wickedness of his uncle Donald, he promoted Edgar to the kingdom; the abovementioned Donald being despatched by the contrivance of David, the youngest brother, and the power of William. Edgar yielding to fate, Henry made affinity with Alexander, his successor, giving him his illegitimate daughter in marriage, by whom he had no issue that I know of; and when she died, he did not much lament her loss: for there was, as they affirm, some defect about the lady, either in correctness of manners, or elegance of person. Alexander resting with his ancestors, David the youngest of Malcolm's sons, whom the king had made a knight and honoured with the marriage of a woman of quality, ascended the throne of Scotland. A youth more courtly than the rest, and who, polished, from a boy, by intercourse and

* "The laws of Henry I. have lately been reprinted in the 'Ancient Laws and Institutes of England,' under the able editorship of Mr. Thorpe."—HARDY.

familiarity with us, had rubbed off all the rust of Scottish barbarism. Finally, when he obtained the kingdom, he released from the payment of taxes, for three years, all such of his countrymen as would pay more attention to their dwellings, dress more elegantly, and feed more nicely. No history has ever recorded three kings, and at the same time brothers, who were of equal sanctity, or savoured so much of their mother's piety; for independently of their abstemiousness, their extensive charity, and their frequency in prayer, they so completely subdued the domestic vice of kings, that no report, even, prevailed, that any entered their bed except their legitimate wives, or that either of them had ever been guilty of any unlawful intercourse. Edmund was the only degenerate son of Margaret, who, partaking in his uncle Donald's crime, and bargaining for half his kingdom, had been accessary to his brother's death. But being taken, and doomed to perpetual imprisonment, he sincerely repented; and, on his near approach to death, ordered himself to be buried in his chains: confessing that he suffered deservedly for the crime of fratricide.

The Welsh, perpetually rebelling, were subjugated by the king in repeated expeditions, who, relying on a prudent expedient to quell their tumults, transported thither all the Flemings then resident in England. For that country contained such numbers of these people, who, in the time of his father, had come over from national relationship to his mother, that, from their numbers, they appeared burdensome to the kingdom. In consequence he settled them, with all their property and connexions, at Ross, a Welsh province, as in a common receptacle, both for the purpose of cleansing the kingdom, and repressing the brutal temerity of the enemy. Still, however, he did not neglect leading his expeditions thither, as circumstances required: in one of which, being privily aimed at with an arrow from a distance, though by whose audacity is unknown, he opportunely and fortunately escaped, by the interposition of his firmly mailed hauberk, and the counsel of God at the same time frustrating this treachery. But neither was the director of the arrow discovered at that time, nor could he ever after be detected, although the king immediately declared, that it was not let fly by a Welshman, but by a subject; swearing to it, by the death of our Lord, which was his customary oath when moved, either by excess of anger or the importance of the occasion. For at that very time the army was marching cautiously and slowly upon its own ground, not in an enemy's territory, and therefore nothing less was to be expected than an hostile attack. But, nevertheless, he desisted not from his purpose through fear of intestine danger, until the Welsh appeased the commotion of the royal spirit, by giving the sons of their nobility as hostages, together with some money, and much of their substance.

By dint of gold, too, he brought the inhabitants of Brittany to his views, whom, when a young man, he had had as neighbours to his castles of Danfrunt and Mount St. Michael's; for these are a race of people, poor at home, and seeking abroad to support a toilsome life by foreign service. Regardless of right and of affinity, they decline not even civil war, provided they are paid for it; and, in proportion to the remuneration, are ready to enter any service that may be offered. Aware of this custom, if, at any time he had need of stipendiary troops, he used to lavish money on these Bretons; thereby hiring the faith of a faithless nation.

In the beginning of his reign he offended Robert, earl of Flanders, from the following cause: Baldwin the Elder, the grandfather of this Robert, had powerfully assisted William, when going to England, by the wisdom of his councils, for which he was famed, and by a supply of soldiers. William had frequently made splendid returns for this; giving, every year, as they report, three hundred marks* of silver to his father-in-law, on account of his fidelity and affinity. This munificence was not diminished towards his son Baldwin; though it was dropped through the evil disposition of Robert Friso, as my history has already recorded. Moreover this Robert, the son of Friso, easily obtained the omitted largess from William the Second, because the one alleged his relationship, and the other possessed a boundless spirit in squandering money. But Henry giving the business deeper consideration, as a man who never desired to obtain money

* "It appears from two charters, printed in Rymer's Fœdera, vol. i. pp. 6, 7, that Henry agreed to pay a pension of four hundred marks, annually, to Robert, earl of Flanders, for the service of one thousand knights."—HARDY.

improperly, nor ever wantonly exhausted it when acquired, gave the following reply to Robert, on his return from Jerusalem, when imperiously making a demand, as it were, of three hundred marks of silver. He said, "that the kings of England were not accustomed to pay tribute to the Flemings; and that he would not tarnish the liberty of his ancestors by the stain of his cowardice; therefore, if he would trust to his generosity, he would willingly give him, as a kinsman and as a friend, whatever circumstances would permit; but if he thought proper to persist in his demand, he should refuse it altogether." Confuted by this reasoning, he, for a long time, cherished his indignation against Henry; but getting little or nothing by his enmity, he bent his mind to milder measures; having discovered that the king might be wrought upon by intreaty, but not by imperious insolence. But now, the change of times had given his son, Baldwin, matter of offence against Henry; for, wishing to place William,* the son of Robert the Norman, in his inheritance, he voluntarily busied himself in the affairs of others, and frequently made unexpected attacks upon the king's castles in Normandy. He threatened extreme trouble to the country, had the fates permitted; but engaging at Arques with a larger party of soldiers than he had apprehended, he accelerated his death; for his helmet being battered with repeated strokes, he received an injury in his brain. They relate, that his disorder was increased from having that day eaten garlic with goose, and that he did not even abstain from carnal intercourse at night. Here let posterity contemplate a noble specimen of royal attention; for the king sent a most skilful physician to the patient, bewailing, as we may believe, that person's perishing by disease, whom, through admiration of his valour, he had rather seen survive. Charles, his successor, never annoyed the king; and first, with a doubtful, but afterwards, a formal treaty, embraced his friendship.

Philip, king of France, was neither friendly nor hostile to our king, being more intent on gluttony than business; neither were his dominions situated in the vicinity of Henry's castles; for the few which he possessed at that time in

* "William, surnamed Clito [the Clito], son of Robert, duke of Normandy, and Sibilla de Conversano, succeeded to the earldom of Flanders upon the death of Charles le Bon, A. D. 1127."—HARDY.

Normandy were nearer to Brittany than France. Besides, as I have said before, Philip growing in years was oppressed by lust; and, allured by the beauty of the countess of Anjou, was enslaved to illicit passion for her. In consequence of his being excommunicated by the pope, no divine service could be celebrated in the town where he resided; but on his departure the chiming of the bells resounded on all sides, at which he expressed his stupid folly by laughter, saying, "You hear, my fair, how they drive us away."* He was held in such contempt by all the bishops of his kingdom, that no one, except William,† archbishop of Rouen, would marry them: the rashness of which deed he atoned for by being many years interdicted, and was with difficulty, at last, restored to apostolical communion by archbishop Anselm. In the mean while, no space of time could give satiety to Philip's mad excess, except that, in his last days, being seized with sickness, he took the monastic habit at Flory.‡ She acted with better grace and better success; as she sought the veil of a nun at Fontevrault, while yet possessed of strength and health, and undiminished beauty. Soon after she bade adieu to the present life: God, perhaps, foreseeing that the frame of a delicate woman could not endure the austerities of a monastery.

Lewis, the son of Philip, was very changeable; firmly attached to neither party. At first, extremely indignant against Robert, he instigated Henry to seize Normandy; seduced by what had been plundered from the English, and the vast wealth of the king. Not indeed, that the one offered it, but the other invited him; exhorting him, of his own accord, not to suffer the nerves of that once most flourishing country, to be crippled by his forbearance. But an enmity afterwards arose between them, on account of Theobald, earl of Blois, son of Stephen who fell at Ramula;

---

* He probably intended a joke on the custom of ringing the bells to scare evil spirits.

† "Ordericus Vitalis attributes this act to Odo, bishop of Bayeux; but Pope Urban II., in his Epistle to Raynald, archbishop of Rheims, ascribes it to Ursio, bishop of Senlis."—HARDY.

‡ "Although king Philip, a few years before his death, entertained some notion of embracing a monastic life, as is seen in the epistle written to him by Hugh, abbat of Cluni, yet it appears that he never carried his design into effect."—HARDY.

Theobald being the son of Stephen by Adala, daughter of William the Great. For a considerable time, messengers on the part of the king wasted their labour, entreating that Lewis would condescend to satisfy Theobald. But he, paying little regard to entreaties, caused Theobald to be excommunicated by the pope, as arrogant and a rebel to God; who, in addition to the austerity of his manners, which seemed intolerable to all, was represented as depriving his lord of his hereditary possessions. Their quarrel being thus of long continuance, when, each swollen with pride, neither would vail his consequence to the other, Lewis entered Normandy, proudly devastating every thing with overbearing violence. These things were reported to the king, who shut himself up in Rouen until the common soldiers infested his ears, by saying, "That he ought to allow Lewis to be driven back; a man who formerly kept his bed through corpulency, but was now, by Henry's forbearance, loading the very air with threats." The king, mindful of his father's example, rather preferred crushing the folly of the Frenchman by endurance, than repelling it by force. Moreover, he kindly soothed his soldiers, by addressing them to the following effect, "That they ought not to wonder if he avoided lavishing the blood of those whom he had proved to be faithful by repeated trials: that it would be impious, in achieving power to himself, to glory in the deaths of those persons who had devoted their lives to voluntary conflicts for his safety; that they were the adopted of his kingdom, the foster-children of his affection; wherefore he was anxious to follow the example of a good king, and by his own moderation to check the impetuosity of those whom he saw so ready to die for him." At last, when he beheld his forbearance wrongly interpreted, and denominated cowardice, insomuch that Lewis burnt and plundered within four miles of Rouen; he called up the powers of his soul with greater effort, and, arraying his troops, gloriously conquered: compensating his past forbearance by a sanguinary victory. But, however, soon afterwards, peace was concluded, "Because there is a change in all things, and money, which is capable of persuading what it lists, extenuates every injury." In consequence William, the son of our king, did homage to the king of France for Normandy, holding that province, in future, by legal right from him. This was the period when the same youth married the daughter of Fulco, earl of Anjou, and obtained, by the careful management of his father, that, through the mediation of money and of affinity, no tumults should affect the son.

At this time, pope Calixtus,* of whom I shall relate much hereafter, approached the confines of Normandy, where the king of England, entering into conference with him, compelled the Romans to admire and proclaim the ingenuity of the Normans. For he had come, as was reported, ill-disposed towards Henry; intending severely to expostulate with him, for keeping his brother, the pilgrim of the Holy Sepulchre, in confinement. But being pressed by the king's answer, which was specious, and by his plausible arguments, he had little to reply. For even common topics may avail, through eloquence of speech; and, more especially, that oratory cannot be despised, which is seasoned with valuable presents. And that nothing might be wanting to the aggregate of glory, he provided some youths of noble family, the sons of the earl of Mellent, to dispute with the cardinals in logic. To whose inextricable sophisms, when, from the liveliness of their arguments, they could make no resistance, the cardinals were not ashamed to confess, that the Western climes flourished with greater literary eminence, than they had ever heard of, or imagined, while yet in their own country. Wherefore, the issue of this conference, was, that the pope declared, that nothing could be more just than the king of England's cause; nothing more conspicuous than his prudence, or more copious than his eloquence.

The father of these youths was Robert, earl of Mellent, as I observed, the son of Roger de Beaumont, who built the monastery of Preaux in Normandy; a man of primitive simplicity and sincerity, who, being frequently invited by William the First, to come to England, and receive, as a recompence, whatever possessions he chose, always declined, saying, that he wished to cultivate the inheritance of his forefathers, rather than covet or invade foreign possessions which did not belong to him. He had two sons, Robert, of

* "Pope Calixtus met king Henry at Gisors on his return from the council at Rheims, held in October 1119."—HARDY.

whom we are speaking, and Henry. Henry earl of Warwick, a man of sweet and placid disposition, passed and ended his days, in occupations congenial to his habits. The other, more shrewd, and of a subtler character, in addition to his paternal inheritance in Normandy and large estates in England, purchased from the king of France a castle called Mellent, which Hugh the son of Gualeraun, his mother's brother, had held. Conducted gradually by budding hope towards fame in the time of the former kings, he attained to its full bloom in Henry's days; and his advice was regarded as though the oracle of God had been consulted. indeed he was deservedly esteemed to have obtained it, as he was of ripe age to counsel; the persuader of peace, the dissuader of strife, and capable of very speedily bringing about whatever he desired, from the powers of his eloquence. He possessed such mighty influence in England, as to change by his single example the long established modes of dress and of diet. Finally, the custom of one meal a day, is observed * in the palaces of all the nobility through his means; which he, adopting from Alexius, emperor of Constantinople, on the score of his health, spread, as I have observed, among the rest by his authority. He is blamed, as having done, and taught others to do this, more through want of liberality, than any fear of surfeit, or indigestion; but undeservedly: since no one, it is said, was more lavish in entertainments to others, or more moderate in himself. In law, he was the supporter of justice; in war, the insurer of victory: urging his lord the king to enforce the rigour of the statutes; himself not only following the existing, but proposing new ones: free himself from treachery towards the king, he was the avenger of it in others.†

Besides this personage king Henry had among his counsellors, Roger‡ bishop of Salisbury, on whose advice he prin-

* This practice is referred to by Henry Huntingdon, when speaking of Hardecanute, who had four repasts served up every day, "when in our times, through avarice, or as they pretend through disgust, the great set but one meal a day before their dependents."— H. Hunt. lib. vi. p. 209

† "Henry of Huntingdon, in his epistle to Walter (Anglia Sacra, pars ii., p. 695) gives a flattering character of Robert. Ordericus Vitalis places his death on the first June, A.D. 1118."—HARDY.

‡ Roger had a church in the neighbourhood of Caen, at the time that Henry was serving under his brother William. Passing that way, he

cipally relied. For, before his accession, he had made him regulator of his household, and on becoming king, having had proof of his abilities, appointed him first chancellor and then a bishop. The able discharge of his episcopal functions led to a hope that he might be deserving of a higher office. He therefore committed to his care the administration of the whole kingdom, whether he might be himself resident in England or absent in Normandy. The bishop refused to embroil himself in cares of such magnitude, until the three archbishops of Canterbury, Anselm, Ralph, William, and lastly the pope, enjoined him the duty of obedience. Henry was extremely eager to effect this, aware that Roger would faithfully perform every thing for his advantage. Nor did he deceive the royal expectation; but conducted himself with so much integrity and diligence, that not a spark of envy was kindled against him. Moreover, the king was frequently detained in Normandy, sometimes for three, sometimes four years, and sometimes for a longer period; and on his return to his kingdom, he gave credit to the chancellor's discretion for finding little or nothing to distress him. Amid all these affairs, he did not neglect his ecclesiastical duties, but daily diligently transacted them in the morning, that he might be more ready and undisturbed for other business. He was a prelate of a great mind, and spared no expense towards completing his designs, especially in buildings, which may be seen in other places, but more particularly at Salisbury and at Malmesbury. For there he erected extensive edifices, at vast cost, and with surpassing beauty; the courses of stone being so correctly laid that the joint deceives the eye, and leads it to imagine that the whole wall is composed of a single block. He built anew the church of Salisbury, and beautified it in such a manner that it yields to none in England, but surpasses many, so that he had just cause to say, "Lord, I have loved the glory of thy house."

entered in, and requested the priest to say mass. Roger began immediately, and got through his task so quickly that the prince's attendants unanimously declared, "no man so fit for chaplain to men of their profession." And when the royal youth said, "Follow me," he adhered as closely to him, as Peter did to his heavenly Lord uttering a similar command; for Peter, leaving his vessel, followed the King of kings; he, leaving his church, followed the prince, and appointed chaplain to himself and his troops, became "a blind guide to the blind." Vide G. Neubrig, 1. 6.

Murcard, king of Ireland, and his successors, whose names have not reached our notice, were so devotedly attached to our Henry that they wrote no letters but what tended to soothe him, and did nothing but what he commanded; although it may be observed that Murcard, from some unknown cause, acted, for a short time, rather superciliously towards the English; but soon after on the suspension of navigation and of foreign trade, his insolence subsided. For of what value could Ireland be if deprived of the merchandize of England? From poverty, or rather from the ignorance of the cultivators, the soil, unproductive of every good, engenders, without the cities, a rustic, filthy swarm of natives; but the English and French inhabit the cities in a greater degree of civilization through their mercantile traffic. Paul, earl of Orkney, though subject by hereditary right to the king of Norway, was so anxious to obtain the king's friendship, that he was perpetually sending him presents; for he was extremely fond of the wonders of distant countries, begging with great delight, as I have observed, from foreign kings, lions, leopards, lynxes, or camels,—animals which England does not produce. He had a park called Woodstock, in which he used to foster his favourites of this kind. He had placed there also a creature called a porcupine, sent to him by William of Montpelier; of which animal, Pliny the Elder, in the eighth book of his Natural History, and Isodorus, on Etymologies, relate that there is such a creature in Africa, which the inhabitants call of the urchin kind, covered with bristly hairs, which it naturally darts against the dogs when pursuing it: moreover, these are, as I have seen, more than a span long, sharp at each extremity, like the quills of a goose where the feather ceases, but rather thicker, and speckled, as it were, with black and white.

What more particularly distinguished Henry was that though frequently and long absent from his kingdom on account of the commotions in Normandy, yet he so restrained the rebellious, by the terror of his name, that peace remained undisturbed in England. In consequence, foreigners willingly resorted thither, as to the only haven of secure tranquillity. Finally, Siward king of Norway, in his early years comparable to the bravest heroes, having entered on a voyage to Jerusalem, and asking the king's permission, wintered in England. After expending vast sums upon the churches, as soon as the western breeze opened the gates of spring to soothe the ocean, he regained his vessels, and proceeding to sea, terrified the Balearic Isles, which are called Majorca and Minorca, by his arms, leaving them an easier conquest to the before-mentioned William of Montpelier. He thence proceeded to Jerusalem with all his ships in safety except one; she, while delaying to loose her cable from shore, was sucked into a tremendous whirlpool, which Paul* the historian of Lombardy describes as lying between the coasts of the Seine and Aquitaine, with such a force of water that its dashing may be heard at thirty miles' distance. Arriving at Jerusalem he, for the advancement of the Christian cause, laid siege to, battered, and subdued the maritime cities of Tyre and Sidon. Changing his route, and entering Constantinople, he fixed a ship, beaked with golden dragons, as a trophy, on the church of Sancta Sophia. His men dying in numbers in this city, he discovered a remedy for the disorder, by making the survivors drink wine more sparingly, and diluted with water; and this with singular sagacity; for pouring wine on the liver of a hog, and finding that it presently dissolved by the acridity of the liquor, he immediately conjectured that the same effect took place in men, and afterwards dissecting a dead body, he had ocular proof of it. Wherefore the emperor contemplating his sagacity and courage, which promised something great, was inclined to detain him. But he adroitly deluded the expectation in which he was already devouring the Norwegian gold; for, obtaining permission to go to a neighbouring city, he deposited with him the chests of his treasures, filled with lead and sealed up, as pledges of a very speedy return; by which contrivance the emperor was deceived, and the other returned home by land.

But my narrative must now return to Henry. He was

* "Paulus Diaconus, also called Winfrid, was secretary to Desiderius, last of the native princes of Lombardy. Paulus wrote his History of the Lombards, in six books, before the empire by Charlemagne was founded "— HARDY. Malmesbury seems to imply that the vessel was lost in the Mediterranean, but if so, he misunderstood Paulus Diaconus, who is speaking of the race of Alderney. Vide Paul. Diac. lib. i. c. 6, ap. Muratori. Rer. Ital. Script t. 1.

active in providing what would be beneficial to his empire;[*] firm in defending it; abstinent from war, as far as he could with honour; but when he had determined no longer to forbear, a most severe requiter of injuries, dissipating every opposing danger by the energy of his courage; constant in enmity or in affection towards all; giving too much indulgence to the tide of anger in the one, gratifying his royal magnanimity in the other; depressing his enemies indeed even to despair, and exalting his friends and dependants to an enviable condition. For philosophy propounds this to be the first or greatest concern of a good king,

" To spare the suppliant, but depress the proud."[†]

Inflexible in the administration of justice, he ruled the people with moderation; the nobility with condescension. Seeking after robbers and counterfeiters with the greatest diligence, and punishing them when discovered; neither was he by any means negligent in matters of lesser importance. When he heard that the tradesmen refused broken money,[‡] though of good silver, he commanded the whole of it to be broken, or cut in pieces. The measure of his own arm was applied to correct the false ell of the traders, and enjoined on all throughout England. He made a regulation for the followers of his court, at whichever of his possessions he might be resident, stating what they should accept without payment from the country-folks; and how much, and at what price, they should purchase; punishing the transgressors by a heavy pecuniary fine, or loss of life. In the beginning of

[*] Of Henry's prudent accommodation to the times, a curious anecdote is related by Ordericus Vitalis, p 815. When Serlo bishop of Sees met him on his arrival in Normandy, he made a long harangue on the enormities of the times, one of which was the bushyness of men's beards which resembled Saracens' rather than Christians', and which he supposes they would not clip lest the stumps should prick their mistresses' faces; another was their long locks. Henry immediately, to show his submission and repentance, submits his bushy honours to the bishop, who, taking a pair of shears from his trunk, trims his majesty and several of the principal nobility with his own hands.

[†] Virg. Æn. vi 853.

[‡] Whilst endeavouring to distinguish good coin from counterfeits, the silver penny was frequently broken, and then refused. Henry's order, therefore, that all should be broken, enabled any one immediately to ascertain the quality, and, at the same time, left no pretext for refusing it on account of its being broken money.—Vide Edmerum Hist. Novor. p. 94.

his reign, that he might awe the delinquents by the terror of example, he was more inclined to punish by deprivation of limb, afterwards by mulct. Thus, in consequence of the rectitude of his conduct, as is natural to man, he was venerated by the nobility, and beloved by the common people. If at any time the better sort, regardless of their plighted oath, wandered from the path of fidelity, he immediately recalled them to the straight road by the wisdom of his plans, and his unceasing exertions; bringing back the refractory to soundness of mind by the wounds he inflicted on their bodies. Nor can I easily describe what perpetual labour he employed on such persons, while suffering nothing to go unpunished which the delinquents had committed repugnant to his dignity. Normandy, as I have said before, was the chief source of his wars, in which, though principally resident, yet he took especial care for England; none daring to rebel, from the consideration of his courage and of his prudence. Nor, indeed, was he ever singled out for the attack of treachery, by reason of the rebellion of any of his nobles, through means of his attendants, except once; the author of which was a certain chamberlain, born of a plebeian father, but of distinguished consequence, as being keeper of the king's treasures; but, detected, and readily confessing his crime, he paid the severe penalty of his perfidy.* With this exception, secure during his whole life, the minds of all were restrained by fear, their conversation by regard for him.

He was of middle stature, exceeding the diminutive, but exceeded by the very tall: his hair was black, but scanty near the forehead; his eyes mildly bright; his chest brawny; his body fleshy: he was facetious in proper season, nor did multiplicity of business cause him to be less pleasant when he mixed in society. Not prone to personal combat, he verified the saying of Scipio Africanus, "My mother bore me a commander, not a soldier;" wherefore he was inferior in

* Suger relates, that Henry was so terrified by a conspiracy among his chamberlains, that he frequently changed his bed, increased his guards, and caused a shield and a sword to be constantly placed near him at night: and that the person here mentioned, who had been favoured and promoted in an especial manner by the king, was, on his detection, mercifully adjudged to lose only his eyes and his manhood, when he justly deserved hanging.—De Vit. Lud. Grossi. Duchesne, iv. 308.

wisdom to no king of modern time; and, as I may almost say, he clearly surpassed all his predecessors in England, and preferred contending by counsel, rather than by the sword. If he could, he conquered without bloodshed; if it was unavoidable, with as little as possible. He was free, during his whole life, from impure desires;* for, as we have learned from those who were well informed, he was led by female blandishments, not for the gratification of incontinency, but for the sake of issue; nor condescended to casual intercourse, unless where it might produce that effect; in this respect the master of his natural inclinations, not the passive slave of lust. He was plain in his diet, rather satisfying the calls of hunger, than surfeiting himself by variety of delicacies. He never drank but to allay thirst; execrating the least departure from temperance, both in himself and in those about him. He was heavy to sleep, which was interrupted by frequent snoring. His eloquence was rather unpremeditated than laboured; not rapid, but deliberate.

His piety towards God was laudable, for he built monasteries in England and in Normandy: but as he has not yet completed them, I, in the meantime, should suspend my judgment, did not my affection for the brotherhood at Reading forbid my silence. He built this monastery between the rivers Kennet and Thames, in a place calculated for the reception of almost all who might have occasion to travel to the more populous cities of England, where he placed monks of the Clugniac order, who are at this day a noble pattern of holiness, and an example of unwearied and delightful hospitality. Here may be seen what is peculiar to this place: for guests arriving every hour, consume more than the inmates themselves. Perhaps, some person may call me overhasty and a flatterer, for so signally celebrating a congregation yet in its infancy; unconscious what future times may produce: but they, as I hope, will endeavour, by the grace of God, to continue in virtue; and I blush not at commending men of holiness, and admiring that excellence in others which I possess not myself. He yielded up the investiture†

* " Compare Malmesbury's character of Henry in this particular with that given of him by Henry of Huntingdon."—HARDY.

† The ceremony of giving possession of lands or offices, was, by the feudal law, accompanied with the delivery of certain symbols. In con-

of the churches to God and St. Peter, after much controversy between him and archbishop Anselm, scarcely induced, even at last, to consent, through the manifold grace of God, by an inglorious victory over his brother. The tenor of these disputes Edmer has recorded at great length; I, to give a completer knowledge of the matter, shall subjoin the letters of the so-often-mentioned pope Paschal on the subject.

"Paschal the bishop to king Henry, health. From your letters, lately transmitted to us by your servant, our beloved son, William the clerk, we have been certified both of the safety of your person, and of those prosperous successes which the divine favour hath granted you in the subjugation of the adversaries of your kingdom. We have heard too, that you have had the male issue you so much desired, by your noble and religious consort. As we have derived pleasure from this, we think it a good opportunity to impress the commands and will of God more strongly upon you, at a time when you perceive yourself indebted to his kindness for such ample favours. We also are desirous of associating our kindness with the benefits of God towards you; but it is distressing, that you should seem to require what we cannot possibly grant. For if we consent, or suffer, that investitures be conferred by your excellence, no doubt it will be to the great detriment both of ourselves, and of you. In this matter we wish you to consider, what you lose by not performing, or gain by performing. For we, by such a prohibition, obtain no increase of influence, or patronage, over the churches; nor do we endeavour to take away any thing from your just power and right; but only that God's anger may be diminished towards you, and thus every prosperity attend you. God, indeed, hath said, 'Those that honour me, I will

---

formity to this practice, princes conferred bishoprics and abbeys by the delivery of a crozier and a ring, which was called their investiture: and as consecration could not take place till after investiture, this, in fact, implied their appointment also. The popes at length finding how much such a practice tended to render the clergy dependent on the temporal power, inhibited their receiving investiture from laymen by the staff and ring, which were emblems of their spiritual office. The compromise of Henry with Paschal enacted, that in future the king would not confer bishoprics by the staff and ring; but that the bishops should perform the ceremony of homage, in token of submission for their temporals. the election by these means, remaining, nominally, in the chapter, or monastery.

honour; and those that despise me, shall be lightly esteemed.' You will say then, 'It is my right;' no truly, it is neither an imperial nor royal, but a divine right; it is His only, who has said, 'I am the door:' wherefore I entreat for his sake, whose due it is, that you would restore and concede it to him, to whose love you owe what you possess. But why should we oppose your pleasure, or run counter to your good will, unless we were aware, that in consenting to this matter, we should oppose the will of God, and lose his favour? Why should we deny you any thing, which might be granted to any man living, when we should receive greater favours in return? Consider, my dearest son, whether it be an honour, or a disgrace that Anselm, the wisest, and most religious of the Gallican bishops, on this account, fears to be familiar with you, or to continue in your kingdom. What will those persons think, who have hitherto had such favourable accounts of you? What will they say, when this gets noised abroad? The very people who, before your face, commend your excess, will, when out of your presence, be the first more loudly to vilify the transaction. Return then to your understanding. my dearest son, we entreat you, for the mercy of God, and the love of his Only-begotten Son: recall your pastor, recall your father; and if, what we do not imagine, he hath in anything conducted himself harshly towards you, and hath opposed the investitures, we will mediate according to your pleasure, as far as God permits: but nevertheless, remove from your person and your kingdom the infamy of such an expulsion. If you do this, even although you should ask very difficult matters of us; still if, with God's permission, we can grant, you shall certainly obtain, them: and we will be careful to entreat the Lord for you, himself assisting, and will grant indulgence and absolution, as well to your sins, as to those of your consort, through the merits of the holy apostles. Moreover, we will, together with you, cherish the son whom you have begotten on your exemplary and noble consort; and who is, as we have heard, named after your excellent father, William, with such anxious care, that whosoever shall injure either you, or him, shall be regarded as having done injury to the church of Rome. Dated at the palace of Lateran, the ninth before the kalends of December."

"Paschal to Anselm. We have received those most gratifying letters of your affection, written with the pen of charity. In these we recognise the fervency of your devotion, and considering the strength of your faith, and the earnestness of your pious care, we rejoice; because, by the grace of God, neither promises elevate, nor threats depress you. We lament, however, that after having kindly received our brother bishops, the ambassadors of the king of England, they should, on their return home, report what we never uttered, or even thought of. For, we have heard, that they said, if the king conducted himself well in other respects, we should neither prohibit the investiture of the churches, nor anathematize them, when conferred; but that we were unwilling thus to write, lest from this precedent other princes should exclaim. Wherefore we call Jesus, who trieth the hearts and reins, as witness to our soul, if ever such a horrid crime, even entered our imagination, since we assumed the care of this holy see." And again below. "If, therefore, a lay hand present the staff, the sign of the shepherd's office, or the ring, the emblem of faith, what have the bishops to do in the church? Moreover, those bishops who have changed the truth into a lie, that truth, which is God, being the criterion, we separate from the favour of St. Peter and our society, until they have made satisfaction to the church of Rome. Such, therefore, as have received the investiture,* or consecration, during the aforesaid truce,† we regard as aliens to our communion and to the church."

"Paschal to Anselm. Since the condescension of Almighty God hath inclined the heart of the king of England to obedience to the papal see, we give thanks to the same God of mercies, in whose hand are situated the hearts of kings. We believe it indeed to have been effected through favour to your charity, and the earnestness of your prayers, that in this respect the heavenly mercy hath regarded the people

---

* The printed copy, as well as such manuscripts as have been consulted, read, "investituras consecrationum." evidently wrong; the true reading, as appears from Edmer, p. 72, where the whole instrument is inserted, being "investituram vel consecrationem."

† On Anselm's return, shortly after Henry's accession, it was agreed that all matters should remain in abeyance, until both parties should have sent messengers to the pope, for his decision on the subject of investitures. See Edmer, p. 56.

over whom your watchfulness presides. But whereas we so greatly condescend to the king and those who seem culpable, you must know that this has been done from kindness and compassion, that we may lift up those that are down. And you, also, reverend and dearest brother in Christ, we release from the prohibition or, as you conceive, excommunication, which, you understand, was denounced against investitures or homage by our predecessor of holy memory pope Urban. But do you, by the assistance of God, accept those persons who either receive investitures, or consecrate such as have received them, or do homage on making that satisfaction which we signify to you by our common legates William and Baldwin, faithful and true men, and absolve them by virtue of our authority. These you will either consecrate yourself, or command to be consecrated by such as you choose; unless perchance you should discover somewhat in them on account of which they ought to be deprived of their sacred honours. And if any, hereafter, in addition to the investitures of the churches, shall have accepted prelacies, even though they have done homage to the king, yet let them not, on this account, be denied the office of consecration, until by the grace of Almighty God, the heart of the king may be softened, by the dew of your preaching, to omit this. Moreover, against the bishops who have brought, as you know, a false report from us, our heart is more vehemently moved, because they have not only injured us, but have led astray the minds of many simple people, and impelled the king to want of charity for the papal see. Wherefore, by the help of God, we suffer not their crime to pass unpunished. but since the earnestness of our son the king unceasingly entreats for them, you will not deny, even them, the participation of your communion. Indeed, you will, according to our promise, absolve from their transgressions and from penance the king and his consort, and those nobles who for this business, together with the king, have by our command been under sentence, whose names you will learn from the information of the aforesaid William. We commit the cause of the bishop of Rouen to your consideration, and we grant to him whatsoever you may allow."

In this manner acted Paschal the supreme pope, anxious for the liberty of the churches of God. The bishops whom he accuses of falsehood, were Girard archbishop of York, and Herbert of Norwich, whose errors were discovered by the more veracious legates, William afterwards bishop of Exeter, and Baldwin monk of Bec. Anselm* the archbishop was now again, in the time of this king, an exile at Lyons, resident with Hugh, archbishop of that city, when the first letter which I have inserted was despatched, for he himself possessed no desire to return, nor did the king, through the multitude of sycophants, suffer his animosity to be appeased. He deferred, therefore, for a long time, recalling him or complying with the papal admonition; not from desire of power, but through the advice of the nobility, and particularly of the earl of Mellent, who, in this affair, running counter to reason more from ancient custom than a sense of right, alleged that the king's majesty must be much diminished if, disregarding the usage of his predecessors, he ceased to invest the elected person with the staff and ring. The king, however, considering more attentively what the clear reasoning of the epistles, and the bountiful gift of divine favours, plentifully showered down upon him, admonished, yielded up the investiture of the ring and staff for ever, retaining only the privilege of election and of the temporalities. A great council, therefore, of bishops, nobles, and abbats, being assembled at London, many points of ecclesiastical and secular business were settled, many differences adjusted. And not long after, five bishops were ordained in Kent, on the same day, by archbishop Anselm: William to the see of Winchester; Roger to Salisbury; William to Exeter; Reinald to Hereford; Urban to Glamorgan. In this manner a controversy, agitated by perpetual dissensions, and the cause of many a journey to and from Rome by Anselm, met with a commendable termination.

Henry's queen, Matilda, descended from an ancient and illustrious race of kings, daughter of the king of Scotland, as I have said before, had also given her attention to literature, being educated, from her infancy, among the nuns at Wilton and Romsey. Wherefore, in order to have a colour for refusing an ignoble alliance, which was more than once offered by her father, she wore the garb indicative of the

* He had been recalled on the king's accession, but afterwards quitted the kingdom again.

holy profession. This, when the king was about to advance her to his bed, became matter of controversy; nor could the archbishop be induced to consent to her marriage, but by the production of lawful witnesses, who swore that she had worn the veil on account of her suitors, but had never made her vow. Satisfied with a child of either sex, she ceased having issue, and enduring with complacency, when the king was elsewhere employed, the absence of the court, she continued many years at Westminster, yet was no part of royal magnificence wanting to her; but at all times crowds of visitants and talebearers were, in endless multitudes, entering and departing from her superb dwelling; for this the king's liberality commanded; this her own kindness and affability attracted. She was singularly holy; by no means despicable in point of beauty; a rival of her mother's piety; never committing any impropriety, as far as herself was concerned; and, with the exception of the king's bed, completely chaste and uncontaminated even by suspicion. Clad in hair cloth beneath her royal habit, in Lent, she trod the thresholds of the churches barefoot. Nor was she disgusted at washing the feet of the diseased; handling their ulcers dripping with corruption, and, finally, pressing their hands, for a long time together to her lips, and decking their table. She had a singular pleasure in hearing the service of God; and on this account was thoughtlessly prodigal towards clerks of melodious voice; addressed them kindly, gave to them liberally, and promised still more abundantly. Her generosity becoming universally known, crowds of scholars, equally famed for verse and for singing, came over; and happy did he account himself who could soothe the ears of the queen by the novelty of his song. Nor on these only did she lavish money, but on all sorts of men, especially foreigners, that through her presents they might proclaim her celebrity abroad; for the desire of fame is so rooted in the human mind, that scarcely is any one contented with the precious fruits of a good conscience, but is fondly anxious, if he does any thing laudable, to have it generally known. Hence, it was justly observed, the disposition crept upon the queen to reward all the foreigners she could, while the others were kept in suspense, sometimes with effectual, but oftener with empty promises. Hence, too, it arose that she fell into the error of prodigal givers; bringing many claims on her tenantry, exposing them to injuries, and taking away their property; by which obtaining the credit of a liberal benefactress, she little regarded their sarcasms. But whoso shall judge rightly, will impute this to the designs of her servants, who, harpy-like, conveyed everything they could gripe into their purses or wasted it in riotous living. Her ears being infected with the base insinuations of these people, she induced this stain on her noble mind, holy and meritorious in every other respect. Amid these concerns she was snatched away from her country, to the great loss of the people, but to her own advantage; for her funeral being splendidly celebrated at Westminster, she entered into rest; and her spirit manifested, by no trivial indications, that she was a resident in heaven. She died, willingly leaving the throne, after a reign of seventeen years and six months, experiencing the fate of her family, who almost all departed in the flower of their age. To her, but not immediately, succeeded Adala,* daughter of the duke of Louvain, which is the principal town of Lorraine.

By Matilda king Henry had a son named William, educated and destined to the succession,† with the fondest hope, and surpassing care. For to him, when scarcely twelve years of age, all the free men of England and Normandy, of every rank and condition, and under fealty to whatever lord, were obliged to submit themselves by homage, and by oath. When a boy, too, he was betrothed to and received in wedlock, the daughter of Fulco‡ earl of Anjou, who was herself scarcely marriageable; his father-in-law bestowing on him the county of Maine as her dower. Moreover, Fulco, proceeding to Jerusalem, committed his earldom to the king, to be restored, should he return, but otherwise,

* "Henry married Adala, daughter of Godfrey, conte de Louvain, in February, 1121."—HARDY.

† "Bromton (col. 1013, x Scrip.) ascribes to Malmesbury words which are no where to be found in this author, 'Willelmus Malmesbiriensis dicit, quod ille Willelmus regis primogenitus palam Anglis fuerat comminatus, quod, si aliquando super eos regnaret, faceret eos ad aratrum trahere quasi boves : sed spe sua coruscabili Dei vindicta cum aliis deperiit.'"—HARDY.

‡ "The nuptials of prince William with Matilda, daughter of the earl of Anjou, were celebrated in June, 1119, before the council of Rheims."—HARDY.

to go to his son-in-law. Many provinces, then, looked forward to the government of this boy: for it was supposed that the prediction of king Edward would be verified in him; and it was said, that now might it be expected, that the hopes of England, like the tree* cut down, would, through this youth, again blossom and bring forth fruit, and thus put an end to her sufferings: but God saw otherwise; for this illusion vanished into air, as an early day was hastening him to his fate. Indeed, by the exertions of his father-in-law, and of Theobald the son of Stephen, and of his aunt Adala, Lewis king of France conceded the legal possession of Normandy to the lad, on his doing him homage. The prudence of his truly careful father so arranged and contrived, that the homage, which he, from the extent of his empire, disdained to perform, should not be refused by his son, a youth of delicate habit, and not very likely to live. In discussing and peaceably settling these matters, the king spent the space of four years; continuing the whole of that time in Normandy. Nevertheless, the calm of this brilliant, and carefully concerted peace, this anxious, universal hope, was destroyed in an instant by the vicissitudes of human estate. For, giving orders for returning to England, the king set sail from Barfleur just before twilight on the seventh before the kalends of December; and the breeze which filled his sails conducted him safely to his kingdom and extensive fortunes. But the young man, who was now somewhat more than seventeen years of age, and, by his father's indulgence, possessed everything but the name of king, commanded another vessel to be prepared for himself; almost all the young nobility flocking around him, from similarity of youthful pursuits. The sailors, too, immoderately filled with wine, with that seaman's hilarity which their cups excited, exclaimed, that those who were now a-head must soon be left astern; for the ship was of the best construction, and recently fitted with new materials. When, therefore, it was now dark night, these imprudent youths, overwhelmed with liquor, launched the vessel from the shore. She flies swifter than the winged arrow, sweeping the rippling surface of the deep: but the carelessness of the intoxicated crew drove her on a

* See page 252.

rock, which rose above the waves not far from shore. In the greatest consternation, they immediately ran on deck, and with loud outcry got ready their boat-hooks, endeavouring, for a considerable time, to force the vessel off: but fortune resisted and frustrated every exertion. The oars, too, dashing, horribly crashed against the rock,* and her battered prow hung immoveably fixed. Now, too, the water washed some of the crew overboard, and, entering the chinks, drowned others; when the boat having been launched, the young prince was received into it, and might certainly have been saved by reaching the shore, had not his illegitimate sister, the countess of Perche, now struggling with death in the larger vessel, implored her brother's assistance; shrieking out that he should not abandon her so barbarously. Touched with pity, he ordered the boat to return to the ship, that he might rescue his sister; and thus the unhappy youth met his death through excess of affection: for the skiff, overcharged by the multitudes who leaped into her, sank, and buried all indiscriminately in the deep. One rustic† alone escaped; who, floating all night upon the mast, related in the morning, the dismal catastrophe of this tragedy. No ship was ever productive of so much misery to England; none ever so widely celebrated throughout the world. Here also perished with William, Richard, another of the king's sons, whom a woman of no rank had borne him, before his accession; a youth of intrepidity, and dear to his father from his obedience: Richard earl of Chester, and his brother Otuell, the tutor and preceptor of the king's son: the countess of Perche, the king's daughter, and his niece the countess of Chester, sister to Theobald: and indeed almost every person of consequence about court, whether knight, or chaplain, or young nobleman, training up to arms. For, as I have said, they eagerly hastened from all quarters, expecting no small addition to their reputation, if they could either amuse, or show their devotion to the young prince. The calamity was augmented by the difficulty of finding the bodies, which could not be discovered by the various persons who sought them along the

* Virgil Æneid. v. 206.
† He is called a butcher by Ordericus Vitalis, p. 867, who has many particulars of this event.

shore; but delicate as they were, they became food for the monsters of the deep. The death of this youth being known, produced a wonderful change in existing circumstances. His father renounced the celibacy he had cherished since Matilda's death, anxious for future heirs by a new consort: his father-in-law, returning home from Jerusalem, faithfully espoused the party of William, the son of Robert earl of Normandy, giving him his other daughter* in marriage, and the county of Maine; his indignation being excited against the king, by his daughter's dowry being detained in England after the death of the prince.

His daughter Matilda, by Matilda, king Henry gave in marriage to Henry emperor of Germany,† son of that Henry mentioned in the third book. Henry was the fifth emperor of the Germans of this name; who, although he had been extremely incensed at his father for his outrages against the holy see, yet, in his own time, was the rigid follower of, and stickler for, the same sentiments. For when Paschal, a man possessed of every virtue, had succeeded pope Urban, the question again arose concerning the investiture of the churches, together with all the former contentions and animosities: as neither party would give way. The emperor had in his favour all the bishops and abbats of his kingdoms situated on this side of the mountains; because Charles the Great, to keep in check the ferocity of those nations, had conferred almost all the country on the churches: most wisely considering, that the clergy would not so soon cast off their fidelity to their lord as the laity; and, besides, if the laity were to rebel, they might be restrained by the authority of their excommunication, and the weight of their power. The pope had brought over to his side the churches beyond the mountains, and the cities of Italy scarcely acknowledged the dominion of Henry, thinking themselves exonerated from servitude after the death of his brother Conrad, who, being left by his father as king of Lombardy, had died at Arezzo. But Henry, rivalling the ancient Cæsars in every

* "The marriage of William, son of the duke of Normandy, with Sibilla, in 1123, was dissolved, at the instance of king Henry, in the following year, by the pope's legate."—HARDY.

† "Matilda was betrothed to the emperor Henry V. in 1109, but was not married to him until the 7th January, 1114."—HARDY.

noble quality, after tranquillizing his German empire, extended his thoughts to his Italian kingdom: purposing to quell the revolt of the cities, and decide the question of investitures, according to his own pleasure. This progress to Rome, accomplished by great exertion of mind, and much painful labour of body, hath been described by David, bishop of Bangor, a Scot; though far more partially to the king than becomes an historian. Indeed he commends highly even his unheard-of violence in taking the pope captive, though he held him in free custody; citing the example of Jacob's holding the angel fast till he extorted a blessing. Moreover, he labours to establish, that the saying of the apostle, "No servant of God embroils himself in worldly business," is not repugnant to the desires of those bishops, who are invested by the laity, because the doing homage to a layman, by a clergyman, is not a secular business. How frivolous such arguments are, any person's consideration may decide. In the meantime, that I may not seem to bear hard on a good man by my judgment, I determine to make allowances for him, since he has not written a history, but a panegyric. I will now therefore faithfully insert the grant and agreement extorted from the pope, by a forcible detention of three weeks; and I shall subjoin, in what manner they were soon after made of none effect, by a holier council.

"The sovereign pope Paschal will not molest the sovereign king, nor his empire nor kingdom, on account of the investiture of bishoprics and abbeys, nor concerning the injury suffered by himself and his party in person and in goods; nor will he return evil to him, or any other person, on this account; neither, on any consideration, will he publish an anathema against the person of king Henry; nor will the sovereign pope delay to crown him, according to the ritual; and he will assist him, as far as possible, by the aid of his office, to retain his kingdom and empire. And this the sovereign pope will fulfil without fraud or evil design."
These are the names of the bishops and cardinals who, at the command of the sovereign pope Paschal, confirmed by oath the grant to, and friendship with, the sovereign emperor Henry: Peter, bishop of Porto; Censius, bishop of Sabina; Robert, cardinal of St. Eusebius; Boniface, cardinal

of St. Mark; Anastasius, cardinal of St. Clement; Gregory, cardinal of the apostles Peter and Paul; also Gregory, cardinal of St. Chrysogonus; John, cardinal of St. Potentiana; Risus, cardinal of St. Lawrence; Remerus, cardinal of Saints Marcellinus and Peter; Vitalis, cardinal of St. Balbina; Teuzo, cardinal of St. Mark; Theobald, cardinal of John and Paul; John, deacon in the Greek School;* Leo, dean of St. Vitalis; Albo, dean of Sergius and Bacchius.

The king also made oath as follows: "I, Henry, the king, will, on the fourth or fifth day of the ensuing week, set at liberty the sovereign pope, and the bishops and cardinals, and all the captives and hostages, who were taken for him or with him; and I will cause them to be conducted, safely, within the gates of the city, beyond the Tiber,† nor will I hereafter seize, or suffer to be seized, such as remain under fealty to the lord Paschal: and with the Roman people, and the city beyond the Tiber, I will, as well by myself as by my people, preserve peace and security, that is, to such persons as shall keep peace with me. I will faithfully assist the sovereign pope, in retaining his papacy quietly and securely. I will restore the patrimony and possessions of the Roman church which I have taken away; and I will aid him in recovering and keeping every thing which he ought to have, after the manner of his predecessors, with true faith, and without fraud or evil design: and I will obey the sovereign pope, saving the honour of my kingdom and empire, as Catholic emperors ought to obey Catholic Roman pontiffs." And they who swore on the part of the king are these: Frederic, archbishop of Cologne; Godebard, bishop of Trent; Bruno, bishop of Spires; Berengar, earl; Albert, chancellor; Herman, earl; Frederic, count palatine; Boniface, marquis; Albert, earl of Blandriac; Frederic, earl; Godfrid, earl; Warner, marquis.

This treaty being settled and confirmed by the oath of the aforesaid bishops and cardinals, and mutual embraces exchanged, the sovereign pope, on Sunday, the fourth before the ides of April, celebrated the mass, "As though just born,"

* The church of St. Maria, in Scuola Græca, is so called, from a tradition that St. Augustine, before his conversion, there taught rhetoric — See Lumisden, 318

† Trastevere, that part in which St. Peter's is situated.

in which, after his own communion, and that of the ministers at the altar, he gave the body and blood of our Lord to the emperor with these words: "This body of the Lord, which the truly holy church retains, born of the Virgin Mary, exalted on the cross for the redemption of mankind, we give to thee, my dearest son, for the remission of thy sins, and for the preservation of the peace and true friendship to be confirmed between me and thee, the empire and the priesthood." Again, on the next day, the pope and the king met at the columns* which are in the Forum, guards being stationed wherever it was deemed necessary, that the consecration of the king might not be impeded. And at the Silver† gate he was received by the bishops and cardinals, and all the Roman clergy; and the prayer being begun, as contained in the ritual, by the bishop of Ostia, as the bishop of Albano, by whom it ought to have been said, had he been present, was absent, he was conducted to the middle of the Rota,‡ and there received the second prayer from the bishop of Porto, as the Roman ritual enjoins. After this they led him, with litanies, to the confessionary of the Apostles, § and there the bishop of Ostia anointed him between the shoulders and on the right arm. This being done he was conducted, by the sovereign pontiff, to the altar of the aforesaid apostles, and there the crown being placed on his head by the pope himself, he was consecrated emperor. After putting on the crown, the mass of the Resurrection of the Lord was celebrated, in which, before the communion, the sovereign pope, with his own hand, gave to the emperor the grant, in which he conceded to him and his kingdom what is underwritten; and in the same place confirmed it by the sanction of a curse.

"Pope Paschal, servant of the servants of God, sendeth health and his apostolical benediction, to his dearest son in Christ, Henry Augustus, by the grace of Almighty God, emperor of the Romans. The Divine disposal hath ordained, that your kingdom shall unite with the holy Roman church,

* Three beautiful columns, supposed to be remains of the temple of Jupiter Stator.

† The principal entrance to St. Peter's church, so called by way of pre-eminence.

‡ The Rota, which seems to have been a part of St. Peter's church, is not enumerated by Fontana, de Basilica Vaticana.

§ The chapel, in which the tombs of the apostles are said to be placed.

since your predecessors, through valour and surpassing prudence, have obtained the crown and sovereignty of the Roman city; to the dignity of which crown and empire, the Divine Majesty, by the ministry of our priesthood, hath advanced your person, my dearest son Henry. That pre-eminence of dignity, then, which our predecessors have granted to yours, the Catholic emperors, and have confirmed in the volume of grants, we also concede to your affection, and in the scroll of this present grant confirm also, that you may confer the investiture of the staff and ring on the bishops or abbats of your kingdom, freely elected, without violence or simony: but, after their investiture, let them receive canonical consecration from the bishop to whom it pertains. But if any person shall be elected, either by the clergy or the people, against your consent, unless he be invested by you, let him be consecrated by no one; excepting such, indeed, as are accustomed to be at the disposal of the archbishops, or of the Roman pontiff. Moreover, let the archbishops or bishops have permission, canonically, to consecrate bishops or abbats invested by you. Your predecessors, indeed, so largely endowed the churches of their kingdom of their royalties, that it is fitting that kingdom should be especially strengthened by the power of bishops or abbats; and that popular dissensions, which often happen in all elections, should be checked by royal majesty. Wherefore, your prudence and authority ought to take more especial care to preserve the grandeur of the Roman church, and the safety of the rest, through God's assistance, by your gifts and services. Therefore, if any ecclesiastical or secular person, knowing this document of our concession, shall rashly dare oppose it, let him be bound with the chain of an anathema, unless he recant, and hazard his honour and dignity. But may God's mercy preserve such as keep it, and may he grant your person and authority to reign happily to his honour and glory."

The whole ceremony of the consecration being completed, the pope and the emperor, joining their right hands, went with much state to the chamber which fronts the confessionary of St. Gregory, that the pope might there put off his pontifical, and the emperor his regal vestments. As the emperor retired from the chamber divested of his royal insignia, the Roman patricians met him with a golden circle, which they placed upon his head, and by it gave him the supreme patriciate* of the Roman city, with common consent and universal approbation.

All this parade of grants and consecration I have taken literally from the narrative of the aforesaid David, written, as I said, with too great partiality towards the king. In the following year, however, a council was assembled at Rome, rather by the connivance than the command of the pope, and the grant was nullified. The authors of its reversal, were, the archbishop of Vienne, who afterwards ruled the papal see ;[†] and Girard, bishop of Angouleme : who stimulated their brother bishops, to make these concessions of none effect. The proceedings of that council were as follow.

"A.D. 1112, the fifth of the indiction, in the thirteenth year of the sovereign pope Paschal the second, in the month of March, on the fifteenth before the kalends of April, a council was held at Rome, at the Lateran, in the church of Constantine ;[‡] where, when pope Paschal, together with the archbishops, bishops, and cardinals and a mixed company of clergy and laity, had, on the last day of the council, taken his seat ; making public profession of the Catholic faith, lest any one should doubt his orthodoxy, he said, " I embrace all the Holy Scripture of the Old and New Testament; the Law written by Moses, and by the holy prophets : I embrace the four Gospels ; the seven canonical Epistles, the Epistles of the glorious preacher St. Paul, the apostle, the holy canons of the apostles ; the four Universal councils, as the four gospels, the Nicene, Ephesian, Constantinopolitan, Chalcedonian : moreover the council of Antioch and the decrees of the holy fathers, the Roman pontiffs ; and more especially the decrees of my lords pope Gregory the seventh, and pope Urban of blessed memory. What they have approved, I approve : what they held, I hold : what they have confirmed, I confirm : what they have condemned, I condemn : what they

* The patrician of Rome appears to have been its chief magistrate; derived from the office of prefect or patrician under the emperors of Constantinople.
† As pope Calixtus II.
‡ The church of St. Saviour, or St. John Lateran, built by Constantine the Great.

have opposed, I oppose: what they have interdicted, I interdict: what they have prohibited, I prohibit: I will persevere in the same in every thing and through every thing." This being ended, Girard, bishop of Angouleme, legate in Aquitaine, rose up for all, and by the unanimous consent of pope Paschal and of all the council, read the following writing. "That grant which is no grant, but ought more properly to be called an abomination,* for the liberation of captives and of the church, extorted from the sovereign pope Paschal by the violence of king Henry, the whole of us in this holy council assembled, with the sovereign pope, condemn by canonical censure, and ecclesiastical authority, by the judgment of the Holy Sprit; and we adjudge it to be void, and altogether nullify it: and that it may have neither force nor efficacy, we interdict it altogether. And it is condemned, on this account; because in that abomination it is asserted, that a person canonically elected by the clergy and the people, shall not be consecrated by any one, unless first invested by the king; which is contrary to the Holy Spirit and to canonical institution." This writing being read, the whole council, and all present, unanimously cried out Amen, Amen: So be it, so be it.

The archbishops there present with their suffragans were these: John, patriarch of Venice: Semies of Capua: Landulf of Benevento: Amalfi, Reggio, Otranto, Brindisi, Capsa, Cerenza;† and the Greeks, Rosanus, and the archbishop of St. Severina; the bishops were, Censius of Sabina, Peter of Porto, Leo of Ostia, Cono of Prænesti, Girard of Angouleme, Galo of Leon, legate for Berri and the archbishop of Vienne, Roger of Volaterra, Gaufrid of Sienna, Rolland of Populonia, Gregory of Tarracina, William of Turin,‡ William of Syracuse, legate for all the Sicilians, and near a hundred other bishops. Siwin, and John bishop of Tusculum, though at Rome, were not present on that day of the council; but they afterwards, on the reading of the condemnation of the grant, assented and approved of it.

These things gaining publicity, all France made no scruple

* MS. pravilegium, a play on the words privilegium and pravilegium
† Cosenza, L'Abbe, tom. x.
‡ Another MS. reads Troianus instead of Turianus.

of considering the emperor as accursed by the power of ecclesiastical zeal hurled against him. Roused at this, in the seventeenth* year of pope Paschal, he proceeded to Rome, to inflict signal vengeance on him. But he, by a blessed departure,† had avoided all earthly molestation, and from his place of repose on high, laughed at the threats of the angry emperor; who having heard of his death, quickened his journey, in order that ejecting John Gaitan, chancellor to the late pope, who had been already elected and called Gelasius, he might intrude Maurice,‡ bishop of Brague, surnamed Bourdin, on the See: but the following epistle of Gelasius will explain the business more fully.

"Gelasius, servant of the servants of God to the archbishops, bishops, abbats, clergy, princes, and other faithful people throughout Gaul, health. As you are members of the church of Rome, we are anxious to signify to your affection what has there lately taken place. Shortly after our election, then, the sovereign emperor coming by stealth and with unexpected haste to Rome, compelled us to depart the city. He afterwards demanded peace by threats and intimidation, saying he would do all he might be able, unless we assured him of peace by oath. To which we replied thus: Concerning the controversy which exists between the church and the empire, we willingly agree to a meeting or to legal discussion, at proper time and place; that is to say, either at Milan or Cremona, on the next feast of St. Luke, at the discretion of our brethren, who, by God, are constituted judges in the church, and without whom this cause cannot be agitated. And since the sovereign emperor demands security from us, we promise such to him, by word and by writing, unless in the interim himself shall violate it: for otherwise to give security is dishonourable to the church, and contrary to custom. He, immediately, on the forty-fourth day after our election, intruded into the bosom of the church, the bishop of Brague, who, the preceding year had been excommuni-

* "*Septimo decimo*] More correctly *octavo decimo*, as the emperor went before Easter in the year 1117."—HARDY.

† "Paschal died in Jan. 1118."—HARDY.

‡ "Maurice Bourdin, archbishop of Brague, was elected pope by the influence of the emperor Henry V, on the 9th of March, 1118, and took the name of Gregory VIII."—HARDY.

cated by our predecessor pope Paschal, in a council at Benevento; and who had also, when he formerly received the pall from our hands, sworn fidelity to the same pontiff, and his catholic successors, of whom I am the first. In this prodigious crime, however, thanks to God, the sovereign emperor had no single Roman associate; only the Guibertines, Romanus of St. Marcellus, Censius, who was called of St. Chrysogon; Teuzo, who for a long time was guilty of many excesses in Dacia; these alone transacted so shameless a deed. We command your wisdom, therefore, on the receipt of these presents, that, deliberating on these matters in common, by the grace of God, you be prepared, by his help, to avenge the mother church, as you are aware ought to be done by your joint assistance. Done at Gaeta on the seventeenth before the kalends of February."

Gelasius after his expulsion, embarking at Salerno, came thence to Genoa, and afterwards proceeded by land to Clugny, where he died.* Then, that is A.D. 1119, the cardinals who had accompanied him, together with the whole Cisalpine church, elevating with great pomp Guido, archbishop of Vienne, to the papacy, called him Calixtus; hoping, from the consideration of his piety and energy, that through his power, as he possessed great influence, they might be able to withstand the force of the emperor. Nor did he deceive their confidence: for soon after calling a council at Rheims, he separated from the churches such as had been, or should be, invested by the laity, including the emperor also, unless he should recant. Thus continuing for some time in the hither districts, to strengthen his party, and having settled all affairs in Gaul, he came to Rome, and was gladly received by the citizens, as the emperor had now departed. Bourdin then, deserted, fled to Sutri, determining to nurture his power by many a pilgrim's loss; but how he was ejected thence, the following epistle explains.

"Calixtus, the bishop, servant of the servants of God, to his beloved brethren, and sons, the archbishops, bishops, abbats, priors, and other faithful servants of St. Peter, clergy as well as laity, situated throughout Gaul, health and apostolical benediction. As the people have forsaken the

* "Gelasius II, died at Clugny, 29th Jan. 1119.—HARDY.

law of the Lord, and walk not in his judgments, God visits their iniquities with a rod, and their sins with stripes: but retaining the bowels of paternal love, he does not desert such as trust in his mercy. For a long time indeed, their sins so requiring, the faithful of the church have been disturbed by Bourdin, that idol of the king of Germany; nay, some have been taken captive, others afflicted, through want in prison, even unto death. Lately, however, after celebrating the festival of Easter, when we could no longer endure the complaints of the pilgrims, and of the poor, we left the city with the faithful servants of the church, and laid siege to Sutri, until the Divine power delivered that Bourdin aforesaid, the enemy of the church, who had there made a nest for the devil, as well as the place itself, entirely into our power. We beg your brotherly love therefore, with us, to return thanks to the King of kings, for such great benefits, and to remain most firmly in obedience and duty to the catholic church, as you will receive from God Almighty, through his grace, due recompence for it, both here and hereafter. We beg, too, that these letters be made public, with all due diligence. Done at Sutri on the fifth before the kalends of May."

How exquisite and refined a piece of wit, to call the man he hated, the idol of the king of Germany! for the emperor certainly held in high estimation Maurice's skill in literature and politics. He was, as I have said, bishop of Brague, a city of Spain: a man whom any one might highly reverence, and almost venerate, for his active and unwearied assiduity; had he not been led to make himself conspicuous by so disgraceful an act: nor would he have hesitated to purchase the holy see, if he could have found as desperate a seller as he was a buyer. But being taken, and made a monk, he was sent to the Den,* for so is the monastery called.

The laudable magnanimity of the pope proceeded still farther in the promotion of justice, to the end that he might repress the boundless and innate cupidity of the Romans.

---

* A monastery near Salerno, inaccessible, except by one passage. Here were kept such as from their conduct had become either dangerous or scandalous: they were supplied with every thing necessary, according to their order, but were held in close confinement. Its name was given from the untameable disposition of its inmates. See Orderic. Vital. 870.

In his time there were no snares laid for the traveller in the neighbourhood of Rome; no assaults on him when he arrived within the city. The offerings to St. Peter, which, through insolence, and for their lusts, the powerful used to pillage, basely injuring such preceding popes as dared to complain, Calixtus brought back to their proper use; that is to say, for the public service of the ruler of the holy see. Neither could the desire of amassing money, nor the love of it when collected, produce in his breast any thing repugnant to justice: so that he admonished the English pilgrims, on account of the length of the journey, rather to go to St. David's * than to Rome; allowing the benefit of the same benediction to such as went twice to that place, as resulted to those who went once to Rome. Moreover that inveterate controversy between the empire and the priesthood, concerning investiture, which for more than fifty years had created commotions, to such a degree, that, when any favourer of this heresy was cut off by disease or death, immediately, like the hydra's heads, many sprouted up afresh; this man by his diligence cut off, brought low, rooted out, or plucked up: beating down the crest of German fierceness by the vigorous stroke of the papal hatchet. This, the declaration of the emperor, and of the pope, will shew to the world in the following words:

"I, Calixtus, bishop, servant of the servants of God, do grant unto you, my beloved son, Henry Augustus, by the grace of God, emperor of the Romans, that the election of bishops and abbats of the German empire, who pertain to the regality, shall take place in your presence without simony, or any violence: so that if any discord shall arise between the parties, you may give your assent, or aid, to the worthier side, by the counsel or judgment of the metropolitan or suffragans: but the elect shall receive the royalties from you, and do whatever, by these, he is lawfully bound to perform to you: but any one consecrated in the other parts of the empire, shall, within six months, receive his royalties from you, by your sceptre, and do whatever, by these, he is lawfully bound to perform to you; all things excepted which are known to belong to the Roman church. Moreover in those matters whereof you have complained, and demanded

* This was a high compliment to the ancient Briton.

my assistance, I will afford you aid according to the duty of my office. I grant firm peace to you and to all, who are, or were aiding you at the time of this dispute. Farewell."

"In the name of the Holy and Undivided Trinity, I Henry Augustus, by the grace of God, emperor of the Romans, for the love of God, and of the holy Roman church, and of the sovereign pope Calixtus; and for the release of my soul, do grant unto God, and the holy apostles Peter and Paul, and to the holy catholic church, all investitures by the ring and staff, and do allow canonical election, and free consecration to take place, in all churches of my kingdom or empire. The possessions and regality of St. Peter, which, from the beginning of this dispute to the present day, have been taken away, either in my father's or my own time, and which I now hold, I restore to the same holy Roman church: and such as I do not possess, I will faithfully assist her in recovering. And of the possessions of all other churches, princes, and others, clergy as well as lay, which have been forfeited in this contention by the advice of my princes, or by course of law, such as I have, I will restore; and such as I do not possess, I will faithfully assist in recovering. And I grant firm peace to the sovereign pope Calixtus, and to the holy Roman church, and to all, who are, or have been on her side: and I will faithfully assist her in every thing in which she requires assistance: and will afford her due justice in such matters whereof she shall have complained. All these affairs were transacted by the consent and counsel of the nobility, whose names are here subscribed. Albert, archbishop of Mentz: Frederic, archbishop of Cologne: the bishop of Ratisbon: the bishop of Bamburg: Bruno, bishop of Spires: the bishop of Augsburg: the bishop of Utrecht: the bishop of Constance: the abbat of Fulda: duke Herman: duke Frederic: Boniface the marquis: Theobald the marquis: Ernulf count palatine: Othbert count palatine: earl Berengar."

The inveterate malady which had disturbed the church being thus cured, every true Christian greatly rejoiced that this emperor, who, in military glory trod fast upon the footsteps of Charles the Great, neither degenerated from his devotion to God: for, in addition to nobly quelling the rebellions of his German empire, he subdued his Italian dominions in such wise as none had done before. Entering Italy thrice, within the space of ten years, he restrained the pride of the cities: at his first coming he exterminated by fire, Novaria, Placentia, Arezzo: at the second, and third, Cremona, and Mantua; and quieted the sedition at Ravenna, by a siege of a few days' continuance: for the Pisans and Pavians, with the people of Milan, embraced his friendship, rather than encounter the weight of his enmity. The daughter of the king of England, who, as I said before, was married to him, resembled her father in fortitude, and her mother in sanctity: piety and assiduity vied with each other in her character, nor was it easy to discern, which of her good qualities was most commendable.

At that time lived William earl of Poitou; a giddy unsettled kind of man; who, after* he returned from Jerusalem, as the preceding book relates, wallowed as completely in the sty of vice, as though he had believed that all things were governed by chance, and not by Providence. Moreover, he rendered his absurdities pleasant, by a kind of satirical wit: exciting the loud laughter of his hearers. Finally he erected, near a castle called Niort, certain buildings after the form of a little monastery, and used to talk idly about placing therein an abbey of prostitutes, naming several of the most abandoned courtezans, one as abbess, another as prioress; and declaring that he would fill up the rest of the offices in like manner. Repudiating his lawful consort, he carried off the wife of a certain viscount, of whom he was so desperately enamoured, that he placed on his shield the figure of this woman; affirming, that he was desirous of bearing her in battle, in the same manner as she bore him at another time. Being reproved and excommunicated for this by Girard bishop of Angouleme, and ordered to renounce this illicit amour, "You shall curl with a comb," said he, "the hair that has forsaken your forehead, ere I repudiate the viscountess;" thus taunting a man, whose scanty hair required no comb. Nor did he less when Peter bishop of Poitou, a man of noted sanctity, rebuked him

* Guibert of Nogent excuses himself from commemorating the valour of many of the crusaders, because, after their return, they had run headlong into every kind of enormity. Opera, p. 431.

still more freely; and, when contumacious, began to excommunicate him publicly: for, becoming furious, he seized the prelate by the hair, and flourishing his drawn sword: "You shall die this instant," said he, "unless you give me absolution." The bishop, then, counterfeiting alarm, and asking leave to speak, boldly completed the remainder of the form of excommunication; suspending the earl so entirely from all Christian intercourse, that he should neither dare to associate, nor speak with any one, unless he speedily recanted. Thus fulfilling his duty, as it appeared to him, and thirsting for the honour of martyrdom, he stretched out his neck, saying, "Strike, strike." But William, becoming somewhat softened, regained his usual pleasantry, and said, "Certainly I hate you so cordially, that I will not dignify you by the effects of my anger, nor shall you ever enter heaven by the agency of my hand." After a short time, however, tainted by the infectious insinuations of this abandoned woman, he drove the rebuker of his incest into banishment: who there, making a happy end, manifested to the world, by great and frequent miracles, how gloriously he survives in heaven. On hearing this, the earl abstained not from his inconsiderate speeches, openly declaring, that he was sorry he had not despatched him before; that so his pure soul might chiefly have to thank him, through whose violence he had acquired eternal happiness. The following verses are a tribute of applause to the life and death of Peter. It was said of him, when alive,—

> Coarse food, his body: and the poor, his store
> Consum'd: while study morals gave, and lore
> Virtues he rear'd, check'd faults, encouraged right,
> And law: in peace, not tumult, did delight.
> Help to the wretch, to sinners pardon gives,
> And, for his friend, his ardour ever lives.
> Busy for man was Martha; Mary's heart,
> Intent on God, assumed the better part:
> So 'twas in him; for God his soul possess'd,
> Unmix'd: his friendless neighbour had the rest.
> Rachael he lov'd. nor Leah's hopes depriv'd
> Of joy: another Jacob, doubly-wiv'd;
> Dotes on the one, for beauty's matchless grace;
> Regards the other, for her numerous race.

And when dead, it was said of him,—

> Poor and confin'd, and exiled from his see,
> The virtuous prelate bore each injury:
> Now rich, free, fix d, his suff'rings are made even,
> For Christ he follows, and inherits heaven.
> His life, religion · and a judgment sound,
> His mind adorn'd, his works his fame resound,
> Reading his knowledge, and a golden mean
> His words, arrang'd . in his decisions seen
> Was law . severity his justice arm'd,
> And graceful beauty in his person charm'd :
> His breast was piety's perpetual stand,
> The pastor's crosier well-became his hand :
> The pope promotes him, but the earl deprives:
> Through Christ to joy eternal he survives.

The contemporaries and associates in religion of this Peter, were Robert de Arbrisil,* and Bernard† abbat of Tyron, the first of whom was the most celebrated and eloquent preacher of these times. so much did he excel, not in frothy, but honeyed diction, that from the gifts of persons vying with each other in making presents, he founded that noble monastery of nuns at Font-Evraud, in which every secular pleasure being extirpated, no other place possesses such multitudes of devout women, fervent in their obedience to God. For in addition to the rejection of other allurements, how great is this! that they never speak but in the chapter: the rule of constant silence being enjoined by the superior, because, when this is broken, women are prone to vain talk. The other, a noted admirer of poverty, leaving a most opulent monastery, retired with a few followers into a woody and sequestered place, and there, "As the light could not be hidden under a bushel," vast numbers flocking to him, he founded a monastery, more celebrated for the piety and number of the monks, than for the splendour and extent of its riches.

And, that England may not be supposed destitute of virtue, who can pass by Serlo, abbat of Gloucester, who advanced that place, almost from meanness and insignificance, to a glorious pitch? All England is acquainted with the considerate rule professed at Gloucester, which the weak

---

* Robert de Arbrisil founded the monastery of Fontevrault in 1099, and died in 1117.

† "Bernard founded the abbey of Tyron in 1109, and died in 1116."—Hardy.

may embrace, and the strong cannot despise. Their leader, Serlo's axiom, was, "Moderation in all things." Although mild to the good, he was fierce and terrific to the haughty; to corroborate which, I shall insert the verses of Godfrey the prior concerning him:—

> The church's bulwark fell, when Serlo died,
> Virtue's sharp sword, and justice's fond pride:
> Speaker of truth, no vain discourse he lov'd,
> And pleas'd the very princes he reprov'd:
> A hasty judgment, or disorder'd state
> Of life, or morals, were his utter hate
> The third of March was the propitious day,
> When Serlo wing'd, through death, to life his way.

Who can in silence pass Lanzo, who flourished at that time, equal to any in sanctity? A monk of Clugny, and prior of St. Pancras* in England; who, by his worth, so ennobled that place with the grace of monastic reverence, that it might be justly declared the peculiar habitation of virtue. As nothing I can say will equal the merits of his life, I shall merely subjoin, in the language I found it, an account of his death; that it may plainly appear, how gloriously he had lived, who died so highly favoured.

"The affectionate Lord who scourges every son whom he receives,—who promises the just, that they shall be partakers of his sufferings as well as of his consolation; permitted Lanzo to approach his death by such bitter sickness, during three days, that if any spot from earthly intercourse had adhered to his pure soul, it must no doubt have been wiped away by that suffering. For, as that great apostle, who reclined on the breast of our Lord, says, 'If we say that we have no sin we deceive ourselves, and the truth is not in us;' and since Christ will judge every sin, either lightly here or more severely hereafter, he was unwilling that any offence should be in the way of him after death, whom he knew to have loved him with all his heart. Wherefore, if there was anything which he thought worthy of examination in Lanzo, he was desirous of consuming it in his lifetime. To this assertion his confidence in death bore witness. For when in full health, on the fifth day of the week before the passion of our Lord, having read the psalter, according

* At Lewes in Sussex.

to the daily custom of Lent, and being about to celebrate mass at the third hour, he had robed himself to the chasuble,* and had proceeded in the service till mass was on the eve of beginning, he was suddenly seized with such an acute disorder, that himself laying aside the garments he had put on, he left them not even folded up.† Departing from the oratory, he was afflicted for two days, without intermission, that is, till the Saturday, having no rest either sitting, walking, standing, lying, or sleeping. During the nights, however, he never spoke to his brethren, though entreating him to break silence; but to this he did not consent, beseeching them not to sully the purity of his vow; for since he had assumed the monastic habit, whenever he had gone out from complines, he had never spoken till primes of the ensuing day. But on the Saturday, though so convulsed as to expect dissolution every moment, he commanded the brethren, now rising for matins, to come and anoint him: and when he was anxious to kiss them, after being anointed, as is the custom, through excess of love he saluted them, not lying or sitting, but, though agonized to death, standing, supported in their arms. At dawn, being conducted to the chapter-house,‡ when he had taken his seat, he asked all the brethren to come before him, and giving them the paternal benediction and absolution, he entreated the like from them. He then instructed them what they were to do in case he died: and so, returning whence he came, he passed the rest of the day with the succeeding Sunday, rather more tranquilly; but, behold, after this, that is, after Sunday, signs of approaching death were discovered; and having his hands washed, and his hair combed, he entered the oratory to hear mass; and receiving the body and blood of the Lord retired to his bed. After a short time he became speechless, gave his benediction to the brethren singly as they came before him, and in like manner to the whole society. But lifting his eyes to heaven, he attempted with both hands to bless the abbat, with all committed to his charge. Being entreated by the fraternity to be mindful of them with the Lord, to whom he was going, he most kindly assented by an inclination of his

* The uppermost garment of the priest, covering the rest entirely.
† Those who officiated were enjoined to fold up their garments.
‡ It was customary to hold a short chapter immediately after primes.

head. After he had done thus, he beckoned for the cross to be presented to him, which, adoring with his head and indeed with his whole body, and embracing with his hands, he appeared to salute with joyful lips and to kiss with fond affection, when he distressed the standers-by with signs of departing, and, being caught up in their arms, was carried yet alive into the presbytery before the altar of St. Pancras. Here, surviving yet a time, and pleasing from the rosy hue of his countenance, he departed to Christ, pure, and freed eternally from every evil, at the same hour of the day on which, for his purification, he had been stricken with disease. And behold how wonderfully all things corresponded; the passion of the servant with the passion of the Lord; the hour of approaching sickness with the hour of approaching eternal happiness; the five days of illness which he endured for purifying the five senses of the body, through which none can avoid sin. Moreover, from his dying ere the completion of the fifth day, I think it is signified that he had never sinned in the last sense which is called the touch. And what else can the third hour of the day, in which he fell sick, and by dying entered into eternal life, signify, than that the same grace of the Holy Spirit, by which we know his whole life was regulated, was evidently present to him, both in his sickness and his death. Besides, we cannot doubt but that he equalled our fathers Odo and Odilo,* both in virtue and in its reward, as a remarkable circumstance granted to them was allowed to him also. For as the Lord permitted them to die on the octaves of those festivals which they loved beyond all other, (as St. Odo chiefly loved the feast of St. Martin, and St. Odilo the nativity of our Lord, and each died on the octaves of these tides), so to Lanzo, who beyond all of this age observed the rule of St. Benedict, and venerated the holy mother of God and her solemnities with singular regard, it happened that, as, according to his usual custom, both on the demise of St. Benedict, and on the festival of St. Mary, which is called the Annunciation, he celebrated high mass in the convent: so on the eighth from the aforesaid anniversary of St. Benedict, being stricken with sickness, he also on the eighth day from the annunciation de-

* Odo, second abbat of Clugny, was founder of the Clugniac rule in the tenth century. Odilo was elected the fifth abbat of Clugny in 994.

parted to Christ. Wherefore, he who is unacquainted with the life of Lanzo, may learn from his death, how pleasing it was to God, and will believe with us that these things, which I have mentioned, did not happen after the common course of dying persons, as he was a man surpassed by none, in the present times, for the gifts of the Holy Spirit."

Nor ought the memory of Godfrey, prior of Winchester, to decay, who was celebrated in these times for his learning and his piety: his learning is attested by many works and epistles composed in his familiar and pleasing style, but principally by his epigrams, written after the manner of satires, and his verses in celebration of the chief personages of England.* Indeed he restored every divine office to its native grace, from the manner in which he treated it, though before it had become obsolete from antiquity. The laws of religion and of hospitality, already happily traced out, he strongly impressed on the monks, who to this day so closely follow the footsteps of the prior in both, that they deserve all or nearly all possible commendation; indeed in this house there is a place of entertainment to any extent, for travellers of every description by sea or land, with boundless expense and ceaseless attention. Among other things this holy man was noted for his humility, so that nothing but what savoured of modesty and sweetness proceeded from this singular depository of philosophy. How great indeed must this commendation seem? for there is hardly any one, even the least tinctured with learning, who does not appear to consider others beneath his dignity, by his haughty gestures and proud gait proclaiming the consciousness of his own erudition. However, that no perfection might be wanting to his pure soul, he kept his lowly bed for many years, equally consuming his vitals and his transgressions in the furnace of lasting sickness.

But why should I enlarge on such characters? There were, indeed, at that time in England many persons illustrious both for learning and for piety, whose virtue was the more commendable in proportion to its constancy and vigour in

* Godfrey was prior of Winchester from A.D. 1082 to 1107. His verses in commendation of the chief personages of England are in the manner of those already inserted on Serlo abbat of Gloucester. Many of his epigrams have very considerable merit.

these degenerate times. By a blameless life, therefore, they gave credibility to ancient histories, and freed them from any suspicion of falsehood, as they produced modern example of the possibility of doing what was there recorded. Moreover, were there any prelates apparently degenerating from the sanctity of ancient times, that is to say, skilled in secular, indolent in spiritual matters? If there were such, I say, they endeavoured to shade their failings by costly ornaments for their cathedrals. Each of them erected new churches, and adorned the bodies of their saints with silver and gold; lavish of expense to secure the good opinion of the beholders. Among these is Ranulf beforementioned, who, being made bishop of Durham, purchased some glory for his name, by new buildings for the monks, and by regard to St. Cuthbert. His fame is exalted by his translation of the holy body, which when taken from its resting-place he exhibited to all who wished to behold it. Radulf, at that time bishop of Sees, and afterwards archbishop of Canterbury, with fortunate temerity, handled and displayed the uncorrupted body; for it had become matter of doubt with certain persons whether the miracle of the incorruption of the corpse, which had formerly been reported, still had effect. About the same time, in the monastery of Ely, under abbat Richard, the virgin reliques of St. Etheldritha, subjects of amaze and reverence to the beholders, were seen entire. This monastery, lately changed by king Henry into a bishopric, had Hervey, as its first prelate; who, from the scantiness of its revenues, had deserted Bangor, where he had been enthroned. And that the bishop of Lincoln might not complain of the mutilation of his diocese, the king made up his loss, out of the possessions of Ely, and satisfied his claim. Indeed, whatever, in his time, was unjustly purloined, or violently taken, from the primacy of the two metropolitans of Canterbury and York, I will relate in its proper place. For having now ended the series of the kings, it seems incumbent on me, to speak of that of the bishops of all England: and here I wish I had abundant matter for relation, in order that such splendid luminaries of the country might no longer be lost in obscurity. Moreover, there will perhaps be many in different parts of England, who may say, that they have heard and read some things differently related from the mode in which I have recorded them: but if they judge candidly, they will not, on this account, brand me with censure: since, following the strict laws of history, I have asserted nothing but what I have learned either from relators, or writers, of veracity. But be these matters as they may, I especially congratulate myself on being, through Christ's assistance, the only person, or at least the first, who, since Bede, have arranged a continued history of the English. Should any one, therefore, as I already hear it intimated, undertake, after me, a work of a similar nature, he may be indebted to me for having collected materials, though the selection from them must depend upon himself. *

Thus much then, my venerated lord, I have had to relate, concerning the history of the English, from their first arrival in this country, till the twentieth year of your father's most happy reign: the remainder will occupy a separate volume, if you condescend a kind regard to these. For when I had finished this work, after contemplating many characters, I determined that it ought more especially to be dedicated to you: as, when I examine others, I observe nobility in one; in another military science; in a third learning; justice in a fourth; but munificence in few indeed. Thus, I admire some things in one, some in another; but in you the aggregate of all. For, if ever any man was truly noble, you certainly excel in that quality; being descended from the most glorious kings and earls, and resembling them in your disposition. From the Normans, therefore, you derive your military skill; from the Flemings your personal elegance; from the French your surpassing munificence. Of your activity in war, who can doubt, when your most excellent father himself looks up to it? For whenever any tumults are reported in Normandy, he despatches you before him, in order that, what is suspicious may be dispelled by your valour, and peace may be restored by your sagacity. When he returns to his kingdom, he brings you with him, as a safeguard to him abroad, a delight at home, and an ornament every where.

So devoted are you to literature, that though distracted by

* He probably has Henry Huntingdon in view, who wrote a History of England shortly after him.

such a mass of business, you yet snatch some hours to yourself, for the purpose either of reading, or of hearing others. Justly do you regulate, indeed, your exalted rank in life, neither omitting the toils of war for literature, nor contemning literature, as some do, for military service. Here, also, the excess of your learning appears; for, whilst you love books, you manifest how deeply you have drunk of the stream. For many things, indeed, are eagerly desired when not possessed, but no person will love philosophy, who shall not have imbibed it thoroughly. The fame of your justice reaches even our parts; for a false sentence has never been extorted from you, either by elevation of rank, or by scantiness of fortune. The person who wishes to subvert justice, finds in your breast nothing conducive to his design, either by the offering of presents, or by the charm of favour. Your munificence and disregard of money, is amply shown by the monastery of Tewkesbury; from which, as I hear, you not only do not extort presents but even return its voluntary offerings. You must be well aware, how noble such a proceeding is, more especially at the present time; how much it redounds to your glory among men, how productive of the favour of God. Happy, then, according to Plato, is the republic whose ruler is a philosopher, whose sovereign delights not in gifts. More could I add on such subjects, did not the suspicion of flattery on my part, and commendable modesty on yours, restrain my tongue. In truth, my design was, not to pass by in silence the things I have uttered, in order that, by my agency, your worth might reach posterity; and that it may continue to proceed from virtue to virtue. Moreover, it was long since my intention, at the instance of certain persons, to subjoin to this work, whatever I may deem of importance, according to the successive years: but it appears advisable rather to form another volume of such matters, than to be perpetually adding to that already completed. Nor can any one say, that I engage in a superfluous work, if I record the transactions of the most celebrated among the kings of his time. Indeed my lowly condition is much indebted to his greatness, and will be still more so, were it for nothing else, than his being able to pride himself on such a son.* For,

* Terentii Andria, i. 1.

when he had most auspiciously begotten, he first commanded you to be instructed, not superficially, as plainly appears at the present day, in science; he next made you master of a most princely fortune; and, at this moment he reposes his paternal regards upon you. Let this volume then, whatever its merits or defects, be altogether dedicated to your fame; in the next my life and my history will terminate together. Farther, kindly accept this my offering, that I, whose judgment has not erred in its choice, may be gratified by the good wishes of my patron.

THE MODERN HISTORY.

PREFACE,

ADDRESSED TO ROBERT, EARL OF GLOUCESTER.

To his most loving lord, Robert, son of king Henry, and earl of Gloucester, William, librarian of Malmesbury, wishes, after completing his victorious course on earth, eternal triumph in heaven. Many of the transactions of your father, of glorious memory, I have not omitted to record, both in the fifth book of my Regal History, and in those three smaller volumes, which I have intituled Chronicles.* Your highness is now desirous that those events which, through the miraculous power of God, have taken place in modern time, in England, should be transmitted to posterity: truly, like all your other desires, a most noble one. For what more concerns the advancement of virtue ; what more conduces to justice ; than to recognize the divine favour towards good men, and his vengeance upon the wicked ? What, too, can be more grateful, than to commit to the page of history, the exploits of brave men, by whose example others may shake off their indolence, and take up arms in defence of their country ? As this task is committed to my pen, I think the narrative will proceed with exacter order, if, going back a little, I trace the series of years from the return of the empress into England, after the death of her husband. First, therefore, invoking the help of God, as is fitting, and purposing to write the truth, without listening to enmity, or sacrificing to favour, I shall begin as follows.

* What these were is unknown, as it is believed there is no MS. of them now to be met with.

BOOK I.

In the twenty-sixth year of Henry king of England, which was A.D. 1126, Henry, emperor of Germany, to whom Matilda the aforesaid king's daughter had been married, died* in the very bloom of his life and of his conquests. Our king was at that time residing in Normandy, to quell whatever tumults might arise in those parts. As soon as he heard of the death of his son-in-law, he recalled his daughter by honourable messengers despatched for that purpose. The empress, as they say, returned with reluctance, as she had become habituated to the country which was her dowry, and had large possessions there. It is well known, that several princes of Lorraine and Lombardy came, during succeeding years, repeatedly into England, to demand her as their sovereign, but they lost the fruit of their labours, the king designing, by the marriage of his daughter, to procure peace between himself and the earl of Anjou. He was certainly, in an extraordinary degree, the greatest of all kings in the memory either of ourselves, or of our fathers . and yet nevertheless, he ever, in some measure, dreaded the power of the earls of Anjou. Hence it arose, that he broke off and annulled the espousals which William, his nephew, afterwards earl of Flanders, was said to be about to contract with the daughter of Fulco, earl of Anjou, who was afterwards king of Jerusalem. Hence, too, it arose, that he united a daughter of the same earl to his son William, while yet a stripling; and hence it was, that he married his daughter, of whom we began to speak, after her imperial match, to a son of the same Fulco, as my narrative will proceed to disclose.

In the twenty-seventh year of his reign, in the month of September, king Henry came to England, bringing his daughter with him. But, at the ensuing Christmas, convening a great number of the clergy and nobility at London, he gave the county of Salop to his wife, the daughter of the earl of Louvain, whom he had married after the death of Matilda. Distressed that this lady had no issue, and fearing

* "The emperor Henry V. died on the 23rd of May, A.D. 1125, and in September, A.D. 1126, king Henry returned from Normandy, with his daughter the empress."—HARDY.

lest she should be perpetually childless, with well-founded anxiety, he turned his thoughts on a successor to the kingdom. On which subject, having held much previous and long-continued deliberation, he now at this council compelled all the nobility of England, as well as the bishops and abbats, to make oath, that, if he should die without male issue, they would, without delay or hesitation, accept his daughter Matilda, the late empress, as their sovereign: observing, how prejudicially to the country fate had snatched away his son William, to whom the kingdom by right had pertained: and, that his daughter still survived, to whom alone the legitimate succession belonged, from her grandfather, uncle, and father, who were kings; as well as from her maternal descent for many ages back: inasmuch as from Egbert, king of the West Saxons, who first subdued or expelled the other kings of the island, in the year of the incarnation 800,[*] through a line of fourteen kings, down to A.D. 1043, in which king Edward, who lies at Westminster, was elevated to the throne, the line of royal blood did never fail, nor falter in the succession.[†] Moreover, Edward, the last, and at the same time the most noble, of that stock, had united[‡] Margaret, his grand-niece by his brother Edmund Ironside, to Malcolm, king of Scotland, whose daughter Matilda, as was well known, was the empress's mother. All therefore, in this council, who were considered as persons of any note, took the oath: and first of all William, archbishop of Canterbury; next the other bishops, and the abbats in like manner. The first of the laity, who swore, was David, king of Scotland, uncle of the empress; then Stephen, earl of Moreton and Boulogne, nephew of king Henry by his sister Adala; then Robert, the king's son, who was born to him before he came to the throne, and whom he had created earl of Gloucester,[§] bestowing on him

---

[*] "The union of the kingdoms under Egbert did not take place for several years after his accession in 802."—HARDY.

[†] This must be understood with the exception of Canute and his sons, between Edmund Ironside, and Edward the Confessor.

[‡] Here seems a mistake. Margaret was given to Malcolm by her brother Edgar Atheling, while in exile in Scotland, A.D. 1067. See the Saxon Chronicle.

[§] "Robert was created earl of Gloucester in the year 1119. On the Pipe-roll, 31 Hen. I., this entry occurs: 'Glœcecestrescire. Et comiti Glœc. xxii. numero pro parte sua comitatus.'"—HARDY.

in marriage Mabil, a noble and excellent woman; a lady devoted to her husband, and blessed in a numerous and beautiful offspring. There was a singular dispute, as they relate, between Robert and Stephen, contending with rival virtue, which of them should take the oath first; one alleging the privilege of a son, the other the dignity of a nephew. Thus all being bound by fealty and by oath, they, at that time, departed to their homes; but after Pentecost, the king sent his daughter into Normandy, ordering her to be betrothed,* by the archbishop of Rouen, to the son of Fulco aforesaid, a youth of high nobility and noted courage. Nor did he himself delay setting sail for Normandy, for the purpose of uniting them in wedlock. Which being completed, all declared prophetically, as it were, that, after his death, they would break their plighted oath. I have frequently heard Roger, bishop of Salisbury, say, that he was freed from the oath he had taken to the empress: for that he had sworn conditionally, that the king should not marry his daughter to any one out of the kingdom without his consent, or that of the rest of the nobility: that none of them advised the match, or indeed knew of it, except Robert, earl of Gloucester, and Brian Fitzcount, and the bishop of Louviers. Nor do I relate this merely because I believe the assertion of a man who knew how to accommodate himself to every varying time, as fortune ordered it; but, as an historian of veracity, I write the general belief of the people.

The remaining years of the life and reign of Henry, I must review briefly, in order that posterity may neither be defrauded of a knowledge of these events, nor that I may seem to dwell on topics little relevant to this history. In his twenty-eighth year, the king† returned from Normandy; in his twenty-ninth, a circumstance occurred in England which may seem surprising to our long-haired gallants, who, forgetting what they were born, transform themselves into the fashion of females, by the length of their locks. A certain English knight, who prided himself on the luxuriancy of

* "The nuptials of Matilda with Geoffrey Plantagenet, afterwards earl of Anjou, were celebrated in the presence of her father, in Sept. 1127."—HARDY.

† "Henry completed the twenty-eighth year of his reign the 4th of August, 1128; but the Saxon Chronicle places his return from Normandy during the autumn of 1129."—HARDY.

his tresses, being stung by conscience on the subject, seemed to feel in a dream as though some person strangled him with his ringlets. Awaking in a fright, he immediately cut off all his superfluous hair. The example spread throughout England; and, as recent punishment is apt to affect the mind, almost all military men allowed their hair to be cropped in a proper manner, without reluctance. But this decency was not of long continuance; for scarcely had a year expired, ere all who thought themselves courtly, relapsed into their former vice: they vied with women in length of locks, and wherever they were defective, put on false tresses; forgetful, or rather ignorant, of the saying of the apostle, "If a man nurture his hair, it is a shame to him"*

In his thirtieth year, king Henry went into Normandy. Pope Honorius dying in this year, the church of Rome was agitated by great contentions about electing his successor. There were, at that time, in the city, two very celebrated cardinals, Gregory, deacon of St. Angelo, and Peter, cardinal-priest, son of Leo, prince of the Romans; both noted for learning, and activity, nor could the people easily discern which of them more justly ought to be elected by the clergy. The party, however, which favoured Gregory took the lead, and ordaining him pope, called him Innocent. Moreover a rumour was disseminated among the people, that Honorius was still just alive, and had commanded this to be done. The promoters of this choice were, William, bishop of Præneste, Matthew of Albano, Conrad of Sabina, John of Ostia, Peter of Crema, cardinal of St. Chrysogonus, and Haimer the chancellor. But the other party, after Honorius was buried, at the instigation of Peter's brothers, who were the most opulent and powerful of the Romans, having elected and consecrated him, gave him the name of Anaclet. The chief adviser and instigator to this ordination was Peter, bishop of Porto, whose letter, if I subjoin it, will disclose the whole controversy; although it inclines rather to Anaclet.

* It is very remarkable what excessive pains were employed to prevail on the young men to part with their locks. In the council held at London by archbishop Anselm, A.D. 1102, it is enacted, that those who had long hair should be cropped, so as to show part of the ear, and the eyes. From the apparently strange manner in which this fashion is coupled in Edmer, p 81, one might be led to suspect, it was something more than mere spleen which caused this enactment. See also Orderic. Vitalis.

"Peter, bishop of Porto, to the four bishops, William of Præneste, Matthew of Albano, Conrad of Sabina, John of Ostia. How great is the tribulation of my heart for you, he only knows, who knows all things; indeed, you would have already been acquainted with it, in part, by my letters, did not the sentence and the common authority of the church prohibit. Of the praise or dispraise of those persons, concerning whom various discourses are at present held, it is not of this world to judge: there is who may seek and judge. But if any be ready to accuse, one will be ready, and who is also bound, to reply; more especially when both in your and my sight, and in that of the whole church, each of them has lived discreetly and honestly; and has hitherto executed his office impartially. It rather concerns you to abstain from idle language and the words of haste. If the question be of report, the business is far different from what your letters to me declare. In addition to this, if you regard the accounts you have published, and the order of proceeding, with due reverence be it spoken, by what boldness, by what assurance, do you presume to call that usurpation of yours an election? Why do you call that man of yours ordained, when there was no order whatever in his case? Have you so learned to elect a pope? What, in a corner, in a hidden place, in darkness, and in the shadow of death? If you were desirous that a living should succeed to a dead pope, why would you give out that the deceased was still alive? It were much better, surely, to pay the last sad offices to the dead, and in this manner provide for the succour of the living: but, behold, while you seek succour for the living from the dead, you destroy both the living and the dead at the same time. Lastly, it was neither your office nor mine to elect; but rather to refuse, or to approve, when elected by the brethren. Since, therefore, in neglect of the ritual, contempt of the canon, and disregard of the very anathema, framed by yourselves; without consulting me, your superior, or your elder brethren and superiors, or even summoning, or waiting for them; when you were inexperienced, and but very few in number, you have presumed to do this; you must be sensible, from your own estimation of the case, that it must be considered void and of no avail whatever. The Lord, however, was quickly present to us, and pointed out a method whereby to obviate your error. For, indeed, your brethren the cardinals, who possess the chief power of electing, together with the whole clergy, at the request of the people, and with the consent of the nobility, openly, in the light of day, have unanimously, and heartily, elected the noble cardinal Peter, as Roman pontiff, by the title of Anaclet. I have witnessed this election canonically celebrated; and confirmed it by the authority of God. The church accepts and venerates him; and, by the grace of God, the bishops and abbats, chief princes and barons, some by themselves, and others by their delegates, acknowledge him in our presence. The robbery and cruelty you mention, I do not perceive: whoever goes to him for consultation, or on business, is kindly received, and still more kindly dismissed. Return, then, return to your understanding, do not make a schism in the church, to the perdition of souls: do not persist any farther; let the fear of God possess you, not worldly shame: does any sleep, will he not add, that he must rise again? Cease now from lies, in which the wicked put their hope. The lord Tiburtius hath testified by oath, in writing, that I have deemed the deacon of St. Angelo, the only fit person for the office of pope: let him look to what he hath said: I have spoken nothing in secret; no person hath ever heard such a word as this from my mouth. My opinion always was, that till the pope was buried no mention should be made of his successor. I have held, and will hold, the unity of the church; I will be careful to adhere to truth and justice; confidently hoping, that truth and justice will set me free."

After this manner wrote the aforesaid Peter, bishop of Porto, rather partial to Peter, the son of Leo. Nor did the other party at all give way; but called Peter himself a lion's whelp,* and his partizans, the leaders of a faction. And they, indeed, acted variously among themselves, under these doubtful circumstances. Innocent, however, excluded from Rome, passed the Alps and went into France. Here he was immediately received by all the churches on this side the mountains; and moreover, even king Henry, who did not very well know how to be driven from an opinion he had once taken up, willingly acknowledged him at Chartres;

* An allusion to his name, which signifies a lion.

and, at Rouen, condescended to honour him, not only with presents from himself, but also from the nobility, and even the Jews. Yet Innocent, though greatly assisted by the kings of England and France, and the emperor of Germany, could never enjoy peace so long as Anaclet occupied the see of Rome. However, Anaclet himself dying in the eighth year of his usurped papacy, as it was called, Innocent enjoys the papal dignity unmolested to the present time. *

In the thirty-first year of his reign, king Henry returned to England. The empress, too, in the same year, arrived on her native soil, and a full meeting of the nobility being held at Northampton, the oath of fidelity to her was renewed by such as had already sworn, and also taken by such as hitherto had not. In the same year † Lewis, king of France, growing aged and unwieldy through extreme corpulency, commanded his son to be crowned as successor to the kingdom; who dying soon after by the fall of his horse, he caused another of his sons to be consecrated king, by the hands of the Roman pontiff. He, as they relate, not degenerating from the ancient valour of the French, hath also acquired Aquitain, as the marriage portion of his wife, which, it is well known, the kings of France have never held in their own right since Lewis, son of Charles the Great.

In the thirty-first‡ [second] year of king Henry, a dreadful murrain among domestic animals extended over the whole of England. Entire herds of swine suddenly perished; whole stalls of oxen were swept off in a moment: the same contagion continued in the following years, so that no village throughout the kingdom was free from this calamity, or able to exult at the losses of its neighbours. At this time, too, the contention between Bernard, bishop of St. David's, and Urban, of Landaff, on the rights of their dioceses, which Urban had illegally usurped, was finally put to

* Pope Innocent died A.D. 1143.

† "Philippe, eldest son of Louis VI, was consecrated by command of his father on the 14th April, 1129; but meeting with an accidental death on the 13th October, 1131, the king, twelve days afterwards, caused his second son, Louis, to be crowned at Rheims by the Roman pontiff, Innocent II "—HARDY.

‡ Both the printed copy and the MSS., which have been consulted, read here tricesimo primo, 'thirty-first,' [1131]; but it should be the thirty-second, 1132.—See Hen. Hunt.

rest. For, after being agitated by so many appeals to the court of Rome, so many expensive journeys, so many debates of lawyers, for a number of years, it was at last terminated, or rather cut short, by the death of Urban at Rome. The pope also, weighing the equity of the case, did justice to the piety and right of the bishop of St. David's by a suitable judgment. In the same year William, archbishop of Canterbury, personally obtained the legation of England, through the indulgence of the see of Rome.

The day after the thirty-second[*] year of his reign was completed, Henry, on the nones of August, the very day on which he had formerly been crowned at Westminster, set sail for Normandy. This was the last, the fatal voyage of his reign. The providence of God, at that time, bore reference in a wonderful manner to human affairs: for instance, that he should embark, never to return alive, on that day on which he had originally been crowned, so long and prosperously to reign. It was then, as I have said, the nones of August; and, on the fourth day of the week, the elements manifested their sorrow at this great man's last departure. For the sun on that day,[†] at the sixth hour, shrouded his glorious face, as the poets say, in hideous darkness, agitating the hearts of men by an eclipse: and on the sixth day of the week, early in the morning, there was so great an earthquake, that the ground appeared absolutely to sink down; a horrid sound being first heard from beneath the surface. During the eclipse I saw stars around the sun: and, at the time of the earthquake, the wall of the house in which I was sitting was lifted up by two shocks, and settled again with a third. The king, therefore, continued in Normandy for

[*] "Malmesbury seems to have committed two oversights here. Henry went to Normandy for the last time on the third before the nones of August, (that is, third, instead of fifth), A.D. 1133. This is evident from the eclipse he mentions, which took place on that day, as well as from the testimony of the continuator of Florence of Worcester, a contemporary writer."—SHARPE. "Although all the MSS. read 'tricesimo secundo,' yet it is evident, from the context, that it should be 'tricesimo tertio;' the completion of Henry's thirty-third regnal year being on the 4th of August, 1133. This, and other passages show, that Malmesbury reckoned Henry's reign to commence on the 5th of August, the day of his consecration, and not on the 2nd of that month, the day of his brother's death."—HARDY.

[†] "The eclipse of the sun took place on the 2nd of August, 1133, at mid-day."—HARDY.

the space of three* whole years, and so much longer, as from the nones of August, on which day, as has been said, he crossed the sea, to the kalends of December, on which night he died. Doubtlessly he performed many things worthy of record while in Normandy, but it was my design to omit whatever did not come authenticated to my knowledge. Divers expectations of his return to England were all frustrated, by some adverse fate, or by the will of God.

He reigned, then, thirty-five years, and from the nones of August to the kalends of December, that is, four months, wanting four days. Engaged in hunting at Lihun, he was taken suddenly ill. His malady increasing, he summoned to him, Hugo, whom, from prior of Lewes, he had made abbat of Reading, and afterwards archbishop of Rouen, who was justly indebted to him and his heirs for such great favours. The report of his sickness quickly gathered the nobility around him. Robert, too, his son, the earl of Gloucester, was present; who, from his unblemished fidelity and matchless virtue, has deserved to be especially signalized throughout all ages. Being interrogated by these persons, as to his successor, he awarded all his territories, on either side of the sea, to his daughter, in legitimate and perpetual succession; being somewhat displeased with her husband, as he had irritated him both by threats and by certain injuries. Having passed the seventh day of his sickness, he yielded to nature about midnight. I waive describing his magnanimous character in this place, as I have been diffuse upon it in the fifth book of my Regal History. In how Christian a manner he departed, the following epistle of the aforesaid archbishop of Rouen, will testify.

"To his lord and father, pope Innocent, due obedience from his servant, Hugo, priest of Rouen. I have deemed it proper to write to your fatherly affection concerning the king my master, never to be remembered but with grief: for, being seized with sudden sickness, he wished for me to console his sufferings, and sent messengers as soon as possible for that purpose. I went, and passed three melancholy days with him. Agreeably to my suggestion, he confessed his sins, he beat his breast, and he laid aside all his animosities. Through the grace of God, and through our advice and that

* From what has been said above this should be two.

of the bishops, he promised to attend to the amendment of his life. Under this promise, according to our office, on the third day, and three days successively, we gave him absolution. He devoutly adored the cross of our Lord, received his body and blood; bestowed his alms thus; saying, 'Let my debts be paid, let the wages* and stipends which I owe be discharged, let the remainder be distributed to the poor.' I wish they who held, and do hold, his treasures had done thus. At last I earnestly stated to him our duty concerning the unction of the sick, which the church adopted from the apostle St. James, and, at his own devout request, I anointed him with holy oil. Thus he rested in peace; and may God grant him the peace he loved." These circumstances relating to the faith of king Henry when dying, were truly attested by the aforesaid archbishop of Rouen.

The body, royally attended and borne by the nobility in turn, was brought to Rouen; where, in a certain retired part of the principal church, it was embowelled, lest, through time, becoming putrid, it should offend the senses of those who approached it. The intestines were buried in the monastery of St. Mary des Prees, near the city, which, as I hear, he had honoured with no mean presents, as it had been begun by his mother. His body was kept at Caen, till the season, which was then very boisterous, became more tranquil. In the meantime, Stephen earl of Moreton and Boulogne, nephew of king Henry, as I have before said, who, after the king of Scotland, was the first layman that had sworn fidelity to the empress, hastened his return into England by Whitsand. The empress, from certain causes, as well as her brother, Robert earl of Gloucester, and almost all the nobility, delayed returning to the kingdom. However, some castles in Normandy, the principal of which was Danfrunt espoused the party of the heiress. Moreover, it is well known, that, on the day on which Stephen disembarked in England, there was, very early in the morning, contrary

* " Liberationes," signifies, sometimes, what we now call liveries, that is garments, sometimes money at stated periods, or, as we should say, wages: it is here rendered in the latter sense, as being distinct from " solidatæ," pay or stipends. Perhaps it was intended to distinguish two orders of persons by this bequest; servants and soldiers: otherwise it may mean garments and wages.

to the nature of winter in these countries, a terrible peal of thunder, with most dreadful lightning, so that the world seemed well-nigh about to be dissolved. He was received, however, as king, by the people of London and of Winchester, and gained over also Roger bishop of Salisbury, and William Pont de L'Arche, the keepers of the royal treasures. Yet, not to conceal the truth from posterity, all his attempts would have been vain, had not his brother, Henry bishop of Winchester, who is now legate of the papal see in England, granted him his entire support: allured indeed by the fullest expectation that Stephen would follow the example of his grandfather William in the management of the kingdom, and more especially in the strictness of ecclesiastical discipline. In consequence, when Stephen was bound by the rigorous oath which William archbishop of Canterbury required from him, concerning restoring and preserving the liberty of the church, the bishop of Winchester became his pledge and surety. The written tenor of this oath, I shall be careful hereafter to insert in its proper place.

Stephen, therefore, was crowned king of England on Sunday the eleventh* before the kalends of January, the twenty-second day after the decease of his uncle, anno Dom. 1135, in the presence of three bishops, that is, the archbishop, and those of Winchester and Salisbury; but there were no abbats, and scarcely any of the nobility. He was a man of activity, but imprudent: strenuous in war; of great mind in attempting works of difficulty; mild and compassionate to his enemies, and affable to all. Kind, as far as promise went; but sure to disappoint in its truth and execution. Whence he soon afterwards neglected the advice of his brother, befriended by whose assistance, as I have said, he had supplanted his adversaries and obtained the kingdom.

In the year of our Lord 1135, on the prevalence of gentler gales, the body of king Henry was, immediately after Christmas, put on ship-board, and brought to England; and, in the presence of his successor in the kingdom, was buried at the monastery of Reading, which he had liberally endowed, and filled with an order of monks of singular piety. Shortly after, a little before Lent, king Stephen went into Northum-

* "The majority of contemporary writers state that Stephen's coronation took place on the 26th December."—HARDY.

berland, that he might have a conference with David king of Scotland, who was said to entertain hostile sentiments towards him. From David he readily obtained what he wished; because, being softened by the natural gentleness of his manners, or by the approach of old age, he willingly embraced the tranquillity of peace, real or pretended.

In the same year, after Easter, Robert earl of Gloucester, of whose prudence Stephen chiefly stood in awe, came to England. While he was yet resident in Normandy, he had most earnestly considered, what line of conduct he should determine upon in the present state of affairs. If he became subject to Stephen, it seemed contrary to the oath he had sworn to his sister; if he opposed him, he saw that he could nothing benefit her or his nephews, though he must grievously injure himself. For the king, as I said before, had an immense treasure, which his uncle had been accumulating for many years. His coin, and that of the best quality,* was estimated at a hundred thousand pounds; besides which, there were vessels of gold and silver, of great weight, and inestimable value, collected by the magnificence of preceding kings, and chiefly by Henry.† A man possessed of such boundless treasures, could not want supporters, more especially as he was profuse, and, what by no means becomes a prince, even prodigal. Soldiers of all kinds, and light-armed troops, were flocking to him, chiefly from Flanders and Brittany. These were a most rapacious and violent race of men; who made no scruple to violate church-yards,‡ or rob a church. Moreover, not only would

* "The author of the Dialogus de Scaccario states that for some time after the Norman conquest there was very little money in specie in the realm, and that, until the reign of Henry the First, all rents and farms due to the king were rendered in provisions and necessaries for his household; but Henry I ordered the payments to be made in money: they were consequently made 'ad scalam,' and 'ad pensum;' 'in numero,' or by tale; and 'per combustionem,' or melting, which latter mode was adopted to prevent payment being made in debased money, hence perhaps it was that Henry's money was of the best quality."—HARDY.

† The progress of some of Henry's treasure is curious. Theobald, earl of Blois, gave many jewels, which had been bestowed on him by Stephen, his brother, to certain abbeys, and these again sold them for four hundred pounds to Suger, abbat of St. Denis. Henry, Suger observes, used to have them set in most magnificent drinking vessels. Suger, ap. Duchesne, t. iv. p 345

‡ Church-yards were, by the canons, privileged, so that persons in turbulent times conveyed their property thither for security.

they drag men of the religious order from their horses, but also make them captive: and this was done not merely by foreigners, but even by the native soldiers, who had abhorred the tranquillity of king Henry's time, because it subjected them to a life of poverty. All these most readily resorted to the prince whom they could easily incline to their purposes, pushing their fortune at the expense of the people. Stephen, indeed, before he came to the throne, from his complacency of manners, and readiness to joke, and sit, and regale, even with low people, had gained so much on their affections, as is hardly to be conceived: and already had all the nobility of England willingly acknowledged him. The most prudent earl therefore was extremely desirous to convince them of their misconduct, and recall them to wiser sentiments by his presence; for, to oppose Stephen's power, he was unable, from the causes aforesaid: indeed he had not the liberty of coming to England, unless, appearing as a partaker of their revolt, he dissembled for a time his secret intentions. He did homage to the king, therefore, under a certain condition; namely, so long as he should preserve his rank entire, and maintain his engagements to him; for having long since scrutinized Stephen's disposition, he foresaw the instability of his faith.

In the same year, soon after the earl's arrival, the bishops swore fidelity to the king, "so long as he should maintain the liberty of the church, and the vigour of its discipline." He himself also swore according to the tenor of the following instrument.

"I Stephen, by the grace of God, elected king of England by the consent of the clergy and of the people, and consecrated by the lord William, archbishop of Canterbury and legate of the holy Roman church, and afterwards confirmed by Innocent, pope of the holy Roman see, through respect and love towards God, do grant the holy church to be free, and confirm to it all due reverence. I promise that I will neither do any thing simoniacally, nor permit it to be done, in the church, or in matters ecclesiastical. The jurisdiction and power over beneficed clergy, and over all persons in orders, and their property, and the distribution of effects of ecclesiastics, I admit to be in the hands of the bishops, and confirm it so to be. I grant and appoint, that the immunities of the churches, confirmed by their charters, and their customs observed from ancient usage, do remain inviolate. All the possessions of the churches, and the tenures which they held during the life, and at the death of my grandfather king William, I grant to them free, and discharged from the claim of all parties: but if the church shall hereafter claim any thing held, or possessed, before the death of the king, of which it is now deprived, I reserve such matter for discussion, or restitution at my will and pleasure. Moreover, whatever, since that king's death, has been obtained by the liberality of kings, or the gift of princes; by offerings, or purchase, or by any exchange of the faithful, I confirm. I pledge myself to keep peace, and do justice to all, and to preserve them to my utmost ability. I reserve to myself the forests which king William, my grandfather, and William the Second, my uncle, have made and possessed: all the rest which king Henry added, I give and grant, without molestation, to the churches, and the kingdom. And if any bishop or abbat, or other ecclesiastical person, shall have severally distributed* his property before his death, or appointed such distribution, I allow it to remain good: but if he shall have been suddenly seized by death, before making a disposition, let the said distribution be made, at the discretion of the church, for the repose of his soul. Moreover, when the sees shall be vacant, let both them, and their whole possessions, be committed into the hands and custody of the clergy, or of lawful men of the same church, until a pastor be canonically appointed. I entirely do away all exactions, mischeningas,† and injustices, whether illegally

---

* It had been the practice to seize, to the king's use, whatever property ecclesiastics left behind them. Henry of Huntingdon relates, that on the death of Gilbert the Universal, bishop of London, who was remarkable for his avarice, all his effects, and among the rest, his boots crammed with gold and silver, were conveyed to the exchequer. Anglia Sacra, ii. 698. Sometimes, even what had been distributed on a death-bed, was reclaimed for the king. Vide G. Neub. 3, 5 "This practice of seizing the property of ecclesiastics at their death seems subsequently to have settled down into a claim on the part of the king of the cup and palfrey of a deceased bishop, prior, and abbat. See Rot. Claus. 39 Hen. III, m. 17, in dorso."—HARDY.

† It seems to have been a vexatious fine imposed on litigants when, in their pleadings, they varied from their declaration. Murder is sometimes taken in its present acceptation; sometimes it means a certain fine levied on the inhabitants where murder had been committed.

introduced by the sheriffs, or any one else. I will observe the good and ancient laws, and just customs, in murders, pleas, and other causes, and I command and appoint them to be so observed. Done at Oxford, A.D. 1136, in the first year of my reign."

The names of the witnesses, who were numerous, I disdain to particularize, because he as basely perverted almost every thing, as if he had sworn only that he might manifest himself a violator of his oath to the whole kingdom. This easy man must pardon me for speaking the truth; who, had he entered on the sovereignty lawfully, and not given a ready ear to the insinuations of the malevolent in the administration of it, would have wanted little in any princely quality. Under him, therefore, the treasures of several churches were pillaged, and their landed possessions given to laymen; the churches of the clergy were sold to foreigners; the bishops made captive, or forced to alienate their property; the abbeys given to improper persons, either through the influence of friendship, or for the discharge of debts. Still I think such transactions are not so much to be ascribed to him as to his advisers; who persuaded him, that, he ought never to want money, so long as the monasteries were stored with treasure.

In the year of our Lord 1137, in the beginning of Lent, the king crossed the sea. The earl, too, having thoroughly sounded, and discovered the inclinations of such as he knew to be tenacious of their plighted oath, and arranged what he conceived proper to be done afterwards, himself embarked on Easter-day, and prosperously reached the continent. Not long after, he had very nearly experienced the malignity of adverse fortune: for the king endeavoured to intercept him by treachery, at the instigation of one William de Ipres. The earl, however, informed of it by one of the accomplices, avoided the snare prepared for him, and absented himself from the palace, whither he was repeatedly invited, for several days. The king, troubled at having succeeded so little by his artifices, and thinking to effect his design by cunning, endeavoured, by a serene countenance and unrequired confession, to extenuate the enormity of his crime. He swore, in words framed at the earl's pleasure, never again to give countenance to such an outrage: and still more to recover his good graces, he confirmed his oath, by Hugo, archbishop of Rouen, giving his hand to Robert. This he did, it is true; but he never bestowed his unreserved friendship on that man, of whose power he was ever apprehensive. Thus, in his presence he would pleasantly and affably call him "earl:" when he was absent, he would vilify him, and would deprive him, clandestinely, of such portions of his estates as he was able. Robert, too, artfully eluding his duplicity, disguised his feelings, and allowing the king to depart peaceably to his kingdom, continued in Normandy, intent on his own concerns. Wherefore while Stephen, perplexed by many commotions in England, and first attacking one, and then another, justly verified, what was said of Ishmael, "That the hands of all were against him, and his hand against all," Robert passed that whole year in Normandy in perfect quiet. The king pointedly, as it is reported, used frequently to say of his rebellious subjects, " Since they have elected me king, why do they desert me? By the birth of God, I will never be called a fallen king!" Robert, placed, as it were, on an eminence, watched the event of circumstances, and earnestly revolved how he might escape, before God and man, the imputation of falsifying the oath he had sworn to his sister.

In the year of our Lord 1138, England was shaken with intestine commotions. For many persons, emboldened to illegal acts, either by nobility of descent or by ambition, or rather by unbridled heat of youth, were not ashamed, some to demand castles, others estates, and indeed whatever came into their fancy, from the king. When he delayed complying with their requests, alleging the dismemberment of his kingdom, or that others would make similar claims, or were already in possession of them; they, becoming enraged immediately, fortified their castles against him, and drove away large booties from his lands. Nor, indeed, was his spirit at all broken by the revolt of any, but attacking them suddenly in different places, he always concluded matters more to his own disadvantage than to theirs; for, after many great but fruitless labours, he gained from them, by the grant of honours or castles, a peace, feigned only for a time. He created likewise many earls,* where there had been none before, appro-

* Earls, till this time, had apparently been official; each having charge

propriating to them possessions and rents, which rightfully belonged to the crown. They were the more greedy in asking, and he the more profuse in giving, because a rumour was pervading England, that Robert earl of Gloucester, who was in Normandy, would shortly espouse the cause of his sister, after first renouncing his fealty to the king. This report was in fact well-founded: for shortly after Pentecost, despatching some of his people to Stephen from Normandy, he, according to ancient usage, renounced his fealty and friendship, and disannulled his homage; assigning as a just reason for so doing, that the king had illegally aspired to the kingdom, and neglected his plighted faith to him, not to say absolutely belied it: and, moreover, that he himself had acted contrary to law; who, after the oath sworn to his sister, had not blushed to do homage to another, during her lifetime. Doubtless also his mind was biassed by the answers of many ecclesiastics, whom he had consulted upon the subject; who declared that he could by no means pass the present life without ignominy, nor deserve the happiness of the next, if he violated the oath made to paternal affection. In addition to this, he contemplated the tenor of the papal decree, commanding obedience to the oath taken in the presence of his father: a copy of which decree I shall be careful to give in my next book. Robert, who had imbibed knowledge by a copious draught from the fount of science, was aware that these things would be of great advantage to him hereafter. But the king, indignant at the spirit of the earl, deprived him, as far as he was able, of all his possessions in England; and levelled some of his castles to the ground. Bristol alone remained, which not only expelled the enemy, but even harassed the king by frequent incursions. But as it may suffice to have brought the first book of modern history, from the return of the empress to her father after the death of her husband, to this period, I shall now begin the second, from the year in which this heroine came to England, to assert her right against Stephen.

---

of a county, and receiving certain emoluments therefrom: but these created by Stephen, seem to have been often merely titulary, with endowments out of the demesnes of the crown. Rob. Montensis calls these persons Pseudo-Comites, imaginary earls, and observes that Stephen had completely im-

BOOK II.

In the year 1139, the venom of malice, which had long been nurtured in the breast of Stephen, at length openly burst forth. Rumours were prevalent in England, that earl Robert was on the very eve of coming from Normandy with his sister: and, when under such an expectation, many persons revolted from the king, not only in inclination but in deed, he avenged himself for this injury, at the cost of numbers. He, also, contrary to the royal character, seized many at court, through mere suspicion of hostility to him, and obliged them to surrender their castles, and accede to any conditions he prescribed. There were, at that time, two very powerful bishops, in England, Roger of Salisbury, and his fraternal nephew, Alexander of Lincoln. Alexander had built the castle of Newark, as he said, for the defence and dignity of the bishopric. Roger, who wished to manifest his magnificence by building, had erected extensive castles at Sherborne, and more especially at Devizes. At Malmesbury, even in the church-yard, and scarcely a stone's throw from the principal church, he had begun a castle. He had gotten into his custody the castle of Salisbury, which being royal property, he had obtained from king Henry, and surrounded with a wall. Some powerful laymen, hurt at the probability of being surpassed by the clergy, in extent of riches and magnitude of their towns, took offence at this, and fostered the latent wound of envy in their bosoms. Wherefore they poured forth their imagined grievances to the king; observing, that the bishops, regardless of their order, were mad for erecting castles: that none could doubt, but that they were designed for the overthrow of the king; for, as soon as the empress should arrive, they would, induced doubtless by the recollection of her father's kindness to them, immediately greet their sovereign with the surrender of their fortresses: that, therefore they ought to be prevented,

poverished the crown by his liberalities to them. Henry the Second, however, on being firmly seated on the throne, recalled their grants of crown lands, and expelled them the kingdom.

and compelled to give up their strong holds; otherwise the king would repent too late, when he saw in the power of the enemy, that which, had he been wise, he might have applied to his own purpose. Such were the frequent insinuations of the nobility. The king, though far too partial to them, for some time pretended not to listen to what gratified his ear so much; assuaging the bitterness of delay, either by his respect for the piety of the bishops, or, as I rather think, from apprehension of the odium he might incur, by seizing their castles. Finally, he only postponed the execution of what the nobles had urged him to, till an opportunity presented itself for his purpose: which was as follows.

A great assembly of the nobles being held at Oxford about the eighth before the kalends of July, the prelates above-mentioned also repaired thither. The bishop of Salisbury set out on this expedition with great reluctance; for I heard him speaking to the following purport: "By my lady St. Mary, I know not why, but my heart revolts at this journey: this I am sure of, that I shall be of much the same service at court, as a foal is in battle:" thus did his mind forbode future evils. Here, as though fortune would seem subservient to the king's wishes, a quarrel arose between the servants of the bishops and those of Alan, earl of Brittany, about a right to quarters, which had a melancholy termination; as the bishop of Salisbury's retainers, then sitting at table, left their meal unfinished and rushed to the contest. At first, they contended with reproaches, afterwards with swords. The domestics of Alan were put to flight, and his nephew nearly killed: nor was the victory gained without bloodshed on the bishops' side; for many were wounded, and one knight* even slain. The king, eagerly seizing the opportunity, ordered the bishops to be convened by his old instigators, that they might make satisfaction to his court, as their people had infringed his peace: that this satisfaction should be, the delivery of the keys of their castles, as pledges of their fidelity. Though prepared to make compensation, they hesitated at the surrender of their fortresses; and in

* The term "miles" is very ambiguous: sometimes it is a knight; sometimes a trooper; sometimes a soldier generally. In later times it signified almost always a knight, but in Malmesbury, it seems mostly a horseman, probably of the higher order.

consequence, lest they should depart, he ordered them into close confinement. He therefore conducted bishop Roger, unfettered, but the chancellor, the nephew, or as it was reported, more than the nephew,* of the bishop, in chains, to Devizes ; a castle, erected at great and almost incalculable expense, not, as the prelate himself used to say, for the ornament, but as the real fact is, to the detriment of the church. At the first summons, the castles of Salisbury, Sherborne, and Malmesbury were yielded to the king. Devizes also surrendered at the end of three days, after the bishop had voluntarily enjoined himself abstinence from all food, that, by his personal sufferings, he might subdue the spirit of the bishop of Ely, who had taken possession † of it. Nor did the bishop of Lincoln act more perseveringly ; for he purchased his liberty by the surrender of his castles of Newark and Sleaford.

This transaction of the king's gave rise to the expression of many different opinions. Some observed, that the bishops were justly dispossessed of their castles, as they had built them in opposition to the injunction of the canons : they ought to be glad preachers of peace, not builders of houses which might be a refuge for the contrivers of evil. Such was the doctrine enforced with ampler reasons and discourses, by Hugo, archbishop of Rouen · as far as his eloquence extended, the strenuous champion of the king. Others took the opposite side of the question. This party was espoused by Henry, bishop of Winchester, legate of England from the papal see, and brother to king Stephen, as I have said before, whom no fraternal affection, no fear of danger, could turn aside from the path of truth.' He spake to this effect : " If the bishops had in anything overpassed the bounds of justice, the judging them did not pertain to the king, but to the ecclesiastical canons : that they ought not to be deprived of any possession but by a public and ecclesiastical council : that the king had not acted from zealous regard to right, but

* " Roger, the chancellor of England, was the son of Roger, bishop of Salisbury, by Maud of Ramsbury, his concubine."—HARDY.

† The author of the "Gesta Stephani," says, the king ordered both bishops to be kept without food, and threatened, moreover, to hang the son of bishop Roger. Gest. Stephani, 944 The continuator of Flor. Wigorn. adds, that one was confined in the crib of an ox-lodge, the other in a vile hovel, A.D. 1138.

with a view to his own advantage; as he had not restored the castles to the churches, at whose expense, and on whose land they were built, but had delivered them to laymen, and those by no means of religious character." Though the legate made these declarations not only privately, but publicly also before the king, and urged him to the liberation and restitution of the bishops, yet, being entirely disregarded, he lost his labour. In consequence, deeming it proper to resort to canonical power, he summoned his brother, without delay, to be present at a council he intended to hold at Winchester, on the fourth before the kalends of September.

On the appointed day, almost all the bishops of England, with Theobald, archbishop of Canterbury, who had succeeded William, came to Winchester. Thurstan, archbishop of York, excused himself, on account of the malady with which he was afflicted; for he was so enfeebled, as to be hardly able to guide his steps: the others apologized for their absence, by letter, on account of the war. The bull of pope Innocent was first read in the council, whereby, even from the kalends of March, if I rightly remember, he had enjoined the administration of his anxious charge to the lord bishop of Winchester, as legate in England. This was received with much good-will, as the bishop had shown his forbearance by the lapse of time, and had not proclaimed himself legate with precipitate vanity. Next followed, in the council, his address, in the Latin tongue, directed to the learned, on the disgraceful detention of the bishops: "of whom the bishop of Salisbury had been seized in a chamber of the palace, Lincoln in his lodgings, and Ely, fearing a similar treatment, had escaped the calamity by a hasty retreat to Devizes:" he observed, "that it was a dreadful crime, that the king should be so led away by sinister persons, as to have ordered violent hands to be laid on his subjects, more especially bishops, in the security of his court: that, to the king's disgrace was to be added the offence against God, in despoiling the churches of their possessions, under pretext of the criminality of the prelates: that, the king's outrage against the law of God, was matter of such pain to him, that he had rather himself suffer grievous injury, both in person and property, than have the episcopal dignity so basely humiliated; moreover, that the king, being repeatedly admonished to amend his fault, had, at last, not refused that the council should be summoned: that therefore, the archbishop and the rest should deliberate what was proper to be done; and he would not be wanting to execute the sentence of the council, either through regard to the friendship of the king, who was his brother, or loss of property, or even danger of life."

When he had gradually expatiated on these matters, the king, not distrusting his cause, sent certain *earls into the council to demand wherefore he was summoned. The legate briefly replied, "that, when he recollected he was in subjection to the faith of Christ, he ought not to be displeased, if, when guilty of a crime, such as the present age had never witnessed, he was required, by the ministers of Christ, to make satisfaction: that it was the act of heathen nations to imprison bishops, and divest them of their possessions: that they should tell his brother, therefore, that if he would deign a patient assent to his advice, he would give him such, by the authority of God, as neither the church of Rome, nor the French king's court, nor even earl Theobald, their common brother, a man of surpassing sense and piety, could reasonably oppose; but such as they ought favourably to embrace: that, at present, the king would act advisedly, if he would either account for his conduct, or submit to canonical judgment: it was, moreover, a debt he owed, to favour the church, by whose fostering care, not by military force, he had been promoted to the kingdom." The earls retiring after this speech, returned shortly with an answer prepared. They were accompanied by one Alberic de Ver, a man deeply versed in legal affairs. He related the king's answer, and aggravated as much as possible the case of bishop Roger, for bishop Alexander had departed; but this he did with moderation, and without using opprobrious language, though some of the earls, standing by, repeatedly interrupted his harangue by casting reproaches on the bishop.

The sum of what Alberic had to allege, was as follows: "That bishop Roger had greatly injured king Stephen; that he seldom came to court, but his people, presuming on his power, excited tumults; that they had, frequently at other

* It has before been related that Stephen made many earls, where there had been none before. these seem the persons intended by Malmesbury in many places, when speaking of some of the king's adherents.

places and very lately at Oxford, attacked the attendants, and even the very nephew of earl Alan, as well as the servants of Hervey de Lyons, a man of such high nobility, and so extremely haughty, that he had never deigned to visit England though king Henry had invited him; that the injury, therefore, of such violence having been offered him, doubly recoiled on king Stephen, through respect to whom he had come hither; that the bishop of Lincoln had been the author of the tumult excited by his followers from ancient enmity to Alan; that the bishop of Salisbury secretly favoured the king's enemies, though he disguised his subtlety for the moment; that the king had discovered this beyond all doubt, from many circumstances, more especially, however, from the said bishop's having refused permission to Roger de Mortimer with the king's soldiers whom he was conducting, when under the greatest apprehensions from the garrison of Bristol, to continue even a single night at Malmesbury; that it was in every person's mouth, that, as soon as the empress should arrive, he would join her party, with his nephews and their castles; that Roger, in consequence, was made captive, not as a bishop but as the king's servant who had administered his affairs and received his wages; that the king had not taken their castles by violence, but that both bishops had surrendered them voluntarily to escape the punishment due to the disturbance they had excited in the court; that the king had found some trifling sums of money in the castles which must lawfully belong to himself, as bishop Roger had collected it from the revenues of the exchequer in the times of his uncle and predecessor king Henry; that the bishop had readily relinquished this money as well as the castles through consciousness of his offences, of which the king did not want for witnesses; that, therefore, he was willing that the conditions entered into by himself and the bishops should remain in force."

It was rejoined by bishop Roger, in opposition to the speech of Alberic, that he had never been the minister of king Stephen; nor had he received his wages. This spirited man, too, who blushed at being cast down by adversity, threatened, that if he could not have justice for the property which had been wrested from him, in that council, he would seek it in the audience of a higher court. The legate mildly, as usual, observed that every allegation against the bishops ought to be made and the truth of it inquired into in an ecclesiastical court, before passing sentence, contrary to the canons, on innocent persons; that the king ought therefore to do as was incumbent in civil courts, that is, re-invest the bishops with their own property, otherwise, being disseized, by the law of nations, they will not plead.

Many arguments of this kind being used on both sides, the cause, at the king's request, was adjourned to the next day; then, on the morrow, prolonged still a day farther till the arrival of the archbishop of Rouen.

When he came, while all were anxious to hear what he had to allege, he said he was willing to allow the bishops their castles if they could prove by the canons that they ought justly to possess them; but as they were not able to do this it was the height of impudence to contend against the canons. "And admitting," said he, " that it be just for them to possess castles, yet most assuredly, as the times are eventful, all chiefs, after the custom of other nations, ought to deliver up the keys of their fortifications to the will of the king, who is bound to wage war for the common security." Thus the whole plea of the bishops was shaken: for, either according to the decrees of the canons, it was unjust for them to have castles, or, if that were allowed by the king's indulgence, they ought to yield to the emergency of the times, and give up the keys.

To this, the aforesaid pleader Alberic added that it had been signified to the king that the bishops muttered among themselves, and had even made preparation for some of their party to proceed to Rome against him. "And this," said he, "the king advises that none of you presume to do; for if any person shall go from England to any place, in opposition to him and to the dignity of his kingdom, perhaps his return may not be so easy. Moreover, he, as he sees himself aggrieved, of his own accord summons you to Rome." When the king had sent such a message, partly advising and partly threatening, it was perceived what was his design. In consequence the council broke up, as he would not submit to canonical censure; and the bishops deemed it unadvisable to enforce it against him for two reasons: first, because it was a rash act to excommunicate the king without the knowledge of the pope; secondly, because they understood, or some of them even saw, that swords were unsheathed around them. The contention was no longer of mere words, but nearly for life and for blood. The legate and the archbishop still, however, were anxiously observant of their duty. They humbly prostrated themselves before the king in his chamber, entreating him to take pity on the church, and to consider his soul and his reputation, and that he would not suffer a schism to be made between the empire and the priesthood. Although he in some measure removed the odium of his former conduct, by condescendingly rising to them, yet, prevented by ill advice, he carried none of his fair promises into effect.

The council broke up on the kalends of September; and on the day previous to the kalends of October, earl Robert, having at length surmounted every cause of delay, arrived with the empress his sister in England, relying on the protection of God and the observance of his lawful oath; but with a much smaller military force than any other person would have required for so perilous an enterprise; for he had not with him, at that time, more than one hundred and forty horsemen. My assertion is supported by persons of veracity; and did it not look like flattery, I would say that he was not inferior to Julius Cæsar, at least in resolution, whom Livy* relates to have had but five cohorts when he began the civil war, with which he attacked the world; though the comparison between Julius and Robert is invidious. For Julius, an alien to the true faith, reposed his hope on his good fortune, as he used to say, and the valour of his legions; Robert, celebrated for Christian piety, relied only on the assistance of the Holy Spirit and the lady St. Mary. The former had partizans in Gaul, in part of Germany, and Brittany, and had attached to him by means of presents all the Roman people with the exception of the senate; the latter, bating a very few who regarded their plighted oath, found the nobility in England either opposing or affording him no assistance. He landed, then, at Arundel, and for a time delivered his sister into the safe keeping, as he supposed, of her mother-in-law, whom Henry, as I have before related,

* It would seem from this passage that he had seen Livy in a more complete state than it exists at present.

had taken to his bed on the death of the empress's mother. Himself proceeded through the hostile country to Bristol, accompanied, as I have heard, by scarcely twelve horsemen, and was joined in the midst of his journey by Brian Fitz-Count of Wallingford. Nor was it long ere he learned that his sister had quitted Arundel; for her mother-in-law, through female inconstancy, had broken the faith she had repeatedly pledged by messages sent into Normandy. The earl, therefore, committed the empress to Henry bishop of Winchester and Waleran earl of Mellent for safe conduct, a favour never denied to the most inveterate enemy by honourable soldiers. Waleran, indeed, declined going farther than Calne, but the bishop continued his route. The earl, therefore, quickly collecting his troops, came to the boundary appointed by the king, and placed his sister in safe quarters at Bristol. She was afterwards received into Gloucester by Milo, who held the castle of that city under the earl in the time of king Henry, doing him homage and swearing fidelity to him; for this is the chief city of his county.

On the nones of October one Robert Fitz-Hubert, a savage barbarian, by night clandestinely entering the castle of Malmesbury, which bishop Rochester had inauspiciously founded, and burning the town, boasted of the deed, as though he had gained a great triumph. But, within a fortnight, his joy was at an end, being put to flight by the king. Stephen, in the meantime, commanded possession to be kept of the castle, until, on the restoration of peace, it might be destroyed. The king, moreover, before he came to Malmesbury, had occupied, and placed a garrison in a small fortress called Cerney, belonging to the aforesaid Milo. In consequence, thinking he should be equally successful elsewhere, as at that place and at Malmesbury, he assailed a castle called Trowbridge, belonging to Humphrey de Bohun, who was of the empress's party, but he departed without success.

The whole country then around Gloucester to the extremity of Wales, partly by force, and partly by favour, in the course of the remaining months of that year, gradually espoused the party of their sovereign the empress. The owners of certain castles, securing themselves within their fastnesses, waited the issue of events. The city of Hereford was taken without difficulty; and a few soldiers, who determined on resistance, had thrown themselves into the castle, were blocked up. The king drew nigh, if possible, to devise means for their assistance; but frustrated in his wishes, he retired with disgrace. He also approached Bristol, and going beyond it, burnt the neighbourhood around Dunstore, leaving nothing, as far as he was able, which could minister food to his enemies, or advantage to any one.

On the third before the ides of December, Roger bishop of Salisbury, by the kindness of death, escaped the quartan ague which had long afflicted him. They assert that his sickness was brought upon him through grief at the severe and repeated injuries he had received from king Stephen. To me it appears, that God exhibited him to the wealthy as an example of the mutability of fortune, in order that they should not trust in uncertain riches, which, as the apostle says, "while some have coveted, concerning faith have made shipwreck." He first ingratiated himself with prince Henry, who became afterwards king, by his prudence in the management of domestic matters, and by restraining the excesses of his household. For, before his accession, Henry had been careful and economical in his expenses, compelled thereto by the scantiness of his resources, and the illiberal treatment of his brothers, William and Robert Knowing his disposition this way, Roger had deserved so well of him in his time of need, that, when he came to the throne, he denied him scarcely any thing he thought proper to ask, gave him estates, churches, prebends, entire abbeys of monks, and, lastly, committed even the kingdom to his fidelity: made him chancellor, in the beginning of his reign, and not long after, bishop of Salisbury. Roger, therefore decided causes; he regulated the expenditure; he had charge of the treasury. Such were his occupations when the king was in England: such, without associate or inspector, when he resided in Normandy; which took place repeatedly, and for a long time together. And not only the king, but the nobility, even those who were secretly stung with envy at his good fortune, and more especially the ministers and debtors of the king, gave him almost whatever he could fancy. Was there any thing contiguous to his property which might be advantageous to him, he would directly extort it, either by entreaty or purchase; or, if that failed, by force. With unrivalled magnificence in their construction, as our times may recollect, he erected splendid mansions on all his estates; in merely maintaining which, the labour of his successors shall toil in vain. His cathedral he dignified to the utmost with matchless ornaments and buildings on which no expense was spared. It was truly wonderful to behold in this man, what abundant power attended him in every kind of dignity, and flowed as it were to his hand. How great was the glory, indeed, what could exceed it, that he should have made his two nephews, by virtue of his education, men of noted learning and industry, bishops; and, not of mean sees; but of Lincoln and Ely, than which, I know not whether there be more opulent in England? He was sensible of his power, and, somewhat more harshly than became such a character, abused the favours of heaven. Lastly, as a certain poet observes of a rich man,*

"He builds, destroys, and changes square for round,"

so Roger attempted to turn abbeys into bishoprics, and bishoprics into abbeys. The most ancient monasteries of Malmesbury and Abbotsbury, he annexed, as far as he was able, to his see. He changed the priory of Sherborne, which is subject to the bishop of Salisbury, into an abbey; and the abbey of Hortun was forthwith dissolved and united to it. These events took place in the time of king Henry, under whom, as I have observed, his prosperity reached its zenith: for under Stephen, as I have before related, it began to decline; except that in the beginning of his reign, he obtained for one of his nephews, the chancellorship; for the other the office of treasurer; and for himself the town of Malmesbury; the king repeating often to his companions, "By the birth of God, I would give him half England, if he asked for it: till the time be ripe, he shall tire of asking, ere I tire of giving." But fortune, who, in former times, had flattered him so long and so transcendently, at last cruelly pierced him with scorpion-sting. Such was that instance, when he saw those whom he dearly regarded, wounded; and his most favoured knight killed before his face; the next day, himself, and, as I said before, his nephews, very powerful bishops, the one compelled to fly, the other detained, and the third, a

* Horat. Epist. i. 1, 100.

young man to whom he was greatly attached, bound with chains: on the surrender of his castles, his treasures pillaged, and himself afterwards, in the council, loaded with the most disgraceful reproaches. Finally, as he was nearly breathing his latest sigh, at Salisbury, the residue of his money and utensils, which he had placed upon the altar for the purpose of completing the church, was carried off against his will. The height of his calamity, was, I think, a circumstance which even I cannot help commiserating ; that, though he appeared wretched to many, yet there were very few who pitied him : so much envy and hatred had his excessive power drawn on him, and undeservedly, too, from some of those very persons whom he had advanced to honour.

In the year of the Incarnate Word 1140, the monks of those abbeys which Roger had unjustifiably usurped, waiting on the king, were permitted to enjoy their ancient privileges, and abbats, as formerly. John, a monk of that place, a man highly celebrated for the affability of his manners and the liberality of his mind, was elected abbat of Malmesbury by the monks, according to the tenor of the privilege which St. Aldhelm had obtained from pope Sergius four hundred and sixty-six years before, and had caused to be confirmed by the kings, Ina of the West Saxons, and Ethelred of the Mercians. The legate approved the claim, but disapproved of the person : for he could not be induced to believe that the king had consented to the election but by a gift in money. And, indeed, a small sum had been promised, on the score of liberating the church, not for the election of the person. Wherefore John, though taken off by a premature death within the year, still left a lasting and laudable memory of himself to all succeeding ages. For no monk of that place, I confess the truth, would have pursued a task of such difficulty, had not John begun it. Wherefore let his successors be praised, if they shall preserve the liberty of that church ; he certainly rescued it from thraldom.

The whole of this year was embittered by the horrors of war. There were many castles throughout England, each defending their neighbourhood, but, more properly speaking, laying it waste. The garrisons drove off from the fields, both sheep and cattle, nor did they abstain either from churches or church-yards. Seizing such of the country vavassours * as were reputed to be possessed of money, they compelled them, by extreme torture, to promise whatever they thought fit. Plundering the houses of the wretched husbandmen, even to their very beds, they cast them into prison; nor did they liberate them, but on their giving every thing they possessed or could by any means scrape together, for their release. Many calmly expired in the midst of torments inflicted to compel them to ransom themselves, bewailing, which was all they could do, their miseries to God. And, indeed, at the instance of the earl, the legate, with the bishops, repeatedly excommunicated all violators of church-yards and plunderers of churches, and those who laid violent hands on men in holy or monastic orders, or their servants: but this his attention profited but little. It was distressing, therefore, to see England, once the fondest cherisher of peace and the single receptacle of tranquillity, reduced to such a pitch of misery, that, not even the bishops, nor monks, could pass in safety from one town to another. Under king Henry, many foreigners, who had been driven from home by the commotions of their native land, were accustomed to resort to England, and rest in quiet under his fostering protection: in Stephen's time, numbers of freebooters from Flanders and Brittany flocked to England, in expectation of rich pillage. Meanwhile, the earl of Gloucester conducted himself with caution, and his most earnest endeavours were directed to gaining conquests with the smaller loss to his adherents. Such of the English nobility as he could not prevail upon to regard the obligation of their oath, he held it sufficient if he could so restrain, that, if they did not assist, they would not injure the cause: being willing, according to the saying of the comic writer, "To do what he could, when he could not do what he would." But when he saw the opportunity present itself, he strenuously performed the duty both of soldier and of general; more especially, he valiantly subdued those strong holds, which were of signal detriment to the cause he had espoused; that is to say, Harpetrey, which king Stephen had taken from certain soldiers of the earl before he came to England, and many others; Sudley,

* The meaning of vavassour is very various: here it seems to imply what we call a yeoman.

Cerney, which the king had garrisoned, as I have said; and the castle which Stephen had fortified over against Wallingford, he levelled to the ground. He also, in these difficult times, created his brother Rainald, earl of Cornwall. Nor indeed did the king show less spirit in performing the duties of his station; for he omitted no occasion of repeatedly beating off his adversaries, and defending his own possessions. But he failed of success, and all things declined, for lack of justice. Dearth of provisions, too, increased by degrees, and the scarcity of good money was so great, from its being counterfeited, that, sometimes out of ten or more shillings, hardly a dozen pence would be received. The king himself was reported to have ordered the weight of the penny, as established in king Henry's time, to be reduced, because, having exhausted the vast treasures of his predecessor, he was unable to provide for the expense of so many soldiers. All things, then, became venal in England; and churches and abbeys were no longer secretly, but even publicly exposed to sale.

During this year, in Lent, on the thirteenth before the kalends of April, at the ninth hour of the fourth day of the week, there was an eclipse, throughout England, as I have heard. With us, indeed, and with all our neighbours, the obscuration of the sun was so remarkable, that persons sitting at table, as it then happened almost every where, for it was Lent, at first feared that chaos was come again: afterwards learning its cause, they went out, and beheld the stars around the sun. It was thought and said by many, not untruly, that the king would not continue a year in the government.

In the following week, that is, during the time of the Passion, on the seventh before the kalends of April, the forementioned barbarian, Robert Fitz-Hubert, a character well calculated for the stratagems of war, surprised the castle of Devizes:* a man, by far the most cruel of any within the circle of this age's memory: blasphemous, also, towards God. He used voluntarily to boast of having been present at a place where twenty-four monks were burnt, together with the church, declaring, that he too would

* This he effected by means of scaling ladders, made of thongs of leather. Gest. Stephani, 951.

frequently do the like in England, and grieve God, by the plunder of the church of Wilton; and the destruction of Malmesbury, with the slaughter of all its monks: that he would return them this good office, because they had admitted the king, to his disadvantage: for of this he accused them, though without foundation. I myself have heard, when, at any time, which was extremely rare indeed, he liberated his captives without torture, and they thanked him for it, on the part of God, I have heard him, I say, reply; "never let God owe me any thanks." He used to expose his prisoners, naked and rubbed with honey, to the burning heat of the sun; thereby exciting flies, and other insects of that kind, to sting them. But, having now got possession of Devizes, he hesitated not to boast, that, he should gain, by means of this castle, the whole district from Winchester to London; and that he would send to Flanders for soldiers to defend him. While meditating, however, such a scheme, divine vengeance overtook him through the agency of one John Fitz-Gilbert, a man of suprising subtlety, who had a castle at Marlborough. For being thrown into chains by him, because he refused to surrender Devizes to his sovereign, the empress, he was hanged, like a common thief. Wonderful was the judgment of God on this sacrilegious wretch, that he should meet with such an ignominious end, not from the king, to whom he was inimical, but from the very persons he appeared to favour. The authors of his death ought worthily to be extolled, for having freed the country from such a pest, and justly despatched an intestine enemy.

In the same year, during Pentecost, the king resided at London, in the Tower, attended only by the bishop of Sees, for the others disdained, or feared, to come thither. Some little time after, by the mediation of the legate, a conference was appointed between the empress and the king, that, if possible, by the inspiration of God, peace might be restored. To this conference, near Bath, were sent on the part of the empress, her brother Robert, and others of her friends: on the king's, the legate, the archbishop, and also the queen. But they wasted words and time, to no purpose, and departed without being able to conclude a peace. Nor was the ground of separation equal on both sides, as the empress, more inclined to justice, had declared, that she was not averse to the decision of the church: but the king most cautiously avoided this; fondly trusting to the counsels of those persons who loved nothing less than peace, so long as they could make their ascendency over him answer their own purposes. In the latter end of September, the legate, who knew that it was the especial duty of his office to restore peace, undertaking the toil of a foreign voyage for its accomplishment, hastened to sail over to France. Here, a long and anxious discussion, for tranquillizing England, taking place, between the king of France, earl Theobald, and many of the clergy, he returned, nearly at the end of November, bringing back counsels wholesome for the country, could they have been carried into effect. And indeed the empress and the earl assented to them immediately, but the king delayed from day to day, and finally rejected them altogether. Upon this, at last, the legate discontinued his exertions, waiting, like the rest, for the issue of events: for what avails it to swim against the stream? and, as some one observes, "To seek odium only by one's labours is the height of madness."

BOOK III.

I now attempt to give a clue to the mazy labyrinth of events and transactions which occurred in England, during the year 1141,* lest posterity, through my neglect, should be unacquainted with them; as it is of service to know the volubility of fortune and the mutability of human estate, God only permitting or ordaining them. And, as the moderns greatly and deservedly blame our predecessors, for having left no memorial of themselves or their transactions since the days of Bede, I think I ought to be very favourably regarded by my readers, if they judge rightly, for determining to remove this reproach from our times.

King Stephen had peaceably departed from the county of Lincoln before Christmas, and had augmented the honours of

* Several MSS., as well as the printed copy, read 1142, but one has 1141, which is right.

the earl of Chester,* and of his brother; of whom the earl, long since, in the time of king Henry, had been married to the daughter of the earl of Gloucester. In the mean while, the citizens of Lincoln, who wished to acquire great favour with the king, certified him by a message, when resident in London, that the two brothers had taken up their abode in security, in the castle of that city: and that, suspecting nothing less than the arrival of the king, they might be very easily surprised, while themselves would provide that he should get possession of the castle as secretly as possible. As Stephen never wished to neglect any opportunity of augmenting his power, he gladly repaired thither. In consequence, the brothers were surprised and besieged, even in the Christmas holidays. This step appeared unjustifiable to many, because, as I have observed, he had left them before the festival, without any suspicion of enmity; nor had he, even now, after ancient usage, abjured his friendship with them, which they call "defying." However, the earl of Chester, though surrounded with imminent dangers, adroitly escaped from the castle. By what management this was accomplished I know not; whether through consent of some of the besiegers, or whether, because valour, when taken by surprise, frequently tries variety of methods, and often discovers a remedy for its emergencies. Not content with his own escape, he earnestly cast about, how to devise the safety of his brother and of his wife, whom he had left in the fortress. The more prudent mode seemed to be, to request assistance from his father-in-law, although he had long since offended him on many accounts, but principally because he appeared staunch to neither party. He sent messengers, therefore, promising eternal fidelity to the empress, if, induced more by affectionate regard than any desert of his, he would rescue those from danger, who were already in the very jaws of captivity.

Unable to endure this indignity, the earl of Gloucester readily assented. Weary of delay, too, as the fairest country was harassed with intestine rapine and slaughter, for the sake of two persons, he preferred bringing the matter to an issue at once, would God permit. He hoped, also, for the Divine

* "Ranulf, earl of Chester, and his uterine brother, William de Romare, were the sons of Lucia, countess of Lincoln."—HARDY

assistance on his undertaking, as the king had molested his son-in-law, without any fault on his part; was at that moment besieging his daughter; and had castellated the church of the holy mother of God in Lincoln. How much ought these things to weigh in the mind of a prince? Would it not be better to die, and fall with honour, than endure so marked a disgrace? For the sake then of avenging God, and his sister, and liberating his relations, he entered on this perilous undertaking. The supporters of his party readily accompanied him; the major part of whom being deprived of their inheritances, were instigated to hostility by rage at their losses, and the consciousness of their valour. However, during the whole extended march, from Gloucester to Lincoln, he studiously concealed his intention, leaving all the army, with the exception of a very few, in suspense, by his mysterious conduct.

At length, on the day of the Purification of the blessed Mary, they arrived at the river flowing between the two armies, called the Trent, which, from its springs, together with floods of rain, had risen so high, that it could not possibly be forded. Here, at last, disclosing his intention to his son-in-law, who had joined him with a strong force, and to those he had brought with him, he added, that, " He had long since made up his mind, never to be induced to fly, be the emergency what it might; if they could not conquer, they must die or be taken." All encouraged him to hope the best; and, wonderful to hear, though on the eve of hazarding a battle, he swam over the rapid river I have mentioned, with the whole of his party. So great was the earl's ardour to put an end to calamity, that he preferred risking extremities to prolonging the sufferings of the country. The king, too, with many earls, and an active body of cavalry, abandoning the siege, courageously presented himself for battle. The royalists began the prelude to the fight, which they call the " joust,"* as they were skilled in that exercise: but when they saw that the consular party, if they may be so called, did not attack from a distance with lances, but at close quarters with swords, and broke the king's ranks with violent and determined onset, the earls, to a man, for six of

* The joust signifies a contest between two persons on horseback, with lances. each singled out his opponent.

them had entered the conflict, together with the king, consulted their safety by flight. A few barons, of laudable fidelity and valour, who would not desert him, even in his necessity, were made captive. The king, though he by no means wanted spirit to defend himself, being at last attacked on every side by the earl of Gloucester's soldiers, fell to the ground by a blow from a stone; but who was the author of this deed is uncertain. Thus, when all around him were either taken or dispersed, he was compelled to yield to circumstances and become a captive. On which the truly noble earl of Gloucester commanded the king to be preserved uninjured, not suffering him to be molested even with a reproach; and the person, whom he had just before fiercely attacked when dignified with the sovereignty, he now calmly protected when subdued: that the tumults of anger and of joy being quieted, he might show kindness to his relation, and respect the dignity of the diadem in the captive. The citizens of Lincoln were slaughtered on all sides by the just indignation of the victors, and without commiseration on the part of the conquered, as they had been the origin and fomenters of this calamity.

The king, according to the custom of such as are called captives, was presented to the empress, at Gloucester, by her brother, and afterwards conducted to Bristol. Here, at first, he was kept with every mark of honour, except the liberty of going at large: but in succeeding time, through the presumption of certain persons, who said openly and contumeliously, that it did not behove the earl to treat the king otherwise than they chose; and also, because it was reported, that having either eluded or bribed his keepers, he had been found, more than once, beyond the appointed limits, more especially in the night-time, he was confined with fetters.

In the meanwhile, both the empress and the earl dealt by messengers with the legate his brother, that he should forthwith receive her into the church,* and to the kingdom, as the daughter of king Henry, to whom all England and Normandy had sworn allegiance. This year, the first Sunday in Lent happened on the fourteenth before the kalends of March. By means of negotiators on either side, the business was so far forwarded, that they agreed to meet in conference,

* That is, as appears after, to acknowledge her publicly as their sovereign.

on an open plain on this side of Winchester. They assembled, therefore, on the third Sunday in Lent, a day dark and rainy, as though the fates would portend a woeful change in this affair. The empress swore, and pledged her faith to the bishop, that all matters of importance in England, and especially the bestowing of bishoprics and abbeys, should await his decision, if he, with the holy church, would receive her as sovereign, and observe perpetual fidelity towards her. Her brother, Robert, earl of Gloucester, swore as she did, and pledged his faith for her, as did also Brian Fitz-count, lord Marcher* of Wallingford, and Milo of Gloucester, afterwards earl of Hereford, with some others. Nor did the bishop hesitate to receive the empress as sovereign of England, and, together with certain of his party, to pledge his faith, that so long as she did not infringe the covenant, he would observe his fidelity to her. On the morrow, which was the fifth before the nones of March, a splendid procession being formed, she was received in the cathedral of Winchester; the bishop-legate conducting her on the right side, and Bernard, bishop of St. David's, on the left. There were present also, Alexander, bishop of Lincoln, Robert of Hereford, Nigel of Ely, Robert of Bath: the abbats, Ingulf of Abingdon, Edward of Reading, Peter of Malmesbury, Gilbert of Gloucester, Roger of Tewkesbury, and some others. In a few days, Theobald, archbishop of Canterbury, came to the empress at Winchester, by invitation of the legate: but he deferred promising fidelity to her, deeming it beneath his reputation and character to change sides, till he had consulted the king. In consequence, he, and many other prelates, with some few of the laity, were allowed to visit Stephen and converse with him: and, graciously obtaining leave to submit to the exigency of the times, they embraced the sentiments of the legate. The empress passed Easter, which happened on the third before the kalends of April, at Oxford; the rest returned to their respective homes.

On the day after the octaves of Easter, a council began,

---

* Marchio: this latterly signified marquis in the sense we now use it; but in Malmesbury's time, and long after, it denoted a guardian of the borders: hence the lords marchers on the confines of Scotland and Wales; though it does not appear very clearly how this should apply to Wallingford, unless it was is his place of birth.

with great parade, at Winchester, consisting of Theobald, archbishop of Canterbury, all the bishops of England, and many abbats: the legate presiding. Such as were absent, accounted for it by messengers and letters. As I was present at the holding of this council, I will not deny posterity the truth of every circumstance; for I perfectly remember it. On the same day, after the letters were read by which some excused their absence, the legate called the bishops apart, and discoursed with them in secret of his design; then the abbats, and, lastly, the archdeacons were summoned. Of his intention nothing transpired publicly, though what was to be done engrossed the minds and conversation of all.

On the third day of the week, the speech of the legate ran nearly to this effect. "That, by the condescension of the pope, he acted as his vicegerent in England: wherefore, by his authority, the clergy of England were assembled at this council to deliberate on the peace of the country, which was exposed to imminent danger: that, in the time of king Henry, his uncle, England had been the peculiar abode of peace; so that by the activity, and spirit, and care of that most excellent man, not only the natives, of whatever power or dignity, dared make no disturbance; but, by his example, each neighbouring king and prince, also, yielded to peace, and either invited, or compelled, his subjects to do the like: moreover, that this king, some years before his death, had caused the whole realm of England, as well as the duchy of Normandy, to be engaged, by the oaths of all the bishops and barons, to his daughter, late the empress, who was his only surviving issue by his former consort, if he should fail of male offspring by the wife he had espoused from Lorraine: and adverse fortune," said he, "was envious of my most excellent uncle, and suffered him to die in Normandy without male issue. Therefore, as it seemed long to wait for a sovereign who delayed coming to England, for she resided in Normandy, we provided for the peace of the country, and my brother was allowed to reign. And although I gave myself as surety between him and God, that he would honour and advance the holy church, and uphold good, but abrogate evil, laws; yet it grieves me to remember, shames me to say, how he conducted himself in the kingdom: how justice ceased to be exerted against the daring; how all peace was annihilated, almost within the year: the bishops made captive, and compelled to give up their possessions; the abbeys sold; the churches robbed of their treasures; the counsels of the abandoned regarded: while those of the virtuous were postponed or totally despised. You know how often I addressed him, both by myself and the bishops, more especially in the council held last year for that purpose, and that I gained by it nothing but odium. Every one, who shall think rightly, must be aware, that I ought to love my mortal brother, but that I should still more regard the cause of my immortal Father. Wherefore, since God has exercised his judgment on my brother, by permitting him, without my knowledge, to fall into the hands of the powerful, I have invited you all here to assemble by virtue of my legation, lest the kingdom should fall to decay through want of a sovereign. The case was yesterday agitated in private, before the major part of the English clergy, to whose right it principally pertains to elect the sovereign, and also to crown him. First, then, as is fitting, invoking God's assistance, we elect the daughter of that peaceful, that glorious, that rich, that good, and, in our times, incomparable king, as sovereign of England and Normandy, and promise her fidelity and support."

When all present had either becomingly applauded his sentiments, or, by their silence, not contradicted them, he added: "We have despatched messengers for the Londoners, who, from the importance of their city in England, are almost nobles, as it were, to meet us on this business; and have sent them a safe-conduct: and we trust they will not delay their arrival beyond to-morrow: wherefore let us give them indulgence till that time."

On the fourth day of the week the Londoners came; and being introduced to the council, urged their cause, so far as to say, that they were sent from the fraternity, as they call it, of London, not to contend, but to entreat that their lord the king might be liberated from captivity: that all the barons, who had long since been admitted to their fellowship, most earnestly solicited this of the lord legate and the archbishop, as well as of all the clergy who were present. The legate answered them copiously and clearly: and, that their request might be the less complied with, the speech of the preceding day was repeated, with the addition, that it did not become the Londoners, who were considered as the chief people of England, in the light of nobles, to side with those persons who had deserted their lord in battle ; by whose advice the king had dishonoured the holy church ; and who, in fact, only appeared to favour the Londoners, that they might drain them of their money.

In the meantime, a certain person, whose name, if I rightly remember, was Christian, a clerk belonging to the queen, as I heard, rose up, and held forth a paper to the legate. He having silently perused it, exalted his voice to the highest pitch, and said, that it was informal, and improper to be recited in so great an assembly, especially of dignified and religious persons. For, among other offensive and singular points, the signature of a person was affixed to it, who, in the preceding year, at a similar council, had attacked the venerable bishops with opprobrious language. The legate thus baffling him, the clerk was not wanting to his mission, but, with notable confidence, read the letter in their hearing ; of which this was the purport. "The queen earnestly entreated the whole clergy assembled, and especially the bishop of Winchester, the brother of her lord, to restore the said lord to his kingdom, whom abandoned persons, and even such as were under homage to him, had cast into chains." To this suggestion, the legate answered to the same effect as to the Londoners. These conferring together, declared, that they would relate the decree of the council to their townsmen, and give it their support as far as they were able.

On the fifth day of the week the council broke up, many of the royal party having been first excommunicated; more especially William Martel, who had formerly been cupbearer to king Henry, and was at that time butler to Stephen ; for he had sorely exasperated the legate, by intercepting and pilfering much of his property. It was now a work of great difficulty to soothe the minds of the Londoners: for though these matters, as I have said, were agitated immediately after Easter, yet was it only a few days before the Nativity of St. John that they would receive the empress. At that time great part of England readily submitted to her government; her brother Robert was assiduously employed in promoting her dignity by every becoming method; kindly addressing the nobility, making many promises, and intimidating the adverse party, or even, by messengers, exhorting them to peace; and already restoring justice, and the law of the land, and tranquillity, throughout every district which favoured the empress; and it is sufficiently notorious that if his party had trusted to Robert's moderation and wisdom, it would not afterwards experienced so melancholy a reverse. The lord legate, too, appeared of laudable fidelity in furthering the interests of the empress. But, behold, at the very moment when she imagined she should get possession of all England, every thing was changed. The Londoners, ever suspicious and murmuring among themselves, now burst out into open expressions of hatred; and, as it is reported, even laid wait for their sovereign and her nobles. Aware of and escaping this plot, they gradually retired from the city, without tumult and in a certain military order. The empress was accompanied by the legate and David king of Scotland, the heroine's uncle, together with her brother Robert who then, as at every other time, shared her fortune; and, in short, all her partizans to a man escaped in safety. The Londoners, learning their departure, flew to their residence and plundered every thing which they had left in their haste.

Not many days after, a misunderstanding arose between the legate and the empress which may be justly considered as the melancholy cause of every subsequent evil in England. How this happened I will explain. King Stephen had a son named Eustace, begotten on the daughter of Eustace earl of Boulogne. For king Henry, the father of the empress, that I may go back somewhat to acquaint posterity with the truth of these transactions, had given Mary, the sister of his wife, the mother of this lady, in marriage to the aforesaid earl, as he was of noble descent and equally renowned for prudence and for valour. By Mary, Eustace had no issue except a daughter called Matilda. When she became marriageable, after the death of her father, the same truly magnificent king gave her in wedlock to his nephew Stephen, and also procured by his care the county of Boulogne for him, as he had before conferred on him that of Moreton in Normandy. The legate had justly proposed that these counties should be bestowed on his nephew Eustace, whom I mentioned, so long as his father should remain in captivity. This the empress altogether opposed, and it is doubtful whether she had not even promised them to others. Offended at the repulse, he kept from her court many days; and though repeatedly sent for, persisted in refusing to go thither. In the meanwhile, he held a friendly conference with the queen, his brother's wife, at Guildford, and being wrought upon by her tears and concessions, bent his mind to the liberation of Stephen. He also absolved, without consulting the bishops, all those of the king's party whom he had excommunicated in the council, while his complaints against the empress were disseminated through England, that she wished to seize his person, that she observed nothing which she had sworn to him; that all the barons of England had performed their engagements towards her, but that she had violated hers, as she knew not how to use her prosperity with moderation.

To allay, if possible, these commotions, the earl of Gloucester, with a retinue not very numerous, proceeded to Winchester; but, failing in his endeavours, he returned to Oxford, where his sister had for some time established her residence. She therefore understanding, as well from what she was continually hearing, as from what she then learned from her brother, that the legate had no friendly dispositions towards her, proceeded to Winchester with such forces as she could muster. Being immediately admitted into the royal castle, with good intentions probably she sent messengers to the bishop, requesting that, as she was upon the spot, he would come to her without delay. He, not thinking it safe to go, deceived the messengers by an evasive manner, merely saying, "I will prepare myself:" and immediately he sent for all such as he knew were well-disposed to the king. In consequence almost all the earls of England came; for they were full of youth and levity, and preferred military enterprise to peace. Besides, many of them were ashamed at having deserted the king in battle, as has been said before, and thought to wipe off the ignominy of having fled, by attending this meeting. Few, however, attended the empress: there were David king of Scotland, Robert earl of Gloucester, Milo de Hereford, and some barons; for Ranulf earl of Chester came late, and to no purpose. To comprise, therefore, a long series of events within narrow limits: the roads on every side of Winchester were watched by the queen and the earls who had come with her, lest supplies should be brought in to those who had sworn fidelity to the empress. The town of Andover also was burned. On the west, therefore, necessaries were procured but scantily and with difficulty; some persons found on the road, being intercepted and either killed or maimed; while on the east, every avenue towards London was crowded with supplies destined for the bishop and his party; Geoffrey de Mandeville, who had now again revolted to them, for formerly after the capture of the king he had sworn fidelity to the empress, and the Londoners, lending every possible assistance, and omitting no circumstance which might distress that princess. The people of Winchester were, though secretly, inclined to her side, regarding the faith they had before pledged to her, although they had been in some degree compelled by the bishop to such a measure. In the meanwhile combustibles were hurled from the bishop's castle on the houses of the townspeople, who, as I have said, rather wished success to the empress than to the bishop, which caught and burned the whole abbey of nuns within the city, and the monastery which is called Hyde without the walls. Here was an image of our Lord crucified, wrought with a profusion of gold and silver and precious stones, through the pious solicitude of Canute, who was formerly king and presented it. This being seized by the flames and thrown to the ground, was afterwards stripped of its ornaments at the command of the legate himself: more than five hundred marks of silver and thirty of gold, which were found on it, served for a largess to the soldiers. The abbey of nuns at Warewell was also burned by one William de Ipres, an abandoned character who feared neither God nor man, because some of the partizans of the empress had secured themselves within it.

In the meantime, the earl of Gloucester, though suffering, with his followers, by daily contests with the royalists, and though circumstances turned out far beneath his expectation, yet ever abstained from the burning of churches, notwithstanding he resided in the vicinity of St. Swithun's. But unable to endure any longer the disgrace of being, together with his party, almost besieged, and seeing fortune inclining towards the enemy, he deemed it expedient to yield to necessity; and, having marshalled his troops, he prepared to depart. Sending his sister, therefore, and the rest, in the vanguard, that she might proceed without interruption, he himself retreated gently, with a chosen few, who had spirit enough not to be alarmed at a multitude. The earls immediately pursuing him, as he thought it disgraceful, and beneath his dignity to fly, and was the chief object of universal attack, he was made captive. The rest, especially the chiefs, proceeded on their destined journey, and, with the utmost precipitation, reached Devizes. Thus they departed from Winchester on the day of the exaltation of the holy cross, which at that time happened on a Sunday, having come thither a few days before the assumption of the holy mother of God. It appeared to some rather miraculous, and was matter of general conversation in England, that the king on the Sunday of the purification of our lady, and the earl on the Sunday of the exaltation of the life-imparting cross, should each experience a similar fate. This, however, was truly worthy of remark and admiration, that, no one, on this mischance, ever beheld the earl of Gloucester either dispirited or dejected in countenance. He breathed too high a consciousness of dignity, to subject himself to the caprice of fortune; and, although he was at first invited by soothing measures, and afterwards assailed by threats, he never consented to treat of his liberation, except with the privity of his sister. At last the affair was thus decided: that the king and himself should be liberated on equal terms; no condition being proposed, except that each might defend his party, to the utmost of his abilities, as before. These matters, after repeated and long discussion, from the exaltation of the holy cross, to the festival of All Saints, then came to a suitable conclusion. For on that day, the king, released from his captivity, left his queen, and son, and two of the nobility at Bristol, as sureties for the liberation of the earl; and came with the utmost speed to Winchester, where the earl, now brought from Rochester, whither he had first been taken, was at this time confined. The third day after, when the king came to Winchester, the earl departed, leaving there on that day his son William, as a pledge, till the queen should be released. Performing with quick despatch the journey to Bristol, he liberated the queen, on whose return, William, the earl's son, was set free from his detention. It is, moreover, sufficiently notorious, that, although, during the whole of his captivity and of the following months till Christmas, he was enticed by numberless and magnificent promises to revolt from his sister; yet he always deemed his fraternal affection of greater importance than any promise which could be made him. For leaving his property and his castles, which he might have quietly enjoyed, he continued unceasingly near the empress at Oxford, where, as I have said before, fixing her residence, she held her court.

In the meantime, the legate, a prelate of unbounded spirit, who was never inclined to leave incomplete what he had once purposed, summoned by his legatine authority a council at Westminster, on the octaves of St. Andrew. I cannot relate the transactions of this council with that exact veracity with which I did the former, as I was not present. We have heard that a letter was then read from the sovereign pope, in which he gently rebuked the legate for not endeavouring to release his brother; but that he forgave him his former transgression, and earnestly exhorted him to attempt his liberation by any mode, whether ecclesiastical or secular: that the king himself entered the council, and complained to the reverend assembly, that his own subjects had both made captive, and nearly killed him by the injuries they inflicted on him, who had never refused them justice. That the legate himself, too, by great powers of eloquence, endeavoured to extenuate the odium of his own conduct: that, in truth, he had received the empress, not from inclination, but necessity; for, that, while his brother's overthrow was yet recent, all the earls being either dispersed or waiting the issue of events in suspense, she had surrounded Winchester with her party: that she had obstinately persevered in breaking every promise she had made pertaining to the right of the churches: and that he had it from unquestionable authority, that she, and her partisans, had not only had designs on his dignity, but even on his life: that, however, God, in his mercy, had caused matters to fall out contrary to her hopes, so that he should himself escape destruction, and rescue his brother from captivity: that he commanded therefore, on the part of God and of the pope, that they should strenuously assist the king, anointed by the will of the people and with the approbation of the holy see: but that such as disturbed the peace, in favour of the countess of Anjou, should be excommunicated, with the exception of herself, who was sovereign of the Angevins.

I do not say, that this speech was kindly received by all the clergy, though certainly no one opposed it; for all bridled their tongues either through fear, or through reverence. There was one layman sent from the empress, who openly forbade the legate, by the faith which he had pledged to her, to ordain any thing, in that council, repugnant to her honour; and said, that he had made oath to the empress, not to assist his brother, unless, perchance, by sending him twenty horsemen at the utmost: that her coming to England had been effected by his frequent letters: that her taking the king, and holding him in captivity, had been done principally by his connivance. The advocate affirmed these and many other circumstances, with great harshness of language, and by no means sparing the legate. However, he could not be prevailed upon, by any force of argument, to lay aside his animosity: for, as I have said before, he was an active perseverer in what he had once taken in hand. This year, therefore, the tragedy of which I have briefly related, was fatal, and nearly destructive, to England; during which, though conceiving that she might now, perhaps, experience some little respite, yet, she became again involved in calamity, and, unless God's mercy shall shortly come to her relief, must there long continue.

It seems fitting that I should commence the transactions of this year, which is A.D. 1142, with certain events which were unnoticed in the former; and, at the same time, briefly recapitulate what has been said, in various places, of Robert, earl of Gloucester, son of king Henry, and submit it, thus arranged, to the consideration of the reader. For, as he was the first to espouse the just defence of his sister, so did he persevere with unshaken constancy in her cause without remuneration; I say without remuneration, because some of her supporters, either following the course of fortune, are changed with its revolutions, or having already obtained considerable benefits, fight for justice under expectation of still further recompence: Robert, alone, or nearly alone, uninfluenced by such considerations, was never swayed, as will appear hereafter, either by hope of advantage, or fear of loss. Let no one, therefore, suspect me of adulation, if I relate these matters circumstantially: for I shall make no sacrifice to favour; but pure historical truth, without any stain of falsehood, shall be handed down to the knowledge of posterity.

It has been related of the earl, how, first* of all the nobility, after David, king of Scotland, he confirmed, by oath, his fealty to his sister, the empress, for the kingdom of England, and the duchy of Normandy, in the presence of his father Henry. There was some contention, as I have said, between him and Stephen earl of Boulogne, afterwards king of England, who should swear first; Robert alleging the preference of a son, Stephen the dignity of a nephew.

It has been recorded too, what reasonable causes, from December, when his father died, till after the ensuing Easter, detained him in Normandy, from coming immediately into England to avenge his sister's injuries. And when at last he did come, with what just deliberation, and with what proviso, he consented to do homage to the king; and how justly, in the following year, and thenceforward, he abjured it.

Nor has his second arrival in England from Normandy, after his father's death, with his sister, been omitted: where, relying on the favour of God, and his innate courage, he ventured himself, as into a desert full of wild beasts, though scarcely accompanied by one hundred and forty horsemen. Neither has it been unnoticed, that, amid such tumult of war, while anxious watch was kept on all sides, he boldly came to Bristol with only twelve horsemen, having committed his sister to safe custody, as he supposed, at Arundel: nor with what prudence, at that time, he received her from the very midst of her enemies, and afterwards advanced her in all things to the utmost of his power; ever busied on her account, and neglecting his own interest to secure hers, while some persons taking advantage of his absence, curtailed his territories on every side: and, lastly, urged by what necessity, namely to rescue his son-in-law, whom the king had

* This seems an oversight, as he had before related, more than once that Stephen preceded Robert in taking the oath to Matilda.

besieged, he engaged in a hazardous conflict, and took the king prisoner. This fortunate event, however, was somewhat obscured by his own capture at Winchester, as I have recorded in the transactions of the former year; though by the grace of God, he showed himself, not so much an object of commiseration, as of praise, in that capture. For, when he saw that the royalist earls were so persevering in the pursuit that the business could not be gotten through without loss on his part, he sent forward all those for whom he was under apprehension, and more especially the empress. When they had proceeded far enough to escape in safety, he followed leisurely, that the retreat might not resemble a flight, and received the attack of the pursuers himself; thus purchasing, by his own detention, the liberty of his friends. And now, even at the moment of his capture, no one, as I have said above, perceived him either dispirited, or humbled in language : he seemed so far to tower above fortune, that he compelled his persecutors, for I am loth to call them enemies, to respect him. Wherefore the queen, though she might have remembered, that her husband had been fettered by his command, yet never suffered a bond of any kind to be put upon him, nor presumed on her dignity to treat him dishonourably. And finally at Rochester, for thither he was conducted, he went freely whither he pleased, to the churches below the castle, and conversed with whom he chose, the queen only being present (for after her departure he was held in free custody in the keep) and so calm and serene was his mind, that, getting money from his vassals in Kent, he bought some valuable horses, which were both serviceable and beneficial to him afterwards.

The earls, and those whose business it was to speak of such matters, at first, tried if he would allow of the king and himself being liberated on equal terms. Though his countess, Mabil, out of solicitude for her beloved husband, would have embraced these terms the moment she heard them, being, through conjugal affection, bent on his liberation, yet he, in his wiser policy, refused : asserting that a king and an earl were not of equal importance; however, if they would allow all who had been taken with him, or for him, to be set at liberty, to this he might consent. But the earls and other royalists would not assent to these terms; they were anxious indeed for the king's liberty, but not at their own pecuniary loss : for earl Gilbert had taken William of Salisbury : and William de Ipres, Humphry de Bohun ; and others had made such captures as they could, at Winchester, greedily expecting large sums for their ransom.

Next attacking the earl another way, they were anxious to allure him with magnificent promises, if so they might effect their purpose. Would he go over to the king's side, and dismiss his sister, he should govern the whole country : all things should await his decision : the crown should be the only distinction between him and the king : over all others he should rule as he pleased. The earl rejected these unbounded promises, with a memorable reply, which I wish posterity to hear, and to admire : "I am not my own master," said he, " but am in another's power ; when I shall see myself at my own disposal, I promise to do every thing which reason dictates on the matter you propound."

Irritated and incensed at this, when they could do nothing by fair means, they began to menace, that they would send him over sea to Boulogne, and keep him in perpetual bondage till death. Still, however, with a serene countenance, dispelling their threats, he firmly and truly protested, that he feared nothing less. For he relied on the spirit of his wife, the countess, and the courage of his partizans, who would immediately send the king into Ireland, if they heard of any foul deed perpetrated against himself.

A month elapsed in these transactions ; so difficult a work was it to effect the liberation of princes whom fortune had fettered with her chain.* But, at length, the supporters of the empress having conferred together, entreated the earl by divers messages, that " as he could not do what he would," according to the comic writer, " he would do what he could :" he should allow therefore, the king and himself to be set at liberty, on equal terms, " otherwise," said they, " we fear lest the earls, inspirited by the consciousness of their great and most distinguished exploit in making you captive, should attack us one by one, reduce our castles, and even make an attempt upon your sister."

Robert, wrought upon at length, assented to the proposal of the legate and archbishop, but still on condition that none

* Virgil, Æn 1. 33.

of the castles, or territory, should be restored, which had come under the power of the empress or of any of her faithful adherents, since the capture of the king: but he could not by any means obtain the release of his friends, as he had given offence to some persons, in rejecting, with a kind of superciliousness their magnificent promises with respect to the government of the whole kingdom. And as they were extremely anxious that, for the royal dignity, the king should be first set at liberty, and then the earl; when he demurred to this, the legate and the archbishop made oath, that if the king, after his own liberation, refused to release the earl, they would forthwith deliver themselves up into Robert's power, to be conducted wherever he pleased. Nor did he rest here; for his sagacious mind discovered an additional security. It might fall out, that the king, as often happens, listening to evil counsel, would consider the detention of his brother, and of the archbishop, as of very little consequence, so that he himself were at his ease. He demanded, therefore, from them both, separately, instruments, with their seals, addressed to the pope, to the following effect; "That the sovereign pope was to understand, that they, for the liberation of the king and the peace of the kingdom, had bound themselves to the earl by this covenant, that, if the king refused to liberate him after his own release, themselves would willingly surrender to his custody. Should it, therefore, come to this calamitous issue, they earnestly entreated, what it would well become the papal goodness voluntarily to perform, that he would release them, who were his suffragans, as well as the earl, from unjustifiable durance." There was something more to the same effect.

These writings, received from either prelate, Robert deposited in a place of safety, and came to Winchester with them and a great company of the barons. The king also, as has been before observed, coming thither soon after, had a friendly interview with the earl. But although he, and all the earls present, eagerly busied themselves in bringing over Robert to their wishes, yet, "firm as a rock amid the ocean" in his resistance, he rendered their attempts abortive, or refuted them by argument. He affirmed, that, it was neither reasonable nor natural, that he should desert his sister, whose cause he had justly espoused, not for any benefit to himself, nor so much out of dislike to the king, as regard to his oath, which, they also ought to remember, it was impiety to violate, especially when he called to mind, that he had been enjoined by the pope to respect the oath he had taken to his sister in the presence of his father. Thus failing of peace, they severally departed.

The reason why I have not incorporated these events with the transactions of the former year is that I did not then know them; for I have always dreaded to transmit anything to posterity, through my narrative, the truth of which I could not perfectly vouch for. What, then, I have to relate of the present year will commence as follows.

The respective parties of the empress and of the king, conducted themselves with quiet forbearance from Christmas to Lent, anxious rather to preserve their own, than to ravage the possessions of others. The king went to a distant part of the kingdom for the purpose of quelling some disturbances Lent coming on gave all a respite from war; in the midst of which the empress came with her party to Devizes, where her secret designs were debated. So much of them, however, transpired that it was known that all her partizans had agreed to send for the earl of Anjou, who was most interested in the defence of the inheritance of his wife and children in England. Men of respectability were, therefore, despatched and such as might fitly execute a business of such magnitude. Not long after, nearly on the Easter holidays, the king, while meditating, as it is said, some harsh measures, was detained by an acute disease at Northampton; so severe, indeed, that he was reported, almost throughout England, as being at the point of death. His sickness continued till after Pentecost, when returning health gradually restored him. In the meantime, the messengers returning from Anjou, related the result of their mission to the empress and the princes in a second council, held at Devizes on the octaves of Pentecost. They said that the earl of Anjou in some measure favoured the mission of the nobility, but that among them all he was only well acquainted with the earl of Gloucester, of whose prudence and fidelity, greatness of mind and industry, he had long since had proof. Were he to make a voyage to him he would, as far as he was able, accede to his wishes: but that all other persons would expend their labour in passing and repassing to no purpose.

The hopes of all the assembly being thus excited, they entreated that the earl would condescend to undertake this task on account of the inheritance of his sister and of his nephews. At first he excused himself, alleging the difficulty of the business, the perilous journey, beset with enemies on either side of the sea; that it would be attended with danger to his sister, as in his absence those persons would be hardly able to defend her, who, distrusting even the strength of their own party, had nearly deserted her during his captivity. Yielding at length to the general desire, he demanded hostages, especially from those who were considered as the chief persons, to be taken with him into Normandy, and to be pledges, as well to the earl of Anjou as to the empress; and that all, continuing at Oxford, should unite in defending her from injury to the utmost while he was absent. His propositions were eagerly approved, and hostages given him to be conducted into Normandy.

Robert, therefore, bidding adieu to his sister, and taking with him his hostages and some light troops, proceeded by safe marches to Wareham, which town and castle he had long since entrusted to his eldest son William. There, soon after the festival of St. John, committing himself, by the grace of God, to the ocean, with such vessels as he then possessed, he weighed anchor. When they were about mid-sea, a tempest arising, all except two were dispersed; some were driven back, and some carried beyond their destination. Two only, in one of which was the earl with his most faithful adherents, keeping their course, arrived in the wished-for port. Proceeding thus to Caen, he sent messengers for the earl of Anjou. The earl came without reluctance, but stated his difficulties, and those not a few, to the object of the embassy when proposed to him; among others that he should be detained from coming into England by the rebellion of many castles in Normandy. This circumstance delayed the earl of Gloucester's return longer than he had intended: for, that he might deprive the earl of Anjou of every evasion, he assisted him in subduing ten castles in Normandy. The names of which were Tenerchebrei, Seithilaret, Brichesart, Alani, Bastenborg, Triveres, Castel de Vira, Placeit, Vilers, Moreton Yet even by this activity, he furthered the end of his mission but little. The earl of Anjou stated fresh causes, as the former were done away, to excuse his coming into England. Indeed, as a very singular favour, he permitted his eldest son, by the empress, to accompany his uncle to England, by whose presence the chiefs might be encouraged to defend the cause of the lawful heir. The youth is named Henry, after his grandfather; may he hereafter resemble him in happiness and in power.

In England, in the meantime, the king seizing the opportunity of the earl's absence came unexpectedly to Wareham, and finding it slightly garrisoned, he burned and plundered the town, and immediately got possession of the castle also. Not content with this, as he saw fortune inclined to favour him, three days before the festival of St. Michael, by an unexpected chance,* he burned the city of Oxford, and laid siege to the castle, in which was the empress with her domestic guards. This he did with such determined resolution, that he declared no hope of advantage or fear of loss should induce him to depart till the castle was delivered up, and the empress surrendered to his power. Shortly after, all the nobility of the empress's party, ashamed of being absent from their sovereign in violation of their compact, assembled in large bodies at Wallingford, with the determination of attacking the king if he would risk a battle in the open plain; but they had no intention of assailing him within the city, as Robert earl of Gloucester had so fortified it with ditches that it appeared impregnable unless by fire.

These rumours becoming prevalent in Normandy, Robert hastened his return. He embarked, therefore, somewhat more than three, but less than four hundred horsemen, on board fifty-two vessels; to these were added two which he took at sea on his return. God's grace so singularly favoured his pious resolution that not one ship, out of so great a number, was separated, but all nearly close together, or gently proceeding one before the other, ploughed the calm bosom of the deep. Nor did the waves violently dash against the

* The garrison having sallied out against him, he suddenly passed a ford which was not generally known and, repelling the enemy, entered the town with them. Gesta Regis Stephani, 958.

fleet, but rather seemed subserviently to further their passage, like that most beautiful appearance at sea when the wave gradually approaching gently breaks upon the shore. Thus making the port of Wareham, these favoured vessels restored the earl and all his companions to the wishes of their friends.

He had at first thought of landing at Southampton, at once to wreak his vengeance both on its inhabitants and on their lord: but this resolution was changed through the repeated entreaties of the Vituli, who were fearful that their dearest connexions, who resided at Southampton, would be involved in the general calamity. These are a kind of mariners, who are known by the name of Vituli; and as they are his faithful adherents he thought fit to listen to their petitions, and desist from his design. Again, it appeared more dignified to return to the place whence he had departed, and to recover by force what he had lost by a similar mode. Reducing, therefore, immediately the port and town, he laid siege to the castle, which by its strength stimulated the spirit, not to call it obstinacy, of those of the king's choicest troops who defended it. Yet, nevertheless, soon after, the garrison, shaken in their resolution by the engines of the earl, and greatly alarmed, begged a truce, that, as is the custom of the military, they might demand assistance from the king, consenting to deliver up the castle if he refused to come by a certain day. This, though he was possessed with the utmost impatience to become master of the fortress, was very agreeable to the earl, as it led him to suppose it might draw off Stephen from besieging his sister. We may imagine what firmness of mind this man possessed who, with little more than three hundred horsemen, and as yet joined by no succours in England, could undauntedly await the king, who was reported to have more than a thousand; for many persons had joined the siege, not so much through dislike to the empress as through the hope of plunder.

However, when it was certified that the king, from that resolution which I have before mentioned, refused assistance to the besieged at Wareham, the earl obtained the castle, and with the same attack subdued the island of Portland, which they had fortified, as well as a third castle, called Lullewarden, which belonged to a certain chamberlain, called William

ESCAPE OF THE EMPRESS.

of Glastonbury, who had lately revolted from the empress. Robert then, at the beginning of Advent, summoned the whole of Matilda's partisans to Cirencester: where all resolving to afford their sovereign every possible assistance, they meditated a march to Oxford; courageously determining to give the king battle, unless he retreated. But as they were on their route, the pleasing account reached them, that the empress had escaped from the blockaded castle at Oxford, and was now at Wallingford in security. Turning aside thither, then, at the suggestion of their sovereign, since the soldiers who had remained at her departure, after delivering up the castle, had gone away without molestation, and the holidays admonished them to repose awhile, they resolved to abstain from battle, and retired to their homes.

I would very willingly subjoin the manner of the empress's liberation, did I know it to a certainty; for it is undoubtedly one of God's manifest miracles. This, however, is sufficiently notorious, that, through fear of the earl's approach, many of the besiegers at Oxford stole away wherever they were able, and the rest remitted their vigilance, and kept not so good a look out as before; more anxious for their own safety, in case it came to a battle, than bent on the destruction of others.* This circumstance being remarked by the townsmen, the empress, with only four soldiers, made her escape through a small postern, and passed the river. Afterwards, as necessity sometimes, and indeed, almost always, discovers means and ministers courage, she went to Abingdon on foot, and thence reached Wallingford on horse-back. But this I purpose describing more fully, if, by God's permission, I shall ever learn the truth of it from those who were present.

---

* One of the MSS omits from, "This circumstance," to the end, and substitutes, ... "but these matters, with God's permission, shall be more largely treated in the following volume."

INDEX.

*A*DULTERY, punished in Old Saxony, 74
Ælla founds the kingdom of Sussex, 92.
Aimar, bishop of Puy, 363, 365.
Alcuin, 62; his epistles, 66, 79, 84
Aldhelm, abbat of Malmesbury, 29, made bishop of Sherborne, 35
Aldred, abp. of York, crowns William I, 281.
Aldrey, William de, account of, 340
Alexander, bp. of Lincoln, imprisoned, 500
Alexius I, emperor of Constantinople, 365.
Alfwold, king of Northumbria, 68
Alfred, king of England, anointed by pope Leo, 99; ascends the throne, 113; retires to Athelney, ib.; assumes the garb of a minstrel, 114; routs the Danes, 116; his personal bravery, 117; his children, ib.; founds various monasteries, 118; his love of literature, ib.; dies, 121
Alfred, the son of Ethelred, 207.
Alfrid, king of Northumbria, 52
Alla, king of Northumbria, 41
Almodis, countess of Toulouse, 416.
Ambrosius, monarch of Britain, 11
Analaf, 129, 136; created king by the Northumbrians, 141
Angles and Saxons invited from Germany, 7, arrive in Britain, 8.
Angle-School at Rome, 99
Anjou, earls of, account of, 265
Anjou, Geoffrey earl of, account of, 261
Anlaf, king of Norway, baptized, 163
Anselm, abp. of Canterbury, quits the kingdom, 338; recalled, 428; his contest with king Henry, 448.
Anschetil, a Norman nobleman, 141
Antioch, description and siege of, 378—382
Aoxianus, governor of Antioch, 379, 381
Arbrisil, Robert de, account of, 471
Architecture, new style of at Westminster, 55; at Salisbury and Malmesbury, 442
Armorica or Bretagne, British settlement of, 6.
Arthur assists Ambrosius, 11; his sepulchre never found, 315
Asia Minor, its ancient fruitfulness, 377
Ass, a man transformed into one, 180
Asser, bishop of Sherborne, account of, 118
Assingdon, consecration of church at, 198
Athelard, abp. of Canterbury, 82
Athelstan, king of Mercia, 128—140
Athelwold, the confidant of Edgar, 159
Augustine, St., converts the king of Kent to Christianity, 12, 26 See Joscelyn
Azotus, siege of, 405

Babylon in Egypt, formerly Taphnis, 390.
Badon, Mount, siege of, 11
Bayeux, city of, burned, 433.
Baldred, king of Kent, 17, expelled, 96.
Baldwin I, king of Jerusalem, 395—412.
Baldwin II, king of Jerusalem, 412.
Baldwin, earl of Flanders, 206
Balista, what, 380
Ballads, ancient historical, 138, 148, 315.
Balso the Short, story of, 145.
Bangor, monastery of, 44
Battles at Aylesford, 194, Antioch, 382 Ascalon, 391, Assingdon, 194, Benaington, 38, Bruneford or Brumby, 129, Degstan, 43; Dol, 291; Eschendun, 111, Gerborai, 291; Hastings, 257, 276, 280, Hellendun, 96, Penn, near Gillingham, 193, Sceorstan, ib; Standford-bridge, 256; Tenersebray, 433, Walesdun, 260, Witgeornesbrug, 20, Wodensdike, 19
Battle abbey, founded by William I, 300
Bede, Venerable, 3, 54, 56, 59
Belesme, Robert de, 430, 433
Benedict Biscop, founder of Wearmouth, 54
Benignus, St. 25; his epitaph, ib
Berefreid, what, 388
Berengar of Tours, account of 311
Bernard, abbat of Tyron, account of, 471.
Bernard, the monk, 385.
Bernicia, kingdom of, 46
Bernulph, king of Mercia, 87, 96.
Berthwulf, king of Mercia, expelled, 88.
Bertric, king of Wessex, 40; expels Egbert, 95; poisoned, 106
Bethlehem, church of St. Mary, at 383.
Bezants, money so called, 372, 406
Bishoprics, extinct or consolidated, 78 Extent of, 22; removal of, 78, 352, precedence of, 22
Bishops, seven, story of, 127, 128.
Blois, Theobald earl of, 438
Blois, Henry de, bishop of Winton, and legate, 501; his treaty with the empress Maud, 517; holds a council at Winton, 518; his quarrel with the empress, 523
Blois, Stephen earl of, joins the crusade, 366, 408; killed at Ramula, 410
Blood, its physical effects, 361; shower of, 67
Boamund, his design in urging the crusade, 356, 365; account of, 413
Boniface, archbishop of Mentz, 73
Boy, Jewish, legendary story of, 314
Bracelets exposed by Alfred on highways, 118.

Briget, St 25.
Britons, avarice and rapine of, 67.
Britons, western, or Cornwallish, 134.
Brithwin, bishop of Wilton, 247
Burgundy, Stephen earl of, 408. Killed at Ramula, 410
Burhred, king of Mercia, 88.

Cadwalla, king of the Britons, 46.
Cædwalla, king of Wessex, 16 Baptized, and called Peter, 31.
Caerleon, or Chester, 43.
Cæsarea, siege of, 405.
Cæsar, Julius, subdues Britain, 5.
Calixtus II, pope, his letter on reducing Sutri, 466, accommodation with the emperor Henry V, 467.
Caine, remarkable accident at, 163.
Canons, secular, expelled Winchester, 149, Attempt to recover their monasteries, 162
Canterbury, see of, attempt to remove it to Lichfield, 78, controversy with see of York, 319.
Canterbury, city of, burnt, 16 Dreadful outrage at, 218.
Canute, elected king by the Danes, 190, lands at Sandwich, 192; divides the kingdom with Edmund Ironside, 195; assumes the sovereignty of England, 196; conquers the Swedes and Norwegians, 198, his epistle from Rome, 199; his death, 205.
Caradoc of Lancarvon, his Life of Gildas, 22, *note*.
Ceawlin, king of Wessex, his character, 18.
Ceolwulf, king of Northumbria, 53; becomes a monk, 61.
Centuries, or hundreds, instituted, 117.
Cenric, king of Wessex, his character, 18.
Ceolfrid, abbat of Wearmouth, 51, 55.
Ceols, vessels so called, described, 8, 18.
Cerdic, founds the kingdom of Wessex, 17
Charles the Great (Charlemagne), 65, 85.
Charles the Bald, king of France, 125.
Charles the Simple, king of France, 124
Charles the Fat, king of France, 102
Charters, Ethelbald's, 76. Ethelwulf's, 107 Edmund's, to Glastonbury, 141 Edgar's, to Glastonbury, 151. To Malmesbury, 153; Canute's, to Glastonbury, 203. Stephen's, 493.
Chartres, siege of, 125. Church of, 204.
Chasuble, meaning of, 473, *note*
Chester, reduced by Edward the elder, 131
Chorges, bishop of, account of, 414, 417.
Christianity, introduced into Mercia, 71.
Chronicle, Saxon, 3, 30, 39, 98.
Churchyards, privileges of, 492, *note*
Cirescet, what, 202.
Cissa, king of Sussex, 92, *note*.
Cistertian order, origin of, 347, observances of, 349.
Clergy, vanity of their dress condemned, 76.

Clerks, two, at Nantes, story of, 268.
Clermont, council of, its enactments, 356.
Clock, mechanical, 175
Cologne, abp of, his exemplary conduct, 183.
Comet, appearance of, 251, 343.
Complines, what, 350, *note*.
Constantine the Great, exhausts Britain, 6.
Constantine, elected emperor, and slain, 6.
Constantine, king of Scots, expelled his kingdom, 129; killed, 130.
Constantinople, described, 372 Its emperors, 374.
Corbaguath, or Corbanach, commander of the Persian forces, 381 His death, 421.
Councils, ecclesiastical, civil, &c 76, 127, 163, 191, 311, 356, 462, 499, 501, 517, 525.
Court, licentiousness of Rufus's, 337.
Courtiers, their insolence to the clergy, 339.
Crida, king of Mercia, 70, *note*
Cross, part of our Saviour's, 118, 136, 390, 411
Crucifix, said to have spoken, 163 Celebrated one at Lucca, 332. At Winchester, 523
Crusaders, march of, 364 Their extreme distress, 377. Their admirable conduct, 387—391.
Cuichelm, king of Wessex, 19, 20.
Cumberland, assigned to Malcolm, 141.
Curfew, supposed abolition of, 428, *note*.
Cuthbert, St. 52 Appears to Alfred, 113. His incorruption, 236.
Cuthburga, abbess of Wimborne, 35
Cuthred, king of West Saxons, 37.
Cynegils, king of Wessex, account of, 20.
Cynewolf, king of West Saxons, 38.

Dancers and profane singers punished, 182.
Danes, invade England, 40, 96. Ravages of, 69, 112, 167. Butchered by Ethelred, 169 Exact tribute, 185
Danube, the river, described, 374.
Daibert, abp. of Pisa, joins the Crusade, 397. Made patriarch of Jerusalem, 398
Dalmatic, garment so called, what, 85.
Danfrunt, siege of, 263 Castle of, 436.
David, St., 26.
David, tower of, at Jerusalem described, 387.
David, king of Scotland, his character, 434.
Decennaries, or tithings instituted, 117
Deira, province of, 42
Den, a monastery so called, 466.
Denmark, succession of its kings, 292.
Devices, on armour or shields, 262, 469.
Devil, visible appearance of, 343
Dionysius the Areopagite, 119
Domesday-book, account of, 291.
Drinking by pegs, account of, 148
Dunstan, abp. of Canterbury, 141, 167, 245.
Durham, privileges of the see of, 303

Eadbert, king of Northumbria, 61—67.
Eadburga, daughter of Edward the Elder, 125, 244.
Eadburga, queen of Wessex, 106.

INDEX. 539

Eadbald, king of Kent, 13.
Eadbert Pren, king of Kent, 17, 87.
Eadgaring, meaning of, 64.
Eadmer, the historian, 3, *note.*
Ealstan, bishop of Sherborne, 106, 108.
Earls, their official honours, 496, *note.*
Earthquake, terrible, 342.
East Anglia, kingdom of, 68. Extent of, 92. Plundered by the Danes, 112 Account of, 240.
Ecclesiastics, their property seized at death, 494
Eclipse, terrific, 488, 511.
Edan, king of Scots, 43.
Edessa, in Mesopotamia, described, 396.
Edgar, king of England, 147—162
Edgar Etheling, son of Edward the Exile, 253. His character, 284.
Edgitha, wife of the Confessor, 216
Edifices, stone, first builders of in England, 54.
Editha, daughter of Edgar, 161, 245.
Edmund, St king of East Anglia, 89. Slain, 112. His incorruption, 236 His boundary, 242 Church built in honour of him, 198
Edmund, king, 141. His death, 143.
Edmund Ironside, 191—195
Edred, king of England, 145
Edric, duke of Mercia, 169, 191, 197.
Edward the Elder, 122. His issue, 124. Education of his children, 125.
Edward the Martyr, 162—165.
Edward the Confessor, 213 Crowned at Winchester, 216. His character, 247. His predictions, 251. Dies, 253.
Edward the Exile comes to England, 253
Edwin, king of Northumbria, 45
Edwin, brother of Athelstan, 139
Edwin, brother of Edmund Ironside, 196.
Edwin and Morcar, earls of Northumbria, 285.
Edwy, king of England, 145—147.
Egbert, king of Kent, 15
Egbert, archbishop of York, 61
Egbert, king of Wessex, 94—97.
Egfert, king of Mercia, 86.
Egfrid, king of Northumbria, 51
Eginhard, his life of Charlemagne, 64, *note*
Eisc, son of Hengist, king of Kent, 12.
Elbert, and Egelbright, 15, 237, 243.
Eleutherius, bishop of Rome, 21
Elfred, the rival of king Athelstan, 128, His singular death, 137.
Elferius, destroys monasteries, 164, 165.
Elfgiva, concubine of king Edwy, 146.
Elfthrida, wife of king Edgar, 159, 161, Causes the murder of king Edward, 164.
Elmer, a monk, flies like Dædalus, 252
Elphege, archbishop of Canterbury, 168, his body translated to Canterbury, 202; its incorruption, 236.
Elward, or Ethelwerd, abridger of the Saxon Chronicle, 3, *note*
Ely, church of, made a cathedral, 476.

Emma queen of Ethelred, 187, her liberality to Winchester, 215, story of the ploughshares, ib. *note*
England, divisions of, geographical and ecclesiastical, 91—93, oppressed state of after the conquest, 235, 253, its lamentable condition in the time of Stephen, 496, 509
Eroonbert, king of Kent, 14.
Ercongotha, St 15, 242
Eric, expelled the kingdom by Canute, 197.
Ermenhilda, St 242
Ethelbald, king of Mercia, 73—77
Ethelbald, king of Wessex, 110
Ethelbert, king of Kent, 12, his answer to Augustine, 14, converted to Christianity, ib.
Ethelbert, St king of East-Anglia, killed, 78.
Ethelbert, king of Kent, Essex, &c 110
Ethelbert, son of Ermenred, murdered, 15, 237, 243.
Ethelburga, queen of Ina, her art, 36.
Etheldrida, St. her incorruption, 242
Ethelfrid, king of Northumbria, 43.
Ethelnoth, archbishop of Canterbury, 203.
Ethelred, king of Mercia, 72
Ethelred, son of Ermenred, murdered, 15, 237, 243
Ethelred, or Ethelbert, king of Northumbria, 68.
Ethelred, king of Wessex, 111
Ethelred II, king of England, 165, 186—193
Ethelfleda, lady of the Mercians, 123.
Ethered, earl, governor of Mercia, 116.
Ethelric, king of Northumbria, 42.
Ethelwald opposes Edward the Elder, 123
Ethelwalch, king of Sussex, 30
Ethelwold, bishop of Winchester, 149.
Ethelwulf, king, 97, his grant of tithes, 98, marries Judith, 99; returns from Rome, 106, his charter, 107, his descent, 109
Euripus, or sea-flood, destroys villages, 191.
Eustace, earl of Boulogne, his affray, 218
Exeter, fortified and walled by Athelstan, 134, burnt, 168, reduced by Wm I, 281.

Famine, ravages England, 170.
Feudal law, practices connected with, 447, *note.*
Fire, sacred, miracle of, at Jerusalem, 384, 404.
Fitz-Hubert, Robert, 506, 511
Fitz-Osborne, William, 288
Flanders, Robert earl of, 366, 436
Formosus, pope, his pretended epistle, 127.
Forest, New, account of, 306
Franks, origin of, 63; their character, 95
France, recapitulation of kings of, 64, 99
Frea, wife of Woden, 8
Frideswide, St. church at Oxford burnt, 191.
Fulcher of Chartres, on Syrian transactions, 395.
Fulbert of Chartres, his character, 204, 314.

Fulda, monastery of, 210; disease at, 318.
Fulk, earl of Anjou, account of, 265.

Gelasius II, pope, expelled Rome, 464
Geoffrey, Martel, account of, 267.
Gerbert, pope Sylvester II, 172—181.
German, St. 24; his miracles, 116
Gildas, the historian, 22, 67.
Girth, or Gurth, son of Godwin, 222, 275.
Glastonbury, antiquities of, by William of Malmesbury, 51; account of, 21; its privileges, 142, 150; Canute's presents to, 203; contention at, 303
Gosfrith, bishop of Coutances, 328, 329
Gloucester, Robert earl of, prefatory epistle to, 1 Conclusion of Regal History addressed to, 477, his character, 478, Modern History addressed to, 480; conduct with respect to Stephen, 492, with respect to his sister, 497, arrives in England, 505—531; his death 1, *note*
Godfrey, duke of Lorraine, account of, 365
Godfrey of Boulogne, account of, 392, joins the crusade, 394; chosen king of Jerusalem, 390, 394, dies, 395
Godfrey, prior of Winton, account of, 475
Godwin, earl, defeats the Swedes, 198, supports Emma, 206, murders Alfred the son of Ethelred, 207, his character and death, 221, his family, 223
Golgotha, church of, 395, *note*
Gothrun, a Danish king, baptized, 115.
Gregory I, pope, 42, dialogues of, 119, 232, his pastoral translated by Alfred, 120
Gregory VI, pope, otherwise Gratian, 223—230.
Gregory VII, pope, otherwise Hildebrand, 298.
Gregory VIII, pope, otherwise Maurice Bourdin, 464
Griffin, king of the Welsh, 214, 256.
Grimbald, abbat of Winton, 118, 120.
Guimund, bp of Avers, his eloquence, 312
Guiscard, or Wiscard, Robert, 294, 413.
Gunhilda, married to Hen, III, 207; accused of adultery, 238
Gunhildis, sister of Swayne, murdered, 185.

Handboc, Alfred's, 120, and *note.*
Hardecanute, 205; dies at Lambeth, 206.
Harold, sends presents to Athelstan, 134.
Harold, son of Canute, 205, dies, 206.
Harold, son of Godwin, 214; banished, 220, 254; seizes the crown of England, 55, 275; his death, 277—280.
Harold Harfager, king of Norway, 256, 257.
Harding, founder of Cistertians, 347.
Hastings the Dane, his ravages, 115.
Hastings, battle of, 276—280
Head, magical, formed by Gerbert, 181.
Hegesippus, a Greek author, 378
Helena, mother of Constantine the Great, 5
Helias de la Fleche, 341
Hengist, king of Kent, his origin, 8; arrives in Britain, 9; his son and brother arrive at Orkney, 10, settle in Northumbria, ib

his massacre of the British nobles, 11; death, ib.
Henry I, king of England, 425; elected king, 427; marries Matilda of Scotland, 428, gets possession of Normandy, 431, his wholesome laws, 434, his transactions with the Scots, ib, subdues the Welsh, 435; quarrel with earl of Flanders, 436, interview with pope Calixtus, 440; passion for exotic animals, 443, recapitulation of his character, 445; his person and habits, 446, espouses Adala of Louvain, 454; transactions till his death, 483—490.
Henry III, emperor of Germany, 208—212.
Henry IV, emperor, excommunicated, 358.
Henry V, his contest with the pope, 457.
Hereford, Roger earl of, rebels, 288.
Herbert, bishop of Norwich, account of, 353
Hildebrand, pope Gregory VII, 295, his conduct to the emperor Henry V, 298.
Hildebert of Mans, verses on Berengar, 312, 367
Hingwar, the Dane, ravages Northumbria, 240
Horsa, brother of Hengist, his death, 10.
Horæ, what, 350, *note*
Hospital, erected at Jerusalem, 385.
Hubba the Dane, brother of Hingwar, 240.
Hugh the Great, brother of Philip, joins the Crusade, 365. His death, 408.
Hugo, abbat of Clugny, his account of Hildebrand, 296 Announces the death of Rufus, 344.
Hugo, abp. of Rouen, his letter, 489
Hunting, right of, restricted by Will II, 339
Hyde monastery, Winton, 122; burnt, 523
Hyrcanus, digs gold from David's sepulchre, 177

Ida, king of Northumbria, 41
Ina, king of Wessex, 31. Abdicates and dies at Rome, 37. His grant to Glastonbury, 32
Indract, St. account of, 26
Investiture of churches, 298, 447 Pope Paschal's epistle on, 448 Contests about, 458
Ipres, William de, his perfidy, 495 Burns the abbey of Warewell, 523
Ireland, converted, 24 Its dependence on England, 443.

Jerusalem, expedition to, or Crusade, 355. Approach to by Crusaders, 383 Description of, 384. Patriarchs of, 385 Siege of, 387. Capture of, 389.
Jews, their insolence, 338.
Jewish youth, anecdote of, 338, *note*.
John XIII, pope, his epistle to Alfric, 151. Confirms the grants to Glastonbury, 153.
John XV, pope, makes peace between Ethelred and Richard duke of Normandy, 171
John Fitz-Gilbert, 512.

INDEX.

Joscelyn of St Bertins, account of, 355
  His translation of St. Augustine, ib.
Jothwel, king of the Welsh, 129
Joust, meaning of that term, 515, *note*
Jutes, a German tribe, settled in Britain, 9

Katigis, son of Vortigern, death of, 10.
Kenelm, St. 87. Murdered by his sister, 238.
Kenred, king of Northumbria, 53.
Kenred, or Kinred, king of Mercia, 72
Kent Its conversion to Christianity, 13
  Annexed to West Saxons, 17 Ravaged by Ina, 31 Its extent, 91
Kentwin, king of Wessex, 30
Kenwalk, king of Wessex, 20, his death, 30
Kenulph, king of Mercia, 79—86.
Kinad, king of Scots, 147, 158.
Knights, order of, among the Anglo-Saxons, 131

Lambert, abp of Canterbury, deprived, 78.
Lamp, perpetual, 234.
Lanfranc, abp of Canterbury, 300, 323.
Lanzo, prior of Lewes, account of, 472.
Laurentius, abp. of Canterbury, chastized by St Peter, 13
Legion, Theban, account of, 136, *note*
Leo III, pope, 79 His epistle, 82.
Leofa, murders king Edmund, 143
Leofric, earl of Hereford, 214
Leonard, St his peculiar power, 415, *note*
Leutherius, bishop, founds Malmesbury, 28
Lewis VI, king of France, account of, 438.
Library, noble one at York, 62, at Jerusalem, 385
Libraries formerly attached to churches, 120
London, ravaged, 97, granted by Alfred to earl Ethered, 116, besieged by Danes, 167, by Canute, 194, dreadful tempest at, 342
Longinus, St. legend of, 136, *note*
Lothere, king of Kent, 15
Lucius, king of the Britons, baptized, 21
Luidhard, bishop, exemplary life of, 12

Mabil, wife of Robert earl of Gloucester, 1, *note*, 433, *note*, 483, 528
Malcolm, king of the Cumbrians, 147.
Malcolm II, king of Scotland, 199
Malcolm III, placed on the throne of Scotland, by Edward the Confessor, 214; receives the English fugitives, 282, slain, 283, 333.
Malger, archbp. of Rouen, account of, 300.
Malmesbury, monastery of, founded, 28, seized by Offa, 78, by Alstan, 98, its possessions restored, 86, monks expelled by Edwy, 146 seized by Roger bishop of Salisbury, 508, singular account of one of its monks, 177
Malmesbury, John abbat of, his character, 509.
Malmesbury, William monk of, his motives for writing history, 1, his history of Glastonbury, 21, his love of learning and fondness for books, 93, of Norman and English parentage, 258, his diffidence, 414, first regular historian of the English after Bede, 477, three small volumes of his works supposed to be lost, 480, *note*, residence at Malmesbury, 28, indignation at oppression of his monastery, 78, 98, 146, 508, his design of writing the lives of the prelates, 148

Magus, Simon, legend of, 180, *note*
Mancus, value of, 82, *note*.
Manse, signification of, 108, *note*
Marchio, its signification, 517, *note*
Margaret, wife of Malcolm king of Scots, her issue, 253, her piety and death, 333
Martin, St his relics cure a leprous person, 116
Matilda, wife of William I, 265, 305
Matilda, wife of Henry I, account of, 253, 428; her piety, learning, and death, 452
Matilda, or Maud, married to Henry V, 457, returns to England, 481, succession of England settled on her, 482, married to Fulco earl of Anjou, 483, succession again confirmed to her, 487, elected queen, 519, designs of, 531; escape from Oxford, 535
Maurilius of Feschamp, account of, 301.
Mayors of the palace, 64, *note*
Maximus, assumes the empire, 6, his expedition to Gaul, and death, ib
Mellent, Robert earl of, account of, 441
Mercia, kings of, 70, extent of, 92, Mercians unite with the Danes, 112, their noble stand in favour of Ethelred, 192
Mice, singular tales concerning, 316, 317.
Milburga, abbess of Wenlock, 243
Miles, ambiguity of that term, 289, *note*, 499
Miracles, Oswald's, 49; of pope Leo III, 65, of St Martin, 116, St Edward's, 164, of St. Magnus, 182, of Ethelred and Ethelbert, 238, of St Kenelm, ib St. Wistan, 239, St. Edmund, 240, St. Milburga, 243, Eadburga, 244; Editha, 245; of Edward the Confessor, 248.
Money, debased state of in time of king Stephen, 511
Montgomerie, Roger, conspires against William II, 329
Morcar, son of Elgar, made earl of Northumbria, 223, defeated by Danes, 256, his death, 285
Moreton, William earl of, rebels against Henry I, 431
Mountain, perforated, tale of, 178
Murrain, dreadful, 417.

Necromancy, 180, 232
Nice, in Bithynia, siege of, 366, 377.
Nidering, or Nithing, signification of, 330.
Normandy, granted to Rollo, 125, distracted state of, 260, 331, 422, 431

Normandy, William I, duke, 143
Normandy, Richard I, duke of, his pacification with Ethelred, 171
Normandy, Richard II, duke of, account of, 188
Normandy, Robert I, duke of, account of, 259, his expedition to Jerusalem, 189
Normandy, Robert II, Curthose, duke of, pawns his duchy, 339; joins the crusade, 366, 410, account of, 420, arrangement with Henry I, 422, imprisoned till death, 423
Normans, subdue part of Gaul, 8; unjust preference of after the conquest, 253, dislike to William II, 329, feuds of with the English, 217, manners and customs of, 280
Northumberland, Robert, earl of, 327, 339.
Northumbria, kingdom of, 41, its extent, 93; yields to Egbert, 96, unites with Danes, 112, subdued by Athelstan, 129.
Norwegian, singular courage of one, 256.
Norway, succession of its kings, 292.

Odo, archbishop of Canterbury, separates Edwy from Elfgiva, 146.
Odo, bishop of Bayeux and earl of Kent, 307; rebels against Rufus and is banished, 328.
Offa, king of Mercia, his character, 77; rapacity, 78; treaty with Charlemagne, 84.
Offa, king of Essex, becomes a monk, 91.
Ordeal, account of, 22, *note*.
Order, monastic, afflicted by Edwy, 146; revives under Edgar, 155.
Organ hydraulic, account of, 175.
Orkney, isles of, subdued by Magnus, 343, Paul earl of, 443.
Osberne, precentor of Canterbury, his life of Dunstan, 146, his skill in music, 148.
Osbert, king of Northumbria, 112
Osred, king of Northumbria, 68.
Oswald, king of Northumbria, 46; his death, 48; miracles, 49, 237.
Oswin, king of Northumbria, 50.
Oswy, king of Northumbria, 50, 51.
Otha, brother of Hengist, settles in Northumbria, 40
Otho, the Great, 66.

Pallas, his body found at Rome, 234.
Palling, a Danish noble murdered, 185
Palms, assumed by pilgrims, and why, 398.
Palumbus, a priest, 233, his death, 234
Paschal II, pope, his letter to Henry I, on investitures, 448, to Anselm, 450, contest with the emperor Henry V, 457.
Paschasius, his story of the Host, 314.
Patrick, St 24.
Patrician of Rome, its office, 462.
Paul, of Samosata, 396
Paulinus, 26, converts the Northumbrians, 45

Peneda, king of Mercia, his character, 70; his death, 71
Peter the Hermit, account of, 366, 381
Peter-pence, origin of, 98, 202
Petrary, meaning of that term, 380, 405
Philip I, king of France, 206. His infatuated conduct, 437
Philip the clerk, account of, 420
Places, holy, account of, 57
Plegmund, abp of Canterbury, 120.
Plough-alms, what, 201
Poison, antidote against, 415
Poitou, Peter, bishop of, account of, 469
Poitou, William, earl of, defeated by the Turks, 408. His licentious conduct, 469.
Prodigy, of the double woman, 235.
Pythagoras, his double path, 172.

Quendrida, murders her brother Kenelm, 87, 238.

Ramula, description of, 383 Siege of, 409
Ranulf, or Ralph, bishop of Durham, his character, 336, 476 Imprisoned, 428. His escape, 429
Raymond, earl of St Giles, joins the crusade, 365 Account of, 416.
Reading monastery, 447
Redwald, king of the East Angles, 41, 88
Repasts, custom concerning in England, changed, 441, *note*
Richard, son of Will I, his untimely death, 306.
Ring, with Solomon's impression, 177.
Ritual, Ambrosian, 350, *note* Gregorian, ib
Robert, archbishop of Canterbury, 217 He flies, proceeds to Rome, and dies, 221
Robert, bishop of Chester, account of, 354.
Robert Curthose See Normandy.
Robert, earl of Moreton, brother of Will I, 307.
Robert Fitz-Hubert, 511
Robert Friso, earl of Flanders, account of, 289
Robert Guiscard, account of, 295.
Robert, king of France, his character, 204.
Robert, son of Godwin, account of, 284.
Roger, bishop of Salisbury, account of, 441. Imprisoned, 500. Death and character, 507
Rollo the Dane, obtains Rouen, 125. His insolence, 126.
Romans finally quit Britain, 6.
Rome, dreadful state of, 224. Citizen of, singular story of, 232 Poetical description of, 367. Account of its gates, churches, &c 368. Schism in church of, 484.
Rome-scot, 98, 202
Ross, in Wales, Flemings settled at, 435.
Rouen, William, archbishop of, account of, 438.

Sabert, king of East Saxons, baptized, 90.
Saints, incorruption of several, after death, 48, 236

Salisbury, tempest at, 343; cath____l, 442.
Saracens, their learning and divination, 173. Defeat of at Ascalon, 407.
Saxons, invited over from Germany, 7.
Saxons, East, kingdom of, 90. Its extent, 92.
Saxons, West kingdom of, 17. Its extent, 92.
Schools instituted in East Anglia, 88.
Scotland, subdued by Canute, 199.
Scots, defeated by the Angles, 9. Characterized, 364. Civilized by king David, 434.
Scotus, Johannes, account of, 119.
Scotus, Marianus, account of, 317.
Selsey, monastery of, 92. Singular circumstance at, 236.
Sepulchre, holy, church of, 384, 389.
Serlo, bishop of Sees, trims the beard of Henry I, 445, *note*.
Serlo, abbat of Gloucester, account of, 471.
Severus, dies in Britain, 5.
Shift of the Virgin, confounds the Danes, 125.
Ship, a magnificent, presented to Athelstan, 134.
Shoes with curved points, 337, *note*.
Sibilla, duchess of Normandy, 421, *note*.
Sigebert, king of Wessex, 38. His death, ib.
Sigebert, king of East Anglia, 89.
Sighelm, bishop of Sherborne, sent to India by Alfred, 118.
Simony, its extensive spread, 357.
Siric, abp. of Canterbury, 167.
Sithtric, king of Northumbria, 129, 132.
Siward, earl of Northumbria, kills Macbeth, 214. Supports Edward the Confessor, 219.
Siward, king of Norway, winters in England, 444. His voyage to Jerusalem, ib.
Slaves, female, prostituted and sent to Denmark, 222. Custom of selling, 279.
Sleepers, seven, story of, 230, *note*.
Solyman, sovereign of Romania, his army defeated, 376. Defeats the Franks, 408.
Sow, a warlike engine so called, 388.
Spear of Charlemagne, which pierced our Saviour, 135.
Spike, used at the Crucifixion, 135.
Statue, in the Campus Martius, 176.
Statue, brazen, at Rome, story of, 232.
Stephen, earl of Moreton, account of, 482. Comes to England and is chosen king, 490. Crowned, and goes into Scotland, 491. His character, 495. His perfidy to Robert, earl of Gloucester, 496. His violent conduct, 500. Contest with his brother the legate, 504. Conflicts with the Empress's party, 506, 507. Besieges Lincoln, 514. Defeated and made captive, 515. Liberated, 524. Plunders Wareham, 533. Burns Oxford, ib.
Stigand, bishop of Winton, 221, 253, 281, 302.
Sugar-cane, account of, 397, *note*.
Suger, abbat of St. Denis, his account of Henry I, 446, *note*.

___ing of that term, 379.
Superstition, singular, 122, and *note*.
Sussex, kingdom of, 92, *note*.
Sweyn, king of Denmark, invades England, 185. His conduct, 189, and death, 190.
Sweyn, son of Godwin, 219, 222. Goes to Jerusalem and is killed by the Saracens, ib.
Swithun, St., bishop of Winchester, 98.
Sword, miraculous, Athelstan's, 130; Constantine's, 135.

Tancred, prince of Antioch, enters Bethlehem, 383; his covetousness, 390; his conduct and death, 419.
Tewkesbury, monastery of, 433.
Thanet, isle of, appropriated to the Angles on their arrival, 9.
Thanet, monastery of, minster, 15.
Theodore, archbishop of Canterbury, 15, *note*, 51.
Thorns, crown of, 136.
Thurkill, the Dane, invites Sweyn, to England, 185; his expulsion and death, 197.
Time, division of by candle, 121.
Tirel, Walter, kills W. Rufus, 345.
Tosty, son of Godwin, expelled by the Northumbrians, 222; retires to Flanders, 223; his attempts against Harold, 256; defeated and slain, 257, 285.
Tower of London, its origin, 341.
Truce of God, why so called, 358, *note*.
Tudites, or Martel, Carolus, 64; his body carried off by evil spirits, 232.
Turks, their extensive dominion, 360; crafty mode of fight, 361; cruelty at the siege of Nice, 376; at Antioch, 379; defeated near Berith, 401; bodies burnt to obtain money they had swallowed, 406, *note*; besiege Baldwin at Rama, 284.

Vavassour, meaning of, 510, *note*.
Vallery, St., his body brought forth to implore a wind, 273.
Ver, Albric de, his harangue in favour of king Stephen, 502.
Vindelici, account of, 208.
Virginity, Aldhelm's commendation of, 29, 36.
Visions, of Charles king of France, 102; of Athelstan's mother, 139; of Edgar, 156; of Edward Confessor, 249; of Constantine the Great, 372.
Vortigern, his character, 7, 11.
Vortimer, the son of Vortigern, 10.
Ulfkytel, earl of Essex, attacks the Danes at Thetford, 69; killed at Assingdon, 170, 194.
Urban II, pope, 299; instigates the first crusade, 357; his speech at the council of Clermont, 359; contests with Guibert, 414.
Utred, earl of Northumbria, 192; defeated and put to death by Canute, 193.

Waher, Ralph de, rebels against William I, 287.

INDEX.

Wales, reduced to a province, 214, pays tribute to Athelstan, 134
Walkelin, bishop of Winchester, 302
Walker, bishop of Durham, murdered, 303
Walwin, nephew of Arthur, his sepulchre, 315
Waltheof, earl, account of, 386, his death, ibid
Warewell, or Whorwell, 160, monastery of, ib
Warwick, Henry earl of, 441
Welsh, subdued by Edward the Elder, 123, by Harold, 256, by Henry I, 435
Werburga, patroness of Chester, 72, 236, 243.
Werefrith, bishop of Worcester, 118
Westminster Abbey consecrated, 255.
West-Saxon kings, geneology of, 109
Wight, Isle of, given to Withgar, 218, converted to Christianity, 71
Wilfrid, bishop of Hexham, expelled his see, 51.
William I, king of England, 253, his early history, 259, his conquests, 268; is crowned, 281, summary of his wars, 282; his issue, 305, munificence to monasteries 308, death, 310.
William II, king of England, his birth and education, 327, contentions with his nobles, 328, seizes castles of Tunbridge and Pevensey, 319, contests and treaty with his brother Robert, 330, his expedition against Wales and Scotland, 333, character, 334, 346, calamitous events of his reign, 342, singular tokens and manner of his death, 344

William of Carilef, bishop of Durham, 304
William, earl of Arches, 263
William Fitz-Osberne, account of, 289.
William, son of Henry I, 454
Winchelcumb, dreadful tempest at, 342
Winchester, church at, 21, 39, Canute's liberality to, 198
Windows, glass, first makers of in England, 54.
Wistan, St. account of, 239
Witch, Berkeley, account of, 230.
Witches, two at Rome, account of, 180.
Withlaf, king of Mercia, 88, 96.
Withred, king of Kent, 16
Woden, account of, 8
Wolves, tribute of, paid to Edgar, 158.
Woodstock Park, menagerie at, 443
Worcester, insurrection at, 207
Wulnod, destroys Ethelred's fleet, 169
Wulnod, son of Godwin, 222
Wulstan, precentor of Winchester, 149 his book on the harmony of sounds, ib
Wulstan, archbishop of York, confined by Edred, 145
Wulstan, bishop of Worcester, account of 303.
Wulfhere, king of Mercia, 71, 72.

York, city of, burnt, 112, besieged, 133 destroyed, 282.
York, see of, controversy with Canterbury 319, with Worcester and Dorchester 323
Youths, from England, exposed to sale a Rome, 42

BIBLIOLIFE

Old Books Deserve a New Life
www.bibliolife.com

Did you know that you can get most of our titles in our trademark **EasyScript**™ print format? **EasyScript**™ provides readers with a larger than average typeface, for a reading experience that's easier on the eyes.

Did you know that we have an ever-growing collection of books in many languages?

Order online:
www.bibliolife.com/store

Or to exclusively browse our **EasyScript**™ collection:
www.bibliogrande.com

At BiblioLife, we aim to make knowledge more accessible by making thousands of titles available to you – quickly and affordably.

Contact us:
BiblioLife
PO Box 21206
Charleston, SC 29413